MANORS AND MARKETS

Manors and Markets:

Economy and Society in the Low Countries, 500–1600

BAS VAN BAVEL

Utrecht University, the Netherlands

OXFORD
UNIVERSITY PRESS

OXFORD
UNIVERSITY PRESS

Great Clarendon Street, Oxford OX2 6DP

Oxford University Press is a department of the University of Oxford.
It furthers the University's objective of excellence in research, scholarship,
and education by publishing worldwide in

Oxford New York

Auckland Cape Town Dar es Salaam Hong Kong Karachi
Kuala Lumpur Madrid Melbourne Mexico City Nairobi
New Delhi Shanghai Taipei Toronto

With offices in

Argentina Austria Brazil Chile Czech Republic France Greece
Guatemala Hungary Italy Japan Poland Portugal Singapore
South Korea Switzerland Thailand Turkey Ukraine Vietnam

Oxford is a registered trade mark of Oxford University Press
in the UK and in certain other countries

Published in the United States
by Oxford University Press Inc., New York

© Bas van Bavel 2010

The moral rights of the author have been asserted
Database right Oxford University Press (maker)

First published 2010

All rights reserved. No part of this publication may be reproduced,
stored in a retrieval system, or transmitted, in any form or by any means,
without the prior permission in writing of Oxford University Press,
or as expressly permitted by law, or under terms agreed with the appropriate
reprographics rights organization. Enquiries concerning reproduction
outside the scope of the above should be sent to the Rights Department,
Oxford University Press, at the address above

You must not circulate this book in any other binding or cover
and you must impose the same condition on any acquirer

British Library Cataloguing in Publication Data

Data available

Library of Congress Cataloging in Publication Data

Data available

Typeset by Laserwords Private Limited, Chennai, India
Printed in Great Britain
on acid-free paper by
CPI Antony Rowe, Chippenham, Wiltshire

ISBN 978–0–19–927866–4 (Hbk.)

1 3 5 7 9 10 8 6 4 2

For Sarah and Noortje

Contents

List of Tables and Maps	xi
Preface	xiii

I. Introduction: Purpose, Context, and Approach — 1

- I.1. The Low Countries in the later Middle Ages — 1
- I.2. Explanations for Pre-industrial Growth and Development — 3
- I.3. Approach and Outline — 8

II. The Emergence of a Regional Framework in the Early and High Middle Ages: Land and Occupation — 15

- II.1. Landscape and Soil — 15
- II.2. Man-made Land: Early Occupation and Reclamation — 27
  - Ethnic Composition After the Roman Era — 28
  - Occupation in the Early Middle Ages — 32
  - Early Medieval Population Numbers — 35
  - Occupation and Reclamation in the High Middle Ages — 38
  - Hydrological Projects — 41
  - Interaction Between Man and Landscape — 44

III. The Emergence of a Regional Framework in the Early and High Middle Ages: Power, Property, and Social Structures — 51

- III.1. King, Nobility, and Other Landholders — 52
  - Royal Properties — 52
  - The *Homines Franci* and Smaller Landholders — 57
  - Properties of Religious Institutions — 61
  - The Rise of Banal and Territorial Lords — 63
- III.2. Manors and Freedom — 75
  - The Rise and Nature of Manorial Organization — 76
  - Reclamation, Manors, and Freedom in the High Middle Ages — 83
  - The Dissolution of Manorialism — 86
- III.3. Village and Town — 93
  - Village Communities — 93
  - Towns in the Early and High Middle Ages — 101
  - Urban Communities and Territorial Lords — 110
  - Urban Elites, Guilds, and Urban Government — 117

IV. The Economy: Agriculture and Industries in the Early and High Middle Ages — 124

IV.1. Agriculture in the Early and High Middle Ages — 124
Organization of Early Medieval Agriculture: Manor, Family Holding, and Village — 126
Cereal Culture and Pastoral Farming in the Carolingian Period — 129
Agrarian Technology in the High Middle Ages — 133
Communal Organizations and Customs — 136
Agriculture and Living Standards — 140

IV.2. Industries in the Early and High Middle Ages — 146
Manors and Early Medieval Production — 146
Industrial Specializations — 149
Industries in Town and Countryside — 152
Technology — 157

V. The Rise and the Institutional Framework of Markets in the High and Late Middle Ages — 162

V.1. The Land Market — 162
Rights to Land and Their Transfer — 162
The Role of Public Authorities — 167
The Exploitation of Land Ownership: The Emergence of Leasing — 170
The Mobility of Land in the Market — 178

V.2. The Capital Market — 181
The Emergence of Capital Markets — 182
Further Institutional Improvements in the 15th and 16th Centuries — 187
Coin Production — 193

V.3. The Labour Market — 200
Emergence of Labour Markets — 200
The Nature of Wage Labour, Labour Relations, and Organization of Labour Markets — 205
Quantitative Indicators — 211

V.4. The Market For Goods and Products — 213
The Institutional Organization of Trade in the Carolingian Period — 213
Towns and Trade in the High and Late Middle Ages — 218
Government Influence on Trade — 228
Improvements in Transport and the Growth of Markets — 234

VI.	**Social Change in the Late Middle Ages**		242
	VI.1.	Social Structures and Change	242
		Social Transformations in the Countryside	242
		Social Transformations in the Towns	252
		State Formation, Fiscality, and Bureaucracy	263
		Social Conflicts	271
	VI.2.	Demographic Change and Urbanization	278
		Population Numbers and Urbanization	278
		Regional Differences in Demographic Development	282
		The Position of Women	292
	VI.3.	Commercialization and Occupational Differentiation	294
	VI.4.	Welfare	304
		Wages and Standards of Living	304
		Poor Relief	307
		Education and Literacy	313
		Living Conditions	320
VII.	**The Economy in the Late Middle Ages: Agriculture and Industries**		325
	VII.1.	Agriculture	325
		Population Pressure and the Growth of Markets, 1100–1350	325
		Population Decline, Transition, and Specialization, 1350–1600	330
		Fishing	338
		Growth and Sustainability	340
	VII.2.	Industries	343
		Industrial Concentrations in Town and Countryside	343
		Different Strategies of Urban Industries: Flanders and Holland	346
		Technological Innovation	350
		Sources of Energy	356
		Rural and Urban Industries in the 16th Century	361
		Scale-Enlargement and Regional Specialization	364
		The Main Lines of Industrial Development	367
VIII.	**Economic Growth and Social Change in the Very Long Run**		372
	VIII.1.	Indicators of Growth	372
		Extensive Growth	372
		Intensive Growth	373
		Real Wages and Standards of Living	376
		Phases and Regional Patterns of Growth	378

VIII.2.	Possible Causes for Regional Variations in Economic Change	380
	Geography	380
	Demography and Urbanization	383
	Polities	385
VIII.3.	Socio-institutional Factors	387
	The Path-dependency of Socio-institutional Arrangements at the Regional Level	387
	The Effects of Socio-institutional Constellations on Economic Development	397
	The Low Countries in European Perspective	406

Bibliography   410
Index   463

List of Tables

2.1	Various regions in the Low Countries	26
2.2	Estimates of population densities in the early Middle Ages	36
4.1	Ages at death as reconstructed from dental remains	144
5.1	Interest rate percentages for Flanders and Holland, 13th to 16th centuries	192
5.2	Coins minted in the Low Countries, 13th to 16th centuries	199
5.3	The skill premium in the Low Countries	212
6.1	Five wealth categories, and their share of total wealth	256
6.2	Estimates of the urbanization rate for various principalities in the Low Countries, 1200–1600	281
7.1	Index of total grain output in the Cambrésis, 1320–1700	330
7.2	Output of wheat in hl/ha of sown land in various parts of the Low Countries, 1325–1600	332
7.3	Estimated number of busses engaged in herring fishing, 1439–1600	339
7.4	Amount of raw peat extracted in the Low Countries, 1200–1599	356

List of Maps

1.	Regions in the Low Countries	16
2.	Main settlements and abbeys in the Early Middle Ages	54
3.	Main towns in the Early and High Middle Ages	104
4.	Towns and villages in the Late Middle Ages	254

Preface

In writing this book, I have been able to build on the great number of studies published on the medieval history of the Low Countries in recent years. The academic flourishing of archaeology and historical geography in the Netherlands and Belgium in the 1980s and 1990s, for instance, has contributed greatly to our knowledge. The research into occupation history, settlement patterns, field systems, and burial practices has done much to enhance our knowledge of the early medieval period, for which written sources are scarce or absent. The 'Kempenproject', begun in the early 1980s, for instance, has made the infertile Campine area one of the best-investigated parts of early medieval north-western Europe. But archaeological research has also greatly increased our insight into early trade, especially the Frisian trade of the early medieval period, by uncovering artefacts, coins, boats, and imported products.

Urban history has also made great progress, with a host of studies on such topics as trade and urban networks, urban elites, status, representation, finances, and town planning. The universities of Ghent and Leiden, with Marc Boone, Walter Prevenier, and Wim Blockmans as their main exponents, have led the way. This progress is matched by that in the field of rural history. Many local and regional studies have provided a clearer understanding of the regional and rural elements of economic development in the Middle Ages. The Wageningen School, led first by B. H. Slicher van Bath and later by A. M. van der Woude, has been especially productive, as well as the scholars in Ghent and elsewhere working in the tradition of Adriaan Verhulst and his successor Erik Thoen. Fine examples of comprehensive regional studies are those by Peter Hoppenbrouwers, devoted to the late medieval people, families, properties, and social organizations of the Land of Heusden, a part of Holland, and by Erik Thoen, who produced an in-depth discussion on demography, agriculture, industry, and social structure in the late medieval countryside of inland Flanders. Erik Thoen facilitated my one-year stay in Ghent, where I became better acquainted with the medieval and rural history of the southern Low Countries, and also through the exchange of ideas and friendship of the people working there.

Another productive line of research is that on economic growth and social inequality over the long run, particularly the period 1000–1800, as practised mainly by the Economic and Social History group in Utrecht. This group, with Maarten Prak, Jan Luiten van Zanden, and Oscar Gelderblom, has principally analysed developments in the Netherlands, although its geographical scope is now becoming broader. Its research focuses especially on the interaction between social structure, institutional organization, and economic growth in the pre-industrial period. Over the last years, this group has offered me a warm, dynamic, and intellectually challenging place to work. Here, I found the right setting for my research project on the rise and organization of markets in medieval Holland, which has generated many ideas for the present book and its analytical framework. Together with the younger generation of scholars in this and subsequent projects, we will try to probe further the possible causes of economic development and social change.

Apart from the people mentioned above, who have offered me academic inspiration and their help, I should like to thank especially those colleagues who have commented on parts of the earlier drafts: Michael Mitterauer read several sections of the book, Hans Middelkoop and Hans Renes read section II.1, Theo Spek read section IV.1, John Munro section VII.2, Jaco Zuijderduijn section V.2, and Jessica Dijkman section V.4. Various anonymous referees have read my book proposal and the manuscript: their suggestions have helped me a lot. My colleagues in Utrecht, Maarten Prak, Jan Luiten van Zanden, and Oscar Gelderblom have read the whole manuscript closely. Their comments, and often penetrating criticism, each made from their own angle, have greatly benefited the book, and show how fertile Utrecht University is in this subject area. A vital contribution to this research fertility has been made by the University Library, and the people there who have tirelessly supplied me with the requested books and journals. I should also like to thank Phyllis Mitzman and Eileen Power for their work on the correction of the English, and Frerik Kampman for his work on the references and the bibliography. The Netherlands Organization for Scientific Research has financially supported this research and offered me the opportunity to write the book. Most of all, however, I want to thank Astrid and our two daughters, Sarah and Noortje, to whom I dedicate this book.

I

Introduction: Purpose, Context, and Approach

I.1. THE LOW COUNTRIES IN THE LATER MIDDLE AGES

The Low Countries—an area roughly embracing the present-day countries of the Netherlands and Belgium—underwent remarkable developments in the Middle Ages. This area experienced strong population growth and, particularly from the 11th century onwards, a continuous increase in the urbanization ratio. At the end of the Middle Ages this was the most densely populated and urban region of Europe, equalling or even overtaking the north of Italy in these respects. At the beginning of the 14th century, a fifth of the population in the Low Countries already lived in the cities, with urbanization concentrated mainly in Flanders. By the late 15th century, the urbanization rate had increased to over a third. Flemish cities such as Ghent and Bruges flourished in the 13th and 14th centuries, Antwerp emerged as one of the main European trading centres in the 15th and 16th centuries, and Amsterdam became the centre of the world economy in the 16th and 17th centuries. The significant extent of urbanization in the Low Countries is an indicator of the strong specialization and commercialization of the economy. This is true not only of the urban sectors, but also of agriculture, which developed and became increasingly specialized from the high Middle Ages onwards. Combined with improvements in agricultural techniques, this resulted in an increase in agrarian surpluses, which in turn enabled and sustained the rise and growth of non-agrarian activities and trade. In some periods there was probably even economic growth in a modern sense, that is, a long-term rise in average per capita income.

This continuous period of development and growth over several centuries set the Low Countries apart from many other parts of western Europe, where economic growth was at best intermittent, and at worst absent. This growth not only came about from the intensification of labour and increasing market-oriented specialization, processes which are assumed to have been present in other parts of pre-industrial Europe, but in several parts of the late medieval Low Countries also resulted from the emergence of highly capital-intensive agricultural and industrial sectors.[1] The large investments in expensive implements, land improvements, hydraulic and industrial works, and other capital goods, often accompanied by increases in the stock of human knowledge, resulted in a reduction of labour input, and hence in higher surpluses and an increase in labour productivity.

Parallel to this quantitative growth, and enabling it, the economy of the late medieval Low Countries developed significantly in a qualitative sense. This is illustrated by the growth of open and flexible markets for labour, capital, goods, and products, the advanced division of labour in agriculture and industry, the emergence of secure and absolute property rights, and—indirectly—the extremely high and increasing level of urbanization. These elements started to develop in the Low Countries in the 11th and 12th centuries and were clearly present as early as the 15th and 16th centuries.[2] In some regions they were accompanied by profound social changes: proletarianization, a rise in wage labour, an accumulation of the means of production in the hands of wealthy entrepreneurs, and a sharp polarization of society.[3] Large segments of the population lost their economic independence and saw their standards of living decline. In these regions, market-oriented production by entrepreneurs using wage labour became dominant by the 16th century, both in agricultural regions such as the Guelders river area and in industrial regions such as Holland. These were the European forerunners in the transition to a modern capitalist economy and society.

At least as interesting as these developments, however, are the sharp regional differences within the Low Countries. Several regions did not experience these rapid developments, and even neighbouring regions often differed widely. In the 16th century, the Guelders river area underwent the final phase in its transition to agrarian capitalism,[4] but neighbouring regions such as the Veluwe saw hardly any fundamental change until well into the 19th century and remained dominated by family-scale peasant farming. In 16th-century Flanders, too, a clear boundary separated different social and economic developments.[5] In coastal Flanders large leased farms and highly specialized, extensive agriculture were dominant, but inland Flanders was characterized by small peasant holdings, intensification of agriculture, and proto-industrial development, subordinated to the interests of the urban merchants and guilds. There were marked variations also between coastal Friesland and Groningen—dominated by large farmers specializing for the market and employing large numbers of wage labourers—and neighbouring Drenthe, where cottagers focused instead on subsistence-oriented agriculture on their smallholdings. These regions in many ways are representative of the various

---

[1] For agriculture: De Vries, 'The transition to capitalism', 78–80.

[2] As observed for 16th century Holland by De Vries and Van der Woude, *The first modern economy*, 62, 196–201 and 665–668.

[3] Brenner, 'The Low Countries in the transition', 309–315, and Thoen, 'Transitie en economische ontwikkeling'.

[4] Van Bavel, 'Land, lease and agriculture', 31–34. [5] Thoen, 'Social agrosystems'.

types of economies and divergent trajectories found in western Europe. This book focuses on these regional differences within the Low Countries. It uses them as an opportunity for a comparative analysis of long-term economic and social development, in order to uncover the underlying causes of growth and development and to establish the reasons for the strong geographical divergences observed.

1.2. EXPLANATIONS FOR PRE-INDUSTRIAL GROWTH AND DEVELOPMENT

The authors involved in the debate on the determinants of pre-industrial growth and development, and the marked regional differences in the form and the timing of this process, have proposed various explanations, some focused on climate or ecology, others on technology or demography. The neo-Malthusian approach, stressing the tension between population development and natural resources—and the resulting population cycles and wage–price scissors as main determinants of socio-economic development—has been particularly influential in recent decades.[6] However, although this and the other approaches help in describing and understanding certain aspects of pre-industrial growth and change, and as such will be used throughout this book, they cannot in themselves offer an *explanation* of developments. They do not explain the marked differences among relatively small areas. This inadequacy is most apparent with respect to explanations sought in climate and demography, since these factors often vary little over wide areas, whereas economic and social developments within these areas may differ widely. The same applies to technological knowledge. While this was often widely available, it is the chronological and geographical differences in the adaptations, applications, and use of this technology that formed the actual differences in economic growth and need to be explained.[7]

The neo-classical focus on commercialization and the rise of markets nor the accessory Thunensian and Christallerian models,[8] which have become almost dominant in present-day historiography, can neither provide this explanation. True enough, this focus has helped to bring about major progress in understanding the rise of markets for products and goods in the pre-industrial era and the effect of these markets—and especially of growing urban demand—on the development of economy and society. It has become clear that as early as the late Middle Ages this influence must have been substantial, leading to increased commercialization and specialization in town and

---

[6] Promoted by such scholars as Postan, *The Medieval Economy*, 27–40, 61–72, and 224–46, and Le Roy Ladurie, 'L'histoire immobile'.
[7] Mokyr, *The lever of riches*, 6–10, and Persson, *Preindustrial Economic Growth*, 124–140.
[8] These economic geographical models conceptualize the patterns of land use around a city with respect to the distribution of urban locations under the influence of market forces.

countryside.⁹ Therefore, for the Low Countries, with its large cities, markets, and intensive trade, it is particularly tempting to focus on commercialization as the main explanation of development and change, but this approach is unable to provide an explanation for the great geographical differences in social and economic development which can be observed there.

Despite the short distances and the fact that market demand was felt almost everywhere in the Low Countries, there was a striking regional variation in economic and social developments within this relatively small area. At first sight, these differences are mainly found between the coastal provinces in the west and the inland provinces in the east, with urbanization and trade concentrated in the coastal areas. The latter were favoured by the inexpensive transport opportunities that took advantage of the sea, cheap energy in the form of peat, and other geographical benefits. But there were more profound regional differences in the Low Countries than the simple division between inland and coastal areas alone. On a smaller geographical scale, social and economic differences among regions may have been even more significant, as has become clear in recent years. A cross-section through the 16th-century Low Countries, by way of the examples cited above, makes this regional diversity very apparent.

It was not only coastal areas that showed rapid development: inland regions such as the Guelders river area and Salland did so too. The availability of raw materials was not the determining factor either: there was very little economic development in Drenthe, which had massive amounts of peat, for instance. Nor were these differences determined by the presence or absence of urban markets, as is shown by the differences in development between coastal and inland Flanders, both situated close to large cities, and by the strong development in the Guelders river area, which was not highly urbanized. In regions where the market was close and reasonably accessible—which was the case in most parts of the Low Countries—specialization for the market can be observed in this period, but the nature and significance of that specialization varied sharply with the region.¹⁰ The extent to which people reacted to market demand and especially the direction they gave to market specialization, and whether this led to extensification or intensification, or stimulated further development and investment, depended on factors other than the presence of market demand alone.

In the search for explanations it is more productive to focus on the institutional organization of the economy, and more specifically on the rules that govern exchange, as proposed by Douglass North and the New Institutional Economics.¹¹ It is now becoming clearer that the market is not a neutral, almost abstract element, but rather a complex and specific set of institutional arrangements, and these are largely responsible for determining the effects on

---

⁹ Britnell, 'Commercialisation and economic development'.
¹⁰ Van Bavel, 'Agrarian change'.
¹¹ North and Thomas, *Rise of the Western World*, and North, *Institutions*.

the economy and the further development of trade: whether markets stimulate growth, or retard or even block it. The specific institutional framework within which market exchange takes place determines to an important extent the risks, opportunities, and costs of marketing, and hence the degree to which markets can develop. By incorporating these elements into the analysis, the geographical differences in the development of trade and markets can be better understood. Institutional arrangements can also help to explain why the market had such a divergent effect on the development of economies. Economic trends or the growth of supply and demand alone cannot explain these divergences, but must be considered within a structural approach to the market. This approach can be particularly fruitful when investigating the genesis of rules for market exchange within a society where non-market forms of exchange were more important, as in early and high medieval Europe. The same focus on the institutional arrangements is, of course, very applicable to the other, non-market forms of exchange, where the issue is again whether the institutional arrangements formed an incentive for effort, and whether they aligned private and public benefits, and thus stimulated growth.

This approach should be applied not only to the emerging commodity market, which is now at the centre of historiographical attention,[12] but also to the markets for land, labour, and capital, which have received comparatively little notice in recent years.[13] Their neglect is surprising because they determine to a large extent the opportunities for investment, specialization, and accumulation, and hence play a crucial role in development. In contrast to the markets for goods and products, which developed rapidly from the high Middle Ages, factor markets were much more restricted, insecure, inflexible, and inaccessible. This is because they were embedded in social organizations and were ruled by non-economic motives, even well into the early modern period. Only very slowly did the factor markets become more open, favourable, and secure, in a process that showed marked regional differences which had a profound effect on economic and social development.

The new institutional approach is applied, for instance, in the recent investigation of the role of emerging markets for land, labour, capital, and goods in late medieval Holland.[14] The investigation analyses how exchange was performed within a very specific institutional framework, and shows that this indeed formed a crucial element in the efficiency, growth, and economic effect of transactions. More important, it also shows how closely the institutions are linked to the people, interest groups, and organizations which shaped the rules, applied them, and enforced their observance. The emergence of this framework was clearly linked

---

[12] Examples of fruitful approaches are those by Britnell, *The commercialisation of English society*, and Epstein, 'Regional fairs, institutional innovation'.

[13] An attempt to balance this is: Van Bavel, De Moor, and Van Zanden (eds.), *Factor markets*.

[14] 'Power, markets and economic development: the rise, organization and institutional framework of markets in Holland, 11th–16th centuries', research project at Utrecht University, 2001–2007.

to the power relations among interest groups, creating great differences among regions.[15] Up to now this social element has not been sufficiently integrated in the institutional economic approach. The same applies to the role of the state, or more generally, to the public authorities that shaped these institutions, at local, regional, and national levels. The high and late medieval process of state formation, and the formation and development of public bodies in general, and its specific nature, thus becomes a principal element for understanding the genesis and further development of institutional arrangements and their effect on exchange.[16] This also brings into the picture the degree of representation of social groups in public bodies, as well as the social power behind these processes of state formation and the increasing influence of authorities. These again are part of the principal explanation of the regional differences observed.

Concentrating on the link between social power and the institutional organization of exchange thus promises to reveal more insightful explanations than do the current descriptive commercialization models. It brings social structure to the fore as a main factor for understanding differences in development. Which social groups were able to influence or shape institutional arrangements in the region in question? And which groups used this institutional organization, with an often divergent effect on economic and social development? Robert Brenner made a clear contribution by pointing out geographical differences in class relations, based on and expressed in social property systems, and showing their divergent effect on economic development. He also drew attention to structural changes in social property systems, as in the rise of agrarian capitalism, and the geographical differences this process shows.[17] By linking the analysis of these structural processes to the insights offered by the New Institutional Economics, a clearer idea can be gained of how these social differences influenced the institutional organization of exchange and shaped the path of economic development.

If the causes of the divergences in economic and social development indeed are mainly to be found in the social and institutional structures of the area in question—lending demographic, ecological, commercial, and technological elements their specific, often divergent effect—we still need to establish where these geographical differences in social structure originated. This issue has not been satisfactorily addressed yet, but study of the Low Countries can help to clarify this matter. First, by showing that it is not the larger national entities but regions which are the relevant geographical units for understanding long-term economic and social development. Aggregative studies at a national level obscure relevant developments and obstruct sound analysis. As recently as the mid-19th century,

---

[15] Cf. for instance: Zuijderduijn, *Medieval capital markets?*, and Van Bavel, 'The emergence and growth of short-term leasing' and 'The land market'.

[16] Epstein, *Freedom and growth*, esp. 6–9. On a local, urban level: Gelderblom, 'The decline of fairs'.

[17] Brenner, 'The agrarian roots of European capitalism', and Thoen, 'Transitie en economische ontwikkeling'.

the region was the most important unit of economic change, and the regional context was far more significant in determining economic development than was the national context.[18] It is, therefore, at this level that the relevant factors must primarily be sought, identified, and analysed.

Second, the evidence from the Low Countries indicates the origin of the regional differences. These differences were clearly present in the 16th century, and many persisted into the 19th century, but their roots can generally be traced back far into the Middle Ages. Many of the socio-economic regions are characterized by specific soil conditions and occupation history, as, for example, the Guelders river area, with its fertile river clay soils which were occupied by large landholders in the early Middle Ages, or the peatland of Holland, which was reclaimed and occupied by peasants only in the 11th to 13th centuries. Similar differences in soil, occupation, and social structure can be observed in Flanders, with its clear dichotomy between the coastal part, consisting of sea clay soils, and the inland part, with its infertile sandy-loamy soils. Here, and in many other cases, there were clear socio-economic boundaries among the regions, coinciding with differences in soil and occupation history. We will investigate the possible link among these elements, but it can at least be presumed that the process of occupation was crucial to the emergence of regional differences, and hence constituted a formative or creative phase.

The book will thus contribute to better integrating the medieval period into the discussion about economic growth and social change. Placing emphasis only on the centuries immediately before the rise of factory industry has often hindered the emergence of a long-term perspective. In those few cases where the medieval period has been integrated into a larger analysis, it is often done in a very cursory way, as by Landes,[19] despite the critical importance he attaches to this period. Still, a significant amount of research in recent years has improved opportunities for a better integration of the Middle Ages. There are now increasing numbers of long-term series of data for wages, prices, population numbers, urbanization ratios, and even income levels, some covering the entire period 1000–1800, or at least large parts of it. These series are available, for instance, for England (1209–1869) and Italy (1000–2000).[20] A long-term perspective has also been brought closer by our new understanding of social and economic developments in the high Middle Ages. Again, the main example is England. Investigations into the processes of commercialization, monetization, and specialization have highlighted the crucial changes in the period 1000–1300.[21] It has also become clear that England then saw a rapid growth of market institutions and physical

---

[18] Cf. for the 18th and early 19th century, Hudson, 'The regional perspective'.

[19] Landes, *The wealth and poverty of nations*, 29–59.

[20] For instance Clark, 'The long march', 97–135, Federico and Malanima, 'Progress, decline, growth', and Malanima, 'Urbanisation and the Italian economy'.

[21] Britnell, 'Commercialisation and economic development', and for institutions also: Campbell, 'Factor markets'.

infrastructure. This knowledge has opened up the possibility of an analytical investigation of the link between the high Middle Ages and 'modern' growth, but only a few authors have made such an attempt. Among these few is Brenner, who links medieval manorial structures to possible transitions of the rural economy in the early modern period and the eventual emergence of industrial capitalism, contrasting the experiences of England and France in these respects. Persson applies the concept of self-sustained economic growth to the Middle Ages and uses the results to present the Industrial Revolution as the culmination of earlier technological development.[22]

For the Low Countries—often hailed as the principal example of pre-industrial economic growth—attempts to integrate the medieval past into the debate have been even scarcer. The grand international studies often discuss only Flanders in the late Middle Ages and Holland in the 16th and 17th centuries, that is, two smaller parts of the Low Countries at the height of their achievements.[23] Also, more specific studies concerning Holland mainly concentrate on its golden age and look for the causes of its economic prosperity in this period.[24] An exception is the work of Jan Luiten van Zanden, who pointed out the possible link between medieval and early modern developments in Holland. Otherwise, even those authors who acknowledge or suggest that the foundation of the exceptional development of Holland was laid in Middle Ages, do not discuss this period,[25] and therefore do not analytically link its medieval history to its later period of prosperity and dominance.

The task of integrating the medieval Low Countries fully into the international debate on the causes of pre-industrial growth and change, and giving it the prominent position it deserves in this debate, is perhaps hindered by the language barrier. Up-to-date overviews of the social and economic history of the medieval Low Countries are lacking,[26] and many studies are available only in Dutch. The present book aims to fill this gap by incorporating the new insights provided by more recent research.

I.3. APPROACH AND OUTLINE

We plan to integrate the results from this recent research on Belgian and Dutch economic and social history into a new, coherent framework of analysis, centred

---

[22] Brenner, 'The agrarian roots of European capitalism', and Persson, *Pre-industrial economic growth*, 135–140.

[23] For instance: Arrighi, *The long twentieth century*, 43–47 and 127–144, or Landes, *The wealth and poverty of nations*, 137–149.

[24] Israel, *Dutch Republic*, 307–315, but for an alternative approach Van Zanden, *The rise and decline*, 19–35, and Van Bavel and Van Zanden, 'The jump-start'.

[25] De Vries and Van der Woude, *The first modern economy*, 159, asserting that this would be entering a terrain 'where quantification is useless and convincing demonstrations are difficult'.

[26] The only overview for the Low Countries as a whole is Van Houtte's *An Economic History of the Low Countries 800–1800*, first published in 1964 in Dutch, and published in English in 1977.

on the thesis that the regional social structures developed in the early and high Middle Ages exercised a determining influence on later development, resulting in distinct paths of regional development.[27] The Low Countries offer ample material for this regional approach. Despite their small area, covering only some 75,000 km^2, they were not a homogeneous unit with respect to economic and social developments. We will first investigate the possible geographical elements in this regional diversity. The variety of landscapes in this part of Europe is huge, probably because of the continuous influence of the sea and rivers in this delta area, and the related geographical dynamics, possibly even enhanced as a result of the intense interaction between landscape and people.[28] We will try to assess to what extent distinct geographical regions in the Low Countries emerged out of this process, and will investigate whether the process of occupation and reclamation, and the creation of man-made landscapes, also resulted in a regional diversity in social systems.

Most parts of the Low Countries were occupied in the early and high Middle Ages, after the post-Roman population low of the 5th to 6th centuries. Because of the huge variety of landscapes, there were clear differences in the timing, method, and organization of reclamation and occupation. In this formative period, an initial distribution of rights to land, labour, and other resources was made, and increasingly also a social and institutional framework for levies, barter, and trade developed. This process will be investigated to assess whether each of these regions developed a distinct social structure, founded on a specific distribution of property rights, and each having its own institutional organization. If so, the interaction between landscape and people in the Low Countries would have resulted in a great regional diversity of social systems—a diversity which often overlapped geographical distinctions. This also offers an opportunity to investigate whether the resulting regional mix of soil, social property systems, and institutional organization exercised a fundamental influence on the path of further development, perhaps even to the beginning of the modern era, and thus to assess the degree of path-dependency at a regional level.

If so, the distinct structure of these regions and its influence on later developments was primarily rural, based on the ownership and exploitation of the land. Therefore, close attention will be paid to social patterns of land ownership, exploitation of land ownership, and the development of agriculture, which was by far the most important sector in the medieval economy. A knowledge of the changes taking place in the countryside in this period is necessary to understand the development of the economy and society, including the rise of trade, industry, and cities. Contemporary changes in the primary sector enabled the development of trade and cities in some parts of the Low Countries, particularly

[27] The terms early, high, and late Middle Ages will be used here to roughly designate the periods 5th to mid-9th centuries, mid-9th to 12th centuries, and 13th to 16th centuries, respectively.
[28] See sections II.1, pp. 25–26, and II.2, pp. 32–34 and 44–50.

in the high Middle Ages. We will investigate to what extent this development and its specific nature were determined by the power and property structures of the region. This applies to the nature of cities and to town–countryside relationships—which differed greatly from region to region—and especially to the social and institutional framework for levies, barter, and trade that developed in this period.

Once this framework was in place, it probably showed strong continuity over the centuries, precisely because it was associated with social positions of power. To test this assumption, we will investigate whether dominant groups in society—whether manorial lords or urban merchants—indeed showed an interest in preserving the existing institutional framework, even when economic circumstances changed and this interest started to hinder further development. When was it possible for institutional change to occur? Was it most likely to happen when a power balance existed between various social groups? We may be able to glean this from what took place when the manorial lords in several regions switched to short-term leasing in the 13th and 14th centuries. These lords were strong enough to retain or even strengthen their control over the land, but perhaps not powerful enough to shackle the peasants or force them to accept unfavourable conditions. This situation opened the way to free, contractual leasing, which was the key to the rise of a dynamic lease market and the rapid development of the rural economy in these regions in the later Middle Ages.[29] In this case, change was possible, enabled by the balanced social relations that existed in the region, and further building on them. If this example can be generalized, the institutional sclerosis and stagnation found in many parts of pre-industrial Europe may thus be at least partly attributed to the absence of such a social balance. In this study we will test whether such a power balance existed in the Low Countries, preventing sclerosis and leading instead to relatively strong development and growth.

By taking a very long-term view, as this study will do, it is possible to determine whether there was scope for flexibility and adaptation, how tenacious the social-institutional framework was, and to what extent it determined the further possibilities for the development of markets, specialization, and economic growth. We will investigate, through regional cases from the Low Countries, to what extent this social structure and framework, which emerged mainly in the early and high Middle Ages, influenced social and economic development over the long term, or even set the boundaries which contained the scope for development, and whether this resulted in regional path dependency. Even if this is the case, it does not mean that economic development occurred solely within the boundaries of the region, nor that national differences in long-term economic development are entirely and directly attributable to additions of regional differences. It is also necessary to see whether the rapid development of

[29] See section V.1, pp. 170–178. Cf. also Van Bavel, 'Leasing'.

the economy of the Low Countries was the result of the successful and probably increasing interaction among these regions with their distinct structures.

We suggest that two elements stimulated this successful interaction. First, if the indirect link between these socio-economic structures and soil conditions holds, and the number of distinct regions in the medieval Low Countries was indeed exceptionally high, these regions with their sharply divergent structures were located much closer to one another than were regions in other parts of Europe. Second, the regional interaction could be facilitated by the absence of strong economic barriers. If so, political unity has played only a modest role, since the Low Countries comprised many independent principalities which in the later Middle Ages were only slowly integrated into the Burgundian-Habsburg Empire.[30] More likely to promote interaction was the rise of open, flexible markets, possibly the result of an equilibrium among a multitude of political powers at all the different levels of society.[31] Linked with this is the question whether the Low Countries experienced the early disappearance of non-economic coercion and to what extent this contributed to economic integration. Finally, we will need to assess whether all these elements had a favourable effect on economic development. Did the Low Countries, and its regional economies, indeed experience exceptional growth? And what qualitative changes did economy and society undergo in this period? Did economic growth lead to higher standards of living for the majority of the people, or was such a possible effect eroded by the negative side-effects of growth? Even if such developments were relatively favourable, we do not aim to advocate some kind of 'Low Countries exceptionalism'. Our main focus is not on comparing the Low Countries with other parts of Europe, but on comparing and explaining the development of particular regions within the Low Countries.

Differences among regions in the Low Countries were significant, and increased even further in the later Middle Ages. Integration played a large role in this, since it led to intense competition among the regions and to a great deal of regional specialization. In this process, the strongest growth probably took place in those regions which offered the most favourable social and institutional frameworks in the economic circumstances of the period. These regions would economically surpass the other ones, even those whose framework had been conducive to economic growth in earlier phases, particularly when attempts to change with economic circumstances were frustrated there by special interest groups, which led to institutional sclerosis.

The process could be expected to result in significant shifts in the economic core in the Low Countries in the course of the medieval period. We will investigate whether such shifts have indeed taken place. At first sight it seems that they did. In the early Middle Ages, the regions along the main rivers, the Meuse and the Rhine, took the economic lead, and this was especially true for

---

[30] Blockmans, 'Voracious states'.   [31] To be investigated in Chapter V.

the Guelders river area and the Meuse valley, which were the core regions of the Carolingian Empire. In the high Middle Ages, the economic core shifted to southern Flanders and later, increasingly to inland Flanders. In the later Middle Ages, Flanders lost its leadership to Brabant and then to Holland. Holland is especially interesting in this context, since it developed from a swampy, backward region in the 11th to 13th centuries to the centre of the world economy only a few centuries later.[32] Investigating and analysing the shifts in economic leadership in the Low Countries through a comparative analysis allows us to assess which socio-institutional mix was most favourable to economic growth in the circumstances prevailing at a particular time and what the underlying causes were for the emergence of this mix.

The search for the factors shaping the regional differences in social and economic development within the Low Countries will carry us far back in time, to the high and even the early Middle Ages. In most other studies dealing with the Low Countries, the focus is on the period of economic flourishing in the late Middle Ages and the early modern period, but economic development probably started much earlier and evolved more gradually than previously thought. This early emergence applies even more to the specific social structures and the institutional framework within which this development took place: these were already in place in the early and high Middle Ages when the particular region was occupied. The aim of the present study is therefore to examine the early and high Middle Ages intensively and to integrate this period into an analysis of the economic and social development of the Low Countries. We begin with the post-Roman population low in the 5th century (when many parts of the Low Countries were virtually deserted and then slowly reoccupied) and end our examination in the late 16th century, when the Dutch Revolt led to a political division between the south (the Austrian Low Countries, Belgium) and the north (the Dutch Republic, the Netherlands).

This study will not use the geographical framework of the Low Countries, let alone the framework of the later national states, Belgium and the Netherlands, in a teleological way, as if the birth of Belgium and the Netherlands were the natural outcome of developments. Rather, it will question the importance of this framework. Despite a certain geographical and traditional unity, the Low Countries are historically made up of a fairly accidental politico-dynastic assemblage of separate areas, cobbled together under the growing power of the Burgundian and Habsburg princes.[33] Moreover, the political assemblage was not completed until comparatively late, and enclaves and independent provinces such as Utrecht and Guelders lost their independence only in the 16th century. Under Emperor Charles V (1515–55), the core provinces did become more united, with some integration in political structure, legislation,

---

[32] Van Bavel and Van Zanden, 'The jump-start'.
[33] De Schepper, 'Die Einheit der Niederlanden'.

and written language, but this integration was never complete or universal. All the local and provincial privileges, laws, and fiscal systems were only partly unified by the Habsburgs, and the short period of integration had already ended in 1568–72 with the Dutch Revolt, bringing a new political rupture.

This regional diversity was even more apparent in economic and social respects, and it increased in the 16th century. As a result of the growing integration and interaction, regional specialization increased greatly, and differences among the regions became even more pronounced. There were interactions with regions outside the Low Countries also. Provinces in the east of the Netherlands, such as Guelders and Overijssel, were very much oriented towards the Rhineland and Cologne. Those in the north, such as Groningen, had ties with the north of Germany and the Hanseatic cities. Flanders had strong economic links with Artois, Picardy, and the north of France. So there is every reason not to view the Low Countries as a sealed box.

This study will not cover all topics exhaustively, but rather will focus on the main themes and the long-term developments. It will emphasize those elements considered essential, either as expressions or as causes of economic growth and social change. Nor will this book be exhaustive geographically, but each main theme will be illustrated by a number of representative regional cases. To develop the main lines of the argument, we will highlight the developments in selected regions: the Meuse valley (showing strong development in the early Middle Ages), inland Flanders (highly urbanized, with strong development in the 11th to 14th centuries), Holland (also highly urbanized, with strong development in the 14th to 16th centuries), Drenthe and the Campine (two agrarian peasant areas), and the Guelders river area (an agrarian area where manorial organization was dominant). These regions are relatively well-investigated, and they are representative of the main types of social and economic regimes in the Low Countries. In a way they represent a *pars pro toto* for all of western Europe, and thus are an appropriate tool for comparative analysis. This will offer a way to identify the main determinants of development, which operated mainly at a regional level.

The book thus aims to offer a new analysis of the social and economic history of the medieval Low Countries. It is based on recent studies, but also integrates and develops new theoretical insights, which will be evident from its regional approach, the analysis of the interactions among people, land, and water, and the emphasis on the specific property and power structures and the associated institutional framework. Covering a period of more than a thousand years will allow us to assess how these structures shaped and determined later social and economic developments within a mainly regional framework or even along a regional path. The focus on the socio-institutional organization will help in understanding the wide differences in the application of knowledge and techniques, as well as explaining how the developments in climate, demography, and ecology were able to have sharply divergent effects on economic and social development. Through a systematic comparison of very different regions in the Low Countries, we hope to identify fundamental causes rather than simply to describe apparent characteristics of regional development.

II

The Emergence of a Regional Framework in the Early and High Middle Ages: Land and Occupation

II.1. LANDSCAPE AND SOIL

The Low Countries are located in north-western Europe, with the northern German plain to the east, the fringes of the central European uplands to the south-east, the Parisian basin to the south, and the North Sea to the west and north. The subsoil of this area slopes from the Ardennes Massif to the north-west. At the end of the Saale Glacial, the second-last Ice Age, glaciers from the north pushed up sand and gravel, and created ridges, especially in the central zone of the present-day Netherlands. During the last Ice Age, large parts of the Low Countries were covered with aeolian deposits, namely sand, sandy loam, and loess. At the coast, sand barriers were formed, and peat moors developed behind them, but these were partly swept away again by the sea or covered by sea clay. This area was traversed by three of the largest rivers of western Europe, the Rhine, the Meuse, and the Scheldt, flowing into the North Sea and depositing alluvial material. This genesis, combined with the dynamic influence of the large rivers and the sea, created a marked variety in landscapes.

Despite their relatively small size of some 75,000 km^2, the Low Countries thus have a varied geographic mosaic. To some extent the mild maritime climate is also varied. Although the climate is characterized by cool summers and mild winters, and with rainfall fairly evenly spread between seasons,[1] there are nevertheless clear climatic differences, particularly between the coastal and the inland areas. The differences are much more pronounced for wind velocity and rainfall than for temperature. The upland region of the Ardennes, with a modified continental climate, has much more precipitation: 100–150 mm per month on average, which is twice as much as most other parts of the Low Countries. It also has the sharpest fluctuations in temperature between seasons: there are 110 frost days per year and the snow cover lasts much longer. These differences have a clear effect

---

[1] Können, *Het weer in Nederland*, 40–43, 51–53, and 75, and *De toestand van het klimaat*.

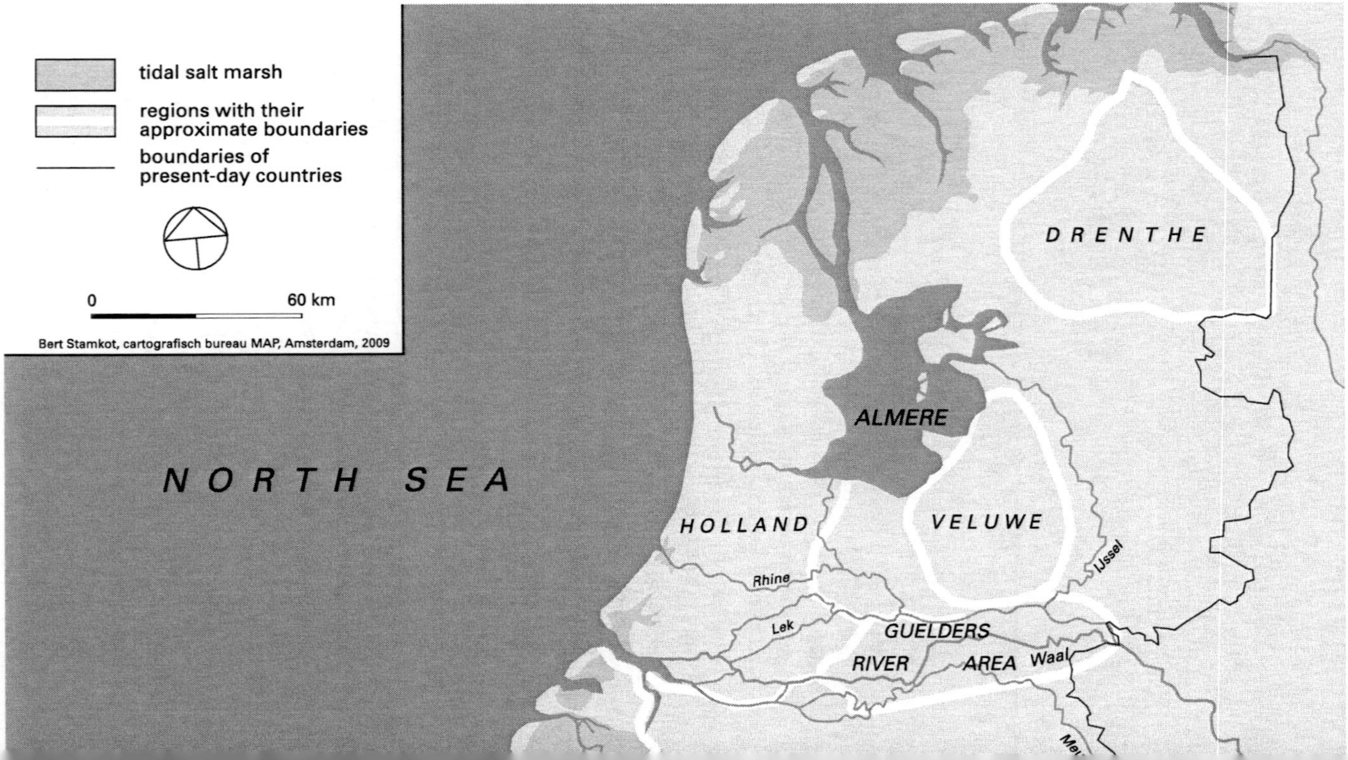
tidal salt marsh
regions with their approximate boundaries
boundaries of present-day countries
0
60 km
Bert Stamkot, cartografisch bureau MAP, Amsterdam, 2009
NORTH SEA
DRENTHE
ALMERE
HOLLAND
VELUWE
IJssel
Rhine
Lek
GUELDERS
RIVER
AREA
Waal

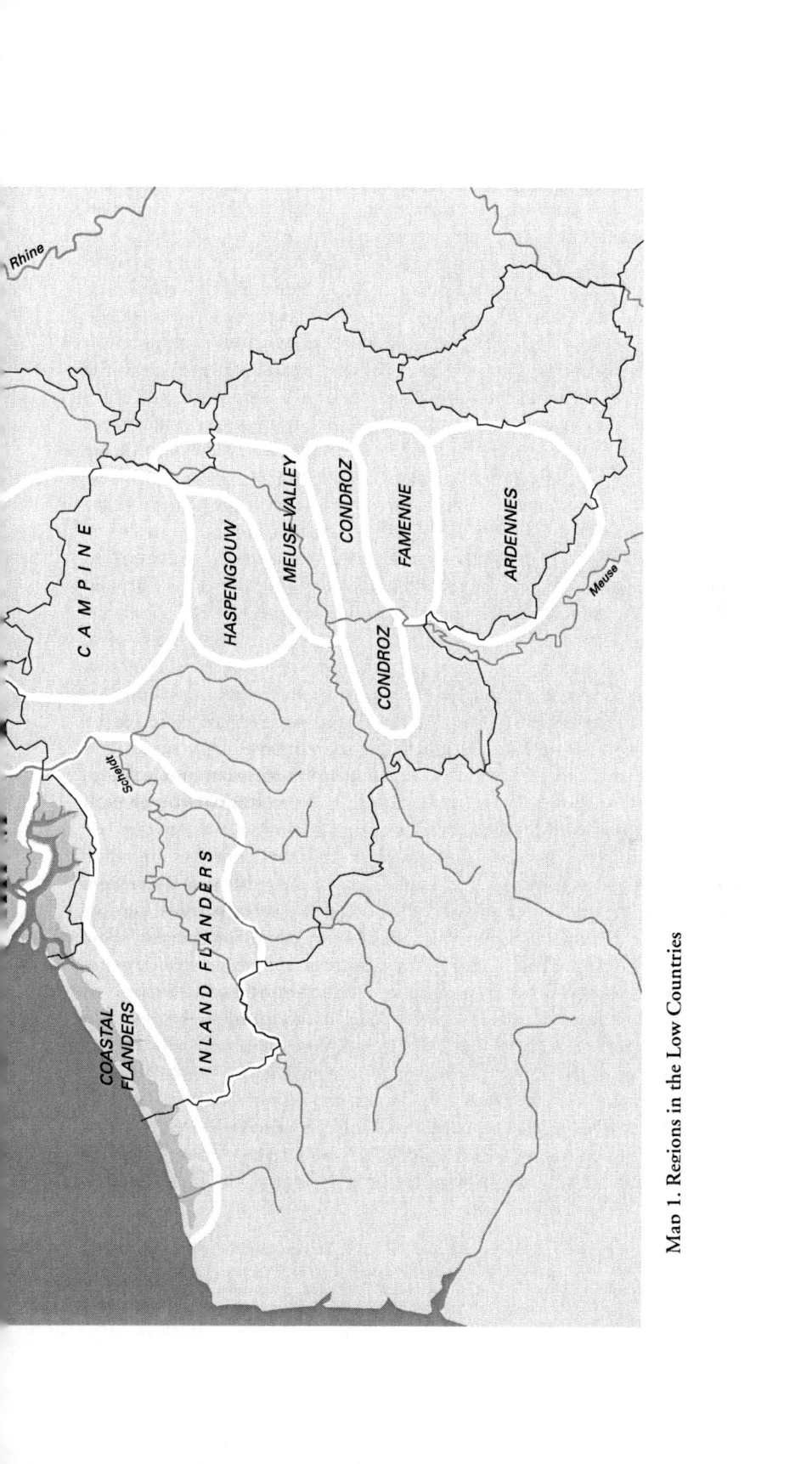

Map 1. Regions in the Low Countries

on potential crops: the growing season is shorter by at least a month and hardly any cultivation of aftercrops is possible.

The climate was not uniform over the entire period of the Middle Ages, but underwent changes, which can be reconstructed from written documents and grain price movements, as well as from pollen analysis and tree ring research. There was a cold period from the late Roman era until the 10th century, followed by a warmer period with mild winters, few temperature extremes, and moderate rainfall starting in the late 11th to 12th centuries. This 'medieval optimum' was followed in the 14th century by a worsening of the climate as a prelude to the Little Ice Age, and the period of cooling reached one of its climaxes around 1600.[2] The late medieval period was characterized by increasingly severe windstorms and sea floods, increasing precipitation, and cooler temperatures. The Little Ice Age averaged almost 1° C lower than the high Middle Ages or the present. These changes had a pronounced effect on agriculture, by far the most important sector of the medieval economy. The precise effects differed from area to area. The growing incidence of storm floods was, of course, most detrimental to the coastal areas, as on the Flemish coast in the second half of the 16th century.[3] The cold most affected the Ardennes, with its already short growing season. But the effects of climate change should not be overemphasized. Not only were the climate fluctuations relatively small, but, more importantly, their effects were not as unilinear and clear as was once thought. They do not explain why developments varied so much among regions: some coastal regions were severely affected by storms and loss of land, and others much less so. Human intervention, and the regional differences in this, which varied according to social organization, played a large part, as shown below (in Section II.2). Straightforward ecological determinism does not work for the Low Countries.

Geographical differences among the regions in the Low Countries are much more pronounced than differences in climate. Despite the small area, differences in soil and landscape are very great. In contrast to many other parts of Europe, where such differences are mainly a permanent or slowly changing element, some of these characteristics have been strikingly dynamic over the last millennia, partly as a result of natural causes, but even more as intended or unintended results of human actions. The interaction between man and nature, further elaborated in the next section, and the natural dynamics in this delta area were very strong, particularly because of the impact of the large rivers and the sea.

The major influence of the rivers and the sea can be observed most clearly in the western, coastal area. The coasts of Holland, Zeeland, and Flanders are protected from the sea by a narrow belt of sand dunes. Around 3000 to 2400 BC, after a rise in sea level in the preceding millennia, the beach barriers

---

[2] Lamb, *Climate, history*, 165–167, 172–182, and 191–199, Buisman and Engelen, *Duizend jaar weer, wind en water*, i, 594–603 and ii, 629–641; and Grove, *Little Ice Ages*, 591–631.

[3] De Kraker, 'A method to assess the impact of high tides', 287–302.

stabilized at their present position. A row of sand banks gradually rose above sea level, and this barrier became covered by sand dunes. But even after this formation, changes and shifts occurred. Starting around 1000 AD, increasingly more sand was deposited, some of it from the older dunes. The movement was caused by erosion, the combined result of an increasing storm frequency, and long-lasting drought, but mainly by cutting and removing trees in the dune area, intensified grazing, and the destructive work of the rabbits introduced there. In the course of the process much steeper dunes were formed, up to 50 m high.[4]

Behind this strip of dunes, the coastal areas consisted mostly of extensive flat peatlands, which were developed particularly in the period from the Atlanticum onwards (from 7,000 BC), as climate conditions changed and the water table started to rise in these poorly drained areas, greatly stimulating peat accumulation.[5] This changed again in the Roman era, as the dynamism of the rivers accelerated, resulting in increased clay sedimentation, which ended the peat formation. In the Middle Ages, the sea started to break through the Zeeland coast as a result of peat digging, salt production, and land reclamation, all of which weakened the peat soils. The incursions of the sea, at different places in different stages, but intensifying from the 13th century onwards, destroyed most of the peatlands in Zeeland, northern Flanders, and the north-west of Brabant, replacing them with sand, silt, and clay, or covering the peatlands, or washing them away.[6] Of all the lowland peat areas, those in Holland remained most untouched and intact, protected by the strength of the dunes; only in some places were they covered by strips of river clay deposited by the rivers.

Palynological research has enabled reconstruction of the vegetation that existed in the peat areas before the medieval reclamations. In the peat fens, where the peat was below the water table, the vegetation consisted mainly of water lilies, bulrush, and reeds. In the shallow waters there was also reed mace and sedge, and on the dry parts of the marsh forest willow and alder.[7] After reclamation, marked pedological changes occurred in the peat areas, particularly the fens. The arduous task of reclamation initially seemed to be worthwhile in a region well suited for agriculture. However, as will be discussed more extensively in the next section, after reclamation, peatlands start to oxidize as a result of being drained and become compressed. In the centuries following reclamation there was ongoing subsidence of the soil and increasing difficulties with groundwater. Here, too, a strong dynamism can be observed.

---

[4] Beets and Van der Spek, 'The Holocene evolution of the barrier', 3–16, and Jelgersma et al., 'The coastal dunes', esp. 94–102 and 130–132.

[5] Pons, 'Holocene peat formation', and Berendsen, *De vorming van het land,* 139–141, 189, and figs on 166 and 180.

[6] Leenders, *Verdwenen venen,* 287–306, and Cleveringa et al., "So grot overvlot der watere". For the human influence in this process, see section II.2, pp. 45–48 and VII.1, p. 342.

[7] Braams, *Weyden en zeyden,* 34–37.

The sea clay areas witnessed an even more violent genesis and pronounced dynamism, from the action of the sea. In these areas the peat was largely swept away by the sea or covered with sea clay in the medieval period. In Zeeland, as a result of the incursions of the sea, a new part of the Dutch delta was formed. In the post-Roman era, the sea invaded this area with force, forming various new, broad estuaries, such as the Zwin, the Ijzer, and in particular the Scheldt river. The Westerschelde was formed from the 9th century onwards as a new branch of the Scheldt between Walcheren and Flanders,[8] making the Scheldt tidal. This led to a considerable widening of the river, as far upstream as near Antwerp. The whole of Zeeland, and to a lesser extent also the coastal part of Flanders, became subject to the influence of the water, except for the narrow strip of dunes and some stream ridges. A huge salt marsh area developed there: a landscape of saltings intersected by meandering creeks and tidal inlets. On the lowest-lying parts, which were flooded by each high tide, the vegetation consisted almost solely of glasswort. The frequently flooded lowest marshes had a vegetation of mainly sea poa, and the higher parts, which flooded only with spring tide or storm surge, contained thrift, sea milkwort, and salt-marsh rush, which was also found in the coastal areas in the north. This vegetation is ideal for cattle grazing.

The northern part of the Low Countries saw the development of a huge inland sea, the Zuiderzee, which was formed as recently as the high Middle Ages. Around 2300 BC, the then inland sea had been sealed off from the North Sea, followed by massive peat formation. In those peatlands some lakes were gradually formed, and they merged into one large lake around the start of our era. This lake, called Mare Flevo in Roman sources, was connected to the North Sea by a small stream. Around 800 AD a wider connection, the Marsdiep, developed, which became ever larger, allowing the sea to intrude more forcefully into this lake, pushed inward by several storm surges, particularly in the 12th and 13th centuries.[9] In the course of this process, large parts of the remaining peat were washed away. The destruction of the landscape led to an increasing enlargement of the Zuiderzee, developing an open connection to the North Sea, with the water becoming increasingly brackish and even saline.

Water played an important role in the formation of the landscape in the river clay areas as well. The upper courses of the Scheldt and Meuse rivers showed only small changes, and the rivers there had less influence on the surrounding landscapes, mainly because the subsoil, consisting of loam, stony loams, sandstone, and slate, did not erode as quickly. But further downstream the influence of the rivers was more pronounced. In addition to the smaller strips of river clay land along the Scheldt and Meuse rivers and a broader strip in Salland

---

[8] Augustyn, *Zeespiegelrijzing*, 191 and 204; and Vos and Van Heeringen, 'Holocene geology and occupation history', 76–78.
[9] Gottschalk, *Stormvloeden*, 80–94 (storm surge of 1170), 121–126 (1196), 174–186 (1248), and 194–197. Compare with the situation in the Roman era: Zagwijn et al., *Atlas van Nederland*, part 13, map 73.

along the IJssel river, the largest river clay area is in the Guelders river area, which is transected by the Rhine and Meuse and several of their arms. The rivers had a decisive role in the formation of landscape and soil in this area, although the sea's influence was increasingly important further west.[10] The restraining effect of the inflowing flood water and the smaller gradient of the rivers in this peri-marine area caused the rivers there to become wide, sluggish, and tidal.

The beds of these rivers were not at all static, with new branches continuously forming and deserted river beds becoming silted up. Especially in the western peri-marine parts of the Guelders river area, avulsions were frequent during the earlier Holocene. The C14-method shows that particularly in the late Roman era drastic changes occurred to the pattern of almost all rivers in this area.[11] This was probably related to the destruction of forests in the catchment areas of rivers and brooks upstream, which caused higher peaks in water discharges and greater river dynamism.[12] There may also be a relationship between the frequency of these riverbed shifts and the sea transgressions, i.e. periods of rising sea levels resulting in an increasing influence of the sea. In this case, these shifts would be related to the beginning of the Dunkirk II transgressive phase, from the late 3rd to 6th centuries. But this relationship is more difficult to assess. Moreover, the earlier rectilinear arguments about transgressions and their rigid periodization, once popular among geographers, are now contested.[13] It now seems that the transgressions date from various periods, and their influence seems to have been a complex process that did not evolve synchronously in the various parts of the Low Countries as a result of the differing geographical circumstances and human intervention. Moreover, the impact of incidental storm surges is now rated as greater than that of assumed general transgressions.

The most important avulsions in this period are those of the Lek and Waal rivers, two arms of the Rhine. The present Lek, for instance, developed only around the beginning of our era, or even somewhat later, when it broke through the Hagestein stream ridge; it greatly increased in importance in the course of the early Middle Ages.[14] Older beds of the Rhine ceased to be active in about the same period. The IJssel River, which had initially only been the lower course of a few small brooks, became a branch of the Rhine in the first century BC, either by a natural breach or by human intervention. Perhaps its formation was the result of a deliberate intervention by Drusus, stepson of Emperor Augustus, who was commander of the Roman Army in Gaul and undertook several military expeditions in this area. According to Tacitus, in

---

[10] Berendsen, *De vorming van het land*, 130, 167–169, and figure on 180.
[11] Törnqvist, *Fluvial sedimentary geology and chronology*, 131–163, and Stouthamer, *Holocene avulsions*, 67–68 and 97–98.
[12] Janssen, ' "Landnahme" and "Landesausbau" ', 181–190.
[13] Gottschalk, 'Subatlantische transgressiefasen en stormvloeden', and Augustyn, *Zeespiegelrijzing*, 191 and 204.
[14] Henderikx, 'De Lek en de Hollandse IJsel', and Berendsen, *De genese*, 183–185.

12 BC he ordered the construction of a canal connecting the Rhine with the Flevo lake to the north. This *Fossa Drusiana* would thus, at least according to some geographers, have constituted the artificial beginning of the upper course of the present IJssel.[15]

So, in the areas transected by the lower courses of the Rhine, Meuse, and Scheldt rivers, covering perhaps a tenth of the Low Countries, the dynamism in the landscape was very pronounced. In the Guelders river area in particular the soil was shaped by the activity and sedimentation of the rivers; not only by big avulsions but also by regular inundation. Until river dikes were constructed in the 11th and 12th centuries,[16] at high-water discharges the water ran freely over the land, leading to deposits of material. The coarser material carried by the river, namely sand and silt, was deposited closest to the river bed, forming sandy ridges. The water that sedimented further away from the river bed contained only fine particles of clay, forming the heavy low-lying backlands or flood basins. This process created the pattern of high stream ridges and low backlands so characteristic of the river clay areas. The pronounced differences in height and soil lent sharply differing features to the stream ridges and the backlands. The backlands are not only low-lying, but as a result of the heaviness of the clay, their compact texture, and absence of sand they are also impervious to water, which often makes them marshy. The stream ridges, on the other hand, are relatively high and well drained on account of their sandier soils. The natural vegetation, which can be reconstructed from palynological research, thus shows clear differences.[17] Before the reclamations in the Roman era, the stream ridges were probably overgrown with oak, beech, hazelnut, elm, and ash, while in the zone between ridges and backlands mainly willow, alder, and ash could be found, and in the lowest backlands there were willow, sedge, reed, bulrush, and reed mace.

A completely different picture emerges for the sandy regions, such as the Veluwe, the Campine region, the Achterhoek, and Drenthe. These were split by the Rhine, IJssel, and Meuse into four separate 'islands', separated by the large rivers and their deposits, which gave each its individual characteristics. They had in common, however, their infertile soils, classified among the poorest in Europe. Not only were the soils very poor in minerals, but also the hydrologic situation was unfavourable, with most land being either too dry or too wet.[18] Large parts of the Campine have a substratum of clay covered with sand, making these parts waterlogged, with the water accumulated on the impermeable clay layer. The

[15] This topic is hotly debated among geologists, archaeologists, and historians. Cf. Teunissen, 'Enkele gebeurtenissen', 321–334, and the ensuing debate between J. E. Bogaers, J. N. B. Poelman, D. Teunissen, and W. J. H. Willems in *Westerheem* 30 (1981).

[16] Cf. below, section II.2, pp. 42–43.

[17] Cf. Braams, *Weyden en zeyden*, 34–37, and Teunissen, *Palynologisch onderzoek in het oostelijk rivierengebied*.

[18] E. Paulissen, *Belgische Kempen*, and Spek, *Het Drentse esdorpenlandschap*, 178–203.

higher parts on the Campine plateau have a cover of some 10 m of sand and gravel, making this an arid area.

The landscape of the Veluwe was mainly formed during the last ice ages. In the penultimate ice age, glaciers penetrated the region from the north and pushed sand and gravel forwards and sideways, resulting in lateral moraines of considerable height, sometimes over 100 m.[19] In the last ice age, the ice sheet did not reach this area, but the climate was so cold that vegetation was almost completely lacking there. The wind had free play, and wind-blown sand was deposited widely. Only gradually did these coarse sands, with their low water-table, become covered again by poor woodland, with oak or beech, and also some linden, hazel, ash, and elm.[20] In the millennia before the present era, these forests were reduced by cutting and burning, and in parts gave way to heather vegetation. In the high Middle Ages, the remaining forest and heather were further affected by human activity, giving drift sands the opportunity to develop and grow further. It is typical of the variety of landscapes in the Low Countries that this infertile sandy region of some 3,000 km² is surrounded by regions with completely different landscape and soil: the Guelders river area with its fertile clay soils directly to the south, the Holland fenlands to the west, the peat areas swallowed by the Zuiderzee to the north, and the river clay basin of the IJssel to the east. This is characteristic of the geographical variety of this part of Europe.

The southernmost part of the Dutch province of Limburg and particularly the adjacent Haspengouw in present-day Belgium consist of loess soils. The area is a north-western offshoot of a zone with areas of loess soils stretching from Normandy to the Ukraine and the edges of the Urals.[21] These are light soils, deposited by the wind, with a thickness in the Low Countries varying from 0 to 8 m. Loess soils are intrinsically very fertile, well drained, and have good water retention qualities, and their lightness of texture makes them easy to cultivate. Thus, they are among the finest agricultural soils of the Low Countries and western Europe, leading to very early occupation, with Haspengouw being one of the oldest cultivated areas of Europe.[22] The terrain in these loess regions is hilly, sometimes with sharp relief as a result of deep dissections made by streams and rivers.[23] Original vegetation on the loess plateaus consisted of oak and beech woods, and in the valleys and streams, of marshy alder woods.

Aeolian soils are also found further west, in Brabant, inland Flanders, and Artois. These soils, however, contain fewer nutrients than the loess soils to the east, and contain more sand, or sand and loam, particularly in inland Flanders, where natural soil fertility is generally fairly poor. The natural vegetation in

---

[19] Heidinga, *Medieval settlement*, 80–81.
[20] Koster, *De stuifzanden*, 25. For erosion in the later Middle Ages see section II.2, pp. 48–49.
[21] Koster, *The physical geography of western Europe*, 140 and 148–149.
[22] Bonenfant, *Civilisation préhistorique*, and Bodson, *L'évolution d'un paysage*.
[23] Segers, *Haspengouw*.

these areas consisted mainly of mixed oak and hornbeam forests, with some beech. In the past millennia, most of these forests degraded, with beech disappearing first. Some were reduced almost to nothing. The latter happened to the large Silva Carbonaria, a zone of forests stretching from the Sambre up to the Dijle Valley, some 50 km north.[24] After an interlude of recovery in the post-Roman period, this forest almost completely disappeared. The present-day Zoniënwoud, situated just south-east of Brussels, is its last main remnant.

The Ardennes, part of the secondary mountain range stretching from the Middle Rhine highlands over the Eifel to the north of France, cover the south-eastern part of the Low Countries. This area is broken up into several regions, with a great diversity of landscapes. The central parts, in particular the Hautes Fagnes or hohes Venn, near the present-day German border, consist of high, flat, wet peat bogs,[25] located 500–700 m above sea level, and form a clearly separate region. There, peat formation took place above the water table in an environment poor in nutrients; this oligotrophic peat was nourished only by rainwater, as was also the case with peat formation in Drenthe in the north. In these plateaus of raised bogs, which are linked to large similar areas to the east in present-day Germany, vegetation consisted mainly of birch, bell heather, bog moss, cotton grass, and sedge, and also some plantain, with hazel, beech, and hornbeam as the main trees. In the southern parts of the Hautes Fagnes, in the transition zone to the Ardennes, beech, hazel, willow, and alder were also important, with ferns and grasses as the main herbs.[26]

Most of the Ardennes, however, is not flat at all, but cut deeply by rivers and streams, and is very uneven. Most soils are shallow and acid, with little natural fertility. In the subsoil, often less than a metre below the cover of stony loam, are granite, some limestone, sandstone, and coal.[27] The coal deposits, part of a long range stretching from the Ruhr area to the north of France, crop out in the valleys of the Meuse and Sambre, as around Liège, offering great possibilities for mining. For agriculture, however, the hydrologic situation is often unfavourable, and soils are difficult to cultivate, consisting of up to 15 per cent rock fragments. Long periods of frost, snow cover, and heavy rainfall severely limit the growing season. Most of the land was covered by trees, with beech being the dominant species, but also some oak and alder.[28] In the Roman era, large parts of the forest were cut down, but after the fall of Roman authority and the dark centuries of chaos and depopulation, the woods returned. In the Middle Ages the Ardennes was by far the largest forest area in the Low Countries, although the wooded areas were not entirely unbroken, even in the early Middle Ages.[29] There were some

---

[24] Noël, 'Deux grandes forêts', 651–657.
[25] Slotboom, 'Comparative geomorphological and palynological investigation', 21–23.
[26] Couteaux, *Recherches palynologiques*, 30–33 and 55–60.
[27] Boulvain and Pingot, *Une introduction à la geologie de la Wallonie*, and Nemery, *La Famenne*.
[28] Couteaux, *Recherches palynologiques*, 55–60.   [29] Wickham, 'European forests', 175–179.

manors, houses, and clearings. The densest woodland was to be found where the forests were protected by royal legislation and, from the high Middle Ages onwards, were organized as a forest county (*comitatus nemoris*) to safeguard royal hunting privileges. In this region the forest remained much more intact than in other parts of the Ardennes.

The Low Countries, despite their small area, thus show a wide diversity of landscapes. This diversity cannot be reduced to a simple partition between Holocene and Pleistocene soils,[30] since the marked differences in lithology, soil fertility, hydrology, relief, and vegetation—elements connected with one another—resulted in much finer regional diversity. Extremes sometimes existed in adjacent areas. Some of the poorest soils in Europe (the sandy soils of Drenthe, the Veluwe, or the Campine area) are situated immediately alongside some of the finest (the loess soils of Haspengouw or the river clay soils of the Guelders river area).[31] Many of the major soils of Europe are represented there, often as an offshoot of a larger zone. Examples are the peat areas, which are part of a zone stretching from Denmark to Belgium; the loess soils, which are part of a zone stretching from the Ukraine to France; and the sand belt of cover sands, stretching from the Polish–Russian border to England.[32] The fact that these large zones all cross the relatively small area of the Low Countries is a main element in the regional diversity of the landscapes there.

Although comparative studies in this field are lacking, this regional diversity seems to have been more pronounced here than elsewhere in Europe. If this is true, an important factor must have been the influence of the sea, with no less than one-third of the Low Countries lying less than 5 m above sea level. The rivers, three of the largest ones of Europe, also caused strong geographical dynamism. The third main factor contributing to this diversity was the strong interaction among land, water, and the population, with human influence having profound effects on the landscape, as will become clear in the next section. This influence was probably greater than elsewhere in Europe because of the Low Countries' relatively high population densities and the vulnerability of the soils to human activity.

The result was a variety of fairly small regions, each homogeneous in landscape and soil, and each averaging 2,000 to 3,000 km² in size. These regions, as multi-dimensional units, sometimes had some common characteristics with neighbouring regions (such as climate), but more often not (soils), resulting in great regional diversity even between neighbouring areas. In the following section it will become apparent that these regional differences are also expressed in occupation history, social structures, and the organization of the rural economy. This makes the regional diversity even sharper and more apparent, and gives each

---

[30] As done, for instance, by De Vries and Van der Woude, *The first modern economy*, 11.
[31] Cf. for Belgium: Christians, 'Belgium's geographical mosaic'.
[32] Koster, *The physical geography of western Europe*, 139–149.

Table 2.1 Some regions in the Low Countries

Name	Soil	Area (km² approx.)	Political entity (late medieval)
The Campine	sandy	5,000	part of the former Duchy of Brabant
Inland Flanders	sandy loamy	4,000	part of the former County of Flanders
Coastal Flanders	sea clay	2,500	including present-day Dutch Zeeuws-Vlaanderen
The Haspengouw	loess	2,000	most of it part of the Prince-bishopric of Liège
Drenthe	sandy	2,500	part of the Oversticht
Guelders river area	river clay	2,500	part of the Duchy of Guelders plus the south-eastern part of the Nedersticht
Holland	peat	4,000	major part of the former County of Holland plus the western part of the Nedersticht
The Veluwe	sandy	3,000	part of the Duchy of Guelders plus the adjacent eastern part of the Nedersticht

region its own distinct character.[33] A crucial aspect in the economic development of the Low Countries is the size of these regions. In many parts of Europe, regions like these would be much larger, although comparisons are difficult, in part because of the different definitions of the term 'region'. The most similar are perhaps the 41 farming counties of England and Wales, amounting to 150,000 km² in total, i.e. almost 4,000 km² on average.[34] Bigger regions are probably found in the north of France and the north of Germany. In some parts of Europe perhaps much smaller micro-landscapes can be found, but their scale is mostly too small to be considered a socio-economic region. Rather, these micro-landscapes together formed one large region, as did the alternating stream ridges and the backlands in the Guelders river clay area, with these very different landscapes fulfilling a complementary role within the economic system. Together they formed a socio-economic unit, just like the stream valleys and the adjacent sandy soils in Drenthe or the Campine.

In total, some 20 to 25 of these regions existed in the Low Countries, some having boundaries that overlapped political boundaries, but most not. The most conspicuous examples are listed in Table 2.1. Other regions are the Condroz, the Famenne, and the Ardennes. Such very distinct regions were numerous in

---

[33] This concept of regions thus links up with the agricultural regions identified by Thirsk, *Agricultural regions and agrarian history in England*, 11–12 and 37–38, or Kerridge's farming counties (*The farmers of old England*), but even more with the social agrosystems analysed by Thoen, ' "Social agrosystems" '.

[34] Kerridge, *The farmers of old England*, 8 and 67–102, although he puts a stronger emphasis on the agricultural aspects than the present study does.

the Low Countries. They formed the main geographical framework of social and economic development in the pre-industrial era.

II.2. MAN-MADE LAND: EARLY OCCUPATION AND RECLAMATION

Much progress has been made in recent years on research into the early human occupation history of the Low Countries. Using various indicators, such as archaeological finds, toponyms, settlement forms, and literary sources, the early medieval occupation of the Low Countries can now be reconstructed fairly well. In the near future this picture may be clarified even further from results of systematic archaeological research, for instance, by excavations performed in preparation for large-scale infrastructure projects, and by palynological research. But our present knowledge makes it possible to develop a broad overview of the medieval occupation.

Most regions in the Low Countries were all but completely deserted after the Roman era, as population declined radically. In some regions this decline had already begun in the course of the 3rd century, particularly in the border regions of the Roman Empire where insecurity and danger increased after the *limes*, a closed system of defence, was abandoned for more flexible depth defences around 270 AD.[35] From the late 4th century onwards, significant population decline occurred in all parts of the Low Countries. Several factors played a role in this decline, the principal ones being the dissolution of Roman power and the associated chaos and insecurity. But increasing problems with water, partly caused by human activity, and perhaps soil exhaustion due to overcropping, also played a role, as maybe did the colder climate. Many regions experienced marked population declines, settlements collapsed, trade and markets disappeared, administration dissolved, and the social organization was disrupted. There were some exceptional regions where at least some continuity remained, such as the Haspengouw and the adjacent Meuse valley.[36] To a lesser extent, the same was true of the southern part of inland Flanders, along the Leie and Scheldt rivers, and the eastern part of the Guelders river area, as well as the highest clay regions in Frisia. Here, some slight continuity remained, although this was mostly geographical rather than functional continuity.[37] Most other parts of the Low Countries were almost completely deserted, as is established for most of the coastal areas in Friesland,

---

[35] Willems, 'Das Rhein-Maas-Delta', and Van Es, 'Volksverhuizingen en continuïteit', 66–69, although the profoundness of this change is sensitively treated.

[36] Lodewijckx, 'On the issue of continuity'.

[37] Willems, 'Romans and Batavians', esp. 76–92, and Knol, *De Noordnederlandse kustgewesten*, 109–110 and 137.

Westerwolde in Groningen, Drenthe, almost all of Holland, the west of the Guelders river area, the Campine, Zeeland, north-west Brabant, and large parts of the Ardennes.[38] In Twente, investigation of pollen and aerosols showed a population low around 500 AD that was much lower than it had ever been during the late Bronze Age or the Iron Age.[39] Most of the Low Countries after the Roman era must have been a *tabula rasa*, in contrast to many parts of Europe further to the south.

Population growth, or reoccupation, started to occur from the 6th century onwards, and in some regions even later. Roughly, and leaving aside regional variations, two phases can be observed in the growth of population and cultivated area in the medieval Low Countries: from the 6th/7th centuries to the 9th century, and from 1000 to 1300. While this pattern was broadly similar to that found in most western European areas, it was much more pronounced in the Low Countries, and its increase far outstripped what occurred elsewhere.[40] It is this period, from the 6th century on, that was the formative phase in which the monumental task of reoccupation and rebuilding of economy and society was undertaken.

Ethnic Composition After the Roman Era

At the start of the first phase of early medieval population growth, various peoples can be found in the Low Countries, albeit in very low numbers. They can be roughly divided into Frisians, Franks, Saxons, and Celts, although this division is not absolute, given the complexity of ethnic formation, mixture, and sometimes affinities among all these peoples. Clear-cut distinctions are often artificial, and earlier writings on this point are heavily tainted by 19th-century nationalism.[41] The Celtic tribes, such as the Belgae, the Menapii, and the Nervii, lived mainly in the southern parts of the Low Countries. Those in the west (in what would later be Flemish territory) were only superficially Romanized, those in the south and east more so. Some of this Gallo-Roman population remained after the disturbances. In the fertile Haspengouw, for instance, in the second half of the 3rd century, the town of Tongeren and many villas fell prey to plunder, which caused part of the Gallo-Roman population to leave and be replaced by Frankish allies. Some remained, however, resulting in a mingling of people. Further south, the Roman element remained more

---

[38] Leenders, *Van Turnhoutervoorde*, 109–115, Groenendijk, *Op zoek naar de horizon*, 235–239, Henderikx, *De beneden-delta*, 41–45, Theuws, *De archeologie van de periferie*, 162, Vos and Van Heeringen, 'Holocene geology', 68, and Ewig, *Spätantikes und fränkisches Gallien*, i, 528–530.

[39] Van Geel et al., 'Holocene raised bog deposits in the Netherlands as geochemical archives', 467–476.

[40] Cf. the estimates and comparisons below in this section, pp. 35–37.

[41] Wenskus, *Stammesbildung und Verfassung*, who unravelled the notion of 'Stamm', and Geary, *The myth of nations*, 15–40.

pronounced, particularly south of the Roman Bavai–Tongeren–Cologne road, which, with castles and watchtowers alongside it, in the 4th century became a kind of border zone. Here, there was more continuity and the villas were often rebuilt after the disturbances of the second half of the 3rd century. Germanic immigrants formed only a small minority, arriving gradually, opening the way to Romanization and linguistic assimilation.[42] North of this zone, on the other hand, discontinuity was much sharper and the proportion of Germanic immigrants higher, with a second massive wave in the 6th and 7th centuries. This was a crucial element in the formation of the linguistic border between the Roman/French and German/Dutch languages, although it remained unstable for a long time, with many language islands on both sides and a broad bilingual zone in the middle of present-day Belgium. From the 7th century on, these zones slowly crystallized into monolingual areas that would remain more or less up to the present.

In several parts of the Low Countries the Frankish element became dominant. The Franks were an association of tribes living in the area between the Weser and Rhine rivers in the Roman era. In the course of the 4th century, several of these tribes, particularly the Salii and the Chamavi, entered the Guelders river area and Toxandria, where they took up defence of the border zone as allies of the Roman Empire, until they migrated further south around the middle of the 5th century.[43] Childeric, leader of the Salian Franks and at that time already Romanized, was buried in 481 with great splendour at Tournai. Later the centre of Frankish power shifted even further south. The influence of the Franks on the composition of the population in the Low Countries was probably fairly significant. Since they migrated in several waves which may have included some 100,000 people, their occupation involved settlement of a substantial agricultural population. In the south, across Gaul, they fanned out and formed at most a small percentage of the total population. Just over the former imperial frontier, however, many Franks had settled. Absorbed in the stream of Frankish immigrants there were probably the Batavians, a Germanic tribe that was an offshoot of the Chatti and had settled in the Guelders river area a few centuries earlier.

In the north-eastern parts of the Low Countries, the Saxons were more important. This is a collective name for several tribes, or bands, that had originally settled in Schleswig-Holstein and around the mouth of the Elbe.[44] From the 3rd century on, these Saxons started to expand; in the following centuries they extended their power south and also overseas to England. This expansion brought them into fierce conflict with the Franks, mainly in Westphalia but also in the north-east of the Low Countries. Around 770, the political border

---

[42] Van Durme, 'Genesis and evolution of the Romance-Germanic language border'.
[43] Blok, *De Franken*, 11–19, and Dierkens and Périn, 'The 5th–century advance of the Franks'.
[44] Wenskus, *Stammesbildung und Verfassung*, 541–550.

between Frankish and Saxon territory was along the Gelderse IJssel, although it is unclear whether the people living there were Saxons, and whether they voluntarily joined the Saxon confederacy or were subjected to it.[45] In the northwest of the Low Countries, the Frisian influence was particularly strong. In the 7th and 8th centuries, Frisian settlements were to be found all along the coast from Zeeland to the present German/Danish border in Schleswig-Holstein, as well as further inland along the branches of the Rhine in the central Dutch river area.[46] The Frisians shared a common language and laws to some extent, but it is not certain what kind of ethnic entity they formed. Also, people of several ethnic backgrounds lived intermixed in this area, as has also been assumed to be the case for Zeeland, in the southern part of this Greater Frisia. Analysis of 19 clusters of medieval skulls from the Zeeland islands shows a great variety in cranial forms, within and between villages. Both dolichocephalics and extreme brachycephalics are present in large numbers, which points to a very heterogeneous population of both Frisian and non-Frisian, 'Alpine', people.[47]

Each of these tribes, or groups of tribes, had some kind of political organization, although it was mostly a rather loose one. The Frisians had a chief, designated as *rex* in Anglo-Saxon sources and by the somewhat condescending term *dux* in Frankish ones; rulers included the 'kings' Aldegisl (*c*.675) and Radbod (*c*.700).[48] Frisian organization was probably loose, but became tighter under pressure from the major build-up of power by their southern neighbours, the Franks. The Merovingians succeeded in extending their power over a large part of Gaul. In particular Clovis, the son of Childeric, who converted to Orthodox Catholic Christianity around 500, was able to transform the more decentralized organization of the Franks into a single, charismatic kingship.[49] Some parts of the Low Countries, such as the loess region of the Haspengouw, were incorporated into this Merovingian kingdom by the end of the 5th century. The period of political disintegration and insecurity after the dissolution of Roman rule was relatively short there. In the north this period lasted much longer. However, the Franks were very interested in gaining control over these northern parts, and particularly over the Dutch river area. As self-proclaimed successors of the Roman Empire, they wanted to control the former Roman *limes*, offering a line of defence, various forts, and more prestige. Their attempts often brought them into conflict with the Frisians, with alternating successes and failures in the second half of the 6th century. Around 690, the Franks gained more control over the river area after Pipin II won an important battle against Radbod at Dorestad.[50] This, and the subsequent campaigns

---

[45] Blok, *De Franken*, 54–56, and Epperlein, 'Sachsen im frühen Mittelalter'.
[46] Halbertsma, *Frieslands oudheid*, 59–79.
[47] Dumon Tak and Van de Velde, 'Beschouwing over de schedelvorm'.
[48] Lebecq, *Marchands*, 110–111, and Van Egmond, 'Radbod'.
[49] Wood, *The Merovingian kingdoms*, 41–49.
[50] Van Es, 'Friezen, Franken en Vikingen', 90–92.

by Charles Martel to the north, resulted in the slow and sometimes painful integration of these areas into the Frankish kingdom, along with a process of Christianization.

The subjection of the Saxons took even longer. They had a peculiar and fairly broad political organization which was not headed by a king or *dux*, but with many *pagi* led by chieftains, and a regular assembly in Marklo on the Weser River. To this assembly each *pagus* delegated 12 noblemen, freemen, and serfs to decide on legal matters, disputes, and matters of war and peace.[51] The Saxons were the Franks' most powerful enemy in the 8th century. The border area between Saxons and Franks in Westphalia and Hesse became heavily militarized, with fortifications on both sides.[52] Franks and Saxons also came into conflict in the eastern parts of the present Netherlands, in Overijssel and Groningen. Charlemagne's war against the Saxons lasted over 30 years, but in 804 he finally achieved a decisive victory, which brought all of the Low Countries under Frankish control.

All in all, the Low Countries contained many different peoples, tribes, and cultures within a small area. In the early Middle Ages, Frisians lived mainly in the north-western part and the western river area, Saxons in the north-east, there were concentrations of Franks in several central regions around the Meuse, Rhine, and Scheldt, with perhaps some Batavian elements in the eastern river area, and Celts to the south, with highly Romanized Celts in the southernmost parts. This diversity was perhaps greater than elsewhere in Europe.

Unfortunately, hardly any research has been done on the effects of the cultural, political, and ethnic diversity on later developments. It would be very interesting to know more about what remained of it after inclusion in the Frankish empire. Did these elements merge or retain much of their diversity? How did the diversity affect later legal systems, property arrangements, and regional differences in the short and long runs? Included in this are differences between collective and individual property arrangements, or between perpetual and fixed-term property rights, possibly influencing later regional variations in the arrangement of the leasing system. And how did this diversity affect later differences in power and social structures? Some regions were characterized by marked social differences, whereas others had a more equal distribution of property and power, with a greater portion of the population involved in political decision-making, as in Frisia and Saxony. And how did this affect differences in freedom or the lack of it, and hence the emergence and layout of the manorial system and its later development and decay? Differences like these, originating in the early Middle Ages, sometimes come to light in later centuries. This happened in the nascent county of Holland in the high Middle Ages, where the south had become more Frankish, whereas the north retained

---

[51] Wood, 'Political and social structures of the Saxons'.
[52] Hardt, 'Hesse, Elbe, Saale', esp. 221–224.

its Frisian characteristics. In this process, and in the subsequent integration of the two areas into one county, these differences in language, inheritance laws, social structure, and community rights led to clashes and even outright warfare lasting for several centuries.[53] Here, as elsewhere, the early medieval situation greatly influenced later developments. Future research will help early medievalists, social historians, ethnologists, and historians of law to join forces to make further progress in understanding the nature and extent of this possible continuity.

Occupation in the Early Middle Ages

The extension of Frankish power, and the associated return of security and peace, was probably one of the key factors in the population growth of the early Middle Ages.[54] Growth can be surmised in many parts of the Low Countries from roughly the middle of the 6th century onwards, resulting in increasing population densities and reoccupation of abandoned regions. Several factors affected whether people were attracted to occupy a particular region. The nature of the soil was perhaps most decisive, although it was not always the soil fertility that determined settlement. Often, the possibilities for easy reclamation were more important, particularly in view of the simple tools available to the occupants. The occupation, and especially its chronology, thus depended largely on the labour needed and difficulties encountered in reclaiming the land, relating to the vegetation, the possibilities for natural drainage, the prospects for habitation, and the accessibility of the area. The regions that were reclaimed first, therefore, often offered a compromise between fertility of the soil and the ease of reclamation and cultivation.[55]

Factors other than geography also affected choices of occupation: power, political stability, security, and the presence of transport routes. Several regions stood out in the 6th to 8th centuries as most suited to reoccupation. Most attractive were the loess soils in the Haspengouw, which were fertile and easy to reclaim and cultivate. Second choices were the stream ridges in the river clay areas; these were harder to reclaim and difficult to work, but highly fertile. Frankish control in these areas was strong at a very early date. This was also true of the sandy, loamy soils in Flanders along the Scheldt and Leie rivers and their tributaries. It was in these regions that habitation was strongly concentrated in the period. The degree of concentration is striking. Unlike the Romans, who cultivated all soils to varying degrees of intensity,

---

[53] Blok, 'Holland und Westfriesland'.
[54] For the other factors, see below section VIII.3 pp. 397–398, and for estimates of population numbers, below pp. 35–37.
[55] Pollard, *Marginal Europe*, 21–24.

the Franks fixed on the soils most suitable for arable cultivation. Research has demonstrated this for the Niederrhein region, immediately across the present German border, as well as the Famenne and Condroz areas, where the heavy concentration of Merovingian burial sites was in sharp contrast with the even distribution of Roman villas.[56] Compared with the Romans, with their diversified agriculture and stress on non-agricultural activities, the Franks clearly focused on grain cultivation, probably associated with their preference for organizing land ownership through a manorial system whose operations were crucially linked to grain cultivation.[57]

These factors resulted in a very different occupation history from region to region. Some remained virtually uninhabited until the 10th and 11th centuries, such as Holland, consisting mainly of peatlands. The land there was then occupied through large-scale reclamation.[58] In the adjacent Guelders river area, on the other hand, there was some continuity of habitation from the Roman era, at least in the eastern parts. The rest of the region was rather densely inhabited in the Roman era, but later became almost completely deserted, and then was resettled in the course of the early Middle Ages. This resettlement of the Guelders river area can be reconstructed fairly well. Population densities were probably low initially, since archaeological indications for habitation from the Merovingian and Carolingian periods are limited in number, and are found only on the stream ridges. These also show that the population was gradually advancing from the highest stream ridges in the east to the lower ones in the west. The date of the place names reflects some of the occupation history, although they do not offer unambiguous insights, certainly in view of the long periods during which most were productive. It is clear, however, that in the western part only the place names of Tricht (from the Roman 'Trajectum'), Maurik (from the Celtic/Roman 'Mannaricium'), and Wadenooijen (from 'Wada', mentioned by Tacitus) show continuity from the Roman era.[59] They thus mirror the slight continuity of occupation in the region, although it should be kept in mind that names represent the lowest level of continuity, not necessarily proving continuity of habitation. Suffixes show that seven other settlements in the area must have existed at least from the 7th century, and thus reflect the first stage of early medieval occupation. Most striking, however, are the large concentrations of place names ending with *-heem*, which were productive mainly in the Frankish period.[60] They testify to a massive early medieval reoccupation, which went hand in hand with the establishment of Frankish power and its local pillars, the *homines franci*. Concentrations like these are found mainly in the west of the

---

[56] Janssen, 'Landerschliessung', esp. 99–113, and Wieger, 'Das Siedlungs- und Agrargefüge', 66.
[57] Mitterauer, *Warum Europa?*, 47–50, and below, section III.1, pp. 40–41.
[58] Cf. below, pp. 40–41. [59] Henderikx, *De beneden-delta*, 43 and appendices IV.a–IV.d.
[60] Blok, *De Franken*, 125–130. For the role and position of the *homines franci*, see also section III.1, pp. 57–59 below.

region, closest to the Holland peatlands and probably completely deserted after the Roman period.

Here, occupation moved westward in the Carolingian period, with this cluster of *-heem* villages forming the western border of the newly occupied area. The relatively large area occupied and the indications of intensive habitation in the Carolingian period, such as the sharp rise of non-tree pollen from a low around the year 500 to a much higher level around 850,[61] show that within a fairly short span of time enormous reclamation projects must have been carried out there. The supposition that mentions of reclamation activity in the Carolingian period indicate only a kind of agrarian clean-up and that large-scale reclamation projects date from the 10th century at the earliest,[62] does not seem to accord with the facts. Big reclamation works were also carried out in inland Flanders, where similar and even larger concentrations of *-heem* names can be found, particularly in the area around and south-west of Ghent.[63]

That the area of arable land in several parts of the Low Countries was greatly extended in the early Middle Ages can also be reconstructed from the toponyms of 'arable'. The names *eng* and *es*, the latter used in the eastern parts of the Netherlands, indicate an open arable field close to an old settlement, for which reclamation generally can be dated to the early Middle Ages. The locations, parcel shapes, and archaeological finds on the *engen* in the Guelders river area show that most of these date from the Merovingian period. A map of the distribution of this toponym in the present-day Netherlands shows more than 200 of these early medieval arable fields, particularly in the Guelders area, the Veluwe, and Salland, indicating the pronounced expansion of arable there in this period.[64] In inland Flanders, the early medieval *akkers* were grouped from the 9th century onwards in similarly large complexes of arable land, which gradually came to be called *kouter*.[65] The *akkers* are thus the oldest arable lands, and they are found mainly in the area between the Scheldt and Dender, the most densely populated part of Flanders in the early Middle Ages. Palynological research can also help with the reconstruction of occupation and reclamation in the early medieval period, especially where written sources are scarce. Pollenograms for Rulles in the Ardennes, not far from Neufchâteau, for instance, clearly show the retreat of habitation in the second half of the 4th century, which saw a low in population until about 800, and then a rapid increase.[66] Along similar lines,

---

[61] Teunissen, *Palynologisch onderzoek*.
[62] Cf. Ganshof, 'Manorial organization', 38–39. This idea has already been criticized by Blok, 'Hoofdlijnen van de bewoningsgeschiedenis', 151–152.
[63] Verhulst, *Landschap*, 119.
[64] Blok, 'De enken', and Edelman, 'Enige ongewone aspecten', 188.
[65] Verhulst, *Landschap*, 120–126. See also below, section IV.1, pp. 128–129.
[66] Couteaux, *Recherches palynologiques en Gaume*, 19–20 and 78–81.

for Bas-Luxembourg as a whole, a definite fall in grain cultivation after the 5th century as well as a simultaneous increase in beech can be observed, with these trends reversing again around 700, providing a clear indicator for a decline in population and its later recovery from the 8th century on.

Early Medieval Population Numbers

These indicators show that there was little or no continuity of habitation from the Roman era to the early Middle Ages in the Low Countries. Population numbers were severely reduced, and started to rise again only slowly from the 6th century, following a low of several centuries. Growing occupation in the 6th to 8th centuries was concentrated mainly in a few regions which offered favourable prospects for reclamation and arable agriculture, but even there population densities were initially very low, although they clearly rose in the course of this period. This is observable, for instance, in the Campine region. From written sources and archaeological investigation of burial sites, it is estimated that the Dutch part of the Campine, some 600 km^2 in size, had some 1,000 to 1,100 inhabitants around the middle of the 7th century, and the Campine plateau in present-day Belgium had a similar number in a comparable area. These were two areas of relatively concentrated occupation: the region between the Scheldt, Demer, and Meuse rivers as a whole may have had no more than 5,000 to 6,000 people on about 10,000 km^2, or only 0.5 persons per km^2.[67] A similar population density is found in the Veluwe, where in the 7th century some 1,500 to 2,500 people lived on 3,000 km^2, while in the 6th century perhaps only several hundred had lived here.[68] In the course of the 7th and 8th centuries, these numbers increased, as was also the case in other parts of the Low Countries. An estimate is available for Drenthe, where in the 7th century some 3,000 to 4,000 people lived on 1,200 km^2 of occupied territory, and on 2,600 km^2 of this infertile region as a whole, or 1.3 persons per km^2.[69] In the 10th century, this had increased to some 4,000 to 5,000 people, or 1.7 per km^2. Growth was greater in the present-day province of Overijssel, where some 2.5 persons per km^2 lived around 700.[70] A century later this probably increased to 3.5 persons per km^2, with the average in the two centres of occupation (Salland and Twente) being 4.5 per km^2. This is similar to the estimate for Groningen.

Other parts of the Low Countries were more densely populated at the time. This probably applies to the Guelders river area, the Meuse valley, the

---

[67] Theuws, *De archeologie van de periferie*, 189–195.
[68] Heidinga, 'De Veluwe in de vroege Middeleeuwen', 192.
[69] Spek, *Het Drentse esdorpenlandschap*, 586–590.
[70] Slicher van Bath, *Een samenleving onder spanning*, 735–737, and 'The economic and social conditions', 100–101.

Table 2.2 Estimates of population densities in the early Middle Ages

		Mid-7th century	800	900
Densely populated (10,000 km²)	Guelders river area, Meuse valley, the Haspengouw, the south of Flanders, the sea clay regions of Friesland	8	14	18
Moderately populated (30,000 km²)	Salland, Groningen, Twente, Condroz, Famenne, etc.	3	4.5	6
Scarcely populated (35,000 km²)	the Ardennes, the Campine area, Drenthe, the Holland fenlands, Veluwe, etc.	0.75	1.0	1.5
Average Low Countries (75,000 km²)		2.7	4.1	5.5
Total population		200,000	310,000	410,000

Haspengouw, the south of Flanders, and the sea clay regions of Friesland. The high population densities in the latter region are reflected in the very high numbers of early medieval terps in Friesland. Based on the number of terps (dwelling mounds), as well as the number of parishes and archaeological finds, it is assumed that these areas (Oostergo and Westergo) were among the most densely populated in Europe, with some 10–20 persons per km² around 900.[71] The other regions mentioned were probably at the same level. Some figures are available for the south of Flanders, which are calculated from the mid-9th century polyptique of St Bertin. Although interpretation of these data is disputed, they show that this region and the adjacent part of Artois had no fewer than 20 inhabitants per km² at the time.[72]

It is difficult to estimate total population numbers and their development from the scattered data, but we may be able to obtain a rough idea by dividing the Low Countries into three parts (relatively densely populated, populated, and virtually unpopulated), and combining all the indicators discussed, including the knowledge that population in the Frankish period was highly concentrated. (See Table 2.2.)

On this basis, population in the Low Countries can thus be roughly estimated at 200,000 people around the mid-7th century, rising to 300,000 around 800, and to 400,000 around 900. Developments in the late 9th to 10th centuries are not very clear. It is probable that the population rise in the Low Countries stagnated and that developments were less favourable than elsewhere in western Europe as a result of the decline of central power, increasing feuding, and the

[71] Slicher van Bath, 'The economic and social conditions', 99–103 and 131–133, and the overview for the Netherlands: Thurkow et al., *Atlas van Nederland*, part 2, map 5. For densities in later centuries, see section VI.2, pp. 283–284 below.
[72] Schwarz, 'Village populations', reducing by some 40 per cent the older calculations by Van Werveke, 'De bevolkingsdichtheid in de IXe eeuw', 107–116.

major impact of Viking attacks in this area, where wealth was within easy reach of raiders.[73] Perhaps the Haspengouw, Condroz, the Famenne, the Ardenne, and other inland regions largely escaped this, and witnessed further expansion in this period.[74] The period 1000–1300 is fairly well documented and witnessed an enormous and continuing population growth, concentrated in regions which had been virtually uninhabited until then, such as the Holland fenlands. Around 1300, the population of Holland had soared to 210,000.[75] The fertile province of Groningen saw its population rise from 12,500 in $c.900$ to 40,000 in $c.1300$.[76] On the sandy soils, which had been occupied much earlier and did not seem to offer much scope for further growth because of their lack of fertility, there was also some population growth, although less pronounced. In Drenthe, for instance, the population increased from about 5,000 in the 10th century to some 12,000 to 15,000 in the late 13th.[77] The first extensive set of concrete data from fiscal records for the Low Countries as a whole is available for the second half of the 15th century. Some 2.5 million people were living in the Low Countries then, a figure that may have been as high in 1300 before the Black Death.

Difficult as it is to compare these figures, they suggest that population growth between the 7th and 13th centuries had been very strong, probably rising by a factor of 10–15. In other parts of Europe this rise had been much more modest: a factor of 3–4 for Europe as a whole and 6–7 for western Europe.[78] Population densities, too, started to far exceed those in most other parts of Europe, rising from 2.5 persons per km^2 in the mid-7th century to 5.5 $c.900$, and no fewer than 30 per km^2 $c.1300$. In the 13th century, the Low Countries, which had been sparsely populated six centuries before, had become the second most densely populated part of Europe, after Italy. Densities there can be estimated at 8 per km^2 in the mid-7th century, rising to 17 around 1000, and 41 around 1300, when the centre and north of Italy had about 48 people per km^2.[79] This was still by far the densest in all of Europe, but the Low Countries were clearly catching up, particularly as a result of the very large reclamations in the 11th to 13th centuries. In this period, various regions were reclaimed which had only been used extensively before. This reclamation took

---

[73] For the factors affecting early medieval population rise and decline, see also chapter VIII.3, pp. 397–398, and for the insecurity in this period, see section III.1, pp. 63–65. For western Europe as a whole, a more optimistic picture of this period is sketched by Devroey, 'Histoire économique', 193–199.
[74] Despy, 'Villes et campagnes'.
[75] Van Bavel and Van Zanden, 'The jump-start of the Holland economy'. For population developments in the late Middle Ages, see section VI.2, pp. 278–280.
[76] Jansen, 'Sociaal-economische geschiedenis'.
[77] Spek, *Het Drentse esdorpenlandschap*, 591–592.
[78] As suggested in the overviews by Slicher van Bath, *Agrarische geschiedenis*, 87, and Russell, 'Population in Europe'.
[79] Federico and Malanima, 'Progress, decline, growth', 446.

very different forms, determined by landscape, habitation, and particularly social context.

Occupation and Reclamation in the High Middle Ages

On the sandy soils, small-scale reclamation by peasants was dominant. There were a few localities where manorial lords held a strong position and organized the reclamation, and some areas where the territorial lord planned reclamation, as in parts of the Veluwe, but small extensions of cultivated land by individual peasant farmers were the norm.[80] Reclamation was often individually undertaken from the *huiskampen*, the arable land near the scattered farms which formed the oldest cultivated land there. This process resulted in irregular, block-shaped parcels, often carved out of the woodland, with some of it formed in the early Middle Ages, but some only later. Only slowly, and particularly in the high Middle Ages, did the separate tracts of arable land in these areas come together in *essen* or *engen*, the open complexes of arable land parcelled out in narrow strips. In Drenthe, for instance, many of the *essen* were formed in the high Middle Ages, simultaneously with a process of nuclearization of settlement and the formation of villages, although many others date only from the 16th century or even the first half of the 19th.[81] This is much later than in the fertile Guelders river area and Salland, where they had developed by the early Middle Ages.[82]

In the sandy, infertile Campine area, there had been some extension to the cultivated land from the early 8th century, but the real acceleration in occupation began in the early 12th century.[83] Pollen analysis shows that from the 11th century onwards oak, beech, and hornbeam receded, while buckwheat, spurry, and in particular rye greatly increased. The reclamation was mainly piecemeal, and undertaken by peasants. The sandy soils were relatively easy to reclaim, and did not require expensive tools. Also, because of their infertility, they were not very attractive to manorial lords. The high cost of monitoring within the manorial system made these soils with their low fertility unattractive to large manors, leaving them to peasants who carved out small bits and pieces from the wilderness.

In the earlier literature, significant value was attached to the role of the newly founded Premonstratensian and Cistercian abbeys in the 12th and 13th-century reclamation of the sandy areas. This applied particularly to the Campine region, where the important abbeys of Tongerlo, Postel, and Averbode were located. In the traditional view, most of these abbeys were founded in deserted wastelands

---

[80] Spek, *Het Drentse esdorpenlandschap*, passim.
[81] Ibid., 672–690. For the villages, see also sections III.3, pp. 93–98.
[82] This is discussed more extensively above in this section, p. 34.
[83] Steurs, *Naissance d'une région*, 211–213, 240–279 and 377–380.

for religious reasons, allowing them to acquire large tracts of unreclaimed land.[84] The abundance of labour power provided by the many lay brethren enabled these abbeys to exploit and expand their properties, without having to have recourse to the labour of others in the form of levies, rents, or tithes, in accordance with the religious ideals of these orders. This traditional view, however, has now been discarded. Almost none of these abbeys appear to have been founded in uninhabited areas, most of the reclamation had already been undertaken before their founding, and in practice the abbeys had no scruples about profiting from other men's labour.[85] An illuminating case is that of Tongerlo, located in the middle of the infertile Campine, where confirmation of the traditional image would have been expected. As the foundation charter of 1130 clearly shows, however, the endowment of this abbey consisted of reclaimed land, some farms let for rents in money and kind, tithes, and a mill. The area was already inhabited and in full development. The actual reclamation here was not primarily undertaken by these abbeys, but rather by local lords and particularly by peasants, who had long held most property rights to land, and the abbeys adapted to this. Similarly, abbeys founded in regions with a strong manorial system came to own complete manors with dozens of serfs, and they mostly left the manorial organization intact.[86] This shows the power of regional structures: even these large and powerful institutions, urged by their religion to follow another road, appear to have adjusted to the social and economic structures, and to have profited from developments already under way.[87]

Reclamation on a larger scale also took place in the high Middle Ages on the fertile loess soils of the Haspengouw. In its eastern extension, the area south-east of Maastricht, the cultivated area was enlarged from one-tenth of the total at the beginning of the 11th century to a quarter $c.1200$ and more than four-fifths at the end of the 13th century.[88] Around 1300, the Haspengouw as a whole had become almost devoid of woodland, except for some steep slopes. Massive reclamation was also carried out in the backlands of the river clay areas. The highest stream ridges in the eastern part of the Guelders river area had been populated since the beginning of the Carolingian period, but now, as population increased further, the arable land on the lower stream ridges was gradually extended. Next, in the 11th to 13th centuries, all the backlands were rapidly transformed to more intensive agricultural use, which was undertaken

---

[84] Duby, *Rural economy*, 70–76.
[85] Despy, 'Les richesses de la terre', esp. 61–65 for the Cistercian houses of Villers, Orval, and Aulne, and Van Bavel, 'Stichtingsplaats, ontginning en goederenverwerving'.
[86] Van Bavel, *Goederenverwerving en goederenbeheer*, 226–264.
[87] This even applies to the fields of diking and the assembling of granges where their particular contribution to the economy was perhaps strongest. See this section below, pp. 43–44.
[88] Renes, *De geschiedenis*, 61–71 and 81.

from existing manors and villages. This process was completed long before 1300, as shown by archaeological finds for the area south of the small town of Culemborg, where the most extensive and lowest-lying backlands of the Guelders river area are situated. Their reclamation can be dated precisely through archaeological, geographical, and literary evidence, such as the mention of a parish church, the levying of new tithes, and the payment of reclamation levies.[89] All the evidence points to a large-scale reclamation campaign, particularly in the first decades of the 12th century. Virtually the last common pasture lands were parcelled out and made fit for more intensive use in the decades around 1300. By that time, all the land in the Guelders river area had been reclaimed.

Elsewhere in the Low Countries, even larger reclamation projects took place in the 10th to 13th centuries, a period of huge population growth, as in the Frisian peatlands, the salt marshes of Zeeland, coastal Flanders, and especially in the Holland–Utrecht fenlands. These regions were a kind of frontier area, difficult to reclaim. The early medieval population growth had largely passed them by. In particular the Holland–Utrecht fenlands, almost uninhabited until then, saw the large-scale occupation of new territory. This reclamation required solid organization, in view of the challenging hydrological tasks lying ahead. Reclamation blocks in this peat area had to be enclosed by two side dikes and a back dike to protect against the upstream water, and drainage canals and ditches had to be dug to drain the marshy peatland. A large and well-organized workforce was needed to carry out these difficult projects and to make these outlays more large-scale, which offered economies of scale.

The organization and planning resulted in the reclaimed lands having a very regular pattern. The width of the parcels was standardized at about 100 m, which was circumscribed by two ditches. These ditches extended parallel to a natural water course or a drainage canal. Sometimes the territorial lord also determined the extent of the reclamation, mostly at 1,250 m, creating rectangular reclamation blocks with very regular parcels, and farms all having about 12.5 hectares of land.[90] The systematic and well-organized reclamation thus resulted in a fixed pattern of equal parcels in the form of strips. This pattern can still clearly be seen in the landscape in Holland and the western part of Utrecht.[91] These large-scale, systematic reclamations covered a vast area from the IJ in the north to the Land of Culemborg in the south-east, no less than 4,000 km² in total. The archbishops

---

[89] Van Bavel, *Transitie en continuïteit*, 62–69.

[90] Van der Linden, *De cope*, 20–25, and Henderikx, 'Die mittelalterliche Kultivierung der Moore', 81–82 and map 7. For the social-political context and effects of this type of reclamation see section III.2, pp. 83–85.

[91] G. Borger et al., *Het Groene Hart*. Cf. for the somewhat different chronology and organization in the Holland peat area north of the IJ: Besteman, 'North Holland AD 400–1200', and Bos, 'The bog area of North Holland'.

of Hamburg–Bremen also attracted settlers from Holland and Utrecht to the marshes at the mouths of the Elbe and Weser rivers in the north of Germany.[92] These settlers, from 1113 on, brought the same methods from Holland, which resulted in a similar, regular landscape.

Hydrological Projects

A specific element in the occupation and reclamation of the river and coastal areas in the Low Countries was the management of the water. In the 11th and 12th centuries, and perhaps even before, some dikes had already been constructed. Earlier, even in the Iron Age, human beings tried to protect themselves against the water by raising mounds. Many hundreds of such artificial hills or terps, perhaps as many as several thousand, can be found throughout the coastal areas: some in Flanders, Zeeland, and Holland, but particularly in Friesland, Groningen, and on the present North German coast.[93] Most of these structures, called *terpen*, *wierden*, or *Wurden*, started as a small elevation for a single farmhouse; in the course of many centuries these were gradually raised further in phases and were sometimes joined together into village terps.

After embankment of the area these mounds could still be useful as defences against the water if the dikes were not sufficient to contain it in winter or during severe storms. Some of these mounds also had a military function, as in Zeeland. Most were built 1–3 m high in the 10th or early 11th centuries, but some were raised further in the 12th and 13th centuries to 5–12 m, and additionally surrounded by palisades. Such constructions gave the *werven* a military function, analogous to the general western European phenomenon of the construction of mottes.[94] In the same period, in Friesland and Groningen, a similar development took place, with the construction of some 100 *stinswieren*, hills with a conical shape, built to a height of 5–10 m and mostly found near the residences of local gentry.[95] These mounds were often constructed by local magnates after the weakening of central comital power. In both Zeeland and Friesland strong central rule was much weakened in this period, and territorial lords were not able to fill the power vacuum. In reaction, local authorities started to build their own strongholds, often using them as a basis for reclamation and a way to control the reclaimed area. This, too, can be observed in other parts of western Europe, as in the Niederrhein area,[96] just east of the present-day Dutch border, where some 300 to 400 mottes were erected in the 10th–13th

---

[92] Van der Linden, *De cope*, 173–182, and Petri, 'Entstehung und Verbreitung der niederländischen Marschenkolonisation', esp. 727–733.
[93] Lebecq, 'De la protohistoire', and Knol, *De Noordnederlandse kustlanden*, 42–45.
[94] Trimpe Burger, 'Onderzoekingen in vluchtbergen', and Dekker, *Zuid-Beveland*, 88–90 and 492–502. For the mottes, see also section III.1, pp. 65–66.
[95] Kramer, 'Onderzoek naar stinswieren'.
[96] Janssen, 'Die Bedeutung der mittelalterlichen Burg', 261–316, esp. 268–276.

centuries; not in areas already occupied and cultivated in the Carolingian era, but in the wetlands near streams and rivers, which came to be occupied in this period. In some cases, pollen analysis can even show that oak and alder immediately declined after the motte had been built, indicating a direct link with reclamation.

The artificial mounds in the coastal areas lost most of their hydrological function after the 10th and 11th centuries when the inhabitants started to construct dikes. Several phases can be discerned in this process, also found in the river areas. At first, people began to protect their settlements against the water by damming up creeks and gullies in the stream ridges and by constructing side dikes. A few small front and side dikes may have been constructed as early as 800, but there was more systematic building, and on a larger scale, in the 11th and 12th centuries.[97] The second phase was building real dikes and joining them, often together with damming of larger creeks and rivers. During the third phase they were linked in a coherent dike system. This can be observed, for instance, in Frisia, but also in coastal Flanders, where in the 11th and 12th centuries the coastal area around Bruges, Knokke, and Damme, and that around the Ijzer estuary, became protected from the sea by a dike system.[98] These dikes were largely defensive measures, necessitated by compression of the soil after reclamation, especially to protect existing agricultural lands. In the fourth phase, the coastal population started constructing offensive embankments, gaining new lands from the sea. In coastal Flanders these new polders were mainly built in the period from 1180 to the second half of the 13th century.[99] In Frisia offensive embankment started in the same period, from 1200 on. These attempts to gain land from the sea, or to regain it, fit with the large reclamation movement of the 11th–13th centuries, and were its specific expression in the coastal areas.

Medieval dikes were not as impressive as some of the modern ones, since they were mostly fairly low, at 1–3 m, and narrow. Only in the 15th and 16th centuries were some of them raised to about 4 m. Nevertheless, in view of the state of technology, it must have required an enormous effort to construct them. This raises questions about the organization of these embankments. Earlier, it was thought that intervention by central authorities or large religious institutions was absolutely necessary to accomplish major water management projects such as ring dikes or long drainage canals.[100] But this was not always the case. Rather, local or regional powers were more decisive, which resulted in regional

---

[97] Harten, 'Stroomrug- en komontginning', 21, and Henderikx, 'De zorg voor de dijken', esp. 182–186.
[98] Tys, 'Domeinvorming', 49–51, and De Langen, *Middeleeuws Friesland*, 30–37.
[99] Tys, 'Domeinvorming'.
[100] Moorman van Kappen, 'De historische ontwikkeling van het waterschapswezen', 14–27, and Borger, 'De ouderdom van onze dijken', 76–80.

differences in the involvement of territorial lords, abbeys, large landowners, or village communities. The role of abbeys in general was not very prominent. The orders traditionally considered to have been heralds of reclamation and building dikes, the Cistercians and to a lesser extent the Premonstratensians, emerged too late to play any role in the first phase of embankment, now dated earlier than previously believed. In later phases they did contribute, not through their own labour or that of their lay brethren, but mainly through their investments. In Zeeland and coastal Flanders in particular, the Cistercians invested heavily in embankment.[101] Together with building up their landed property and granges, the Flemish Cistercian abbeys of Ten Duinen and Ter Doest extensively used their capital in the late 12th and in the 13th centuries to take the final and most expensive steps in offensive embankment and damming of large gullies, for which financial resources would have otherwise been lacking.

Territorial lords sometimes played an important part in water management, as the counts of Flanders did on the Flemish coast, where comital estates were systematically embanked and tidal channels were drained on comital initiative in the 11th and 12th centuries.[102] But their role was not absolutely necessary. Smaller projects, and even some of the larger ones, were often carried out within a local framework. This can be seen in the western part of the Guelders river area, where central rule was almost absent until the 14th century. This did not block completion of major hydrological projects, as appears from the construction of long drainage canals traversing various jurisdictions. Where these drainage canals discharged into the river or the sea, first culverts and later wooden sluices were placed, as happened in the Guelders river area and in various coastal regions from the 11th century on. By the 13th century sluices had fully developed, with widths of several metres and complex chamber designs, requiring great skill of the carpenters.[103] Organization of maintenance and control of hydrological works was sometimes provided by local aldermen, or by meetings of landowners or villagers, as well as by separate organizations for water management which started to emerge. In the 12th and 13th centuries, these developed an elaborate and formal structure, such as the water boards on the Flemish coast, with sluice masters acting as an executive board, levying taxes, keeping accounts, and appointing or hiring labourers.[104] In Holland, regional water boards, or *hoogheemraadschappen*, developed early, but their operational responsibilities were considerably smaller, leaving much of the actual organization to the village communities.[105] The

---

[101] Dekker, *Zuid-Beveland*, 137–162, 168–182 and 201–212. Cf. for Friesland Mol, 'Middeleeuwse kloosters en dijkbouw'.
[102] Tys, 'Domeinvorming', 51–58.
[103] Van de Ven, *Leefbaar laagland*, 88–98, and Van Dam, 'Ecological challenges'.
[104] Soens, 'Explaining deficiencies', 37–38.
[105] For the rise of the village communities, see also section III.3, pp. 93–95.

count of Holland had only a very limited influence in this field, contrary to the situation in Flanders, for instance. The organization of water management thus differed greatly according to the social and political constellation of the region, and in several regions much of the population participated in administration.

Initially, construction and maintenance of these water management projects was mainly carried out by the people who were directly involved. The regular work on the dikes was often divided among the owners and users of the neighbouring parcels of land. In the course of centuries, however, this system proved increasingly inadequate, since water management required increasingly more labourers, and also more specialized workers, who were rewarded with money wages for constructing and maintaining the expensive water mills and sluices. At the same time, regions such as coastal Flanders saw a shift from peasant land ownership to leasing out large landholdings to tenant farmers, and from a peasant society to agrarian capitalism. This went hand in hand with undermining communal organizations for water management, so that their administration was increasingly controlled by large landowners,[106] a development which could have negative consequences for the quality of water management.

Interaction Between Man and Landscape

The occupation and reclamation of the land caused intense interaction between landscape and human activity, resulting in a landscape which was to a large extent man-made and which underwent drastic changes in the medieval period. For several reasons, both these observations are more true of the Low Countries than of any other part of Europe. First, the presence of rivers and the sea, increasing the intensity of interaction and requiring all kinds of measures to control the water. Second, the nature of the soils, which were relatively susceptible to erosion and change, such as the peatlands and the sandy soils. Then there was the dense population, the increasingly higher population pressure, and the intensity of land use, which was greater than anywhere else in Europe.

The major extent of these changes caused by human actions can be observed throughout the Low Countries, but especially on the peat soils. After reclamation of the peatlands, which had been an arduous task because of their marshiness and the rough, wild landscape, the region initially seemed to be well suited to

---

[106] For this process and the increasing specialization in water management, see section VI.3, pp. 300–301 below. For the effects on water management, see also below, pp. 47–48.

agriculture. However, after reclamation, peat soils oxidize and become compressed as a result of the drainage, leading to subsidence of the soil.[107] This may amount to up to 1 m per century and in some cases to 2 m or more in total, and it caused serious and increasing problems with groundwater. Moreover, both in Zeeland and in the Zuiderzee area, the compression of the soil seems to have enabled the sea to advance further inland. Large parts of the peatlands were swept away by sea water, causing massive loss of land, particularly in the 11th and 12th centuries.

In Holland, the peat areas remained in place, thanks to the protection offered by the wide belt of dunes, but compression of the soil made farming of the arable land increasingly difficult in the course of the 13th and 14th centuries. Cultivation of bread grains became especially difficult as a result of the rising water table, causing a shift in agriculture to barley and oats, and increasing the importance of livestock farming.[108] But it would probably be wrong to resort to ecological determinism in order to explain the development of the rural economy in Holland. In many places, and certainly when peasants were prepared to invest a great deal of labour, cultivation of oats and barley was still possible. Moreover, technical devices were available for draining the land, particularly using wind-watermills, which were introduced in the early 15th century. Whether windmills were used was to a large extent determined by profitability—or rather lack of profitability, in view of the relatively low food prices of the period. Organizational and institutional barriers also played a role. Only when clear arrangements and rules were developed for dividing the costs and the risks of water storage and for aligning the interests of all parties involved could these technical skills be employed.[109] Ecology was thus certainly not the only factor in this.

In the course of the 15th and 16th centuries, particularly as agricultural prices started to rise again and as institutional problems were gradually solved, the wind-watermill was improved and mills were built in large numbers. At that time, however, new ecological problems were caused by the growing importance of peat digging and the application of new techniques of cutting peat in Holland, in particular the *slagturven*, as scoops were used to extract peat deep under water. Intensive peat cutting destabilized the banks of inland lakes and contributed to a lowering of the ground level. The excavated land was often subject to inundation, resulting in a massive crumbling away of shores and an alarming

---

[107] For more on this process see Braams, *Weyden en zeyden*, 150–154, and Pons, 'Holocene peat formation', 54–70.

[108] De Boer, 'Graaf en grafiek', was the first to underline the effects of this process on the rural economy in Holland.

[109] Van Bavel and Van Zanden, 'The jump-start of the Holland economy'. On the introduction of wind-watermills, see also section VII.2, p. 358.

growth in the Holland lakes, particularly the Haarlemmermeer.[110] In the battle against the water, the Holland population thus remained on the defensive. Real change began only from *c*.1560, as food prices rose rapidly and a large group of financially powerful entrepreneurs emerged in the Holland cities who were willing to provide large-scale investments to improve the windmills and enlarge their numbers. These allowed for improving the agricultural potential of existing land. Extensive use of windmills also enabled draining of shallow lakes or newly embanked areas to gain new lands,[111] which resulted in the creation of thousands of hectares of new polderland.

The river clay areas also experienced major changes in landscape in the centuries following the occupation, when the contrast between stream ridges and backlands became more pronounced. As a result of their greater height and better quality of soil, the stream ridges were more suited to habitation and arable agriculture, whereas the backlands were largely used as meadows or hay fields, or to cultivate willows. In particular the parts of the stream ridges which were settled and used first, the 'ancient settlement soils', had become increasingly fertile and suited to intensive cultivation from the artificial raising and enrichment of the soil.[112] This resulted in the rise of intensive horticulture and fruit growing in the later Middle Ages. In the backlands, on the other hand, the agricultural situation had increasingly deteriorated. Some of the backlands had peat in the subsoil, which was compressed after reclamation. Moreover, after embankment of rivers, from the 11th century on, all sedimentation took place within the dikes, raising the river beds ever higher and necessitating further raising of the dikes. As the level of the backlands soil fell and the river beds rose, the danger of major flooding increased, and water seepage became an even greater nuisance. In the centuries following reclamation, the backlands increasingly suffered from the water, causing a shift to more extensive types of land use. Moreover, the soil there degenerated when used for growing hay, losing nutrients to the farms and subsequently in the form of manure to the arable lands on the stream ridges.[113] In all respects the contrast between stream ridges and backlands became ever greater.

This development is reflected in the settlement history. In the 11th century, when the occupation and reclamation started here, the backlands still seemed well suited to agrarian use. Even arable husbandry was possible, as is shown by the decision to settle and build farmhouses in the parcels in the backlands. But increasing difficulties in their attempt to hold back the water prompted the inhabitants to move away in the 12th and 13th centuries, resulting in deserted settlements, even despite increasing population pressure in this period. Other

---

[110] Van Dam, *Vissen in veenmeren*, 58–70.
[111] Cf. De Vries and Van der Woude, *The first modern economy*, 27–30; or, for a more specific instance, Baars, *De geschiedenis van de landbouw in de Beijerlanden*, 27–88.
[112] Egberts, *De bodemgesteldheid van de Betuwe*, 17–19.
[113] Braams, *Weyden en zeyden*, 155–157, and Edelman, 'Enige ongewone aspecten', 190–192.

indicators, too, show the deterioration of the situation. Several drainage canals and dikes were constructed only after reclamation, as can be seen from the fact that they traversed the existing parcel structure. The later drainage canals all ran east–west, whereas almost all those cut during or preceding reclamation ran north–south or south–north, directly to the large rivers. At some point after reclamation the original drainage system apparently no longer functioned adequately, probably because after embankment the river beds of the Linge and Waal became ever higher, requiring construction of new drainage canals. All this resulted in mounting expenses for constructing and maintaining dikes and other hydrological projects.

The effect of the water on landscape and soil, and its interaction with human action, can also be observed in the sea clay areas, both in the north (Friesland and Groningen) and in the south (Zeeland and Flanders). The Flemish coast along the North Sea was particularly badly affected as a result of the destruction of dunes. In the period of rising population pressure the dunes were increasingly used for pasturing, which led to erosion. Problems mounted in the 14th century, perhaps partly because of the transgressive phase of the sea, but mainly because monitoring the agricultural use of the dunes declined as a result of social, political, and economic turmoil.[114] This led to further erosion of vegetation and destruction of the coastal dunes, leaving the coastal areas unprotected. Also, the risks from inundation had risen as a result of increasing embankment and creation of new polders, reducing the water storage capacities. At times the water piled up behind the dikes and burst over the land when the dikes were breached.

The second half of the 14th century was a time of catastrophes in the north of Flanders and Zeeland, with severe inundations in 1357, 1375–6, 1394, and 1404.[115] Apart from ecological problems, the declining profitability of agriculture as a result of the 14th-century population decline may have played a role in this, making the high costs of water management difficult to bear. Also, there was poor management and lack of control, caused by the fact that the senior dike officials in Zeeland, the *dijkgraven*, were often absentee landowners who collected job titles, without having much knowledge of the field. They often considered this post to be honorific and gave priority to their own interests as large landowners and their own profits.[116] The increasingly skewed property distribution added to the difficulties, with large landowners more interested in short-term gains than in long-term sustainability. In Zeeuws-Vlaanderen in the 16th century, large landowners disposed of their property in areas under threat where water management taxes were high. They concentrated their property inland, thus

---

[114] Augustyn, 'De evolutie van het duinecosysteem'.
[115] Gottschalk, *Historische geografie van westelijk Zeeuws-Vlaanderen*, i: 162–168, 181, 192–194, and 201.
[116] Dekker, *Zuid-Beveland*, 537–548.

further damaging the financial basis for responsible management of the dikes.[117] At times, large landowners were even able to benefit from a catastrophe, since they were the only ones with sufficient resources to bear the great expense of reclaiming the abandoned inundated land. These cases demonstrate how the human influence on the environment can only be understood by including the social structure of the region, sometimes resulting in positive and sometimes in negative ecological changes.

In the sandy areas the effects of human influence on the landscape may have been less dramatic, but they did exist. This was most apparent in the impact of overintensive use of the forest, overgrazing, and the felling of forests. In the Veluwe region as early as the 10th century, deforestation caused by iron manufacture resulted in the decline of the industry and increasing difficulties from drifting sand, further exacerbated by the severe drought in this period.[118] Some parts of the Veluwe became a desert-like landscape, which is now one of the last active inland sand drifts in western Europe. In the later Middle Ages, other sandy areas had similar problems, as in the Campine region, where drifts were mainly due to extensive sod cutting for manure. Lords, village communities, commoners, and, in the later Middle Ages, also the authorities, reacted to these ecological problems by increasing regulation and legislation. These attempted to prevent over-intensive use of the wastelands by recording communal rights, as in the Veluwe, or in other cases by direct supervision exercised by a public servant.[119] The latter was the case, for instance, in the (Neder-)Rijkswald, a relic of the large, old Ketelwoud, formerly a royal forest east of Nijmegen. The local duke appointed a forest count, who was responsible for the sale of oak timber and osiers from the forest, supervision of the foresters and their servants, monitoring regulations, collecting fines, and the general protection of the Rijkswald.[120]

Attempts like these, however, were often unsuccessful. In the first half of the 15th century there were clear signs of exhaustion or degradation of forests in some areas. In the Rijkswald it was the Duke of Guelders himself who, to meet his financial needs, ordered the felling of almost all the larger trees and gradually reduced the minimum number of trees to be left from 75 to 13 per hectare.[121] In practice, around 1430, hundreds of hectares were denuded of trees each year. Similar situations were found in all Guelders forests, such as in the Veluwe, as well as in present-day Limburg. In the late 16th century the Netherlands with

---

[117] De Kraker, *Landschap uit balans*, 269–291, and Soens, 'Explaining deficiencies of water management'.
[118] Heidinga, *Medieval settlement*, 75–81 and 105–127. For the iron industry, see below, section VII.2, pp. 353–355.
[119] Buis, *Historia forestis*, 36–52 en 304–307. Cf. for the commons (*marken*), see below, section III.3, pp. 98–102.
[120] Roes, 'De waldgraaf van het (Neder)Rijkswald'.
[121] Wartena, 'Vier eeuwen bosbeheer in Gelderland', 33–40, 94–100, 182–191, and 256–269.

England and Scotland had become the least forested part of Europe, with about 4 per cent of the area forested, as compared to about one-third in France and Germany.[122] This made wood to be used for fuel, building, and other purposes increasingly rare. The cutting of trees and sod also caused sand to drift over large areas of heath and even arable land.

Attempts were made to stop the drifting by stricter regulation and an active reforestation programme, when, around 1560, the Guelders Audit Office and some entrepreneurs developed plans for controlling the drifting by replanting the Rijkswoud with thousands of young oaks.[123] However, it proved impossible to curtail existing usage rights. Also, knowledge about how best to accomplish reforestation was lacking, and many of the saplings planted were simply stolen, so most of these attempts failed and the process of deforestation advanced ever further. More successful was preservation in regions where almost all forest had already disappeared, increasing the value of the few remaining woodlands. In Flanders the forest of Nieppe became protected by clearly defined property rights, restriction of usage rights, and a strong authority willing to enforce restrictions,[124] resulting in a forest of 2,600 hectares that survives to the present day. On the other hand, in regions where forests were large and seemingly inexhaustible, as in the Ardennes, deforestation advanced much more quickly. Only in the 16th and 17th centuries was stricter legislation enacted, but maintenance remained difficult, and degradation advanced ever further. Moreover, growing industrial need for fuel worked against such efforts.[125] By 1800, following many centuries of cutting, many parts of what was once the largest forest in the Low Countries were almost completely devoid of trees and most of the land consisted of rough sheep pastures. It was only then that serious reforestation programmes were started.

The negative aspects of human activity have been stressed here, but this picture should be more balanced. In general, human beings have fairly successfully maintained a delicate balance with nature in the medieval Low Countries. This equilibrium was more precarious than elsewhere because of the ever-present threat of flooding, the extreme dynamism of natural geographical change, and the relatively high population densities with the associated intensity of land use. Problems were sometimes made worse by the self-interest of particular social groups, but could also be alleviated by institutional arrangements. Sometimes these were aimed at aiding the interests of a particular group, as with the protection of forests by the king and nobility for preserving hunting privileges; sometimes at aiding a more general interest, as with the restrictions on the use of common wastelands imposed by an assembly of commoners. Moreover, positive measures were undertaken to improve the quality of the land or to

---

[122] P. Warde, 'Fear of wood shortage', 34. [123] Buis, *Historia forestis*, 307–315.
[124] Sommé, 'Réglements, délits et organisation'.
[125] Hoyois, *L'Ardenne et l'Ardennais*, 443–483. Cf. also section VII.2, pp. 353–355.

undo unintended results of human action. In several regions the positive effects were predominant and made the land increasingly more suitable to the needs of agriculture. This was the case, for instance, when drainage canals, ditches, and sluices were constructed, or when agricultural land was enlarged by embankment. Also, in several regions the fertility of the arable soil was greatly increased by the use of manure, night soil, marling, or sod manure, and by mixing soils, as was the case in inland Flanders. These regions were not very fertile originally, as they consisted largely of poor sandy-loamy soils, but as a result of century-long use and fertilization, often by very labour-intensive methods, they became increasingly more fertile.[126] Combined with the very intensive cultivation of the soil, this sometimes resulted in very high yields in the late Middle Ages, perhaps the highest in Europe.

Both the negative and the positive aspects of human action appear most sharply in the course of the 12th and 13th centuries, as a result of the growing population pressure. On the one hand, there was an enormous extension of cultivated land through embankment, reclamation, and increasing fertilization, which increased the yields. On the other hand, the pressure on natural resources became very great, intensifying ecological problems. Extra labour input was needed to feed the growing number of mouths and to obtain more output from the land. Extension of cultivated land was becoming increasingly difficult because almost all the suitable land had been reclaimed, and only more marginal lands were still available. On these poorer soils, ecological problems occurred sooner and were more severe than on soils that had been cultivated longer and were more fertile. This can be seen from the soil exhaustion, sand drifting, and difficulties with the water, leading to further pressure on the remaining agricultural land. The fact that people from the coastal areas in the Low Countries could be tempted to emigrate to the north of Germany as early as the 12th century was an indication of this; there was also emigration even further away, to the area between the Elbe and Saale south of Magdeburg,[127] inhabited mainly by Slavs. In the course of the 13th century more direct signs of increasing tension between population numbers and agrarian resources start to appear, culminating in the terrible famine of 1315–22.[128]

These later developments, and the interaction between landscape and people, show distinct regional differences. These are connected with the differences in soil and landscape, but also with the marked differences in occupation and reclamation during the phases of population growth in the 6th–8th centuries and again in the 10th–13th centuries. These produced very different social structures from region to region, and this is the subject to which we will turn now.

---

[126] For agricultural development and productivity, see also section VII.1, pp. 331–333. For the relation with population density and property structures, see also section VI.2, pp. 282–286.
[127] Schlesinger, 'Flemmingen und Kühren'.   [128] Cf. section VI.2, p. 279, below.

III

The Emergence of a Regional Framework in the Early and High Middle Ages: Power, Property, and Social Structures

Landscape and soil were main factors determining the timing, method, and organization of occupation and reclamation for a region. Along with the rights to the reclaimed wilderness, social-political power over the region, and the relative availability of land, labour, and capital, geography was the main element in the process of occupation. This chapter will look at how these elements, in their turn, determined how the rights to land and labour in the newly occupied region were distributed across the social groups. In later chapters it will become clear how these social structures, despite changes in the articulation of rights, showed strong continuity through the centuries and shaped later social and economic developments.

We will first investigate how the rights to land and labour were distributed across the social groups in the (re-)occupation of regions during the early and high Middle Ages, how these rights were organized and used, and how they helped to constitute the socio-economic structures and power balance among the various social groups. We pay special attention to the property rights to land, which were a major source of wealth and power for the elite.[1] In the course of the early Middle Ages, in combination with the emergence of new systems of land ownership such as the manorial system, land became increasingly important as a source of revenue for the elite, as in other parts of western Europe. Land was equally vital for those outside the elite, since holding or using land constituted access to the main source of subsistence.

Rights to land in the Middle Ages differed from the absolute and exclusive property rights that became dominant in north-western Europe in the modern period. In the medieval situation, several persons and parties could have several types of overlapping rights to the same plot of land and its produce. These included rights of usage, inheritance, access, and alienation, and various rights to the produce. There was no single, exclusive owner of the land. Under manorial organization, both the lord and the serf had solid rights to the land, and in

---

[1] Theuws, *Images of the past*, 301–302, and Davies and Fouracre, 'Conclusion', 245–250.

the case of common lands, lords, territorial princes (or the state), villagers, and/or commoners could all claim some rights. Besides these rights, there were additional, overlapping rights to the same land exercised by family members, neighbours, and village communities, as well as by the former owners of the rights.[2] This variety of overlapping claims and rights allowed for stability and continuity, and thus brought long-term security for the parties involved. It also allowed for some flexibility, offering various instruments for the transfer and distribution of land outside the market, and it permitted the holders to translate these rights into whichever element was most valuable to them: status, power, or the production of food. In this sense, the possession of these various rights was fairly effective for all parties involved. As happened in other parts of Europe, these rights only slowly became more absolute and exclusive. In the Low Countries this process was generally more rapid than elsewhere in Europe, since it occurred particularly in the course of the late Middle Ages,[3] but after the period under consideration in this chapter.

In the early and high Middle Ages, therefore, land was not primarily a commodity to be freely bought and sold, but was embedded in social networks and relationships, and landed property formed the main instrument constituting such social relationships and could be used in several ways as a source of power. It opened ways to extract a surplus or levy tribute from the agricultural cultivators, and returns from the land served the consumption needs of the powerful, but land was also a component of socio-political relations. A gift of land, a temporary grant, or a fief created or consolidated these relations. Landed property was thus the main indicator and the basis of social relations and power relationships.

III.1. KING, NOBILITY, AND OTHER LANDHOLDERS

Royal Properties

We begin our analysis with the royal estates. These should not be seen as fixed properties, but rather as complexes of shifting claims, rights, and positions of authority, for the king as an institution, his person, and his family. These royal complexes are relatively well represented in early medieval sources, and their presence and organization exerted a strong influence on the further development of large land holdings and the use of property at that time, particularly in the Low Countries, where they were more strongly represented than in other parts of Europe. The Low Countries was one of the main centres of gravity of

---

[2] Van Bavel and Hoppenbrouwers, 'Landholding and land transfer', 14–16.
[3] Cf. for this and for developments towards more exclusive property rights section V.1, pp. 164–169.

the Carolingian empire,[4] with the Pippinids and the Carolingians possessing a concentration of wealth and influence there. The royal estates there originated from several sources. First, the Frankish kings, who considered themselves the successors to the Roman emperors, appropriated with the conquest of this area all goods formerly belonging to the emperor and the Roman state.[5] Particularly in the southern parts of the Low Countries, belonging to the province of Gaul, they acquired several estates and the areas along roads, as well as the military fortifications in the Limes area in the north along the Rhine. On the basis of the *ius eremi*, the king acquired the rights to uninhabited wastelands. Forfeited and expropriated lands were also added to the royal estates, and there were the 'private' properties of the royal family. The early Carolingians owned many properties in the Meuse valley, which were gradually merged with other royal property.

The royal estates were concentrated in two areas, associated with the origins of the royal property and the attractiveness of the regions. First, there was a belt stretching from the Ardennes, through Liège and the Meuse valley, the Haspengouw and Maastricht, to Aachen and Cologne; and second, a belt stretching from Utrecht, over the Guelders river area and Nijmegen, to the Rijkswoud (the Imperial Forest). Both belts had a good transport network based on the rivers and both had fertile soils. The Meuse valley formed a nucleus of early Carolingian power; the Pippinid branch had its power base in the region around Liège.[6] Several prominent families of the Frankish elite also originated from this area and it had several early royal palaces and *villae*, such as Theux, Herstal, and Jupille, and the Chèvremont fortification near Liège. Several large properties of the early Carolingians were situated here, often bordering on one another and forming huge complexes.[7] These properties descended partly from family holdings, but some were Merovingian fiscal goods acquired by the Carolingians in the late 7th century. This fiscal property probably derived in part from Roman imperial possessions.[8]

The same region also included several religious institutions closely associated with Frankish or royal power, such as St Servaas in Maastricht, the bishopric of Maastricht/Tongeren, and the Abbey of Lobbes. The Pippinids also founded several monasteries, or facilitated their foundation, as in Nivelles, Andennes, and Fosses.[9] The more important of these institutions were situated on the border between the archbishoprics of Rheims and Cologne and between the Frankish kingdoms of Neustria and Austrasia, providing for their founder/protector a

---

[4] Gerberding, *The rise of the Carolingians*, 116–140, and Fouracre, *The age of Charles Martel*, 34, 45–49, and 61–64.
[5] Schlesinger, *Beobachtungen*.   [6] Ibid., 258.
[7] Werner, *Der Lütticher Raum*, 420–421 and 442–455.
[8] Müller-Kehlen, *Die Ardennen*, 67 and 115, asserts this Roman origin, but hardly gives concrete proof. Cf. also the discussion by Werner, *Der Lütticher Raum*, 458–468.
[9] Dierkens, *Abbayes et chapitres*, esp. 320–327.

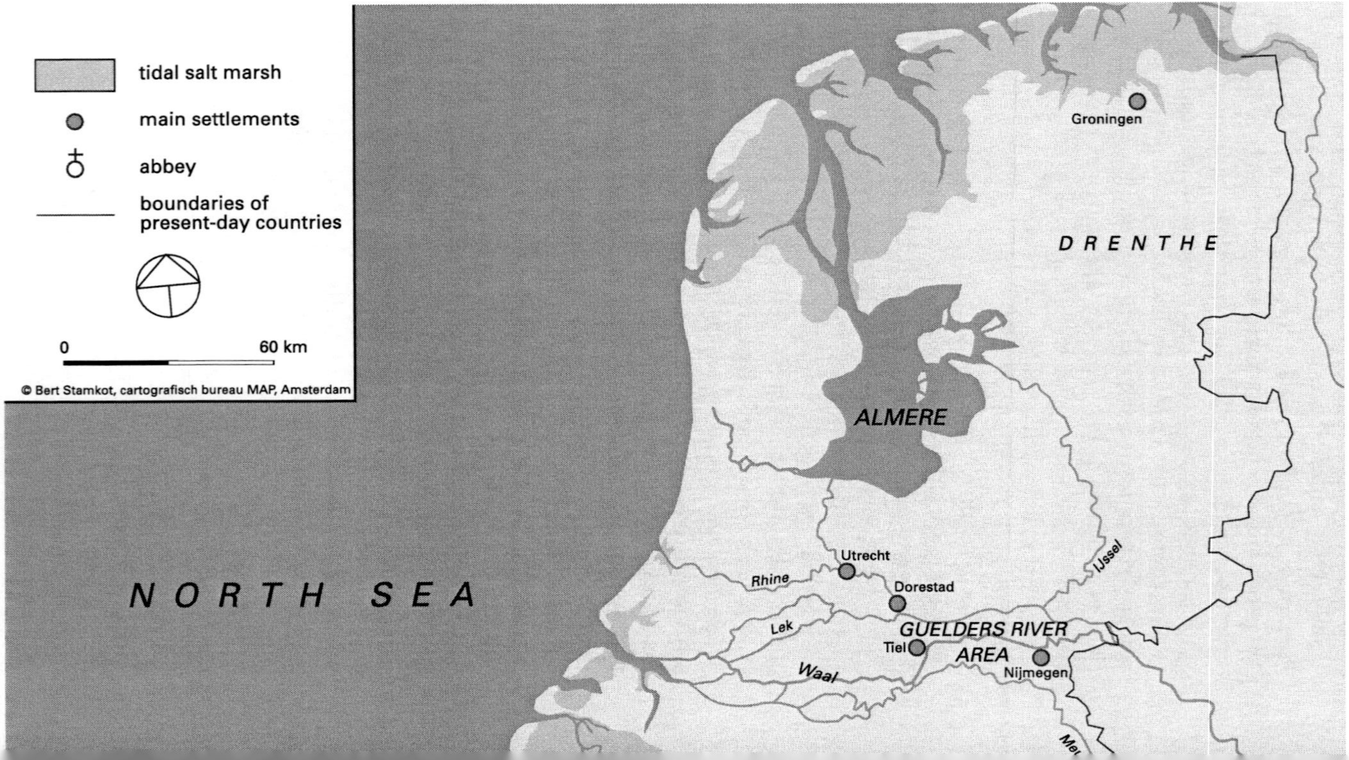
tidal salt marsh
main settlements
abbey
boundaries of present-day countries
0
60 km
© Bert Stamkot, cartografisch bureau MAP, Amsterdam
NORTH SEA
Groningen
DRENTHE
ALMERE
Utrecht
Rhine
Dorestad
IJssel
Lek
GUELDERS RIVER AREA
Tiel
Nijmegen
Waal

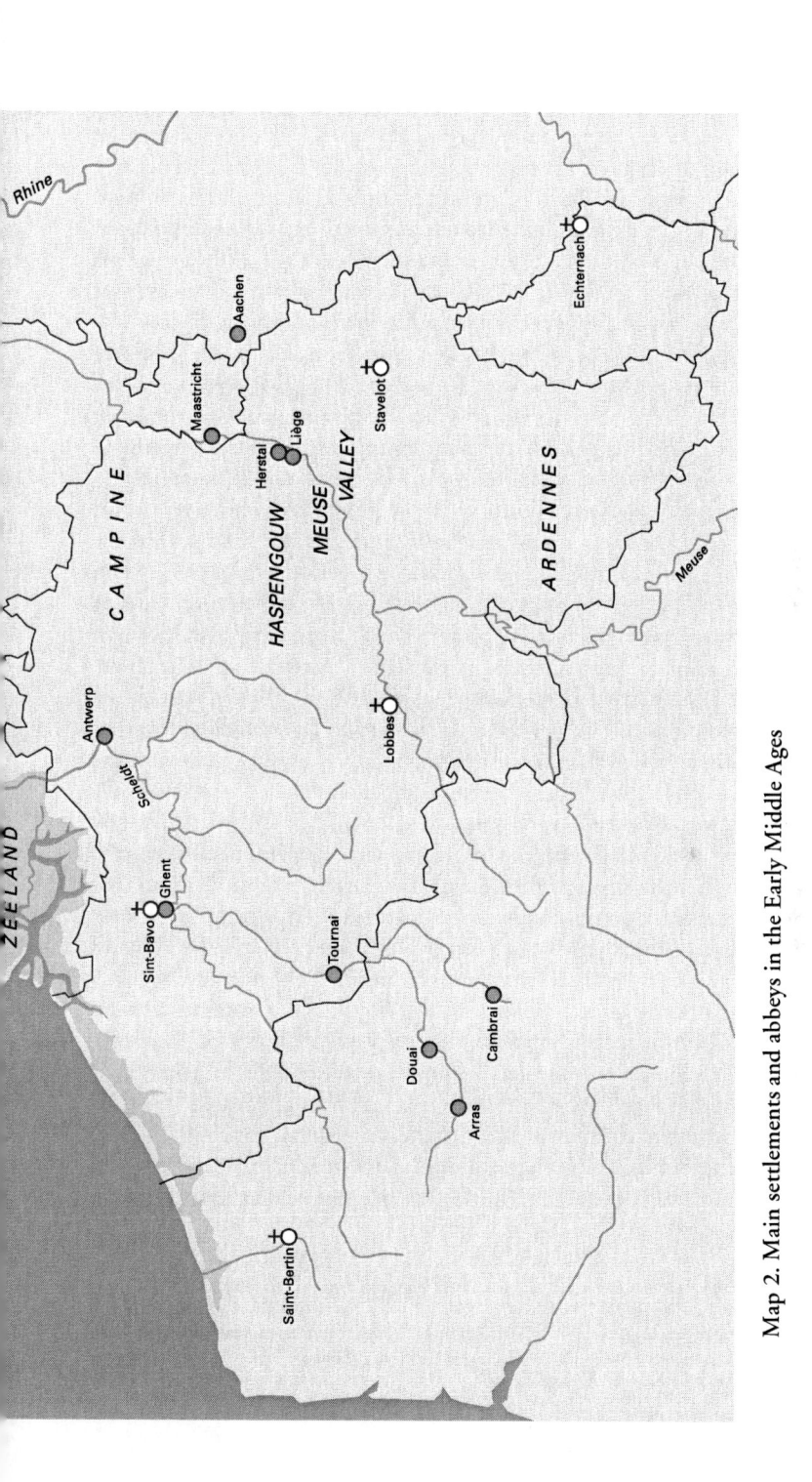

Map 2. Main settlements and abbeys in the Early Middle Ages

powerful position in these strategic locations. Another centre in this royal belt was Aachen, Charlemagne's seat, and the site of the coronations of several kings. Near this belt was the forest area of the Ardennes, probably acquired together with the province of Gaul by the Frankish king, on the basis of the *ius eremi*.[10] This area was one of the king's favourite hunting grounds, and he collected levies on pigs, grazing, and tilling, and had the authority to initiate and direct reclamation there. From the Merovingian period on, administration of the forests in the Ardennes was in the hands of royal *forestarii*. By the 10th century it was organized as a forest county, and its institutions survived well into the modern era.

The second important belt of royal estates was further north, in the Guelders river area. One of its main centres was Nijmegen. The *palatium* there, the Valkhof, was refurbished and extended by Charlemagne into one of the most impressive residences of the period. He and his successors often visited the Valkhof, and it lost its high status only in the course of the 11th century.[11] There was no capital city in the Frankish Empire, with the king and his itinerant court constantly on the move, but Nijmegen was one of the most important residences, sharing this position in the Carolingian period with Aachen and Herstal, again indicating the importance of this area within the empire. Utrecht was also an important base of Frankish power, and the remains of the Roman castle formed the point of departure for the missionary activities of Willibrord, which laid the foundation for the later episcopal see of Utrecht.[12] Almost all the area between Utrecht and Nijmegen was in royal hands. Located close together were the *curtis imperatoria* Tiel, the *caput* (administrative centre) Heerewaarden, and the *villa* Zaltbommel with its royal mint, and there were three royal tolls linked to these centres. Royal estates were also located in Tuil and Varik, directly across the Waal, opposite Zaltbommel and Heerewaarden, forming clusters with the river as the main link. North of the Guelders river area, too, some important concentrations of royal properties were found. There was a large complex of royal estates near IJsselstein, extending along both banks of the Lek and the Holland IJssel, and in the area between the Kromme Rijn and the Lek, around Dorestad, as well as the district Opgooi, probably a large royal estate administered by a separate official.[13] Apparently, Frankish authority placed great political and military value on this region, understandable given its strategic location, as it was situated on the border zone between the areas inhabited by Franks, Frisians, and Saxons, and was vital for transport and trade. In general, concentrations of royal domains were found at important waterways and roads, particularly where different landscape types bordered one another, as in the Guelders river clay area,

[10] Müller-Kehlen, *Die Ardennen*, 99–102, and Kaspers, *Comitatus nemoris*, 32–39 and 93–97.
[11] Binding, *Deutsche Königspfalzen*, 115–116 and 245–252.
[12] Van Vliet, *In kringen van kanunniken*, 71–89 and 101–110; and for the river area: Rothoff, *Studien zur Geschichte des Reichsgutes*, 46, 83–84, 89–91, 128–131, 138, and the map.
[13] Dekker, *Het Kromme Rijngebied*, 370–390.

which was surrounded by sandy regions to the north and south and a peat region to the west, and crossed by several rivers.

Most of these royal estates were probably no longer controlled by the king when they first appear in the sources, since they were often distributed to his vassals, usurped by local potentates, or donated to religious institutions. Still, the royal estates left a clear legacy in later property structures. After the 11th century hardly any royal estates can be found in these regions, but many large properties belonged to religious institutions, territorial lords, or noblemen, who had taken over the royal rights through feudal tenure, usurpation, or donation. In Groningen, in the high Middle Ages the royal properties came into the hands of the Bishop of Utrecht, the Abbey of Werden, the cathedral church, a monastery, two urban parishes, and the castellan.[14] In late medieval sources the origin of these properties and the former important position of the king can still be recognized in property structures, as well as in ecclesiastical, administrative, and economic institutions, and even in the relationship between town and countryside. In general, the influence of royal property on later large land ownership was probably most pronounced in the area of use. Since the properties of the Frankish king were pre-eminently organized in manors,[15] the institutions and authorities that took over the rights of the king, acquiring his goods and often taking their example from the king, showed a predilection for the manorial system.

The *Homines Franci* and Smaller Landholders

Closely associated with royal power were the *homines franci*, found particularly in the Guelders river area. These were men of some standing, closely linked with Frankish authority and being able to exercise military power, buttressed by their medium-sized properties. Their precise status and origin have provoked long and, so far, unresolved discussions.[16] Some see them as Frankish colonizers, placed by Pipin II from the year 690 in the Guelders river area after the defeat of the Frisians, and perhaps also in Zeeland and Brabant. Their arrival would then be part of the Frankish immigration or even colonization, perhaps from the Meuse region. Others, however, suggest instead that Frankish rulers tried to establish links with the local population, and particularly with the local elite, tying its members to their rule, as is confirmed by recent investigation for Toxandria in the Campine region.[17] The same would apply to the Guelders river area, which already had a strong Frankish element in the Chamaves who had long been

---

[14] Noomen, 'Koningsgoed in Groningen', 97–144. This process is discussed in a more general sense below. For more on Groningen, see also section III.3, p. 116.
[15] Cf. section III.2, pp. 80–81 below.
[16] Blok, *De Franken*, 43–46 and 93–96, and Van Winter, 'Homines franci', 346–351. For discussion on the *homines franci*, see also Van Bavel, *Transitie en continuïteit*, 446–458.
[17] Costambeys, 'An aristocratic community', 39–62, although with the misconception that he sees this as a border region, thus overlooking the Guelders river area.

settled there, and thus did not require colonization. The term *franci* could then refer to their Frankish origin, but in other cases such as the Campine perhaps also to their link to Frankish rule, or to the free status of the *homines franci*. Their freedom was used by some authors to designate the *homines franci* as royal freemen, whose free status was created and protected by the king in exchange for taxes and particularly military service.[18] This interpretation has now been abandoned, since royal freedom is increasingly seen as a construction of legal historians with little foundation in the sources.[19] Moreover, the *homines franci* in the Guelders river area and elsewhere do not seem to have been soldier-colonizers, but rather a local elite with a military function.

The Frankish rulers had a clear interest in binding to them a powerful, loyal group of people in the Guelders river area because it was a highly strategic location on the border of the Frankish Empire, at the confluence of the Rhine and the Meuse. The *homines franci* served these interests, by organizing the defence. Perhaps the large concentrations of *heem-* names (from the Frankish *haim* or home) which were found in exactly this part of the river area are the silent witnesses to some kind of defensive complexes laid out by the Franks at strategic locations, as is also suggested for the area along important roads in Westphalia and the eastern Netherlands, such as the road between Putten, Deventer, Ootmarsum, and Coevorden.[20] In the river area, this interpetation is supported by the concentration of Frankish names with the root *heri* (army), such as Herwijnen, Herwen, and Heerwaarden (army watch).[21]

Examples of *homines franci* whose position was strengthened by the king because they received property for reclamation near a royal fisc, either in property or in feudal tenure as royal vassals, are known from various parts of western Europe. They date mainly from the period around 800, and are found especially in the border areas of the Frankish Empire.[22] In the Low Countries this process may have occurred a century earlier, when this area formed a border region of the empire, as in the Guelders river area, forming the border with the Frisian sphere of influence, and also around the estuary of the Scheldt in Zeeland. There, *homines franci* were mentioned in the property list of the Abbey of St Bavo (*c*.810), apparently placed under this religious institution by the king some time earlier, together with the property they lived on, to better organize the defence of this area.[23] The nearby fort of Antwerp, mentioned in 694, was the centre of a *marca regni*, a border district of the Frankish Empire. Antwerp and its toll provided the Frankish fisc with substantial revenues, and from the fort, as

---

[18] Van Winter, *Ministerialiteit*, 25–33 en 45–57.
[19] Schmitt, *Untersuchungen zu den Liberi Homines*, esp. 36–39, 135–136, and 178–179.
[20] Slicher van Bath, *Mensch en land*, i:184–187, and ii: 62–63, 102–104; and for Westfalia: Hömberg, *Westfälische Landesgeschichte*, 28–43, although qualified by Droege, 'Fränkische Siedlung', 271–288. See also section II.2, pp. 33–34 above.
[21] Blok, *De Franken*, 76.   [22] Leupen, 'De Karolingische villa Beek', 379–381 and 389.
[23] Verhulst, 'Das Bezitzverzeichnis', 215–216 and 234.

stronghold on the Frisian border, the Scheldt estuary was guarded by a fleet. In the early Middle Ages this region and other border areas of strategic value were characterized by large royal properties, strong royal influence, and a prominent position of the *homines franci*.

In the reclamations undertaken in these regions during the Frankish period, the *homines franci* played an important part. As local men of standing they were singled out to encourage and lead the reclamation. Moreover, they had a special bond with the Frankish king, who could grant land for reclamation by virtue of his regalian wilderness rights. Their interests and those of the king were completely parallel, creating a solid structure of power and authority. Thus, the *homines franci* acquired a robust position there, buttressed by their medium-sized properties which they retained until the late Middle Ages, particularly where they remained outside the control of the emerging territorial lords. The west of the Guelders river area was brought under princely rule only in the 13th century, and in the late Middle Ages free knights formed no less than 5 per cent of its population.[24] They did not belong to the nobility, nor were they *ministeriales*, but free men of standing, having their roots as a social group in the early medieval *homines franci*. Their survival as a group demonstrates the continuity of social structure through the Middle Ages.

Because there are hardly any relevant sources available, little is known of the properties of smaller landholders in the early Middle Ages, and this is particularly true of the peasants or cultivators of the land. The general impression is that in this period their position became increasingly precarious as a result of the extension of large land ownership, the rise of manorial exploitation, and decreasing freedom. Small family holdings were gradually integrated into large estates and a substantial part of the population became dependent on landlords. In the Campine, for instance, the large landowners considerably increased their control over social and economic life in the 8th century.[25] However, there was one significant group whose position probably improved in this period: the slaves, who gradually were integrated into the group of serfs.

Some idea of the position of non-noble people can also be obtained from the Carolingian legal codifications. Each tribe had its own customary law, transmitted orally, but now codified by Frankish rule. Some Frankish modifications were made, but in general these laws reflected fairly well the regional and ethnic differences within the Low Countries. These are normative sources and insufficient to illustrate the entire diversity of legal-social positions, but they do seem to bear a relation to the actual situation and they offer us some idea of the diversity of ethnic social structures in this period.

---

[24] Cf. Van Bavel, *Transitie en continuïteit*, 446–457.
[25] Theuws, 'Landed property', 346–347. For the decline of slavery and the rise of manorialism, see also section III.2, pp. 76–82 below.

The *Lex Salica* provides an impression of the structure of Frankish society,[26] and particularly relates to most of the central parts of the Low Countries. Social mobility was possible, but what is most striking in this law is the great inequality between the various social groups, as reflected in the amount of the *wergild*, the compensation for homicide to be paid to the heirs of a slain man. This shows that among the Franks freemen and nobles had identical status, with a wergild of 200 shillings. Half-freemen had a wergild of 100 shillings, and serfs and unfree only 35 shillings. The lowest position was held by slaves, who had almost disappeared from the Low Countries, but they are estimated here at the same value as a horse or an ox, and liable to severe punishment (including mutilation) if they broke the law. Regional differences within Frankish society are revealed by the *Ewa ad Amorem*, also known as the *Lex Chamavorum Francorum*, from *c*.800, probably associated with the central part of the Guelders river area, one of the areas earliest occupied by Franks.[27] In this source, as would be expected, the *homines franci* figure prominently as a separate group, with a wergild three times as high as that of the *ingenui* or freemen.

Among the Saxons, found in the north-eastern Low Countries, the *liber* and *nobilis* are clearly separated, at least according to the *Lex Saxonum*, promulgated by Charlemagne in 802/803 after the defeat of the Saxons by the Franks. The nobles held lordship rights, and the freemen subordinate to the nobles, although freemen could own land, serfs, and slaves.[28] The separation of the nobles is also evidenced by their very high wergild, six times that of a freeman, and the highest amount in the whole of Europe, being the equivalent of some 700 cows. The elevated position of the noble was part of a process started in the 8th century, but certainly further enforced by Charlemagne. On the other hand, the difference between freemen and serfs was very small, as evidenced by the 4:3 relationship of their wergild. There were also other democratic or egalitarian elements among the Saxons before the Frankish conquest; most notably the general meetings at Marklo, south of Bremen, where from each district an equal number of noblemen, freemen, and serfs participated in legislation and political decision-making.[29] Charlemagne abolished this system and gave the nobles a monopoly on power and a much higher position in Saxon society.

The *Lex Frisionum* was codified by royal Frankish authority around 802, but despite Frankish influence is assumed to have an old Frisian core. It relates to the Frisians in the north and north-west of the Low Countries and shows the nobles, freemen, and serfs (*liti*) as distinct social groups. As is also shown in a capitulary from 807, there was an aristocracy in Frisia able to afford horses and armour,

[26] Staab, 'Die Gesellschaft des Merowingerreichs', 479–484.
[27] Niermeyer, 'Het middenNederlands rivierengebied', 146–169.
[28] Hagemann, 'Die Stände der Sachsen', 402–445, and Epperlein, 'Sachsen im frühen Mittelalter'.
[29] Goldberg, 'Popular revolt', esp. 472–473. Cf. also above section II.2, pp. 29–31.

but there were also many freemen with free properties, and the sources place more weight on the difference between free and unfree than between noble and non-noble.[30] In addition to these groups, apart from the diversity of legal and social positions hidden behind the terms, there were *mancipia* and *servi*, both probably designating slaves.

After *c.*800, apart from the slaves, the legal-social position of large segments of the population in the Low Countries seems to have deteriorated. In many regions freemen were relegated to the position of dependants or unfree. This was linked to the further rise of the manorial system in this period. The manors of the Abbey of St Bertin in the 9th century were still absorbing formally free, medium- and small-sized properties. There is some controversy about the extent of this process and the generality of this example,[31] but it is clear that it took place, leading to further loss of freedom for many. On the other hand, free peasant ownership remained more intact in infertile, marginal regions, such as Drenthe, and in those further distant from power bases and outside the reach of Frankish authority. These were unattractive to lords and remained outside their scope, or were occupied and reclaimed later, with the peasants obtaining a firmer position there.[32] Where the Franks had less power, as in the northern regions Frisia, Holland, and Drenthe, there were more free people than in the Guelders river area or regions further south. But it is difficult to say how numerous the remaining freemen were, partly because their dealings were largely outside the scope of written sources. The term *allodium* can provide some indication, since it seems to designate land or property held in free ownership by nobility as well as ordinary peasants, partly going back to early medieval free property. Several areas, such as the north-east of Namur, had clear concentrations of these peasant allods.[33] The peasantry thus were not a single homogeneous group, but showed definite differences in wealth, ownership of land, freedom, and status, with some clear regional variations.

Properties of Religious Institutions

Much more is known about the properties of religious institutions. Donations by the elite greatly augmented their property in the early Middle Ages. Many of them, including the abbeys of Lobbes, Stavelot-Malmedy, and St Servaas in Maastricht, and the bishoprics of Utrecht and Maastricht/Liège, were ruled

---

[30] Timmer, 'Restanten'; Lebecq, *Marchands*, 134–135; and kind communication from Wolfert van Egmond dated 5 July 2007.
[31] Genicot, 'Sur le domaine de St–Bertin', 69–78, and Morimoto, 'Autour de grande domaine', 69–70.
[32] See below, section III.2, pp. 81–82.
[33] Genicot, *L'économie rurale, passim*, for example, i: 69–84, and Leenders, *Van Turnhoutervoorde*, 200–240—although both mainly focus on all kinds of high medieval allods, not necessarily all going back to the early Middle Ages.

by clients or relatives of the king and were granted substantial parts of royal estates. Distant religious institutions were also greatly favoured, both by the king and by the local elite. In the early period of Christianization large abbeys in northern France and western Germany acquired properties in various parts of the Low Countries, reflecting both the spheres of political power and their role in missionary activity. For instance, the abbeys of Prüm, Lorsch, Werden, Thorn, the Paderborn Abbey of Abdinghof, Echternach, and the Aachen St Adelbert chapter, all situated far to the east and south-east, had properties in the Guelders river area.[34] This, and the notable absence of properties of West Frankish institutions there, point to the fact that this region was Christianized from the east, from the middle reaches of the rivers Rhine and Meuse. Equally, Echternach, the private abbey of Willibrord and under the protection of Pippin II, received numerous properties in the Campine, where Willibrord had been very active as a missionary.[35] Especially in the early 8th century, Echternach acquired parts or all of estates, as well as forested areas and serfs there.

The introduction of the Christian faith had strong influences on social and economic life. Christianity buttressed the power of the elite, and particularly the position of Frankish rule. The interaction among regional elite groups, religious institutions, and the king in the early Middle Ages has been investigated in an exemplary way for the Campine, showing the role of Christianity in increasing integration.[36] Some elite networks, particularly those where the Frankish kings were not in control, were replaced by networks centred on religious institutions, which were often under the control of the rulers. Christianity also stimulated the emergence of the manorial system and the increasing power of manorial lords, as highlighted below. It also allowed the introduction of a new type of exaction: the tithe, destined for the sustenance of the parish priest, maintenance of the church, and poor relief. This levy, generally one-tenth or one-eleventh of the grain production, and sometimes also levied on cattle and other crops, was strongly supported by Frankish rulers such as by Pipin III in 764/5, and later was even made compulsory by Charlemagne and Louis the Pious.[37] At first, it was mainly the Church that profited from these payments, but increasingly most of the tithes came into the hands of those locally powerful, such as noblemen who founded the parish church or monastery or 'protected' it. The levying of tithes was a heavy burden on the peasantry, and provoked complaints and sometimes even resistance. Many peasants will have welcomed the appeal made around 1100 by Tanchelm, an itinerant preacher, to refuse payment of certain tithes in

---

[34] Van Bavel, *Transitie en continuïteit*, 157–158, 263–264, 299, 314, and Knichel, *Geschichte des Fernbsitzes*, 16–37. Cf. below, section IV.4, pp. 223–224, for the disposal of these distant properties in the high Middle Ages.
[35] Theuws, 'Landed property', 321–324 and 338–344, and Costambeys, 'An aristocratic community'.
[36] Theuws, 'Landed property'. [37] Semmler, 'Zehntgebot und Pfarrtermination'.

Zeeland, where the distant Utrecht chapters owned tithes,[38] just as the peasants constantly tried to escape payment of the tithes by fraud, embezzlement, legal procedures, or even outright refusal. The structural success of such resistance was very limited, however, particularly where the tithe owner held a powerful position, through his jurisdictional power or other instruments.

In the early Middle Ages, religious property and revenues were thus extended further and further. This also brought about new types of administration. The properties of large institutions, generally spread over wide areas, were often administered through inventories and polyptiques, detailed lists of properties and incomes. The example was set by Charlemagne in a capitulary known as the *Brevia Exempla*, intended as a model for the layout of inventories of estates. Royal estates in Artois are listed as one of the three examples in this capitulary. Other 9th-century polyptiques are those of the abbeys of Lobbes (mainly listing properties in Hainaut and also some in Brabant), St Pieter at Ghent (first half of 9th century in Flanders), and St Bertin at Saint-Omer (in southern Flanders, 844–8).[39] Less elaborate documents were also used, such as lists of possessions or inventories, nearly all compiled and kept by large religious institutions. These documents allowed firmer control of the possessions, perhaps changes in their structure and exploitation, and an improved use of the potential they offered.

Shortly afterwards, Western Francia saw the emergence of the cartulary, used mainly by religious institutions, such as the bishop of Utrecht (914), the Abbey of St Peter in Ghent (945) and the Abbey of St Bertin (961), and then more widely in the next century.[40] From the 12th century on, a steep rise in the number of charters issued can be observed, throughout western Europe, but concentrated at first in the regions with large land holdings, particularly of religious institutions. This was followed, especially in the 13th century, by increasingly sophisticated access to written documents, with the introduction of indexes, tables of contents, cross-references, and the reorganization of archives, combined with the development of inventories and catalogues, where again the religious institutions took the lead, later followed by secular lords and towns.[41] This more efficient administration contributed to the security of property rights to land, which slowly became more absolute and exclusive from this period on.

The Rise of Banal and Territorial Lords

In the second half of the 9th century changes in political power started to occur, as the Carolingian monarchy slowly lost influence as a result of the division

---

[38] Teunis, 'De ketterij', esp. pp 161–164. For more in general on resentment against the payment of tithes: Epperlein, *Bauernbedrückung*, 45–47 and 62.
[39] Devroey, *Le polyptyque*.   [40] Declerq, 'Originals and cartularies'.
[41] In general: Mostert, 'Lezen, schrijven', esp. 218–219. For more on the link with property rights, see section V.1, pp. 166–167 below.

of the empire and internal conflicts.[42] Perhaps Carolingian authority had been somewhat superficial, plagued as it was by a lack of material sources and by communication difficulties: its stream of regulations and pronouncements on economy and society were difficult to enforce and often ineffective in practice, but it had worked as a stabilizing factor and offered some security. After the empire was divided, the Low Countries came mainly under the Middle Kingdom ruled by Lothar and Lothar II, which were weak empires with little political cohesion. The central authority was destabilized just when the area experienced invasions and Viking raids, starting around 800 and dramatically increasing from 830 and again at the end of the 9th century. The raiders destroyed and plundered especially the areas along the coast and the rivers, as in the expeditions in the years following 880, first in southern Flanders and northern France, and later when they sailed up the rivers and raided Utrecht, Maastricht, Aachen, Jülich, Cologne, and many other towns, monasteries, and trading stations.[43] In an attempt to stabilize the situation, the Frankish authority granted substantial parts of the Low Countries, particularly in the coastal zones, to Viking leaders, who then in theory became vassals of the king. Harald in Walcheren, a part of Zeeland, and Rorik in the southern part of Frisia, including the Guelders river area, were granted authority by Emperor Lothar, on condition that they would resist further attacks by the Norsemen.[44] At the same time, this situation offered some members of the regional elite the chance to strengthen their position, taking advantage of the decline of central power and the insecurity of the times and filling the power vacuum. Next to them, and especially in this coastal area on the border of the Empire, horizontal associations could then assert themselves better. Peasant associations, whose aid was sometimes even invoked in the battles against the Norsemen, probably strengthened their position. Out of this situation grew a new political equilibrium, which in the following centuries offered increasing stability at local and regional levels, and scope for dynamism—perhaps more than the Carolingian empire would ever have been able to do.

The changes in authority were reflected in the building of fortifications, which were crucial in the developments of the high Middle Ages. After the 6th to 10th centuries, in which offensive, dynamic warfare had been dominant, and mounted horsemen were crucial, a switch to defensive warfare occurred. Defensive structures, such as fortresses, castles, and later towns, gained in importance. This happened all over western Europe, but to a great extent also in the Low Countries, where many hundreds of strongholds were built. At first the fortifications were an expression of central authority, but increasingly they were built by regional and local potentates to buttress their power and strengthen

[42] A nuanced picture is offered by Maclean, *Kingship and politics*, 11–22 and 232–235. The older literature rather seems to have overemphasized the negative sides of this process.
[43] D'Haenens, *Les invasions normandes*, 45–59. For the effect on urban development, see section III.3 (Villages and Towns), p. 107 below.
[44] Halbertsma, 'The Frisian Kingdom', esp. 78–83.

their position with respect to a population who sought security. In the early 9th century, for instance, defence against the Normans was at first still coordinated centrally. Several times Charlemagne personally inspected coastal defences in the Low Countries, ordered a war fleet built, and stationed warships and organized fortified watches manned by garrisons to guard the river mouths.[45] After the Frankish Empire became weak and fragmented, however, and the Frankish armies disbanded, defences against the Normans became a regional matter, often organized and led by counts acting fairly independently. This can be observed from the construction of circular fortresses erected at strategic places where the Normans invaded the country, particularly on the estuaries of the major rivers. These refuge fortresses have circular ramparts ranging from 150 to 300 m in diameter and were built in the second half of the 9th century. The counts took the lead in this in Flanders (where at least four fortresses were built), in Holland (at least two), and perhaps also in Zeeland (several), although the king in his capacity as manorial lord of Walcheren was more involved there than elsewhere.[46]

As central rule disintegrated, the minor lords may have gained even more power than the counts. This can be observed in Zeeland and Friesland, where numerous strongholds built on mounds were erected by local lords.[47] Elsewhere, too, hundreds of small lordly strongholds were constructed from the late 11th century. These sometimes served as residences, as status symbols and representative buildings, but primarily they had a military function. Most notable among them were the motte castles, which sprang up in this period all over Europe. These were artificial mounds surrounded by a dry or wet ditch and reinforced by palisades. Sometimes they had a palisaded courtyard below, where horses and livestock could be kept and residential quarters were located, and a central tower made of wood was used as a sentinel post or residence. Particularly in Guelders, the adjacent Niederrhein area, and Limburg, areas characterized by political fragmentation, ongoing warfare between members of the dynasties, and strong feudal power, many hundreds of motte castles were built in the 12th century,[48] often in or near reclamation areas to control the reclamation and establish authority there. They allowed the castle lords to command the surrounding area and control the population. Although the line between public and private was less clear-cut than it is today, the construction of the hundreds of fortifications in the Low Countries might be interpreted as an expression of the privatization and fragmentation of public authority.

The construction of these strongholds was accompanied by the emergence of banal lordships. After the decline of royal authority, smaller lords succeeded in

[45] Sproemberg, 'Die Seepolitik', esp. 19–24, and Eickhoff, 'Maritime defence'.
[46] Henderikx, 'Vroegmiddeleeuwse ringwalburgen', 94–101.
[47] See also section II.2, pp. 41–42, above.
[48] Janssen, 'Tussen woning en versterking', 32–45, and Besteman, 'Mottes in the Netherlands', 211–224.

appropriating parts of the central jurisdictional role, aided by the insecurity of the times and their new military power. The *bannum* (the right to impose fines) and *districtus* (the right to arrest) were appropriated by local lords. This type of banal lordship, which developed in the 10th and 11th centuries, was often associated with large land holdings. When the *seigneurie banale* overlapped the *seigeneurie foncière* and the lord also had a strong military position backed by his arms and castle, this made him very powerful at the local level.

Often the lords profited from their position of power by assembling many different older levies, reviving certain obligations and imposing new exactions and extortions on the peasantry. The resentment they created among the population was reflected in clerical sources, which labelled them as *malae consuetudines*. These 'bad customs' had a mixed origin.[49] Some were usurped regalian rights, such as the exercise of high and low justice, the levying of excise duties and tolls, fishing and fowling rights, the right of ferrying, the right of accretion, the right of the wind, and rights over the wastelands. Sometimes the process went together with privatization of access to local water, and the lord placed restrictions on where, when, and even how to fish. Perhaps deriving from older custom, but formulated more clearly from the mid-10th century, were the banalities, the right of the lord to compel people to use his mill, oven, and brewery, and to exact a fee for this use.[50] An exaction which appears in the 11th century sources was the *tallia*, a direct tax, arbitrarily imposed and often very high. Specific groups, such as the unfree, bastards, and immigrants, were also taxed by personal impositions such as the heriot, to be paid at death, or a chevage, and encountered restrictions on marriage and the alienation of property. Finally, some public charges devolved upon these local lords, such as the right to demand food and accommodation, requisitioning men, horses, and carts, and tasks involving the construction or maintenance of castles or fortifications.

This amalgam of diverse levies and obligations was increasingly becoming a block of exactions and remunerative rights, which in contrast to the earlier, mainly personal levies, were now largely levied on a territorial basis. They were impressed on every person living in a specific area, excluding only nobles and priests. In the later Middle Ages this block was so uniform and fixed that there was almost no need to enumerate each element, since the designation as appurtenances of the lordship sufficed. The extent of such impositions, however, shows clear regional diversities. An attempt to calculate it was made for the county of Namur in the 13th century.[51] The amount of the tallage, depending on the size of the holding or the number of horses, was a few shillings per holding, equalling a few days' wages for a specialized craftsman. The heriot consisted mostly of a horse or cow,

---

[49] Genicot, *L'économie rurale Namuroise*, iii: 3–5 and 19–35, Genicot, *Rural communities*, 62–68, and Stephenson, 'The origin and nature'.
[50] See also section IV.2, pp. 148–149 below.
[51] Genicot, *L'économie rurale Namuroise*, iii: 78–118. Freedman, *Origins of peasant servitude*, 10.

amounting to several shillings per year, and the use of the banal mill required a levy of 6.25 per cent of the grain. Each of these levies in itself was bearable, but the total was probably burdensome. In Flanders, on the other hand, banal duties were low and most of them had died out early, although at times lords tried to revive them, as in the decades around 1400.[52]

These regional differences were linked to power variations among banal lords, who had the greatest opportunities to establish their position where central royal authority had suffered most, or the new authority of territorial lords emerged latest, as in Zeeland. In Flanders or Holland, on the other hand, where powerful territorial lords emerged early, banal power was weaker and banal levies were less onerous. These regional differences may shed some light on possible causes of the particular strength of banal authority. In addition to the counterweight offered by territorial lords and the local population, there also seems to have been a link to soil conditions and the importance of grain cultivation. Where grain cultivation was well developed, the lord's authority had already been strong in the early Middle Ages, also because of arable farming it fitted well in the manorial system. Moreover, population numbers were highest in places with intensive grain cultivation, and in their turn these allowed a reduction in monitoring costs, a crucial element in this complex of duties and levies. In infertile regions banal authority was generally weaker.

Can the effects of the rise of banal authority be evaluated? The rise of banal lords contributed to the process of territorialization, with personal ties being replaced by territorial ones, promoting uniformity and even integration. This could be seen as the emergence of miniature, stable states where political authority was much more real and effective than in the giant Carolingian Empire. The lord could also bring justice and security, although generally he did so on his own terms. The castles, which embodied the power of these lords, can be seen as instruments of oppression, but they also offered protection to the peasantry. Similarly, the banalities can be regarded as a way of oppressing the population, but also as a means of bearing the costs of expensive investments in mills, ovens, and breweries.[53] Hence, the rise of banal lords may have promoted economic growth to some extent. On the other hand, those regions where banal lords were weak, such as coastal and inland Flanders and Holland, were the ones which experienced the greatest growth from the 11th century on. This suggests that the contribution of banal lords was at best a mixed one.

The social effects of the rise of banalities are clearer. First, since banal power extended over everyone in the same way, many of the differences between types of freedom and unfreedom were now increasingly eroded. At the same time, the divide between lords and other people became sharper. Second, the economic position of most of the population was adversely affected by the rise of banal

---

[52] Thoen, *Landbouwekonomie*, 454–474.   [53] See also section IV.2, pp. 148–149 below.

lords, even where exactions were relatively low.[54] This was mainly because new exactions were introduced, more instruments of extraction could be applied by the banal lords, and more people were affected, since the free or semi-free were also subject to them. If a lord also had a strong military position backed by his weaponry and his castle, he became very powerful at the local level, which could lead to many uses and abuses—even apart from the misery and havoc that resulted from the increased feuding among the nobility.

In some regions, the excesses were prevented by growing resistance, and increasingly the authority of these lords was restricted or counter-balanced in various ways. One of these was the rise and further strengthening of village communities,[55] both in regions occupied by free peasants (such as Holland) and in highly feudalized regions, partly as a reaction to the oppression by banal lords. Because the banal obligations were territorial and imposed on everybody in that particular area they indirectly stimulated the unity and solidarity of the ordinary population. In some regions, as in Holland, the village communities even obtained some control of local administration and jurisdiction. Moreover, some counter-balance against the excesses of lordly aggression was offered by the emergence of the feudal system, that is, the system of reciprocal obligations between vassals and lords,[56] which helped bind the lords in a larger social framework and reduce feuding. The practice of rewarding with land or income those men who performed services of aid or counsel to their lord, by granting a *beneficium* or *feodum*, had developed in the course of the early Middle Ages and was used by the kings. In the 9th and 10th centuries, the system of feudal tenure as practised by the king using mainly royal properties won him the support of the regional authorities and prevented the disintegration of the Carolingian Empire. In the longer term, however, it weakened central royal authority. In practice the vassals enforced the inheritance of fiefs, acquiring strong rights to the fief so that royal power was diminished, as happened from the 11th century.

In the Low Countries a substantial part of the jurisdictional rights were integrated in the feudal system, but only a minor part of the land, in contrast to areas in France to the south. The extent of feudal land could vary according to region, but in general it was only a small part of the total area. In Holland, for instance, almost all of the land was non-feudal, whereas in the Guelders river area about one-fifth and in Flanders more than a quarter was feudal.[57] In the Low Countries, and particularly in the north and west, the feudal system was never very important.

In the 12th and 13th centuries the territorial lords used the feudal system effectively as an instrument to develop bonds with the noble elite and strengthen

---

[54] In general: Taylor, 'The year 1000', 187–236, esp. 201–209.
[55] See also section III.3, pp. 93–96 below.
[56] Here the term 'feudalism' is used in its narrow sense; Ganshof, *Feudalism*, is still the authority. See also Wickham, 'The feudal revolution', 196.
[57] Van Bavel, *Transitie en continuïteit*, 217 and 279–281.

their territorial rule. These territorial lords, or princes, emerged in this period and increasingly rose above the rest of the nobility. In addition to other instruments they used to strengthen their territorial rule, they forged feudal bonds by granting in feudal tenure manors, revenues, tolls, and seigneurial rights, which had often been former royal properties, but sometimes also their own estates. Besides this, many properties were commended by the local lord/vassal to the territorial lord/feudal lord and feudalized, with the former often urged or even forced to do so by the latter. In the Guelders river area the Count/Duke of Guelders held the feudal overlordship over half the feudal land. Feudal tenure was thus used to develop semi-public bonds and forge new rule on a territorial basis.

The territorial lords were particularly keen on obtaining feudal lordships over castles, seigneuries, and high justice in order to have their authority recognized and reduce the military and jurisdictional authority of the lesser lords. In Flanders, the territorial lord, rising to power early, came out on top as early as the 11th century, although he succeeded in acquiring permanent control over the last of the local authorities only in the course of the 12th–13th centuries.[58] After this system was established, there was less in-fighting among the elite, which contributed to peace and security in society.

In 1000 another force against the anarchy, or perceived anarchy, of the period was the Peace of God movement. Starting in Aquitaine and Burgundy, this movement brought thousands of people together in assemblies, encouraged by the church and organized mainly by bishops, abbots, and other religious leaders, often aided by relics brought to the place of assembly. Castle lords and noble warriors felt compelled to take an oath of peace and to renounce feuding against defenceless, unarmed people, such as ordinary men or clerics.[59] This was one of the first mass movements in which 'the people' played an active role, even though many of the nobility also sponsored it. But the territorial lords had an even greater interest in promoting it, since it helped them subdue and control the local nobility. Hence, it was no coincidence that the movement appeared first in Flanders, where territorial lords were strong. It was introduced and sponsored by the counts, such as Baldwin IV, who introduced it in 1024 in Douai and in 1030 in Oudenaarde, often in collaboration with the local bishops and the archbishop, and supported by the rapidly growing Flemish towns, which also had good reason to turn against the feuding nobles and their arbitrary power.[60]

In these developments the territorial lords played an important part. They emerged in the high Middle Ages, often from the group of Carolingian counts, administering as representatives of the king the counties, *gouwen*, or *pagi*. These were the administrative units of the Carolingian Empire, whose development

[58] Warlop, *De Vlaamse adel*, 78–95, and Koch, *De rechterlijke organisatie*, 30–73. Cf. also below pp. 72–73.
[59] Head and Landes, *The peace of God*, 1–20, esp. pp. 2–9 and 14–18.
[60] Kozial, 'Monks, feuds', and Platelle, 'La violence', esp. 116–123. For more on the role of cities, see section III.3, pp. 111–112 below.

began in the Merovingian period. Further south, in Artois and southern Flanders, the counties were more closely allied with the concept of the Roman *civitates*, and often consisted of a town and its surrounding area, as in the counties of Tournai, Cambrai, Arras, Ghent, Kortrijk, and Boulogne. In most of the Low Countries, however, where urban life had disappeared after the end of the Roman era and there was little occupational continuity, the earliest *pagi* grew out of nuclei of occupation and their formation was strongly influenced by landscape and soil.[61] The Franks chose such territorial units, situated as inhabited islands in a sea of wastelands, as a basis for administrative organization. Hence, the counties are often linked to the regions identified above, as with the counties of Haspengouw, Toxandria (the Campine), Salland, Drenthe, Twente, the Veluwe, Teisterbant, and the Betuwe (the Guelders river area), as well as in the south-east with the Condroz, Famenne, and the Ardennes. These counties embody the links between soil, occupation, and political administration, further strengthening the identity of the separate regions in the Low Countries.

The Low Countries and the adjacent Niederrhein area had some 40–60 *pagi* in the 8th–9th centuries, and the number increased in the course of the 9th century as a result of divisions.[62] This figure is high compared with the 300–800 counties in the Carolingian Empire as a whole, and perhaps indicates the economic and political importance of this part of the Empire, or the high degree of fragmentation of inhabited areas. These counties, with their somewhat fluid boundaries, were headed by the counts, who were initially royal officers appointed by the king as his political, military, fiscal, and judicial representatives, and held full authority in these fields. They were responsible for the maintenance of law and order and could summon people for military service.

From the end of the 9th century, and particularly in the 10th, the most powerful counts were beginning to accumulate comital rights. An example was Reginar I, who held comital power in Maasgouw, Haspengouw, and probably also in Liège county and Lommegau. The counts also became increasingly independent of the king and passed on their power to the next generation. Thus, their office became de facto hereditary, although never fully allodial. Increasingly, they began to act independently, using royal rights to further build their power base. All this was aided by the weakening of central authority and the chaos resulting from the Viking attacks.[63] Everhard Saxo, who fought the Normans in the late 9th century as *dux* or military commander, founded the lineage of the Hamaland counts, who succeeded in holding the county of Hamaland, but often also those of the Veluwe, Salland, and Drenthe.[64] Regional potentates like these who emerged from this chaotic situation succeeded in building regional

[61] Nonn, *Pagus und Comitatus*, esp. 203–205, and Heidinga, *De Veluwe*, 198–201.
[62] Ganshof and Berings, 'Staatsinstellingen', esp. 249–251.
[63] Boshof, 'Königtum und adelige Herrschaftsbilding'.
[64] Heidinga, *De Veluwe*, 215–217, and Van Winter, 'Die Hamalander Gräfen'.

seats of power consisting partly of royal properties and rights, combined with their own estates. They also forged blood ties with the Carolingians: Wichman of Hamaland married the great-granddaughter of Charles the Bold. Such ties not only offered them prestige, but also legitimized their control of royal strongholds, royal properties, and lay abbacies of royal monasteries. Their authority became increasingly crystallized, although they were not true territorial lords, since their authority was neither territorial nor exclusive, but consisted of various overlapping rights and claims, all with a clear personal element.

In the course of the high Middle Ages, some of these regional potentates did become territorial lords, slowly removing rival claims within their territory. This protracted process, which is well documented for the Niederrhein area in the 12th century,[65] included elimination or subordination of local lords, who became subject to the suzerainty of the territorial lord and were often forced to feudalize their properties and commend themselves to him. Also, the nascent territorial lords often used their rights over the properties of distant religious institutions, particularly in their role as *advocatus*. Advocacy or stewardship over religious institutions enabled them to acquire rights of high justice and thus to strengthen their sovereignty, which was a principal element in creating a territorial *Flächenstaat*, as happened in northern France and the southern Low Countries from the middle of the 11th century.[66] The Duke of Brabant offers a somewhat later example of this policy. He supported the rise of the Premonstratensian abbeys such as Park, Averbode, Tongerlo, and Grimbergen in the 12th century, over which he acquired stewardship, and subsequently used these abbeys as a weapon in his politics as a territorial lord to eradicate the property and jurisdictional rights of 'foreign' abbeys.[67] In Flanders, the territorial lord did the same in the 11th century, but collaborated with the cities, using them as allies against the nobility—and with similar success.

However, not all Carolingian comital families or regional *potentes* succeeded in becoming territorial lords. Some families were eliminated in the 11th and 12th centuries. After the death in 973 of Count Wichman II, who died without a male heir, a fierce battle over the Hamaland heritage broke out, destroying its power and opening the way for other territorial lords, such as the Bishop of Utrecht and the Counts of Cleves and Guelders.[68] Many smaller enclaves of independent lords remained throughout the Low Countries long after the rise of territorial principalities, even up to the modern period, such as the lordships of Culemborg, Vianen, Buren, and IJsselstein,[69] which were between

---

[65] Aubin, *Die Entstehung der Landeshoheit*, 380–422, and Janssen, 'Niederheinische Territorialbildung', 95–113.
[66] Mayer, 'Zur Geschichte der Vogteipolitik'.
[67] Bijsterveld, 'Een zorgelijk bezit', esp. 17–18 and 26–28. And for Flanders, see section III.3, pp. 110–113 below.
[68] Kos, 'Machtsstrijd in Hamaland'.
[69] Gijswijt-Hofstra, *Wijkplaatsen voor vervolgden*, 44–56.

the principalities of Holland, Utrecht, and Guelders, and remained independent up to 1795–8. All in all, in the Low Countries the process of crystallization of the near exclusive authority of the territorial lords took many centuries, and it resulted in a fairly large number of principalities. This differed from the situation in England, where central royal authority became stronger, and was closer to the situation in Germany, although the process in the Low Countries did not result in as much fragmentation.

The properties of such territorial lords were very diverse. Some originated from their base as landlords, comprising manors, land, rents, and labour services. In addition, there were the rights connected to their comital power and advocacies, especially that of high justice. But regalian rights became ever more important as a source of income and authority. These were taken over, granted, or usurped from the king, or taken over from smaller lords through force or enfeoffment, although some smaller lords managed to retain them. They consisted of tolls, customs dues, minting rights, fishing rights, ferrying rights, and the right of accretion. Most valuable of the regalian rights, however, were the rights to the wastelands. These formed the basis for the organization of large-scale reclamations, with the associated extension of authority and establishment of territorial rule, which was most clearly seen in the coastal region of Flanders and the peat areas of Holland.[70] The territorial lords also increasingly came to rely on new sources of revenues, such as excises and taxes that were levied not on a personal basis but on a territorial one, and these rapidly grew in importance in the course of the late Middle Ages. In this respect, Holland was an exceptional case, since manorial properties had never been important there, and the large-scale reclamations of the high Middle Ages led to many subjects paying taxes and excises, making the Count of Holland a 'modern' ruler almost from the outset.

The rise of the territorial lords is also reflected in the building of strongholds. From the middle of the 12th century, castles were increasingly built of stone or brick, but only territorial lords and the highest nobility could afford to do this. Some territorial lords even started a complete building programme, as did the Bishop of Utrecht in the 12th century and the Count of Holland, Floris V, at the end of the 13th century, after having suppressed a rising of the West Frisians. These series of castles were both a symbol of princely power and military instruments to control contested areas.[71] The most successful of the rising territorial lords in the Low Countries, however, was the Count of Flanders. Flanders had already been a solid group of counties in the Carolingian period, with several *pagi* already united under a single authority.[72] The position of the Flemish counts was further strengthened by their role in the defence against the Vikings. By the beginning of the 10th century the conglomeration of territories

---

[70] Cf. above, section II.2, pp. 40–41, and below, section III.2, pp. 83–85.
[71] Janssen, 'The castles of the bishop', esp. 142–143.
[72] Nicholas, *Medieval Flanders*, 13–18 and 46–47.

they held under their authority was sufficiently established for the whole to be designated under one name: Flanders.

The strength of the Flemish counts was built in part on the early development of a robust administrative apparatus, in Europe equalled only by that of the Duke of Normandy and the later Anglo-Norman rulers. Since 1089 day-to-day control had been in the hands of a senior official, the chancellor of Flanders. In the 12th century further strides were made in central administration in Flanders, and the chancellor grew in authority to become a kind of prime minister as head of administration and finance for the county.[73] The county was divided into castellanies, an organization first used in the late 10th century and further extended in the 11th–12th centuries, often overlapping the older Carolingian division of *pagi*. The castellans exercised military and judicial power as representatives of the count and held their office as fiefs from him.[74] Associated with the division into castellanies, which increasingly covered the whole of the county, castles were built as centres of military and administrative control. Near them larger cities often developed, such as Ypres and Lille. In the late 12th century, the office of bailiff was introduced, as a salaried chairman of the court of high justice, forming a counter-balance to the quasi-hereditary function of the castellans. The nobility was increasingly incorporated into this emerging Flemish state, by offering the nobles functions in this princely apparatus and rewarding them with feudal estates as vassals of the count, but also by sheer force.[75] As part of the new political landscape and the rise of territorial principalities, the production and preservation of administrative texts and charters were often rearranged, particularly from the 10th century onwards, on a regional territorial basis.[76] There was a decline in the number of royal charters, and increasing production by territorial princes, most notably the Count of Flanders.

The Count of Flanders was helped in his early state-building by the substantial income from his extensive estates, acquired by taking over royal properties and by using his regalian rights to gain from the reclamation of uncultivated lands in coastal Flanders.[77] The fact that Flanders as well as Holland still had extensive unreclaimed wastelands in the 11th and 12th centuries as territorial rule was emerging there greatly helped the territorial lords to gain and develop their power almost unhindered by rival feudal parties, and it allowed them to draw revenues from the reclamation process and its results. It is no coincidence that Flanders and Holland were the areas where the territorial lords acquired a robust position.

---

[73] Verhulst and De Hemptinne, 'Le chancelier de Flandre', 267–311.
[74] Koch, 'Die flandrischen Burggrafschaften', 65–79. For the cities developing around these castles, see section III.3, p. 108 below.
[75] Warlop, *De vlaamse adel*, 320–343. Cf. for the further build-up of a civil service in the later Middle Ages also section VI.1, pp. 263–270.
[76] Vanderputten, 'Transformations'.   [77] Thoen, 'The count', esp. 260–262.

Territorial rule in Flanders was exceptional for its strength and early development, but elsewhere in the Low Countries, too, territorial lords started to emerge and establish their more or less exclusive authority over entire areas. The late medieval Low Countries had about 15 territorial principalities. Among them were principalities of bishops, such as Utrecht and Liège, and also some personal unions of principalities, such as Holland and Hainaut. In addition, a number of smaller lords held their positions and their (semi-)independent status, particularly if they were situated in the border zones between larger principalities, such as Arkel, Culemborg, and Bergen op Zoom. Some areas remained outside the authority of territorial lords altogether, such as to some extent Zeeland, and particularly Friesland, where comital authority disappeared. Local potentates, the *hoofdelingen*, acquired a dominant position, with extensive land holdings, jurisdictional authority, and fortified dwellings. Moreover, the Frisian lands had a solid communal organization, with the political bodies formed by the associated members, comparable to the situation in parts of Switzerland.[78] Similar regional assemblies, the *warven*, were found in Westfrisia, in the north of Holland. This situation was associated with the tradition (partly invented) of Frisian freedom, with Frisia being directly under the king without interference from any territorial lord. Princes with territorial pretensions in Frisia, such as the Count of Holland, encountered fierce resistance until the beginning of the 16th century.[79]

A special case bordering the Frisian lands and exemplifying a different political development was the city of Groningen. This non-Frisian town remained free of the territorial lord, the Bishop of Utrecht, and in 1338 allied with some Frisian communities, but this association did not last long. Building on its royal heritage, Groningen retained its semi-autonomous position and even aspired to dominate the surrounding countryside,[80] coming close to forming a city-state.

Despite its small area, the 14th-century Low Countries had a large variety of political formations: independent, small lordships; federations of urban and rural communities; an autonomous city with its hinterland; ecclesiastical principalities; territorial principalities; and personal unions of principalities. We can discern 12 types of states in late medieval Europe,[81] of which no fewer than 6 were represented in the Low Countries, all medium-sized types. Only the smallest and the very largest organizations were absent. The latter is in contrast to France and particularly England, where political unification was more pronounced and a central government gradually asserted its authority over all regions. In the Low Countries, no single overarching central power emerged. The authority of

---

[78] Vries, 'Staatsvorming', 26–42, and *De Friese vrijheid*, 17–20. Cf. section III.3, p. 96 below, which is useful also for perspective on the political role of the urban and rural communities.

[79] Janse, *Grenzen aan de macht*, 29–70, 81–83, and 159–173, and for rural self-organization in Westfrisia and Friesland, see Van Bavel, 'Rural revolts'.

[80] See section III.3, p. 116 below.

[81] Blockmans, 'Van private naar politieke macht', 17–18. For the later period, see also section VI.1, pp. 263–267 below.

the Holy Roman Empire and the German king was only nominal there. For centuries this part of Europe was characterized by a multitude of medium-sized states, mainly principalities. Sometimes it is assumed that political integration and undivided sovereignty were principal elements in economic growth,[82] but the Low Countries do not seem to support this assumption. No larger political entity or empire came into being in the Low Countries, at least not until the Burgundians and Habsburgs started assembling this patchwork of political entities in the 15th and 16th centuries.

III.2. MANORS AND FREEDOM

From the position of the elite and the social distribution of property and power in the early and high medieval Low Countries, we now turn to the use of landed properties. In the organization of large land holdings, the manorial system became increasingly important in the course of the early Middle Ages. In this system the manorial lord exercised far-reaching control over the dependent peasants living on the manor. Serfs were not allowed to leave the manor without the lord's consent and owed part of their labour and specified products to him. This system developed throughout western Europe, but the area between the Loire, Meuse, and Rhine rivers was the core area of manorialism, and the southern part of the Low Countries was situated within it. The 'classic' manors here were bipartite, split into tenures or holdings (*mansi*) given out to the serfs (*mancipia*), and the demesne land. The main obligation of the serfs consisted in performing labour services on the lord's demesne, but they also often owed carting services and had to deliver produce such as chicken, eggs, wax, pigs, and cloth. In some cases, though more rarely, they also owed a money payment. Alongside the classic manors, which were probably only in the minority, there was a diversity of other forms of manorial organization. In such cases the stress was more on levies than on labour services, and the manor did not have a large demesne, but served more as an administrative centre.

Even within this core area, the precise organization of the manors showed wide regional differences, depending on the extent of large properties, the power of the lords, and the former position of the serfs. There were many degrees of freedom or unfreedom, resulting in diversity, in law and in practice, even after people were integrated into a manorial regime.[83] Characteristic of all forms of manorialism, however, is its non-economic coercion, i.e. the exploitative, non-contractual relation between the lord and the occupants of the land, which contrasts with voluntary arrangements or more impersonal contractual relations

---

[82] See e.g. Epstein, *Freedom and growth*, 36–37, 167, and 173–174. For the relation between economic growth and political organization, see section VIII.2, pp. 385–387 below.
[83] Goetz, 'Serfdom'.

negotiated through the market. Moreover, to a certain extent the lords controlled the working power/labour of the serfs/producers, although there was less control in the non-classic types of manorialism. Third, the producers were tied to the land, which limited their mobility, but at the same time offered them some control over their tenures, as they could not be easily separated from the land and had enduring access to its use.

The Rise and Nature of Manorial Organization

The manors in the Low Countries were not the linear successors to the Roman *villae*. Although manors in the early Middle Ages may have used examples from the more thoroughly Romanized south, such as corvées or labour services introduced in the late Roman era, there is probably no direct link. The social and economic discontinuity in the Low Countries in the 4th to 6th centuries was too fundamental to allow such a link, except perhaps to some extent in the Haspengouw and southern Limburg, where early integration in the Merovingian kingdom provided some continuity. But even there most *villae* seem to have been abandoned after the 4th and 5th centuries, even in the fertile loess areas, except perhaps for the area around Maastricht.[84] Although most of those workers on the land remaining after the period of chaos must have been slowly integrated as serfs, direct continuity between the late Roman *coloni* and slaves and the early medieval serfs cannot be assumed, and it is likely that the Low Countries did not see real continuity between the Roman and early medieval *villae*.[85] The important formative period in the emergence of manorial organization was from the late 6th century onwards, as this system developed out of heterogeneous elements, such as the existing estates worked by slaves, the newly developed labour services, and the integration of smallholdings. Under the stimulus of kings and large abbeys the system grew in importance in the Carolingian period.[86] This process has been well investigated for the Campine, integrated late into the Carolingian Empire, where manorial organization only gained a firm foothold in the second half of the 8th and in the 9th centuries, and for the Abbey of St Bertin in southern Flanders, which still incorporated small land holdings among its manors in the 9th century.[87] It can also be observed in 9th-century Saxony after the Frankish conquest. In all these cases this process was accompanied by an increase in the authority of the lords and consequent loss of freedom for large parts of the population.

There was, however, one large group whose position improved: slaves. Slavery very gradually disappeared after the Roman era, especially from the 7th and 8th centuries. In the Low Countries and northern France, this process seems to have

---

[84] Kooistra, *Borderland farming*, 10 and 89–90. [85] Verhulst, 'La diversité'.
[86] Goetz, 'Serfdom', 29–51, and Verhulst, *Carolingian economy*, 33–37.
[87] Theuws, 'Landed property', 338–347. For St Bertin, see also section III.1, p. 63 above.

been more rapid and complete than in other parts of Europe like southern France and Italy, where large numbers of slaves were employed up to the 10th century.[88] After the 7th century, the slaves in the Low Countries were replaced by tenants and serfs providing labour services, except perhaps for Frisia, where they remained until the early 9th century. But the slave trade did remain, particularly in the southern Low Countries, as in Arras (where the 11th-century toll list mentions slaves as a commodity under the heading 'animals') and in Cambrai.[89] Again, the Frisians played a particular role in this, importing slaves from Scandinavia and the Slavic countries and shipping them on to southern Europe, specializing in this trade at least up to the 9th century. Such trade, however, increasingly dealt with exotic slaves for domestic service, while over centuries the indigenous agricultural slaves were probably gradually integrated among the serfs. In this group they merged with parts of the free population whose circumstances had deteriorated and who had also became serfs.

In the possible causes for the relatively rapid decline of slavery in the Low Countries, Christianization probably played a role, with its prohibition against enslaving Christians and its promotion of manumission. But this role cannot have been a determining one, as can be deduced from the much slower decline in the areas that had experienced early Christianization in the south of France and Italy. Other factors must also have played a role. For instance, in contrast to areas further east, after the 9th century there were no large-scale wars in this region. It was warfare and taking of captives that allowed for enslavement of large numbers of people. But socio-economic factors were more likely the principal reason.[90] One main element was probably the success of the manorial system, which formed an alternative to slavery and was better attuned to the weakness of trade and markets, making large-scale slavery on large estates less profitable. Also, there was the successful introduction of labour-saving instruments in the 9th to 12th centuries, such as water mills, sickles and scythes, heavy ploughs, and horses.[91] This made maintaining large numbers of slaves less useful and remunerative; while, conversely, investments in labour-saving instruments was stimulated by the absence of large numbers of agricultural slaves. An additional factor may have been the tradition of freedom for a relatively large segment of the population in the coastal areas of the Low Countries. Although there were probably slaves in Frisia up to around 800, and Frisia did have a fairly prominent elite, still relatively many people were free in that region: they held free property and had full access to offices and political participation. Perhaps this notion of freedom was too robust to allow for massive slavery. Elsewhere in the Low Countries, however, the successful introduction of manorialism seems to have been the crucial element in the decline of slavery.

[88] Verhulst, 'The decline of slavery'.
[89] Bonnassie, 'The survival and extinction', and for the Frisians, Lebecq, *Marchands*, 22–23 and 134–135.
[90] Bonnassie, 'The survival and extinction', 37–40.   [91] Cf. section IV.1, pp. 133–136 below.

The differences in the influence and nature of manorialism in the Low Countries were marked. We will first reconstruct these differences, and then use this reconstruction to uncover the main factors in the rise of manorialism. Traditionally, it was believed that manorial organization in the Low Countries was especially strong in the south, near its core area, and decreased from south to north.[92] It was assumed that there were few, if any, classical bipartite manors in the north. The preoccupation of Dutch historians with the county of Holland, and particularly with the large-scale peat reclamation and the absence of manorialism there, reinforced this belief, since the findings for Holland were often projected on the Netherlands as a whole. In the light of recent studies, however, this traditional view has come to be questioned; in the early and high Middle Ages manorial organization appears to have been important in several parts of the north. Many of the detailed studies of the Guelders river area and the adjacent part of the Nedersticht of Utrecht have revealed clear traces of the substantial presence of large manors in this fertile region of river clay soils.[93] In the western part, an area of some 150 km^2, there were at least 25 *curtes*. In almost every settlement a manor could be found and some settlements even had two or three. These manors, which were owned by religious institutions, territorial lords, and nobles (and probably earlier by the king), mostly appear only in late medieval sources or through late medieval relicts such as labour services; but it can be argued that in general they go back far into the high or even early Middle Ages.

What was the nature of these manors in the northern parts of the Low Countries? Were there only manors of the *type dispersé*, with the dependent tenements scattered over large areas around the manors, making it practically impossible to have a demesne worked by the serfs, which made the manor no more than an administrative centre? Direct mentions of classic bipartite manors in this area are few, but indirect indications do exist. The manor of Frethebold in Hier, in the Guelders river area, was donated in 996, along with its serfs, to the Cathedral Church of Utrecht.[94] Three tenements were exempted from this donation, including the 25 serfs living on them and working on the demesne itself. From the number of serfs, the demesne of this manor must have been fairly large. Time-consuming cartographic reconstruction carried out for Vleuten near Utrecht also shows that manors could indeed consist of large complexes of demesne, tenements, and feudal lands, sometimes covering several hundred hectares and situated closely around the centre of operations.[95] Manors were not

---

[92] Verhulst and Bock-Doehaerd, 'Het sociaaleconomische leven', esp. 179, echoed in international studies such as Brenner, 'The agrarian roots', 107.

[93] Cf. the studies by Dekker (1983), Van Bavel (1993), Buitelaar (1993), Palmboom (1995), and Braams (1995).

[94] Van Bavel, *Transitie en continuïteit*, 437–446.

[95] Huiting, 'Middeleeuws grootgrondbezit', 62–77, and a partial reconstruction for Beusichem by Palmboom, *Het kapittel van Sint Jan*, 342–350.

territorial and consisted of all kinds of overlapping, scattered rights, but in cases like these they covered a substantial, fairly serried area.

In the south of the Low Countries, several regions saw the emergence of manorialism. In the south-western part of Flanders there were some bipartite vills, as shown by the late 9th-century sources of the Abbey of St Bertin, for instance.[96] In the Meuse valley and the Ardennes, manors often covered a much larger area, up to thousands of hectares, such as the royal manor of Jupille near Liège,[97] but there most of the area consisted of forest and uncultivated land. Other regions in the Low Countries, however, did not have many manors. In the northern parts of Flanders, bipartite manors were scarce: the polyptique of St Pieter at Ghent lists small settlements, separate farms, and even separate parcels of land. There is no suggestion of an organization of lands into vills. This source is very early, and manorial organization may have only just begun to develop there, but it seems likely that in large parts of Flanders the classical manorial system was not important.[98] This is even more the case for Holland, where hardly any manors existed.

In Friesland, on the other hand, manors—or at least large land holdings—were probably more important than had earlier been assumed. In the older literature it was assumed that Friesland was a kind of farmers' republic, free from feudalism, territorial lords, and manors. Indeed, feudalism was weak and territorial rule absent, but now ample proof has been brought forward for the existence of large land holdings and the presence of a large and fairly powerful nobility.[99] Before the Frankish conquest and the Christianization, up to the 7th century, estates worked by serfs and probably by slaves were found on the artificial mounds, the *terpen*, similar to a Scandinavian type of estate. After the conquest, serfdom probably continued until the 11th century.[100]

The general picture for the Low Countries is thus very mixed, not along a north–south divide, but rather showing clear differences among the various regions. Some regions did have many large bipartite manors, such as in the Haspengouw and the Guelders river area. In the sandy inland regions, such as the Veluwe, Twente, Salland, Drenthe, and the Campine, there were manors, but not in high densities. Compared to the classic manors from the Frankish core area, these manors probably had a smaller demesne, more scattered tenements which owed fewer labour services, and contained more unfree personnel on the demesne itself, with manorial services being only supplementary. In the Frisian territories the manors were probably not of the classical type, but they were important. In other coastal areas, on the other hand, most notably in Holland and coastal Flanders, manors were few.

---

[96] Ganshof, *Le polyptyque*, 129–131, but more cautious: Morimoto, 'Essai d'une analyse'.
[97] Josse, *Le domaine de Jupille*, 131–143.
[98] Thoen, 'The medieval roots', 3. See also below, p. 85.
[99] Noomen, 'De Friese vetemaatschappij'.
[100] Postma, *De Friesche kleihoeve*, and kind communication from Hans Mol (Fryske Akademy) dated 6 July 2007.

This reconstruction of the wide regional differences in the manorial system in the Low Countries allows us to investigate possible factors in the rise of this system and of serfdom. The land–labour ratio probably played a role in this. Good-quality land became increasingly occupied and reclaimed from the late 6th and 7th centuries. As a source of power and income, land became more important, surpassing mobile wealth in this respect. This land, however, had to be exploited through labour, which was scarce. Nor could labour easily be attracted to areas of large land holdings, since many unreclaimed areas remained and offered an alternative for settlement. From the landlord's perspective, people had to be bound to the land, making serfdom attractive. Nevertheless, the scarcity of labour and the ample availability of land cannot have been the only factors in the rise of serfdom. In other situations the scarcity of labour rather led to high wages and a favourable position for labourers, as in the Holland peat areas reclaimed in the 11th to 13th centuries (cf. below). Thus, we need to look for other factors.

One factor strengthening the position of the lords in the early Middle Ages was insecurity. This forced men to commend themselves, together with their land, to a local authority who had the power to protect them. Even more important, perhaps, was the will of the central authority, i.e. the Frankish king, to create and/or maintain a strong elite. One clear example of the king's desire to do so was his support for the emergence of the *homines franci*. Since ample free land, scarce free labour, and a large non-working elite cannot co-exist simultaneously,[101] and serfdom provides a much higher return for the 'employer' than free peasants do when land is amply available, this royal aim resulted in an outspoken preference for enserfment of labour and its incorporation into the manorial system. This could only succeed if the power base of the king and the elite was firm enough to obtain strong control of land and labour, since the system could only work with the peasants' consent, either compulsory or acquiescent. Also, the presence of royal estates and the influence of the king played a role in the propagation of manorialism through royal ideology, with aristocrats and religious institutions using the example of his method of exploitation.[102] In the case of the Campine the king led this development on his large estates, followed by religious institutions and aristocrats, often closely associated with the king. In the Guelders river area, too, a correlation of widespread manorialism and prominent royal presence can be observed.

The presence of Frankish authority thus strongly stimulated the emergence of bipartite manors using unfree labour. Another factor in the rise of manorial organization was the influence of missionaries and the Christian faith they brought. Manorial organization was seen by the missionaries and by the king who supported them as a way to establish an equilibrium between rulers and the

---

[101] Cf. Domar, 'The causes of slavery'.
[102] Devroey: 'Réflections sur l'économie', esp. 477–479, and 'Les premiers polyptyques', 93–95.

ruled on the basis of peace, or at least it was presented as such. It was an attempt to create a fixed society, a reflection of the order God wanted. Willibrord was a clear example of this in his missionary activities in the Campine, sponsored by the Pippinids. These activities promoted the development of manors worked by dependent peasants. The same period also saw the shift of the elite's graves to new burial sites, stressing their separation from the rest of the community and their increasing power over the local population, often set out in charters introduced by the Church.[103] The construction of a *sala* and a church made the power of the lords clearly visible. The success of missionaries like Willibrord thus contributed to increasing social differentiation and the strengthening of manorialism.

In terms of physical geography, three factors stimulated the emergence of bipartite exploitation: the concentration of property around a manorial centre, a high population density, and the availability of fine arable lands, especially since vill organization was often linked to the seigneurial preference for cereal production. A more dense, concentrated settlement, i.e. in regions with ample possibilities for grain cultivation, was easier to supervise and control and offered better opportunities to exploit unfree labour.[104] Regions with infertile or marshy soils where pastoral farming was dominant were less suitable since they did not allow an easy check on production, and were more sparsely populated. The development of manorial organization, control, and supervision were costly and required energy and investment by the lord, and hence would be undertaken only if rewarding. These rewards were highest in fertile, cereal-producing, and relatively densely populated regions.

Less clear is the influence of economic factors on the rise of manorialism: the proximity to markets, the presence of flourishing trade, and the availability of money. On the one hand, the presence of such elements made the development of manors with their obligations and levies in kind and labour less necessary,[105] but on the other, the lords seem to have placed great value on the building of manorial bases close to trading centres. A large number of bipartite manors were situated very near two of the main trading centres of the north of the Low Countries, Dorestad and later Tiel. Conversely, the low number of bipartite manors in Holland seems not to have been a result of flourishing Frisian trade there, but rather to have been determined by the wet soil, the low population density in this period, the weakness of Frankish influence, and the near absence of large land holdings. In general, these factors appear to have been determining for the emergence of bipartite manors, with the presence of royal estates and royal and missionary influence as additional elements.

---

[103] Fouracre, *The age of Charles Martel*, 128–129, and Theuws, 'Landed property'.
[104] In general: Mitterauer, *Warum Europa?*, 16–28 and 40–58.
[105] Van der Linden, 'Het platteland', 53, following Alberts and Jansen, *Welvaart in wording*, 62–66.

On closer inspection all these factors appear to be closely related. Frankish influence stimulated the formation of large land holdings organized in manors.[106] This influence was strongest in those regions where some continuity of occupation existed and where population densities in the early Middle Ages were relatively high.[107] This was the case on the most fertile lands, such as stream ridges and loess areas, as found in the Guelders river area and the Haspengouw, where most of the large land holdings and royal domains were located. In other parts of the Low Countries, land holdings consisted mostly of complexes of small, scattered holdings. The fertile soil also offered the most suitable arable land, thus combining all relevant factors.

In some regions the absence of these factors resulted in the near absence of manorial organization. This was most clearly the case in Holland. Only in the most fertile parts, the narrow strips of clay along the rivers, were some traces of manorial organization found.[108] There were none in the large peat areas, again confirming the link to soil conditions. In Drenthe, too, there were few manors. The soil was too poor to make this system profitable and the position of the landowning peasants had become too strong because of their leading role in the process of gradual reclamation in the preceding centuries. In the 13th century the peasants in Drenthe demonstrated their robust position by successfully resisting the episcopal attempts to introduce manorial organization after all (cf. below).

In the Low Countries the strength and importance of manorialism showed strong regional diversity, with extremes sometimes directly bordering on one another, as was the case for the Guelders river area, dominated by manorialized large land holdings, and the region directly to the west, the Holland peat area, where these were absent alltogether. Regional differences in the nature and importance of the manors are thus marked and were determined by regional context rather than by the ideas or strategies of the manorial lord.[109] The Bishop of Utrecht and the Utrecht chapters were a clear example, with their holdings scattered throughout the Low Countries, in some cases organized as bipartite manors but in others not. The Utrecht chapter of St Jan, for instance, had bipartite manors with some 75 hectares of demesne and many fairly concentrated tenements, but it also had manors with small demesnes of some 25–30 hectares with small parcels scattered over a wider area, while some manors functioned only as administrative centres.[110] Lords clearly had to adapt to the existing structures, geographical as well as social and economic.

---

[106] Cf. Verhulst, 'La diversité', 133–134 and 142–143.
[107] Cf. Willems, 'Das Rhein-Maas-Delta', 40–45.
[108] Van der Linden, 'Het platteland', 52–53.
[109] Cf. Kuchenbuch, *Grundherrschaft*, 51.   [110] Palmboom, *Het kapittel*, 491–493.

Reclamation, Manors, and Freedom in the High Middle Ages

Differences in manorialism continued to have a strong influence on regional development in later centuries. This can be clearly observed in the reclamations undertaken in the high Middle Ages and their effect on social property structures in the newly reclaimed land. In areas where manorial organization was well developed, reclamation was undertaken within a manorial setting, with the existing structures projected on the newly reclaimed area. Participants in the reclamation each received an area of reclaimable land in proportion to their share in the collective usage rights to these lands, a share being determined by the area of land possessed for the existing cultivated land.[111] Except for the poorest, who had no formal rights and had often formerly been allowed to use the wasteland but now lost that possibility, the distribution of rights to land remained unchanged after reclamation. This was also true of social organization, since those who settled on the new land as unfree on semi-free retained their legal status.[112] The process of settlement resulted in an extension of manorial land, with lords having well-established rights to labour and land. In view of the favourable conditions for settlement they could offer and the population pressure in the already inhabited parts, there was no need for the well-positioned manorial lords to attract settlers by granting them freedom and/or ownership of the land. The manorial lord and his steward also profited from the reclamation by retaining part of the reclaimed land and certain rights, such as the jurisdiction and tithes. All in all, social and economic relationships to the newly reclaimed land were the same as they were to the older settled land.

Reclamations undertaken after dissolution of the manors or in regions where the manorial system had never gained a firm foothold resulted in a totally different situation. This can be seen in the large-scale reclamation works of the 11th to 13th centuries, with the Holland–Utrecht peat areas as the most noticeable example in the Low Countries. This huge fen area was difficult to penetrate and unattractive for settlers, and had been virtually uninhabited until then. In Holland only some small strips of river clay lands and the fertile *geest* soils directly behind the dunes were reclaimed during the early Middle Ages,[113] but the extensive peatlands were reclaimed only from the 11th century. This was done through large-scale reclamation projects, firmly organized from above and carried out in a relatively short period, from the 11th to the 13th centuries.[114] The main organizers were the territorial lords, the Count of Holland and the Bishop of Utrecht giving their vassals or stewards, religious institutions, or others the right to develop the organization on the ground as entrepreneurs.

---

[111] Dekker, *Het Kromme Rijngebied*, 159–161 and 265–270.
[112] Buitelaar, *De Stichtse ministerialiteit*, 148–150 and 212, showing that this even applied to larger reclamations, at least when they were carried out from existing settlements/manors.
[113] Henderikx, *De beneden-delta*, 54–62.
[114] Henderikx, 'Die mittelalterliche Kultivierung', and TeBrake, *The making*, 138–179. See also section II.2, pp. 40–41, above.

The reclamations in this extensive wilderness were carried out in a kind of no man's land, where hardly any settlements or manors existed. No existing structures were copied there. Moreover, after the 9th century there were no longer any large numbers of agricultural slaves in the Low Countries, thus closing the option of occupying and reclaiming the region with slave labour. Therefore, people had to be attracted to occupy this inhospitable area. The territorial lords had to lure people from outside by granting them favourable conditions for settlement. Thus, the numerous colonists who carried out the hard clearing work were granted freedom and in practice became owners of the land. They paid only a small nominal rent in recognition of the right of the count as territorial lord.[115] The issuer (or 'seller'/*vercoper*) of the land, a territorial lord or large institution, retained only the tithes and jurisdiction, often granted in feudal tenure to the person or institution actually organizing and leading the reclamation, the *locator*, as well as the small recognition fee. The land itself came almost completely into the hands of the peasant-colonizers, who also acquired their freedom.

In other regions of 11th and 12th century north-western Europe, too, large-scale reclamation resulted in the freedom of the peasants.[116] This was most notable in the marshlands of northern Germany, where many of the settlers had come from Holland and other parts of the Low Countries and several features of the occupation in Holland were copied, such as the small recognition fee, the ownership rights of the settlers and the jurisdictional organization, although the extent of freedom obtained was less clear and less general than in Holland.[117] For several reasons Holland was exceptional. First, there was the huge area reclaimed, some 5,000 km^2. Next, the fact that the reclamation of the peat soil required a hydrological *tour de force* made it necessary to strictly organize the occupation. The extent of the reclamation also brings a time factor into the picture, in this case the development of techniques of cultivation and hydrology, such as with the introduction of horse traction, heavier ploughs, and better instruments, but also the innovation of sluices and dikes.[118] These developments made it possible to undertake large-scale reclamations in areas with difficult geographical conditions. Another time-linked factor was the rise of territorial lords who possessed the wilderness regalia, the territorial authority, and the will to make the reclamations a success. Their goal was different from that of the earlier manorial lords: they did not want a private-personal control over the labour and surplus, but public-territorial authority over the revenues from their subjects.[119] They thus benefited from the occupation of the region, not because they owned the

---

[115] Van der Linden: *De cope*, 93–95 and 160–182, and 'Het platteland', 69–78.

[116] TeBrake, *The making*, 27, and Lyon, 'Medieval real estate'.

[117] Schlesinger, 'Flemmingen und Kühren', Petri, 'Entstehung und Verbreitung', and Van Winter, 'Das Herkunftsland der Ostsiedler'.

[118] Cf. sections II.2, pp. 41–44 above, and IV.1, pp. 133–136 below.

[119] As suggested by Van der Linden: *De cope*, 89–99, 318–325, and 348–354, and more explicitly in 'Het platteland', esp. 69–78.

land or controlled the manorial labour, but through fiscal, military, and judicial revenues. In contrast to the goals of the Frankish king in the early Middle Ages, which resulted in increasing unfreedom, the goals of the territorial lords now promoted the freedom of the colonizers.

The weakness of 'feudal' structures and presence of a free, landowning peasantry in Holland was still a characteristic feature of the region in the late medieval period, since no less than two-thirds to three-quarters of the land was held in free property by the peasants in the 15th century, and the nobility had a weak position.[120] These features had their roots in the period of occupation. Here, too, the organization of occupation and reclamation was mirrored in the social property structures in the region, which show strong continuity. In the nearby Guelders river area, where robust lordly power and numerous manors had emerged in the early Middle Ages, most of the land remained in the hands of the former manorial lords. In the 15th century three-quarters of the land there was owned by nobles, territorial lords, and religious institutions. The differences in occupation thus resulted in wide social and economic differences among regions that remained for many centuries.

The simultaneous developments on the Flemish coastal plains were in some ways similar to those in the Holland peat area, in particular the freedom offered to the *hospites* attracted to this area and the near absence of manorial organization. But there were also differences. The Flemish count was not only territorial lord, but also a large landowner on the coastal plain from the 9th century, on the basis of the royal properties and the power base he acquired there.[121] He handed over much of these holdings to religious institutions and rich burghers, often by selling them. Later embankments and new polders were mainly accomplished through investments by rich burghers and institutions (1180–1300). The result was that many more large land holdings developed there than in the Holland peatlands, mainly exploited through short-term leases. Situations which occurred at about the same time and in similar soil conditions could thus result in different outcomes, depending on the relative power of the social groups in or near the region in question. In coastal Flanders, cities and urban elites emerged early and obtained strong positions, in contrast to Holland. A similar difference can be observed in the reclamations in northern Germany. Despite external geographical similarities to the Holland reclamation areas and some social-institutional ones in property rights and jurisdiction, personal bonds and even elements of unfreedom existed there, in contrast to Holland. The difference with Holland was a result of the context in which the reclamations took place, since they were influenced by the surrounding territory, which had already been occupied under lordly authority. This was even clearer in the Guelders river region, where the large-scale reclamations of the backlands in this period

---

[120] Cf. for late medieval property structures in this section, pp. 91–92; and section VI.1, pp. 243–247.
[121] Tys, 'Domeinvorming', 35–38, and Thoen, 'A commercial survival economy', 125–126.

were undertaken from long-inhabited stream ridges and incorporated in an existing social context characterized by large land holdings and manorial organization.

On the infertile sandy soils, such as those in Drenthe and the Campine, reclamation took place very gradually, slowly advancing and sometimes retreating again over many centuries. Manors were not really profitable there and remained weak, if present at all. Extensions to the cultivated area were small, mainly from existing farms scattered over the area. This resulted in small peasant land holdings, mainly cultivated by the peasants themselves, under weak manorial influence. The social context in which reclamations were undertaken thus played a large part in determining how occupation and reclamation would result in various forms of ownership and exploitation of the land.

The Dissolution of Manorialism

In the high and late Middle Ages, the exploitation of landed property underwent fundamental changes, including the decline and dissolution of manorialism. This was a very gradual process, but in most regions in the Low Countries it proceeded earlier and faster than in the rest of north-western Europe. In some regions the decline had been completed by the 11th to 12th centuries, and in most it took place before the Black Death. A few regions, however, retained some manorial elements into the 18th century. These regional diversities did not necessarily coincide with the strength of manorial organization. In Flanders and Brabant there was indeed an early decline in an area of weak manorialism. There the dissolution accelerated in the second half of the 11th century through the redemption of labour services.[122] In Namur, where manorialism was much stronger, the process of decline started at about the same period, but evolved more gradually.[123] Already in the 11th century the serfs' obligations had been relaxed, with labour services being fixed at a maximum and services at harvest time increasingly abolished. In the 13th century most labour services were converted to money payments, and at the end of the 14th century serfdom had practically disappeared, partly as a result of individual or collective franchises.

In the heavily manorial Guelders river area, the decline started later but probably occurred relatively rapidly, particularly in the second half of the 13th century. In 1259 the Abbey of Mariënweerd had difficulties with 70 men on the manor of Zoelmond, who refused to acknowledge their position as serfs of the abbey and deserted the manor.[124] In Arnhem the manorial elements still present on the manor of the Count of Guelders were abolished with the granting

---

[122] Despy, 'L'exploitation des "curtes"', 192 and 204.
[123] Genicot, L'économie rurale Namuroise, i: 106–118, and iii: 214–238.
[124] Van Bavel, Mariënweerd, 227–228.

of the urban charter in 1233.[125] The manors of Prüm and Elten in the city of Arnhem, on the other hand, remained partly intact after 1233, and only dissolved later. After the middle of the 14th century, however, only a few remnants of unfreedom still existed in the Guelders river area, in the form of some services and manorial rents,[126] but these no longer fulfilled any real function within a system of manorial exploitation.

The nearby Achterhoek, however, was not heavily manorialized, but nevertheless retained elements of the system into the modern era. In the 18th century the serfs had obtained an almost impersonal right to the land, but they were still set apart from the rest of the population through their own hereditary law, the fine they had to pay on transfer or inheritance of the land/tenement, and their obligation to attend manorial court sessions.[127] Regional differences in the chronology of dissolution were thus clear, and offer possibilities for a comparative investigation into the causes of decline.

These causes are not to be found in the reduction of population numbers from the Black Death. For England, where the dissolution of manorialism took place mainly in the decades around 1400, i.e. after the dramatic population losses of the Black Death, this explanation is often given. Many large landowners there encountered difficulties in finding labour at that time, and this strengthened labour's bargaining power. Still, the population decline cannot really explain the decline of manorialism. In the Low Countries this decline took place mainly during a period of marked population growth in the 12th and 13th centuries, with high population pressure and an abundance of labourers, which was exactly the opposite of the English situation during the decline of manorialism. A reverse argument may even be more to the point: it was not population decline but population increase which contributed to the disappearance of serfdom, since wages became very low and free labour was cheap, making it attractive to the lords to replace serfs with free labour. In addition, using free labour would probably result in higher productivity and lower costs of control and monitoring. Both theoretically and empirically it is not feasible to link the decline of manorialism and the 14th-century population crisis in a unilinear way. Nor did the importance of manorialism determine the chronology of its dissolution, as is shown by the examples of the persisting elements in the Achterhoek as opposed to their early decline in the highly manorial Guelders river area.

More important was the power of the manorial lords with respect to the new authorities rising in this period: the territorial lords and the cities. In Flanders, where these new powers became very strong as early as the 10th and 11th centuries, they succeeded in undermining the power of the manorial lords, and that of the rural nobility in general.[128] Territorial lords aimed to bring everyone

---

[125] Verkerk, *Coulissen van de macht*, 42–49.
[126] Dekker, *Het Kromme Rijngebied*, 152–157, and Van Bavel, *Mariënweerd*, 237–264.
[127] Aalbers, *Het einde van de horigheid*, 26–31 and 37–38.
[128] Thoen, 'A commercial survival economy', 106–110 and 130–131.

within their principality under a union of free subjects, eliminating all rival claims such as those of the manorial lords. This could be accomplished indirectly, by chipping away at the power of rural lords and taking over or curtailing part of the banal powers, as well as directly by granting charters to towns and villages which offered freedom or at least relaxed manorial duties. The Duke of Brabant did so in charters granted to villages in 1180 and 1182, abolishing the heriot for all serfs there, and a similar policy occurred in Hainaut around 1200.[129] The competition between different lords and the growing strength of the territorial lords limited the power of the nobility over the rural population and contributed to an early dissolution of manorialism. The resistance of the serfs themselves to the manorial system also played a role. Although major revolts against manorialism did not occur, Drenthe's struggle against the Bishop of Utrecht can be viewed as resistance against a feudal intruder in a generally free peasant region. Minor rebellions, disobedience, and flight were common, however. Around 1200 in the Niederrhein region, there were several cases of rebellious serfs who succeeded in obtaining a reduction in their duties.[130] Particularly as manorial force was declining and possibilities of success became greater, the serfs' resistance seems to have grown.

Most determinant, however, were the alternatives for both serfs and manorial lords. Perhaps the rise of banal lordships was such an alternative to the lords, since it offered large and growing revenues without the need for a manorial system. Attractive alternatives for the serfs were available near areas of large-scale reclamation and cities. The reclamation areas, as in the Holland peatlands or the Flemish coast, formed open frontiers with possibilities for serfs to improve their position and acquire their own holdings as freemen.[131] Cities, too, offered serfs freedom. Many cities had obtained the privilege of freedom for their citizens in their urban charter, and residing in a town for a year plus a day in most areas offered this free status to former serfs who had moved there. The attraction for a serf in fleeing to a town must not be overestimated, since it did not automatically bring work and income, and meant giving up the certainty of having a dwelling and plot of land, but it did provide freedom and the prospects of a new life. The fact that both cities and reclamation areas developed greatly in the 11th to 13th centuries led to the possibility of flight of serfs and sped up the decay of the manorial system in these and adjacent regions.

That serfs ran away to the cities is evidenced in the treaties signed between several territorial lords in the Niederrhein region in the 13th century which were intended to stop this practice: for instance, between Guelders and Cleves following the complaint by the Count of Guelders in 1242 that his serfs were

---

[129] Nazet, 'La condition des serfs', 83–103. Cf. for the rise of territorial lords, section III.1, pp. 71–73, and for the freedom obtained by urban charters, section III.3, pp. 111–112.
[130] Epperlein, *Bauernbedrückung*, 59–65. See also for the Drenthe resistance this section, pp. 91–92.
[131] As already noted, in a more general sense, by Lyon, 'Medieval real estate', 57–59. For the towns cf. section III.3, pp. 111–112.

migrating to cities in Cleves.[132] Treaties like these had to be constantly renewed, and do not seem to have been very successful. Moreover, in their capacity of manorial lord, the territorial lords were concerned only about their own serfs, and were even pleased to see such departures when the process undermined a rival's authority; hence they were not very energetic in stopping the process. This can be seen from the manors of the chapter of Xanten, which was mostly left to its own devices by the territorial lords of Guelders and Cleves, at least up to a treaty concluded in 1307 in which Guelders and Cleves towns were forbidden to accept Xanten's serfs. Perhaps even more important to the territorial lords was the fact that the rise of cities and markets offered interesting economic possibilities to them, both for marketing and buying products without needing to have recourse to the manorial system. Particularly where the physical and institutional framework of markets developed well and allowed for open and favourable market exchange,[133] this became an attractive alternative to manorialism. At the same time the development of more exclusive and absolute property rights and the rise of the short-term lease offered the lords an instrument to make better use of these options, especially since land in this period of population growth became ever scarcer.[134] Instead of services and direct levies of goods, the lease yielded substantial sums of money, allowing the lords to make their own choices in the market, while at the same time offering secure control over their land holdings. Elsewhere in western Europe, as in large parts of England and especially Germany, such developments took place later, or even much later, but in Flanders, Brabant, the Guelders river area, and Frisia, lords started to employ these options already in the 13th century.

These regional differences are reflected in the chronology of the dissolution of manorialism. This dissolution took place early in Flanders, with its early and pronounced urbanization, proximity to large-scale reclamations on the coastal plain, strong territorial lord, and early loss of the rural lords' power. In the Guelders river area the process occurred somewhat later than in Flanders, but it was still early and evolved rapidly. This was probably due to the proximity of large-scale reclamation areas in the Holland–Utrecht peatlands, offering peasants their freedom and a firm hold on the land. The rapidity of the dissolution was also brought about by the intense urbanization and the growth of markets, particularly in adjacent Holland, but to a lesser extent also in Guelders itself. In areas like Luxembourg and the Achterhoek, on the other hand, cities remained small and few, and reclamations were only piecemeal and took place within the existing structure, thus explaining the long persistence of manorial elements there.

---

[132] Cf. Epperlein, *Bauernbedrückung*, 67–75, and Spiess, 'Zur Landflucht', 174–176 and 182–185.
[133] See section V.4, pp. 226–230 and 236–238 below.
[134] For the rise of the lease and the development towards more exclusive property rights to land, see also section V.1, pp. 164–170 below.

Following its decline, manorial organization did not vanish altogether, since it left important traces in the social and property systems, and particularly in the distribution of land ownership. There was a fairly strong correlation between the intensity of the manorial system in the high Middle Ages and the large land holdings of the elite in the late Middle Ages. This correlation developed along various lines. In several parts of the Low Countries, the manors and their demesnes occupied substantial areas. The land was partly granted in feudal tenure to local nobles or usurped by stewards, but it remained in the hands of families which formed the knightly class in the late Middle Ages. Moreover, the lords did not passively witness the decay of their manors, but energetically reacted to it and continuously searched for new opportunities to maintain their revenues. Leasing out their property or direct farming through wage labourers proved to be suitable alternatives for manorialism, and especially in periods with high grain prices and relatively low wages the latter option proved very attractive.[135]

Such opportunities stimulated the lords to enlarge their former demesnes, either for direct exploitation or to lease out, and they were aided by the revenues from redemption of manorial services. These services had not vanished with the decay of manorialism, but were bought off by the serfs, as demonstrated by some manors around Brussels, where the serfs were allowed to redeem agricultural labour services as early as the late 11th century.[136] The money this yielded could be used by the lord for buying land. Some of this land might be part of the holdings of former serfs, who probably often had to surrender or sell part of their holding to redeem their labour services and bondage. Lords probably also used such resources to redeem land granted earlier in hereditary tenure. This process did not evolve everywhere along similar lines or at an equal pace, but it is clear that with the dissolution of the manorial system the possessions of the former manorial lords greatly changed, so that their portfolio contained increasingly fewer personal levies and labour services and more property rights to land, either consisting of rights to formerly manorial land or rights newly acquired.

In the 12th and 13th centuries the lords largely lost their control of labour, but increased their hold on the land just when it became increasingly scarce and valuable as a result of the mounting population pressure. In this process the lords as large landowners were aided by the wage–price scissors. During almost all of the period 1100–1350, and particularly in 1250–1350, grain prices rose as a result of rapid population growth, and wages were relatively low, allowing large landowners opportunities through direct exploitation and leasing to obtain large surpluses/incomes, which they subsequently spent on buying even more land. A specific example of this process was the acquisition of large land holdings by the new religious institutions founded in the 12th century, which were often endowed and favoured by their benefactors with large tracts

---

[135] Verhulst, 'Aspekte der Grundherrschaftsentwicklung', esp. 17–25.
[136] Despy, 'L'exploitation', esp. 188–192.

of land. Such institutions patiently and consistently bought ever more land, assembling it into large granges. The Premonstratensian Abbey of Mariënweerd in the Guelders river area, for instance, acquired no less than 3,500 hectares in the period 1129–1350, and numerous abbeys in Frisia and Groningen acquired about a thousand hectares each, accounting for about one-fifth of the total area in these regions and often including the best agricultural lands.[137] The religious institutions no longer gave their land in manorial, hereditary, or feudal tenure, but directly farmed most of it. The Cistercians were particularly noted for their successful use of the land in granges, using lay brethren as well as labour services and wage labourers, but they were certainly not unique in this. Abbeys of other orders, and even some older institutions and chapters, in the 12th century increasingly changed over to direct farming and the formation of granges.[138] In the decades around 1300 further changes were made, and such institutions gave almost all of their holdings out in short-term leases, which rapidly became the dominant way of exploiting large land ownership.

The result was that regions formerly dominated by manorial organization, from the 13th century on, were dominated by large land holdings which were to a large extent in the hands of the former manorial lords. This is documented for the Guelders river area, where around the mid-16th century the large land holdings of sovereign lords, nobles, and religious institutions covered about three-quarters of the land, mainly the best agricultural lands.[139] In the area immediately to the west, which was part of the Holland peatlands, the peasants in the 15th century held about three-quarters of the land, as had been the case from the period of occupation in the 11th to 13th centuries. Changes in the exploitation of land ownership had not been very significant there, since Holland remained dominated by peasant landholdings cultivated by the peasants themselves, and short-term leasing never became very important.[140] In Drenthe, where the slow occupation of the infertile sandy soils had led to the peasants possessing most of the land, the same stability can be observed. Attempts to change this from without were fiercely and successfully resisted, as the Bishop of Utrecht experienced in 1225 and subsequent years. The Drenthe peasants feared that the bishop, by increasing his authority, wanted to reduce them to dependence or even serfdom, and strongly opposed him. The bishop tried to crush their resistance with a large army of nobles, including the counts of Holland, Guelders, Bentheim, and Cleves, but they were defeated by the Drents, who killed the bishop and some 400 noblemen, hunted down in the swamps by peasant men and women,

---

[137] Van Bavel, *Mariënweerd*, 202–211 and 281, and Mol, *Grootgrondbezit*, 51–59 and 67.

[138] Cf. Lohrmann, *Kirchengut*, 166–167, 198–206, and 211–226. Cf. for the incorporation of manorial elements in these granges section II.2, p. 39, and for the later shift to leasing section V.1, pp. 170–178.

[139] Van Bavel, 'Land, lease and agriculture', 13–14.

[140] At least not up to the 16th century, as the situation drastically changed there. Cf. section VI.1, pp. 249–250 below.

'fighting like wild animals'.[141] In 1240 this struggle came to a provisional end, with the bishop having to give in and the few elements of manorialism decaying in the following years. Their firm position enabled the Drenthe peasants to withstand even a large coalition of feudal lords, which showed how stable such regional social structures were.

This was also true of the Guelders river area where large landowners were dominant and remained so, but there was a rapid shift from manorial exploitation to short-term leasing in the 13th and 14th centuries, very early by north-west European standards. The relatively quick dissolution of manorialism in the 13th century, in combination with the remaining strength of the former manorial lords, was probably a crucial factor in the successful shift the lords were able to make to leasing out large holdings. Manorial lords may have had more difficulties maintaining their position in regions where the dissolution started earlier and evolved more slowly, or almost invisibly, as was the case in inland Flanders. The fact that the rural lords there were confronted by powerful opponents, with the territorial lord and cities arising early, further weakened their position.[142] Moreover, at the early date when the manors in Flanders dissolved, there were not yet any clear and absolute property rights, advanced administration of rights, or a system of short-term leasing; these developed only in the 13th to 14th centuries[143]—hence, the manorial lords had no alternative and lost some control over the land to the peasants.

The Flanders case is exceptional, however. In general, almost all regions in the Low Countries during the high and late Middle Ages experienced clear stability in the social structures of property ownership, i.e. the distribution of rights to land across social groups. At the same time, transformations in the exploitation of land holdings could be pronounced, showing sharp regional contrasts closely allied with differences in the structure of ownership. The differences among regions that emerged during the respective periods of occupation are clearly reflected in the late medieval situation. Notwithstanding changes in form, as happened with the dissolution of manors and the development of more absolute property rights, the essence of the social power relations remained, and in most cases can still be seen centuries later in the property structures. A region earlier dominated by manors of large landholdings, following the dissolution of manorial organization, often became dominated by large landholdings worked by wage labourers or (more commonly) given out in short-term leases. The lords mostly succeeded in consolidating their position and lending it new substance. Therefore, despite the disappearance of manorialism, it is not possible to call these developments a change in the class constellation in favour of the tenants.[144]

---

[141] Slicher van Bath, 'Drenthe's vrijheid', esp. 170–171.
[142] Thoen, 'Commercial survival economy', 109–110 and 127.
[143] Section V.1, pp. 170–178 below.
[144] Contrary to Kriedte, 'Spätmittelalterliche Agrarkrise', 61–62.

The power balance among the social groups in a region showed a great deal of continuity and stability despite the changes in form such relations took.

III.3. VILLAGE AND TOWN

In the preceding section we emphasized vertical social relations within the elite and between the elite and the rest of the population. These vertical relations became more prominent and elaborate in the course of the early and high Middle Ages, first with the rise of manorialism and later with that of the feudal system and banal seigneurialism. But in the high Middle Ages social organizations in which horizontal ties were important developed also, perhaps building on the tradition of sworn associations that already existed in the countryside, such as the *coniurationes servorum*, the associations of serfs bound by oaths, mentioned in the 9th century for southern Flanders, coastal Flanders, and other coastal areas.[145] These were sometimes tolerated by the lords, but more often suppressed, for example, by Emperor Louis the Pious in 821. This early medieval tradition of association received a new impetus and gained enormous strength, and a more formal organization, in the high Middle Ages, in a general trend felt throughout the whole of society, particularly in the 11th century. The two main examples are the village communities and the towns which developed parallel to, and sometimes overlapping with, the emerging organizations for poor relief, administration of commons, juridical affairs, and water management. In the high Middle Ages both village and town developed their specific forms, which greatly influenced social and cultural life, as well as economic development, far into the modern period.[146] In this section the analysis will concentrate on their institutional organization and the social relations within the rural and urban communities.

Village Communities

The village community, as a corporate polity of villagers with legal, political, and economic functions within a relatively closed settlement, emerged in various parts of the Low Countries in the 9th to 13th centuries. Generally speaking, this development was more pronounced and took place earlier than in many other parts of western and central Europe, perhaps building on the early medieval tradition, especially in the coastal areas. In central and southern Germany, for instance, the crucial phase did not take place until the 13th century, with further development in the later medieval period.[147]

---

[145] Oexle, 'Gilden als soziale Gruppen', 304–308.
[146] For the social and economic effects of these organizations cf. sections IV.1, pp. 136–142, V.4, pp. 218–228, and VII.2, pp. 343–348, below.
[147] Blickle, *Deutsche Untertanen*, 23.

People wanted to join forces for obvious reasons, but in the 9th to 13th centuries several factors accelerated the process in the Low Countries and stimulated its formalization. These included the increasing nuclearization of settlement—with scattered farmsteads being rearranged into villages[148]—and the growing density of population, both compelling and enabling the villagers to work more closely together, particularly in coordinating agricultural activities and regulating access to ever scarcer resources. Sometimes this more nucleated settlement was associated with the rise of manors. But, although the village community could grow out of the jurisdictional organization of the serfs of a manor, it consisted of free people and was organized on a territorial basis, not shaped by personal ties. The territoriality of the village was enhanced by the fact that it often overlapped with the parish. Parishes each had their own district for levying tithes, generally introduced in the 9th century and necessitating a clear demarcation of the boundaries of the parish, and thus of the village.[149] In some regions the rise of village communities can also be seen as a reaction to the growing pressure of banal seigneuries. The fact that the banal obligations were territorial and impressed on everyone in that particular area stimulated a sense of unity and solidarity in the populace, as well as a desire to form a counter-weight against rising banal power. On the other hand, when lordly power was too strong it could prevent the emergence of well-developed village communities.

Although the strength of rural communities in the Low Countries has not been systemtically investigated yet, the scattered data support the main lines set out above. The role of the village community was fairly prominent in Holland where manorialism, coercion, and personal ties had always been weak, and which was dominated by a territorial lord who strove for a modern union of free subjects with equal rights and obligations within his territory.[150] This lent village communities a solid position from the beginning, i.e. the 11th to 13th centuries, when the region was opened up by large-scale reclamation. The same, though perhaps to a lesser extent, was true of areas to which Holland colonizers exported their organization, such as parts of the Niederrhein region and the districts around the mouths of the Elbe and Weser rivers in northern Germany.[151] Village communities also acquired a strong position in some other peasant-dominated regions where manorialism had never been important, such as Drenthe. There their role was further strengthened by the elements of communal farming and the extensive commons used by the community. In Hainaut, the village communities were strongest in the north of the Thiérache, a largely pastoral area, where a high value was placed on the regulation of grazing rights.[152] In the

---

[148] Section II.2, p. 38 above.   [149] Semmler, 'Zehntgebot und Pfarrtermination', 33 and 37–42.
[150] Van der Linden, 'Het platteland', 64–78.
[151] Wunder, *Die bäuerliche Gemeinde*, 35–36 and 44–45, and Petri, 'Entstehung und Verbreitung', 723–734.
[152] Sivéry, *Structures agraires*, 275–292.

grain-producing areas of Hainaut, where lords were powerful, hardly any village communities developed, and those that did were less able to assert themselves. This links up with the situation in the Guelders river area, which was dominated by large landholdings and/or powerful lords, where village communities were weak, with little organization and hardly any formal responsibilities, and where little or no commons or communal farming existed. If the lord there also possessed extensive banal rights, and/or a stronghold enabling him to dominate the village there were few possibilities for village communities to exercise influence or to develop at all.

Communities had many functions, particularly in regions where they obtained a powerful position. They acted as a legal body in voluntary juridical affairs: making agreements, buying, selling, and contracting debts. Often the village community owned some property, mainly land, and public facilities such as a mill, an oven, a market, or even a village hall, and received revenues from leasing out common properties, as well as from fines and local taxes. The revenues covered expenses incurred in maintaining its properties and in paying its personnel. A village often employed a common herdsman, a police officer, and sometimes a clerk, a forester, a fireman, or a servant.

In some regions, as in Holland, the community was also active in collecting taxes, organizing military duties, and maintaining internal order. To some extent this role was encouraged by the seigneurial and/or territorial lord, who was thus relieved of the duty of organizing these tasks himself. On the other hand, lords resisted any usurpation of authority, loss of revenues, or reduction of power that was too far-reaching. In some regions the village communities also obtained some control over local jurisdiction, sometimes even despite the resentment or opposition of the seigneurial lord. The acquisition of authority to administer low justice was the pearl in the crown of village development. Sometimes villages exercised local justice almost autonomously, but more often in cooperation with the lord. Village justice was usually administered by the *schout*, chairman of the village court, who often was both confidential agent of the lord and representative of the village community.[153] Even in the Land of Heusden, part of the Holland peat area where village communities were well developed, administration of justice was not completely autonomous since the initiative was the prerogative of the holder of the *bannus*, i.e. the territorial or seigneurial lord, represented by the schout.[154] On the other hand, the village could exercise some power directly by way of the tribunal, consisting of jurors elected as representatives by the community. They generally functioned as a village court, operating on the basis of customary law. The fact that village communities also developed village bylaws (*decretum villae*) formed another element of self-organization.

---

[153] Bader, *Dorfgenossenschaft*, 297–321 and 364–366.
[154] Hoppenbrouwers: 'Een middeleeuwse samenleving', 507–524, and 'Op zoek naar de "kerels" ', 230–231.

The rural communities especially aimed to protect customs, or perceived ones, against encroachments by the lord or others, as well as wanting to obtain or retain self-government for administration, justice, and taxation. Infringements on these rights were a main cause of rural revolt, as in Westfrisia in the 13th century. The village community also fought the arbitrariness of levies and exactions, aiming to transform them to fixed, general duties. In many cases they were successful, particularly with respect to one of the most hated banal levies, the *tallia* or tallage, which became fixed from the late 12th century, as in Namur and Flanders.[155] These attempts were often supported by the territorial lord, who wanted to break the power of feudal lords, particularly in areas where his own authority was weak. A clear expression of this were the franchises granted to villages by the territorial lord in Brabant and Namur. In the duchy of Brabant, some 130 franchises were granted to communities, in most cases village communities, mainly in the first half of the 13th century.[156] They clearly show the policy of the territorial lord was to strengthen the position of the communities at the expense of local lords, retaining high justice for himself and thus confirming his own position.

In most cases the local seigneurial lord was the main adversary of the village communities, and they often acted against him in cooperation with the territorial lord, but occasionally they struggled against the advancing power of territorial lords. This can be observed most clearly in various parts of Frisia, including East Friesland.[157] Because feudal organization was weak and the territorial lord had very little authority, free yeomen acquired a strong position there. Claiming they were directly under the king's authority, they had begun to organize their autonomous communities in the 11th century. There was broad participation by free farmers in public matters as early as the 12th century. Unlike elsewhere in the Low Countries, the timing of this did not coincide with the rise of territorial lords and shared interests, but largely occurred before the territorial lords started their attempts to acquire authority in Frisia. The rural associations thus had little to gain by aiding the territorial lords' rise, or rather they feared to lose by this, and therefore resisted his ambitions. In the 13th century, the organization of communities developed further, with the appearance of the *redjeven/grietmannen*, judges and representatives, appointed by the community.[158] Also, in the Frisian districts some 25 *terrae* or lands developed, with their boards consisting of the joint representatives of the land. This was the height of self-government for the Frisian communities, and remained in place until the 15th and 16th centuries.

---

[155] Thoen, *Landbouwekonomie*, 411, and Genicot, *L'économie rurale namuroise*, iii:78–79. Cf. also section III.1, pp. 66–68.

[156] Steurs, 'Les franchises' and Id., *Naissance d'une région*. In all these respects, there is a clear parallel with the urban communities (which will be discussed further below).

[157] Schmidt, 'Hochmittelalterliche "Bauernaufstände"', esp. 416–428. See also section III.1, p. 74.

[158] Ehbrecht, 'Gemeinschaft', 154–160.

Village communities could also operate in religious matters, since they often overlapped with the parishes. Villages often wanted to form their own parish instead of having a chapel subordinated to another parish church, a desire which could result in funding their own and providing for the maintenance of the priest. The fact that tithes were levied on a particular territory, with well-specified boundaries, further contributed to the territorialization of the village community. In some cases, the village retained its hold on the administration of church properties, exercised by churchwardens elected by the villagers/parishioners, and sometimes they even controlled the choice or appointment of the priest, verger, and schoolmaster. The right to nominate the priest, often rooted in the foundation of the church, was mostly firmly in the hands of nobles or abbeys, in the Guelders river area, for instance, but the 'Genossenschaftspatronat' or communal right to do so, was very common in Frisia, Groningen, and East Friesland. It was not linked to the early medieval foundation of churches, but was a later development, connected to the wave of communal association there.[159] It was also found in Drenthe and the Campine, regions where, of course, peasants and their communities were also powerful. The community sometimes also administered the village poor box and regulated distributions.

In some of the coastal areas, the village communities often overlapped with the organizations for water management,[160] frequently formed as *coniurationes* of colonist associations, most clearly in peatland Holland and the adjacent parts of the Nedersticht Utrecht. There, in the 12th century, and perhaps even earlier, free confederations were responsible for water management, under the constant threat of flooding which necessitated cooperation and communal organization. The territorial lord tried to gain greater control over these organizations, particularly from the 13th century on, but his control remained limited to formal recognition or regulation. In Holland, even the regional water management boards remained largely autonomous: in the large district of Rijnland in the 13th century, *communis terrae consiliarii* comprised the common council. This council was not appointed by the Count of Holland, but it had the right of co-optation, again pointing to its communal roots.

Communal association, however, was not the only possible solution here. Often it was precisely in water management that the role of the state or central authority was strong: whether for big empires such as China or Iraq, or to a lesser extent also in some regions within the Low Countries. In coastal Flanders the role of the territorial lord was greater than in other regions, as a result of the different roots of water management there. Water control in Flanders had always been under the authority of the Carolingian counts, and subsequently the Count of Flanders. The authority and jurisdiction over even the smallest water management districts remained in the hands of the bailiff and

---

[159] Van Apeldoorn, *De kerkelijke goederen*, 1–12, and Mol, 'Friesische Freiheit', esp. 197–212.
[160] Van der Linden, *Recht en territoir*, 10–26, and Fockema Andreae, *Studiën*, iv:2–7.

the comital tribunal, allowing less overlap with the village community. In some cases, particularly in Flanders, the water management organization increasingly operated in competition with the village community, especially if every villager had an equal say in decisions of the latter. Water management costs, however, were assessed on the basis of landholding, which was not at all equal. This situation caused friction and often resulted in water management boards operating independently of the village community and becoming dominated by landowners, especially wealthy landowners, making the boards in part instruments for defending their own interests.[161]

In several regions, village communities also played a role in the organization of open-field farming and the maintenance of the 'Flurzwang', the collective sowing and harvesting, and collective cattle grazing on the stubble after harvesting.[162] Organizations for the management of meadows, wastelands, and woods used in common also developed. Properties used in common run a high risk of becoming exhausted unless there are clear restrictions and limitations imposed on the users. To avoid overexploitation and to allow the use of the commons to be sustainable, rules, supervision, and sanctions were necessary, as well as a clear decision-making process.[163] Some rules probably existed traditionally, but in the high Middle Ages formal organizations developed to uphold rules and adjudicate disputes. These were called *marken* (in the eastern Netherlands) and *gemeenten* or *vroonten* (in north-western Brabant). In many regions, including Drenthe, the Gooi, and northern Brabant, the commons developed in close association with the village communities and were managed by the village boards.[164] This was the case particularly where peasants were free and held firm property rights to the land. In other regions, where manorialism had been more pronounced, the commons often developed from manorial roots, and they were originally separate from local communities, although in the course of time some overlap started to occur.

There has been some debate on the chronology and origin of such communal organizations. Earlier, they were often seen as the remains of a prehistoric primitive communism, but now their rise is dated as relatively late. It is assumed that the communal organization in Drenthe, for instance, developed together with the village community in the high Middle Ages, and saw its rules formalized only in the period 1250–1350,[165] although data to confirm this are scarce. Reasons for the emergence of common organization are also sought in this

---

[161] Cf. below p. 102, and also section II.2, pp. 47–48, for the disastrous effects this could have on flood defences.
[162] See also section V.1, pp. 163–165 below.
[163] De Moor, 'Common land'; and for the commons in the wider context of medieval associations: De Moor, 'The silent revolution'.
[164] Hoppenbrouwers, 'The use and management', 92–93.
[165] Slicher van Bath, *Mensch en land in de middeleeuwen*, 55–88, and for regional differences also 113–114 and 120–121. Spek, *Het Drentse esdorpenlandschap*, 102–104, following Heringa, rather stresses the earlier, gradual character of their emergence.

period, mainly in the effects of increasing population pressure: the intensification of agriculture and the growing pressure on the wastelands. The rise of new agricultural systems,[166] such as 'perpetual' rye cultivation with sod-manuring, and the growing importance of pasturing sheep made it crucial to acquire control over the common wastelands. Another factor was the rise of territorial lords, who often attempted to obtain rights to the wastelands/commons on the basis of their regalian power. If a lord was successful, he could organize the rights to the commons; if he failed, the attempt usually prompted formal organization by the villagers or commoners.

The sharp regional contrasts in the distribution of power and property across social groups caused a divergent development of control and organization of the commons in the later Middle Ages. In Holland the territorial lord was successful in obtaining nominal rights to the wilderness, and he subsequently granted all of it for reclamation to individual farmers, leaving none for common use. In the large-scale reclamations there, the boundaries of the reclamation were fixed beforehand, and all land within these boundaries was divided into farms, each reclaimed and cultivated individually. At the edges of the newly reclaimed land some commonly used wastelands may have remained, but with the advance of the reclamation movement, almost fully completed in the 13th century, they gradually disappeared. In the Campine, in north-eastern Brabant, the territorial lord also gained formal control over the wastelands, but in the decades around 1300 the duke sold his control to the village communities or the commoners through *gemeynte-brieven* (community charters).[167] By this sale the duke also abandoned his right to issue parts of these commons to third parties. In north-western Brabant, on the other hand, the local lords retained firm control over the common wastelands. The commoners were allowed only usage rights, and the lords continued to issue parts of these lands at a good return for reclamation or for use as private wasteland. This resulted in a rapid decay of these commons, already completed in some villages around Breda in the late 15th century, whereas further east they continued to exist until well into the modern era.

The different genesis is reflected in the management of the commons. In the Guelders river area and in other parts of Guelders and Overijssel where large manorial land holding was strong, the (former) manorial lords were often dominant in the organization, administration and use of the commons, and the ordinary commoners had only some usage rights. By contrast, in those parts of the eastern Netherlands where both manorialism and territorial power had been weak, such as in Drenthe, the village communities, which included most of the villagers, held a firm control over the common wastelands. This is also reflected in the laws of the commons, which show the goals of common organization.

---

[166] Cf. section VII.1, pp. 328–329 below.
[167] Leenders, *Van Turnhoutervoorde tot Strienemonde*, 469–472.

In the eastern Netherlands, with laws that come down from the 14th century, preventing over-exploitation was clearly the primary goal. The subsistence needs of the peasants and the continuity of the village or peasant economy were central to the organization of the commons there.[168] In regions such as Drenthe and the Campine, where the peasants were dominant and there were few if any large land holdings, and where commons played an important part in the agrosystem, these laws were widely accepted, and this organization survived into the 19th century.[169]

This regional diversity also applies to the power balance within the village communities. Not all villagers were by definition members of the village community. In many cases the landless were excluded and only those owning or holding land were considered to belong to the village community with all the rights attached to this,[170] including a say in the decisions made by the village assembly, such as in the appointment of a village herdsman, control over resources, or settling disputes. In the Holland peatlands this meant broad participation, since virtually the entire rural population possessed land, but in the Guelders river area land ownership was highly polarized, creating a sharp divide in eligibility. A growing polarization in social–property structures and proletarianization of large segments of the population, as in 14th-century coastal Flanders or 16th-century Holland,[171] had momentous effects in this respect. Loss of land could mean exclusion from the decision-making process. This can be seen from the water management in coastal Flanders,[172] where the participation of peasants in general meetings and broad consultation were increasingly limited, and decision-making came into the hands of an ever smaller group of landowners, some of them absentees.

Administrative functions and membership of local or regional boards were also linked to ownership of a minimum quantity of land: to become eligible for appointment as an alderman or reeve on a water management board required at least 10 or 15 hectares. Again, the example of water management in coastal Flanders is instructive. Sluice masters and board members were installed at a general meeting of landowners, which endorsed them, but in the 15th and 16th centuries these members increasingly came from the wealthiest group, and in the largest districts they often owned at least 50 hectares. Moreover, fulfilling such functions could further broaden a power base. Holding the office of local tax assessor could enhance an individual's influence in the community. Village offices could thus become an instrument of the village elite to strengthen its control over fellow villagers. Power within the community, therefore, could be very unevenly distributed. Still, compared to the previous situation, the rise

---

[168] Van Zanden, 'The paradox of the marks', esp. 130–135, and De Moor, 'Common land', esp. 124–127.
[169] Section V.1, p. 165 below.
[170] Cf. the illuminating discussion by Hoppenbrouwers, 'Op zoek naar de "kerels" ', 232–236.
[171] Sections II.2, pp. 47–48, and VI.1, pp. 259–260.
[172] Soens, 'Polders zonder poldermodel?'.

of village communities in the high Middle Ages allowed for relatively broad participation of people in local administration.

Towns in the Early and High Middle Ages

In the course of the Middle Ages the Low Countries became one of the most urbanized parts of Europe. The first full overviews are available for the 15th century. At that point, there were sharp contrasts in urbanization among the regions, varying from 10 to 40 per cent, but as a whole the Low Countries was clearly characterized by the importance of the cities; not only demographically, but also economically, politically, and culturally.[173] This situation had largely emerged in the high Middle Ages. By the 12th and 13th centuries the Low Countries had become by far the most urbanized part of Europe, first catching up with and later overtaking Italy in this respect, so the decisive take-off in the urbanization process is to be found in the preceding centuries. In this process the access the urban population had to agricultural surpluses was pre-eminent. The largely non-agricultural population of the cities had to be fed, not an easy task in view of the small agricultural surpluses and the difficult transportation of the period. Crucial also was the success of the urban population in channelling the surpluses to the city. This could be done by economic means such as purchase (with the purchasing power of urban dwellers enhanced by the services they provided in religion, administration, industry or trade), or by using property rights of the town and its burghers (the possession of land, tithes, mills, or jurisdictional rights in the countryside), or in non-economic ways (force exercised by the city or some of its inhabitants, i.e. the presence of powerful people possessing coercive means or the transfer of such means to the city itself). There was generally a mixture of the three instruments, varying according to the region.

We will return to the economic foundations of the town in our analysis of the development of trade and industries.[174] Here we will concentrate on another aspect, that is, the town as social-institutional organization and its internal and external relationships. The development of the town as a social-legal body took place in the same period as that of the village, in the 10th to 12th centuries, and it retained most of its characteristics for many centuries afterwards. The importance of the town as an institution, and the extent to which towns were separated from the countryside, may have been overemphasized in the older literature, but it is a characteristic feature of the Middle Ages, up to the French Revolution or even, in the Netherlands, to legislation of 1851, when institutional-legal differences between town and countryside were finally abolished. Earlier, the specific institutional arrangements of towns were crucial in determining

---

[173] For the process of urbanization and its effects, cf. section VI.2, pp. 278–282.
[174] Sections IV.2, pp. 155–157, and V.4, pp. 224–228.

economic and non-economic possibilities for the town and its access to surpluses, as well as for the economic potential of the region as a whole.

Almost all towns in the Low Countries had emerged only in the Middle Ages itself; pre-existing urban presence was broken off in the post-Roman period. The only exception was in the extreme south-west, where large walled *civitates* such as Cambrai, Arras, and Tournai survived the discontinuity of the post-Roman period.[175] But even they declined greatly in the early Middle Ages because of the general chaos, the diminishing importance of neglected and decaying land routes—on which most of them were situated—in favour of waterways, and the decreasing integration between town and countryside. The limited continuity in the south-west links up with more southern areas in France and Italy, where Roman cities lingered on and remained important aristocratic bases. But to the north, i.e. in almost all of the Low Countries, most Roman settlements were deserted during the invasions of the late 3rd or 5th centuries.

It is striking, nevertheless, how often the Roman site of settlement was repopulated in the Merovingian or Carolingian periods, as has been shown for several Flemish cities.[176] The same is even more true for the towns in the Meuse valley: Huy, Namur, Tongeren, and Maastricht were early medieval centres with an ancient location and sometimes even a slight continuity of occupation.[177] The same applies to Utrecht and Nijmegen, which are in or near the Guelders river area. It is not coincidental that both are located on large rivers, enabling them to become pivotal in early medieval transport. Often the focal point of continuity was a Roman fort. A *castellum*, because of the prestige it had and the protection its walls offered, enhanced topographic continuity. Several missionaries chose the remains of a Roman fort as a basis for their activities, as Willibrord did in Utrecht. The establishment of an episcopal see in the early medieval period was the main element in urban continuity there, and also in Tongeren/Maastricht/Liège, and Cambrai. Often, such centres were also mints, royal fiscs, and home to some aristocrats. In a few cases continuity was more than topographical alone, since the political organization of the *pagi*, which developed in the Merovingian period, was sometimes linked to the Roman administrative subdivisions, again particularly in the south-west of the Low Countries.[178] However, in the course of the process the role of towns clearly changed: administration was no longer almost exclusively based in the *civitates* and their central position was clearly diminished.

Some early medieval centres had no Roman antecedents, but grew out of an important manor, abbey, or lord's residence. The Flemish town of Aalst, for instance, developed from a bipartite manor of the Abbey of Lobbes, with its manor house, demesne, and mill situated on the Dender river, and protected

---

[175] Wickham, *Framing the Middle Ages*, 606–609 and 677–681.
[176] Verhulst, *Rise of cities*, 8–11 and 33–37.
[177] Verhulst, 'The origins of towns', esp. 16–18, Devroey and Devroey—Zoller, 'Villes, campagnes', 223–260, and Theuws, 'Maastricht', esp. 187–188.
[178] Cf. above, section III.1, pp. 69–70.

or fortified by a ditch, probably in the 9th century.[179] Larger settlements of merchants and craftsmen emerged around abbeys in Nijvel, Gembloux, and Sint-Truiden. The merchants living there were often part of the *familia* of the abbey—many as ministeriales. Despite their unfree status in many cases they formed the elite in these urban centres, as for example in Louvain with its Sint-Pietersmannen ('the men of Saint-Peter's') or in Sint-Truiden.[180] In the 11th and 12th centuries, when the *familia* of the abbey began to disband and the town of Sint-Truiden obtained its charter, the former ministerial merchants, perhaps complemented by free merchants, formed the urban patriciate and most aldermen came from their ranks.

This type of early medieval centre, like those with Roman antecedents, was primarily a centre of consumption. They owed their position to the presence of a bishop, large abbey, or king's palace; these institutions and lords owned large properties, increasingly organized within the manorial system. Some of these lords had several or even dozens of manors, sometimes scattered over large areas around the centre. For instance, the Abbey of Echternach, founded on a former Roman settlement, in the period around 700 acquired numerous churches, tithes, and dozens of *villae* all over the Low Countries. These were in Luxembourg, around the Mosel river, as well as more distant, in the Campine, along the river Waal near Nijmegen, in Holland, and in Frisia. They guaranteed the abbey a constant flow of surpluses, either in kind or in cash. This flow stimulated demand for trade and crafts in its immediate surroundings, forming the basis for growth of a market, which may have emerged as early as the 8th to 9th centuries, as well as the town of Echternach.[181] Similar developments can be seen around the abbeys of Gembloux, Saint-Hubert, and Sint-Truiden in the 9th to 11th centuries. Such manorial property provided the main access to surpluses, sometimes gleaned from a large area, acquired on the basis of certain religious, political, and other functions, as well as from non-economic compulsion which the lords exercised over unfree or semi-free peasants. Since the importance of these urban centres was associated with the presence of this elite, such centres were indirectly linked to the success of the manorial system. It is not surprising that in the 7th–12th centuries urban centres particularly developed in the two nuclear regions of manorialism in the Low Countries: the Meuse valley and the Guelders river area.

In addition to this predominant type of centre in the early medieval Low Countries, there were also the trading posts, not founded in Roman times and not closely linked to the surrounding countryside. Some farmers lived in these settlements, which had contact with surrounding manors, but they primarily owed their prominence to their trade networks, both international and regional.

---

[179] Callebaut, 'De topografische groei van Aalst', 227–249.
[180] Petri, 'Die Anfänge', esp. 272–277, and Charles, *La ville de Saint-Trond*, 101–145 and 283–285.
[181] Trauffler, 'Klostergrundherrschaft und Stadt', 219–238, Bijsterveld, ' "Sinte Willibrordus eygen" ', and Wampach, *Geschichte der Grundherrschaft*, 347–404.

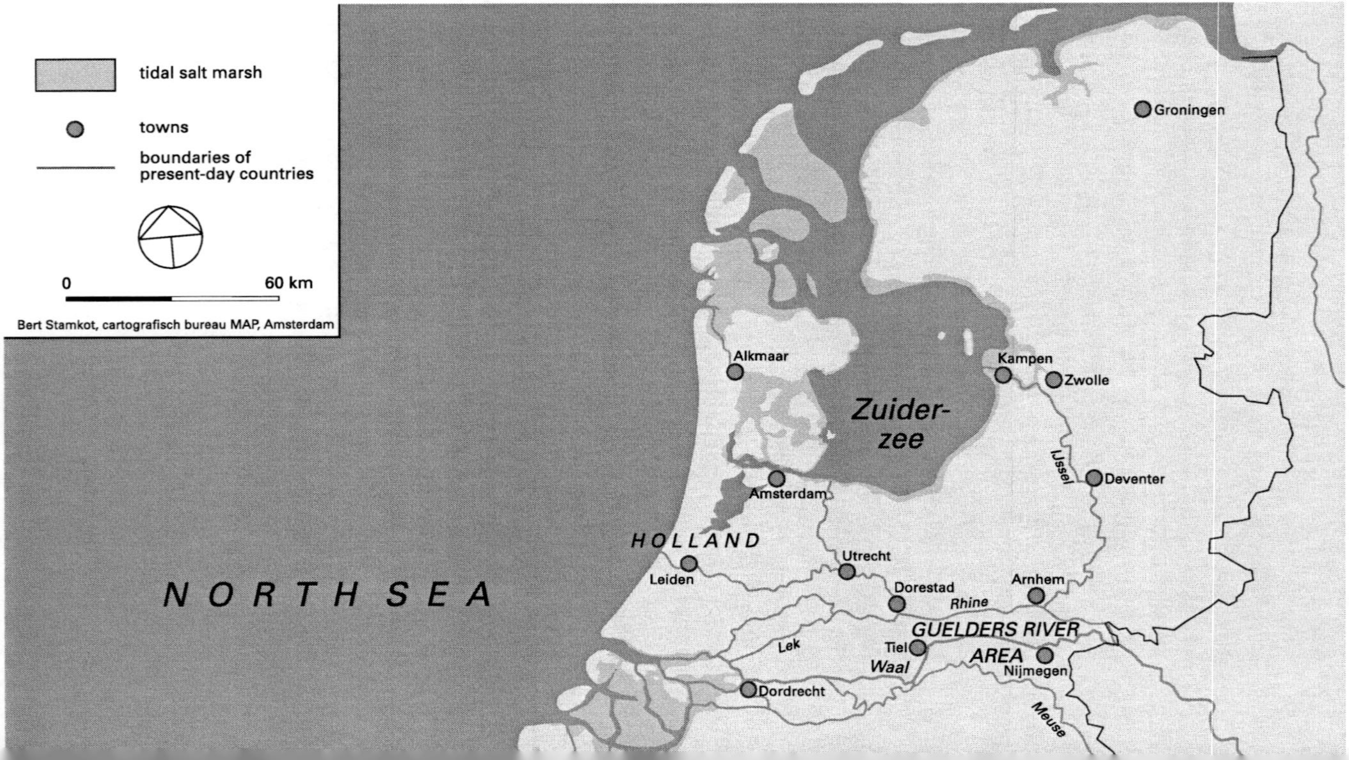
tidal salt marsh
towns
boundaries of present-day countries
0
60 km
Bert Stamkot, cartografisch bureau MAP, Amsterdam
Groningen
Kampen
Zwolle
Zuider-zee
IJssel
Deventer
Alkmaar
Amsterdam
HOLLAND
Leiden
Utrecht
Dorestad
Rhine
Arnhem
GUELDERS RIVER AREA
Tiel
Nijmegen
Lek
Waal
Dordrecht
Meuse
NORTH SEA

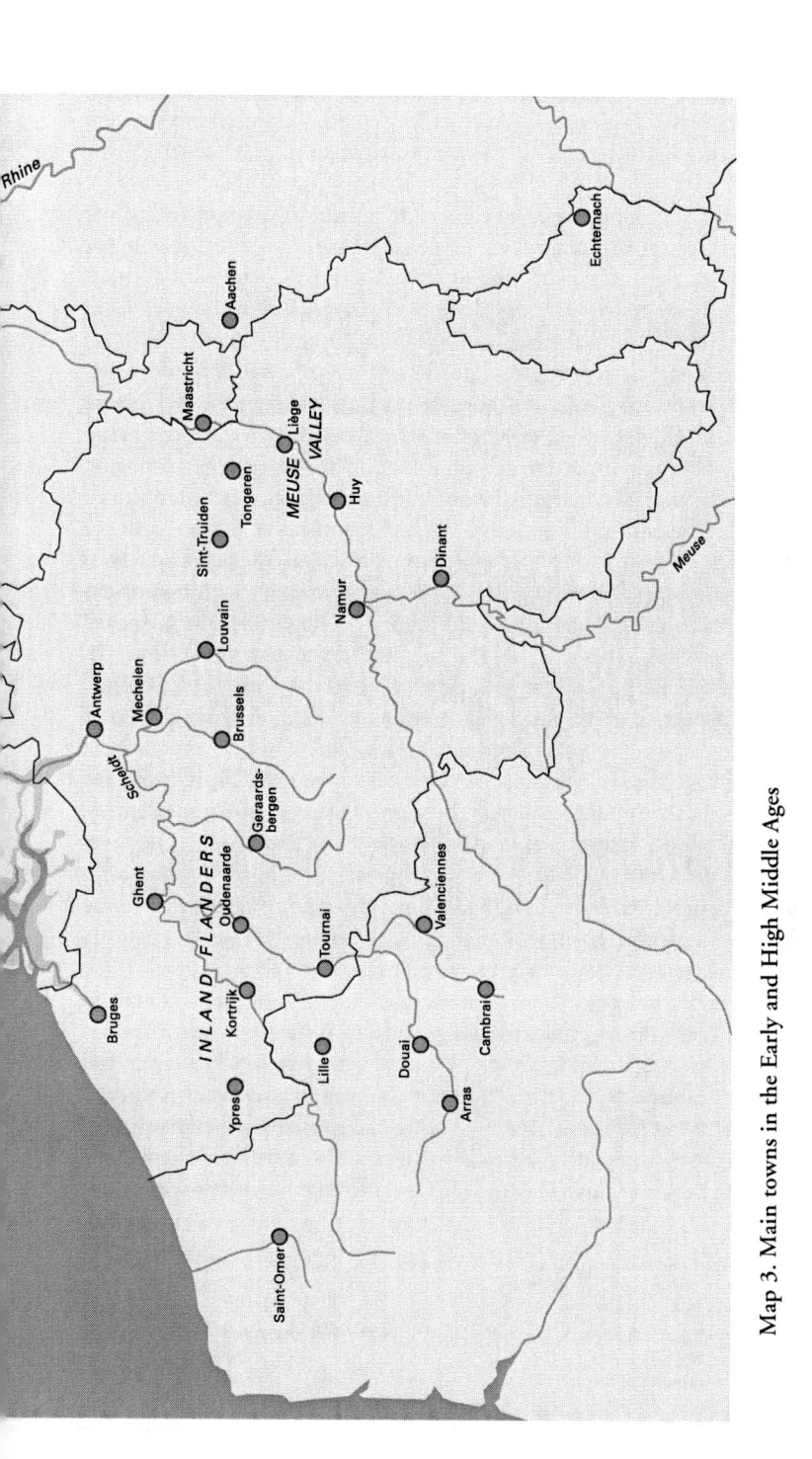

Map 3. Main towns in the Early and High Middle Ages

They are designated in the sources as *emporium* or *portus*, indicating their commercial character. The main example is Dorestad, but there are also the smaller regional centres of Frisian trade, such as Medemblik, Domburg in Zeeland at the mouth of the Scheldt, and Witla near Rotterdam at the mouth of the Meuse.[182]

These settlements were not primarily centres of consumption, but owed their position to trade. One of the main elements in their rise was their favourable location for transport, on the delta of large rivers and at the boundaries of political spheres, between Frankish, Frisian, English, and Saxon territories, allowing them to function as gateways. The integration of Frisia and Saxony into the Frankish Empire in the 8th and 9th centuries benefited such centres as Dorestad, since they were ideally placed in this border zone to channel exchange. Royal power was also a major factor in their development. Dorestad was only a little south of a royal estate, where an important mint functioned before 650 and again after 690. It was located in a highly strategic military region, with many royal properties.[183] The Frankish king established a collection point in Dorestad for royal tolls on imports and exports to and from the Frankish Empire; it was one of the four principal points on the borders of the empire. A *procurator reipublicae* was appointed as a special royal officer to collect tolls and safeguard royal interests. The inhabitants of Dorestad, mainly merchants, were under the close protection of the king and were assigned a wergild three times higher than a free man. All this was part of the royal attempts to channel flows of luxury goods through such trading centres in order to control them, to profit from them through tolls, and to guarantee the supply of luxuries to the royal court. Dorestad was not unique in its prominent royal presence; among the smaller trade centres, for instance, Medemblik included royal property, a mint, and a toll, which was partly donated to the Utrecht Church.[184] Royal presence, and the protection it offered, was clearly preferred by traders. Merchants also profited from protection from treaties agreed between kings or their officers, as in the late 8th century between Charlemagne and Offa of Mercia, the Anglo-Saxon king.

Many of the people living in these centres, and determining their character, were merchants. The non-merchant element is more difficult to identify, but it has been demonstrated through archaeological research for Dorestad and other centres. In Dorestad some 60 farmhouses with granaries were found, as well as numerous traces of industries indicating the presence of craftsmen.[185] Dorestad also exercised some administrative and ecclesiastical functions, having the second oldest church of the bishopric, but the merchant element was clearly

---

[182] Hodges, *Dark age economics*, 39–43 and 74–77, and Hodges, *Towns and trade*. Cf. also section V.4, pp. 214–215.

[183] Cf. above, section III.1, p. 56.

[184] Besteman, 'Carolingian Medemblik', esp. 47–48. Cf. for royal property and interests in these places: Blok, *De Franken*, 75–78 and 101–103.

[185] Van Es, 'Dorestad centred', 158 and 173–177.

predominant. In the 8th century trade flourished under a firm, secure central authority; its decline in the next century was caused by destabilization, insecurity, and Viking raids.[186] It was no accident that this decline occurred as Frankish power was weakened by internal struggles and a shift of focus to areas further south. Raiders took advantage of this, particularly hitting rich trading centres in the delta area. Dorestad was plundered in 834 and in each of the following years. After repeated restoration and looting, by the third quarter of the 9th century its decline could no longer be reversed.

In this period of insecurity, military protection became more important. Many settlements started to protect themselves with walls, such as Tournai, where the wall of the Roman *civitas* was repaired; the monasteries in Arras and Ghent (St Bavo), and Middelburg, with its circular fort, did likewise.[187] To build and protect such strongholds, a secure authority and organization were required. Since the king was no longer able to provide this protection, local lords and the increasingly powerful territorial lords were needed; protection was strongest in regions where princely authority developed early, such as inland Flanders. In the 10th and 11th centuries, with the further weakening of central royal power and the rise of feuding lords, insecurity remained and the process of fortification proceeded. Merchants, craftsmen, and shopkeepers withdrew inside the walls for security, but they were also attracted to such places because the elite, who were their main customers, lived there.

Such changes were most clearly manifested in the new type of city developing in regions such as inland Flanders and Brabant from the 9th century on. They came to dominate the urban scene in the following centuries. Such cities had fortifications and military protection, and thus were able to defend themselves. Moreover, in the 11th and 12th centuries they acquired further rights and privileges, including some independence from lordly capriciousness, self-organization, and also some hold over trade and the surrounding countryside, often confirmed by territorial lords. To a large extent these towns built their dominant position vis-à-vis their rural surroundings on their previous, early medieval role as seat of a viscount, centre of a large manor and early parish centre. In these roles, the central settlement often exercised its influence over a large area, which in several cases in the high Middle Ages seems to have developed into the urban district (*libertas*) or the urban *banmijl/banlieu*. This is argued, for instance, for Brussels and Louvain, where the urban banlieu in the later Middle Ages comprised some 30 hamlets and villages.[188] In the urban district, the urban aldermen had the monopoly of administering law and validating transactions in rural immovables. People living within the banlieu were compelled to work on the urban fortification of the castellan and to pay urban excises. Moreover, urban

---

[186] In a nuanced way: Verhulst, 'The origins of towns', 20–21 and 32. Cf. for the Viking attacks also section III.1, pp. 64–65.
[187] Verhulst, *Rise of cities*, 59–67.   [188] Van Uytven, 'Imperialisme of zelfverdediging'.

merchants and industries held various privileges in this area and rural activities in these fields were often restricted or even prohibited, as is apparent in the first written evidence from the late 13th century on. This type of urban power thus largely went back to the manorial and administrative structures of the early medieval period, explaining why it was largely absent from Holland.

The position of the towns was further butressed by the emerging princes, who provided security and protection, and often strengthened the dominance of the towns over the surrounding countryside through the confirmation of privileges, often formalized from the 13th century on. In turn, the cities were natural allies of the emerging territorial lords against the feuding nobles, and a key to opening up new revenues through tolls and excises. Through their economic power, but also through the privileges and military power that they acquired, the cities were capable of building trading networks, attracting industries and acquiring agrarian surpluses, also available through the manorial system and the burgher properties in the countryside.

With a few exceptions such as Dordrecht in Holland and Groningen in the far north, exercise of non-economic power and the development of staple rights can be seen mainly in Flanders, in cities such as Ghent, Bruges, and Lille, and on a smaller scale in smaller cities such as Geraardsbergen. This urban power in Flanders was linked to the rise of the territorial lord. From the late 10th century, the Count of Flanders administered the county through comital functionaries, the castellans. Associated with this administrative, military, and judicial organization, and the administration of their own manors and other properties, the counts erected castles at strategic points as seats for the castellans, often where merchant communities had already developed. Such castles existed in Lille and Ypres from the middle of the 11th century, and they often formed a nucleus for further urbanization.[189] The developing cities also had their own moats and walls, constructed either on their own initiative or combined with that of the count, to enhance their military protection, but also as a symbol of their position and power. This process started with the largest cities in Flanders and other principalities. In the 11th century Bruges, Ghent, Tournai, Namur, Liège, and Utrecht were already walled. In addition to its comital castle, the town of Ypres was fortified before 1127 and had a new wall built in 1214. The new wall had included a double moat, as well as an earthen rampart and wooden gates, which were later replaced by stone walls and gates at the initiative of the burghers. In Hainaut the process of walling accelerated in the 12th century, when the counts of Hainaut took the initiative in fortifying the towns. In the 13th century, when the cities began to play a larger role in this process and also in bearing the expenses, all 22 cities of the county

---

[189] Nicholas, *Medieval Flanders*, 117–119, and for Ghent: Laleman and Raveschot, *Inleiding*, 202–207. Cf. also section III.1, pp. 72–73.

were walled.[190] This massive construction of walls and fortifications in the high Middle Ages mirrors the fragmentation of royal power and the rise of territorial lords, but also exemplifies the building of separate, smaller zones of authority. The same development can simultaneously be observed in the countryside with the proliferation of motte castles in the 11th century and particularly in the 12th.

Urban fortification often took place together with the acquisition of privileges and power over the surrounding countryside, most clearly in Flanders. Non-economic factors were crucial in a city's access to agricultural surplus, alongside its economic means. Flemish cities were already favoured because surpluses there were large owing to the early specialization of the agricultural sector in Flanders and the extensive grain-growing regions in northern France, which arose partly in response to the demand of growing urban populations.[191] The surpluses could be obtained through the market or the burghers' rural land holdings, the latter particularly from the 13th century, as the Flemish bourgeoisie greatly increased its rural property.[192] But additionally, the cities had access to this surplus via non-economic means. A clear example of this was the staple rights of the large cities and most particularly of Ghent; the rights to force producers from the surrounding countryside to sell their grain in Ghent and the preferential right to buy the grain transported over the Leie and Scheldt rivers through Ghent, associated with the enforced trans-shipment there. These rights probably originated in the early 12th century and were further developed and formalized before the mid-14th century as they were confirmed by the count.[193] A similar large grain staple existed in Douai (formalized in the late 14th century at the latest), but even small towns such as Hulst and Eeklo were able to dominate their countryside and ensure a steady flow of grain from the surrounding villages. By the 12th and 13th centuries, and aided by further growth in their coercive powers in the 14th century, the cities had access to relatively cheap grain, and it was sometimes even resold by the urban elite to the Flemish peasants in times of famine.[194] Because they were able to direct trade and industry, partly through coercive means, over their hinterlands or more widely, the cities developed into important sources of revenue. They thus became places where surpluses could be tapped through tolls, excises, or artificially low prices in buying and high prices in selling, either by the territorial lord or by the urban elite. Cities were used by the territorial lords and urban elites as ways to extract surpluses.[195] This process was most pronounced in the regions which in the high Middle Ages became

---

[190] Piérard, 'Les fortifications médiévales', i: 199–229.
[191] Cf. below section VI.1, p. 337.   [192] Thoen, *Landbouwekonomie*, 512–527.
[193] Bigwood, 'Gand et la circulation des grains', 397–460, Stabel, *Dwarfs among giants*, 168–170, and Nicholas, *Medieval Flanders*, 218–219. Cf. also section V.4, pp. 229–230.
[194] Nicholas, 'Of poverty and primacy', 32–33.
[195] Cf. for Italy: Epstein, 'Cities, regions', 14–15.

urbanized the earliest and most profoundly, inland Flanders and southern Flanders, similar to the other urbanized part of western Europe, the centre-north of Italy.

Long-distance trade thus was not the key factor in the growth of Flemish cities. Trade in the Flemish cities did indeed start to grow in the 9th century, reflected in the fact that the first towns in the Scheldt Valley acquired the name *portus* at that time. The military and institutional protection of the territorial lord offered more security to trade and traders than the older centres in the delta area, especially since central royal power had weakened. But although the second half of the 9th century was a turning point, the initial importance of trade was not dominant. Functions of defence and comital administration, as well as the presence of consumers, were probably more important. In the earliest period international trade was on a very small scale, and only really started to grow in the 11th century.[196] At that time also industrial activities greatly expanded, and became increasingly concentrated in the Flemish cities.[197] Thus, these cities did not owe their existence entirely to the development of long-distance trade, but emerged gradually from a variety of foundations, including their administrative and defensive functions, and the presence of wealthy consumers, drawing surpluses from their manors, lands, and other rights in the countryside. In these respects many similarities existed between a Flemish city such as Bruges, renowned for its role in trade, and the other, older centres of the early and high Middle Ages. Only gradually in the course of the high Middle Ages did trade substantially begin to boost the positions of the Flemish cities, with their growing international trade allowing them to eclipse most other urban centres in western Europe. To this was added the rise of export industries and coercive power that such centres started to exercise over trade, as well as over the surrounding countryside.

Urban Communities and Territorial Lords

The composition of the urban elite often reflects the genesis of a particular city. In many cities which developed from a manor the elite consisted of ministeriales of the bishop, abbey, or secular lord, for example, in Sint-Truiden and Louvain; this was also the case in the episcopal towns of Utrecht and Liège. In the rising towns of Flanders, with their early territorial rule, part of the elite was linked to the count. The viscounts, who were often descended from an early nobility or even the highest rural elite, came to live in the towns from the late 10th century on as representatives of the count, and were mostly based at an urban castle, as in Kortrijk, Ghent, and the other major Flemish towns.[198] In all of

---

[196] Nicholas, 'Of poverty and primacy', esp. 23–24.
[197] Cf. sections IV.2, pp. 155–157, and VII.2, pp. 343–344. Cf. for the non-economic factor in the area of industries section VII.2, p. 346.
[198] Warlop, *De Vlaamse adel*, 113–156.

these centres, but particularly in the growing centres of commerce, the merchant element became increasingly dominant among the elite. In the 11th century this elite strove to gain its freedom from the manorial or feudal lord, often in cooperation with the territorial lords. Only from the 12th and 13th centuries did the interests of counts and urban elites start to diverge, when the cities and urban elites began to gain power bases of their own and to rival comital power.

This interplay or power contest among territorial lords, seigneurial lords, and the elite in the cities can best be seen from the development of urban freedom and the granting of urban charters. In many cities, both older and newer, in the 11th and early 12th centuries burgher associations began to emerge, with French Flanders, Liège, and Hainaut taking the lead, certainly compared with the less urbanized north. In some cases, as observed for the Caritet in Valenciennes, the burgher associations had their roots in a merchant guild aimed at offering mutual support and security.[199] The much broader *coniurationes* or communes, and their representatives, the *iurati*, also first appeared in the south, in Tournai, Saint-Omer, and Cambrai, at the same time as similar associations or confederacies emerged in the countryside. The main goal of such communes, which contained a strong merchant element, seems to have been to ensure internal peace and offer security to people living in the growing centres and conducting trade. Such goals also often entailed freedom from seigneurial arbitrariness and some self-government.[200] In their struggle to achieve these goals, the communes could adopt an aggressive, sometimes even revolutionary, aspect as most clearly in Cambrai in 1077, where the bishop was forced to flee, and later had to grant concessions to the commune, established in a privilege. In other cases more peaceful compromises were reached, mainly through charters establishing the mutual rights and duties of urban lord and commune. Sometimes confirmation of urban freedoms was bought from the lord, as in 1066 in Huy, the first town in the German Empire to receive a formal urban charter, in this case issued by the Bishop of Liège, with the first mention of the term burghers (*burgenses*) in the Empire.[201] The burghers, mainly merchants involved in long-distance trade, paid no less than half of their movable goods to the bishop, thus aiding him to strengthen the city as a stronghold against competing territorial lords. In Valenciennes, with the recognition of the commune in 1114, the burghers also made a payment, in this case to the Count of Hainaut. The emphasis that was included in the *Paix*, the resulting privilege, on peace for the market and security for visiting merchants clearly points to the merchant background of the movement in Valenciennes.

Territorial lords had a strong incentive to support or recognize such communes, since the cities were valuable allies against the feudal lords, who were their main

---

[199] Blockmans, 'Formale und informelle soziale Strukturen', 1–15, and Godding and Pycke, 'La paix de Valenciennes'.
[200] Dhondt, 'Les "solidarités" médiévales', 529–560, and Vermeersch, *Essai sur les origines*.
[201] Ammann, 'Huy an der Maas', 210–213, and Joris, *La ville de Huy*, 107–120.

adversaries in their quest for territorial power. The support offered by territorial lords is reflected in the first major wave of urban charters, which often confirmed earlier customs and rights. In the 12th century, in the county of Namur alone, eight cities (both large and small) received a charter. The rights confirmed or granted to the urban communities were similar in many respects to those desired and often acquired by the rural communities at the time. Most prominent among them were personal freedom, the abolition of manorial duties and banal levies, liberation from the arbitrary power of the lord, the conversion of arbitrary exactions into fixed levies, their own jurisdiction, and the ability to settle disputes between themselves according to their own law, without the lord's intervention or ordeals. Also, the urban communities desired more autonomy in administration, such as the right to appoint the members of the city council and to have them choose the burgomasters. Such elements, which can be seen in all urban charters, increased the legal security and independence of the inhabitants and stimulated economic traffic. In most cases the urban or territorial lord did not abandon all rights, but often retained some influence or revenues, such as market dues, some excises, other non-arbitrary taxes, the profits of courts, and the appointment of officers.

In the later 12th and 13th centuries the initiative for developing urban charters shifted from the urban communes to the territorial lords, and increasingly included northern Flanders, Brabant, and Holland. This could result in more standardization of urban charters by the territorial lord, as happened in Flanders around 1175, when the count granted charters to the seven largest cities in the county, all modelled on the example of Arras. The most extreme form of princely initiative was the foundation of 'new' towns, such as those established by the counts of Flanders in coastal Flanders in the second half of the 12th century in places such as Nieuwpoort and Gravelines. Both the physical infrastructure (city, walls, market, and harbour) and the urban institutions created there were linked to the political reorganization of the coastal plain under the authority of the count.[202] In Brabant in the 12th and 13th centuries, similar developments can be observed with the foundation of *villes neuves* by the duke. These towns, although often not wholly new but already emerging, were 'founded' by the territorial lord mainly to increase his influence in contested border areas. The process was associated with the simultaneous grants of franchises to villages. In this, political goals were predominant, and only as the territories were settled in the 13th century did economic goals start to become more important to the territorial lord, especially promoting trade and industries to profit from them through excises and taxes.

In the 12th and 13th centuries the alliance between the territorial lords and the cities, as observed most clearly in Flanders, started to break up. The cities acquired greater political power, and this became apparent in Flanders in the crisis

---

[202] Rutte, *Stedenpolitiek en stadsplanning*, 59–77.

of 1127–8, following the assassination of the count and the ensuing instability, as the towns and their burghers came to play an almost decisive role in the choice of a new count.[203] Cities also became a threat to princely authority because they started to operate collectively to form power blocs. Inter-urban associations, often crossing territorial boundaries, started to emerge in the 12th century, growing out of associations of merchants or merchant guilds trading in the same market. Such personal associations became leagues of cities, which were often dominated by the merchant elite, with the town governments combining urban with merchant interests. An example of such an association which developed to guarantee common interests in trade was the Hansa of the XVII towns, uniting cities in Flanders, Hainaut, Liège, Artois, and the Champagne, particularly those whose merchants traded in the Champagne fairs, principally exporting cloth.[204] Increasingly, the elites of these cities also started to cooperate in legal and corporate matters, for instance, in recognition of masterships and the collective exclusion of rebellious craftsmen. A similar association of merchants, with common interests for trading in England—especially for procuring wool—which grew into an association of Flemish cities, was the Hanse of London.[205] This, too, had its heyday in the 13th century, although it was not very successful and declined around 1300.

The most noticeable and enduring example of such a formal network among cities, primarily aimed at safeguarding trading interests, was the German Hansa. A private organization of merchants, this association emerged in the 11th and 12th centuries, and fits in with the general rise of merchant guilds in the period. These merchants collectively obtained legal security and privileges in various regions. Gradually, in the 13th and 14th centuries, the Hansa grew from an association of merchants into a semi-political network of Hansa cities, coinciding with the growing autonomy of the cities and the merchants' increasing political dominance in town governments. Gradually, a relationship developed between various cities in the north-east of the Low Countries and the German Hansa. Merchants from Deventer and Kampen, trading centres on the IJssel river, were among the first in the Low Countries to become associated with the Hansa, followed by a group of other cities. In 1285, for instance, the town governments and burghers of Kampen, Deventer, Zwolle, Zutphen, Harderwijk, Groningen, Leeuwarden, Muiden, and Stavoren were notified by Wismar, situated on the Baltic Sea, of trade conflicts with Norway, a notification which indicated their desire to cooperate as well as their common trading interests. The formal incorporation of these cities into the Hansa did not take place until at least the second half of the 14th century.[206] In total, some twenty cities in the Low

---

[203] Nicholas, *Medieval Flanders*, 62–66.   [204] Laurent, 'Nouvelles recherches', 81–94.
[205] Perroy, 'Le commerce anglo-flamande', 3–18.
[206] Alberts, *De Nederlandse Hanzesteden*, 18–41, Seifert, *Kompagnons und Konkurrenten*, 92–113, and Weststrate, 'Abgrenzung durch Aufnahme'. Cf. section V.4, pp. 224–234, for the institutional organization of trade.

Countries had been members or associates of the Hansa at some point, although membership was fluid and seldom well defined.

All of the Hansa towns were situated in the north-east of the Low Countries; only one was in Holland and none in Zeeland or Flanders. Geographical proximity to northern Germany and the Baltic, and thus to the Hansa towns, was important, of course. But it is striking that many of these towns were imperial cities or at least cities with a royal background in the early and high Middle Ages, such as Groningen, Deventer, Tiel, Zaltbommel, and Muiden. All had been centres of trade already for several centuries and most also had a weak territorial lord from whom they succeeded in obtaining a relatively autonomous position. These cities thus had several elements in common, and they flourished contemporaneously, in the 10th to 14th centuries. After this, stagnation or relative decline set in, especially compared with the rising towns in Holland.

Associations of cities like the Hansa may have been a problem for the territorial lord, since the bonds among such cities could conflict with their loyalty to the prince and could result in the cities refusing to fight one another. More dangerous, however, was an association of cities within a lord's own principality: it could aim to dominate provincial politics and become a counterweight to princely power. From the early 13th century on, which was the heyday of urban collectives, such urban confederations emerged throughout the Low Countries. One was in the prince-bishopric of Liège (1229–1231), which was the first region north of the Alps where cities within one principality united; the next associations were in Brabant (1261–2) and Holland (1299).[207] Particularly in times of crisis, when there were problems of succession, weakness of princely authority, or war, such cities took advantage of these situations to acquire power, which was a precursor of the power of the later third order in the Estates. Most successful were the large cities in Flanders, where cities of the high medieval type emerged earliest and urbanization was strongest. There the largest cities united in the *scabini Flandrie*, which in the end included only Ghent, Bruges, and Ypres. Their association gained substantial political power from the late 13th century. The cities deliberated with the count about economic, legal, and administrative matters, and at times even ruled the county autonomously, as in 1339, when the powerless count decided to leave the county. They came to dominate the provincial estates,[208] which to a somewhat lesser extent also happened in Liège, Brabant, and Holland, the other urbanized provinces.

In this way the cities, or urban elites, started to threaten comital power. Moreover, the rise of horizontal associations within the city, such as the communes and later the guilds,[209] was increasingly perceived as undesirable by the territorial lord. An expression of the shifting relationship and the emerging struggle between the cities and the territorial lords can be seen in the development

---

[207] Töpfer, 'Die Rolle von Städtebünden'.
[208] Prevenier, *De Leden en de Staten*, 27–41.
[209] Cf. section V.3, pp. 205–206.

of 'out-burghership'. This institution gave men from the countryside the right to be burghers of a town, with the related rights and privileges, thus removing them from control by their rural lord. This right could be obtained by inheritance or removal to the countryside as well as through purchase. The cities that emerged early, that is, more or less simultaneously with the development of territorial principalities, obtained from the territorial lord many such rights because of their common interest in breaking the authority of the rural nobility.[210] This was the case in Ghent and other Flemish cities, and to a lesser extent in the cities in Hainaut, but in the north only Dordrecht, one of the oldest towns, was able to take advantage of out-burghership. Data from the 14th century, after the heyday of this institution, show that even then there were still large numbers of out-burghers: Dordrecht had a few hundred, but the Flemish cities had many thousands each, and Kortrijk as many as 10,000. This greatly increased the dominance of such cities over the countryside. At that time, however, the growing power of the cities was increasingly recognized by the territorial lords as a threat rather than a blessing, and they also found that out-burghership was detrimental to their fiscal revenues and military obligations. So, from the 13th century they tried to counter this practice. Although this was difficult in existing cases, in those regions where cities were only starting to emerge, as in almost all of Holland, the territorial lords no longer used this instrument. The cities which in the formative period of out-burghership were under the rule of the centralizing French king, such as Lille, Arras, and Douai, also had very few out-burghers. In Flanders, on the other hand, the struggle of the territorial lord against that privilege was won only in the late 15th and 16th centuries.[211] Ghent lost the right to have out-burghers only after the defeat of the city by the Burgundian prince, Philip the Good, and more decisively in 1540, by Charles V.

In Holland the relationship between territorial lord, city, and countryside was very different from that in Flanders. The authority acquired by cities over the countryside was much less important and up to the 16th century, urban privileges and coercion played only a minor role.[212] With the exception of Dordrecht, once more, with its staple rights on the Rhine and Meuse and its market force formalized in 1299, the separation between town and countryside was less strict, the coercive power used by the cities over the countryside was less extensive, and the urban privileges were less clear-cut. This difference was reinforced by the fact that Holland towns hardly had any noblemen among their residents, reflecting the general weakness of the nobility there. Since the cities in Holland emerged later than those in the south and east, in a period when the territorial lord had already established his power, they also received fewer privileges and less

[210] Verbeemen, 'De buitenpoorterij', 81–99 and 191–217. And for common interest with the territorial lord: Thoen, 'Rechten en plichten', esp. 480–486.
[211] Stabel, *Dwarfs among giants*, 100–101, and Blockmans, 'Voracious states'.
[212] Hoppenbrouwers, 'Town and country', though he perhaps overestimates their effect for Holland.

political power than their Flemish counterparts. Only at a second stage in the later Middle Ages, as a result of their growth in size and economic importance, did the Holland cities gain more political influence, particularly through the provincial Estates, but that was more along economic lines and through their fiscal contribution. It was not until the 16th century that the Holland towns started to attempt to exercise non-economic power over the countryside and limit non-agricultural activities there in a systematic way.[213]

Another situation, with a weak territorial lord, existed in Groningen in the far north. This town had emerged as a manorial centre with royal properties, and hence a firm position with respect to the surrounding countryside. When royal authority declined, the Bishop of Utrecht as territorial lord was unable to fill the void. This allowed the town to enforce its position. Before 1040, in cooperation with the king, the merchants had probably already obtained their personal freedom, a formal market, and market peace.[214] Later, particularly in the 13th to 15th centuries, the Groningen region became completely dominated by the city, which exercised strong staple rights, had a compulsory market, and had jurisdictional power over very large parts of the surrounding countryside.[215] Groningen remained aware of its ancient royal heritage and proudly presented itself as a royal city; this image became even more pronounced when it started to become a semi-autonomous city-state in the 15th century. Of all the cities in the Low Countries, Groningen perhaps came closest to creating a city-state.

Cities such as Groningen and those in Flanders, however, were exceptions. Generally, territorial lords succeeded in containing communal tendencies, urban autonomy, and urban control over the countryside.[216] Urban privileges were partly revoked or suppressed after some time. A situation like that in northern Italy, especially in Tuscany, where the cities almost completely dominated the surrounding countryside by eliminating all rival powers, such as those of rural feudal lords, never came into being in the Low Countries. There the feudal lords in most regions probably held a firmer position than in northern Italy, and the village communities were also better able to withstand this process, but it was the rising territorial lords in particular who curbed possible aspirations of the cities.[217] Chronological differences in the rise of cities were probably a main factor: autonomy came closest to being achieved in Flanders, where the cities of the new high medieval type emerged earliest, and in Groningen, where territorial rule emerged later than elsewhere, if at all. In the 15th and 16th centuries, further state formation and centralization under the Burgundians and Habsburgs finally

---

[213] Aten, '*Als het gewelt comt . . .*', 37–63 and 275–297. Cf. also section V.4, p. 232.
[214] Noomen, 'Koningsgoed in Groningen', 141–144. Cf. also section III.1, pp. 57 and 74.
[215] Bos, *Het Groningsche gild- en stapelrecht*, esp. 74–75, 94–95, and 106–134, and Van den Broek, *Groningen*, 63–72 and 291.
[216] Cf. also section VI.1, pp. 263–266.
[217] Van Bavel, 'Markets for land, labour, capital and goods'.

broke many of the remaining urban privileges, sometimes after hard battles, as in the struggle between Emperor Charles V and Ghent.

Not all cities were adversely affected by the process of state building; some profited in their role as residences or even capitals. Until the 14th century, the territorial lords continuously travelled between their scattered residences with part of their court. As a result of increasing territorialization, the growth of agrarian surpluses, improved transport to collect the surpluses at a single point, and development of an administrative apparatus, the royal and aristocratic residences gradually became fewer in number and more fixed. The Duke of Guelders in the 14th century started to restrict his residences to two or three places, and around 1440 Arnhem clearly became his favourite. He built a court there, established a fixed chancellery, held meetings, received envoys, and organized tournaments.[218] Emerging capitals like these were used as a showcase of princely splendour and power, and provided a strong incentive to the urban economy. This was even more the case for the residences of the Burgundians and Habsburgs, which slowly acquired authority over almost all of the Low Countries. Cities such as Brussels, the favourite residence, and Mechelen, where central institutions such as the Great Council were established, profited greatly from the rise of central power. But the difference between this loosely knit unity and centralized kingdoms such as England and, to a lesser extent, France remained very significant. No capital like London or Paris emerged in the Low Countries to dominate the urban landscape.

Urban Elites, Guilds, and Urban Government

In towns which grew out of a manor or had a manorial background—the majority of those that emerged in the 11th and 12th centuries—ministeriales held strong positions, and many of them were active in trade. In general, merchants made up a large part of the urban elite. The social position they had earlier held in the manorial organization and the economic wealth they had acquired through trade were important formative elements for the elite. Possessing urban land was added to these. As cities received more freedom, the possession of land was often restructured, mainly because the urban or manorial lord gave it in free hereditary tenure, often for small sums. The elite benefited most from this because of the powerful position its members already held in the manorial period, which enabled them to acquire control over most of the urban land. This conferred status and also became a valuable asset as urban population and pressure on the land within the city walls were growing. Thus, it provided the elite with capital to be invested in trade. Possession of land also became a criterion for playing a role in urban government and holding certain functions, just as it had in the rural communities. In many cities the rise of this elite in hereditary possession of

[218] Nijsten, 'De ontwikkeling van residenties', 119–149.

the land can be observed, and the term for the elite often contains a reference to this. Examples are the *viri hereditarii* in Ghent, the *legitimi homines et in villa sua hereditarii* in Saint-Omer, or the owners of *ouderve* in Utrecht.[219] An exception was Bruges, where membership of the Hanse of London was the criterion for becoming an alderman.

The urban elite thus held a secure position from the beginning, often founded on its pre-urban position and sometimes confirmed in the urban charter. Its position became even stronger and more distinct in the 13th century as its members started to distinguish themselves socially and legally from other groups.[220] They increasingly monopolized political power, by making offices quasi-hereditary and by using, or misusing, their right of co-optation. From the early 13th century they appointed their own successors, largely without interference from the rest of the urban population or the territorial lord. This applies most particularly to the college of aldermen, which developed from the 11th century as the most important court in criminal and civil cases. This college of 6 to 14 members often also assumed administrative and legislative tasks, as well as organizing the taxation, and membership was sought after by the oligarchic families. In many cities oligarchies of only a few dozen families emerged which took over all power. On their hereditary land they also built large stone houses which often had towers and crenels, and resembled castles—showing their power and prestige.[221] They lived there surrounded by their relatives, friends, retinue, and servants. In other respects, too, these families sought a noble lifestyle, and they generally married only within patrician families and the nobility. Often, they formed supra-familial clans, and these sometimes became rivals within the town. The clans often went back to the organization of the manorial period, as demonstrated by Arnhem. There, two clans of some 40 heads of households each dominated politics in the late Middle Ages. Even in 1364 they still owned almost half the urban land, with their position and the division over two groups going back to their role as ministeriales of the two separate high medieval manors that came to form Arnhem.[222] Many cities, such as Groningen in 1227 and Ghent several times,[223] were scourged by feuds between patrician clans much like the strife among nobles in the countryside.

The elite's hold on the towns also extended to urban finances. Like the rural communities which rose at the same time, the cities obtained authority over the administration of properties and finances. The revenues of the towns were diverse

---

[219] Blockmans, *Het Gentsche stadspatriciaat*, 64–97.

[220] Prevenier, 'La bourgeoisie en Flandre', 407–428, and Van Uytven, 'Stadsgeschiedenis', 188–253, esp. 222–245.

[221] Laleman and Raveschot, *Inleiding tot de studie*, 167–175 and 213–219, and Blockmans, 'Formale und informelle Strukturen'.

[222] Verkerk, *Coulissen van de macht*, 16–19 and 280–309.

[223] Cf. the popular rendering by Blockmans, *Een middeleeuwse vendetta*. See also section VI.2, pp. 287–288.

and consisted of fines, entry levies for acquiring burghership, lease sums from urban land, mills, stalls, and fisheries, payments for using the urban cranes or scales, and direct taxes and excises, with this last category making up the bulk of revenues.[224] Some of these sources of revenue were donated, given in lease, or at least confirmed by the territorial lords, and some originated in the proto-history of these towns. In the 13th century the high expenses of walling and other infrastructure and public services greatly expanded the scale of urban finances, and the sale of rents became a principal instrument for broadening financial possibilities for investment. In the late 13th century, many cities witnessed a sharp growth in outstanding debts, mainly in rents: in Bruges, debts quadrupled from 1283 to 1299.[225] In turn, the payment of rents pressed towns to further increase regular revenues, which in the larger cities often equalled those of a territorial lord. These developments required better administration, as reflected in the creation of urban accounts.[226] However, control of financial administration, although crucial to the city as a whole, became increasingly restricted to an ever smaller circle of magistrates, with no external surveillance. This led to all kinds of abuses, fraud, and favouritism. Moreover, the same small group determined the organization of taxes. They clearly favoured indirect impositions on consumer goods such as bread, beer, and wine, which fell relatively heavily on ordinary people, rather than direct taxation of wealth or income. In the later Middle Ages indirect taxes made up three-quarters of urban revenues on average. The resulting regressive taxation increased economic polarization within the urban population. In addition, the patriciate was able to fix industrial wages through urban legislation, which was another instrument used for its own advantage.

The abuses, self-enrichment, monopolization of power, and favouritism among the elite increasingly provoked hostility and resistance among the rest of the urban population. This resulted in struggles, at times bloody, between this elite and the craftsmen, often supported by the *homines novi*, the new groups of merchants and entrepreneurs who had become wealthy in the 13th century but were not able to make their way into the now closed patriciate. From the middle of the 13th century tensions between the two groups occurred in the cities of the Meuse valley, such as Huy, Dinant, and Liège, as well as in Douai, Ghent, and later in several other Flemish cities.[227] The craftsmen demanded better working conditions and social improvement, but also reform of city governments and a loosening of the hold of the oligarchy of this small elite. In their demand for greater control of urban finances, they were sometimes supported by the territorial lord, who had the same desire for better control, too, as in late 13th-century Flanders.

---

[224] Marsilje, *Het financiële beleid van Leiden*, 111–121, and Van Uytven, *Stadsfinanciën Leuven*.
[225] Sosson, 'Finances communales'.   [226] Section V.2, p. 186.
[227] Blockmans, 'Regionale Vielfalt im Zunftwesen', 51–63. Cf. more extensive section VI.1, pp. 252–253 and 271–272.

In this struggle the craftsmen in the Meuse valley and Flanders increasingly organized themselves into guilds. In the 12th century proto-guilds started to emerge in cities as religious and charitable fraternities organized according to occupation. By *c.*1150 Arras had such fraternities of tailors, minters, and shearers.[228] In the next century these organizations developed as genuine professional guilds, exercising social and economic pressure, around the middle of the century in Huy and Dinant, and later also in the Flemish cities. In the north, guilds emerged in only a few cities, including Dordrecht and Utrecht, which were among the oldest cities there. The guilds were sometimes successful in their struggle for reform, helped by their numbers and the economic weight of the craftsmen and the new rich, particularly in cases where the ruling elite was divided. In Utrecht in 1274, the guilds even acquired control of urban government, and held it for two years until defeated in a bloody battle won by the episcopal troops. This was typical behaviour for the patriciate and the princes at the time. In Brabant, attempts by the guilds were bloodily repressed by the territorial lord, and in northern France by the king. In Flanders, however, the guilds were successful in achieving their political aims, particularly after 1302, as a Flemish army with a substantial guild element defeated the French king, who was in his turn supported by the patriciate. The Flemish victory in the 'Guldensporenslag' greatly strengthened the position of the guilds. Its effect also spread to other parts of the Low Countries, such as Utrecht, where the guilds became victorious in 1304.

One of the guilds' greatest successes in this period was gaining the recognition of the urban authorities and obtaining an autonomous position. Their right to choose their own heads was definitively established, as well as the right to assemble, to own property, and to decide cooperatively on the internal rules of the guild. With respect to urban government and administration, a compromise was often made, with some participation of the guilds, or only the masters, in urban government. Utrecht was an extreme case, where in 1304 the guilds obtained almost full control over the election of urban magistrates, and this happened also in the other episcopal town, Liège.[229] There, in 1312, guild members attacked the patricians and their troops, defeated them, set fire to the church where they took refuge, and killed 10 of the 14 patrician aldermen. In 1384 guild members succeeded in establishing their political power in Liège even more definitively. Mostly, however, the magistrates' functions were distributed over different segments of the urban population, with the territorial lord or his representative appointing some magistrates and the guilds or masters others. In Flanders, after the revolutionary wave of the decades around 1300, the aldermen were no longer co-opted but chosen by electors through systems of indirect

---

[228] Bijsterveld and Trio, 'Van gebedsverbroedering naar broederschap'.
[229] Van Uytven, 'Stadsgeschiedenis', 233–239, and Vercauteren, *Luttes sociales à Liège*, 33–39, 75–77, and 97–105.

vote.[230] Other towns had large meetings of burghers who were consulted on special issues, such as the imposition of a new tax or military service, with all, or many, heads of households participating in the decision-making. In Tournai, for instance, sometimes all heads of households met, but the meeting was usually limited to the 300 most prominent, which was still a fairly extensive representation.

These changes in urban government, however, should not be seen as a complete break. Taxes remained regressive, participation by the guilds in town government was mostly limited to the masters, and in most cities the patriciate regained most of its former dominance after a while.[231] To some extent this was even true for Liège, the most 'democratic' of all towns in the late medieval Low Countries, where participation in politics again became limited at the beginning of the 15th century, when the position of the patriciate and guild masters was strengthened by the intervention of the Duke of Burgundy, while at the same time the middle-class burghers and craftsmen tried to exclude the workers from political participation. It was in Flanders that guilds wielded their greatest influence, and their firm position remained intact for the next two centuries, buttressed by the military power of the guilds. These often formed the core of the communal army, as in Liège and many Flemish towns, and possessed their own arms and war banners. The military role of the guilds was reinforced by the fact that in many towns, as in Ypres in 1276 and in Bruges in 1292, the urban militias were no longer organized on a territorial basis according to city quarter, but rather according to guild.[232] Exceptions in the south, where the territorial organization remained, were Saint-Omer and Douai, perhaps not coincidentally the towns where guild autonomy had been repressed. Elsewhere, because of their political and military power, the guilds were able to keep the elite in check, as well as stimulate and enforce the non-economic power that cities exercised over the countryside. This was used mainly to combat rural competition in industries, sometimes literally, by marching into the countryside and destroying industrial tools, as happened in Flanders.

Guilds in Holland were far weaker than their southern counterparts because they generally lacked political power. Most were not formed in the 13th and 14th centuries, but only as part of a secondary wave in the 16th and 17th centuries. The later rise of cities and industries in Holland than in the Meuse valley and Flanders played a role in their having less power, but the deliberate policy pursued by the territorial lord also helped determine the difference. Leiden, the Holland textile centre *par excellence*, is the clearest example of this: the Count of Holland prohibited the foundation of guilds there in 1313 and helped to suppress the second attempt by craftsmen to obtain more political power in

---

[230] Dumolyn, 'Dominante klassen', 89–90.
[231] Van Uytven, 'Plutokratie', 373–409. Cf. section VI.1, p. 272–275.
[232] Wyffels, *De oorsprong der ambachten*, 105–116.

1393.[233] His support for the urban patriciates in their policy to repress guild development was decisive. Around 1400, aside from the old town of Dordrecht, so often the exception in Holland, only two guilds are known to have operated in the seven largest cities in Holland.[234] Most were founded in the first half of the 16th century or even later. By then, merchants and entrepreneurs, in cooperation with the territorial lord, had acquired such a firm hold on urban government that guilds were not able to compete with them politically let alone acquire political power. The Leiden guilds which were founded late remained under the strict supervision of the municipal authorities, and their function was mainly restricted to developing a training programme and some work rules, as well as social and religious activities.[235] Neither did they have the power to push through acquisition of coercive power over the countryside: the interests of merchants and entrepreneurs which profited from rural industrial activities remained dominant in Holland.

In the current literature the separateness of the medieval city from the countryside is often qualified, with the emphasis now more on a fluid crossover of economic functions between town and countryside and the need to analyse them in their interaction and symbiosis. Moreover, there were many parallels in the social and organizational developments of town and village, particularly in the 11th and 12th centuries, such as the desire for self-organization, freedom, and reduction of the arbitrary powers of the lord. But this does not change the fact that in the high Middle Ages deliberate steps were taken to create institutional differences between town and countryside, particularly by the urban elites, the craft guilds, and the territorial lords. As a result, the cities and their burghers were then more separate from the countryside institutionally and legally than ever before or afterwards. Regional differences were, however, very clear. The cities of inland Flanders and Groningen were very specific cases. They were strong, had important privileges, and held power over the surrounding countryside. In Flanders this occurred in cooperation with the rising territorial lord.

In the following chapters we will investigate how the economy of town and countryside in Flanders was becoming increasingly integrated because of the cities' power, and what the effects of this integration in a territorial framework were. It can be surmised that in the high Middle Ages this was economically the most successful mix, as indicated by the growth and prosperity of the Flemish towns.[236] Compared to the earlier, alternative combinations, this one

---

[233] Marsilje, 'Het economische leven', ii:95–103, and Blockmans, 'Regionale Vielfalt im Zunftwesen'. Cf. the similar, successful policy of the French king in the north of France.

[234] Lourens and Lucassen, 'De oprichting en ontwikkeling'.

[235] Cf. sections V.3, pp. 205–207, and V.4, p. 232, for the effects of this on the organization of the labour market and the market for goods and products, and section VII.2, pp. 346–349, for the effect on industrial development in town and countryside.

[236] For indicators of economic success cf. sections, VI.2, pp. 280–282 (urbanization) and VIII.1, pp. 372–380.

seems to have had a favourable influence on economic development, despite the importance of non-economic force exercised by the cities and the territorial lords aimed at trade and industry—or perhaps even because of it. The next chapter will, among others, investigate how the economy in Flanders as a whole developed greatly in both town and countryside, even where growth was subordinate to the interests of the urban merchant elite or the guilds. The urban economies in particular expanded greatly. Such cities flourished in the 11th to 14th centuries, but in almost all cases their foundations were laid in the 9th to 11th, when a concentration of consumers and capital first developed there, probably fostered by the protection they offered, but when there was also security and a favourable framework for industry and trade, both physical and institutional. In addition, extensive markets started to develop there, partly extended by easy access to raw materials and foodstuffs, partly through the presence of consumers and traders, and partly through force and privileges. This process will be further analysed in the following chapters.

IV

The Economy: Agriculture and Industries in the Early and High Middle Ages

IV.1. AGRICULTURE IN THE EARLY AND HIGH MIDDLE AGES

Information on early medieval agriculture is scanty. Traditionally, written sources have mainly been used, but such materials are very scarce and mostly deal with large estates, thus offering an unbalanced picture. In the Low Countries in recent years, however, a great deal of progress has been made by using alternative sources, such as archaeological finds, animal bones, and plant remains which have been excavated from cesspits and wells. Such finds provide insight into consumption patterns, and indirectly into agricultural production. Pollen analysis has also proven useful, and historical geography and toponymics are increasingly used to provide more information on land use.

In the early Middle Ages, food was not produced in large quantities, but the low population pressure probably made what was produced sufficient. The sources of food were very diverse: foraging, fishing, and fowling in the extensive wastelands were very important, as well as gathering fruits, nuts, vegetables, and roots in the wild. Radishes, onions, leeks, carrots, cabbage, spinach, and all kinds of herbs were not only gathered but also cultivated, as were various kinds of fruit such as raspberries and strawberries. Grapes, introduced in the Roman era, were cultivated as far north as Brabant and the Meuse valley. Ducks, chickens, and geese were widely caught in the wild or kept in the backyard, and some partridge, pheasant, and other wild birds such as wigeon and wood pigeon were consumed.[1]

Hunting game was not as important a source of food, as evidenced by the low percentages of wild animal bones found in settlements. Exceptions to this were some high-status settlements, such as Gennep on the Meuse, probably an elite Frankish settlement, where large wild animals, particularly red deer, accounted

---

[1] IJzereef and Laarman, 'The animal remains from Deventer', esp. 429–434, Ervynck and Van Neer, 'Dierenresten uit een waterput', and Wouters et al., 'Archeologisch en ecologisch onderzoek', 97–109.

for one-fifth of the animal bone remains.[2] Brown bears, badgers, and aurochs were also hunted in the forests around Gennep. In the dunes and coastal areas roe deer, wild boar, beavers, otters, and hares were hunted, and on the beaches seals.[3] The status associated with hunting game was reflected in the role of game in gift exchange as well as in the social restrictions on hunting. In the early Middle Ages, hunting was open to all free men, but increasingly restrictions were imposed, not only because game became less plentiful as a result of reclamation of wastelands and forests, but also because the right to hunt became an aristocratic privilege.[4] In the early Middle Ages, the kings started to exercise exclusive hunting rights in their royal forests, such as the Rijkswoud or the Ardennes. Later, territorial lords used hunting as a regalian right and noblemen increasingly considered it to be a status symbol or even a privilege, although those lower down the social scale often resorted to poaching.

Pastoral farming also had a fairly high status, and cattle, in particular live cattle, were often the object of gift exchange. Horses, and also horned cattle, were an important status symbol among German tribes.[5] Some idea of the composition of livestock herds can be obtained from the analysis of animal bones. Sex ratios and ages at which animals were slaughtered, for instance, tell us whether they were reared primarily for meat, pulling heavy loads, or dairying and shearing. Pigs were very important in the early Middle Ages, and were perhaps the most numerous farm animals, particularly where oak or beech woods were available to provide acorns and beech mast as pig fodder. On an imperial villa near Lille, according to the *Brevia Exempla*, no fewer than 1,025 pigs were kept and 645 salted carcasses were stored, indicating a high turnover and showing that pigs, kept only for meat, were bred quickly and slaughtered young. In early medieval Dorestad, two-thirds of the pigs were killed before they were 24 months old. Cows, oxen, and sheep, however, in the early Middle Ages were generally kept longer,[6] indicating their use for milk, dairy, pulling loads, and wool rather than for meat. Even in an exceptional centre of trade and industry like Dorestad, where it would be expected that prosperity would make meat consumption (especially veal and lamb) more important, most cattle were slaughtered only after 42–8 months.

Up to the 8th century, pastoral farming was very important and sometimes even dominant, not only in the coastal areas but also in the inland parts of the Low Countries. On the basis of the animal remains, relative bone weights, and calculated ages at slaughter, it is estimated that for the six people living on a hypothetical farm in 7th and 8th century Dorestad, 30–50 per cent of their

---

[2] Heidinga and Offenberg, *Op zoek naar de vijfde eeuw*, 88–93.
[3] Clason, *Animal and man*, 30–31, 51, 55, 57, and 61–75.   [4] Spiess, 'Herrschaftliche Jagd'.
[5] Roymans, 'The South Netherlands project', 231–244.
[6] Besteman, 'North Holland', 106, and Prummel, *Early medieval Dorestad*, 152–159 (cattle) and 202–213 (pigs).

energy requirements and 75–100 per cent of protein were provided by animal products. Almost half consisted of cow and sheep milk, cheese, and butter, a quarter of beef and almost a quarter of pig; a small percentage was provided by poultry, eggs, and game.[7] The remainder was supplied by vegetal foodstuffs: mainly grain and some pulses. Even in this relatively densely populated river clay area, animal foodstuffs were amply available, leading to a clear surplus of protein.

Among the cereals most prominent in the 6th to 8th centuries were emmer wheat and barley, while in sandy regions such as Drenthe rye increased even further in importance, after its introduction and rapid rise in the Roman era.[8] Beans, flax, and rape seed were also widely cultivated. Arable agriculture was often practised on separate parcels (*kampen*), which were irregularly shaped and surrounded by hedges or wooded banks, situated close to individual farms. The sandy regions, such as Drenthe and the Campine, often had small arable complexes of some 3 to 8 hectares, consisting of separately enclosed block-shaped parcels. Dispersed settlement consisting of hamlets and isolated farmsteads was dominant. Agriculture was very diverse, with all kinds of farming and keeping cattle, combined with hunting, gathering, and foraging in the extensive wastelands. A wide spectrum of food was consumed.

Organization of Early Medieval Agriculture: Manor, Family Holding, and Village

Agriculture and its social framework underwent significant change in the Frankish period. In those regions where manors became dominant, as in the Haspengouw or the Guelders river area, they exerted a profound influence on the organization of agricultural activities, since serfs had to perform ploughing and harvesting duties on the demesne land, transport grain, wood, and dung, and produce products to deliver to the lord of the manor. For agriculture, the main effect of the rise of manorialism was the increased importance of grain production. The manorial system not only emerged mainly on the finest agricultural lands where grain cultivation was already important, but also manorial lords had an interest in greater population densities made possible through concentration on grain production; moreover, grain output was easier to supervise and control.[9] The labour force on the manors may have been less highly motivated, particularly when working the demesne land, since it was coerced and the serfs were not really able to benefit from greater production. This applied less to the work done on the serfs' own holdings, particularly if the levies were fixed. The manorial system can also be assumed to have counterbalanced negative effects on production by

---

[7] Kooistra, *Borderland farming*, 79–83, and Prummel, *Early medieval Dorestad*, 248–256.
[8] Spek, *Het Drentse esdorpenlandschap*, 586–589. For rye, see below, pp. 130–131.
[9] Section III.2, pp. 81–82.

exercising a certain pressure on the agrarian population to generate surpluses. In addition, the manor offered a framework for sharing risks and pooling capital, making greater investments possible and enabling the purchase of expensive capital goods such as oxen, horses, and ploughs. The heavy plough, increasingly used from the 9th century on, is a case in point, since it was not only costly, but also needed a large team of oxen or horses to draw it, and thus could only be afforded by a larger unit than the average family farm.

An exceptional insight into the large scale of the manors is offered by an inventory dating from 810 of four royal fiscs in the region of Lille, comprising four large and two small manors in total. These covered some 8,000 hectares, including forest and wastelands. The lord's demesne on these manors alone produced about 1,800 hectolitres (hl) of spelt, 2,500 hl of barley, and a few hundred hl of wheat, rye, and oats.[10] The large numbers of pigs kept for meat production (more than 1,000) and the 1,500 sheep, mainly kept for wool, indicate that the demesne also included large forests and heaths for fattening the pigs and for grazing. There were many stables, sheds, granaries, and some fortifications, providing security for the inhabitants. Of course, this was a very specific type of unit, and these findings cannot be generalized or projected for all manors, and emphatically not for the non-manorial sector. A similar caveat applies to the effect of Carolingian regulations for the administration and agricultural exploitation of manors.[11] In the *Capitulare de villis*, dating from the last quarter of the 8th century, for instance, it was ordained that ample supplies of grain and of seed for sowing should be kept, in order to feed the army and alleviate possible famine, a measure perhaps dictated by the severe famines of 792 and 805. These provisions probably did stimulate grain cultivation, although the cohesiveness and the practical effects of these instructions should not be overestimated.

In this period, and associated with the emergence of manorialism, the family-sized farm, the *mansus* or *hoeve*, comes to the fore in various parts of western Europe.[12] The mansus appears in sources from the second half of the 7th century, and was used as a unit of assessment for payments and services to be delivered both by the tenant to the lord and by the lord to the king. These farms were of approximately the same size, consisting of a farm building, farm land, and usage rights to the pasture lands and wastelands. They were adequate for the labour and consumption needs of a single family, as indicated by the contemporary definition *terra unius familiae*. The size of the farm land was often some 5–10 hectares, but this depended on soil fertility and on the social and legal status of the tenant. In many regions, the mansus had already emerged, but now it became

---

[10] P. Grierson, 'The gold solidus', 437–461, and Slicher van Bath, *Agrarische geschiedenis*, 75–77 (the latter with an incorrect calculation of the quantities of grain).
[11] Verhulst, 'Karolingische Agrarpolitik', 175–189, and Dygo, 'Capitulare de villis'.
[12] Herlihy, 'The Carolingian mansus', 79–89.

formalized as a standard holding. To some extent, this formalization was linked to the rise of the manorial system, since labour services and other obligations were attached to each family farm. The manorial system thus enforced a standard family holding as an agricultural unit and often prohibited fragmentation. The rise of the mansus had several consequences. It was an expression of stronger, permanent rights of the peasant family to the land, as shown by the name, which was derived from *manere*, meaning 'to remain'. Formalized in a manorial setting, the system forged a strong link between dependent peasants and the land. Also, there were clear demographic effects, since this system strengthened the development that led to the nuclear family.[13] The area of the farm was well suited to a conjugal family, and the manorial obligations associated with it could and were intended to be borne by that family, as well as the non-manorial levies such as taxes and military services. Indeed, from the 9th-century documentation from the Abbey of Prüm, it can be observed that the mansi on its manors in the Ardennes and elsewhere were primarily held by nuclear families consisting of the parents and their children, typically one or two parents with three or four children. Only in a quarter of the cases were workers, relatives, or other residents added to the nuclear family. It is striking that in the pastoral region of sea clay Frisia, where the manorial mansus system did not exist in its strict form, patrilineal links and the influence of kin remained much more important.

In most regions the single-family farm retained its importance after the early Middle Ages, and after the dissolution of the manorial system, and was also used as a standard in large reclamation projects from the 11th century. In the reclamation areas in Holland, for instance, a farm of 13 hectares, called a *hoeve*, was used as a standard.[14] There, too, the rights of peasant families to the land were strong, or even stronger, especially since the land was held in free ownership, without manorial rights and duties. The standardization of holdings was taken to an extreme, since each family held exactly the same area of land. Only in the course of many centuries did this equal distribution of land disappear as a result of sales in the market and inheritance transfers which often led to a fragmentation of holdings owing to population growth.

Another organizational change in the Frankish period was the tendency towards more concentrated habitation. In various parts of the Low Countries, the dispersed hamlets and farmsteads of the earlier period were gradually replaced by larger groupings of farmsteads. In some cases, this was linked to the formation of a manor, resulting in nuclearization; it was also driven by the desire of manorial lords to better control the people on their lands. In some non-manorial regions, such as Drenthe, however, the same situation can be observed. The main arable land of these nuclear villages was grouped in

---

[13] Mitterauer, *Warum Europa?*, 70–76 and 87, and Kuchenbuch, *Bäuerliche Gesellschaft*, 76–94. For the different situation in Friesland cf. also sections V.4, p. 220, and VI.2, pp. 287–288.

[14] Section II.2, p. 40.

a single large complex situated on the best-quality lands, called *es* (in other regions *eng*, *dorpsakker*, or *kouter*), and similar to the German *Gewann* or the English open field, with the settlement consisting of a more or less closed group of 5–20 farmsteads situated at the edge of this complex. The oldest of such open fields date from the 7th and 8th centuries, but most are later. Their parcels were mostly very small, and shaped as blocks, or later increasingly as strips.[15] They were not fenced off separately, but divided only by a small ditch, a double furrow, or a grass border. The arable complex as a whole was surrounded by a common ditch or fence protecting the crops from straying cattle. The functioning and further development of these open fields will be analysed below, but it is clear that the nuclearization of settlement, like the formation of manors, enabled a better pooling of resources among the villagers.

The way in which agriculture in the 8th to 11th centuries was topographically organized can be reconstructed fairly well, particularly through toponyms.[16] In the Guelders river area and the adjacent Utrecht river clay lands, which were densely populated from the Carolingian period, agriculture on arable land was practised mainly on the *engen*, which was fertile well-drained land, located on high stream ridges close to the villages and often already occupied in the Merovingian era. The *akkers*, mostly situated on lower lying land, came into use later than the *engen* as arable land, mostly in the Carolingian era. Lower still, on wetter and heavier soils, were the communal hay and pasture lands, called *weide* (meadow) and *made* (hayland). The lowest and wettest parts of the village lands, deep in the back swamps, were wastelands. These wastelands were by no means without value to the village economy, since they were used for obtaining firewood and reeds, for hunting, fishing, and fowling, and for extensive pasturage. A similar geographical arrangement can be found in most villages located on the sandy soils, such as Drenthe. The arable land was concentrated near the village, on the later *essen*, and used mainly for rye with some barley and oats, with the land situated around it, called *dries*, being sown only occasionally. The green lands along the river or stream were used for pasturing, and the heaths and wastelands surrounding the whole were used for grazing sheep, fattening pigs on acorns, hunting hares and partridges, cutting sods, collecting wood, and gathering wax and honey supplied by swarms of bees.[17]

Cereal Culture and Pastoral Farming in the Carolingian Period

The most striking agrarian development in the Frankish period was the growth of arable agriculture, with cereals largely replacing meat and forage in the diet.

---

[15] Spek, *Het Drentse esdorpenlandschap*, 672–687.
[16] For instance: Buitelaar, *De Stichtse ministerialiteit*, 123–125.
[17] Spek, *Het Drentse esdorpenlandschap*, 28, 575–578, and 580–585, although this mostly relates to the later Middle Ages.

Livestock production became less important, except in some coastal regions, and was increasingly subordinated to grain production within a system of mixed farming. This process of 'cerealization' was partly linked to the rise of the manorial system, with its preference for concentrated habitation and intensive land use. These phenomena were also linked to the formation of villages and to population growth in the same period, with the cultivation of cereal grains being both a response to the increasing population pressure and the cause of further growth. In turn, this process increased the need for mills, which was associated with the increased number of water mills observed in this period (see below), often within a manorial setting.

At the same time, the composition of the grains cultivated changed. Palynological and palaeo-botanical research shows that the ancient hulled grains like emmer and hulled barley became less important. Spelt, also a hulled grain, remained important for a while longer. In the south-eastern parts of the Low Countries, no less than 50–80 per cent of grain production in the 9th century consisted of spelt.[18] Further north, the cultivation of spelt receded. The main advantages of spelt were that it could be kept for several years and its cultivation entailed less risk because it was robust and winter-hardy, important elements when food supplies are precarious. Because of its keeping qualities, the production of spelt may have been encouraged by Roman authorities, as food for the army, and later by the Frankish authorities on the royal fiscs. On the other hand, spelt yields were low and its processing, particularly husking, was difficult and time-consuming. Its long dominance in the Ardennes can be understood because of the severe winters and the abundance of land; its decline elsewhere may have been a result of the growing pressure to save land, and perhaps time, but may also have been a result of the extension of grain cultivation and improvement in transport, making long storage less vital. Moreover, other grains yielded higher profits as markets started to emerge. Wheat had higher yields, was better quality, and did not have to be husked before milling, so it did not require extra labour and expense, but it was a riskier crop, both in cultivation and storage. It is striking that in areas with less favourable conditions, where development was more restricted, such as the Ardennes, spelt remained an important crop until the early modern period and even later.

Wheat, highly valued as a crop, was increasingly cultivated in the early Middle Ages, particularly on the fertile soils. But the most spectacular rise then was that of rye, which became the dominant bread grain in several regions with sandy soils, especially in the north of the Low Countries. Finds of pure rye from the Roman period in Noordbarge, Peelo, Dalen, and Zeijen (all in Drenthe) and Ede (Veluwe) show that these regions, as well as some sandy areas in northern

---

[18] Devroey, 'La céréaliculture', and De Waha, *Recherches sur la vie rurale*, 55.

Germany, pioneered the intentional cultivation of rye in western Europe.[19] In the early Middle Ages the dominance of rye in these regions grew even further; in Odoorn in Drenthe some 90 per cent of the grain finds are rye. Perhaps this is a coincidence, but these are all regions with hardly any royal influence, hardly any manorialism, and dominated by a relatively free peasantry. Also, there is the geographical element. Since rye tolerates cold, dry weather better than other grains, and does not require high soil fertility (it grows well on poorer sandy soils), it was well suited to more marginal areas in the Low Countries, such as the sandy regions of Drenthe or the Campine.

Rye, therefore, not only pushed out other grains, but enabled grain cultivation in regions where this had been difficult before. This contributed to the fact that sandy, sandy-loamy, and limestone soils in the early Middle Ages came to be used more intensively than the more fertile peat and clay soils. The heavier soils were more difficult to cultivate and only later came into more intensive use, after the spread of the heavy plough in the 9th century. In the earlier period it was the loess soils that were particularly sought after for agricultural use. Not only are they fertile, but they are also fairly light and can easily be tilled, even with the primitive wooden ploughs in use in the early period, such as the scratch plough or *ard*.

Yields from cereal cultivation were probably low in this period, although a lack of data leaves much scope for debate. While some scholars suggest a yield ratio of 1:1.6–2.2 for the Carolingian period, others are more optimistic, seeing indications for a ratio of 1:3.[20] We have no clear data about regional and chronological patterns. Even if yields were low, the increasing dominance of arable farming made land more productive, since it produced more calories per hectare, grain being the most land-efficient supplier of calories, at least before the early modern introduction of the potato. At the same time, the more intensive grain cultivation also required much more labour, perhaps resulting in a decline of labour productivity. In general, agricultural growth in this period was the result of reclamation, the extension of arable land, and the introduction of more intensive rotation systems, rather than of increased efficiency. Extensive growth (in area) and intensification (in land use) were thus more important than a rise in labour productivity. However, the number of people fed per km^2 rose sharply. Larger surpluses could also now be gathered, particularly owing to organizational changes such as the rise of the manor and the nucleated village. At the same time, in most parts of the Low Countries, a switch took place from hulled grains

---

[19] Spek, *Het Drentse esdorpenlandschap*, 509–510, and more generally Watson, 'Toward denser and more continuous settlement', esp. 68–69, Mitterauer, *Warum Europa?*, 18–24 and Behre, 'The history of rye cultivation'.

[20] Duby, *Guerriers et paysans*, 37–40, is a pessimist, while Slicher van Bath, *De agrarische geschiedenis*, 76, is more of an optimist.

to naked grains, such as wheat and rye. Instead of being crushed or pounded in a mortar, and consumed as porridge, gruel, or beer, which happened with the bulk of the hulled grains, the naked grains were more suitable for milling and baking into bread. This far-reaching shift required the massive introduction of mills and ovens, which occurred in exactly this period, often within a manorial setting.

Cereal cultivation thus became more important, but there were some regions where cattle raising remained dominant, or became even more important, as on the Frisian coast, in Zeeland, and in coastal Flanders. The dominance of the pastoral sector in 9th- and 10th-century Frisia is evidenced by the dues paid by holders of the properties of the abbeys of Fulda and Werden: cattle, sheep, cheese, butter, and many hundreds of pieces of cloth.[21] Also, surfaces of land areas here are not generally expressed in *mansi*, but in areas used for grazing a number of heads of cattle or producing a number of cartloads of hay. This dominance of pastoral farming was rare in early medieval Europe, but in the Low Countries it can be observed in several regions. Geography played a crucial part, since the open salt marsh areas, where the lowest saltings were covered with sea poa, and the higher parts with thrift, sea milkwort, and saltmarsh rush, were ideal for cattle grazing. In Zeeland and along the Flemish coast sheep farming was particularly important, and was concentrated in specialized large sheep farms (*bercaria*) on the saltings.[22] Perhaps the oval, nuclear embankments found in coastal Flanders date from the period before systematic embankments were developed to create protected hay lands for such large-scale pasturing of sheep. Some of these embankments were constructed by free farmers with individual farms formed around a collective terp settlement, but most of them were located on large land ownership. At the beginning of the 9th century, the count of Flanders and abbeys such as the St Bavo Abbey of Ghent and its vassals, and in Friesland the abbeys of Fulda and Werden, owned extensive saltings, *marisci*, for thousands of sheep. Perhaps these large institutions could better bear the risks inherent in the specialization in large-scale sheep raising.

Market demand must have played a role in this. The numbers of sheep and cattle raised there were so large that this sector must have been aimed at the market. Conversely, grain probably had to be imported. Grain cultivation on the salt marshes was restricted to some higher creek levees, and mainly limited to barley, since rye, emmer, spelt, and wheat were not suited to saline conditions.[23] In view of the high density of population on the Frisian coast, at least some bread grains had to be imported, an import as evidenced from the finds of rye pollen and non-native field weeds in Wijnaldum, Leeuwarden, and elsewhere

---

[21] Lebecq, *Marchands*, ii: 382–383 (Fulda), ii: 384–386 (Werden), and ii: 387 (Werden); and Postma, *De Friesche kleihoeve*, 100–114.

[22] Tys, 'Domeinvorming', esp. 51–55, and Verhulst, 'Das Besitzverzeichnis', esp. 225–226. For the natural vegetation: section II.1, pp. 18–20.

[23] Behre & Jacomet, 'The ecological interpretation', 81–108, esp. 88–91.

from Merovingian times. This system could only work through exchange, showing some economic sophistication and specialization, as also evident in the rise of specialized production and marketing of cloth, the famous *pallium Fresonicum*.[24] In the 11th to 13th centuries, however, wool production declined in Flanders, Zeeland, and Frisia, as the saltings were increasingly embanked, became desalinated, and were used for more intensive sectors, such as raising cattle or even arable farming.

Agrarian Technology in the High Middle Ages

In the 9th to 12th centuries agricultural development gained further momentum, in parallel with the introduction and application of new techniques. The chronology of technological change is difficult to determine exactly because of the problems in distinguishing the availability of techniques from their dispersion and use. Often, techniques were already known and show up occasionally in early medieval sources, but were only used widely when political and economic conditions became more favourable, and when manors and emerging village communities enabled coordination and pooling. This wider diffusion applies, for instance, to the three-field rotation system, first mentioned in late 8th-century sources in southern Germany. This system became important in the Low Countries in the first half of the 9th century, as evidenced by mentions in the administration of the Abbey of Lobbes, for instance. Its spread can also be seen from pollen analysis in Drenthe, where hardly any winter grains were found before the Carolingian period, but from the 10th century a balance emerges among barley, oats, and rye, pointing to a three-field rotation system.[25] Because of the lack of sources it is impossible to arrive at a more precise chronology, but it is striking that the system seems to have emerged both in manorial and free peasant contexts.

When compared to the earlier alternation of cereal cultivation with grass or more or less permanent types of summer grain cultivation, this system increased the proportion of winter grain, mainly oats. Thus it provided more fodder to make up for the decreasing availability of pasture in the process of converting to cereal cultivation, and it fitted with the increasing use of horses as draught animals, because they consumed large quantities of oats. It also increased the land under cultivation by about one-sixth. Labour input probably also increased somewhat, since more labour was needed for sowing, planting, and harvesting, although three-field rotation saved ploughing time since fallow land was ploughed more frequently than land that was cultivated.[26] It had two further advantages. It

[24] Cf. sections IV.2, pp. 153–154 and V.4, pp. 214–216.
[25] Spek, *Het Drentse esdorpenlandschap*, 510–513 and 587–590, and in general Hildebrandt, 'Historische Feldsysteme'.
[26] Watson, 'Toward denser and more continuous settlement', esp. 72–73.

spread the risks by increasing the variety of cereals sown and by using different growing seasons, and the peaks of agricultural tasks were spread more evenly over the year, allowing more rational use of labour.

There was also wider diffusion of new techniques in ploughing, especially in the regions with heavy, clayey soils.[27] An important element in this was the increasing use of the heavy plough with a mould board from the 9th to 10th centuries. This plough was better able to turn the soil, thus reducing the need for cross ploughing, compared with the scratch plough, which used more labour. In addition, the harness, shaft, and girth were further developed, allowing a better transfer of the power generated by the horse. This series of changes was completed in the 11th century and went along with the gradual replacement of oxen as draught animals by horses. In Flanders, the use of horses seems to have been widespread as early as the 12th century. These horses were slender and fairly small (at a shoulder height of 1.28 to 1.38 m), but had greater stamina than oxen, allowing for quicker and deeper ploughing, and this too saved labour.[28] It is unclear whether these horses, which were fed with the oats from the three-field rotation, were also butchered and eaten.[29] The missionary Boniface was ordered by the pope in 732 to prohibit consumption of horse meat, and it was not eaten in England, but the evidence for the Low Countries is inconclusive. At some Carolingian sites, such as the Veluwe village of Kootwijk, complete horse skeletons were found, suggesting that the horses were not eaten, but in the Holland sites of Medemblik and Den Burg clear butchering marks were discovered. In such places, therefore, the change from oxen to horses did not greatly reduce meat supplies.

Together, these innovations opened up possibilities for cultivating the heavy and intrinsically more fertile soils in the river clay and peat areas, and to use them more intensively. The earlier scratch plough had been unable to cope with these soils. Heavy ploughs with fixed mould boards were used on the clay soils in the Guelders river area already in the 11th century, as is apparent from the long, S-shaped fields there, developed because of the difficulty of turning these ploughs.[30] They were drawn by a large number of oxen, possibly as many as eight. In this region, with its highly developed manorial organization, these large numbers of draught animals could be easily assembled. Combined with the then available techniques this allowed the intrinsically fertile land on the lower stream ridges to be better cultivated than before, resulting in an extension of arable lands and rapid population growth.

The loess soils, and even more the less fertile sandy soils, then gradually lost their dominant position in agriculture. New regions were occupied and reclaimed, or at least used more intensively, such as the river clay areas and

---

[27] In general: White, *Medieval technology*, 41–48 and 57–65, and Comet, 'Technology'.
[28] Langdon, *Horses, oxen*, 266–267, and Thoen, 'Le démarrage économique'.
[29] IJzereef, 'The animal remains', 39–51.   [30] Pleijter and Vervloet, 'Kromakkers'.

the Holland peat area. Also, the importance of arable farming in the Low Countries increased further, both in newly occupied regions and in the older inhabited ones. In the latter case, this was coupled with the bringing together of smaller fields into one large open field per village, as can be seen in inland Flanders (*kouter*), Walloon-Flanders, Hainault, and the Haspengouw (*couture, coultre*). This occurred mainly in the early 12th century, together with the further consolidation of village communities and the formalization of the communal organization of agriculture.[31]

Dominant patterns in the development of farm buildings in this period are harder to find because buildings and settlements were very different from one another in status and size, even within regions, making it difficult to interpret the fairly scarce data. For the Merovingian period some settlements can be reconstructed. Around the year 600 the village of Brebières, in the extreme south of Flanders near Douai, consisted of some 12 sunken huts of only 7–8 m² each.[32] There were no larger buildings there. Elsewhere in the southern Low Countries, too, very small and flimsy buildings have been found, as in Proville and Vitry, all near Douai and Arras. Further north, farms were much more extensive. In Zelhem in the Achterhoek, the settlement from the 6th to 7th centuries contained four farmhouses of about 6.5 × 15–20 m, with smaller auxiliary buildings, three granaries, and three large storage pits.[33] In the Merovingian period Kootwijk on the Veluwe was a hamlet, with a few farm buildings of some 15–16 m long and a byre area with room for 5 or 6 head of cattle, plus some outbuildings and sunken huts.[34] The Merovingian settlements at the mouths of the Rhine and Meuse rivers in Holland are very varied, with a mixture of flimsy structures and larger, more solid ones.

In general, except in the northernmost areas, the buildings were too small to house more than a nuclear family of parents, children, and occasionally perhaps one relative, showing that extended families were rare in the Merovingian period. In many settlements each farm had its own well, rather than depending on common wells, underlining the individuality of these nuclear families. Two other patterns can be discerned from the scattered information. First, farm buildings seem to have been more substantial in areas where pastoral farming was important, as in the north and west of the Low Countries.[35] Cattle farming was especially associated with larger buildings. Second, in several regions there was a shift to more solid and larger farm buildings at the start of the Carolingian period. Kootwijk already had some larger buildings in the Merovingian period, but these clearly grew in number. In the 9th century the settlement counted some twenty

---

[31] Verhulst, *Landschap*, 120–126. For the village communities, see section III.3, pp. 98–99.
[32] Demolon, *Le village Mérovingien*, 212–225.
[33] Van de Velde, 'A Merovingian settlement', 194–211.
[34] Heidinga, *Medieval settlement*, 17–21, and for the Carolingian habitation, 24–39. For Holland: Bult and Hallewas, 'Archaeological evidence', esp. 82–83.
[35] Demolon, 'L'habitat', 165–179.

large, boat-shaped farmhouses, at least 15 m in length and with a floor surface of 80–165 m², which included a dwelling area and a byre. Most farmhouses had a barn, sunken huts, a well, a shed, and a small granary, surrounded by a wooden fence. In Drenthe the comparatively small farm buildings of the 7th and 8th centuries, with a total surface of no more than 100 m² and room for some 10 head of cattle were gradually replaced by larger farms with some 300–500m² in total, as found in the 11th century. These offered more storage capacity, several barns and sheds, and room for about 16 head of cattle, and sometimes even up to some 20 to 30 head.[36] The large numbers of cattle found on these average farms confirm the pastoral character of agriculture in Drenthe in the period. A similar shift can be observed in the Campine in Dommelen, where the small and flimsy buildings of the period around 700 were replaced by more solid, three-aisled buildings with a floor surface of 75–130 m², or twice the surface of their Merovingian predecessors,[37] although still much smaller than the buildings found in Drenthe, and only just large enough to house 2–5 head of cattle.

The introduction of new techniques and instruments was far from universal. For instance, oxen were not immediately replaced everywhere, but rather there was an increasing division between those regions that used horses and those that continued to use oxen in the course of the high and late Middle Ages, depending on the ecological and socio-economic context.[38] Non-diffusion of a new technique is not necessarily a sign of technological backwardness, as is shown by the choice between the sickle and the scythe. The long-handled scythe, appearing in the 12th to 13th centuries, was much more labour-saving than the sickle which had been used earlier in harvesting, but it used more iron, was more expensive, and could only be wielded by men. Another disadvantage was that it could only cut low and caused more ears to fall, leading to a loss of grain.[39] Moreover, the practice of leaving the stubble in the field to feed the cattle made using the sickle more advantageous, whereas the scythe produced large quantities of straw, increasingly needed in stables and cowsheds, and when mixed with dung could produce a high-quality fertilizer. Each implement boasted advantages in particular circumstances. A compromise was the Flemish reaping hook, or short-handled scythe, which became popular at the end of the 13th century. It avoided some of the drawbacks of the scythe, while still doubling labour productivity compared with the sickle. This turned out to be the instrument which offered the optimal mix in the Flemish context.

Communal Organizations and Customs

The high Middle Ages saw several organizational changes, occurring in association with the population rise and the growing importance of cereal cultivation, as

[36] Spek, *Het Drentse esdorpenlandschap*, 589–591.   [37] Theuws, *Images of the past*, 357–362.
[38] Langdon, *Horses, oxen*, 273–276.
[39] Comet, 'Technology and agricultural expansion', esp. 24–25.

well as with social changes. In some regions, manors remained important, but in others they had already started to decline. At the same time, there was a rise of the power of local lords and the emergence of communal associations, all operating on a territorial basis. In these centuries, and connected to these developments, there was also a further nuclearization of settlement, which became more fixed in location. In the sandy regions dispersed groups of farms had become more nucleated in the early Middle Ages, but still occasionally shifted their location and were rearranged. The first phase of such shifts was associated with the chaos and population decline of the 5th and 6th centuries. The second and third phases were linked to agrarian and social changes, in the 7th to 8th and 12th centuries respectively, and entailed an increasing nuclearization of settlement. In the Campine this process can be clearly observed, as in Geldrop, where by 660 the dispersed farms were concentrated in one hamlet that contained 7 or 8 farmhouses.[40] In the 12th century, in Drenthe, many settlements became fixed villages, with a more regular structure and common roads and fences, and with the grass and hay lands now permanently incorporated into the agricultural system.[41] In the Campine, too, in the 12th and 13th centuries, the smaller Carolingian settlements had grown to larger agglomerations, often at a new location on the banks of small rivers and streams. Further nuclearization of settlement in this period was associated with population growth, introduction of three-field rotation, more intensive use of stream valleys, and the simultaneous rise of sod manuring in some more densely populated regions starting in the 10th to 12th centuries, as elaborated below.[42] There were exceptions, however. On the Veluwe, in the 11th and 12th centuries, there were a few concentrated villages, but many scattered farmsteads and smaller nuclei.[43] In the Holland peat area, there was a completely different pattern, since habitation in this newly occupied region was planned as a ribbon along the canal, in marshland villages, with each farmhouse sitting on its own separate holding. This is a physical expression of the strongly individualized agriculture practised there. The developments characteristic of nucleated villages that supported the communal element of agriculture were hardly found in Holland.

In most of the other regions, especially in Drenthe and the Campine, these communal elements were strengthened over time. Particularly in the 13th century, as a result of the increasing pressure on wastelands, formal organizations that regulated use of the commons arose from informal arrangements.[44] The customs enforced by such organizations strictly limited the quantities of wood that could be cut, the amount of peat or sod to be dug, and the number of cattle to be grazed. In the eastern Netherlands (Drenthe, for instance) custom

---

[40] Theuws, 'Proloog van Brabant', esp. 29.   [41] Waterbolk, 'Mobilität von Dorf'.
[42] Below Section VII.1, pp. 328–329. Cf. also Hoppenbrouwers, 'Agricultural production', esp. 94–96.
[43] Heidinga, *Medieval settlement*, 43–45.   [44] Cf. above, section III.3, pp. 98–99.

also forbade commercial use of the commons, restricting or even prohibiting the selling of wood or peat from the commons or the pasturing of outsiders' cattle. The subsistence needs of the peasants and the continuity of the village or peasant economy were thus central to the organization of the commons.[45] In the Campine the organization of common rights offered more possibilities to outsiders than in Drenthe, and allowed them to settle on newly divided common lands relatively easily, and this promoted population growth.

Communal arrangements to use the arable land collectively and to coordinate the cropping patterns also developed, associated with the nuclearization of settlement and the formation of village communities. These arrangements, too, emerged from more informal, looser customs from the 9th and 10th centuries, reaching their mature, fully developed form particularly in the 12th and 13th centuries.[46] In its most rigorous form, a collective rotation system was compulsorily applied to a group of contiguous parcels without fences or hedges (an open field), covering the arable land of the entire village. For three-field rotation, this meant that the arable soil was split into three large, adjacent, open fields or 'breaks' (*slagen*). These were devoted to one compulsory crop every year, usually alternating a spring grain, winter grain, and fallow field. Each peasant had to till at least one plot in every field, and typically a farm consisted of several small plots scattered across these fields. The lord sometimes had his demesne in separate small open fields, but it too was often divided into numerous plots situated among the peasants' plots. This system ensured that in these open fields, with their tiny individual parcels, all tillage was performed more or less at the same time of the year, which prevented a cultivator from damaging other cultivators' crops by taking implements or draught animals across their plots.[47] This allowed optimal use of the area, made it possible to create communal stubble, and allowed for easier control of the harvest by village law enforcers, tithe collectors, and manorial lords. At the same time, firm regulation was required to enforce rules and customs by the village community or the manorial lord.

This system of common agriculture on open fields did not develop everywhere in the Low Countries, and where it did, it showed a clear diversity.[48] In the northern and western parts of Hainault, the Cambrésis, Ostrevant, and in the neighbouring parts of Artois, as in most of northern France, cereal cultivation on large, open fields was clearly the dominant pattern.[49] The system was also introduced in inland Flanders, Brabant, and the Haspengouw, although with a

---

[45] Van Zanden, 'The paradox', esp. 130–135, and Hoppenbrouwers, 'The use and management of commons', 98–106.

[46] Hoffmann, 'Medieval origins', esp. 45–52. Cf. section III.3 (on villages), pp. 93–94.

[47] Thoen, *Landbouwekonomie*, 772–773.

[48] This diversity in the Low Countries is apparent in a European perspective. Cf. the map by Hoffmann, 'Medieval origins', 26—although this map should be used with some caution.

[49] Sivéry, *Structures agraires*, 83–86, 98–105, and 138–142, but further nuanced by Derville, 'L'assolement triennal', 337–376 and Dupont, 'Les pratiques agraires', i: 403–422.

more flexible variant of smaller complexes of plots. These miniature open fields or *kouters*, each some 15 to 50 hectares in size and divided by roads, hedges, or streams, were sown homogeneously and cultivated identically.[50] In inland Flanders and even more clearly in the Guelders river area, the system of common agriculture on open fields went out of use early, since farms were enclosed from the 13th century. In inland Flanders the fixed collective rotation had lost much of its importance by the second half of the 13th century.[51] In the peatland of Holland, this system was never introduced, since from the outset this region had a highly individualized type of agriculture, with each farmer holding an individual consolidated farm in full property. It consisted of one single plot of land, separated from neighbouring farms by ditches and water courses, and the farmers practised their own rotation as they chose, with no common land and no common regulation.

These regional differences can be understood by examining the factors underlying the formation of common open-field agriculture. First, the system reduced the risks in farming since it allowed for dispersing the holdings of each farmer in several plots over the fields, thus helping to avoid the full impact of crop failure or other disasters.[52] It thus fitted very well in a peasant economy since it helped maintain a certain level of production for everyone in the village and mitigated the uncertainty of farming. Moreover, the communal rules associated with it reinforced the role of the community. Group solidarity was chosen over the possible gains for an individual farmer, which would perhaps threaten the livelihood of others. This was not an irrational choice in a period when most lived on the edge of subsistence.[53] In regions where markets and commercially oriented agriculture developed early, such as Holland, Frisia, or the Guelders river area, this peasant system was less suitable, and was either not adopted or went out of use early. Also, the importance of the system lessened as the capital market developed and became accessible to peasants, and as interest rates declined. The possibility of obtaining cheap credit formed an alternative to open fields in coping with risks, but mainly in those regions where a favourable rural capital market emerged, such as Holland and inland Flanders.[54] A third important factor in the rise of open fields was population growth and the increasing scarcity of arable land. Open fields allowed an optimal use of the area available. There was no need for any roads, since the work was done simultaneously, and the system created a communal stubble field, limiting the pressure on the ever scarcer pastureland. It also reduced the space that would have been taken up by barriers between plots. It is thus understandable that the system developed mainly in times (the 12th and 13th centuries) and regions of population pressure.

However, this system was not the only possible solution to the increasing scarcity of land. Agricultural innovation and intensification on a more individual

---

[50] Thoen, *Landbouwekonomie*, 762–772 and 775.　　[51] Thoen, *Landbouwekonomie*.
[52] McCloskey: 'The persistence', esp. 113–119, and 'The enclosure of open fields', 15–32.
[53] Hoffmann, 'Medieval origins', 27–33 and 61–63.　　[54] Cf. section V.2, pp. 189–192.

basis were another possible response, and might have included the introduction of fodder crops, flexible rotation, new techniques, stall feeding, or using more labour, which became more common in inland Flanders after the 13th century.[55] A main factor in the choice between this option and open-field farming could be the local lord, since he had the authority and power to impose the more general and structural changes required for open-field farming, possibly in collaboration with the village community.[56] Lords were in a position to enforce the change and obedience to the extensive regulations of open-field farming. They had an interest in enforcing this system, since it was land-saving. By reducing the need to construct barriers between the plots and by allowing the grazing of cattle under communal supervision, it also saved labour, although travelling to the various scattered plots did take more time. Lords benefited from the more efficient use of land and labour, resulting in more surpluses to be extracted. Indeed, in western Europe a clear overlap can be observed between the areas of strong lordly power and nucleated villages on the one hand, and the open-field system on the other. At the same time, open-field cultivation severely restricted flexibility and individual decisions on land use, probably limiting growth in the long run. It worked against the opportunities for specialization and the cultivation of industrial crops offered by growing market demand.

Agriculture and Living Standards

The development of agriculture, by far the most important sector in this period, was thus determined not only by geography, but also by population developments and social organization in the region in question. The influence exerted by social organization is particularly relevant to the extent and form of manorialism, the specific organization of village communities, the amount of large land holdings and granges, and, increasingly, from the 11th and 12th centuries, the influence of cities and markets. After the chaotic, insecure situation in the post-Roman period, these organizations, combined with the security offered by Frankish rule, seem to have provided a framework that allowed for the growth of agriculture through the Carolingian period and the high Middle Ages. This growth is evidenced by the extension of cultivated land, the introduction of new crops, new techniques, and rotation systems, and the rise of more intensive forms of grain cultivation. All this allowed higher agricultural output and more people to be fed from the land, but did not necessarily entail a rise in labour productivity.

The above findings on reclamation and population numbers show that most growth of agricultural output in the early Middle Ages took place in the regions along the Meuse and the Rhine, as in the Guelders river area, where ample large land holdings and well-developed manorialism existed. Agricultural development in the Carolingian period also took place in Frisia, Zeeland, and coastal Flanders,

[55] Thoen, 'The birth'.   [56] Campbell, 'Commonfield origins', 112–129.

where the existing dominance of pastoral farming was further extended, enabled by specialization within organizations such as abbeys or by market exchange. Real growth in labour productivity and agricultural surpluses may have taken place there, at least temporarily, next to the growth in output found more generally.

In the high Middle Ages the loess soils and the sandy regions saw less conspicuous development. In the river clay areas, on the other hand, growth continued in the 10th and 11th centuries, with the wider use of new techniques and implements, such as heavy ploughs. The substantial progress in the early and high Middle Ages came about there because the soil was intrinsically very fertile, though difficult to cultivate, and manorialism that emerged there allowed for investment in the technology needed to work this soil. As a result of these new techniques and the ongoing population growth, from the 10th century also new regions were opened up to agriculture, most particularly the peat areas. There, in the Holland peatlands and coastal Flanders, for example, growth in agricultural output was very pronounced. This went along with a growing importance of cereals, both there and elsewhere. Pastoral farming remained dominant only in a few coastal areas, such as coastal Frisia, although even there cereal cultivation became more important after the embankments of the 11th and 12th centuries. This process of cerealization was part of a more general intensive land use, raising land productivity but requiring more labour, which fitted well with the rising population pressure. More people could thus be fed from the land, and population numbers in the 13th century were 10 to 15 times higher than they had been in the 7th century, although surpluses did not necessarily rise. Indeed, where population pressure became very great, with much labour applied to the scarce land, this resulted in high physical yields but decreasing surpluses. In some regions greater surpluses were generated by employing new techniques, especially in the 10th to 12th centuries, and increasing specialization because of better transport and growing market exchange sometimes allowed for greater land and labour productivity, as perhaps most clearly throughout Flanders, but in the longer run these surpluses, too, were largely eroded by population growth.

Growth in this period thus mainly consisted of growth in output, which took place both at the extensive and the intensive margin of cultivation. The latter form was found especially in inland Flanders, where intensification in the high Middle Ages was pushed furthest, even in a European perspective. Agricultural development, intensification, and specialization were pronounced there, with the famous Flemish husbandry developing some of its basic traits in this period. Agriculture there witnessed a bipartite development: specialization aimed at the market combined with intensification aimed at the consumption needs of the resident peasant household. This formed the foundation of the commercial survival economy characteristic of rural inland Flanders in the later Middle Ages.[57]

[57] Thoen, 'A "commercial survival economy"'.

Agriculture thus showed distinct change in these centuries, with the assembly of an ever greater stock of implements, techniques, crops, agricultural systems, and organizations, to be used selectively in line with regional characteristics, both ecological and social-economic. At the same time, the emerging market enabling more exchange allowed the population to adapt agriculture to special regional characteristics and to take advantage of these. The effects also differed by social group. The landowning elite probably profited from the greater land productivity and the growing possibilities of exchange and transport, whereas peasants with fragmented holdings under population pressure did not, or indeed were confronted with a decline in their standard of living, especially in regions where strong manorialism and high population densities were combined, such as the Guelders river area and the Haspengouw. The resulting social polarization must have been particularly evident in the nutritional value and variety of food, with the elite in an increasingly more favourable position. An example can be found by comparing the animal remains from a comital castle in Namur with those from the urban settlement and the hospital from the 11th to 13th centuries.[58] The castle dwellers ate a great deal of pork, some beef, and smaller quantities of small game (birds, hare, rabbit) and large game (deer, boar, and brown bear), freshwater fish, as well as saltwater fish (cod, haddock, flatfish), and mussels. Large quantities of butter and cheese may have added to the diversity of their diet. In the urban settlement of Namur, game and saltwater fish were absent, except for the cheaper herring, and consumption of meat and dairy products was certainly much lower. In the high Middle Ages, with its growing population pressure, the diet of ordinary people increasingly consisted of grain, consumed as bread, beer, and porridge. For the lower groups in society, who relied on grain for as much as three-quarters of their caloric intake, this would certainly have caused deficiencies in protein and health problems.

From the few sources it is impossible to make a systematic analysis of the incidence of crop failures, hunger, and famine, but we know that the north of France and the Low Countries were hit by severe famines in 779, 792/3, and 805/6. Perhaps these were accidents of growth resulting from a rapid extension of cultivated area and population growth, which caused temporary tensions in the food supply, followed by rapid demographic recovery.[59] This interpretation may be supported by the fact that later, in the 9th and 10th centuries mentions of severe famines are rare. Although the picture may be distorted because of the increase in the availability of sources, famine seems to have increased and become more general in the course of the high Middle Ages, and particularly in the 13th century, as population pressure grew further. In 1272, for instance, the people in the northern parts of the Low Countries desperately tried to buy grain in Denmark and eastern Europe, but when this attempt failed

---

[58] Boone, De Cupere, and Van Neer, 'Social status', 1391–1394.
[59] Verhulst, *The Carolingian economy*, 25–26 and 123–124.

they were driven to eat nettles, dock, plantain, and grass, and many died of hunger.[60]

The archaeological investigation of dental remains shows that life expectancy in this period, although it fluctuated sharply and was depressed in these periods of famine, in the very long run remained more or less at the same level. The average person in the early medieval Low Countries lived for some 30–35 years. Leaving aside infant mortality, and including only those aged at least 12 years, the non-weighted average for men and women is about 37 years (calculated from Table 4.1). This is comparable to the average age of death for adults (over 15 years old) calculated for the Roman period: 40.2 for males and 34.6 for females; and for the period around 1400: 37.7 for males and 31.1 for females.[61] Regional or chronological patterns are difficult to discern: data are scarce and it is difficult to assess the representativeness of the excavated remains compared to the total population with respect to age, sex, and social position, but the picture may become clearer as research in this promising field continues.

It is difficult to assess how developments in agriculture affected living standards in the early Middle Ages, particularly those of the average population. The best indicator is provided by biological findings, and more specifically, stature, since this can offer a proxy of modal well-being or living standards, and also because this indicator is sensitive to inequality.[62] Stature can be reconstructed from excavated human bones, as has been done for several Merovingian burial sites.[63] Bones from the site at Ciply in the fertile Hainault area, where grain cultivation was important and population density probably relatively high, indicate that men were around 1.71 m tall, and women were much shorter, at 1.57 m on average. In Torgny in the Ardennes forest, where meat consumption was more important, men in the 6th and 7th centuries were no less than 1.75 m on average and women relatively even taller, compared to those at Ciply, at 1.65 m. More or less similar heights are found in Oosterbeintum in Friesland, where the men buried in the period 450–750 measured on average 1.74 m, and the women 1.58 m.[64] In those instances where the social background of these people is analysed, differences between social groups appear to be pronounced. In early medieval Maastricht, the men investigated measured 1.74 m and the women 1.62 m.[65] Men of high status measured 1.75–1.80 m on average, those of intermediate status 1.73–1.76 m, and those of low status only 1.69–1.71 m.

[60] Jansen and Janse, *Kroniek van het klooster Bloemhof*, 448–453.
[61] Hassan, *Demographic archaeology*, 102–103 and 122–123.
[62] General: Steckel, 'Strategic ideas', 803–821.
[63] Polet and Orban, *Les dents et les ossements*, 131, 141, and 147, Polet, Leguebe, and Orban, 'Estimation de la stature', 111–123, Buchet, 'La recherche des structures sociales', and Orban, 'Longueurs'.
[64] Knol et al., 'The early medieval cemetery', esp. 300–302.
[65] Panhuysen, *Demography and health*, 168–171.

Table 4.1a Ages at death as reconstructed from dental remains

Place Region Period	Dorestad Utrecht 8–9C.		Koksijde coast Fl 4–10C.	Nijvel Brabant 5–17C.	Ronse inld Fl 11–12C.	Achet Namur Frankish	Spy Namur Frankish	Ciply Hainaut Frankish
		< 6 yr.	[–?]	[–?]	[–?]			
< 12 yrs.	4 %	6–12 yrs.	[2 %]	[5 %]	[8 %?]	24 %	9 %	3 %
12–17 yrs.	0 %	12–18 yrs.	10 %	5 %	6 %	40 %	4 %	3 %
17–25 yrs.	42 %	18–30 yrs.	27 %	17 %	18 %	10 %	9 %	3 %
25–35 yrs.	41 %					12 %	6 %	6 %
35–45 yrs.	13 %	30–50 yrs.	43 %	62 %	48 %	10 %	53 %	40 %
>45 yrs.	0 %	>50 yrs.	17 %	10 %	21 %	5 %	19 %	45 %
n =	83		427	168	145	42	53	156
Est. average	26		[35]	[35]	[35]	15	34	43
Ave. excl <12	27		35	36	39	30	38	46

Table 4.1b

Place Region Period	Gutshoven Haspengouw Merovingian	Rosmeer Haspengouw Merovingian	Torgny Luxembourg Carolingian	Lent Guelders river 630–750	Oosterleintum Friesland early M.A.
<6 yr.	17 %	2 %	5 %	19 %	
6–12 yrs.	14 %	2 %	11 %	11 %	
12–18 yrs.	6 %	0	11 %	14 %	
18–30 yrs.	8 %	15 %	21 %	23 %	
30–50 yrs.	32 %	51 %	37 %	31 %	
>50	23 %	29 %	16 %	5 %	
$n =$	111	41	19	64	46
Est. average	30	42	31	24	30
Ave. excl <12	41	43	35	32	36

Sources: Brabant and Twiesselmann, 'Etude de la denture', 561–588, Perizonius and Pot, 'Diachronic dental research', 369–413, Brabant, 'Observations sur la denture humaine', 169–296, Van Es and Hulst, *Das Merowingische Gräberfeld*, 207–213, Knol et al., 'The early medieval cemetery', esp. 300–302.

The bones from these Merovingian burial sites show that people were fairly tall. In the case of the skeletons excavated at Torgny, in the midst of the sparsely populated Ardennes forest, both men and women in the 6th to 7th centuries were almost as tall as they are today. These scarce data, if they are representative, confirm the impression that standards of living in the early Middle Ages were fairly high, and the diet probably very varied. Average height decreased between the 12th and 18th centuries,[66] or possibly even a little earlier, as a result of population increase, the related emphasis on cereal cultivation, and the increasing imbalance in the diet. The biometric data, although scarce, also support the more general thesis of this section that changes in the agricultural sector in the early and high Middle Ages did not produce economic growth and rising living standards, but mainly resulted in increases in cultivated area and in physical yields, and hence an increase in the number of people to be fed. Only in a few times and places did these changes also result in real growth in a modern sense, when combined with technological change and specialization, in their turn increasing labour productivity and standards of living. Particularly where specialization, market orientation, and technological change were pronounced, aided by the growth of the market and the formation of manors and later granges in regions dominated by large land holdings, surpluses available for the market increased, and these surpluses facilitated the growth of specialized industries, trade, and towns.

IV.2. INDUSTRIES IN THE EARLY AND HIGH MIDDLE AGES

Manors and Early Medieval Production

In the early Middle Ages most non-agricultural goods were made within the peasant household, and were aimed at the consumption needs of the same household. People brewed their own beer, used hand mills to produce flour, and made simple tools of wood or bone.[67] Cloth and linen, the most important non-agricultural products in the Middle Ages, were probably also largely made within the household. Textile production was a common side activity of women, whereas men prepared the wool and fulled the cloth. These peasant activities were usually a sideline to agriculture. There was also some small-scale local production by craftsmen, who usually also farmed a holding, and such products were exchanged within the settlement. The craftsmen made leather shoes and saddles, some glass and pottery, furniture, and simple iron and wooden tools. The goods produced were coarse and simple, rather than luxurious.[68]

---

[66] Cf. the data for this period in section VIII.1, p. 378.
[67] Hägermann and Schneider, *Landbau und Handwerk*.
[68] Hamerow, *Early medieval settlements*.

The manors which emerged from the 7th and 8th centuries in several parts of the Low Countries played an increasing role in the production of non-agricultural goods, sometimes even on a somewhat larger scale. Manors were important in assembling surpluses of industrial products. Tenants often had to deliver a few pieces of linen or woollen cloth, or some bundles of flax to the manorial lord. Flax cultivation and processing were widespread in the Carolingian Low Countries, as we can tell from the scarce sources, mostly from religious institutions. On the manors of the Abbey of Lobbes, situated in Hainault and the south of Brabant, peasants had to deliver some 30 bundles of flax on average per holding,[69] totalling some 20,000 bundles per year. Similar dues had to be paid by the peasants on the tenements of the Abbeys of St Bertin, in the south of Flanders, and Lorsch, in the 9th century. These deliveries of bundles of flax and woollen or linen cloth were explicitly designated as the produce of women's work, showing the prominent position of women in early medieval textile production.

Products other than textiles are seldom mentioned among the manorial levies. Occasionally serfs had to deliver wooden poles and roof boards, or wooden dishes and basins, as did a serf of St Bertin in Poperinge in Flanders, while a serf in Houmont in the Ardennes delivered iron pots and pans to the Abbey of Prüm. However, these were clearly exceptions, showing that such products were generally produced by specialized craftsmen, not by unspecialized serfs.[70] On each manor, presumably in a dependent or servile position, there were a few craftsmen, such as a blacksmith or a carpenter. In the Carolingian period, some concentrations of specialized craftsmen were found around monasteries, which were their main clients. We know, for instance, that in 831 St Riquier in Picardy had 4 millers, 13 bakers, as well as blacksmiths, saddlers, shoemakers, butchers, fullers, tanners, and brewers settled around the abbey.[71] This was probably the situation at other large monasteries then also. At St Riquier these craftsmen were probably serfs and they belonged to the *familia* of the abbey, but they seem to have possessed at least some economic independence. In some cases manors even became the focal points of larger-scale industry, such as salt production. The relationship between manor and market is thus ambiguous. On the one hand, the organization of manors enabled the exchange of products from producer to consumer without markets, but on the other hand manors also brought together larger quantities of products and allowed for larger-scale production, and such products were often transferred to the market, as will be shown below.

The manorial element is particularly clear in the main industry: milling. Mills, driven by water or horses, and from the 12th century also by wind, were used mainly for processing food, in particular for milling grain and husking barley, but

---

[69] Devroey, *Le polyptyque*, Kuchenbuch, '"Opus feminile"', esp. 140–141, and Sabbe, *De Belgische vlasnijverheid*, 42–46.
[70] Verhulst and De Bock-Doehaerd, 'Nijverheid en handel', 184–188.
[71] Schwind, 'Zu karolingerzeitlicher Klöstern', 115–117, and Lebecq, 'The role of monasteries'.

also for pressing oil, and from the high Middle Ages increasingly for industrial work such as fulling, metalworking, or sawing wood. In Roman times water mills had existed but were not widespread, perhaps because of the availability of cheap and/or forced labour and the preferred use of hand querns. In the early Middle Ages, however, water power became ever more important. This energy source was especially suited to regions with fast-flowing small rivers and streams, as in the Ardennes, Twente, the Achterhoek, and the Haspengouw.

Particularly in the 7th and 8th centuries, as grain cultivation expanded—and especially the cultivation of naked grains for bread production, such as rye and wheat, much better suited to milling than the earlier hulled grains—many mills were constructed. In the 9th century, polyptiques such as those of Lobbes and St Bertin show that almost every manor (except the smallest) possessed at least one mill, sometimes several.[72] Some of these must have been large, like the one Lobbes owned in Thuin, situated in Hainault, which yielded an annual rent of 120 muds (about 50–70 hl) of flour. Taking account of the income of the miller, and the fact that the milling fee was probably one-twentieth to one-tenth of the grain, this mill must have processed many hundreds of hectolitres of grain annually. In total, the 13 manors of St Bertin in the south-west of the Low Countries, each having 400–650 ha of arable land and some 150–250 inhabitants, contained 14 mills, yielding an annual rent of 50 muds of flour on average. This could mean a total production of 500–1,000 muds (= 250–500 hl) of flour, or the processing of 600–1,200 hl of grain per manor. Each hectare of arable land (including the land left fallow) apparently yielded 1.5–2 hl of bread grain, after sowing seed had been deducted and excluding non-bread grains sown and grain used for brewing and making gruel. This allowed each person about 2 hl (120 kg) of flour per year, which would produce almost 200 kg of bread, or more than half a kilo of bread per day per person, or about a thousand kcal. Additional grain was consumed as beer and gruel. These figures again point to the predominant position of grain in the diet, at least in this relatively densely populated region.

The construction of such a mill was a costly operation that only a large organization could afford. The spread of mills must thus be linked to the nuclearization of villages, enabling an association of peasant villagers to assemble the funds for construction, and particularly to the rise of manorialism. The manorial lord had the capital needed for building, and the manor offered a suitable unit for use of the mill and guaranteed that the lord would be able to force his serfs to use it. The same probably applied to baking in the oven and to brewing, often centralized at the manor, with the mill used for crushing malt. From the 9th century, brewery and malt mills were sometimes mentioned

---

[72] Lohrmann, 'Le moulin à eau', i:367–404, esp. i:389–392, and Devroey, *Polyptyque*, xcvii–c. For the conversions of the following calculations: Devroey, 'Units of measurement', 68–92. Cf. also this section, pp. 158–160, and section VII.2, pp. 352 and 358–359, for mills in the high and later Middle Ages.

as standing side by side, a practice becoming widespread in the 11th and 12th centuries.[73] The earlier situation when peasants consumed most of their grain in the form of gruel, potage, or homemade beer, now gave way to bread and beer made by specialists. The rise of mills, ovens, and breweries brought a fundamental change in diet, but also a strong impetus for specialization and the rise of professional millers, bakers, and brewers. From the 10th century, the rise of banal lords and the formal obligation to grind all grain at the lord's mill caused a further increase in the number and capacity of mills.

Industrial Specializations

In the early Middle Ages most industrial production thus took place within the household, village, or manor, with local self-sufficiency in most goods. Luxury goods, destined for the elite, formed the main exception. Amber, for instance, was imported mainly from the Baltic Sea area, and partly worked in the Low Countries, as in Dorestad, where thousands of amber fragments have been excavated.[74] Goods which could not be produced in the Low Countries for lack of raw materials were imported. An example were quern stones made from volcanic basalt, which was mined near Mayen in the Eifel. Many of these stones have also been found in Dorestad, where they were finished off for further export. In addition to these specific industries, in the early Middle Ages a few important industrial specializations existed in the production of more common goods that were partly destined for export. These industries often had clear regional concentrations, and were almost all located in the countryside: the iron industries (in the Veluwe and later in the Walloon area), pottery (in the Meuse valley), salt production (in Zeeland), and textile production (in Frisia and Flanders).

In the coastal peat areas, particularly in Zeeland, but probably also in West Friesland, Friesland, and Ost Friesland, salt was produced in the early Middle Ages. It was extracted there from drowned silty peat bogs, by burning the turf, mixing the salty ashes with seawater, and then boiling and further refining it.[75] Several salt pans are mentioned as belonging to distant religious institutions, such as the Abbey of Lorsch, which owned 17 pans for producing salt on the Zeeland island of Schouwen from the late 8th century on, and the Abbey of Nijvel, which owned 'terram et mancipia ad salem' there.[76] Apparently, in the latter case, production was organized within a manorial setting, with serfs providing the labour. Whether this was common practice cannot be ascertained, since these sources relate only to large land holdings and are not representative. Ibraham ibn Ya'qub, a Jewish adviser to the caliph of Cordoba, travelling in that region

---

[73] Bautier, 'Les plus anciennes mentions', ii:567–626, esp. ii:601–603.
[74] Kars and Wevers, 'Early-medieval Dorestad', 61–81.
[75] Leenders, 'The start of peat digging', 107–110. Cf. for the loss of land possibly connected to this industry: section II.2, pp. 45–46.
[76] Besteman, 'Frisian salt', 171–174.

around 965, wrote that the land was permeated by salt, and that shepherds dug out blocks of soil, dried, and then burnt them. This can be interpreted as shepherds being engaged in salt production as a side activity, although it might also relate to their digging peat as fuel. The salt industry grew in the 11th and 12th centuries in Zeeland as well as in the north of Holland and in Friesland. This may have resulted in ecological problems, since the process required digging and burning the peat to obtain the salty ashes and the fuel for the refining process. These required digging up large tracts of peat, sometimes close to dikes, and endangering the land, which may have been a main factor in the incursions of the sea and loss of land in Zeeland, as evidenced by the submersion of the *Zelnissepolder* (*zel* means the salty ashes) in 1134.

Iron, a vital material for agricultural, industrial, and military use, was produced in several rural areas of the Low Countries. In the early Middle Ages, in regions such as Drenthe and the north of Brabant, bog iron was used on a small scale. Production was on a much larger scale in the Veluwe and adjacent Montferland, where ore was mined from lumps of limonite or rattlestone.[77] Next to southern Sweden, this was the main iron-producing area in early medieval Europe. There are hardly any written records of this industry, so it is necessary to rely almost solely on material from archaeological investigations: dozens of slag heaps and iron pits. The slag was tapped off in wind furnaces used until the 13th century; these were very small and operated for only a short time. They could readily be abandoned and others built where ore and fuel were available. Nevertheless, total quantities of iron produced here were significant and the scale of these sites was larger than anywhere else in Europe. One of the early medieval slag heaps investigated in the Orderbos, admittedly a large one, was formed of waste material from the production of 325 tonnes of iron, produced from about 1,235 tonnes of ore. This iron was enough to forge 50,000 heavy axes, 120,000 horse shoes, and the accompanying nails. Over 70 slag heaps have now been identified in the Veluwe and Montferland. Since many have been cleared away or have not yet been uncovered, these provide some minimum indication of the total production of iron here. Probably some 55,000 tonnes of iron were produced in total from these smelting sites during the early Middle Ages.[78]

These quantities of iron must have been destined for export. The relatively large quantities of imported pottery found there also point to the existence of external trade links. It is probable, but not certain, that this type of export-oriented, large-scale production was organized by professional smelters, perhaps working independently. What is clear, however, is that noblemen from surrounding regions and several distant institutions (the Abbeys of Lorsch, Paderborn,

---

[77] Moerman, 'Oude smeedijzerindustrie', (1968/9) 1–30 and (1970), esp. 1–24: and Heidinga, *Medieval settlement*, 194–203.

[78] Joosten and Van Nie, 'Vroeg-middeleeuwse ijzerproductie', 203–212 and revised calculations in Joosten, 'Technology', 31–32 and 71–87.

Werden, Deutz, and Prüm) owned manors and parts of the forest in this region. Their properties here, which were hardly suitable for agriculture, seem to have been associated with a desire to obtain iron or to profit from the iron production and trade. The same applies to several large forts constructed in the 9th century by the most powerful lords of the time at strategic places between the iron-producing areas and waterways, probably aimed at channelling the trade in iron to control and profit from it.[79] A similar situation can be seen in the Ardennes, where a concentration of no less than six royal fiscs encircled an area in the valleys of the Amblève and Salm rivers where gold ore was extracted.[80] Control over the production of these key goods must have given the lords considerable power.

Following a decline starting in the 9th and 10th centuries, large-scale production of iron ended in the Veluwe in the 12th century. Among the causes were competition from regions such as the Siegerland, and the exhaustion of the easily accessible veins of rattlestone. The increasing shortage of wood may also have played a role in the decline.[81] Production of iron used charcoal as fuel, consuming large amounts of wood. The production from the one slagheap mentioned above required felling no fewer than 100,000 trees on the Veluwe, mainly oak. In total, iron production on the Veluwe used 105,000 tonnes of charcoal, for which tens of thousands of hectares of forest were needed over a period of 250 years. Perhaps forests could regenerate after a smelting site had been temporarily abandoned, but such massive consumption of trees may well have led to deforestation. It is clear that the forested area declined from the 7th century and deforestation and sand drifting caused problems in the Veluwe from the 10th century.

Metal mining and industry were also important in Wallonia.[82] There were rich ore deposits in the Condroz, in the area between the Sambre and Meuse rivers, and south-west of Namur, where mining was practised from Roman times. In the early Middle Ages mining and processing of ore became less important here, but rapidly gained importance again from the 10th century on. Ore was found in thin veins, close to the surface, easily dug out with pickaxe and hammer in opencast mining. There were iron mines in Clermont-sur-Meuse and Florennes, next to the stronghold of a powerful lord. Lead, used for making glass, leaded windows, pipes, vats, and in roofing, was taken from the mines in Gimnée, between the Sambre and Meuse. It was probably imported as well, for instance from England and from the Rammelsberg mine in the Harz, which was opened up before 1000. Calamine was mined in large quantities in Moresnet (Altenberg), where it was easy to dig up.[83] The mining of metals was organized particularly on the larger estates of religious institutions and on lands owned by lords. Mining itself was rather small scale, and the processing was not yet a large export industry.

---

[79] Heidinga, *Medieval settlement*, 199–206.   [80] Theuws, 'Centre and periphery', 51.
[81] Heidinga, *Medieval settlement*, 135–136, but the environmental effects of iron production are nuanced by Joosten, 'Technology', 91–92. For the ecological problems, also see above, section II.2, p. 48.
[82] Joris, 'Probleme', 58–76.   [83] Engelen, 'Delfstoffen'.

This started to change in the 11th century, with the main example being copper production, which expanded rapidly but now within an urban context, as in the cities in the Meuse valley such as Huy and Dinant (cf. below).

Pottery production became increasingly specialized in the early Middle Ages. As a result, the quality of ceramics from the Carolingian period was clearly higher than those of the Merovingian period. The homemade, plain, coarse pottery was gradually replaced by harder fired, wheel-turned, mass-produced pottery. This suggests better organization, probably within a manorial setting.[84] Products were increasingly exported, as evidenced by the larger portion of imported wheel-thrown pottery compared to handmade native pottery found in excavations. In Zelhem in the Achterhoek, 27 per cent of the pottery in the Merovingian period was imported, while in Kootwijk on the Veluwe, this had already reached about 80 per cent at the time,[85] with the proportion further growing in the Carolingian era. Linked to this growing trade, some centres of pottery production emerged, among them Mayen in the Eifel. In the 9th to 13th centuries pottery production became further concentrated regionally, mainly in the quadrangle bounded by Namur, Roermond, Cologne, and Bonn.[86] Production in this area was favoured by the old clays found there, allowing for firing at high temperatures and producing a strong ceramic. Brown coal was also found nearby. Often these pottery centres were linked to regional power centres, as many were situated near fortifications, such as the fortified manor in Xanten, the motte castle of Hoverberg, or the episcopal residence in Siegburg. The powerful lords often helped to diffuse the products across their widespread properties.[87] The largest pottery centres in the region, such as Schinveld, Andenne, Raeren, and Pingsdorf, sometimes had several kilns (as many as 17) that produced massive quantities of cooking pots, pipkins, and jugs, mainly for export. These products, particularly the heavier ones or those produced in larger quantities, were transported mainly by water. Ships built in this period were relatively small compared with Roman and later medieval ships,[88] but small cargo ships like the hulk and the cog were increasingly used to travel up the Rhine, and also along the coast, forming a main link in the process of the increasing industrial specialization of the period.

Industries in Town and Countryside

In contrast to the Roman period when industries were mainly located in cities, the early medieval industries were all located in the countryside or concentrated in royal, monastic, or aristocratic centres. In many cases they were situated in

---

[84] Verhulst, *Carolingian economy*, 79–80.
[85] Van de Velde et al., 'A Merovingian settlement', 194–211, and Heidinga, *Medieval settlement*, 20.
[86] Janssen, 'Gewerbliche Produktion', and Heege, 'Rheinische Keramik', 18–41.
[87] Janssen, 'Die Bedeutung der mittelalterlichen Burg', esp. ii: 304–308, and McCormick, *Origins*, 656–663. Cf. also section VII.2, p. 344.
[88] Unger, *The ship in the medieval economy*, 58–61 and 78. Cf. also below, p. 158.

large estates or manorial organizations, sometimes owned by distant abbeys. Their location seems to have been determined mainly by the proximity of raw materials. This applies particularly to heavy materials (clay, ore, quartz) or where large quantities were needed (wood, turf, brown coal), especially since transport in the early Middle Ages was difficult and costly. Proximity to raw materials became less important in the succeeding centuries, as transport became easier and cheaper.[89] In other industries, where raw materials were much lighter (linen, wool) or had a higher value relative to their weight (textiles and copper), and were thus relatively cheaper to transport, proximity was not essential and the social and institutional context may have been more important for determining production location than the availability of raw materials.

However, cloth production in the early Middle Ages was still found mainly in the regions along the coast dominated by pastoral farming and sheep farming in particular, as was the case in Frisia, and to a lesser extent in Zeeland and coastal Flanders. The dominance of pastoral farming in this period is an indication of the economic sophistication and specialization of these regions, since it depended on exchange. The numbers of sheep and cattle were so large that this sector must have been aimed at the market, especially since most of the grain to feed the people living there probably had to be imported. An important element in this specialization was the production and marketing of cloth. Frisian cloth had a high reputation: when Charlemagne planned to send gifts to Harun al-Rashid, the caliph of Baghdad, he included some *pallia Fresonica*. Frisian cloth was exchanged throughout western Europe, and was traded by the Frisians together with other products such as salt and fish; in exchange they bought cereals, timber, and wine, for instance along the middle and upper courses of the Rhine.[90] The Frisians obtained the dye stuffs needed for cloth production at least partly through trade, as testified by the presence of Frisian merchants to buy madder—used to produce a red colourant—at the fair of St Denis in the second half of the 9th century.[91] Woad, used to obtain blue pigment, was cultivated throughout western Europe, for instance in southern Flanders around Lille and in inland Flanders.

The exact geographical origin of Frisian cloth is debated: some believe that it was produced in Flanders, or in monasteries in the area between the Meuse and Rhine, or even in England, and then bought by Frisian merchants to resell elsewhere as Frisian cloth. Archaeological finds in Frisia, however, now demonstrate that production indeed took place in the region itself, as well as in coastal Flanders, which in the early Middle Ages was sometimes also referred to as belonging to 'greater Frisia'. This is shown from finds of loom weights, spindle whorls, combs, and parts of looms, as well as pieces of high-quality cloth. The early medieval Frisian law code also points to the importance of cloth making there, since crimes committed against goldsmiths, harpers, and women

---

[89] Cf. below p. 158, and section V.4, pp. 234–237.
[90] Verhulst, 'Der frühmittelalterliche Handel'.   [91] Lebecq, *Marchands*, 25–26.

who knew how to make *fresum* (Frisian cloth) were fined more heavily than those against others,[92] demonstrating the high value attached to these occupations.

Cloth was produced in the countryside, often by serfs/tenants, sometimes on manors owned by distant religious institutions. Around 800, for instance, the Abbey of Fulda received annually some 850 pieces of cloth from the abbey's property in Frisia, by way of ten men, presumably acting as intermediaries, and the abbey of Werden in the 10th century collected a thousand pieces of cloth annually in Frisia.[93] There was probably some specialization there, but elsewhere textile production was local and small-scale, and was usually a side activity within the households, mainly performed by women. Most production stages entailed only simple acts, requiring patience and tenacity, and were apparently seen as well suited to women. Larger quantities were assembled by monasteries, receiving them from their tenants and serfs. A few monasteries and royal manors also had *gynaecea*, places where servile women or female slaves were put to work at textile production, carrying out the entire production process from the processing of raw material to finishing the product, as in Tournai.[94] These production centres, however, were major exceptions, since most of the early medieval textile production was performed by unspecialized women within the household.

Textiles were often made in sunken-floored buildings found by the dozen in every early medieval settlement.[95] Kootwijk in the Veluwe, inhabited from the late 7th to the early 11th centuries, had 45 farm buildings and no fewer than 177 sunken-floored huts. These were dug out several decimetres deep. Such constructions were found all over the Low Countries, except for the coastal areas, where the subsoil was too damp. The importance of the sunken-floored huts in textile production is attested by the large numbers of spindle whorls and loom weights found. The humid and cool atmosphere of the huts helped to prevent the fibres from breaking and made processing them easier.

In other industrial sectors, and in the high Middle Ages, castles began to play focal roles. With the fragmentation of central power and the rise of banal lordship, hundreds of castles were built, particularly in the 11th and 12th centuries; these occupied positions as centres of power and consumption, and often also of industrial production. Meer Castle near Neuss in the Niederrhein area, for instance, was the centre of highly developed woodworking and plumbing, with two lead smelting furnaces, whereas around the comital castle in Ghent specialized leatherworking emerged.[96] This production was partly for use in the castle itself, but surpluses were also produced for the market. As markets grew,

---

[92] Pertz, *MGH Legum*, iii: 698–700.
[93] Lebecq, *Marchands*, i: 131–134, and ii: 382–386.
[94] Claude, 'Aspekte des Binnenhandels', Kuchenbuch, '"Opus feminile"', 152–153, and Sabbe, *De Belgische vlasnijverheid*, 42–46.
[95] Wüstehube, 'Das Grubenhaus', and Chapelot, 'Le fond de cabane'.
[96] Janssen, 'Gewerbliche Produktion' and Id., 'Die Bedeutung der mittelalterlichen Burg', esp. ii: 282–283 and ii:304. Cf. for the rise of castles in this period: section III.1, pp. 64–65.

the effect was further concentration of industrial production. Particularly in the 10th to 14th centuries, during the heyday of localized banal power, castles seem to have played such a role, although perhaps not for long in the urbanized areas, when the cities took over that function.

In the high Middle Ages, in a long, gradual, and incomplete process, industries increasingly shifted from the countryside, where the main producers were peasants, manors, and their serfs, and craftsmen around monasteries and later around castles, to semi-urban localities and the rising cities. Only in a few cases in the far south-west of the Low Countries had there been some urban industrial continuity from the Roman period on, as in Arras, where as early as the 9th century wool was brought from the countryside to be processed by some kind of semi-urban cloth industry.[97] Tournai had hosted one of the state *gynaecea* in the Roman era, and in the early Middle Ages had a group of professional female textile workers on former royal property. But genuine, functional continuity from the Roman period cannot be demonstrated, and elsewhere it was clearly absent. Instead, new urban centres emerged, as with the concentration of textile production in Flemish cities such as Douai, Ypres, and Ghent, mainly developing in the 11th century. The increasing specialization, and the presence of markets, security, and privileges were important elements in this shift.[98] But why did the cities emerge as textile centres exactly in Flanders?

The availability of wool and dye stuffs may have played a role, although wool increasingly had to be imported after the embankment of saltings, the switch to cattle farming in coastal Flanders, and the reclamation of heath inland, under mounting population pressure.[99] From the second half of the 12th century, wool was thus mainly imported, especially from England, whereas dye stuffs were cultivated in many places and were relatively easy to transport. More important in the emergence of industries in the Flemish cities was probably the Flemish count's efficient government and the advantages available in the cities. Under the protection of the count's castles, the cities could offer producers a higher degree of security, markets, contacts, privileges, and more scale advantages than elsewhere. The rise of the woollen industry in the Flemish cities was also accompanied by a change in weaving techniques.[100] The primitive vertical loom used in the early Middle Ages and mainly worked by women was replaced from about 1100 by the horizontal loom. This larger loom, although more costly, raised labour productivity, but it required more skill and specialization, making weaving a man's job to an increasing extent and promoting its shift to the towns, where more capital and more scope for the division of labour was available. In these cities cloth was mainly produced by independent craftsmen, but by the 13th

---

[97] Hägermann, 'Grundherrschaft', 364–365, and Verhulst, 'On the preconditions', 33–41.
[98] Cf. below, p. 157, and also section VII.2, pp. 343–344.
[99] Verhulst, 'La laine indigène', esp. 301–303.
[100] Jansen, 'Een economisch contrast'.

century there was already some concentration in the cloth sector, with Jean Boinebroke in Douai as the most noticeable example of a powerful figure making textile workers more dependent on merchant capital.[101]

In the high Middle Ages, other industries were also increasingly relocated from the countryside to the cities, a process made possible by the growth of market exchange of raw materials, finished products, and food. In pottery production this shift occurred in the 12th century, when pottery was exported on a much larger scale. The rural pottery centre of Andenne, for instance, grew into a town, and pottery of the same type came to be produced in the cities of Namur and Liège. Another example of a rising urban industry was copper production, which already existed in early Middle Ages, but grew much larger in the 11th and 12th centuries in cities of the Meuse valley such as Liège, Namur, Dinant, and particularly in Huy, when copper, bronze (an alloy of copper and tin), and brass (copper and zinc) were produced. The fast-growing copper industry there exported its products mainly to Cologne, Koblenz, and further up the Rhine, and to France. Location was partly, but not entirely, determined by the availability of raw materials. The potter's clay needed for making casting moulds was available there. Calamine was found not too far away, in Moresnet and the area between Namur and Liège, and wood, and later coal, were also found nearby. The fast-flowing streams could be used for the propulsion of hammers.[102] Copper had to be imported from afar, either directly from the production sites in the Harz (Goslar) or through intermediate markets such as Cologne.[103] Tin also had to be imported, perhaps from the market in London, where merchants from Huy were active at least from the 11th century. Because it was necessary to import at least some of the raw materials, locating the copper industry in the cities was logical, since merchants and markets were vital for production. Also, demand by a relatively large and wealthy elite was concentrated there. This combination led to the rise of urban specialists working at a high level, of whom Renier de Huy was the most brilliant example. The copper baptismal font he made around 1115 for a church in Liège is considered one of the high points of Romanesque art in Europe, and shows enormous skill, both technically and artistically.[104] After 1200, copper production declined in Huy, and was increasingly outstripped by the textile industry, but in Dinant it remained prominent, and the town obtained a virtual monopoly on copper production and even lent its name to the 'dinanderies' that were exported to England and elsewhere.

In the high Middle Ages, the number of mills in the cities also dramatically increased. Huy possessed some water mills in the early Middle Ages, but around

---

[101] Derville, 'Les draperies flamandes', esp. 357–361.
[102] Joris, 'Probleme der mittelalterliche Metallindustrie', esp. 58–63, and Jansen, 'Een economisch contrast', esp. 5–6.
[103] Hillebrand, 'Der Goslarer Metallhandel', esp. 36–37.
[104] Timmers, *De kunst van het Maasland*, 200–205, and Collon-Gevaert, Lejeune, and Stiennon, *A Treasury*, 73–80 and 182–191.

1100, 4 new ones were constructed by the chapter and the Abbey of Saint-Hubert. In the 14th century, Huy had about 15 water mills, 10 of them located within the city walls.[105] In the suburbs of Arras, in the extreme south of Flanders, at least 17 mills were constructed from the early 11th century on, mainly by the Abbey of St Vaast.[106] Use of these mills was guaranteed by seigneurial ban, since the bakers of Arras were legally compelled to use these mills.

It is not surprising that this shift of industries to the cities happened exactly in this period, the 12th century. Agrarian surpluses per area were probably relatively large in this period, and these could be more easily moved because of the improvements in overland transport. The availability of food surpluses offered further possibilities for specialization in non-agricultural production, particularly in regions where agricultural development had been rapid or access to surpluses was easy, as in Flanders. A shift to the cities also became more feasible when transport of raw materials from distant sources became easier and cheaper. But most important, cities offered many advantages to producers. They had large concentrations of people, enabling lower transaction costs. There were more possibilities for specialization and division of labour. Moreover, they offered physical protection with their walls, particularly important as capital goods needed for production, such as brewing kettles, larger looms, and dye stuffs, became more expensive. Cities also provided markets and a favourable institutional setting for trade and industrial production, protected by the urban government, urban militias, and often the territorial lord.[107] Along with the presence of wealthy consumers, these markets enabled the rise of specialized production. Also stimulating production was the fact that some cities and burghers enjoyed certain privileges with respect to the countryside, granted particularly by the territorial lords in their desire to stimulate the cities. This complex of factors was most pronounced in inland Flanders from the 11th to 12th centuries on. This region had a relatively strong territorial lord, an advanced administration, early specialization, and strong urban growth. At the same time, the example of Flanders shows that in this process it was not only the pure forces of supply and demand that determined development, but power was also important: initially mainly protective power, but in the 13th and 14th centuries the power to compel the rural population was increasingly used.

Technology

Industrial technology had declined sharply, especially in the north of the Low Countries, in the centuries after the Roman era, when specialized industrial

---

[105] Joris, *La ville de Huy*, 298–301. On the diffusion of mills, see also below, pp. 158–160, and section VII.2, pp. 358–359.
[106] Lohrmann, 'Entre Arras et Douai', 1012–1050.
[107] Cf. also section III.3, pp. 120–122, and below section V.4, pp. 218–225.

production fell and techniques were lost. In the Carolingian period, however, there was clear technological progress, albeit slow and intermittent. Archaeological finds show that the average quality of ceramics from this period, for instance, improved.[108] The homemade, plain, coarse, poorly finished pottery of the Merovingian period was gradually replaced by harder fired, wheel-turned, mass-produced pottery.

Changes in shipbuilding techniques are harder to discern, although archaeology increasingly reveals more details. The numerous rivers, lakes, and inlets to the sea of the Low Countries were ideally suited to shipping, and the decay of Roman roads after the 4th century increased the importance of water transport. Still, boats were clearly smaller than those used in the Roman era. At the same time, this increased flexibility, further enhanced by the ships' flat bottoms, enabling them to land on beaches and shallow mud flats. Shipbuilding techniques varied little in the course of the early Middle Ages, but excavations in and around Utrecht have shown that the size of ships increased in the late 10th century. An early 11th-century logboat found there was almost 18 m long, and made out of a 14 m tall oak trunk with a diameter of some 1.5 m, shaped with axe and adze. This boat was able to carry about 6.5 tonnes of cargo, and its strength made it well-suited to the dangerous rapids of the Middle Rhine and the surf of the North Sea.[109] Perhaps these advanced logboats were the predecessors of the later hulks. In the last quarter of the 12th century, a major shift in shipbuilding techniques occurred, when the Hansa towns started to use cogs that were wider, had greater volume, and a higher board, making them more seaworthy.[110] Also, around 1200, a stern-mounted rudder was introduced, replacing the earlier, simpler steering oar or side rudder, and increasingly becoming dominant in European shipping.

Even more pronounced was the gradual improvement and enlargement of mills and their further diffusion from the 7th and 8th centuries onwards. As discussed above, many more water mills were built, and they also became larger and more efficient. The horizontal mills were small, simple, and relatively cheap, but were gradually replaced in the 9th and 10th centuries by vertical mills, thereby increasing their energy efficiency from 5–15 per cent to 15–30 per cent. The vertical mills were more complex and required a professional miller, thus promoting occupational specialization. From the 13th century overshot waterwheels were introduced on a large scale. Such mills, with the water channelled to the top of the wheel, further increased efficiency to 50–70 per cent, and could also be used with weaker water flows, but they were much larger and more complex than the earlier undershot mills. They required larger investments and higher maintenance costs as well as canalization of the water course and construction of a mill pond, water race, and sluice gates to guarantee

[108] Verhulst, *The Carolingian economy*.   [109] Van de Moortel, 'Shipbuilding and navigation'.
[110] Ellmers and Schnall, 'Schiffbau', esp. 353–359. Cf. also section V.4, pp. 222–223.

a regular water supply entering the mill from above.[111] Particularly in or near towns and near abbeys, these mills were increasingly used not only for milling grain or crushing malt, but also for industrial purposes such as fulling cloth or tanning.

Tide mills were constructed in the inlets of the sea. Probably known in western Europe by the 10th and 11th centuries, there were many of them in the estuary of the Scheldt. The earliest mention of a tide mill in the Low Countries is in 1146 in Antwerp, where the tide reaches 4.5 m. Many were built in Zeeland, near Zierikzee, and Tholen, and on the north Flanders coast around the mid-13th century.[112] In Zeeland Flanders, several were built by Cistercian abbeys, linked to their granges in the region and often used to power oil presses. Following their introduction in Normandy, England, and Picardy, windmills came into use in the southern parts of Flanders and Hainault in the late 12th and early 13th centuries.[113] In Holland the earliest mentions date only from the second half of the 13th century, but their later diffusion was enormous: indeed, they became the hallmark of Holland. Initially wooden standard mills, they offered some special advantages. They were cheaper than water mills and important where no fast streams existed or where water flows were too weak to power mills, as in the flat coastal plains. In these regions, where the wind was often strong, they made wind energy available for milling, industrial activities, and, later, pumping water.

From the 7th century on, there was thus a continuing increase in the number, size, and type of mills, driven by water, or later by wind, and they became ever more expensive to build. An important factor in their development was the increasing density of population and the parallel growth of cereal agriculture. This increased the quantities of grain, making construction more profitable, as in densely populated inland Flanders and the grain-growing north of present-day France, where windmills indeed made their entrance early and in large numbers. The high wages in Holland and Flanders in the period stimulated the building of mills, making it more rewarding to save on labour and avoid time-consuming hand milling, but the availability of capital was also important. Mills are very costly and exploitation is risky, requiring major capital reserves. Their construction was thus often linked to manorial and, later, banal power, which helped in concentrating the resources to build them, or to the availability of capital or capital markets, as found later in Holland.[114] Where this power was weak, or capital difficult to obtain, hand mills remained important, as they did also in the coastal areas where no fast-flowing water was found.

---

[111] Derville, *Douze études*, 74, Gies & Gies, *Cathedral, forge and waterwheel*, 33–35, 48–49, and 113–117, and Reynolds, *Stronger than a hundred men*.
[112] Lohrmann, 'Frühe Gezeitenmühlen', 517–528.
[113] Rivals, *Le moulin à vent*, 53–55, and Bautier, 'Les plus anciennes mentions', esp. ii: 606–620, and Malanima, 'Energy systems'.
[114] Lohrmann, 'Antrieb von Getreidemühlen', 221–232. For capital markets, seesection V.2, pp. 191–192.

The seigneurial right to compel people under his jurisdiction to use his mill was often enforced by severe penalties such as the seizure of wagons, draught animals, and grain, as happened in 13th-century Namur. This made the construction of a mill a profitable investment for the lord or the entrepreneur who obtained or leased such rights from him. It made this costly investment safer because of the stable revenues, and stimulated construction, which would otherwise have been impossible in such an insecure period with only small resources. But there was widespread aversion to banal mills and their forced use, as evidenced by fraud, evasion, and the willingness to pay substantial sums to redeem this obligation. Although a water or wind mill was much more labour productive than a hand mill and saved the peasants long hours of milling, the surplus it generated mostly accrued to the lord.[115] Moreover, the peasant had to carry his grain to the banal mill, often several km away, and endure long waiting hours, sometimes even days, rather than milling at home or nearby. The main beneficiary of the banal mills, therefore, was the lord, who gained from the high milling dues, the multure, usually 5 or even 10 per cent of the grain, which often formed a substantial part of seigneurial revenues.

This example again shows that the specialization, scale-enlargement, and innovation in industrial production during the early and high Middle Ages were often linked to the power of lords and religious institutions. Larger-scale production in the early Middle Ages was increasingly influenced by manorial lords: they required deliveries of products and organized production in their manors, and they tried to control the large-scale production and/or trade in industrial products. In several cases, particularly those that used difficult-to-obtain raw materials, production was embedded in large land holdings of distant lords or religious institutions. Thus, they secured access to costly or scarce materials (salt, iron, cloth) or profited from their production, as observed for iron production in the Veluwe. In the 9th and 10th centuries this development continued, with the lords further strengthening their control over industrial production, either by organizing production, introducing levies on part of the output, or obtaining control of raw materials (in their capacity as manorial lord or territorial lord). They increasingly controlled the trade in products and the energy sources (water mills, windmills, firewood, and furnaces) as well, mainly on the basis of banal rights.

Social organization also played a role in the specialization of industrial production, with large landowners and manors enabling and stimulating exchange and, as a consequence, regional specialization. This process of specialization, however, must not be overemphasized: it was slow and protracted and really gained pace only in the high Middle Ages, as the market gained more importance

---

[115] Cf. the discussion and calculations by Dockès, *Medieval slavery*, 174–196, and Genicot, *L'économie rurale*, iii: 99–103.

in industrial production.[116] In addition, the scale of production increased, albeit as a very gradual and intermittent process, and industries increasingly shifted from the countryside to the cities, aided by the protection afforded, the concentration of consumers, the possibilities for division of labour, and the presence of markets offered by the cities, especially in inland Flanders and to a somewhat lesser extent in the Meuse valley. In the development of industries, as well as that of agriculture, therefore, the role of emerging markets grew in importance, not only for goods and products, but also for land, labour, and capital. This is the area to which we now turn.

[116] Section VII.2, pp. 344–345 and 364–367.

V

The Rise and the Institutional Framework of Markets in the High and Late Middle Ages

In the 10th to 16th centuries the Low Countries experienced the rise of market exchange in land, labour, capital, and goods, albeit as a slow, protracted, and uneven process. This type of exchange became dominant in several regions by the end of the Middle Ages. In accordance with a growing historical understanding that the rise and effects of market exchange were to a large extent determined by the specific institutional framework in which this exchange took place, whether favourable or unfavourable, we will begin with an analysis of how this framework developed and the regional differences that occurred in each of the markets. Subsequently, we will use several indicators to assess the effects of the specific institutional frameworks on the growth and functioning of each market. The wider social and economic effects of the rise of market exchange and its specific organization will be treated in subsequent chapters.

V.1. THE LAND MARKET

Rights to Land and Their Transfer

There were no modern land markets in the Low Countries in the early and high Middle Ages. Much, perhaps even most, of the exchange of land took place within the family, shaped by informal or formal arrangements among family members, and hereditary practice. As in the other parts of Europe, exchanges outside the family were generally regulated by the multitude of social organizations we saw developing in the early and high Middle Ages, such as the manor, the village community, and the commons. Exchange of land among the elite was also largely dominated by non-economic motives, as with gift exchange—establishing a lasting bond between the two parties involved, with benefactors making a donation of land to a religious house, or with the establishment of a feudal relationship, where the social, political, and ideological implications of the exchange were predominant.[1] In the 11th to 14th centuries (earlier than in

---

[1] Bijsterveld, *Do ut des*, 18–27 and 32–36. Cf. more generally Rosenwein, *To be the neighbor*, 48 and 130–135.

most areas of Europe), this practice started to change in some parts of the Low Countries with the emergence of a land market. Until then, land transfer was primarily a social instrument, firmly embedded in social organizations and in the formal and informal rules they had developed.

Associated with this type of land transfer in the high Middle Ages, and in some regions until well into the modern period, there was an enormous variety of types of rights to land. In many cases several people could have firm rights to the same plot of land. Parts of the bundle, including the right to use, inherit, access, or harvest, were in separate hands, and even these could be divided among various parties. Thus, a single owner did not have full property rights to a plot of land, since these rights were never absolute or exclusive. This organization of land rights had all kinds of social and ecological advantages, since it prevented any individual party from reaping short-term benefits at the expense of all other parties or to the detriment of long-term social, ecological, or economic sustainability. Thus, it offered more long-term security to all parties involved, and to society as a whole. At the same time, however, it prevented the rise of a land market. The fact that several parties or individuals had to agree before a sale could be concluded must have hindered the closing of rapid and clear agreements, pushing up information and other transaction costs so that hardly any transactions could take place. Moreover, the parties involved often also imposed direct restrictions on the buying and selling of land on the market.

First, with respect to the sale of the land, the family had great influence among the overlapping claims and rights to land, and the prevailing belief was that land belonged to the family as a whole and should be kept within it. Restrictive inheritance customs and family claims clearly limited the possibilities to sell land. Relatives, sometimes even distant ones, could resist or annul the sale of land to anyone who was not a family member, and the family had to agree to the sale. It was also possible to claim back the land which had been sold by a relative, or buy it back for the same price, often as long as a year and a day after the original sale,[2] thus increasing insecurity for buyers. Neighbours and the village community also exercised some influence. Particularly in peasant-dominated regions such as Drenthe all neighbours or villagers had a right of withdrawal on the sale of land located within the village, and could buy it for the agreed price.[3] The feeling was that land should remain within the village community and not be sold to outsiders. Opportunities to sell land were even more restricted with respect to the commons. Often, rights to common land were linked to the farmyards in the village, and could not be sold separately, particularly to outsiders. Common lands were characterized by immutable rights to the land or periodic redistribution of the land by the community, the villagers, the commoners, and/or the lord.

---

[2] Moorman van Kappen, *Met open buydel*, 4–11.
[3] Heringa, *De buurschap*, 10 and 16 (examples from 15th century Drenthe). For the village and the commons, see above, section III.3, pp. 93–94 and 98–99.

These systems of inheritance and redistribution, as well as the communal and family restrictions on the sale of land, can be linked to peasant behaviour. Although peasants were not necessarily averse to buying or selling land, in general the family and communal restrictions on the alienation of land indeed fitted a peasant society where land formed the long-term security of the community and the family against the risks of life, and this security was valued above short-term economic gains.

With respect to feudal land, of course, there was also the influence of feudal lords. Until the beginning of the 13th century, it was, in theory, forbidden to sell a fief, and until late in that century, at least the permission of the feudal lord was required.[4] Later in the Middle Ages, when the practical function of the feudal system had largely disappeared, feudal lords still wanted to retain some control over the transmission of their feudal land. Transmission in their court and the payment of a relief on the investiture of the new vassal was obligatory, and feudal lords often tried to prevent feudal land from being granted to those outside the ranks of the nobility, or to religious institutions.

But most important of all the restrictions on the sale of land were those imposed by manorial lords, at least where manorial organization was strong. The lord had to agree to every sale of land (for example, in the county of Namur up to the 13th century),[5] and he often blocked the sale completely. In addition, manorial customs often prohibited the accumulation of land and the possession of multiple villeinage holdings, as well as splitting up standard land holdings, in order to prevent fragmentation of the obligations associated with them, thus curbing the growth of the land market indirectly. Lords were also entitled to collect a fine from the seller and an entry fine from the buyer of the land. These fines could amount to very substantial sums, thus making buying and selling land less attractive. In the coastal areas of the Low Countries, and particularly in Flanders and Holland, where there had always been few manors, or they had disappeared early, these restrictions were not very pronounced, but in the Guelders river area and the Meuse valley, for example, it can be assumed that in the high Middle Ages this influence was important because of the powerful position of the manorial lords.

Hence non-commercial systems of land allocation were predominant in the high Middle Ages, and the rules associated with them were often efficient in serving social and other aims. At the same time, they obstructed the rise of a modern land market. In the following centuries, however, at least in several parts of the Low Countries, rights to land became more absolute and exclusive, and restrictions and the non-market mechanisms for distributing land were gradually replaced by market transactions. This was a long and protracted process, but it started earlier here and evolved more quickly than elsewhere in Europe.

[4] Opsommer, *'Omme dat leengoed'*, ii: 422–456, and on restrictions ii: 516–531.
[5] Genicot, *L'économie rurale*, i: 125–159.

An important element in this change was the decline of the manorial system, which occurred in the 11th to 13th centuries in many parts of the Low Countries.[6] In some north-eastern areas, such as the Achterhoek, on the other hand, manorial remnants remained in place up to the 18th and 19th centuries, and continued to influence land transfers there. Another important change was the dissolution and privatization of common lands, making them much easier to buy and sell. But again there were significant regional differences. In Drenthe, the Campine and the Ardennes, characterized by poor soils and dominated by peasants and village communities, extensive common wastelands and village restrictions survived until the 19th century,[7] despite difficulties in surveillance and enforcement, increasing population pressure, and the growing opportunities for commercialization and the lure of short-term gains from more intensive use of the commons for market production.

In most regions, however, the dissolution of the commons advanced much more rapidly. Once Holland had been occupied, there were no longer any common lands of any importance, and in many other parts of the western and central Netherlands the commons were also privatized and parcelled out by the 13th century. In the Guelders river area, only very small remnants remained in the 16th century.[8] Population pressure and agricultural intensification played a role in the disappearance of the commons, but it was not a decisive one, since elsewhere, for example in Drenthe and the Campine, increasing pressure had been a cause for formalizing and strengthening a common organization. Rather, the early dissolution of the commons was found in regions where market demand was clearly felt, and there was a greater stimulus to commercialize the land. Second to this, the socio-political balance probably played the most decisive role. For example, the territorial lord could use his power and hold over the unreclaimed territory to push reclamation and privatization of these lands, as happened in Holland,[9] or the same process could take place in regions dominated by large landowners not interested in sustaining a peasant economy, as in the Guelders river area. Particularly after the dissolution of the manorial system, as the common lands lost their indirect value to the former manorial lords, these lords often opted for privatization of the commons, and they largely succeeded where village communities were weak and could not offer a sufficient counter-balance.

Another element was the disappearance of kin control over the land in most parts of the Low Countries, particularly in the 15th century, as the influence of relatives over marriage choices, inheritance, and property was reduced in favour

---

[6] Cf. the extensive survey in section III.2, pp. 86–92.

[7] Cf. the overviews by Hoppenbrouwers, 'The use and management', esp. 98–108, and De Moor, 'Common land', esp. 113–127. For the link with peasant strategies see section III.3, pp. 98–100.

[8] Van Bavel, *Transitie en continuïteit*, 356–368.

[9] Cf. sections II.2, p. 40, and III.2, pp. 83–85.

of the nuclear family and the individual.[10] In addition, real vassalage began to disappear, and from the 13th century onwards there was a relaxation of feudal restrictions on the investiture of those who were not nobles. The effect of this can be observed, for instance, in the Land of Heusden, a part of Holland. There, the share of comital feudal land in the hands of burghers from the city of Heusden increased from 2 per cent in 1375 to no less than 40 per cent a century later.[11]

Behind these apparent changes were the deeper, more fundamental developments of the period, changing the role of land in economic and social organization. Among these were population growth, increasing the value of the land, and making clear property rights to land more desirable, along with the territorialization process of villages in the high Middle Ages. In addition, the rise of the state and other mechanisms that created new social bonds became more important than those forged from shared property rights to land. Last, but perhaps most important, there was the rise of the alternative system of allocation provided by the market, with labour and capital markets making social actors less dependent on the land as a binding element, security, or instrument; the emerging land market offered to some actors a more attractive option, slowly eroding the importance of other ways of allocating and redistributing property rights to land in a continuous feedback cycle.

The regional differences in this process were associated with differences in the formulation and social distribution of property rights. In Holland, the early settlers already held clear rights to the land from the period of occupation in the 11th to 13th centuries, which was the consequence of the specific goals of the organizer of the occupation, the territorial lord.[12] Although these rights were not totally exclusive—since property rights to the harvest in the form of tithes, a small recognition fee, and territorial taxes were in the hands of others—these other rights were at least clear and largely fixed. There were no arbitrary levies or interference by lords, feudal elements were very weak, and manorial organization was never very significant. What little influence it had was further eroded from the 13th century onwards. Thus, overlapping claims and restrictions on the buying and selling of land were few, almost from the outset.

Because rights to land became clearer and more exclusive and absolute in this period, it became easier to delineate and record them. The first organizations to take steps in this respect were the religious institutions. From the 12th century onwards, more and more institutions proceeded to develop a full inventory of their land ownership and the revenues from it. They also tried to solidify their property rights by having written legal contracts of their acquisitions and donations, or by having their land ownership regularly confirmed in charters

---

[10] Hoppenbrouwers, 'Maagschap', esp. 94–96. Cf. also section VI.2, pp. 287–289.
[11] Hoppenbrouwers, 'Een middeleeuwse samenleving', 368.
[12] Van der Linden, *Recht en territoir*. Cf. also section III.2, pp. 83–85.

issued by the pope, bishop, or king, often copied in well-ordered cartularies.[13] This provided the landowners with strong legal weapons to defend their property if necessary against rival claims.

The Role of Public Authorities

In the succeeding centuries, states started to play a greater and sometimes even crucial part, in this process. The strong protection of property rights to land provided by the authorities, at least from the 14th century onwards, is clear from the opinions issued by courts of justice, the security against risk of confiscation by lords or other powerful authorities, and the protection enjoyed by tenants and landlords.[14] This strong protection, and the close involvement of the authorities in the registration of land transfers (see below), are closely related to the tax system. In contrast to the situation in England, for instance, where landlords succeeded in limiting the fiscal burden on land ownership, in the Low Countries, from the 14th century, most taxes were levied on immovable wealth—particularly land—in part because of the strong and successful opposition of merchants and urban governments to indirect taxes, and taxes on trade in particular.[15] In the coastal and river areas, such as Holland and Frisia, taxes for water management were also often levied strictly according to the area of land ownership. Because the authorities had increasing fiscal interests in land ownership, they were very keen to secure, clarify, and register property rights. This protection, however, was very different from the intervention of the state in the land market in early modern Germany and France, where territorial princes and the king protected peasant land ownership against the land hunger and claims of noblemen and burghers beginning in the early 16th century. This *Bauernschutzpolitik*, and the related support for peasant land ownership, was aimed at protecting the fiscal basis of the states, which increasingly consisted of taxes precisely on peasant land. In most parts of the Low Countries, however, in contrast to western Europe generally, fiscal exemptions for noblemen, clerics, and religious institutions were increasingly limited or even abolished. This had occurred in Holland and Zeeland from the late 14th century, and in other areas, where the socio-political influence of noblemen and abbeys was more pronounced, in the 15th.[16] For the state there was therefore no longer any fiscal need to protect peasant land ownership against these groups.

When direct taxation on land and other real property was put on a firm and regular footing—in the Low Countries generally from the 14th century—the state had to decide whom it should assess. This led to all kinds of hereditary and

---

[13] Lohrmann, *Kirchengut im nördlichen Frankreich*, 37–49. For the increasing use of written documents, see section V.2, pp. 185–188.
[14] Van Bavel, 'The land market', 129–130.
[15] Blockmans, 'The Low Countries in the Middle Ages', esp. 284–288.
[16] Bos-Rops, *Graven op zoek naar geld*, 76–77, 96–99, 225–226, and 234.

feudal tenure being regarded as simple property, aided by the gradual introduction of Roman law, with its emphasis on absolute, exclusive property and its strict division between property and usage rights. It should be noted, however, that this was more an instrument than an autonomous motor of change. It was only where non-economic coercion, control by lords, and unfreedom disappeared, and a commoditization of land occurred, often with the state playing a more prominent role, that it became possible to employ Roman law as a significant instrument.[17] Alongside the role of the state, the most important factor in the rise of modern property rights to land was thus the swift pace of the transition of society and economy in most parts of the Low Countries, and the increasing commercialization. Hence, in contrast to many other parts of Europe, from the 16th century onwards the only distinction that still mattered in practice was between property and short-term leasehold.

The crucial role of public authorities in the further growth of the land market can also be observed in the practical organization and registration of land transfers. During the Middle Ages, and in some regions even afterwards, transfers of land could be made legally valid and registered in many ways, depending on the legal status of the land: for allodial property a simple written agreement between private individuals or a notarial charter could be sufficient, for villein tenures transfer was by declaration before a local lord or manor court, and for enfeoffed land transfer was accomplished in a feudal court. When registration took place before a lord, it was often because the lord wanted to retain some control over the transaction of land and levying a transaction fee on the sale of feudal land or land under his jurisdiction, as was the case in many parts of the south. In inland Flanders, this fee amounted to some 8–16 per cent of the sale price.[18] The lord's hold was even stronger with respect to villein land, where manorial lords vigorously enforced registration of all transfers in their manor courts, not only because of the need to keep track of the obligations associated with the land, but also because of the entry fine they were entitled to charge. These fees were often substantial.

Contrast this with regions such as the Guelders river area and Holland. Here, manors had disappeared by the end of the 13th century or had never been important, and the role of lords in the regulation of land transfers was insignificant. Nor were notaries prominent in these regions. Unlike Brabant and the prince-bishopric of Liège, there were only a few of them, and sometimes the authorities even excluded them from registering land and rent transactions, leaving this task to the public courts.[19] Both urban and rural communities played an important part in organizing legal and administrative matters in this way, so

---

[17] Cf. Immink, '"Eigendom" en "heerlijkheid" ', esp. 76–83.
[18] Opsommer, *"Omme dat leengoed"*, ii: 533–553.
[19] Van den Bichelaer, 'Het notariaat in Stad en Meierij', 27–41, and Oosterbosch, 'Van groote abuysen'.

there was a dense network of public courts, often later recognized or incorporated by the territorial lord. Registration of private land transfers before public rather than manorial courts started relatively early in Holland, the Guelders river area, and the adjacent parts of the Niederrhein area. Initially, from the 14th century onwards, registration in aldermen's books became common usage in the towns, where the transactions from the surrounding countryside were also recorded. From the late 15th century, separate courts for rural districts started to produce similar records. The parties engaged in transactions of land increasingly preferred to have the transfer take place in a public court of justice, and to have it registered there, rather than doing this privately, mainly because of the greater legal security with respect to third parties.[20] The court books or protocols had legal validity and evidentiary value.

In some principalities, the authorities went a step further by making seizure after sale before a public law court compulsory, sometimes even on penalty of nullification of the sale. Also, the authorities increasingly compelled local courts to register all deeds enacted, not so much because of the direct revenues involved, but because of the fiscal interests of the government.[21] Through these registers the government was able to check the property returns of all taxable persons. In most of the north and the adjacent Rhineland, the registration of such transactions before a public law court had been made obligatory somewhere between the early 15th and the mid-16th century, which is relatively early compared to other parts of north-western Europe. A beneficial effect of compulsory registration was that information about land, and rents as well, was easily accessible from one central location, as opposed to the fragmented information from notarial records. Even worse was the situation in the Groningen Oldambt,[22] where not only notaries, but also pastors, city councils, and bailiffs recorded land transfers.

The authorities also reduced transaction costs by having areas surveyed. Again, fiscal needs promoted this, since state and water management taxes were levied in proportion to the area owned or used, thus giving a strong incentive to measure and register land. In Holland, public authorities took a lead in this by appointing official surveyors from the first half of the 14th century, and water management boards followed. In the 1540s almost all land in Holland was measured by professional surveyors, using advanced instruments such as the surveying chain and methods such as triangulation.[23] The results were almost as precise as the cadastral surveys of the 19th century. Since registers with numbered plots were drawn up at the same time, often accompanied by maps, major steps towards a modern cadastral register were already being made in the mid-16th century.

---

[20] Nève, 'De overdracht van onroerend goed', 27–29.
[21] Van Bavel, 'The land market', 131–132.
[22] Hartgerink-Koomans, 'Levering van onroerend goed', and information kindly provided by Otto Knottnerus, 9 June 2004.
[23] Van Amstel-Horak, 'De Rijnlandse morgenboeken', esp. 90–94, and Pouls, *Landmeter*.

There were also changes in the ways potential buyers and sellers of land, or landlords and potential leaseholders, were brought together. *Sub rosa* arrangements, such as those between landlords and sitting tenants or their sons, or implicit renewals of the lease, were increasingly replaced by selling or leasing through public bids, assuring landlords of the best possible lease price, and probably also increasing the mobility of land. In Holland, leasing by public auction of tithes, mills, tolls, and all sorts of excises began to take place as early as the 14th century, and for land this method became more common at the end of the 16th. Shortly after the Reformation, the provincial Estates of the new Dutch Republic even made this procedure compulsory for all leasing of possessions of former religious institutions. In several provinces, around 1580, it was decreed that public leasing should be announced in church well in advance, that the bidding should take place in the presence of government officials, and that no pact or arrangement should be made in advance.[24] All these measures taken by the authorities greatly reduced the insecurity and the transaction costs on the land and lease markets, and thus contributed to the rapid growth of these markets in the north of the Low Countries during the 15th and 16th Centuries.

The Exploitation of Land Ownership: The Emergence of Leasing

The emergence of more exclusive rights to land enabled changes in the way in which landowners used these rights. Modern short-term leasing in an open and competitive lease market did not exist in the high Middle Ages, mainly because of the lack of clear property rights. A medieval landowner had many opportunities to benefit from his ownership, but these were all embedded in a variety of social frameworks. For a peasant landowner by far the most common option was to use the land himself, often under firm influence of his family, his neighbours, and the village community. This practice predominated in peasant regions such as Drenthe and the Campine, and continued to do so until the modern period. Large landowners, on the other hand, did not work the land themselves, because their estates were simply too extensive, or because to do so would impinge on their noble status. In regions where the manorial system had developed, the work could be done by the serfs having their own tenements and working the demesne of the manorial lord. A landowner could also decide to hire wage labourers to work his fields, and either manage them himself, or have someone else do so. An owner could also let out his land for a fixed rent (*census*) or on hereditary lease, but by doing this he would lose the right to sell the land, to encumber it, or to pass it on to its heirs. He was entitled to collect a yearly sum, but the land itself was used by the rent payer or hereditary tenant, who could in practice be considered the new owner.

[24] Kuys and Schoenmakers, *Landpachten*, 26 and 34.

In addition to these options, in the high Middle Ages several forms of temporary grants of land existed, such as the *precaria*, mainly employed by religious institutions, or the *usufructus*. There were also the 'peasant fiefs', where the term of the grant was often limited and payment of a rent was specified.[25] But not much is known about these fiefs. This is also true of the *coloni* that appear in late medieval sources. Perhaps in some cases these held the land on some type of lease for a limited period, as suggested by the fact that from the 13th century onwards the term *coloni* is sometimes used for short-term tenants. But these temporary grants of land were clearly not identical to the modern short-term lease. The relationship between tenant and lord was largely non-contractual, determined by manorial custom, and it had clear overtones of dependency, sometimes even close to serfdom. In general, lease relations were personal relations, often of an unequal nature. Even if there was a kind of contract, this does not mean that these tenancy agreements were contracted completely voluntarily between two equal and free parties. Also, in practice these temporary grants for the most part allowed for inheritance of the holding, even if in theory the agreement was made for a limited period only.

Only from about 1200 onwards were these semi-permanent, personal, customary, and often unequal elements reduced, as the modern short-term lease of land started to emerge in some regions. Earlier, leases of complete manors had existed, as well as of mills and tolls, but now separate farms and, more importantly, parcels of land were leased out for short terms, creating much more mobility, flexibility, and competition in the lease market. In north-western Europe there were a number of adjoining regions where the short-term lease was introduced at an early date, from the first half of the 13th century onwards.[26] This area, which included several regions in the Low Countries, stretches from the southern part of the Lower Rhineland in the east, the Haspengouw and Brabant, and to the Flemish coast in the west, and then to the south, over Artois and Cambrésis, to Upper Normandy. The short-term lease became the common method for exploiting large land ownership there as early as the second half of the 13th century.[27] In the neighbouring regions of Hainaut, Zeeland, and Holland, short-term leasing was also introduced fairly early.[28] Outside this belt, short-term leasing was introduced later, in the Guelders river area (first half of the 14th century), in the county of Cleves (14th century), and in the county of Namur, where the real breakthrough did not take place until the beginning of the 15th century.[29]

---

[25] Reynolds, *Fiefs and vassals*, 62–63, 89–95, and 100–103.
[26] Van Bavel, 'The emergence and growth of short-term leasing'. For the social and economic consequences of competitive leasing of parcels of land, see sections VI.1, pp. 246–248, and VII.1, pp. 334–335.
[27] Thoen, *Landbouwekonomie*, 307–310 and 331–346, Despy, 'L'exploitation des *curtes*', 196–210, Reinicke, *Agrarkonjunktur*, 98–104 and 109, and Brunel, 'Leaseholding'.
[28] Delmaire, 'A l'origine du bail', 529–539.
[29] Genicot, *L'économie rurale Namuroise*, i:277–279 and 287–296.

Regional contrasts in the further development of the lease in the later medieval period were even sharper, and regions where it was introduced early were not always those where the share of leased land in the late Middle Ages became greatest.[30] Around the middle of the 16th century, the portion of total land leased out in the Low Countries varied from about 25 per cent to more than 90 per cent, with the average at about 60 per cent. The Holland peatlands, being largely peasant owned, and peasant dominated Drenthe, were below this average, at about a quarter to a third. The ratio in inland Flanders was somewhat higher, but still below the average, at about half. There were also regions where the figure was 75 per cent or more, sometimes reaching 90 per cent: the Guelders river area, the Frisian sea clay areas, the river clay area of Salland, and the sea clay area of coastal Flanders. In these regions, where large land ownership was prevalent, the short-term lease was often introduced relatively late, but quickly became very important time.

Apparently, a solid link existed between the social distribution of land ownership and the growth of short-term leasing in the 14th to 16th centuries. This link followed from the different choices made by the different social groups.[31] The peasantry was the only group where leasing continued to play a marginal role. Widows with orphans were practically the only ones among them who let out their lands on lease. Even at the end of the 16th century, the peasants still directly exploited as much as 80 per cent of their lands. Town dwellers also farmed the majority of their holdings themselves as late as the 15th century, when they were relatively modest in size and situated close to the towns. These towns were generally small and had retained many agrarian traits, including the direct use of the surrounding land by the burghers. The large Flemish cities formed the greatest exception to this. In the course of the 16th century, however, burgher land ownership in several regions became increasingly large scale, and town dwellers began to invest in locations that were further away.[32] This resulted in a substantial increase in the leasing ratio of burgher property, to more than two-thirds. In the south of Holland, where the growth of towns was exceptionally strong in this period, and where a financially powerful group of merchant-entrepreneurs arose who made large-scale investments in lands—primarily at the expense of peasant land ownership—the expanding lands of town dwellers were almost wholly let out on lease.

The sovereign lords, nobles, and large religious institutions, on the other hand, had leased out most of their lands for short terms as early as 1400 and usually retained only one home farm, which was worked by wage labourers or lay brothers. Thus, these large landowners, for the most part former manorial

---

[30] See Van Bavel, 'Emergence of leasing'.
[31] The following figures are calculated for the Guelders river area by Van Bavel, *Transitie en continuïteit*, 499–527. Cf. section VI.1, pp. 242–243, for the social distribution of land ownership.
[32] Van Bavel, 'People and land'. Cf. also below, section VI.1, pp. 259–260.

lords, had within a century almost fully switched to leasing. Apparently, this was more attractive to them than direct use of their land using wage labour. The social groups which could use their own manpower—peasants and some townsmen—were the only ones who did not switch to leasing. The social distribution of land ownership thus played a large part in the regional differences in short-term leasing observed within the Low Countries.

But why did these large landowners shift to short-term leasing so quickly? Sometimes the effects of demographic changes, such as high wages or lack of wage labourers (for example, after the dramatic population losses of the Black Death) are advanced as an important factor. This type of explanation, however, does not hold.[33] Many large landowners encountered difficulties in finding labourers at that time, and perhaps leasing seemed to offer a solution, but in the long term leasing was not a profitable alternative, since real lease prices rapidly declined in the period as a result of decreasing demand for land and declining food prices. Moreover, a lack of labourers cannot offer an explanation for the switch to leasing. This is clearly shown in the chronology observed in the Low Countries, where the rise of leasing took place during a period of population growth in the 13th century, with an abundance of labourers and probably low wages.

It is more likely that geographically more concentrated phenomena, such as the growth of cities, trade, and a monetarized economy, exercised an influence on the switch from direct use to leasing and the regional diversities observed in this, although money was not indispensable for the lease, which could also be fixed and paid in kind. The development of trade and cities, however, also indirectly exercised an influence on the rise of lease holding through the growth of burgher land ownership in the countryside. This burgher ownership was increasingly leased out, with coastal Flanders providing one of the earliest examples of this process.[34] Even more important was the influence of the rise of cities on the decay of the manorial system. This, together with the way the manorial system decayed, was probably one of the most crucial factors in the regional differences observed in the emergence of the lease. In regions where manorial organization was important, and the main instrument for directly exploiting land ownership, the lease became an atractive alternative means of exploitation when the manorial system was dissolving. In this period of dissolution, the former manorial lords often strengthened their hold over the land, partly through the crystallization of property rights, with the emergence of absolute and exclusive property rights to the land. This not only applied to demesne land, over which they had always had firm control, but in many cases also to the tenements, as demonstrated for the Guelders river area,[35] where the former manorial lords emerged as the main owners of the land.

---

[33] Cf. section III.2, p. 87, for the supposed relation between population decline and the dissolution of manorialism.
[34] Soens and Thoen, 'Leasing'.   [35] Section III.2, p. 92.

This situation was well suited to the introduction and rise of the lease. Alternative possibilities for exploiting land ownership had lost most of their attraction for the former manorial lords. This applies especially to exploitation through fixed rents. Large landowners, and particularly ecclesiastical institutions, in the course of the 12th and 13th centuries became increasingly aware of the risk of losing control over the land. This risk was enhanced by the use of fixed rents rather than rents that could be regularly adjusted, the latter reminding both parties of the nature of the rights to the land in question. Also, fixed rents such as most customary rents or hereditary leases became less desirable because of inflation. The period between the late 12th and early 14th centuries was especially notorious for its rising prices.[36] This rapid rise caused large landowners to investigate adjustable rents. Inflation also had a strong indirect influence on regional differences in the rise of leasing. If the decline of the manorial system took place before the beginning of the period of inflation, as happened in many parts of northern France and Flanders in the 11th to 12th centuries, exploitation through fixed rents still seemed an attractive alternative for manorial lords. In regions where the manorial system gradually disappeared, much of the tenements there, and perhaps even part of the demesne, was probably given out against fixed rents and was henceforth controlled by the peasants, who largely used the land themselves. The portion of leased land in regions like these often remained limited until the 18th and 19th centuries, as was the case, for instance, in inland Flanders. If, however, the collapse of the manorial system took place after this period of huge price rises, as in the Guelders river area, the option of fixed rents was no longer attractive, and the landowners—now well aware of the risk—immediately chose short-term leases for exploiting their demesne and the tenements, when they acquired control over these. Hence, the inflation of the 13th century indirectly determined some of the regional differences in the growth of short-term leasing.

In several regions, the lease offered the former manorial lords an instrument for securing their social and economic positions during the decline of manorialism. They did not necessarily lose from the dissolution of manorial system,[37] but instead in the 13th and early 14th centuries, by using the remaining manorial elements, engaging wage labourers, strengthening and enlarging their land ownership, and introducing short-term leases, they were able to secure their positions. The emergence of short-term leasing enabled the large landowners to abandon the manorial system, and at the same time to preserve and even increase their control of the land, as well as to earn a substantial income from the lands, just as the new large burgher landowners in Flanders did, because

---

[36] Fischer, *The great wave*, 17–29. See also section V.2, p. 195.
[37] Although this is often suggested in literature, for instance by Kriedte, 'Spätmittelalterliche Agrarkrise', 61–62, who argues that these developments 'veränderten die Klassenkonstellation entscheidend zugunsten der Bauern' (changed the class constellation decisively in favour of the peasants).

lease prices were greatly increasing at the time.[38] In regions such as the Guelders river area, where the manorial lords had a strong position during the high Middle Ages, they became large landowners who had successfully made the transition to short-term leasing in the later Middle Ages.

However, in cases where the large landowners/lords were too powerful, this would have prevented the rise of the short-term lease, since the preservation of the manorial system or other types of coerced labour, or even the (re)introduction of a manorial system, in many cases was more attractive to the large landowners than leasing out the land. As can be observed in parts of eastern Europe, the manorial system, enserfment, and labour obligations were introduced in the later medieval or modern periods, even where they had not previously existed, and this precisely in a context of growing trade and increasing demand for agricultural goods.[39] In regions where this occurred, the importance of short-term leasing remained limited. If, on the other hand, peasants were dominant in land ownership, they largely farmed the land themselves and short-term leasing did not develop either. The amount of land leased out in these regions stagnated at about a quarter of the total area, with leased land remaining an addition to owned land within a peasant structure. The further growth of short-term leasing thus largely depended on the power balance between lords and peasants, requiring a kind of equilibrium, backed by clear and secure property rights for the first group, and by clear and secure use rights for the second. It also depended on the lords losing their non-economic power over the peasant labour, and the peasants losing their direct, non-market access to the land. The rise of a capital market may have further improved the position of the tenants and given them some independence, thus also contributing to this balance.

Only where this balance existed did short-term leasing quickly grow in importance during the later medieval period. This shows how the introduction and availability of an innovative set of institutions does not automatically lead to its diffusion. This rather depends on the different interests of the social groups and their relative position. In the Guelders river area, a balance between these interests did emerge. The factors highlighted above were present there by around 1300, and the social balance was enhanced even further by the fact that neighbouring Holland offered the peasants freedom in its new reclamation areas and its booming cities. This reduced the opportunities of the large landowners in the Guelders river area to preserve or reintroduce forms of unfree labour in their region or to gain non-economic control over the land and its produce.

The organization of short-term leasing of land, too, was intimately connected to power and property structures. The exact arrangement of the lease system could differ greatly. The most modern form was the economic lease for a limited,

---

[38] Cf. for instance Irsigler, 'Die Auflösung', 295–311, and Thoen, *Landbouwekonomie*, 307–346 and 359–380.
[39] Sundhausen, 'Zur Wechselbeziehung'.

short period. In this type of lease, contracted voluntarily between two free parties, the length of the contract was generally from 5 to 12 years. The leased land, divided into smaller plots of some hectares in size, was given out for an adjustable, economic rent, more or less reflecting the real value of the land on the lease market. The tenant had no permanent rights to the land, and lost his right to farm it after the expiration of the contract. On the other hand, he had the right to be compensated for all the improvements he had made during the term. This type of leasing was found, for instance, in the Guelders river area.

In some regions, however, the tenants claimed stronger and more permanent rights to the land. This was the case where the practice of silent reletting or post-letting of the tenancy existed, with the tenant expecting that the lease would be continued under the same conditions, even without having to seek the consent of the landowner.[40] In Holland, tenants on short-term leases claimed this right of releasing, and their interpretation was backed by customary law. In some cases, tenants even sold the right to releasing to third parties or made it an item in marriage or inheritance settlements. To remain in possession of the leasehold, ex-tenants sometimes threatened or even attacked their successors, destroyed their crops, or injured their cattle.

In the north, in parts of Overijssel, Friesland, and especially in Groningen, tenants also had firm rights to the land they leased, especially if they owned the farmhouse, trees planted, and other improvements.[41] Lease prices there were almost frozen and leases were normally renewed or transmitted by inheritance, although in theory they were granted only for a limited term. In practice, this system of leasing led to a kind of hereditary lease or even outright ownership for the tenant. This contrasts with the situation in the Guelders river area, where the end-limit of the lease was strictly upheld from the earliest period of short-term leasing in the 14th century. Continuation of the lease there was possible only when the tenant had a strong economic position in the lease market. The system encouraged high mobility of land at the user level and open competition, but also offered security to both owner and tenant, unconstrained use of the land, and stimulus for investments. This system had grave social consequences, since it resulted in sharp social polarization, but at the same time also promoted the development of the rural economy.[42] In the course of the 16th century, this situation also began to apply to an increasing degree in Holland. This was associated with the disappearance of the original peasant character of the Holland countryside. The Holland authorities sped up this process by prohibiting claims to reletting or inheritance of leases and acting more severely against them, as one can see from the verdicts of courts and legal councils.

---

[40] Kuys and Schoenmakers, *Landpachten*, 23–25, and De Smidt, *Rechtsgewoonten*, 104–106 and 126–133.
[41] Formsma, 'Beklemrecht en landbouw', esp. 13–27.
[42] Sections VI.1, pp. 244–246, and VII.1, pp. 335–336.

The lease sum was usually fixed, either in money or in kind, but other arrangements were possible. Most important among these alternatives was sharecropping, with the tenant paying a share of the yields (usually half, or in less fertile areas, a quarter or a third), and the landlord providing a large part of the implements, cattle, and seed. This type of lease became dominant in many parts of southern Europe, as well as being in fairly wide use in the Low Countries in the 14th century, and its choice seems to have been connected with access to capital. It must have been difficult for a short-term tenant to procure working capital or obtain credit unless there was a well-functioning capital market. This difficulty was even greater for tenants than for other farmers, since they could not offer their land as security, and thus did not have the collateral to obtain loans. This problem could be partially solved through a sharecropping system. Of course, the tenant still had to bring in capital, usually half of it. Another possibility was to borrow working capital from the lessor through cash advances or the advance of assets, cattle, seed, or crops in the field, as in the Flemish system of *lating*.[43] Like sharecropping, this combined elements of the capital and lease markets, with the landowner providing capital to the farmer who also leased the land from him. This situation created ample opportunities for the landowner to exploit his strong bargaining power. It placed the tenant in a difficult situation of dependence and was much like a paternalistic leasing relationship,[44] rather than one that was determined by the market. Also, it could be one way to bind the tenant to the land or make him pay more than its economic value. Moreover, sharecropping resulted in high monitoring costs, including the need to control the quality of farming, prevent exhaustion of the holding for short-term profits, and enforce the correct sharing of the crops.

In most parts of the Low Countries, however, working capital seems to have been fairly readily available. There was a functional and accessible capital market, even in the countryside, and tenants were assured that the landlords would be lenient in remitting the lease sum in case of calamities, which could help reduce risks for the tenant.[45] Arrangements for the reimbursement of investments, careful registration of mutual obligations, and a good working system of guarantees must have further facilitated the procurement of capital, since this reduced the risks for the creditor and increased the credit-worthiness of the tenant. It is significant that in the later Middle Ages sharecropping disappeared almost completely from most parts of the Low Countries. Exceptions were found only in extreme situations, after the Black Death, and during or after wars, or in some of the most infertile regions, such as the Veluwe with its poor, sandy soils, where the practice

---

[43] Thoen, *Landbouwekonomie*, 575–588. More generally: Toch, 'Lords and peasants', esp. 168–177.
[44] Cf. Thoen, 'A "commercial survival economy" ', 128–129.
[45] Van der Woude, 'Large estates and small holdings', 193–194 and 204, and Van Bavel, *Mariënweerd*, 367–385. Cf. for the rural capital market section V.2, pp. 189–192.

of sharecropping persisted up to the 19th century.[46] Elsewhere in the Low Countries, the capital market offered sufficient scope to reduce risks and procure capital. The ample opportunities to obtain working capital also contributed to a stronger economic position for tenants, and further strengthened the balance between tenants and landlords.

The Mobility of Land in the Market

Price movements and the mobility of land in the land and lease market have not yet been extensively investigated for the Low Countries. A relatively inelastic supply is typical for all land markets. Consequently, shifts in demand as a result of changes in population size and technological developments are highly price sensitive. Only long-term changes in the demand for land can cause any substantial adjustment in supply. When demand increases persist, and prices of land rise for a considerable period of time, the pressure to extend the quantity of agricultural land through reclamation increases. Similarly, permanent desertion of land can follow in the wake of serious and protracted demographic contraction.

This pattern, which links the dynamics of land markets to long-term shifts in the land–labour population ratio, can generally be observed in the Low Countries. Both in the 13th and 16th centuries, rising population and increasing scarcity of land resulted in increased land and lease prices: in Holland nominal lease prices in the period 1500–70 increased by 28 per cent per decade.[47] This was indeed a period of huge population growth, as well as of technological innovations and increasing land productivity. Nevertheless, the link between demographic, economic, and technological developments and the price evolution of the land market is not as straightforward as it may at first seem—as is demonstrated by the strong regional variation in price movements. The pre-modern lease and especially land markets were influenced by a host of non-economic elements, such as familial restrictions, manorial customs, and power relationships, which interacted with the forces of supply and demand.

Ownership of land was not only economically vital but also lent prestige and social esteem, certainly to non-agricultural landowners. Besides its symbolic value to a noble, land ownership was an integral part of his power position, even up to the early modern period.[48] Land also provided social prestige for bourgeois landowners, who were eager to emulate the nobility. Emulation became less a factor in the course of the later Middle Ages, as shown for the entrepreneurs in 16th-century Antwerp, who invested heavily in landed properties for economic reasons, but earlier it must have been a strong impulse, as shown for patricians in

---

[46] Nicholas, *Town and countryside*, 337–338, Roessingh, 'Garfpacht, zaadpacht en geldpacht', and Van Bavel, *Mariënweerd*, 388–394.
[47] Kuys and Schoenmakers, *Landpachten in Holland*, 35.
[48] Marshall, *The Dutch gentry*, 93–115.

14th-century Ghent and Bruges.[49] Peasants, too, would have been very attached to their land, perhaps even as part of their identity, and they derived status from land ownership. This attitude was enforced by the fact that in the late Middle Ages local positions and functions, and sometimes also voting rights (most clearly in Friesland), often depended on ownership of land.[50] Only owners of land were considered members of the village community and could have a say in the decisions made by the village assembly or water management board.

Since land markets are immovable and land is very heterogeneous, they were never really open markets with large numbers of anonymous sellers and buyers.[51] Certainly, in medieval society, with its predominantly local and rural character, transfers of land, and especially buying and selling land, were governed as much by social and cultural considerations as they were by economic calculation. Often, there was a special relationship between the buyer and seller: they may have been kin or fellow villagers, or perhaps the seller was not free to act as he liked, but was constrained by customary preferences, pressure from a lord, or simply dire circumstances. The land market was segmented along the lines of legal categories of land and, related to this, according to the social background of the parties involved.

Between the high Middle Ages and the modern era, however, as part of the general economic and social transition, non-economic factors have gradually lost most of their influence on land markets. It can be assumed that in the course of this process, with markets in various parts of the Low Countries becoming more open and land transfer becoming less restricted, the volume of land markets grew and mobility of land ownership increased. It is possible to calculate the mobility of land in terms of its annual turnover on the market in a particular region, expressed as a percentage of the total area of cultivated land. In the Guelders river area, on average, 1.5 per cent of the total area was transferred in the market each year in the period 1515–57. This turnover was fairly high compared with the few instances calculated for other parts of western Europe.[52]

We are only just starting to understand regional differences in the mobility of land in the market. The degree of security and accessibility offered by the institutional market framework must have played a large role in these differences. It is clear, for instance, that public auctions of lease land must have increased mobility significantly more than *sub rosa* arrangements, and that the increased security and exclusivity of property rights to land did so too. Other factors influencing mobility of land in the market, however, have hardly been investigated. Among such factors would have been the influence of inheritance laws, and particularly the dominance of either monogeniture or partible inheritance. The role of the capital market in land mobility is clearer,

---

[49] Soly, 'Het verraad', and Nicholas, *Town and countryside*, 259–266.
[50] Hoppenbrouwers, 'Op zoek naar de "kerels" ', 232–236. Cf. also section III.3, p. 100.
[51] Van Bavel and Hoppenbrouwers, 'Landholding and land transfer', 20–21.   [52] Ibid., 28–31.

since the potential buyer had to find money or other assets to finance the purchase. Small plots of land were paid for in available cash, but the larger ones were financed principally and often even completely, through credit.[53] Also, the rise of the capital market in the 13th and 14th centuries, and the use of land as collateral, made it more of a commodity. Credit was thus crucial to the mobility of land and the development of smoothly functioning land markets. This did not produce a rosy outcome for all participants, however, since the close ties between credit and land markets could result in increasing dependency or loss of ownership by peasant landowners, as is shown for coastal Flanders.[54]

Among the factors influencing land mobility, population pressure also played a role. In general, there was a positive correlation: the land market appears to have been particularly mobile in times of land scarcity, high grain prices, and population pressure. Around the middle of the 16th century, a period of great population pressure, mobility in the land market became very significant, as we can see in the Brabant area around Antwerp and the Flemish village of Herzele.[55] This was particularly true for regions dominated by peasant landowners, who were desperately in want of land. More generally, land mobility was highest among peasants. Land ownership among the nobility consisted mainly of large complexes, often attached to an aristocratic mansion or jurisdictional rights, making them expensive and difficult to sell. Peasant land ownership was in some instances more than twice as mobile,[56] especially in periods of population pressure, probably as a symptom of stress within peasant society.

Perhaps even more crucial in social and economic developments was land mobility at the level of the user. The main determinant in this was the importance of leasing: the rise of short-term leasing greatly increased the mobility of land, as the turnover of land in a lease market was much higher than in a sales market. In the 14th century, the lifelong lease was still important, yet short terms of 1, 3, or 6 years were often used. In the 15th and 16th centuries, 10-year terms became predominant in the north.[57] From the middle of the 16th century onwards, there are also terms of 8, 6, or even 3 years, resulting in a reduction to less than 8 years on average. Longer terms can be found in the county of Namur (9 to 24 years), but these were still much shorter than the intervals between sales in the land market.

In practice, however, the length of leases could be longer than the nominal term, since the lease agreement could be extended. Moreover, in some regions, and particularly where peasant elements were strong, there existed the practice of silent reletting or post-letting of the tenancy, as observed above. As a result,

---

[53] For the capital market, see section V.2, pp. 191–192.
[54] Thoen and Soens, 'Appauvrissement et endettement'.
[55] Limberger, 'Merchant capitalism and the countryside', esp. 172–173, and Scholliers and Daelemans, *De conjunctuur van een domein*, 175–176.
[56] Van Bavel, *Transitie en continuïteit*, 418–423.
[57] Ibid., 536–537, and for Namur: Genicot, *L'économie rurale*, 280–281.

leased lands often remained in the hands of the same tenant, or his widow or son, for a long time; such lands did not enter the market, and their mobility decreased. This is also true of many of the large tenant farms in Flanders and adjacent parts of northern France. Here, too, continuity was often the rule and farms did not really enter the market, not so much because of customary claims by the tenants, but as a result of the personal relationship between tenants and landlords.[58] Landlords there often used the leased farms as a feudal status symbol and a rural retreat, and they relied heavily on such large farms for providing food. All of these required a secure, personal long-term relationship with the tenant.

This contrasted greatly with many other parts of the Low Countries, where the mobility of leased land was very high, not only formally but also in practice. This was the case in the Guelders river area, in the adjacent northern parts of Brabant, and in the county of Namur. In these areas, in the 15th century, a competitive, market-determined situation existed. Plots of land were rarely let for a second time to the sitting tenant or his son.[59] The landlord granted the lease to the highest bidder, regardless of the wishes of the previous tenant and of the rights he claimed to have. This applied particularly to situations where land was let by public bidding. In these regions, markets for leased land were much more mobile and accessible than sales markets. In the Guelders river area and surrounding regions, the mobility of leased land was greatest. There, leased land entered the market on average every 6 to 10 years, whereas land in the sale market was sold on average only once in 50 to 70 years.

The rise of the lease can be considered one of the keys to understanding the social and economic developments in the later Middle Ages in some parts of the Low Countries, not only because of the mobility it afforded, but also because of the strong competition it encouraged, and the opportunities it offered for accumulation and investment. The rise of modern land and especially lease markets thus formed a main element in the economic and social transition from feudalism to capitalism and the commercialization of the rural economy in these regions.

V.2. THE CAPITAL MARKET

Credit was vital in the emergence of a land market, since most of the land was being paid for by credit. Conversely, credit was often obtained by using land as collateral. Land and capital markets were therefore intimately linked. The same applied to the lease market, since the choice of type of leasehold, whether fixed rents or sharecropping, was related to the accessibility of the capital market. Sales of goods and products also often depended on credit. Credit thus formed

---

[58] Thoen, *Landbouwekonomie*, 567–574.
[59] Jansen, *Landbouwpacht*, 77–80. For Namur: Genicot, *L'économie rurale*, 283–285 and 292.

a crucial element in the commercialization process and in the rise of the market for goods in the high Middle Ages and the markets for land and lease in the 13th and 14th centuries. Further, the availability of credit could promote investments in capital goods, and, on the other hand, inaccessible capital markets or high interest rates could impede investments in agriculture and industries. This is not to say that these investments could not be made without a formal capital market. Resources could be concentrated by some type of coercion, as in the manorial system or banal lordship, or be voluntarily pooled, as done by village communities or water management organizations in the Low Countries from the 11th to 13th centuries, in order to allow for costly investments. Also, credit could be arranged in informal ways—between relatives or friends, or between lord and peasant. Since creditors in these informal systems were well-informed about the creditworthiness of the debtors, risks were limited, and credit was relatively cheap.

These types of pooling resources or informal credit, however, became less feasible as the inequality of wealth distribution grew and the scale of economic operations became bigger. This required more formal capital markets, with new credit instruments and the institutions offering protection and security to the participants in the market. More anonymous forms of credit and larger credit operations now became possible. The formal capital markets, starting to emerge in the high Middle Ages, reduced information asymmetries and the transaction costs of formal credit operations, which would otherwise have prohibited them. Moreover, a favourable institutional framework would help to lower interest rates, and combined with a growing accessibility of the capital market this would stimulate investments. This section concentrates on the emergence of the institutional framework of capital markets, and largely omits the informal forms of credit, of which we know little because sources are lacking.

The Emergence of Capital Markets

Accessible and secure capital markets emerged in the Low Countries from the 11th century onwards in a slow, protracted process. As was true elsewhere in Europe, their rise was impeded by the insecurity inherent in providing credit, condemnation by the Church of interest on money loans, contempt for credit operations, and, partly associated with this, the weak institutional framework of the capital market. These elements led to high transaction costs and high interest rates, slowing the growth of the capital market. These obstacles were gradually overcome in the Low Countries, as in some other parts of Europe. In the 11th century, a formalized type of credit appeared in the Low Countries, called the *mortgage*,[60] which was first used in the Meuse valley, and later extended to Flanders, Hainaut, and beyond. In this system, the debtor offered as security

---

[60] Vercauteren, 'Note sur l'origine'.

for the loan some immovable property to be used by the creditor. Formally, the creditor did not receive interest, and thus did not break the usury laws. At the same time, this type of pledging of real estate offered the creditor ample security, since he had a firm hold on the pledge. Religious institutions in particular used this instrument, mobilizing capital otherwise invested in land. In 1163, however, the Council of Tours condemned this method, because the income from the pledged property was not subtracted from the principal sum and thus constituted interest. Still, this instrument retained some importance, and it was heavily used in the 14th century by territorial lords, who pledged land, tolls, offices, and revenues to raise the liquid capital they needed for wars and state building.[61] The method eventually became redundant as new developments in the capital market increased trust and security, and allowed credit to be obtained without the need to hand over the security to the creditor.

Indeed, profound changes took place in the late 12th to early 14th centuries, a crucial period in the rise of a more open and extensive capital market in the Low Countries. In the first phase, these changes were led by foreigners, particularly Jews and Lombards, who offered credit not in an anonymous market but on a personal basis. Jews, being exempt from Christian usury laws, started to operate in the Low Countries in the early 13th century, although not in as large numbers as elsewhere in western Europe. They were mainly concentrated in Brabant, Hainaut, the Meuse valley, and the (north-)east. Their position was always precarious. As outsiders, often viewed with contempt or even hatred, they could only hope to rely on the protection of the territorial lord, which was exercised on the basis of his right to rule over the Jews. He profited from them by imposing annual fees and taxes, but often he was also one of their largest debtors, and prone to cancel debts he owed them.

As Lombards started to take over from the Jews the larger loans to elite debtors in the decades around 1300, Jewish moneylenders increasingly concentrated on local business, lending small sums of money for short terms on pledge or on security of movables, with interest rates being very high, around 65 per cent. Some exceptional documents from 1349 concerning Jews in Hainaut, show that 7 out of 9 Jews were active in the money market, among them one Jewish woman, and they had 390 outstanding debts in total, mainly smaller sums of a few pounds. Up to half of the debtors were female, and many of them lived in the countryside.[62] The economic hold of Jewish creditors over such poverty-stricken people, combined with latent anti-Semitism, provoked hatred of the Jews, which flared up from time to time: for example, in the pogroms of 1309 and 1348–9. Associated expulsions and massacres reduced the number of Jews in the Low Countries to virtually nil.[63] Some continued to live in the county of Luxembourg

---

[61] Kuys, *Drostambt*, 71–74 and 129–131 (pledging of offices). Cf. also section VI.1, pp. 266–267.
[62] Cluse, *Studien zur Geschichte der Juden*, 18–38, 50–58, and 132–160.
[63] Speet, 'Joden in het hertogdom Gelre'.

and the Duchy of Guelders, as well as in the neighbouring German territories, where they remained present in somewhat larger numbers and also held their position as moneylenders to the upper social segment, at least until *c.*1450 when virulent anti-Semitism forced them to leave, or to move to the countryside and small towns.

In the 13th century, Lombards gradually took over the role of Jews, and also settled in the regions where Jews had never obtained a strong position, such as Flanders and Holland. The first wave of Lombards came mainly from Asti, Chieri, and other Piedmontese towns, and often operated in consortia whose membership changed, primarily formed through strong family bonds. They opened dozens or perhaps even hundreds of small banking houses in the Low Countries, particularly in the last quarter of the 13th century. Around 1300, there were some 40 of them in Brabant alone, but also many in Luxembourg, even in the smallest cities, where they had bought a concession to operate from the territorial lord.[64] Lombards operated at all levels of the money trade, from the lowest to the highest. They lent smaller sums for short terms, mainly on security of movable goods or on promissory notes, as well as larger sums to patricians, nobles, and higher clergymen. By pooling money within their consortia, Lombards were also able to lend large sums, up to thousands of pounds, to territorial princes, to finance their state-building projects, at a time when fiscal instruments had not yet fully developed or were resisted. The Lombards provided the princes with the liquid capital they needed in their political and military competitions. Sometimes Lombards even succeeded in climbing the social ladder, by administering tolls and mints, entering the service of a territorial lord, and becoming members of the patriciate. This was the path followed by the Aretio and Solari families in 14th-century Maastricht.[65] Although the Lombards' position was slightly better than that of the Jews, it still was not secure. At best, their activities were tolerated, but if the debtor was too powerful and the debt too large, he might still default or have the creditor arrested on the charge of usury. Moreover, there always remained a threat of violence. In Utrecht, in 1267, for instance, three Lombard bankers were murdered by a mob in the cathedral.[66] This danger and insecurity resulted in very high interest rates. The three Utrecht bankers had charged 87 per cent per annum in the first four-year period of their concession, and 65 per cent in the following years.

High interest rates in turn often caused social problems. The authorities tried to counteract this by reducing insecurity and increasingly binding the short-term loans provided by Lombards to a maximum interest, mostly fixed at 43 per cent. At times, sometimes rather arbitrarily, creditors were condemned for exceeding this maximum: in 1280–1 in Ypres, two Lombards and eight Flemish

---

[64] Tihon, 'Aperçus', and Reichert, 'Lombarden zwischen Rhein und Maas'.
[65] Van Schaïk, 'On the social position', esp. 181.
[66] Melles, *Bisschoppen en bankiers*, 31.

burghers were condemned for usury.[67] Condemnations like these, however, became rarer as ecclesiastical courts lost their influence and secular authorities became increasingly reluctant to follow ecclesiastical exhortations on this point.

The Ypres example shows that the Lombards did not have a monopoly on credit operations. To an increasing extent local people became involved, and between 1249 and 1291 in Ypres no fewer than 5,500 debt recognitions are recorded by the aldermen.[68] These were mainly promises of payments at a future time, often at one of the Flemish fairs, for goods delivered or services rendered, almost always between inhabitants of the town. The role of local people extended even to high finance, as testified by the many large bankers from Liège, Artois, and Flanders, of whom the financiers from Arras were the most notable examples. From the early 13th century, at the latest, the Arrageois were advancing large sums to cities, lords, and kings. In the late 13th century, burghers from Arras, and especially the Crespin family, had advanced huge sums to dozens of cities in Artois and Flanders in the form of loans and life annuities. In 1275 the city of Ghent had debts amounting to 38,500 pounds, of which 37,700 were held by six Arras burghers. In 1304 Bruges owed 140,000 pounds, mainly to the Crespins.[69] Although default remained a problem, these loans were relatively secure for the creditors, certainly compared with those offered by the Lombards. This is reflected in the interest of about 10–12 per cent, which was generally considered acceptable, and up to 20 per cent at most.[70] An interest rate of 10 per cent at the time also applied to the capital of orphans deposited with the cities in the Low Countries. Because this rate was fixed and determined by the debtor (the city), it even found favour with some theologians, such as the Dominican Gilles de Lessines from Hainaut in his treatise *De usuris* (c.1280).

Thus, the attitude of ecclesiastics to interest slowly became more nuanced, as well as less relevant, as a result of the emergence of new instruments allowing for advancing credit without violating the usury laws. Most important were the perpetual annuities and life annuities secured on real property, mainly land. In western Europe the sale of life annuities by towns emerged in the first half of the 13th century in the border zone between the north of France and the south of the Low Countries, i.e. Picardy, Artois, the south of Flanders, and Hainaut. The extensive and detailed contracts for the six life annuities sold by the town of Tournai to burghers of Arras and Saint-Quentin in 1228–9 are among the oldest examples.[71] Since this method involved the sale of rent, and not interest on money lent, it was not generally considered usury by the Church. The theologian Gilles de Lessines, for instance, considered life annuities to be no more than an ordinary sale, provided they were sold for a just price. His fellow theologian and contemporary from the south, Henry of Ghent (1217–93), disagreed with de

---

[67] Wyffels, 'L'usure en Flandre', 867–871. [68] Nicholas, 'Commercial credit'.
[69] Bigwood, 'Les financiers d'Arras', and Derville, 'La finance Arragoise'.
[70] Wyffels, 'L'usure en Flandre', esp. 861–863. [71] Tracy, 'On the dual origins'.

Lessines; he remained clear in his condemnation of the selling of life annuities as sinful, based on the fact that the buyer hoped to get more from the transaction than he had paid.[72] De Lessines countered this argument by introducing the new concept of time preference, arguing that the money the seller of the annuity received at the sale was more valuable to him than future payments, even if the total of these payments was higher. This opinion would prove to be crucial.

Not until the 15th to 16th centuries did most of the resentment among canonists against lending money for interest disappear. Although the disapproval of unjust interest and taking advantage of other people's distress always remained, the selling of life annuities remained largely outside ecclesiastical criticism, apart from zealots such as Henry of Ghent. Around the middle of the 13th century, towns such as Arras, Douai, Saint-Omer, and Ghent were already heavily involved in life annuity sales, with the Arras burghers using them as a main instrument to advance credit to the towns. The practice spread to Brabant and Holland around 1300 and to the rest of the German Empire from the mid-14th century onwards.[73] This clear chronology raises questions about the underlying causes. Why was it that this instrument emerged first in the area of Artois and Flanders? One main reason was the formation of the towns as corporate associations, acquiring legal personhood in the 12th to 13th centuries and able to own property, enter into contracts, and sell annuities, and this development was strongest precisely in these regions.[74] Apparently, there was then enough trust that the town magistrates would honour the towns' obligations. The increasing expenses incurred by these growing towns in financing walls, infrastructure, civil service, and military duties must have been relevant too, and the apparent financial power of the Arras burghers, and the comparative stability of currency there, also stimulated the rise of the life annuities.

Life annuities were sold in the Low Countries in massive numbers from the early 14th century onwards, making credit at relatively low interest available to towns and other sellers. Short-term debts could be converted into medium-term obligations, while at the same time offering ample security to the purchaser of the annuity. Religious institutions in particular, with ample capital available, were attracted to buy annuities to secure a steady income flow, and they found numerous potential sellers in the cities and among private individuals needing to attract capital. The importance of this instrument, and the security it offered, becomes evident from the huge numbers sold. Dordrecht sold hundreds or even thousands in the 15th century, in order to finance works on its harbour, town walls, and bridges, and to fulfil its fiscal duties to the central government.[75] Each

---

[72] Wood, *medieval economic thought*, 196–197 and 213–215.
[73] Bangs, 'Holland's civic lijfrente loans' and Houtzager, *Hollands lijf- en losrenteleningen*, 19–27. For the effects, see also section VI.1.
[74] Tracy, 'On the dual origins', 13–24, and section III.3, pp. 111–112, for the towns as corporations.
[75] Dokkum and Dijkhof, 'Oude Dordtse lijfrenten'. Cf. section VI.1, for the dominance of Brabantine and Flemish creditors.

year, the town paid out between 400 and 1,100 annuities, usually taken out on two lives, sold in Brabant and Flanders. It is clear that in the same period private individuals also started to sell life annuities in large numbers in the market, but how developments in private and public markets influenced or reinforced each other remains a question to be investigated in the future.

Further Institutional Improvements in the 15th and 16th Centuries

A more favourable institutional framework for the capital market developed, first in the south-west (Artois, Flanders) in the 13th century, with Arras as the main financial centre, and then in the 14th century spreading to Brabant and Holland and later to the other parts of the Low Countries. This must have increased the security and accessibility of the capital market, and lowered interest rates in its various segments (see below). In the following centuries, that framework's functioning improved further, resulting in a larger, more open, and anonymous market, no longer dominated by creditors specializing in money trade, such as the Jews and Lombards. Intervention by the authorities played a large part in this. From the 14th century onwards, urban authorities especially became aware of the negative aspects in the massive creation of annuities and the overburdening of land and houses with interest obligations, and they started to make perpetual annuities redeemable, including the older annuities which had no redemption clause.[76] This measure improved the position of the rent payers. Increasingly, the option of redemption was even made compulsory, as ordained by central legislation for Flanders in 1529. Moreover, as capital and possible creditors became more widely available, the debtors acquired more freedom in bargaining and became less dependent on the creditors.

Some authorities also increased security by registering sales of annuities, a practice that was well established in Holland, the Guelders river area, and elsewhere as early as the 15th century, as was also the case with respect to transfers of land. In 1529, Charles V even made registration of the creation of annuities by public courts compulsory. Again, as with transactions in the land market, this legislation was partly inspired by the fiscal needs of governments, as they started to tax annuities. Because registration was undertaken by public courts, the role of notaries in this field was not significant, in contrast to early modern France, for example, where they played a vital part as intermediaries in the capital market.[77] The public registration of land and annuity sales in most parts of the Low Countries, and the monopoly local authorities held on ratification, offered the strong advantage of enabling possible creditors to see how many annuities were already funded on a plot of land or other collateral, since it was

---

[76] Godding, *Le droit foncier à Bruxelles*, 205, 213–216, and 220–231.
[77] Hoffman, Postel-Vinay, and Rosenthal, 'Information and economic history', 69–94.

clear what the jurisdiction was for every transaction.[78] This reduced information costs and increased security, thus further facilitating the development of a more anonymous market where personal trust was less vital.

In some parts of the Low Countries, as in Holland and the Guelders river area, it also began to be possible to sell annuities without land as collateral, funded on movables alone. This innovation was particularly important for tenant farmers, who did not own land to offer as collateral. In the Guelders river area, where short-term leasing became especially widespread, tenants in the 16th century were indeed selling annuities with only their movables as a security, sometimes even for substantial sums.[79] In some other areas, as in most of western Europe, on the other hand, ownership of land or a house continued to be required to obtain credit, except from Lombards at a high interest. This even applied to some big cities, such as Brussels: in 1606 it was still prohibited to sell an annuity without real property as security.[80] Urbanization, and the fact that land ownership was only one of the many forms of property there, were not enough, as security in the capital market and the guarantees offered by the authorities were also needed to make this instrument available.

In the 15th century, further innovations were made, as letters obligatory or IOUs became popular in the Low Countries, and these were increasingly made payable to bearer and thus transferable.[81] Debt assignment was initially not fully secured by legal enforcement, thus limiting the circulation of such IOUs to narrow circles of acquaintances. Decisive steps in offering full security were made in Antwerp in 1507, in Bruges in 1527, and by central decree for the Low Countries as a whole in 1537/41. The bearer now received all the rights of the principal, fully secured by legislation, thus greatly increasing the security for the person who took over the letter. From that point such titles could pass through dozens of hands before payment in cash took place. These IOUs were increasingly used to raise money for commercial or industrial enterprises, for medium terms, with not only land but also ships, merchandise, and even jewellery used as security. A main centre of financial transactions, remittance of bills obligatory, insurance, and other financial operations became the new Antwerp Bourse, opened in 1531. The Antwerp money market at that point held supremacy in north-western Europe.[82]

In the same period, certain types of credit emerged for smaller sums and transactions by retailers and craftsmen. From the late 15th century, we have the first concrete evidence that customers often maintained a current account with retailers, settled only from time to time. It is highly likely that this practice had

---

[78] Zuijderduijn, *Medieval capital markets*, 50–52 and 138–166.   [79] Van Bavel, 'Leasing'.
[80] Godding, *Le droit foncier à Bruxelles*, 284–296.
[81] Van der Wee, *The growth*, 337–349, Munro, 'The medieval origins', and Gelderblom and Jonker, 'Completing a financial revolution'.
[82] Van der Wee, 'Antwerp and the new financial methods', and Id., *The growth of the Antwerp market*, 199–207.

started much earlier. Probably in the 13th century tallies came into use in the Flemish towns to record debts and mutual obligations between bakers, butchers, innkeepers, and their customers,[83] and institutional landowners maintained current accounts for transactions involving up to hundreds of tenants, written down in paper registers. The tenants settled their bills only once a year or so, in cash or kind, with credit often amounting to more than the yearly lease sum.[84] Formal credit, too, became available for a large sector of society, particularly in Holland, where it was on offer even to peasants, at relatively low cost. In the Zeevang—not among the most advanced parts of the Holland countryside—around the middle of the 15th century, one-quarter of all rural households participated in the capital market, rising to 43 per cent in 1563, and they were able to borrow money at an interest rate of only about 5.5 per cent.[85] Holland increasingly took the lead in this area, not through sophisticated innovations and refined techniques, but through the high security and accessibility offered by the regular capital market and by the public authorities enforcing its rules.

To improve the position of the poorer people in the capital market, *montes pietatis*, or pawnshops, were set up, where only a modest interest was charged for loans. These were established in many Italian cities from the second half of the 15th century onwards, but they made their appearance in the Low Countries only from *c*.1550.[86] They were found only in the south, and even there many attempts failed. Probably this can partly be taken as showing that the capital markets were mature and worked well, particularly in the north, which meant this type of charitable credit was not as necessary as elsewhere.

Some authorities in the Low Countries tried to ban the activities of the Lombards, as in acts propounded in 1451, 1457, 1473, and 1511. These bans were generally revoked after some time, and perhaps were mainly used to levy new taxes and raise octrois, but still the authorities gradually acquired greater control over the Lombards for fiscal as well as social motives.[87] The maximum interest they could charge was further reduced to 32 per cent in 1549. At that time, the number of Lombards was already drastically reduced, particularly in the north, where this decline was evident before the early 15th century. By then, the high levies on Lombards and the limitation of maximum interest had reduced their profits, amd the growth of poor relief and alternative ways of obtaining credit had also made their services less crucial. These elements were apparently less developed in the south. In the principality of Liège, for instance, Lombards remained in large numbers, also in smaller towns including Visé, Maaseik, and Thuin, where they retained their monopoly on loan tables up to the late 16th

---

[83] Wyffels, 'De kerfstok', and Van der Wee, 'Monetary'.
[84] Van Bavel, *Mariënweerd*, 361–385.   [85] Zuijderduijn, *Medieval capital markets*, 171–178.
[86] Soetaert, *De bergen van Barmhartigheid*, 67–89.
[87] Boone, 'Geldhandel en pandbedrijf', 767–791, Van Uytven, 'De Lombarden in Brabant', 21–36, and Somers, 'Het laatmiddeleeuws pandbedrijf'.

century.[88] In the north, as a result of the development of formal, secure, and open markets, there was less need for such professional moneylenders who operated on a personal basis, at high risks. Instead, burghers, religious institutions, and princes now entered an anonymous capital market in massive numbers. This is reflected, for instance, in the declining role of Lombards in furnishing liquid capital to the counts of Holland and Zeeland. While their role must have been important around the middle of the 14th century, with 2,650 pounds of outstanding debts for the brothers Jan and Pieter Pussabini alone, in the following century the counts relied more and more on loans provided by the towns and by civil officers, and on life annuities sold to private individuals.[89] In the 15th century, they appealed to Lombards only when in extreme need, once all other options were exhausted.

This example shows that in the late Middle Ages the authorities developed new ways of financing their debts, which were needed to cover their rapidly rising expenses. As an alternative to taxes on capital, some cities regularly requested, and sometimes even forced, their own burghers to provide credit at low interest rates. This method can mainly be found in the older cities where non-economic power was strong, most notably in the Flemish cities. In Bruges, in 1297, such a semi-voluntary loan was used to pay for the construction of fortifications. In the late 15th century, there was again a wave of forced loans to the Flemish cities, often converted into perpetual annuities, as well as in Utrecht, where in 1481, 1492, and 1495 hundreds of burghers were each forced to make loans to the city.[90] Most of them were patricians and derived some benefit from the situation, including opportunities to exercise influence on the town government and the use of public resources, and perhaps also to take preference over others as excises were leased out or public works were put out to contract. This has been detailed for Bruges in the late 15th century, where a small group of urban creditors used their leading participation in the urban debt in order to strengthen their political power.[91] Moreover, because some of the town's funds were used to finance representation, clothes and travel expenses of the same elite, this could produce an undesirable mix of interests.

Thus, the urban capital market sometimes tended to shift towards forcing and profiteering. Most cities in the Low Countries tried to avoid this, however, preferring to sell life and perpetual annuities in the open market. In the long run this strategy potentially offered much better opportunities for obtaining credit. Despite huge debts, and interest payments which often absorbed 30–50 per cent of the urban revenues, as in 's-Hertogenbosch, Antwerp, and Dordrecht

---

[88] Lejeune, *Le formation du capitalisme*, 69–75.
[89] Bos-Rops, *Graven op zoek naar geld*, 39, 93, 208, 232, and 240–241.
[90] Berents, 'Gegoede burgerij in Utrecht', and Blockmans, 'Nieuwe gegevens'.
[91] Derycke, 'The public annuity market', 176–177.

Manors and Markets 191

c.1500, towns still succeeded in selling new annuities.[92] Also, they were able to attract credit at low costs, at interest rates of 5 per cent (as in Bruges in the late 15th century) or 5–6.7 per cent (in 's-Hertogenbosch), rates also found in the southern German towns, for instance. In the 16th century, the annuity market in Holland had become very open, and about half the annuities were sold to people living outside the province, often in Brabant and Flanders,[93] perhaps because individuals there had accumulated more wealth, but also because the institutional organization of Holland capital markets offered these creditors the security they desired. In the later 16th century these sales from Holland to non-residents declined; in Haarlem and Dordrecht 80 per cent of annuities were sold within Holland, mainly to buyers resident there. Perhaps this was the result of the wealth accumulation now taking place in the Holland towns and the firmer grip secured by the local elite on the town finances, but the topic requires further investigation.

Since cities had hardly any land to offer as collateral, urban excises were used to fund the annuities, in Flanders and Artois as early as the second half of the 13th century, and even more significantly from the 14th century onwards in Holland, where cities were less able to force their burghers to advance them credit. It is exceptional, from a European perspective, that annuities were also developed for use at a higher political level: that of the province, again most notably in Holland.[94] Central authorities in the Low Countries were not able to force their subjects to advance credit because their power was fragmented and various interest groups exercised influence, so they also entered the open market and tried to offer security to creditors to attract capital. The provincial estates of Holland were especially successful in this respect. Already in the 14th century the count of Holland had used the cities as intermediaries to sell annuities in the capital market, but in the course of the 15th to 16th centuries the estates of Holland developed the instruments to directly fund debts on future tax revenues at the provincial level. These debts would total as much as 12 times the annual provincial revenues, and this at low cost, usually 6.25 per cent interest, reflecting the trust placed in this organization.

There are other quantitative measures of the functioning of the capital market. Differences in interest rates between town and countryside were negligible in Holland. There were no differences between the interest rates in the town of Edam and the surrounding countryside of the Zeevang, for instance.[95] In the first half of the 16th century, average interest rates in Edam were 5.6 to 5.7 per cent, and in the Zeevang they fluctuated between 5.3 and 5.8 per cent. The near

---

[92] Hanus, *Tussen stad en eigen gewin*, 35–39.
[93] Van der Heijden, *Geldschieters van de stad*, 152–189 and 197–203, and Hanus, *Tussen stad en eigen gewin*, 51–57.
[94] J. Zuijderduijn, *Medieval capital markets*, which nuances and extends the pioneering work by Tracy, *A financial revolution*. For more on political fragmentation, see section III.1, pp. 72–75.
[95] Zuijderduijn, *Medieval capital markets*, pp. 242–246.

Table 5.1 Interest rate percentages for Flanders and Holland, 13th to 16th centuries (perpetual annuities, redeemable, secured on landed property, and sold in the private market)

Century	Flanders	Holland
Late 13th	10 %	10 %
Early 14th		10
Mid-14th		10
Late 14th		8 (approx.)
Early 15th	8	7.5 (approx.)
Mid-15th		7 (approx.)
Late 15th		6.2
Early 16th		5.6
Mid-16th		5.6
Late 16th	6.3	

Sources: Thoen and Soens, 'Appauvrissement et endettement', 709–712, Thoen, *Landbouwekonomie*, 911–916, Zuijderduijn, *Medieval capital markets*, 175–179.

absence of rent differentials shows how the capital market was better integrated in Holland than elsewhere, both between town and countryside and among the various areas, confirming our observations about its favourable institutional framework. More generally, the interest rates in the Low Countries show a clear decline from the 13th century to the 16th (see Table 5.1).

Figures on interest rates are difficult to compare between regions and countries, since they relate to different types of annuities and their purchasers, but it is clear that the sharp decline in the cost of capital was a general pattern in Europe in the late 14th and early 15th centuries. Probably the rapid decline in interest rates after 1350 can to a large extent be ascribed to the population decline of the Black Death and the changing balance between population and capital, found all over Europe. However, the decline in the Low Countries and England was much more pronounced than in France and Italy. And, even more interesting, there was no rise in interest rates in the Low Countries in the 16th century as population numbers started to rise again. Instead, the rates declined even further, in contrast to developments in Italy, for instance.[96] This points to the fact that institutional changes and increasing security in the capital market were more crucial in the decline in interest rates than were population developments. This applies most clearly to Holland, where the population decline after 1350 was very limited compared to other parts of western Europe, and numbers increased rapidly from the 15th century onwards,[97] yet interest rates declined there to

---

[96] Van Zanden, 'Common workmen', and Clark, 'The cost of capital', esp. 271–276.
[97] For the exceptional demographic developments in Holland, see section VI.2, p. 283.

a level even lower than elsewhere, making capital cheap and investments an attractive option.

Coin Production

In monetary transactions the lack of availability of coins was a serious problem. In early medieval western Europe, the supply of precious metals was limited and few coins were available. Particularly from the middle of the 6th century, very few were minted. Gold and silver were hoarded, used as status symbols or gifts, or for political payments. The total number of coins struck is difficult to estimate, but must have been small. Perhaps the scarcity of coins was less severe in the Low Countries than elsewhere, however, since they were relatively well-endowed with mints and coins in the early Middle Ages. In the Merovingian period minting was organized by *monetarii*, private entrepreneurs, possibly authorized by the king to supervise a mint. A relatively large number of these *monetarii* were active in the regions that were becoming the heartlands of economic and political power: the Meuse valley and the Guelders river area. Twelve apiece are known for Merovingian Huy and Maastricht, and some also for Dinant, Namur, Nijmegen, Dorestad, and Tiel.[98] Particularly at the end of the 8th century, as coin production increased further, Dorestad became the most prolific mint in the north of the Frankish Empire, producing some larger golden coins (the *tremisses*, worth one-third of a shilling), and from the second half of the 7th century also millions of small silver coins (the pennies).

At that time, from Pepin onwards, minting was brought under royal control and remained a royal prerogative, except in Frisia, where central power was weak and minting remained a private enterprise. The minters there operated like entrepreneurs, and members of the public were free to bring bullion to the mint. The only check on quality was the social control exercised by the community and the market.[99] Elsewhere, however, minting was increasingly centralized and brought under state control. This control was also apparent in the regulation of the monetary system, as Charlemagne introduced an account system of 1 pound = 20 shillings = 240 pennies, which remained dominant for the next millennium. In practice, only the silver penny was actually being minted at that time. Gold coins were very seldom struck in the Carolingian Empire, except in the royal palace at Aachen (mainly to enhance imperial prestige) and at Dorestad, where gold shillings were minted from 830 to 900.[100] In Frisia, on the other hand, a large number of imitations of the gold shilling were struck, probably mainly for commercial purposes in international trade. But, apart from

---

[98] Dhondt, 'L'essor urbain', Spufford, *Money*, 19–30, and Pol, 'De verspreidingsgebieden'. For the central position of these regions, see section III.1, pp. 53–56.
[99] Henstra, *The evolution*, 86–91.
[100] Grierson, 'The gold solidus', and Coupland, 'Dorestad in the ninth century'.

this, silver coins became dominant and remained so until far into the late Middle Ages. The Carolingian coins were highly uniform, since weight and thickness were fixed by the king. Also, minting within the empire was centralized and the number of mints limited to better control minting. At times, a complete recoinage was ordered as part of the monetary policy and to stop counterfeiting. Minting offences were severely punished. Partly because of their uniformity, these coins circulated over very large distances, as shown by the origin of coins found in hoards. For instance, the 145 coins found in the Drenthe peatland were probably lost there around 890 and originated mainly from Dorestad, but there were also coins from Visé and Bastogne, and even from Auxerre and Milan.[101] The hoard contained only one gold coin, reflecting the shift to silver in the Carolingian period.

Total numbers of coins in circulation in the Carolingian period remained rather limited, just enough to allow money to function as a standard of value and a means to store wealth, but only to a lesser extent was it used as a medium of exchange. In the next century the numbers of coins struck stagnated or even decreased, at least up to the 960s, until veins of silver were found at Goslar in the Harz Mountains. These coins were now minted by a variety of polities, since the right of minting, along with the other regalia, came into the hands of the territorial lords, or sometimes of abbeys or cities, producing all kinds of coins in small numbers. The fragmentation of central power thus led to a decentralization of monetary policy. The uniformity of coins gave way to a diversity in weight, appearance, and thickness. Total numbers struck dwindled, particularly in Frisia, where production in the 10th and 11th centuries was still considerable but then decreased rapidly. In this period relatively many coins came to be struck in the developing towns in the Meuse valley, by the bishop of Liège, and from the beginning of the 11th century, to a lesser extent, in Artois and Flanders by the count of Flanders.[102] Within the Low Countries, there was thus a shift of minting to the south. Flanders in this period apparently had a favourable trade balance, and hence the silver available for minting, but elsewhere there seems to have been a decline in coin production, mainly because of lack of silver.

The scarcity of coins was felt more sharply when demand rose as a result of the growth of population and economic activities in the 11th to 12th centuries. Ways were developed to circumvent this scarcity. Payments were concentrated at times and places where money was available, most notably at fairs. This resulted in chains of payments. Precious stones and valuable objects were also used in transactions. The Bishop of Liège, when buying properties from Godfried of Bouillon in 1098, paid in gold plates taken from the shrine of the patron saint of the bishopric, as well as in chalices and gold crosses, thus making hoarded precious metals available for economic traffic. Horses, fine textiles, pepper, and even books

---

[101] Van Gelder and Boersma, *Munten in muntvondsten*, 38–41.
[102] Spufford, *Money and its use*, 85–86 and 96–97.

were also used as payment. Many monetary obligations, such as lease sums, were paid in kind, a practice that remained important far into the late Middle Ages, and even longer in regions where trade was weak and markets scarce.[103] But even if payments were not made in coins, the value was still expressed in money. People were aware of the monetary value of goods and services, even if barter was used.

From the 1160s onwards, coining started to gain momentum again, particularly in Flanders and Artois. The influx of silver from newly opened mines in the Harz and Hungary alleviated the scarcity of silver, especially in Flanders and Artois, where growing economic activities made it possible to attract bullion. The right to mint became one of the main sources of income for territorial lords, accounting for anything between 10 and 70 per cent of their total revenues. Around the middle of the 14th century, for instance, the Count of Flanders received 15–20 per cent of his income from this lucrative prerogative.[104] The actual minting was done by private entrepreneurs, paying to the territorial lord for their concession a sum that varied between 1 and 12 per cent of the nominal value of the coins struck. This sum, the seignorage, and the profit of the moneyer were obtained from the difference between the nominal and intrinsic value of the coins. Hence the territorial lord could gain by reducing the intrinsic value, about which he could decide himself, as well as from the thickness and exchange rate of the coins and the extent of the seignorage. This situation, and the scarcity of silver, resulted in a constant reduction in the weight or silver content of coins. Around the year 1000 in Flanders, for instance, the penny weighed 1.2 g, but around 1200 only 0.45 g. From 1180 to the early 14th century, prices kept rising, at about 0.5 per cent per annum.[105] This inflation brought an additional advantage to the territorial lord, since it reduced the relative weight of his debts.

Debasements could also be an instrument of monetary warfare: including those by Philip the Bold in late 14th century Flanders, which in turn were forced by debasements in France. This caused a bullion flow from Brabant to Flanders, and destabilized the monetary structure of Brabant.[106] Currency instability was detrimental to economic growth, and awareness of this in the late Middle Ages was articulated most clearly in the handbook *De moneta*, written by the Norman cleric Nicolas Oresme in 1358. He showed how increases in the nominal supply of money enriched the territorial lord at the expense of his subjects and the development of trade. He argued that it was not the prince, but only the community which had the right to decide about alterations to the coinage. His contemporary, Philip of Leyden, the legal adviser to the Count of Holland, on the other hand, fiercely defended the right of the territorial lord to act as he pleased in monetary matters.[107]

---

[103] Ibid., 98–99, and for the late Middle Ages: Van Bavel, *Transitie*, 558–562.
[104] Van Werveke, 'Currency manipulation', 115–127.   [105] Fischer, *The great wave*, 17–19.
[106] Cockshaw, 'A propos de la circulation', nuancing the deliberateness of this action.
[107] Wood, *Medieval economic thought*, 104–107, and Leupen, *Philip of Leyden*, 223–224.

The clash of interests between the territorial lord, who gained from devaluation, and entrepreneurs and merchants, hurt by this policy and desiring a strong, stable currency, was fought not only in theory, but also in practice. From the 13th century, both in Holland and in Flanders, count and city governments regularly deliberated on these matters,[108] with the latter representing the interests of entrepreneurs and merchants. The counts recognized that the cities were crucially important in providing tax revenues and credit to them, and therefore that they could not unilaterally change the coins or exchange rates, despite Philip of Leyden's advice. The counterweight offered by the cities was strongest in Holland and Flanders as a result of the significant urbanization, the cities' economic and fiscal power, and their political influence on monetary policy through their position in the estates.[109] Minting came to be regarded as a public service there and hence monetary stability was relatively high, forming a contrast with the soaring inflation elsewhere. The opportunistic behaviour of the territorial lords in this field was becoming more the exception than the rule. This shows, once again, the importance of an equilibrium between interest groups in the development of favourable economic institutions.

Thus, the fragmentation of minting proved positive, since urban governments and merchants were better able to promote their interests within their relatively small principality rather than facing one strong central ruler who would dismiss possible opposition. However, this fragmentation also resulted in a huge diversity of coins, which led to uncertainty about unfamiliar coins and high information and exchange costs. The exchangers and the speculators tried to profit from changes in exchange rates. Money changers appeared in the Low Countries from the late 12th century onwards. They were granted a concession by the territorial lord or city, often on payment of a rent or tax. There were changers in Arras from 1180 onwards, in Nivelles in 1182, and in other cities in Artois, Flanders, and Brabant they appeared in the 13th century.[110] In Bruges, 4 exchanges operated around 1320, and another 16 were sublicensed by the holders of the concession. At the Torhout fair, 28 exchange booths were erected, testifying to the growth in the numbers of changers. Their main occupation was changing coins at a rate fixed by the authorities, and they were expected to destroy counterfeit coins. They were allowed to charge a small commission (0.5 to 3 per cent), although some probably engaged in fraud. Some money changers also developed into financial intermediaries and cashiers, particularly at the local level. In Bruges, centre of international commerce and finance and host to Italian merchant bankers, some changers even adopted an advanced system of deposit banking, with money on deposit assigned to creditors. As early as the 14th century, these money changer/bankers each had

---

[108] Wyffels, 'Contribution'. [109] Spufford, 'Coinage', and Blockmans, 'La participation'.
[110] Van Uytven, 'Geldhandelaars en wisselaars'.

dozens or even a few hundred accounts.[111] Women played a prominent role as partners, managers, or even independent money changer/bankers. This system developed in Bruges not only because of the available financial institutions, but also because Flemish inheritance law and its concept of limited partnership helped reduce the risks and effects of bankruptcy in this insecure business. Findings for Bruges, however, cannot be generalized. Methods of banking were not very advanced in other late medieval cities, not even in a large city such as Ghent, and the number of money changer/bankers remained small.

From the late 14th century onwards, the number of money changers in the Low Countries declined. Monetary unions and the increasing dominance of a single gold coin reduced demand for their services. In the north in particular, urban and central authorities started to appoint official city changers, who often had a monopoly in this area and whose activities were strictly regulated through a multitude of laws. Since they also played a role in the sale of annuities and levying urban taxes, they often had ample capital at their disposal and were better placed to develop into cashiers, thus replacing the earlier private money changers.

In this period, the possible problems resulting from the political fragmentation and the absence of a single strong, stable coinage minted in the Low Countries were increasingly overcome. The monetary stability forced by interest groups played a positive role, as did the increasing dominance of foreign gold coins, such as the French écu from the first half of the 14th century, the English noble, and the Rhine guilder.[112] This period saw the rise of the gold coin for paying larger amounts, after silver had been dominant for centuries. A select group of foreign gold coins became widely used in the Low Countries as real coins used for payment, but even more as a measure to express monetary amounts, helping to lower information costs. Most of the long-term financial obligations were expressed in these coins because of their stability. Territorial lords from the Low Countries were increasingly minting their own versions of these gold coins, although these were devalued in the course of time. Ways were also developed to get around the difficulties of comparing coins by using money of account, which was often linked to a strong foreign coin.[113] In addition, monetary unions and conventions were developed, such as those between Flanders and Brabant from 1299 onwards. The two started to mint a common silver groat, the *leeuwengroot*, which was very successful, with no fewer than 60 million struck by 1365.[114] This monetary union was later undermined by Philip the Bold, but the unification of Flanders, Brabant, and Holland under the Burgundians around 1430 brought a final solution to monetary problems here. This applied even more to the first half

---

[111] De Roover, *Money, banking and credit*, 202–205 and 247–283. See also Aerts, 'Middeleeuwse bankgeschiedenis', nuancing the generality of De Roover's findings, and Murray, 'Family, marriage and moneychanging', 115–125, for the social context.
[112] Spufford, *Money and its use*, 267–282 and 320.   [113] Henstra, *The evolution*, 140–149.
[114] Baerten, *Muntslag en muntcirculatie*, 37–41 and 78–81.

of the 16th century, when most of the Low Countries were conquered/united by the Habsburgs and the stable carolus guilder became dominant. There was a risk that minting in the Low Countries might now become an instrument of dynastic and imperial policy, not necessarily favourable to trade and economic interests, but in practice this did not happen. Apparently, counter-balances in the Low Countries, found also in the estates-general, were still sufficient to avoid this.

Although barter, payment in kind, or delayed payment reduced the need for money, the demand for coins must have greatly increased in the later Middle Ages as a result of the growth in trade and wage labour. The rise of fiscality further pushed up the demand for coins, since taxes can be assumed to have been almost always paid in coins. This growing demand was met by a growing supply in the Low Countries beginning in the late 12th century, both locally produced and imported. Ever larger numbers of coins became available, as exemplified by the production of the leeuwengroot as well as the silver *esterling*, of which some 90 million pieces were struck in the Low Countries in 1290–1300 alone.[115] These coins were struck in the princely workshops that employed large numbers of people: in 1300 there were 40 workers in the mint in Hasselt, 100 in Namur, and 200 each in Leuven and Brussels.[116] Moreover, the ever larger numbers of coins found in hoards demonstrate their growing availability; the massive hoard from *c*.1264 in Brussels consisted of 140,000 silver pennies. Louise of Male, Count of Flanders (1346–84), struck an impressive total of some 15 million gold and some 135 million silver coins, or 150 pieces of gold and 1,350 pieces of silver per Flemish household, in his 40-year reign.[117] The mints in Flanders were probably the busiest in Europe in this period. But many of these coins ended up in England, particularly for wool purchases, or they were hoarded. As silver from the mines dried up in the late 14th century and resulted in a bullion famine, most mints in the Low Countries, and throughout north-western Europe, were temporarily closed.[118] Those in the Low Countries shut down completely in the periods 1447–54 and 1460–7, resulting in a decline in the availability of coins per person. It was only around 1470 that this problem was solved, as new silver mines were opened, but until that happened, the scarcity of coins may have been an obstacle to growing market exchange. (See Table 5.2.)

On the one hand, credit was adversely affected by the scarcity of coins, since possible creditors were reluctant to grant credit if they doubted the ability of the debtor to repay.[119] Territorial lords or towns might have difficulties levying taxes or excises used as security for a loan if coins were scarce, and thus could be forced to default. Town authorities could also prohibit credit transactions in order to combat coin scarcity. In 1399, the town government of Bruges suspended the

[115] Mayhew, 'The circulation', 61. Data for the 15th and 16th centuries: Lucassen, 'Wage payment', 21.
[116] Baerten, *De munten*, 38 and 59.
[117] Van Werveke, 'Currency manipulation', and Day, 'The great bullion famine', 15–18.
[118] Munro, 'Mint policies', and Spufford, *Monetary problems*, 46–54.
[119] Fryde and Fryde, 'Public credit'.

Table 5.2 Coins minted in the Low Countries or in parts of the Low Countries (13th–16th centuries)

Name	Principality	Period	No. ($\times 10^6$)	No./yr ($\times 10^6$)	(No./yr)/person
Silver					
esterling	Low Countries	1290–1300	90	9	4
leeuwengroot	Fland+Brabant	1299–1365	60	1	1
various	Flanders	1346–1384	100	2.9	6
various	Flanders	1384–1424	95	2.7	5
various	Flanders	1424–1434	40	4	8
various	Flanders	1434–1474	55	1.4	3
various	Flanders	1474–1484	30	3	6
various	Burg. Low Coun.	1433–1447	33	2.2	1
various	Burg. Low Coun.	1447–1466	0	0	0
various	Burg. Low Coun.	1466–1485	83	4	2
various	Burg. Low Coun.	1486–1496	44	4	2
Gold					
various	Flanders	1346–1384	15	0.4	0.8
various	Burg. Low Coun.	1433–1496	5	0.1	0.04

Sources: Lucassen, 'Wage payment', 21; Spufford, *Monetary problems*, 46–54 and 190–192; Munro, 'Petty coinage'.

payment of bills of exchange by bank transfer, hoping that this would force the coins out of hoards into circulation, and a year later it even instructed merchants to settle all transactions in cash,[120] although this measure may not have been really effective. The logic could also work the other way round. Using credit helped to circumvent payment in cash and to solve the problem of scarcity of coins. Current accounts, tallies, bank transfers, as well as the bill of exchange, were used as a way to transfer capital or make transactions without having to use or transport coins. Scarcity of coins could therefore promote credit operations. In the development of these instruments, and the capital market in general, efficient administration was essential. Proper bookkeeping not only increased security and made it easier to check transactions, but also offered an overview of complex credit operations. Again, developments in the 13th century were crucial. Rudimentary accounts for religious institutions are found from then onwards. One of the first examples is the overview of expenses made by the Charité de Tournai, an organization that emerged from an association of merchants in 1240–3.[121] But the cities were even more interested in drawing up accounts, which started—probably not coincidentally—from the time they started selling annuities and their long-term obligations grew rapidly. The territorial lords and the local population also felt a growing need to exercise some control on the

[120] Day, 'The great bullion famine', 17.   [121] Verriest, 'La charité Saint Christophe'.

dealings of the urban magistrates and pressed them to keep proper accounts. The earliest remaining examples from the Low Countries are from Arras (1241), Mons (1279), Bruges (1280), Ghent (1280), and Dordrecht (1283), but from then on there was a huge increase in annual urban accounts.[122]

Private individuals, probably even small tradesmen and retailers, also saw the need for bookkeeping, but almost all of these records are lost. Part of the administration of two Bruges money changer/bankers from around 1370 has been preserved; one consists of a single ledger, and the other of five ledgers, two journals, and indexes.[123] These books were public and offered legal security to their customers, thus rendering it unnecessary for the parties involved to write receipts, find witnesses, or draw up charters. However, they did not lead to a real balance or a clear overview of profit and loss, since they were kept as single-entry books, thus requiring additional calculation of all open balances. Double-entry bookkeeping was promoted in the 16th century, for example, in the manual published in Antwerp by Jan Ympyn (1543).[124] This method allowed for distinguishing between capital and revenue, and was well suited to an economy in which credit had become vital. It made it easier to obtain an overview of profit, even with many delayed payments, bills of exchange, and credit operations. But, although the theoretical knowledge was available in the Low Countries, and people there closely followed the Italians, who were leaders in this field, in practice the method of double-entry bookkeeping was not very widely used. Like most of the advanced Italian techniques, this method was far too ponderous to play the decisive role in credit, trade, and economic development that was attributed to it in the older literature; much more important were the gradual improvements in the capital market observed from the late 12th century onwards, in their turn induced by the scale-enlargement of the economy. These improvements, combined with the increasing supply of money, enabled the further rise of markets for land, labour, goods, and products, especially where the capital market offered much security, as in Holland.

V.3. THE LABOUR MARKET

Emergence of Labour Markets

Wage labour, defined as economically dependent but legally free contractual labour performed for an employer for payment of a wage, perhaps existed in the early and high Middle Ages, and other forms of labour performed for a reward with a monetary value certainly did. Among these were probably forms

---

[122] Burgers and Dijkhof, *De oudste stadsrekeningen*, and Dijkhof, 'Goatskin and growing literacy'. For the pressures of population and territorial lords, see section III.3, p. 119.
[123] De Roover, *Money, banking and credit*, 210–213 and 250.
[124] De Roover, 'Aux origines d'une technique'.

of reciprocal exchange: informal agreements in which the labourer was rewarded in kind or by being allowed to use an employer's capital goods. Concrete data from this early period are very scarce, however. In the 9th-century registers, such as the polyptyque of the Abbey of Lobbes, the labour services owed to the abbey are often expressed in equivalent amounts of money, showing that there was an awareness of the monetary value of labour. Moreover, it can be reasoned indirectly that some kind of wage labour must have existed on the manors of Lobbes. Many hundreds of *haistaldi* and *sessi* are mentioned there, as well as in various other sources from the 9th–11th centuries, mainly for Brabant and Hainaut, but also for other manorialized areas. Such labourers lived on the manor and were personally bound to the lord, but had no land of their own, or only a small garden, and no usage rights in woods or pasture; therefore they must have been largely dependent on work performed on the demesne or on larger farms, probably for wages.[125] But almost all the evidence on wage labour is indirect and often in a situation of dependency, as in the Lobbes example. In the 12th century, more concrete data are available from Cistercian granges, where wage labourers (*mercenarii*) were employed alongside lay brothers.[126] But, even though people must have been available for hire as wage labourers at these early dates, and indeed were hired, this does not signify the existence of a genuine, extensive labour market. Wage labour at the time was probably unimportant, influenced by all forms of personal dependency, and only complementary to forced labour, services, and internal labour supplied by the households.

Several interrelated elements were required to allow the rise of labour markets: freedom of labour/people, a growing inclination for individuals to hire themselves out for wages, and a growing demand for wage labour. Freedom of labour, or its absence, in the high Middle Ages is to a large extent linked to the importance of the manorial system, in which the people are tied to the land and required to provide forced labour services. In some regions, such as Holland, this system had never been important, and in most others it declined in the 11th to 14th centuries. Some remnants survived in the late Middle Ages in the form of labour services owed to the former manorial lord. In the Kromme Rijngebied, part of the river area, some carting duties remained up to the 14th century, although they were mostly commuted into money payments shortly afterwards.[127] A few other types of customary services also persisted. Often, tenant farmers had to perform labour services, largely transport duties, for the landowner; some of these may have originated within a manorial context, but in other cases there was no direct link.[128] They are found in regions where the bond between tenant and

---

[125] Devroey, *Le polyptyque*, xcv–xcvi, cvii–cviii, cxvii, and cxxi, and Kuchenbuch, *Bäuerliche Gesellschaft*, 249–260.

[126] There is a very brief mention by Rösener, 'Zur Wirtschaftstätigkeit', 137.

[127] Dekker, *Het Kromme Rijngebied*, 153–156, and Schuur, 'Late sporen van onvrijheid', 85. See also section III.2, pp. 88–90.

[128] Jansen, *Landbouwpacht*, 16, 18, 55–56, and 99.

landowner was personal, as in Flanders, or where manorialism had been strong, as in the Guelders river area or Namur. Some services owed to the seigneurial lords survived also. In the Land of Heusden, between Holland and Brabant, all non-noble and lay countrymen had to perform three days of labour per year for the lord, either with the spade or, for those who owned a horse, with horse and cart.[129] Moreover, there were services owed to public authorities. These could be owed to the territorial lord, such as work on fortifications, or collective conscription, such as the *heervaart* (military conscription) in Holland, probably established in the Carolingian era for defence against the Vikings. But these services could also be owed to the city, by its own burghers or the inhabitants of the surrounding villages.[130] In 1425, for instance, several villages in West Friesland were ordered to help the city of Enkhuizen for two or three days to dig fortifications.

For the most part, these late medieval labour duties were light, requiring only a few days per year, except perhaps for the military obligations, and they became increasingly commercial and convertible into a fixed money payment. Conscription in Holland, for instance, from the second half of the 14th century was replaced by money payments—the *soldij* (soldier's pay) tax—used to hire mercenaries. The same applied to the contribution of surrounding villages to the fortification of cities, which were largely converted to a monetary tax.[131] Only in a few, exceptional cases, as in some villages in the Land of Heusden, did these labour services of a few days for the local lord remain in force even to the 18th century.

The second, but completely different, factor limiting the growth of wage labour was the dominance of peasant holdings, either manorial or free. These were family holdings, mainly worked by labour supplied by the individual household, and seldom using additional wage labour. Their dominance thus indirectly curbed the rise of wage labour. In the cities, too, production by craftsmen was mostly small-scale and performed by household labour. Only as scale-enlargement and proletarianization increased did a labour market emerge.[132] This interactive process can be assumed to have started in the 11th to 13th centuries, but direct sources are very scarce.

The picture becomes clearer in the late 13th and 14th centuries. In the growing cities, labour was still mostly small-scale and independent, but some sectors witnessed a clear increase in wage labour, especially where relatively large numbers of labourers were needed, for example in building, public works, and transport. Dozens of carpenters, masons, hodmen, and slaters could be

---

[129] Hoppenbrouwers, 'Een middeleeuwse samenleving', 590–594.
[130] Jansma, 'Het economisch overwicht', 35–53, esp. 42, and Verlinden, 'Le balfart'.
[131] Jansen and Hoppenbrouwers, 'Military obligation'.
[132] Cf. sections III.2, pp. 88–90 (on the dissolution of manorialism), and VI.1, pp. 244–246 and 256–258 (scale-enlargement and proletarianization).

employed as wage labourers in the massive building of churches. Even larger numbers were employed in public works, and especially the construction of walls and gates, undertaken in many cities in this period. In 1382 in Bruges, up to 150 master masons, 160 journeymen masons, and 720 diggers were employed in the construction of fortifications, although most only for some six days a month on average.[133] From this small number of average workdays, and the seasonal nature of building works, it is clear that these labourers were not exclusively dependent on this wage, but must have had other sources of income or access to poor relief to finance periods of unemployment. In other urban sectors as well, wage labour increased from the 13th century onwards, since some artisans expanded their production and required labour from outside the household. The most common solution to this, however, was probably to use apprentices and journeymen within a guild system. In exceptional cases, perhaps larger numbers of wage labourers were employed in a workshop, as suggested for the Flemish textile centre of Douai. In the 13th century the merchant and entrepreneur Jehan Boinebroke had brought many artisans into economic dependence there, although it is unclear whether he really employed them as wage labourers or they retained a more independent position, for instance as subcontractors.[134] But, generally, small-scale commodity production remained dominant in the cities, certainly in production and services aimed at the local market, but even in export-oriented industries, especially in towns where the guilds held a firm position.[135] Although the practice of subcontracting offered flexibility to entrepreneurs even within the guild system, and thus led to some scale-enlargement and the rise of wage labour, a very substantial number of producers in the Flemish and Brabantine cities remained independent.

In the countryside, the importance of wage labour increased in the later Middle Ages, stimulated by changes in both supply and demand. The supply of wage labourers can be assumed to have drastically increased in the 13th and early 14th centuries because of the increasing population pressure, which led to a fragmentation of holdings or even landlessness, and the need for those who lived in the country to find additional sources of income. This certainly applied to times of scarcity, as for example in Groningen, where the famine of 1272 forced people who had formerly cultivated their own fields to work for wages, in the countryside or in the towns.[136] Particularly in the 15th and 16th centuries, in coastal Flanders and later in the Guelders river area, Salland, and coastal Frisia, the demand for wage labour increased as a result of the emergence of large farms,

---

[133] Sosson, *Les travaux publics*, 232–255.
[134] Cf. the careful analysis by Derville, 'Les draperies Flamandes', 357–360.
[135] Dambruyne, *Corporatieve middengroepen*, 59–83, and DuPlessis and Howell, 'Reconsidering the early modern economy'. Lis and Soly, 'Corporatisme', however, puts more emphasis on the role of subcontracting. Cf. also section VI.1, pp. 253 and 257–259.
[136] Jansen and Janse, *Kroniek*, 453.

which required additional labour, either at peak times during the harvest or all the year round.[137] In regions dominated by peasants, where the smaller family holding retained its importance, on the other hand, the need to hire additional labour remained small.

For the countryside some calculations of the importance of wage labour are available for the 16th century. Around the middle of the century, in central Holland, almost half of all rural labour was performed as wage labour, and in the Guelders river area as much as 60 per cent, but in inland Flanders only a quarter. The substantial rise of proto-industries in inland Flanders, although they were strongly market oriented, did not lead to an increase in wage labour, since small-scale, independent producers remained dominant there.[138] This applies even more to agriculture there: amid the mass of small peasant holdings, there were some large farms that used the cheap labour offered by impoverished peasants, but these were an exception. Despite the commercialization of some rural sectors, the strong urbanization, and the presence of markets in inland Flanders, there was no substantial rise in rural wage labour, in contrast to Holland and the Guelders river area. The number of wage labourers was probably even lower in peasant-dominated regions such as Drenthe or the Campine: even in the late 17th century, only 25–30 per cent of the people worked for wages in Drenthe.[139]

All in all, in the 16th century probably more than a third of the labour in the Low Countries was performed for wages. Compared with estimates for other parts of north-western Europe,[140] this is relatively high. The share of wage labour in the rural Guelders river area was higher than in more urban regions such as Holland and inland Flanders. This suggests that the determining factor in the rise of rural wage labour, and wage labour in general, is not found in the degree of urbanization in a region. Until more research on this point has been done for the urban economy, it must remain an open question whether the cities in these regions had a greater degree of wage labour than the countryside did. Proto-factories were absent in the cities, and most workshops were small, whereas more large-scale production with wage labourers was often found in the countryside, for example in mining, peat digging, and brick production. To better understand the differences in the importance of wage labour observed, for which the degree of urbanization apparently cannot offer an explanation, we will turn to the nature and organization of wage labour.

---

[137] Cf. section VI.1 pp. 244–246.
[138] Van Bavel, 'Early proto-industrialization'. Cf. also sections VI.1, pp. 247–250, and VII.2, pp. 361–362.
[139] Bieleman, *Boeren*, 132–135 and current research by J. Lucassen at the International Institute of Social History (IISG) in Amsterdam.
[140] Van Bavel, 'Wage labour as an indicator'.

The Nature of Wage Labour, Labour Relations, and Organization of Labour Markets

In many regions various non-economic elements can be found in the institutional framework of labour markets, even after the dissolution of the manorial system. Although at the end of the Middle Ages forced labour was largely a thing of the past, the wage labour market was not open and free, but often coupled with unequal power relationships, artificially fixed low wages, or all kinds of restrictions.[141] Clear elements of the labourer's subjection to the authority of the master, restrictions on mobility, and indenture can be found in inland Flanders, both in town and countryside. Wage relations in the countryside there were mainly characterized by a personal relationship, inequality, and dependence of the wage labourer on the employer. This can be observed, for instance, in the relations between the large landowners and their tenants, on the one hand, and the small peasants hiring out their labour to them, on the other. The small peasants were often dependent on the employer because they were heavily indebted to him or needed to use or rent his capital goods, such as horses or wagons, but also because of his dominant social and administrative position within the village community.[142] This had negative aspects, but the personal relationship also offered the labourer some security and the advantages of reciprocal exchange. These positive aspects were smaller in the proto-industrial sectors, where personal links were weaker and the power of the mainly urban-based employers over rural labourers was instead buttressed by urban privileges, restrictions on rural activities, and non-economic market forces.

In the Flemish cities, too, many restrictions can be found in the labour market. The urban governments had a strong tradition of intervention—often at the instigation of the guilds.[143] These guilds emerged in a proto-form in the 12th and 13th centuries, and were formalized as autonomous bodies in the late 13th and early 14th centuries. They soon acquired substantial political power in several Flemish cities.[144] In addition to organizing the training of craftsmen through the apprentice system, they also decided (often ratified by the urban bylaws) how many journeymen could be employed, the conditions for hiring journeymen, which days were workdays and which holidays, and the length of workdays. In textile centres where the drapers were very powerful, for instance, they pushed the town governments to have a bell rung at the beginning of the working day, and to force labourers to start work at these fixed times on penalty of a fine, as ordered in Aire-sur-Lys in Artois in 1355.[145] Regulation of time, and control over working

---

[141] Cf. Lis and Soly, 'Policing the early modern proletariat', esp. 170–172.
[142] Lambrecht, 'Reciprocal exchange', 242–245, although this mainly discusses the 18th century.
[143] Van Houtte and Van Uytven, 'Wirtschaftspolitik und Arbeitsmarkt', esp. 48–58.
[144] Cf. for the political power of guilds section III.3, pp. 120–121.
[145] Le Goff, 'Le temps du travail'. For the link with the rise of the mechanical clock and measurement of time, see section VII.2, pp. 351–352.

times, now became an issue as wage labour was increasing. Especially in the 16th century, guild masters succeeded in lengthening the working day and cutting the number of holidays substantially. Guilds also tried to fix wages, as did the urban legislation on this point, which had begun in the 13th century, often on the advice of or influenced by the craftsmen and their organizations.[146] All in all, the guilds played an important part in structuring the labour market, mainly serving the needs of the independent masters and protecting small-scale commodity production, but sometimes dictated more by the bigger guild masters.

Moreover, in several Flemish and Brabantine towns the guilds restricted professional mobility by making it difficult for outsiders to enter a trade. Access to a profession in a city was often only possible after having acquired citizenship and guild membership, since many guilds held a professional monopoly. Securing membership could be costly because of the high entrance fees. In early 16th-century Ghent, the entry fee was about 170 summer days' wages for a skilled journeyman, on average, and added to this was a payment to the town, a silver cup to be presented to the guild, a banquet for the guild members, and often also some presents for the members of the board—as well as the investments required to set up the enterprise.[147] Fees for outsiders were even higher. Sons of masters, on the other hand, did not have to pay this entry fee, but only a very small registration fee. Moreover, the authorities sometimes limited the number of workers in particular sectors, as happened with the carters and transporters in Antwerp around the middle of the 15th century. To become a member of the guild, and thus have access to work in this sector, it was necessary to purchase a position from a resigning member, which required a large sum, in addition to the sums to be paid to the city and the guild.[148] In 1544 Charles V took steps to abolish these monopolies and reduce entry fees, mainly in order to break the political power of the guilds, but a few decades later the system was re-established and remained in effect until the 19th century. Moreover, places in public halls were limited, thus restricting the numbers of butchers and fishmongers. In Flemish and Brabantine cities, where guilds were powerful, in practice some of these professions became hereditary, particularly in periods of economic stagnation. All this resulted in a lack of mobility and segregation of the labour market, as well as a strengthening of some masters at the expense of journeymen and labourers.

In the north-west, labour markets were much more open than in Flanders. There, too, the power of the lords over labour had dissolved early, or had never been strong, but the authorities made fewer attempts to restrict freedom in the labour market. Moreover, especially in Holland, guilds were far weaker

---

[146] Wyffels, *De oorsprong der ambachten*, 46–49 and 86–89, and Boone and Brand, 'Vollersoproeren', discussing several 15th-century conflicts about wages. For wage stickiness, see below, p. 211.
[147] Dambruyne, *Corporatieve middengroepen*, 184–213.
[148] Deceulaer, 'Institutional and cultural change', esp. 31–34.

than their southern counterparts, mainly because they lacked political power, and were unable to influence and shape the labour market to the extent their southern counterparts had done. The Leiden guilds, for instance, were under the close supervision of the municipal authorities, and their function was mainly restricted to training programmes and some work rules, but they had no political power. In Flanders and Brabant, on the other hand, the guilds remained strong. Even in Antwerp, a booming metropolis in the 16th century, large entrepreneurs such as Gilbert van Schoonbeke tried to break the restrictions imposed by guild regulation, but production remained dominated by small-scale independent units.[149] Only in sectors where guild organization was absent or weak, such as building, brick production, and brewing, did scale-enlargement, concentration, the decline of independent masters, and the rise of free wage labour take place in Antwerp. Although it is now argued that guilds offered more flexibility than had once been thought,[150] the point remains that they did influence and restrict the labour market, particularly in the Flemish cities where they acquired political power.

A particular aspect of the restriction and segmentation of labour markets was the position of women and their economic role more generally. Throughout western Europe, the guilds seem to have excluded women and suppressed their independent activities. In the Low Countries, this was especially the case in Flanders, where, in 1302, the guilds took decisive steps in this direction, probably because they now acquired political power and there was resistance to women playing a political role.[151] Women were banned from plenary meetings or board membership, and prohibited from training apprentices, forming a business partnership with their husband, and sometimes even from operating as a master after the death of their husband. In general, only low-paid, unskilled, and insecure jobs were open to women, such as spinning or carding, or some small-scale retailing.

In the north, women seem to have had more opportunities in the wage labour market and to some extent as independent entrepreneurs. They had access to the guilds, although often as assistants to their husbands or as widows continuing their husband's business. In 15th-century Leiden, the largest textile centre in Holland, there was no explicit regulation against the activities of women, and a substantial number seem to have been active as entrepreneurs in this sector, albeit sometimes on a smaller scale.[152] In the decades around 1400, about one-fifth of the drapers and cloth retailers in Leiden were female, showing that women had access to capital and skills. Among the cornmongers, tailors, and bonnetmakers, for instance, independent female masters can also be found in the north, but the

---

[149] Soly, 'Nijverheid en kapitalisme', 331–352. See also section VI.1, pp. 258 and 276.
[150] Farr, 'On the shop floor', 24–54, and Prak, 'Politik, Kultur'.
[151] See Farr, *Artisans in Europe*, 37–41, and the nuanced discussion with regard to Flanders by Stabel, 'Women at the market'.
[152] Kloek, 'De arbeidsdeling'; Howell: 'Women, the family economy' and *Women, production*, 70–75.

situation then changed, and in 1508, for instance, women in Leiden were banned from the cloth-shearers' guild, which previously had been open to both men and women.[153] Still, their position within the economy was less weakened than in the south,[154] perhaps because the guilds in the north were weaker, as was their political power, and because women had a more independent material position there, in part through marriage settlements and hereditary laws.[155] Foreigners, such as Guicciardini, who visited Holland and Zeeland in 1567, were struck by the economic independence of women and their activities, particularly in trade, but also in production. Despite this, and despite the near absence of formal restrictions, in practice there was often an implicit division of labour between the sexes, even in Holland. In the textile industries, spinning and combing were almost exclusively performed by women, and weaving and fulling exclusively by men. Technological innovations such as the introduction of larger looms often intensified this pattern. With the rise of a more capitalist organization of production, the position of women seems to have further worsened: their earlier position was to a large extent based on their position within the family and the household economy, whereas now household production was undermined.[156] Women had more difficulty competing with large entrepreneurs, and increasingly only simpler activities, such as piecework done at home or low-paid wage labour jobs, became available to them.

There were also regional differences in the nature of the wage relationship. One of these differences was the extent of full-time proletarianized labour in total wage labour. In the 16th century, perhaps as much as half of all rural wage labour in the Guelders river area was performed by proletarians, mainly working in agriculture on the large farms. In Holland, many more of the rural population had at least a smallholding, and the semi-proletarianized peasants often combined this with working in proto-industries. This resulted in a seasonal labour cycle which combined work on their own small farms with some hunting and fowling, spinning, and other proto-industrial work in winter (often for wages), work on the land and peat digging in spring (almost all for wages), mowing and harvesting on larger farms in summer (for wages), and fishing in autumn (increasingly also for wages).[157] In inland Flanders, the small amount of rural labour performed for wages could to a large extent be supplied by servants and semi-proletarianized peasants. The servants, perhaps making up some 8 per cent of the population,[158] were mainly young men and women who left home when they were about 15 to work in another household as wage labourers until they were ready to start their own families. This type of wage labour was part of a life cycle, often a peasant life cycle, and not fully proletarian at all.

[153] Van Nederveen-Meerkerk, *De draad in eigen handen*, 152–159.
[154] Quast, 'Vrouwen in gilden', 26–37, and Panhuysen, 'Maatwerk'.
[155] Cf. section VI.2, pp. 292–293. [156] Howell, 'Women, the family economy', esp. 215–216.
[157] Lucassen, *Naar de kusten*, 122–124 and 164–168. Cf. also section VI.3, pp. 301–302.
[158] Vandenbroeke, *Prospektus*.

A specific element of rural wage labour in the north was the role of migrant labourers, very important there as early as the 16th century: in digging and diking (in most coastal and river regions), as well as in harvesting, threshing, mowing, pollarding, transporting, and sawing (Guelders river area), and in peateries, fisheries, brick production, and other rural industries (Holland).[159] The rise of migrant labour in Holland, which is often dated from the Golden Age,[160] appears to have had much earlier roots in the late Middle Ages, and is associated with the scale-enlargement and the increasing demand for wage labour in proto-industries and later in agriculture, and the high seasonal peaks in the demand for labour in these regions. The migrant labourers working there and in the Guelders river area seem to have been mainly from the peasant regions to the east and south-east, sometimes 100–150 km away. In inland Flanders, migrant labour was much less important and the much lower amounts of wage labour were mostly supplied from within the village itself.

Also, it seems likely that in the 15th to 16th centuries in the Guelders river area, Frisia, and Holland, the wage relationship had become less personal than in inland Flanders. Sometimes, partly because of the much wider area of labour recruitment, this relationship was even impersonal. Arrangements between employer and labourer were formal and based on the payment of a money wage, which was paid regularly on a daily, weekly, or monthly basis. Regular payment was possible because of the massive minting of silver coins suitable for small wage payments. From the late 13th century onwards, millions of silver coins, appropriate for paying the daily wage of labourers, were minted in the Low Countries each year.[161] This massive coining avoided a coin shortage, which otherwise would have necessitated payment of wages in kind, through the use of capital goods or in the form of credit. These alternatives, or the truck system, were generally hated by workers, but often profitable for the employer, who asked high prices for his goods or products. Also it could lead to dependency or even debt bondage for the labourer. In Leiden, attempts to introduce the truck system were resisted by the fullers, who organized strikes and even left town in 1435 and 1478. The town government was sensitive to their arguments and stipulated that wages should be paid each Saturday, in silver coin only. In the north, wages in the 16th century were indeed generally paid in coin,[162] and labour contracts in these regions were mostly formal and for short terms. They could be verbal agreements for the day or written one-year contracts. Around 1570 Rienck Hemmema, a larger farmer in Frisia, employed two servants and two maids, who rarely stayed for more than a year, and at times a foster-mother

---

[159] Van Bavel: *Mariënweerd*, 415–416 and 428–429, and 'Early proto–industrialization', esp. 1156–1157.

[160] Lucassen, *Naar de kusten*, 159–172, and Van Zanden, *The rise and decline*, 157–167.

[161] For the link between minting and wage labour see Lucassen, 'Wage payments', 21–23; and for minting see section V.2, pp. 198–199.

[162] Munro, 'Wage stickiness', 202–203, and De Vries, 'An employer's guide'.

for about a year, as well as an additional servant for half a year, and numerous day labourers at peak times.[163] Mobility of labour was very strong on his farm, and there were no signs of an intimate, personal relationship between master and servant. Also in Holland and the Guelders river area, wage labour seems to have been relatively free, with few restrictions on the mobility of labour and no additional non-economic elements, in contrast to the personal and long-lasting wage relationships in inland Flanders.

The differences between Flanders and some other regions in the south from those in the north-west are also reflected in the 16th-century debate on wage levels and the possible role of public authorities in fixing these. Especially in the towns, the authorities often played a role here, either stimulated by some pressure group or as an intermediary formalizing the outcome of collective bargaining. In 1423, Duke Philip the Good, for instance, fixed the salary of fullers in Ghent, thus confirming a compromise between their demands and the offer made by the drapers, as his predecessors had often done and his successors would do.[164] But around 1560 some authorities and provinces in the south wanted to go a step further. They proposed to limit maximum wages more generally, for rural labourers also. Such attempts were resisted by the authorities in the north, especially those in Holland and Utrecht. The Utrecht city government, dominated by merchants and entrepreneurs, stated that wage setting is entirely God's work, which man should certainly not impose on.[165] This can be seen as a plea that the forces of supply and demand should function freely in the labour market. On the other hand, the authorities in Utrecht and Holland often combined this position with measures to increase the supply of labour in the market to indirectly push down wages, for example, by limiting poor relief to the elderly, disabled and those who were involuntarily unemployed, and by prohibiting begging and vagrancy. In Holland, a new type of forced labour was introduced from the second half of the 16th century: spinning houses were erected where 'idle' poor were forced to work. It was precisely in regions such as Holland and Utrecht that new, and often harsh policies in this field first took root.[166] The reforms in poor relief there from the 1530s onwards offered a safety net, and people who depended solely on wage labour knew they would no longer have to fear dying of hunger when the demand for labour dwindled, but these measures were also employed as ways to increase the labour supply and discipline labour. They cannot be seen apart from the early importance of wage labour and the demand for proletarianized labour, and the absence of non-economic means for entrepreneurs to keep wages down in these regions.

[163] Slicher van Bath, *Een Fries landbouwbedrijf*, 114–116 and 126.
[164] Boone, Brand, & Prevenier, 'Revendications salariales'.
[165] Verlinden & Craeybeckx, *Prijzen- en lonenpolitiek*, 10–12, 76–90, and 105–108. The statement of the Utrecht government is dated 22 March 1561.
[166] Cf. Lis & Soly, *Poverty and capitalism*, 82–96. See also section VI.4, pp. 311–313, also for the reforms in poor relief.

Quantitative Indicators

The effects of this institutional framework on the labour market can also be measured. The specific organization of the labour market was one of the main reasons that wage labour became so important, for instance, in Holland and the Guelders river area, as early as the 15th to 16th centuries, when it accounted for at least half the total labour input. The freedom and integration of labour markets in most parts of the Low Countries were also reflected in the slight differences in nominal wages between town and countryside. In Italy, because of restrictions on immigration and entry into urban occupations, and greater price differentials in the cost of living, this difference could amount to 100 to 150 per cent for similar occupations/tasks. In the southern parts of the Low Countries, there were also some restrictions on mobility. Moreover, entry into the urban wage market became much more difficult for countrymen because of the guild restrictions on certain occupations. In inland Flanders, nominal wages in the countryside were still close to urban wages in the early 14th century, but in the late 14th to 15th centuries an urban/rural wage differential of some 50 to 70 per cent emerged, probably because it was then that urban and guild restrictions became tighter. In Holland, on the other hand, the urban/rural difference was and remained very small, if it existed at all.[167] For the 14th century, this can still be attributed to the small size of the cities, but after the dramatic growth of Holland towns in the 15th and 16th centuries, the absence of institutional barriers was the main cause.

The few restrictions on migrant labour and the many migrant labourers available probably also helped to iron out wage differences among regions to some extent, but this has not been investigated yet. It would also be interesting to know whether the differences in wages for men and women were smaller in the Low Countries than elsewhere in Europe.[168] Another indicator of the flexibility and openness of labour markets is the extent to which wages adapted to changes in supply and demand. Wages did change, but customs and conventions caused some lag in this, and entrepreneurs or authorities prevented the rapid rise in nominal wages, even in periods of very high inflation, thus adversely affecting the real wages of labourers. Conversely, customs and collective action by workers often prevented reductions in nominal wages, even in periods of deflation. In Bruges, from 1398 to 1476, the daily wage of a town policeman remained fixed at 5 pennies, although declining consumer prices prevailed for most of this period.[169] It was especially the unorganized, unprotected workers, such as

---

[167] Malanima, 'Wages, productivity', Stabel, *De kleine stad*, 185–192, Thoen, *Landbouwekonomie*, 955–960 (Flanders), and Van Bavel & Van Zanden, 'The jump-start', 512–513 (Holland).

[168] Cf. DuPlessis, *Transitions to capitalism*, 19–20, for examples of wage differentials in the south of France.

[169] Munro, 'Wage-stickiness'.

seasonal, migrant labourers in agriculture, who were subject to more rapid shifts and to cuts in nominal wages in periods of deflation.

Another indicator of the functioning of labour markets and capital markets was the skill premium, which is the differential in wage payment between skilled and unskilled labourers. This is influenced by the availability of skilled labourers, with greater availability reducing the premium, and by the absence of obstacles in the labour market and easy access to skilled jobs with high wages, which further reduces the premium. A decline in the premium is often connected with falling interest rates in the capital market, making it more attractive for households to forgo earning money during training and to invest in human capital.[170]

The skill premium declined in western Europe from about 100–150 per cent in the first half of the 14th century to some 50–60 per cent around the middle of the 15th century, where it remained until the 19th century. In southern Europe, after a similar decline, it gradually started rising again to a level of about 75 per cent in the 17th century.[171] Similar geographic differences can be observed within the Low Countries. Calculations of the skill premium by comparing wages of hodmen/labourers with those of craftsmen in the same sector show the exceptional position of Holland. In Antwerp, Bruges, and Nijmegen, the skill premium around 1500 appears to have been fairly high, at 65–80 per cent, whereas in Holland it was only about 25–50 per cent. (See Table 5.3.)

This decline in the skill premium, which was most pronounced in Holland, can be explained by the favourable organization of the capital market in the Low Countries, and in particular, the easy accessibility of the capital market in Holland. Also, there was a link to the favourable organization of the labour market and the near absence of privileges, making entry into skilled jobs relatively

Table 5.3 The skill premium in the Low Countries (expressed as a percentage of the wages of unskilled labour in the same sector)

	Bruges Flanders	Antwerp Brabant	Amsterdam Holland	Nijmegen Guelders	Zutphen Guelders
1350–1400	–	–	–	–	–
1400–1450	–	–	–	–	60–70%
1450–1500	65%	–	–	60–90%	65–80%
1500–1550	–	65–80%	25–50%	–	50–65%
1550–1600	–	75–80%	25–50%	–	45–50%

Sources: Scholliers, 'Prijzen en lonen', 379–386, 409–413, 445–446, and 471–475, Lis & Soly, 'Different paths of development', 227, Van Schaïk, 'De bevolking van Nijmegen', esp. 17–19, Noordegraaf & Schoenmakers, *Daglonen in Holland*, 55, Van der Wee, *The growth*, I: appendices 27–33, Allen, 'The great divergence', 428, Kuppers and Van Schaïk, 'Levensstandaard', 9 and 21.

[170] For this and the following discussion, cf. Van Zanden, 'Common workmen' and 'The skill premium'.
[171] Van Zanden, 'The skill premium'.

easy. It is uncertain whether the guilds played a positive role by way of their part in the education and training of labour. Perhaps, in the late Middle Ages, the organization of apprenticeships by the guilds in the Low Countries formed a positive factor in the training and development of skills, although they also barred entrance to certain skilled professions.[172] In addition to the guilds, there were other ways of improving human capital: schools became very numerous and well run in the Low Countries, even in rural areas, resulting in a high level of literacy. In the 15th century this rose to a level higher than anywhere else in Europe, reaching perhaps 30 per cent at the beginning of the 16th century.[173] If a skilled job required reading and/or counting, these schools probably contributed to building the human capital needed. The labour market itself must also have offered the opportunities to acquire skills, as can be deduced from the low skill premium in Holland, where guilds were weak. Apparently, investment in human capital was high there and entrance into skilled jobs easy, with a positive effect on the region's economic growth potential.

V.4. THE MARKET FOR GOODS AND PRODUCTS

The Institutional Organization of Trade in the Carolingian Period

In the early Middle Ages, exchange of goods and products was limited, and most of this exchange was not commercial trade. Gift exchange, barter, forced transfers from peasants to lords, distributions by the powerful to clients, or closed exchange between the various possessions within the economies of large landowners were more important forms of exchange.[174] This limited importance of market trade was caused by lack of coins, lack of markets, and lack of security and market institutions. But there was some commercial exchange, and it usually concerned goods and products rather than land, capital, and labour. Hence, some of the relevant institutions for this market had already been formed in the early Middle Ages, in contrast to the factor markets, which emerged only from the high Middle Ages on.

Market exchange of goods and products started increasing in the Low Countries in the 7th century and particularly in the 8th. Compared with other parts of north-western Europe, this growth was strong in the Low Countries, as is shown by the relatively large numbers of coins circulating there.[175] When roads had fallen into disrepair and land transport declined in the post-Roman period, the relative importance of water transport grew correspondingly, and the Low Countries benefited from being close to the sea and having many rivers and

---

[172] Cf. in general Epstein, 'Craft guilds'.   [173] Section VI.4, pp. 317–319.
[174] Claude, 'Aspekte des Binnenhandels', esp. 10–14.
[175] Grierson and Blackburn, *Medieval European coinage* i:135–138 and 149–154. See also section V.2, p. 193.

natural harbours. The diversity in soil and resources between regions, and the resulting comparative advantages, must also have stimulated trade there. From the beginning of the 7th century, the North Sea developed into a commercially more united area, in which traders from the Low Countries played a major role.[176] In absolute terms, trade was not yet impressive, but a wide variety of goods was traded in the early Middle Ages, including luxuries, such as salt, silk, spices, glass, and weapons purchased by lords and monasteries. There were also the surpluses sold by large landowners, mainly built up within the manorial system.[177] This system increasingly generated and concentrated surpluses of wine, grain, wool, and flax, of which a part was sold in the market.

Much of this exchange was done by agents of monasteries and lords, and only some of it was in the hands of professional merchants. In contrast to the more southern parts of the Carolingian Empire, Jews and Syrians played a minor role in north-west European trade, except for a few merchants who supplied the royal court in Aachen.[178] Only in the 11th century do some Jews start to appear in Arras and other more northern cities. More important were the traders from the Meuse valley: Huy, Dinant, Namur, and Maastricht in the 8th and 9th centuries were designated as *portus* and *vicus*, pointing to their role in trade. These centres all had tolls and mints, and the relatively many coins minted there are found all over Europe.[179] But an even bigger commercial role in north-west European trade was played by the Frisians, who traded as far afield as Scandinavia and the Upper Rhine. These people lived in the coastal areas stretching from Flanders to Zeeland, Holland, Friesland, and Groningen to Ost Friesland. They were already engaged in international trade in the late 7th century, and they became dominant, at least in the North Sea and on the Rhine, in the 8th and 9th centuries. Their trading role is recorded in written sources, which mention their presence at the fairs of St Denis and their trading colonies throughout western Europe, as far away as York. Their role is also testified by archaeological evidence of Frisian trading products, and mainly by numismatic evidence.[180] Gold coins, principally used for international trade, were minted in relatively large numbers in Frisia, as well as the Frisian silver sceattas found throughout Europe, and in Friesland and Groningen large numbers of gold coins minted elsewhere have been found, all pointing to intensive Frisian involvement in trade.

Frisia produced goods well suited to international trade, such as cloth and salt, and its location on the borders of the Frankish Empire also made it perfectly suitable as a trading link among the Empire, England, and Scandinavia. The Frisians had a network of trading places, with the emporium of Dorestad

---

[176] Lebecq, 'The northern seas', 639–659.
[177] Cf. sections IV.1, pp. 146–147, and VIII.1, pp. 325–326.
[178] Devroey, 'Juifs et Syriens', 51–72, and Lebecq and Costambeys, 'The role of monasteries'.
[179] Section V.2, pp. 193–194.
[180] Lebecq, *Marchands et navigateurs*, 23–34 and 49–97, and Verhulst, 'Der frühmittelalterliche Handel'.

at the top of the hierarchy, and regional hubs such as Witla, Stavoren, and Medemblik, situated only some 50–100 km from one another. The Guelders river area, crossed by the lower branches of the Rhine and the Meuse, had a dense concentration of trading centres; in addition to Dorestad, Tiel, Zaltbommel, and Utrecht developed international trading activities in the course of the 7th to 10th centuries. Dorestad developed into a gateway where foreign goods entered the Empire. The area had increasingly come under Frankish control in the 7th to 8th centuries, and profited from the protection offered by the Frankish king. Dorestad and the other trading centres all had a strong royal presence, with a Carolingian mint, toll, and market offering the framework and security necessary for trade.[181] The Carolingian elite, with the king at their head, were very interested in protecting and channelling trade there. The king taxed this trade at Dorestad through a toll of 10 per cent, one of the most important in the whole Empire, and the elite were similarly anxious to control this trade in order to secure a steady flow of foreign luxuries from northern Europe, such as furs, amber, walrus ivory, and slaves—all of which were status symbols and could be used in gift exchanges or as tribute, or displayed for prestige. Trade centres like these were thus still firmly embedded in a pre-market society.

Excavations in Dorestad also throw light on the physical infrastructure of this trading centre, which was the most important in north-western Europe at the time.[182] This town was some three km long. Apart from the agrarian and industrial quarters, and a fort that went back to the Roman castle, it had a commercial quarter, the *vicus*. This was a kilometre in length, and consisted of some 150 houses in two or three rows along the harbour. The bank of the river was extended by a series of jetties, each group of buildings having its own causeway to the river bank. In other trading centres, boats were simply beached or moored on the shore, with hardly any infrastructure, so Dorestad was exceptional.

A variety of boats were used in trade. The Frisians used small boats for short distances, but also had larger, more stable vessels for long-distance trade, such as the hulk-type boats of up to 18 m long.[183] Such boats, mainly used in the trade with Britain and on the Rhine, as far upstream as Strasbourg and Mainz, had no keels and could not support strong masts able to carry a large sail. Thus, they largely depended on oarsmen, up to 24 per boat, and on being pulled along by men on the river bank or punting in shallow water. There was scarcely room for bulky cargoes; long-distance trade was principally light commodities that had a high value. The Frisians traded in fur from north-east Europe, wine, pottery, and grain from the Rhineland, honey and quern stones from the Eifel, salt and fish from the Frisian coast, glass and spices from the Mediterranean, and also slaves

---

[181] Blok, *De Franken*, 75–78 and 101–103, and also section III.3, p. 100.
[182] Van Es, 'Dorestad centred', and Clarke and Ambrosiani, *Towns in the Viking Age*, 25–27.
[183] Van de Moortel, 'Shipbuilding and navigation', 39–50. Cf. also section IV.2, p. 158.

bought in England.[184] But the main Frisian trading product was cloth from their homelands, made from wool produced by the large numbers of sheep in Frisia, and in coastal Flanders and Zeeland. Most grain had to be imported, because of the relatively high density of population on the Frisian coast and the difficulties of grain growing in these marshy lands. This system could therefore only work by way of exchange. In their trade with ports that had tidal harbours, mainly in the eastern parts of the North Sea and Jutland, the Frisians often used a different type of boat, the cog, which was more suited to those circumstances.[185] The cogs had sails, hesitantly applied in the 7th century, and only to supplement the work of the oarsmen, but more generally used in the 8th century and later. This encouraged sea traffic, although the scale and scope of its growth should not be overestimated, in view of the low surpluses, lack of capital, insecurity, and poor organization of trade.

Transaction costs were probably reduced in the Carolingian period. The rule of the Carolingian kings increased security within the Empire, and they also tried to standardize coins, measures, and weights, as ordered in the *A Admonitio generalis* of 789 and enforced by the introduction of new weights and measures by Charlemagne.[186] This fitted with the Carolingian pretensions to strong sovereign power and unification of the empire. The right to determine measures was seen as a prerogative of the ruler, and the legislation of Carolingian kings on this point was clearly inspired more by political motives, as proof of their authority, than by economic ones. The same was true of their concern for good, stable money. The impact of their decrees was limited, since in practice there remained a diversity in weights and measures, but at least some steps had been taken towards achieving more uniform, equal, and public weights and measures, thus reducing transaction costs and stimulating trade. In addition, the minting of silver coins made a positive contribution to trade. Before the late 7th century, only small numbers of mainly large gold coins were minted, which were only suitable for long-distance trade in luxuries. Now, silver coins became available in large numbers, and were appropriate for smaller transactions. The Carolingian rulers were also concerned with maintaining the infrastructure and improving transport by repairing old Roman roads and constructing new ones, although their resources and technical capabilities remained very limited.

Around the year 800 state authorities, followed by ecclesiastical leaders, also formulated a grain policy, fixing maximum prices and prohibiting the build-up of stocks for speculation while themselves amassing public stocks of grain to

---

[184] Lebecq, *Marchands et navigateurs*, 126–131.
[185] Ibid., 163–176, Unger, *The ship in the medieval economy*, 58–67, and Ellmers, *Frühmittelalterliche Handelsschiffahrt*, 149–150.
[186] Verhulst, *The Carolingian economy*, 117–118, 124–125, and 129–131, Kula, *Measures and men*, 18–19, 80–82 and 161–162, and Portet, 'Remarques sur les systèmes'. For coins see also section V.2, pp. 193–194.

bring onto the market at low prices when shortages arose.[187] This strategy was part of the concept of a 'just' price (*justum pretium*), expressed in a capitulary issued by Carloman in 884, and later incorporated in canon law. In general, the market price was considered to be a just price according to this concept, except when famine, speculation, or monopoly drove up prices, and then public authorities had the duty to step in.[188] But again, the Carolingian policy on this point was not really the result of a long-term economic plan, but was rather aimed at political prestige, inspired by religious and moral considerations and by experience. Moreover, it is questionable to what extent the Carolingian authorities could achieve their high ideals in practice, in view of their meagre resources and the few men who were part of the state apparatus.

Royal intervention in trade can also be seen in tolls and markets. The great increase in the number of markets in this period is clear, as in the Meuse valley and the Ardennes, where in the late 10th century at least five regular markets were held. The oldest was the fair of Saint-Hubert, held next to the monastery, which was mainly visited by merchants from the towns in the Meuse valley.[189] Many of these markets had been established privately, by monasteries or lords, but were later authorized by the king, and thus proclaimed legitimate or public markets. Authorization offered more security to the merchants, through the protection guaranteed by the king for the duration of the market. Many of these early fairs took place in the grounds of religious institutions, which became focal points for trade, not only because of their role as consumers and collecting points for surpluses generated by the manorial organization of their large estates, but also because of the security, regular markets, privileges, and freedom from toll they offered. For merchants it was, therefore, advantageous to be members of the *familia* of the monastery as serfs and to have these advantages, as was the case with the slave and gold merchants in 9th-century Arras, who belonged to the *familia* of the abbey of St Vaast.[190] Away from markets and protected areas, and without the personal protection of king or monastery, it often remained unsafe to trade. All this led to regional concentrations of trade, which was increasingly found where large estates, royal power, and, later, princely power prevailed, most especially in the Meuse valley.

King and lords also aimed to concentrate trade in certain markets to profit from them through tolls, which became more important, as they were levied not only at key points on roads, but also at ports, markets, and bridges.[191] The levying of tolls, which certainly dates from the 6th century and perhaps goes back to the Roman period, was in principle a royal prerogative and exercised

---

[187] Devroey, 'Réflexions', esp. 480–481, and a more negative view by Verhulst, *The Carolingian economy*, 123–125 and 128–129.
[188] De Roover, 'The concept of the just price'.
[189] Despy, 'Villes et campagnes', and Irsigler, 'Grundherrschaft'.
[190] Irsigler, 'Grundherrschaft', 68–69, and also section III.3, p. 103.
[191] An overview is offered by Adam, *Das Zollwesen*, 39–68. See also Verkerk, 'Les tonlieux carolingiens'.

by the counts as royal officers. In the high Middle Ages, however, this power largely passed to the territorial lords. Market tolls were also levied by private lords and monasteries, often as the founder of a market. In the 8th century, tolls were still mainly linked to services provided, such as the use and maintenance of bridges, roads, markets, and ports, but from the 9th century onwards they were increasingly used as a lucrative source of income, with a significant growth in the amount and number of tolls, and so they became an obstacle to trade. Further, it was a small step from the levying of tolls to semi-legal brigandage, a step often taken by local lords, especially as central rule began to wane after the 9th century.

Even more detrimental to trade in this period were the attacks by the Vikings, who looted goods and created insecurity. Particularly rich trading centres like Dorestad were hard hit, as they were raided many times, especially in the decades around 850. Even after some measure of security returned, however, the Frisians were unable to regain their former position in trade. There was still some Frisian trade in the 10th to 11th centuries, including some in new centres such as Groningen and Stavoren, but the Frisians lost their dominant position to towns in northern Germany, and to the emerging towns in Flanders and the Meuse valley. Apparently, more structural factors than the Viking attacks alone were responsible for shifting the balance. The determining factor was security, which was stronger in the Flemish cities that were protected by castles, walls, and later the power of the territorial lord.[192] Such protection was absent in the former heartlands of Frisian trade, especially in Friesland, Groningen, and Ost Friesland, but also in Zeeland, since no territorial rule emerged there after the central power had dissolved. In Flanders, however, the early emergence of a strong territorial lord offered security through his military and administrative organization. Moreover, institutions were more favourable to trade in the Flemish cities: clear rules governing trade, freedoms, and privileges were inserted in the urban rights, often under the pressure of merchant guilds, and confirmed by the territorial lord.[193]

Towns and Trade in the High and Late Middle Ages

The emerging urban settlements, which sometimes grew up near monasteries but more often near castles, became the main centres of trade, and traders increasingly organized themselves through guilds, voluntary associations of merchants of a particular town. Guilds had existed before, in the early Middle Ages as organizations of clerics and laymen. Some of these guilds must have included merchants, as evidenced by the guild-like organization mentioned in 779 in the Capitulary of Herstal, in which the members swore to assist one

---

[192] Verhulst, 'The origins of towns' and Id., *The rise of cities*, 59–69 and 88–110. See also sections III.1, p. 71, and III.3, pp. 120–123.

[193] See also section III.3, pp. 111–112, and below pp. 219–221.

another in the event of fire or shipwreck.[194] Guilds explicitly denoted as merchant organizations were first mentioned at the beginning of the 11th century. Some elements of these guilds, such as the communal meals and convivial drinking, almsgiving to the poor, fraternal loyalty, duty to carry arms, and expulsion from the community as penalty, seem to point to a Frisian or German origin.[195] These elements, and the oath sworn to provide mutual assistance in case of emergency or poverty, encouraged solidarity and gave the merchant the security he would otherwise lack. Also, this organization could offer a counterweight to rulers, and command some protection from them as well as deter them from attempts at confiscation, thus promoting the security of trade.

These organizations, however, did not find favour with everybody, as can be seen from the vicious description by the cleric Alpertus van Metz in about 1020 of the merchant guild of Tiel, one of the heirs of Dorestad and centre of trade with England.[196] Alpertus van Metz did not turn against trade as such. Although the Church was somewhat suspicious of profiting from a non-productive activity, it mainly condemned particular types of trade, specifically speculation in times of famine and slave trade, and the greed sometimes involved in trade. Alpertus frowned upon the way the Tiel merchants distinguished themselves from others, made their own rules, paid for their drinking bouts from their own communal funds, and administered justice according to their own judgement, a right they claimed had been granted them by the emperor. It was therefore their legal, financial, and administrative autonomy and independence that he particularly disliked. And perhaps he was also disturbed by the fact that the guild was a completely secular organization, not under the control of any ecclesiastical authority.

In this period, and particularly in the 11th century, the institutions governing market exchange became increasingly territorialized. At first, the customary rules of trading of the Carolingian period developed along with the trade privileges and liberties issued by the king into a *ius mercatorium*. From the late 10th century onwards this body was extended, along with property and inheritance law and rules on jurisdiction and market usage, to emerge as a market law.[197] Next it became increasingly embedded in urban regulations, often later recognized in an urban charter issued by the territorial lord. In Saint-Omer, for instance, the merchant guild saw its rules and public functions gradually integrated into those of the town community in the 11th century, during which process the *ghildhalle* transformed into the town hall; these rules were confirmed by the Count of Flanders in 1127.[198] In Saint-Omer and elsewhere, these charters met

---

[194] Oexle, 'Gilden als soziale Gruppen', esp. 301.
[195] But see the different views expressed by Oexle, 'Die mittelalterlichen Gilden', Lebecq, *Marchands et navigateurs*, 260–263, and Bijsterveld and Trio, 'Van gebedsverbroedering', 28–33.
[196] Künzel, *Beelden*, 91–92, and Akkerman, 'Het koopmansgilde'.
[197] Schulze, *Grundstrukturen der Verfassung*, ii: 155–156.
[198] Derville, *Histoire de Saint-Omer*, 44–48.

the requirements of the merchants to limit the arbitrary rule of the lord and increase security. A clear example of increased security was the abolition of the trial by ordeal. The ordeal by fire or water—but for property disputes mainly by battle—had been widely used in the 9th to 12th centuries. Abolition of judicial battle was promoted by the Church, but also by merchants and town communities, and it greatly increased the security of commercial activities.[199] Preparing for a duel and finding a champion were much too time-consuming for a visiting merchant, and he was probably scared off by the possibility of having to prove he was right in such an irrational way. At the beginning of the 11th century, the merchants of Tiel already possessed an imperial privilege exempting them from the judicial duel and this exemption was also included in urban charters of around 1100 for several Flemish cities. Evidence, testimonies of witnesses, and judicial verdicts replaced the duel in trade conflicts.

The tradition of compurgation in conflicts had always been strong in Frisia,[200] and was part of the ordeal as applied there. It was also often possible to make reparations through a monetary payment, which compared favourably with practices in other regions. But from the 11th to 12th centuries onwards, Frisia started to lose its lead in this field as cities in Flanders developed even more rational solutions. In Frisia, the ordeal remained in use much longer. In 1219, Emo, a Frisian abbot, even attributed the storm surges that hit the area to the fact that ordeal by hot iron was still practised there. A factor in the survival of the ordeal was the weakness of central power in Frisia; elsewhere, central authorities were able to enforce anti-ordeal legislation. In the absence of a monopoly on the use of violent force by the state, the clan structure and feuds remained important in solving conflicts in Frisia. Personal elements thus remained crucial. Moreover, trials in Frisia often depended on oaths sworn by the parties involved and their oathhelpers, with the judges having only a passive role. There was a reluctance to accept written evidence, affidavits, and the systems of authenticated evidence that were developing elsewhere.[201] This was an obstacle to trade, particularly when long-term obligations and agreements were involved. Also, in Frisia, the burden of proof remained with the suspect rather than the plaintiff. Oaths sworn by family and clan members could avert suspicion, which fitted with a clan structure and worked within closely-knit communities, but was not very suitable for a merchant operating outside his community. Elsewhere, and especially in Flanders, much more security was available to the merchant, specifically where urban and/or central authorities enforced a clear legal system with transparent rules and increasingly used written evidence. This difference surely played a part in the decline of Frisian trade in the period.

---

[199] Bartlett, *Trial by fire*, 13, 24–27, 55–61, 132–133, and 164.
[200] Kalifa: 'Ebauche d'un tableau' and 'Note sur la nature'.
[201] Algra, *Oudfries recht*, 27–29, 113—124, and 156–184, and Noomen, 'De Friese vetemaatschappij'. See also section III.1, pp. 96–97, for the social and political situation in Frisia.

Territorial lords were also involved in encouraging and controlling trade by establishing markets and fairs, or formalizing existing ones. The early 12th century saw the development of four networks of fairs in north-western Europe: besides the famous Champagne fairs and those in eastern England there were two groups in or near the Low Countries. By 1127 there were already four fairs in Flanders: at Ypres, Lille, Mesen, and Torhout, and soon afterwards also in Bruges. A similar system emerged in the 12th century along the Lower Rhine, with fairs in Utrecht, Duisburg, Aachen, and Cologne. These were all sequential fair systems, with each fair lasting some two to four weeks, with a fixed number of days for entry, display, sale, and payment, and programmed in a cycle, with some days between fairs, allowing the merchants to travel from fair to fair.[202] This cycle enabled periodic concentrations of merchants, merchandise, and information, vital in this era of limited trade; it also allowed for lowering information and other transaction costs. These fairs and their participants were under the protection of the territorial lord, who proclaimed a market peace and offered safe conducts to local and foreign merchants travelling to and from the fairs. The merchants also benefited from the suppression for the duration of the fair of rights of reprisal, pursuit, and escheatage, and generally of all claims not originating from the fair itself. Moreover, protection and certain privileges were granted by the territorial lords to collectives of merchants, or more particularly to the Hansa associations, which emerged in the 12th century as associations of merchants from a particular town, or groups of towns, trading in the same foreign market.[203] All this encouraged long-distance trade, particularly in regions of strong territorial rule, such as Flanders.

Trade in these fairs was mainly over land, made possible by simultaneous improvements in land transport. In the early Middle Ages, Roman roads still played an important part, at least in the Romanized south of the Low Countries, the main example being the road from Cologne to Bavai (*Bavacum*, near Valenciennes), which ran through Haspengouw and Hainaut. Lack of maintenance and organization, however, caused these roads and bridges to decay. Water transport was already much cheaper, especially for bulk goods, but now its dominance was further strengthened, and improvements in shipbuilding techniques favoured it also. Trading centres in the early Middle Ages were thus almost all situated on a river, or at the mouth of a river. In the high Middle Ages, however, many bridges and roads were built, making land transport easier. Among them the new Cologne–Maastricht–Louvain–Ghent–Bruges axis through Brabant and Flanders opened in the 12th century,[204] outstripping the older, more southern Roman road from Cologne to Bavai. The emergence of this new road reflects the changing trade patterns and the growing role of

---

[202] Van Houtte, 'Les foires', Irsigler, 'Grundherrschaft, Handel und Märkte', 72–78, and Feenstra, 'Les foires'.
[203] See section III.3, pp. 113–114.   [204] Bonenfant, 'L'origine des villes brabançonnes'.

Flanders in trade. This area now became even more attractive as a point of entry for English and French goods on their way to markets in the German Empire, and in particular to the booming market in Cologne. A road linking the Flemish fairs was opened in the early 12th century. Although roads like these were rarely paved, and were hardly more than lanes, they still encouraged traffic.

Land transport was also improved by the increase in the number of places to stay overnight. In the 11th century such accommodation was found mainly in the hospices of the new religious houses and in the 12th to 13th centuries in the hospitals and commercial inns in the emerging cities, often located only short distances from one another. New bridges, and those that replaced fords, were also very much improved in this period. For instance, bridges over the wide river Meuse already existed in the 10th century in Maastricht, Dinant, and Liège, but around 1100 bridges were also built in Givet, Namur, Andenne, Huy, and Visé, and that at Dinant was rebuilt in stone. This is roughly one bridge every 15–20 km as the crow flies. At the same time, and particularly in the 12th to 13th centuries, ferry crossings over the main rivers became more numerous,[205] a service promoted by the territorial lords, who held the right on these ferries as one of their regalia. In the first half of the 14th century there were dozens, or perhaps even hundreds of ferries in the Low Countries. Land transport was also speeded up by the introduction of horses in place of oxen as draught animals. New technology made this possible: the horse collar, horse shoe, and four-wheeled cart, which gained importance from the 11th century onwards.[206] Horses were more expensive, but saved time because they were twice as fast as oxen. Horses and bridge-building were both integral to the growing trade and commercialization of the high Middle Ages, making more markets accessible to producers and consumers.

Although land transport thus became increasingly competitive, partly because there were fewer tolls on land than on rivers, water transport in the Low Countries remained important, or even preponderant for bulk goods carried over longer distances. This dominance continued to favour the Low Countries as a centre of trade, especially for locations on its rivers and coasts. Water transport was also stimulated by the construction of canals. In 1122, for instance, the Kromme Rijn, an old branch of the Rhine that had become silted up and difficult to navigate, was dammed by the Bishop of Utrecht to allow reclamation of the surrounding area. Pressed by the Utrecht merchants, he replaced this route with a new canal linking the marketplaces there to the new branch of the Rhine, constructed over a distance of 10 km.[207] Similar canals were dug in the 12th century linking Saint-Omer to Gravelines, and Bruges to Damme, and hence to the sea. In

---

[205] Fuchs, *Beurt- en wagenveren*, 5–9.
[206] Langdon, 'Horse hauling', for England. See section IV.1, p. 134, for the increasing use of the horse in agriculture.
[207] Dekker, 'De dam bij Wijk'.

the peat areas, numerous smaller canals were dug for transporting peat. Further improvements were also made in seafaring vessels in the 11th and 12th centuries, particularly in the design and size of the cogs, which became larger, up to 100 tonnes in the mid-13th century. This strengthened the economic position of ports near the sea or on estuaries, such as Antwerp, Dordrecht, and Middelburg, particularly because of the deeper draught of these ships, which was up to three m. The construction of quays, introduced in the early 11th century, and later built in all major ports, helped in the unloading of large cargoes, providing increased efficiency and making the ports accessible to larger ships.[208]

The advantages the Low Countries held because of their numerous rivers and navigable watercourses, therefore, were used even more extensively, particularly in the areas close to the sea, and problems caused for land transport by these same rivers were increasingly solved by bridges and ferries. Transport in the 11th and 12th centuries, both over land and water, became much quicker, easier, and cheaper. All this probably had a significant effect on the volumes traded and the extent of commercialization. Only indirect evidence is available, but it points to a substantial growth in commerce. One indicator is the increasing replacement of payments and levies in kind by money payments. Moreover, large landowners started to dispose of their distant properties, which had previously been used to obtain specific products directly from specific regions, such as wool, cloth, salt, or wine, outside the market. Many abbeys in the Low Countries, such as Stavelot, Nivelles, and Sint-Truiden, had acquired significant properties along the Middle Rhine and the Moselle in the early Middle Ages to provide themselves with wine, often within a manorial organization and later through sharecropping. These vineyards produced tens of thousands of litres per abbey per year, which were transported to the abbeys using the toll exemptions they had acquired. Starting in the 11th century, but gaining momentum from the early 13th century onwards, these lands were exchanged, sold, or leased out for monetary rents.[209] Apparently, purchasing wine from professional merchants in the rising markets nearby now became more attractive for the abbeys than organizing production, processing, and transport of these crops.

Such markets were increasingly found within the growing cities. The growth of urbanization, starting in the 11th and 12th centuries,[210] can also be seen as an important indicator of expanding trade, since most of the urban population had to rely on markets for selling their products and obtaining food. In the 12th and 13th centuries, the abbeys of the new Cistercian and Premonstratensian orders played an important role in supplying food to towns, since they were able to generate enormous surpluses through acquisition of vast tracts of land and reorganizing this land in large granges, often comprising several hundred

---

[208] Unger, *The ship in the medieval economy*, 109 and 146–147, and Jansen, 'Een economisch contrast', esp. 17–18.
[209] Van Rey, 'Der deutsche Fernbesitz'.   [210] See section VI.2, pp. 280–281.

hectares. The abbeys linked the granges to mansions erected or bought in nearby towns, of which each abbey had some 5–10.[211] Through these mansions agrarian surpluses were brought to market, often helped by the abbeys' trade privileges and toll exemptions. One of the most striking examples of this is the row of mansions belonging to the Premonstratensian abbeys in 's-Hertogenbosch, linked to their vast granges in the Campine, and used for storing and marketing wool and oats in this rapidly rising town.

In the subsequent centuries, trade greatly increased. Main elements in the rapid development of the market for goods and products were the growing numbers of coins minted and the emergence of an open and favourable capital market from the 13th century onwards.[212] Sophisticated instruments used in international trade became available, such as the bill of exchange, but perhaps more important for local and regional trade were the chances of obtaining credit on a smaller scale, such as with the tally, the creation of annuities, or other credit instruments. Most loans in the late Middle Ages were probably for small sums in the context of retail transactions. Credit was also widely used, sometimes for large amounts, by merchants who dealt in horses, hides, cloth, jewellery, or other expensive items.

In the late Middle Ages, cities grew further as the principal places of trade. Fairs became relatively less important and were overtaken by weekly markets and permanent marketplaces and shops. The number of regular markets, granted or confirmed by the territorial lords or by other lords having or claiming that right, rose steadily in this period, but there were important regional differences. In Holland, which had no large metropolises but a very large number of smaller towns, a correspondingly dense network of markets emerged in the late Middle Ages, and there was a relatively large number of village or semi-urban markets, as well as villages that held markets without an explicit or formal charter.[213] In Flanders, on the other hand, and to a lesser extent also in Brabant, there was a much clearer hierarchy to the urban network, dominated by a few giant cities, most notably Ghent and Bruges, and few medium-sized towns, with a corresponding reduction in the number of market towns.[214] The large cities often used non-economic power and privileges to crush the competition of rural markets. In the 11th and 12th centuries, rural markets were still significant in inland Flanders, in villages such as Drongen, Wormhout, and Torhout, and even grew in number with the extension of reclamations and the growth of market exchange, as witnessed by new markets in Kemzeke and Kluizen. Around 1200, however, new markets were founded in large cities such as Kortrijk and Bruges, the latter created by the count, and rural markets then started to decline or even

---

[211] Van Bavel, 'Schakels tussen abdij en stad'. See section VII, pp. 325–326, for the building of granges.
[212] Section V.2, pp. 191–192.
[213] Noordegraaf: 'Het platteland', esp. 13–15, and 'Internal trade'. Dijkman, 'The development'.
[214] Stabel, *Dwarfs among giants*, 27–31.

disappear, except for some fairs.²¹⁵ Rural markets saw their functions being taken over by urban ones, but sometimes they were also suppressed by the towns, or even prohibited outright. In the late Middle Ages daily and weekly markets no longer took place in Flemish villages, except for a few in the remote corners of the Quarters. The negative effects of the limited number of markets in Flanders only became apparent in the later Middle Ages. Earlier, in the 13th century, this partly artificial concentration of transactions had apparently been favourable to trade. Since there was not a great deal of merchandise, only few merchants, and not much information at the time, agglomeration made relatively strong growth possible. The same was true for Cologne, which acquired extensive staple rights, became the main trading metropolis on the Rhine and extended its commercial influence over the eastern parts of the Low Countries from the 12th century onwards, and also for Bruges in the 13th and 14th centuries.

In the 13th century, Bruges became the centre of international trade in the Low Countries and of a larger network spanning north-western Europe. It did not have an exceptionally favourable geographical location: access to the sea was improved by the construction of the canal to Damme in the 12th century, but big ships still had difficulties getting to the town. However, Bruges had the general advantages of all Flemish towns, such as physical and institutional security and protection, and it really stood out because of its many networking institutions.²¹⁶ There were the money changers, who offered financial services; the organizations for foreign merchants (the *nations*), which gave cohesion and security; and the taverns that provided meeting space. The houses of the mendicant orders also played a role, providing religious services for groups of merchants, offering meeting places, and keeping the archives of the nations. Most important, however, were the hostellers, some 100 in total. Besides offering lodging and warehousing facilities, they acted as brokers and local agents for the merchants, and provided them with information about local customs, laws, measures, and merchandise, as well as financial services.²¹⁷ Since all these institutions were concentrated in a specific part of town, this brought together an enormous amount of information, merchants, and merchandise, allowing for exponential growth of trade.

It was precisely in this period, when Bruges was growing, that active trade by Flemish merchants declined. Foreign merchants, from England, France, the German Hansa, Italy, and particularly from Spain and Portugal, came to Flanders, looking for consumers and products. Many hundreds (and perhaps as many as a thousand during the trade season) were present in Bruges around 1400. Elsewhere in western Europe, foreign traders sometimes obtained their own space in trading centres, a compound with legal immunity and their own

---

[215] Yamada, 'Le mouvement des foires'. For the later Middle Ages: Stabel, *De kleine stad*, 256–257 and 275–277.
[216] Murray, 'Of nodes and networks'.
[217] Greve, 'Die Bedeutung', and Murray, *Bruges, cradle of capitalism*, 178–205.

jurisdiction, as was the case with the Hansa merchants in London, Venice, and Bergen. The Hansa traders attempted to get a similar exclusive enclave in Bruges, but were unable to do so.[218] The development of Bruges, its urban institutions, and the political power of the town and the county of Flanders were already too advanced to allow such a privilege to the foreign merchants. Nevertheless, they acquired some collective privileges, as the German traders did in 1252–3, obtaining toll reductions and increased legal security, and they formed their own organizations, the nations. The German traders had their own nation in the early 14th century, followed by the Venetians, who were the first to establish a formal consulate in Bruges. Some twelve nations emerged, each having its own board, representing the group of merchants in their dealings with the authorities and other parties, defending the merchants in conflicts, settling internal disputes, often according to their own law, and keeping in touch with the authorities at home.[219] At times the nations, which often made membership compulsory for compatriots, also operated as pressure groups, threatening to leave Bruges collectively, either because of political conflicts or to extort certain privileges or concessions from the town, as happened when the Hansa temporarily removed its staple and merchants to Dordrecht (1388–92), Antwerp (1437–8), or Deventer (1490–2). These nations thus offered the foreign merchants protection, a collective identity, and economic-legal advantages. The nations were much less important in 16th-century Antwerp and no merchant guilds or foreign nations developed in Amsterdam,[220] and their absence is indicative of the growth in the institutional framework of exchange and the higher security of trading in these newer centres. The high quality of this framework made these organizations apparently redundant.

Antwerp was the successor to Bruges in international trade. The foundation of its trading position was laid with the Brabantine fairs established in the 1320s, and held in Antwerp and Bergen-op-Zoom.[221] Trade there remained linked to the periodic fair system, in the shadow of the metropolis of Bruges, until *c*.1500, when Antwerp assumed a more permanent character as centre of international trade and was associated with a number of simultaneous structural changes. New trade routes started to emerge, first over land through Germany, and increasingly using the Atlantic, which opened up the field to new traders, such as those from southern Germany, from Spain and Portugal, from Holland and Zeeland, and the Merchant Adventurers of London.[222] The Hanseatic and Italian merchants were losing ground and remained in Bruges, but the new groups focused on Antwerp, bringing their spices, silk, gold, silver, colonial wares, butter, and cheese there. Antwerp became the new commercial metropolis of western Europe, with

---

[218] Murray, *Bruges, cradle of capitalism*, 220–221.
[219] Vandewalle, 'Vreemde naties', 27–42, and Gelderblom, 'The decline of fairs', 207–210.
[220] Gelderblom, 'The decline of fairs', 219 and 223–225. For Amsterdam, see below, pp. 239–240.
[221] Slootmans, *Paas- en koudemarkten*, 6–37, and Coopmans, 'De jaarmarkten'.
[222] Van der Wee, *The growth*, ii: 119–131, and Harreld, *High Germans*.

the Zeeland ports such as Middelburg and Veere as outports. Around the middle of the 16th century, no fewer than 2,000 merchants were active there, of whom only about 500 were from the southern parts of the Low Countries.

The rise of Antwerp, and the simultaneous decline of Bruges, was not the result of the silting up of the Zwin and declining access to the port of Bruges, as is often suggested in the older literature. This process had also been taking place in the 13th and 14th centuries, during Bruges's heyday, and, moreover, it could be countered by dredging, canals, and the availability of outports such as Sluis and Damme. The situation in Antwerp was not much better, with a similar use of outports and the need to trans-ship the cargo on smaller ships. Rather, an important factor in the shift to Antwerp was the political turmoil, temporarily forcing the merchants out of Bruges, and the rise of new products, routes, and groups of merchants which triggered change.[223] The change became permanent as the merchants who had been uprooted or new ones experienced the structural advantages that Antwerp offered in trade, specifically its better physical infrastructure, including the stalls for specialized merchandise in the courtyards of convents and the Exchange (Beurs) newly built in 1531. Antwerp also had a more favourable institutional organization. The adaptation and combination of institutions—insurance techniques, commercial bills, post services, bookkeeping techniques, the presence of long-distance hauliers—all concentrated in this one town as the centre of a giant commercial network, offered clear advantages of agglomeration.[224] The concentration of merchandise, merchants, and information, and the easy access to capital, transport, and knowledge offered greater efficiency in trade, attracted more merchants, and induced an even greater concentration of trade.

From the high Middle Ages onwards, larger cities generally had an advantage in developing trade because of their better and more extensive physical infrastructure, consisting of harbours, quays, cranes, warehouses, markets, public scales, and halls. Quays, built with wooden or stone walls, are found from the 11th century onwards. These allowed a harbour for bigger ships, with a deeper draught, which could be unloaded with levers, which were in use from the 12th century and made it easier to unload merchandise.[225] Cranes were introduced around the middle of the 13th century, as in Damme, where they were built to unload wine casks, and in Bruges, Utrecht, and Antwerp. These huge wooden constructions, powered by a circular treadmill, were an ingenious adaptation of windmill technology. The crane of Bruges, able to lift 1,800 kg of cargo, was famous.[226] Infrastructure like this was very costly, and it was mainly funded by urban governments. With respect to funding, cities had some major

---

[223] Van Uytven, 'Stages of economic decline', 259–269, stressing the political, and Van der Wee, *The growth*, ii: 124–136 and ii: 177–186, stressing changes in trade.
[224] Limberger, 'Economies of agglomeration'.
[225] Ellmers, *Frühmittelalterliche Handelsschiffahrt*, 150–169.
[226] Degryse, 'De oudste houten kranen'.

advantages over the countryside: large numbers of people, as well as the fiscal organization and the framework needed for the sale of annuities, enabling the procurement of larger sums of money. Moreover, the costly infrastructure was relatively safe, protected by the city walls. The result was an enormous growth in fixed capital goods, starting with the rise of cities in the 11th to 12th centuries in Flanders, where urbanization and territorial protection were strongest. The effect of this infrastructure, combined with their institutional framework, was a further concentration of trade in the largest cities. Building such an infrastructure, therefore, led to the continuity of trade centres over the centuries, unlike their early medieval predecessors which were more ephemeral. But the main effect of the infrastructure improvements, and the reduction in transport and transaction costs they brought, was to allow for the growth of trade and specialization.[227] The fruits of these largely collective investments, funded by flat-rate or even regressive taxes, largely accrued to a small group of merchants, who kept their capital floating. In most of these towns the same merchants could decide on extensions to the urban infrastructure because they held a dominant position within the urban government.

Government Influence on Trade

The concentration of trade was in many cases furthered by the power politics pursued by town governments. These tried to concentrate trade within the town walls by suppressing rural markets nearby, prohibiting forestalling and forcing country dwellers to buy and sell in urban markets. The most blatant examples of these policies can be observed in Flanders.[228] Ghent in the late 14th century, for instance, did not allow grain, meat, or fish to be sold within a radius of up to 30 km around the town. Urban politics also aimed at getting a grip on transit trade, which was often done in concert with the territorial lord. An early example was the series of measures the Counts of Holland took to give Dordrecht a firm hold on river trade beginning in the 11th century. This was partly for political reasons and the hope that tolls would enable them to profit from the rise of the town. In the 13th century, Dordrecht became crucial to the count for obtaining credit also: the town made direct loans to him as well as borrowing on his behalf, providing its burghers' property as security. The count first boosted the position of Dordrecht through a toll system in the delta of the rivers Rhine, Meuse, and Scheldt, focused on Dordrecht, and then, beginning in the late 13th century, by offering privileges to foreign merchants visiting Dordrecht, such as safe conduct, reduction in tolls, and respect for their jurisdiction in the event of

---

[227] Van der Wee, 'Continuïteit en discontinuïteit', 273–280, and Antunes and Sicking, 'Ports on the border'.
[228] Dijkman, *Commodity markets*, ch. 3, and Stabel, *Dwarfs*, 163–170. See also section III.3, pp. 107–109.

internal conflicts.[229] Further, from 1299 onwards, staple rights were granted to the town, forcing almost all ships on these rivers to unload their cargo of wine, wood, grain, and salt in Dordrecht to offer it for sale there.

Cities were very keen to obtain the staple right on transit trade, in order to safeguard the provisioning of their urban populations, but perhaps even more, to concentrate trade and to artificially lower prices in their markets, offering employment for burghers and profits to their merchants. Saint-Omer had a compulsory staple on the river Aa by the late 12th century and Cologne had started to build a staple on the Rhine in the second half of the 12th century and obtained a formal staple right in 1259. At that time, compulsory staples in the Low Countries multiplied. The first staple right in the Meuse valley was granted in 1317 in Liège for sea fish, followed by staples in Huy and Maastricht in the late 14th century, and in Namur and Dinant in the 15th.[230] Compulsory staples were strongest in areas where towns had emerged early and had acquired political-military power, as in Flanders, where Bruges, with its staples for Flemish textiles and wine, and Ghent, with its grain staple, were the main examples.[231] In Holland, on the other hand, staples and compulsory markets did not really develop, except in the oldest town, Dordrecht.

Some were established by the seller: the staple on English wool was the only place where English merchants sold their wool destined for the Continent. In the 12th and 13th centuries, the Flemish merchants came to England to buy the English wool there, but in the late 13th century they were pushed aside by English merchants. Their activities in the wool trade were increasingly concentrated at one location on the Continent. The wool staple, preferential from the 1270s and compulsory from about 1310, was established by the English crown as an economic, fiscal, and political instrument.[232] This also explains the sharp shifts in the location of the staple, mainly as a result of political conflicts and the desire to use the staple as a political ploy in making alliances. It moved from Dordrecht to Antwerp to Saint-Omer, where the first compulsory staple was established in 1313, and subsequently to Antwerp, to Bruges, to several English ports (1326–37), then to Bruges again, to English-occupied Calais (1363), to Middelburg (in 1348 and 1383–8), and then back to Calais. The establishment of this staple strengthened the position of English merchants in the wool trade and helped them sell their merchandise at higher prices, but it also had indirect effects, such as bolstering the position of large merchant-entrepreneurs in the Flemish, Brabantine, and Holland cloth industry, which depended on the fine English wool to a large extent. At that time it could only be obtained in a

---

[229] De Boer, 'Florerend vanuit de delta'. For the background of this policy: Dijkhof, 'De economische en fiscale politiek'.
[230] Suttor, 'Le contrôle du trafic fluvial', and Derville, *Histoire de Saint-Omer*.
[231] Nicholas, *Medieval Flanders*, 218 and 292–295. See also section III.3, pp. 107–110.
[232] Power, *The wool trade*, 52–55 and 86–103.

few places, and the staple opened up possibilities for monopolies in the further distribution and processing of the wool.

Compulsory staples in the earlier period had perhaps a positive effect—they allowed for a concentration of trade and a related increase in transparency and reduction of information costs and other transaction costs—but this advantage disappeared as the the institutional framework of markets became more secure and the volumes traded became bigger. In the 15th to 16th centuries, this artificial concentration of trade tended to lead to monopolies, price squeezing, and rent seeking by the merchants, both in buying and selling. Even if this caused inefficiencies, urban governments often kept on defending the staple rights of their towns, pressed to do so by their merchant elites who often held a firm grip over local government. An example is the continuous obstruction of trading activities in Aardenburg and Sluis by the Bruges government, pushed to do so by the mercantile elite, and even leading to the occupation of Sluis by a Bruges army and the reduction of the aldermen of Sluis to local deputies of Bruges.[233]

Governments also interfered in trade by regularly promulgating export restrictions, or even total bans. These were issued in the 14th century, applying to strategic materials such as alum, sulphur, and saltpetre, mainly in times of war, but also to grain in times of famine. With the expansion of public power in the late Middle Ages, the intervention of the government in the provision of foodstuffs became ever greater, both in the cities and at a central level. Concern for maintaining peace and order played a role, as did a moral sense of responsibility for the population and concern for fiscal revenues. The authorities' attention was primarily focused on grain and bread, the main staple foods. From the 15th century onwards, stocks of grain, including private ones, were checked and counted, public stocks were built up, grain provisioning was organized, grain exports were prohibited in times of scarcity, and speculation was punished. Moreover, when a grain shortage was anticipated, the urban authorities would subsidize imports by reimbursing some of the transport or transaction costs of grain merchants. All this was meant to prevent sharp price rises and famine in times of scarcity, and indeed seems to have had some effect in reducing price volatility. Even earlier, urban authorities generally started to fix bread prices, first in the largest cities, such as in Liège in 1252, Bruges in 1291, and Utrecht in 1341.[234] For each grain price, a corresponding bread price was fixed and publicly announced. The effect of this was to stabilize prices, although increasing market integration perhaps also played a role in the stabilization of bread prices.

The authorities also influenced the market by levying tolls and excises. Levying tolls was a regalian right, and in the course of the high Middle Ages came

---

[233] Dijkman, *Commodity markets*, section 5.1, and Nicholas, *Town and countryside*, 118–122, 135, and 161–162.
[234] Van Schaïk, 'Marktbeheersing', and Zylbergeld, 'Les régulations du marché'. For grain distributions to the poor see section VI.4, p. 310.

mostly into the hands of the territorial lords. The number of river tolls greatly increased, particularly in the 13th and 14th centuries, as has been demonstrated for the principalities of Liège and Namur where the territorial lords and lords with the rights to high justice established dozens of tolls at rivers, bridges, roads, and markets.[235] In Holland, strategically located in the delta of three large rivers, elaborate systems of river toll stations were devised to prevent ships from circumventing these tolls. They developed into a main source of income for some of the territorial lords: in the late 14th century the Duke of Guelders received a quarter of his revenues from the river tolls and the Count of Holland relied on them for a third of his.[236] The amounts levied were not arbitrary, but fixed, and from the 12th to 13th centuries were recorded in bills of tariffs. These levies were not very high, often about 1–2 per cent of total value, but some tolls were higher, and the large number of successive toll stations put pressure on river trade.

In addition to tolls on the transport of goods, indirect taxes were levied on the production and sale of consumption goods, mostly by the urban governments. In the late Middle Ages, excises developed as the most important source of income, by far, for most cities. Usually excises on most products were no more than a few per cent of the market value, but with wine and especially beer the total taxes on production and excises on the sale could vary between 8 and 50 per cent of the retail price.[237] Sometimes excises were also levied on hides, shoes, textiles, iron, and other industrial products. Since these were mainly basic necessities, except for wine, such excises were regressive taxation. The levying of excises also affected the organization of trade, since trade was concentrated and monitored by the authorities to allow for their proper levying. Sworn porters were appointed to act on behalf of the tax collectors. Often a strict separation of production, transport, and sale was enforced to allow maximum control and prevent tax fraud.

Excises were also used by the urban government as an instrument to protect local industries, as was most clearly the case for the brewing industry. From the 14th century, towns raised taxes on imported beer to protect local breweries, although the central government tried to prohibit this protectionism for political and fiscal reasons. This clash of interests can be clearly observed around 1500, as towns throughout the Low Countries levied high excises on beer imported from Gouda, the largest beer producing and exporting centre.[238] The town of Gouda took its case to the Grote Raad, and was victorious in court, but the authorities in importing towns immediately reacted by employing other excuses to hinder the import of Gouda beer, such as quality regulations or setting maximum prices on the pretext of protecting the poor burghers.

---

[235] Fanchamps, 'Etude sur les tonlieux', esp. 237–242.
[236] Verkerk, 'Tollen en waterwegen', and Weststrate, 'Laat-veertiende-eeuwse Gelderse tolrekeningen', esp. 228–229.
[237] Unger, *A history of brewing*, 140–157. For the importance of excises in urban finances see also section III.3, p. 119.
[238] Egmond, 'De strijd', and Unger, *A history of brewing*, 42–43, 54–55, 66–67, and 189–198.

When it suited them, the urban authorities encouraged open competition in the market, prohibiting forestalling, monopolization, and speculation, supported in this by canon law that condemned these activities as usurious.[239] The formation of secret partnerships or cartels in trade was usually prohibited, as in many 15th-century by-laws of the Holland towns.[240] Since markets were not fully integrated and flows of information were uneven and slow, large merchants had significant opportunities to use their inside information, especially if access to the market was restricted. Urban bylaws often tried to prevent this by concentrating trade at fixed times and fixed locations, such as in cloth halls in Flemish textile centres, to guarantee transparency and provide an equal opportunity to all participants in the market, including the consumers.[241] At the same time, the authorities wanted to control trade, protect local traders, and safeguard fiscal revenues. Town governments dominated by industrial interests tried to keep wages and costs of production low, promote exports, and protect their industries. Opportunism played a major role when considering which of these conflicting aims would be most important in a given situation, with the final result often depending on the power balance within the city among entrepreneurs, craft guilds, and merchants. Urban government in Gouda, for instance, was dominated by the large brewers, making the town's policies to a large extent subordinate to their interests.

Government interference was also evident in weights and measures. The public scales, or weigh house, were an important source of revenue through the weighing tax. It was an instrument to maintain control over trade, partly for fiscal purposes. At the same time, the weigh houses increased security in trade, since buyers could be certain of the size and volume of the traded goods, and they concentrated trade flows. Some of the weigh houses remained in the hands of territorial lords, as in Antwerp, but this right was usually granted to the urban government, which jealously guarded it, particularly with respect to villages, claiming the right to weigh.[242] Some towns, such as the Frisian towns of Sneek and Leeuwarden in the early 16th century, obtained the privilege of banning weigh houses in their rural environs. In Holland opportunities for weighing and trading in the countryside remained open much longer, especially in the north, where in the 15th and 16th centuries there were at least ten rural weigh houses. But in the late 16th century even in Holland the towns started to take coordinated action against the rural freedom of trading, and in 1597 a proclamation by the Estates of Holland was issued, aimed at banning most of the village scales and concentrating weighing in the official urban weigh houses.

---

[239] Wood, *Medieval economic thought*, 138–143, and Stabel, *Dwarfs*, 162–163.
[240] Cornelisse, *Energiemarkten*, 88–95.
[241] Stabel, 'Marketing cloth', esp. 23–28. Persson, *Grain markets*, 73–76, provides a more general perspective.
[242] Van der Wee, *The growth*, i: 75–76, and Noordegraaf, 'De waag'. For weigh houses in Holland: Dijkman, *Commodity markets*, section 4.3.

The variety of measurements was enormous in the Middle Ages, and because self-determination in these matters was seen as an expression of power and authority, each lord or town clung to its own measures. The fragmentation of measures led to disagreements, uncertainty, and a rise in information costs. But still, there was some progress, particularly from the 14th century onwards. Towns started to devise systems of measurements and organize the stamping of weights and measures, as Breda and several other Brabantine towns did from the 14th century.[243] Measures were displayed to the population in public places, cut in stone or cast in heavy metal. Sworn inspectors were appointed, such as the corn measure controllers who were present in all towns. Further, from the 15th century onwards, weights and measures were increasingly listed in conversion tables, either in private or public administrations, or in merchant manuals, as printed in the tens of thousands from about 1540 onwards.[244] With the unification of the Low Countries under the Burgundians and Habsburgs, the central government began to intervene in these matters in order to standardize them. In 1502, for instance, the troy ounce was made obligatory for all goldsmiths. More important for trade, probably, was the standardization and stabilization of coins in this period.

Increasing security on roads and rivers also had a positive influence. Safe conducts, greatly increasing in number in the 13th and 14th centuries, were offered or sold to merchants, and increasingly enforced through stronger governmental power. Moreover, territorial lords entered into treaties with one another to offer safe conducts for longer distances; for example, in 1344 the Count of Luxembourg entered into treaties with five other territorial lords that covered a large part of the main Basel–Bruges road, which ran through his territory.[245] In return, these lords would profit from the tolls and payments made by merchants for safe conduct. The increasing political unification of the Low Countries under the Burgundians and later the Habsburgs was not in all respects an advantage for security. The process of unification caused many disturbances, the most serious occurring around 1540, as Guelders strongly resisted Habsburg rule and its forces went on the rampage throughout the Low Countries. After this, there was only a short interval of quiet before the Revolt broke out in 1567. Moreover, incorporation in imperial dynastic policy was not always easy to reconcile with trading interests, whereas provincial estates and earlier territorial lords of such trading regions as Flanders and Holland were more inclined to give trade interests priority from self-interest. In these smaller political entities, merchants had more relative weight, and they successfully used that to influence policy.

At sea, security probably increased in the 15th and 16th centuries, when attempts to counter piracy and remove other obstacles to trade by organizing convoys and defending important trade arteries were undertaken. Holland,

---

[243] Scherft, 'Het stedelijk ijkwezen', and Van der Wee, *The growth*, i: 65–68.
[244] Mertens, 'Een niet bewaard XVIde-eeuws handboekje'.
[245] De Craecker-Dussart, 'Une grande route'.

rapidly becoming the main shipping region of the Low Countries, with many hundreds of seafaring ships, even undertook expeditions to prevent blockades of crucial arteries, such as the Sound, which formed the link between the North Sea and the Baltic and was particularly important for Dutch trade.[246] The Holland Estates did hesitate to undertake offensive military measures, as in 1438, when Holland, with a fleet of more than a hundred ships, waged war on the six main Hansa cities in northern Germany. Expenses for equipping a temporary fleet were borne mainly by the merchant towns and villages, which preferred to incur these costs than the otherwise possible losses in trade. Burgundian and Habsburg governments were largely reluctant to support Holland in these conflicts, since they set greater store by their dynastic and political interests. On the other hand, the Holland Estates, and the towns, were reluctant to support financially the building of a permanent Habsburg fleet that would accommodate the growing Habsburg desire to dominate the seas, partly for reasons of political prestige.[247] It was only around the middle of the 16th century that the various aims were temporarily aligned, as the Habsburg government proved willing to devote part of its tax income to sustain this fleet, and the defence of trade was incorporated in Habsburg maritime policy. This Habsburg fleet, using Veere in Zeeland as its naval base, indeed came to dominate the North Sea, foreshadowing the Dutch Republic's maritime dominance in the golden age. Around 1560, however, this central project dissolved, and Holland again steered its own course—able to do so because of its maritime strength.

Improvements in Transport and the Growth of Markets

After the big advances made in the 11th and 12th centuries, transport costs in the late Middle Ages were further reduced because of growing security and technical improvements. These costs still remained a major obstacle for transporting relatively cheap goods over large distances: for example, around 1400 they accounted for almost half the price of Baltic grain that was sold in Bruges.[248] For expensive goods and transport over shorter distances, however, transport costs comprised only a few per cent of the price in the market. Land transport was several times more expensive than water transport, but it remained important in the late Middle Ages.[249] For goods that had a high value and low weight, transport over land had always been competitive, but even for heavier goods it had some advantages. It was more flexible, could go directly from the point of origin to its destination, and was less hindered by tolls or compulsory staples, because it was less easy to monitor. Moreover, transport over land could often use

---

[246] Seifert, *Kompagnons und Konkurrenten*, 275–320, and Sicking, 'Die offensive Lösung'.
[247] Sicking, *Neptune and the Netherlands*, 105–121, and Tracy, 'Herring wars'.
[248] Unger, *The ship in the medieval economy*, 163–169.
[249] Blondé and Van Uytven, 'Langs land- en waterwegen'.

the merchant's own horses and wagon, which made it more competitive. Land transport was further facilitated by the improvements on roads. Transport on smaller rivers, on the other hand, sometimes became more difficult as a result of the competing use of the waterways for fishing, drainage, and generating power. Increasingly, fishing nets, sluices, and mills obstructed navigation. Sometimes sluices were even built or portages constructed to hinder access to competing market centres, which in 16th-century Holland led to conflicts between towns.[250] In some cases, as in the silted upper course of the river Leie in southern Flanders, where lack of water was the problem, sluices were built to make navigation possible, by damming up the water.[251] Since these sluices were often opened only twice a week, transport remained difficult.

Despite these potential problems, the many waterways in the coastal and riverine areas made transport easy and relatively cheap. In the 13th and 14th centuries the toll registers show busy traffic on the rivers. In 1306, more than 2,000 cargo ships passed the toll at Lobith on the river Rhine, mostly from Nijmegen, Arnhem, Zutphen, Duisburg, and Cologne.[252] In the 15th century, Holland extended its commercial position and acquired a pivotal role in inter-regional transport. As early as 1500, Amsterdam had 83 cogs and Rhine ships active in river trade, Dordrecht had some 140, Hoorn 114, Alkmaar 100, and even a small town such as Weesp had 30.[253] The total Holland fleet plying the rivers must have comprised perhaps a thousand large ships at the time.

Trade was further facilitated by institutional innovations such as the *beurtvaart*, mainly developed in Holland and the north-west. Barges departed on fixed days and at fixed times, in a system first developed through private initiative in the 15th century, for example, between Amsterdam and Utrecht and Dordrecht. From the beginning of the 16th century, however, cities started to establish them, first unilaterally and later bilaterally. Agreements were set up between towns, appointing the skippers who would take turns (*beurten*) transporting passengers and goods between the two towns according to an agreed schedule, with the first documented example being the service from Amsterdam to Hoorn (1529).[254] This was particularly beneficial to traders who did not have enough goods to hire an entire ship.

As a result of physical and institutional improvements, trade in the Low Countries kept on growing over the centuries. In the 13th to 15th centuries this growth took place mainly in inter-regional trade, in tandem with the regional specializations emerging in agriculture and industries,[255] and facilitated by the low transport costs over these relatively short distances. The region coming to

---

[250] Aten, *"Als het gewelt"*, 22–60.   [251] Derville, 'Rivières et canaux'.
[252] Alberts, *Het Rijnverkeer*, 8–9.
[253] Lesger, *Handel in Amsterdam*, 48–49, also for the data on the Gouda toll.
[254] De Vries, *Barges and capitalism*, 17–18, and Fuchs, *Beurt- en wagenveren*, 13–15, 31–39, 43, and 69–72.
[255] See also section VII.1, pp. 333–336.

the fore in this field, especially in the second half of the 14th century, was Holland, which developed a massive trade in its characteristic products, such as peat, bricks, beer, butter, and fish, and acquired a key role in trade with its huge fleet. Within this fleet, the role of Amsterdam increased steadily. At the sluice toll of Gouda, on the inland route through Holland, 6,880 ships were recorded in the single year 1543–4, with Amsterdam the most frequent place of origin.[256] Some areas, such as the inland regions in the infertile Ardennes, remained largely outside the growing exchange, however. Volumes traded there remained much more limited, as shown by toll registers, even from the late 16th century. In 1599–1600, over a period of 18 months, only 1,700 hectolitres (hl) of grain, 246 head of cattle, 7,700 sheep, 169 pigs, and 120,000 pounds of wool passed the toll near Bastogne—one of the most important in the Ardennes region.[257]

In the coastal and riverine areas the declining transaction costs and growing trade volumes allowed for increasing integration of markets, probably by the high Middle Ages. In the market for grain, the staple food, this integration was particularly important, since it resulted not only in an increasing correlation of prices in different markets, but also in reducing price fluctuations, thus having a positive effect on the stabilization of food consumption. International grain markets in northern and western Europe became integrated only in the 16th century,[258] but the process was established much earlier at a more regional level: probably, for example, in the 12th and 13th centuries between the western parts of the Low Countries and the grain-producing regions in the north of France, such as Artois and Picardy. Around 1300, hundreds of thousands of hectolitres of grain were already being exported from these regions to the north.[259] When price data become more abundant, in the years around 1400, it appears that the markets for wheat and rye in Artois, Flanders, Brabant, and Holland had become almost fully integrated. Year-on-year differences in grain prices within this area in the 15th century were rarely more than 15 per cent and generally lower than 10 per cent, even in a small and land-locked town such as Mol in the Campine, which was 50 km from the nearest large town.[260] The integration of markets helped to keep price volatility down: even in a region like Holland, which could not feed itself with grain because of the unfavourable soils, the coefficient of variation of annual wheat prices in the 15th century did not exceed 10 per cent on average. In this inter-regional trade, Holland shippers and merchants assumed an ever greater role. In 1461, for instance, half of the 454 grain shipments passing Abbeville on the river Somme, totalling 50,000 to 60,000 hl, belonged to Holland merchants.[261]

---

[256] Lesger, *Handel in Amsterdam*, 49–51.   [257] Yante, *Trafic routier en Ardenne*, 49–51.
[258] Unger, 'Integration of grain markets', and Id., 'Feeding Low Countries towns'.
[259] Derville, 'Le grenier des Pays-Bas'. See also section VII.1, p. 337.
[260] Tits-Dieuaide, *La formation des prix*, 43–44 and 251–256, and Dijkman, *Commodity markets*, chapter 9, which also contains information on price volatility.
[261] Van Tielhof, *De Hollandse graanhandel*, 12–20.

At that time, in the late 15th and 16th centuries, ever larger distances were covered and progress was notable also in ocean-going shipping. The size and design of sea-going vessels was improved, and cogs became larger, up to 200 or even 300 tonnes. The reduction of transport costs now made it attractive to transport bulk goods such as grain, timber, and herring over large distances, stimulating trade with the Baltic in particular. At first it was mainly the Hansa merchants who took advantage of this, but later Hollanders did as well, and they came to be responsible for more than half of all shipments through the Sound in the 15th century. Increasing numbers of ships were used, particularly in the seaports of Holland, and these ships became more specialized. The so-called busses had earlier been used for transport, fishing, and privateering, but in the 16th century they were designed and used especially for the herring trade, and *c.*1550 the combined herring fleet of Holland, Zeeland, and Flanders numbered some 700 of these busses, of which 400 had their home ports in Holland.[262] Holland also had a merchant fleet of many hundreds of large vessels: in 1477, it numbered 230 to 240 large ships, with a total tonnage of 38,000 tonnes. By then, Holland had far surpassed the maritime tonnage of Flanders and other parts of the Low Countries, as well as that of the republics of Genoa (some 20,000 tonnes) and Venice (20,000 to 30,000 tonnes). In the following centuries, the maritime power of Holland would grow dramatically. By 1530, in the Baltic trade alone, some 270 large ships were used by Dutch merchants, increasing to 700 in 1565.[263]

These ships were very costly, and fitting them out was expensive as well. In the 16th century the increasing size of the ships and the longer distances covered made the expense of fitting them out for voyages even more costly. The accessibility of the Dutch capital market, which offered credit at low interest rates, facilitated investment in large ships.[264] Another solution used to finance them was the *partenrederij*, the 'share shipping company', with the ownership of the ship divided between several individuals, often including the shipper. This system was introduced in north-western Europe in the late Middle Ages and became particularly widespread in Holland. By the 15th century ownership of ships in Holland was often split into as many as 32, 64, or even 128 shares. This offered ordinary people opportunities to invest in ships, and it also contributed to spreading the risk, with some individuals owning shares in as many as two dozen ships at the same time. The division of shares must have given rise to some type of limited liability, although there is no concrete proof of this.[265] The

---

[262] Kranenburg, *De Zeevisscherij*, 25–40. Cf. also section VII.1, pp. 338–340.
[263] Sicking, *Neptune and the Netherlands*, 42–44, and De Vries and Van der Woude, *The first modern economy*, 350–358.
[264] Gelderblom and Jonker, 'Completing a financial revolution', 644–648, and Hart, 'Rederij'. See also section V.2, pp. 191–193.
[265] Kind communication by Heleen Kole, Utrecht University, 21 Jan. 2008. For the advantages of this system see Hart, 'Rederij'.

partenrederijen originally settled their accounts after each voyage, as expenses and revenues were calculated and profits or losses were distributed among the shareholders. However, in the 16th century, the partnerships became more permanent, operating more than a single trip, and equity shares were sometimes sold or transferred. This was in contrast to Flanders and Brabant, where actual ownership of a ship was generally in the hands of a single individual, making financing investments more difficult and risks much greater.

The greater risks may also explain why trade insurance became widespread in Flanders and Brabant, in contrast to Holland where there was no system of insurance before the late 16th century.[266] In Italy, insurance contracts had developed around 1350, and they were also employed for trade voyages to the Low Countries. One of the oldest contracts, from 1347, concerned the shipment of alum from Genoa to Sluis, an outport of Bruges. Shortly afterwards, insurance contracts were also used in Bruges. Premiums remained fairly stable over the centuries, at some 4–5 per cent of the insured risk for shipments from Bruges or Antwerp to Bordeaux (although they rose in times of insecurity); the rates were 7–10 per cent to Seville and 10–18 per cent to Genoa. By 1549, and again in 1563, the Habsburg rulers started to regulate the insurance system by standardizing policies and prescribing standard forms.[267] This system helped to reduce the risks in investing in long-distance trade. On the other hand, by using partnerships the Holland shipping sector avoided the high overhead costs of these insurances, forming a crucial element in their competitive edge, as explicitly noted by observers around 1530.[268]

Helped by this, and by the flexible capital and labour markets, Holland shippers and merchants became ever more prominent in long-distance sea transport, especially in the Baltic trade. By *c.*1500, already 600 of the 1,000 ships passing through the Sound annually, and transporting hundreds of thousands of hectolitres of grain, were from Holland, with Amsterdam assuming the most prominent position.[269] The massive imports of rye from the Baltic to Holland went along with integration of grain markets at a European level. Grain prices in Lübeck and Utrecht in the first half of the 16th century already showed some correlation (with a coefficient of 0.52), and even more between Utrecht and more distant Danzig in the second half of the century (0.69). At the beginning of the 17th century, grain prices in Danzig and Amsterdam were almost fully correlated (0.88).[270]

---

[266] Davids, 'Zekerheidsregelingen', and De Groote, *De zeeassurantie*, 9–10, 102–103, and 135–138.
[267] Davids, 'Zekerheidsregelingen', 196–198, and De Groote, *De zeeassurantie*, 28–29 and 33–36.
[268] Van Tielhof, *De Hollandse graanhandel*, 116.   [269] Ibid., 86–106.
[270] Achilles, 'Getreidepreise und Getreidehandelsbeziehungen', 46–49.

Reconstructions have been made of international trade for the early 1540s,[271] showing the decline of Flanders and the dominance of Antwerp, but also the already firm position of Amsterdam, with more than 6 per cent of all international exports from the Low Countries. This share increased subsequently, partly complementary to the role of Anwerp in international trade. Much more important for Holland, however, was intra-regional and inter-regional trade. The growth of trade is reflected in the high levels of commercialization of economic activities there, as early as the 14th century.[272] In the 16th century, almost all the output of Holland agriculture and industries was destined for the market. Markets in Holland were evidencing many advantages, such as an absence of non-economic forces and restrictions, relatively high security, and a very dense network of markets in both town and countryside. This lowered transport and information costs, and stimulated commercialization and commercial integration. These elements are found particularly in Amsterdam, which never received staple force or privileges comparable to Dordrecht's, but still supplanted Dordrecht as the principal trading centre in Holland from the early 16th century. Market exchange there was free of compulsory staples and non-economic coercion, up to the early 17th century, as this influence was eventually developed by the Dutch East India Company, at least overseas.[273] Also, Amsterdam did not have fairs but developed a permanent market, where the institutional framework of exchange and the guarantees offered by the authorities allowed merchants to operate without the support of corporate bodies, such as merchant guilds or foreign nations.[274] As volumes traded on the markets increased in the 15th and 16th centuries, the open and dense network of markets in Holland became more attractive to trade than those where agglomeration was aided through the use of power and privileges, most notably in Flanders, where this artificial concentration had been an advantage in the earlier situation of thin markets.

Moreover, trade in Holland profited from the well-functioning capital market there, making capital available at low cost, for investments in ships, merchandise, and physical infrastructure. The flexible labour market in Holland proved an additional advantage, especially with the scale-enlargement in shipping and the growing need for wage labour. This favourable institutional framework of markets had already emerged in Holland in the late Middle Ages, and was largely a result of endogenous factors, more specifically the absence of feudal elements and non-economic power of cities or interest groups. This enabled Holland

---

[271] Lesger, *Handel in Amsterdam*, 31–50, and Gelderblom, 'From Antwerp to Amsterdam', 250–254. For levels of commercialization, see section VI.3, pp. 294–300.
[272] Van Bavel and Van Zanden, 'The jump-start'.
[273] De Vries and Van der Woude, *The first modern economy*, 382–396.
[274] Gelderblom, 'The decline of fairs', 229–230.

shippers and merchants to have a growing role in trade, from the 14th century at the latest. Hence the dominance of Holland in international trade, and the rise of Amsterdam to a position as central international staple market, as completed in the late 16th century,[275] did not come out of the blue but were clearly built on a late medieval foundation.

Some authors explain the commercial rise of Amsterdam, and the simultaneous decline of Antwerp, in terms of the religious troubles of 1566 and afterwards, the fall of Antwerp in 1585, and the blockade of the river Scheldt, with the subsequent split in the gateway system of the coastal Low Countries and the emigration of hundreds of Calvinist merchants to Holland.[276] In this view the rise of Holland, with Amsterdam as its commercial heart, would not have been inevitable, but rather the effect of these events. But the preceding does not support this view. The economic and commercial rise of Holland appears to have started much earlier, with the decisive take-off as early as the second half of the 14th century; followed by further growth in the 15th century and a second acceleration in the late 16th century.[277] Transport and fishing, and the emergence of open and favourable markets, played an important part in this take-off, with Holland acquiring maritime dominance in the North Sea in the 15th century, in terms of the number of commercial ships, active merchants and shippers, and naval power. Amsterdam, as gateway within Holland, benefited most from this development, and began to rival Antwerp in the transit trade between east and west as early as 1540. By 1520—long before 1585—Antwerp started to show signs of decline, such as its failure to retain its hold over the European spice trade and the stagnation of its German trade. The commercial situation in Antwerp worsened in the 1550s and was further aggravated by the religious turmoil in the decades after 1566.[278]

The final stage in the rise to commercial dominance of Amsterdam only occurred in the period 1590–1610, and was probably hastened by the political and religious events and the problems Antwerp experienced in this period, but this rise was firmly built on fundamental advantages developed in earlier centuries. These advantages were to a large extent located in the organization of markets, and allowed Holland—and Amsterdam in particular—to develop gradually from a marginal position in trade to a dominant one. In Holland, the social structure and the absence of non-economic power allowed for flexible, open, and favourable markets for goods, as well as for capital, labour, and land. In other parts of the Low Countries, these were more restricted, and offered

---

[275] Davids and Noordegraaf, *Dutch economy*, and De Vries and Van der Woude, *The first modern economy*, 366–382.
[276] Israel, *The Dutch Republic*, and Lesger, *Handel in Amsterdam*, 110–137. Cf. also the discussion by Gelderblom, 'From Antwerp to Amsterdam', 247–249.
[277] Van Bavel and Van Zanden, 'The jump-start'. See also section VI.1, pp. 247–251.
[278] Van der Wee, *The growth*, ii:153–161 and ii:216–243.

less flexibility and security. Other ways of redistribution or transfer outside the market, determined by social relations rather than by economic ones, remained more important there. These differences had a strong effect on the potential for economic growth and the path of social change in the later medieval period, topics to which we will now turn.

VI

Social Change in the Late Middle Ages

VI.1. SOCIAL STRUCTURES AND CHANGE

Social Transformations in the Countryside

Despite the relatively small area of the Low Countries, regional differences in social formation at the beginning of the late Middle Ages were quite marked, especially in the countryside, where they usually dated from the time when an individual region was first occupied.[1] The variable timing and organization of occupation and reclamation resulted in sharp contrasts in the social distribution of power and property between the regions, and these contrasts remained for many centuries. For instance, in Holland, the large-scale reclamation work carried out at considerable distances from existing manorial structures by free colonizers in the high Middle Ages was still reflected many centuries later in the weakness of feudal, coercive power, the weak position of the nobility, and the strong presence of a free landowning peasantry. On the other hand, in the neighbouring Guelders river area, where numerous manors had emerged in the early Middle Ages, most of the land in the 14th century was in the hands of the former manorial lords. Noblemen and religious institutions held a firm grip over economic, social and political life there. The boundary between Holland and the Guelders river area, and the distinction in social organization, was still as clear-cut as it had been in the high Middle Ages.

These regional differences, most clearly expressed in the social distribution of the ownership of land, were found all over the late medieval Low Countries.[2] In some regions no less than 80–90 per cent of all cultivated land was owned by peasants, as in Drenthe, where the social structure was dominated by peasant landowners, with strong village communities and extensive common lands. In late medieval Holland and inland Flanders, too, probably two-thirds or more of the land was in the hands of peasants, and was fairly evenly distributed over a large number of holders of small and medium-sized plots. In sea clay Frisia,

---

[1] Cf. sections II.2, pp. 32–35 and 38–40, III.1, pp. 51–59 and III.2, pp. 78–86.
[2] Van Bavel, 'Structures of landownership', table 6.1, largely reconstructed backward from 16th-century data.

Salland, and the Guelders river area, on the other hand, some three-quarters of the land was owned by large landowners, including territorial lords, nobles, and religious institutions.

Differences among towns in various regions were less pronounced than those in the countryside, and there was greater variation among towns within a region, but regional differences can still be observed. This holds in particular for those elements going back to the earliest phases of the towns, such as the composition of landed properties and revenues of the urban elite, the political organization, the extent of formal privileges and monopolies, and the relationship with its rural hinterland.[3] To a large extent, these reflect the rural context out of which these settlements emerged, and they therefore show the same regional variations.

In the late Middle Ages several parts of the Low Countries saw great social changes, but in the course of these one factor generally remained constant: the social distribution of land ownership. Regional differences in ownership patterns remained essentially intact in the period from the beginning of the 14th to the middle of the 17th century.[4] This was especially true of the ratio between the land owned by peasants, common burghers, and small ecclesiastical institutions on the one hand, and territorial princes/sovereign lords, nobles, large institutions, and wealthy burghers and patricians on the other. Although there were changes in the exploitation of land ownership, particularly as a result of the rise of the lease, this prime aspect of the social distribution of land ownership showed great stability in almost all regions. Although the land market, investment strategies, and population development brought dynamism at the micro level, they did not produce any fundamental changes in landowning structures at the regional level.[5]

The social distribution of land ownership and property, which was formed in the early and high Middle Ages, in its turn was a main element in shaping the extent and direction of social change during the late Middle Ages. It formed the regional prism which refracted the various dynamic forces of the period, chief among which was the rise of markets for land and lease, labour, capital, and goods, which increased mobility of production factors and intensified competition. To a lesser extent, the late medieval process of state formation can be considered a motor, and population developments could also contribute to social and economic dynamism.[6] However, changes did not take place in all regions, and when they did, their direction could vary widely as a result of the divergent effect of the existing regional structure of power and property. In the later Middle Ages, therefore, distinctions between regions became even more pronounced.

---

[3] See section III.3, pp. 107–110.   [4] For instance, Van Bavel, *Transitie en continuïteit*, 427–432.
[5] Van Bavel, 'Structures of landownership', esp. 135–139. For Holland, the main exception in the Low Countries, see below, pp. 259–260.
[6] For the effects of population development see section VI.2, pp. 282–287.

Here we will look more closely at some of the possible processes of social change in the late Middle Ages, whose clearest example was probably the rise of large tenant farmers. In the Guelders river area, coastal Frisia, and coastal Flanders, in the 15th and 16th centuries the land increasingly came into the hands of a small group of wealthy tenant farmers.[7] This development occurred at the expense of the farmers of small and average-size tenanancies, who gradually lost their leased lands and largely disappeared from the scene, as has been documented for the Guelders river area. The agrarian landscape there became dominated by large tenant farmers, with 35 to 70 hectares. At the beginning of the 15th century, there had been no huge tenant farms in this area, but by around 1580 there were hundreds of them, and farmers with more than 25 hectares occupied 40 per cent of the total cultivated land.

This process had far-reaching consequences for the rural population. Many thousands of families in such regions lost their leased land and hence the possibility of operating an independent farm. They now depended on income from wage labour, which did not amount to much because of falling real wages. As a result, many suffered extreme poverty, particularly around the mid-16th century, when the developments described above increased in pace and the large tenant farmers were able to strengthen their position further with respect to their less fortunate fellow villagers. The socio-economic polarization among the rural population in these areas was strong. Village communities increasingly lost their homogeneity and cohesion, and became divided into a large group of impoverished farm workers and a small group of well-to-do lease farmers. These *coqs du village* also monopolized village offices and local decision-making.[8] Impoverished villagers also became dependent on the large farmers for their income, since they were often hired by them to work as wage labourers alongside seasonal workers. A three-tier hierarchy consisting of large landlords, large tenant farmers, and landless wage labourers emerged to take the place of the earlier structure dominated by large landlords and medium-sized family farms.

This scale-enlargement of farms did not occur everywhere in the Low Countries: instead fragmentation took place in Drenthe and even more so in inland Flanders and Holland. In these regions of peasant land ownership, most farms were very small, ranging from a half to four hectares.[9] Many people had direct access to land through their smallholding, and this remained the case. In the course of the 15th and 16th centuries, fragmentation proceeded even further, most clearly in inland Flanders. Around 1570 some 80 per cent of rural households there had a holding smaller than 5 hectares.

---

[7] Van Bavel, 'Land, lease and agriculture', 31–34.
[8] For the dominance of these farmers within the village communities see also section III.3, p. 100.
[9] De Vries, *The Dutch rural economy*, 63–67, and Thoen, 'A "commercial survival economy"', 113–116.

This divergence in the development of farm size is associated with differences in the social distribution of land ownership. The crucial element in this link is the availability of lease land. In parts of the Low Countries dominated by large landowners who had lost their non-economic power with the dissolution of the manorial system, the landowners started to use short-term leasing as an instrument for exploiting their land from the late 13th century onwards. They stopped using customary or hereditary tenure, and since they could no longer rely on manorial organization, they started to lease their land ownership out for short terms, making leased land amply available from the middle of the 14th century.[10] In the Guelders river area, for instance, c.1400 more than half the cultivated land was leased for short terms, and this had increased to three-quarters by the end of the 16th century. In coastal Friesland and Salland, also dominated by medium and large landownership, this share was even greater: around 1520 some 80–90 per cent of the land was leased. Consequently, farmers in these areas were almost completely dependent on the lease market to obtain land. At the other end of the spectrum were regions such as Holland and Drenthe, dominated by small and medium-sized peasant landholdings, where only a quarter to one-third of the land was leased out,[11] and this was used by the peasants only as an addition to land held as property within a structure dominated by small-scale peasant agriculture. Therefore, the differences in the availability and role of leased land were closely associated with the social distribution of land ownership.

A second element in the divergence between regions was the specific organization of the short-term lease. In regions such as the Guelders river area, this resulted in strong competition and mobility. The lease contract, with terms between 5 and 12 years, offered the tenant no permanent rights to the land, and he lost his right to use the land after expiry of the contract. The contract was offered to the highest bidder, resulting in great mobility. In most other regions, however, there was a close, more personal relationship between landlord and tenant, with the latter often claiming the right of silent reletting, as in Holland and inland Flanders.[12] But in the Guelders river area, lease land became the object of fierce competition and changed hands very often; extending the lease was exceptional, and happened only for economic reasons.

Farmers there were obliged to compete continually against one another for the lease land. Such competition forced them to reduce costs, increase market orientation, and specialize to increase profits. The large investments made jointly by tenants and their landlords, partly from credit obtained on the capital market, resulted in increasing specialization, changes in land use, and technological

---

[10] See section V.1, pp. 172–175. For the figures that follow, see Van Bavel, 'The emergence and growth of short-term leasing', and Slicher van Bath, *Samenleving onder spanning*, 612–620.

[11] Bieleman, *Boeren op het Drentse zand*, 252–261 (figures for 1630), and Diepeveen, *De vervening*, 57–65.

[12] See section V.1, p. 176.

innovation, in most cases aimed at reducing labour input and thereby maximizing surpluses and profits.[13] Properly functioning labour markets were also needed to achieve this: the emerging large farms were too large to work with family labour alone, so wage labourers had to be hired. Markets for labour, capital, and goods were thus a vital and necessary precondition for the emergence of large tenant farms. If combined with the rise of a competitive type of short-term leasing and the availability of large amounts of lease land, the competition for land in a context of open and extensive markets in the long run led to a significant accumulation of land and the rise of large tenant farms. In the regions where this happened, in some parts of the Netherlands in the 15th–16th centuries, and in the 17th–18th centuries in parts of England, the rise and specific arrangement of the short-term lease thus resulted in the proletarianization of large parts of the rural population and a rise in wage labour.[14] In the Guelders river area in the mid-16th century, indeed, some 50 per cent of the population was mainly or fully proletarianized, and 60 per cent of labour was performed for wages, which may have been higher than anywhere else in Europe.[15] In these parts of the Low Countries the transformation from a medieval to a modern capitalist society took place as early as the 16th century.

Other regions in the Low Countries were characterized instead by the fragmentation of farms, which took place, for instance, in Twente, Holland, inland Flanders, and parts of Brabant, where peasant landowning was dominant and land users often divided their farms among their children. The link between average farm sizes and demographic developments stayed intact, with an inherent tendency towards population growth and fragmentation of farms. A relatively large group there thus had the prospect of owning at least some land, securing their subsistence and the possibility of supporting a household so that they could marry and establish their own families early, compared to children in regions dominated by large landownership.[16] Moreover, the land ownership there was divided fairly evenly among the owners, a situation which offered many people access to a plot of land large enough to support a family. This gave rise to a demographic regime characterized by relatively high rates of marriage, early marriage, and rapid population growth, combined with the subdivision of farms.

Small freeholders who had little land strove to increase its physical output, and they achieved this by turning to intensive agriculture.[17] If their region was

---

[13] Van Bavel, 'Land, lease and agriculture', esp. 29–31 and 35–39, and Brenner, 'The Low Countries', 296–302 and 308–315.
[14] Cf. Brenner, 'The agrarian roots of European capitalism', esp. 83–99 (for England), and Van Bavel, 'Elements in the transition' (for the Netherlands).
[15] Van Bavel, 'Rural wage labour'. See also section V.3, p. 204.
[16] For more details see section VI.2, pp. 285–286.
[17] See Thoen, 'A "commercial survival economy"', 111–122, and Van Bavel, 'People and land', esp. 22–27.

suitable for market orientation, for example, as a result of favourable market structures and a location close to large urban markets, as in inland Flanders and Holland, this went along with specialization for the market. Specialization became labour-intensive there, since these peasant farmers aimed to use the relatively plentiful labour available within the household. In inland Flanders and Holland, for instance, they specialized in labour-intensive commercial crops such as flax, hemp, mustard, and hops.[18] When specialization and intensification were successful, they opened the way to an even further fragmentation of the holdings and enabled ever smaller holdings to survive.

This situation of numerous peasants owning small holdings and seeking additional revenue through intensification of labour was ideal for protoindustrialization. Labour-intensive cottage industries were a logical extension of the peasant economy. They enabled the peasants to employ the surplus labour of all household members, using raw materials produced partly on their own holdings and inexpensive tools which they mostly owned themselves. The rise of market-oriented, non-agricultural activities in the countryside took place in a few regions during the late Middle Ages. Among them were the Pays de Herve and the Vesdre valley east of Liège, where metallurgical activities, and in particular textile industries, developed, the latter mainly from the 15th century,[19] but the main examples were inland Flanders and Holland. In inland Flanders proto-industrial activities became increasingly important in the late Middle Ages, employing a quarter of the labour input around 1570. In Holland the proportion was even higher, at $c.$ 40 per cent. On the other hand, proto-industries did not develop in those regions which came to be dominated by large tenant farmers and wage labourers, such as the Guelders river area, where only a small percentage of total rural labour input was engaged in such activities.[20] Markets and capital were easily available there, but the main basis for proto-industries—the presence of numerous peasants who owned small amounts of land and who could offer their surplus labour and that of family members—was lacking. The erosion of this peasant base and subsequent disappearance of proto-industrial activities can be clearly seen in coastal Flanders in the 13th and 14th centuries and in Holland in the late 16th and 17th centuries with the transition to large-scale capitalist agriculture.[21]

In the peasant regions with small holdings where proto-industrialization developed, it may have been a motor of social transformation. This effect is often suggested for proto-industries, assuming that the producers would become more and more dependent on the merchant-entrepreneurs, the accumulation of capital would increase, the division between labour and the means of production would

---

[18] Bieleman, *Boeren in Nederland*, 82–84 and 91–96, and Thoen, *Landbouwekonomie*, 722–725 and 982–1000. See also section VII.1, pp. 326–327.
[19] Dechesne, *Industrie drapière*, 21–24.   [20] Van Bavel, 'Proto-industrie'.
[21] Van Zanden, *The rise and decline*, 36–40 and 116–125.

grow, and a class of entrepreneurs would emerge. The rise and development of proto-industry would thus have played an important part in the advance of proto-capitalistic production relationships in the countryside and have functioned as a forerunner for the Industrial Revolution.[22] In this respect it is instructive to examine the two examples of strong proto-industrialization in the Low Countries, Holland and inland Flanders, showing that this process could be both a motor of change/transition (Holland), and an element of involution (inland Flanders).[23]

The two regions had different types of proto-industrial activities. The textile sectors were predominant in rural inland Flanders,[24] where many tens of thousands of men, women, and children worked in this sector. In Holland, on the other hand, the sectors that flourished were not industrial in the strict sense; they were fishing, shipping, and peat digging, as well as brick production, bleaching, and shipbuilding. In these sectors, as well as in Holland textile industries, activities were generally less labour intensive than in Flemish proto-industries. Significant in this respect was the use of labour-saving spinning wheels, iron cards, and the growing import of yarn for use in the textile industries in Holland.[25] To an increasing extent semi-finished goods were also imported and labour-intensive production stages were avoided. Capital-intensive sectors, on the other hand, were much more important than elsewhere, and increasingly so in the period under investigation. Most non-agricultural activities in the Holland countryside were thus more capital oriented than labour oriented, and increasingly so; an aspect which had drastic consequences for organization and dynamics within the sector. Another marked difference between the regions is that non-economic coercion in these sectors played a much smaller role in Holland than it did in Flanders, which applied to both production and trade. In Holland a consistent and long-standing policy of suppression of rural activities operated only in the brewing industry. Urban privileges were either insignificant or did not apply to the same extent as in Flanders. Associated with this was the fact that division of labour between town and countryside was less clear-cut than it was in Flanders. In those cases where such a division existed in Holland, it was mostly the result of economic developments and caused by growing capital intensity and scale-enlargement, as, for instance, can be observed in the shipbuilding sector, rather than artificial and enforced by urban coercion and privileges, as in Flanders.

In the Flanders region, in general, producers were independent peasants who owned their small farms and the main means of production, which were relatively cheap. Most of these producers worked independently, on their own account.

---

[22] Mendels, 'Proto-industrialization', and Schlumbohm, 'Produktionsverhältnisse', esp. 210–232.
[23] There is a more extensive discussion in Van Bavel, 'Early proto-industrialization'.
[24] Sabbe, *De Belgische vlasnijverheid*, 74–85 and 125–129, and Thoen, *Landbouwekonomie*, 980–1020.
[25] Van Bavel, 'Early proto-industrialization', 1130–1135. See also section VII.2, p. 362.

In the linen sector, for instance, most of the producers were small peasants who organized the cultivation and processing of the flax, as well as the spinning and weaving by themselves, within their own household. Thus, in the Flemish linen industry there was no putting-out system in the strict sense, but a *Kaufsystem*, in which the role of the merchants was more limited to the commercial sphere.[26] At the same time, the producers were limited in production and trade by the privileges and prerogatives of the cities, merchants, and guilds, which were strong in Flanders. The urban-based groups used their privileges to suppress certain rural activities and to stamp out possible competition from the countryside, which was a concern of guilds and guild-dominated city governments. Market coercion and control over trade were also used to skim off the surplus of proto-industrial activities. Merchants and other mainly urban-based groups were able to do so through their strong control over sale, distribution, export, and raw materials, often founded on privileges and force. It was the merchants who held the strongest position in the proto-industrial sector, buttressed by staple and market privileges, restrictions on export of raw materials, and trade and production regulations, and also by their control over the final production stages and marketing of the product.[27] They had direct access to the surplus value through trade, so they had no need to interfere directly in property relations or the organization of production.

In Holland, however, the urban merchant-entrepreneurs at an early stage had already obtained control over the (often costly) means of production through their investments, aided by the accessibility of the capital market and the low cost of credit there. The Leiden patriciate, for instance, in the 14th century had already acquired large interests in brick and lime ovens.[28] Both industries were capital intensive: they required relatively expensive capital goods as well as land and fuel. The latter made it attractive for urban investors to combine such activities with peat digging operations, which required huge investments in drainage canals and transport facilities. In the course of the processes of scale-enlargement, capital intensification, and accumulation, which were characteristic of activities in Holland, most sectors became controlled by urban capital as a result of the investments made in costly fixed capital goods and materials. This offered the urban elite the opportunity to profit from the work of rural wage labourers without having to use coercion or non-economic privileges.

In both regions, proto-industrial activities were originally performed by semi-independent peasants who combined such activities with small-scale farming, often with the family as the principal unit of production. Most products were destined for non-local or even non-regional markets, and the organization,

---

[26] See for instance Van der Wee and d'Haeseleer, 'Ville et campagne', esp. 764–767, and Haagen, ' "Uitbuiting-door-handel" ', 215–243.

[27] See Sabbe, *De Belgische vlasnijverheid*, 199–203, 212–213, and 230–243, and Stabel, 'Urban markets', 148–150.

[28] Van Kan, *Sleutels tot de macht*, 89–90, and Brand, *Over macht*, 184–187.

finishing, and marketing were partly controlled by others than the producers themselves. In inland Flanders, where the position of the peasants in the production process was relatively stable because of their control of the land, the tools, and often the raw materials, this situation remained in place, even during the period of sharp growth of proto-industries in the 16th century. In Holland, however, there were significant changes in this period. Non-agricultural activities were on an increasingly larger scale, and peasant producers lost their semi-independent position when they lost control over the means of production and became subjected to urban capital as wage labourers. Also, production within the household, combined with subsistence farming, was increasingly replaced by wage labour performed by individual family members outside the household farm. Around 1550, no less than 65 per cent of proto-industrial work in Holland was performed for wages, compared with only 28 per cent in inland Flanders.[29]

These divergent courses of proto-industrialization were determined by the specific institutional arrangement of markets, the social position of the participants in the market, and the general socio-political context in which they operated. Markets in Holland were more open, flexible, and efficient, and offered a more favourable framework than in Flanders. This applied to the market for goods, as well as to those for capital and labour. Associated with this, and probably partly resulting from it, were the differences in interest rates on the capital market and differences in the attractiveness of making investments in fixed capital goods between the two regions. In addition, differences in relationships between town and countryside and between urban merchant-entrepreneurs and rural producers are part of the explanation. In inland Flanders the peasants held a firm grip on landownership, whereas the urban elite was dominant in finishing and trade, which induced both to cling on to this situation. As a result, in Flanders the organization of proto-industrial activities showed stability, whereas in Holland they were very dynamic. Peasants in Holland lost control of their means of production, and the link between non-agricultural activities and subsistence farming on their smallholdings was almost completely severed, leading to an erosion of the proto-industrial base. From that time, industries moved to the cities, as did the proletarianized countrymen.[30] In Holland the rise of proto-industry contributed to the transition of the rural economy; in inland Flanders this was not the case, despite its quantitative importance. There, it strengthened the existing peasant situation.[31] Small-scale, peasant-owned farms remained viable because of the highly intensive, horticulture-like sectors of specialized agriculture and

---

[29] Van Bavel, 'Rural wage labour', 55 and 59.
[30] Van Zanden, *The rise and decline*, 31–41. For migration and urbanization, see also section VI.2, pp. 284–287.
[31] Thoen, 'A "commercial survival economy"', 119–122. For the demographic effects, see section VI.2, pp. 290–291.

the additional income obtained from proto-industrial activities, both requiring enormous labour inputs by the peasant families.

But even if the organization of markets were similar, the social distribution of property and power of the region in question could lend the functioning of markets a divergent effect on rural development. Commodity and lease markets, for instance, emerged early in both the Guelders river area and inland Flanders. In the former region, dominated by large landownership, they facilitated the rise of large tenant farms, since specialization for the market was one of the main instruments by which the tenant farmers maximized profits and strengthened their position in the lease market. In Flanders, characterized by peasant land ownership, the effect was the opposite. The presence of markets there facilitated intensification and further fragmentation of holdings. Leased land remained an addition to the peasant ownership structure, and was divided over the multitude of small peasants. The market for goods and products in Flanders was dominated by the urban merchant elite, through non-economic as well as economic force, further contributing to this divergence. The institutions were not determining in themselves, but their specific organization and the social context in which they developed produced these divergences.

Similar divergences can be observed for the rise of credit, in some cases strengthening peasant society and in others undermining it. The interlink of credit and land markets could produce many losers. Credit supplied by burghers to peasants might produce a situation in which the rents absorbed all the surpluses from the countryside and led to impoverishment of the peasants. Moreover, this weakened the bargaining position of these peasants; for instance when they were indebted to urban merchant-entrepreneurs who also supplied raw materials or organized proto-industrial activities with them. In the final resort the peasant was sometimes compelled to sell his land, often to the creditor. Such forced sales were not an automatic result, however, since the effect of urban capital on the countryside depended on the wider social and economic context. This can be observed in inland Flanders and coastal Flanders, two adjacent regions where significant differences existed in the use and effect of credit.[32] In coastal Flanders, as a result of the increasingly skewed social property structures, further aggravated by ecological problems, credit was an element in the loss of peasant landowning, whereas in inland Flanders credit increased flexibility in sustaining small peasant holdings and supported the existing structure. In some circumstances the credit obtained in the market could even be beneficial to the peasant, for instance, by offering him the opportunity to invest in his holding,[33] particularly when credit was not obtained for consumption or distress, but because of favourable opportunities to invest.

---

[32] Thoen & Soens, 'Appauvrissement et endettement', 703–720.
[33] Thoen, *Landbouwekonomie*, 896 and 926–935.

Developments in the agricultural and proto-industrial sectors varied according to region, but mining was one rural sector where social developments were very pronounced everywhere. As can be seen from the stone quarries in Soignies, in calamine mining in Vieille Montagne/Altenberg, and in coal mining, capitalist production relations rapidly advanced as early as the late Middle Ages. The nature of coal mining required large-scale organization and high capital input, which led to a clear dominance of capital and the use of relatively large numbers of wage labourers. In the 16th century, as the easily accessible seams became exhausted and more investment had to be made to dig deeper and pump out the water, this process was further accelerated.[34] At the time, thousands of workers were employed in the coal pits around Liège, with the investments being borne by partnerships of wealthy urban brewers, drapers, merchants, and entrepreneurs, such as the famous arms manufacturer Jean Curtius, as well as by civil servants, lawyers, and nobles, who often reaped huge profits from mining activities. A similar development can be observed in Walloon metallurgy.[35] The costs of the ever-larger ovens and blast furnaces became too expensive for individual workers, forcing them to form associations, but also to attract external capital and sell shares. In the course of this process the ownership of most ovens and furnaces came into the hands of a small number of urban investors. This tendency was most pronounced in the rural sectors requiring large capital investments, such as metallurgy and mining.

Social Transformation in the Towns

In the cities of the Low Countries, generally speaking, social transformation in the later Middle Ages was less fundamental than in the countryside. Most changes in the cities had taken place earlier, in the 11th to 13th centuries, with the first acceleration in the urbanization process and the rise of urban merchants and entrepreneurs. Sectors in which relatively large numbers of labourers were needed, such as building, public works, and transport, then witnessed a clear rise in wage labour. Wage labour had also increased in some urban industries, particularly in cloth production, since some artisans expanded their production, mainly for export, and required extra-household labour. Also, in the 13th century the power of the urban elites in the towns of the Low Countries had become stronger and more distinct.[36] The members of the urban elite distanced themselves socially and legally from groups they perceived as inferior, and they monopolized political power by making offices semi-hereditary and employing their right of co-optation. In many cities, oligarchies of only a few dozen families

---

[34] Lejeune, *La formation du capitalisme*, 129–137, 142–144, and 251–253; unfortunately, more recent in-depth studies on this interesting sector are lacking.

[35] Gillard, *L'industrie du fer*, pp. 235–237, and Gutmann, *Toward the modern economy*, 49 and 58–60.

[36] See also section III.3, pp. 117–119.

emerged. They also used their authority to avoid taxes on capital goods and promote indirect imposts on consumer goods as the main fiscal instrument in the cities, which was a relatively heavy burden on the ordinary population. The resulting regressive character of taxation increased economic polarization in the urban population.

This situation provoked more and more resistance. Around the year 1300 many cities in the Low Countries saw the emerging guilds agitating against it and sometimes even coming to power in this struggle, most particularly in Flanders. Where guilds obtained influence in urban government, they did not change the market orientation of urban production, but tried to control the negative side-effects of market competition and to block the process of scale-enlargement of production structures. The main goals of the guilds and guild-influenced governments were full employment, guaranteeing a decent living for small masters or guild members, and securing independence for the producers. Therefore, they protected small-scale commodity production by independent masters who had their own workshops and tools and employed only a few labourers, often partly from their own household. Guild regulation and corporatism, however, did not exclude all wage labour. Production in the cities was often concentrated through subcontracting, with networks of small-scale workshops under a central organization led by a wealthy entrepreneur.[37] This can be seen in the cloth industry in late medieval Bruges, where subcontractors were employed to bypass the restrictions on the maximum size of workshops; these were mainly craft masters themselves, with the wage labourers consisting of journeymen and impoverished craft masters. Similar arrangements can be seen in public works, as in the building and masonry sector in Bruges, where in the period 1388–1401 the entrepreneur Jan van Oudenaarde accumulated 44 per cent of the town's contracts, equalling some 80,000 days of work. But, although the effect of corporatism must be nuanced, in general the rise of wage labour in the cities seems to have remained more limited than in the countryside. Small-scale production for the market, organized by independent small masters, remained dominant over the centuries, even in export-oriented textile centres.[38] This can be seen in a medium-sized town such as 15th-century Lier, which had some 1,200 households, where weaving of cloth was organized by about 230 independent weavers, mostly possessing their own loom and each employing one journeyman. But the same was also true of large centres such as Lille.

The wealth distribution in the towns, which can be reconstructed from fiscal registers, reflects the above outline, although the link to social structure is not always easy to establish. The poor, who probably comprised a quarter

---

[37] Lis and Soly, 'Subcontracting', and Sosson, 'Les métiers', 339–348.
[38] Van der Wee, 'Die Wirtschaft der Stadt Lier', and Duplessis and Howell, 'Reconsidering the early modern economy', esp. 50–51 and 83–84.

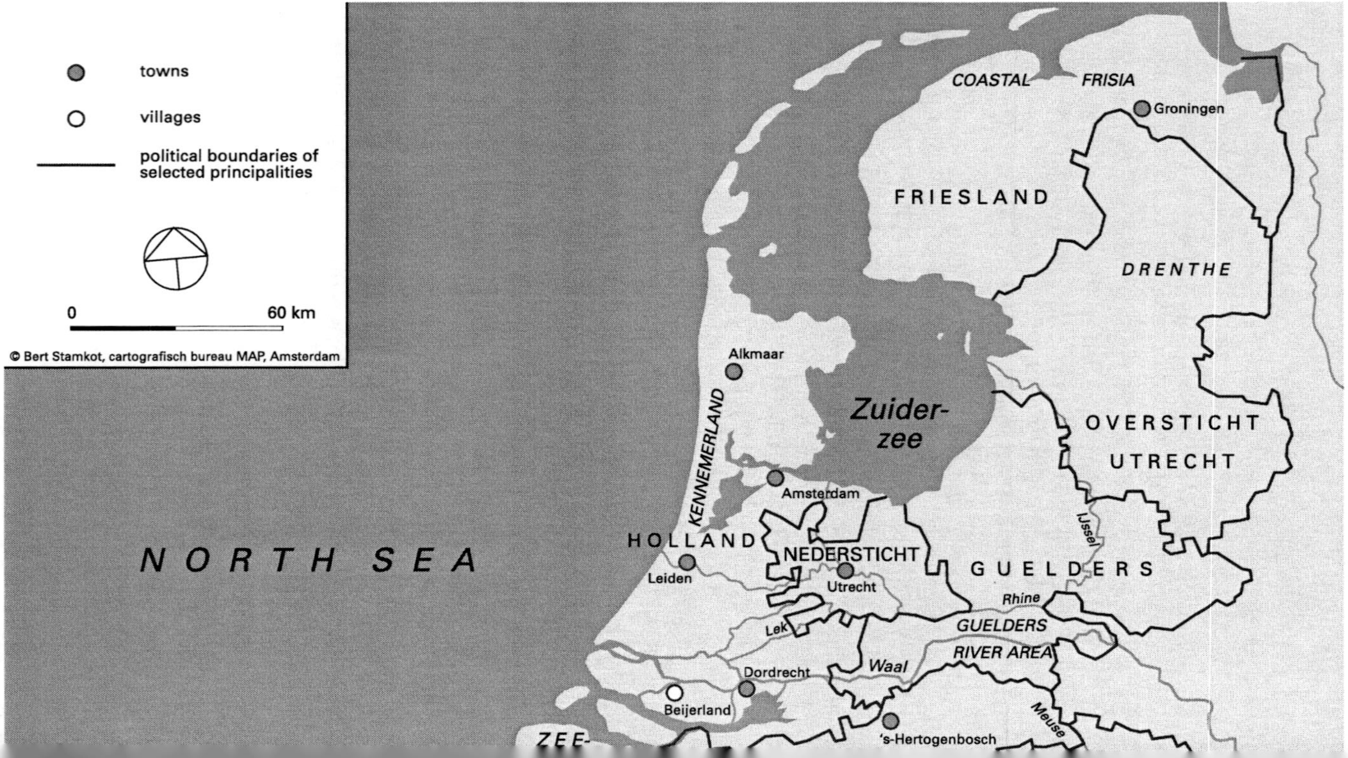
towns
villages
political boundaries of selected principalities
0
60 km
© Bert Stamkot, cartografisch bureau MAP, Amsterdam
COASTAL
FRISIA
Groningen
FRIESLAND
DRENTHE
Alkmaar
KENNEMERLAND
Zuider-
zee
OVERSTICHT
UTRECHT
Amsterdam
IJssel
HOLLAND
NEDERSTICHT
GUELDERS
NORTH SEA
Leiden
Utrecht
Rhine
Lek
GUELDERS
RIVER AREA
Waal
Dordrecht
Beijerland
Meuse
's-Hertogenbosch
ZEE-

Map 4. Towns and villages in the Late Middle Ages

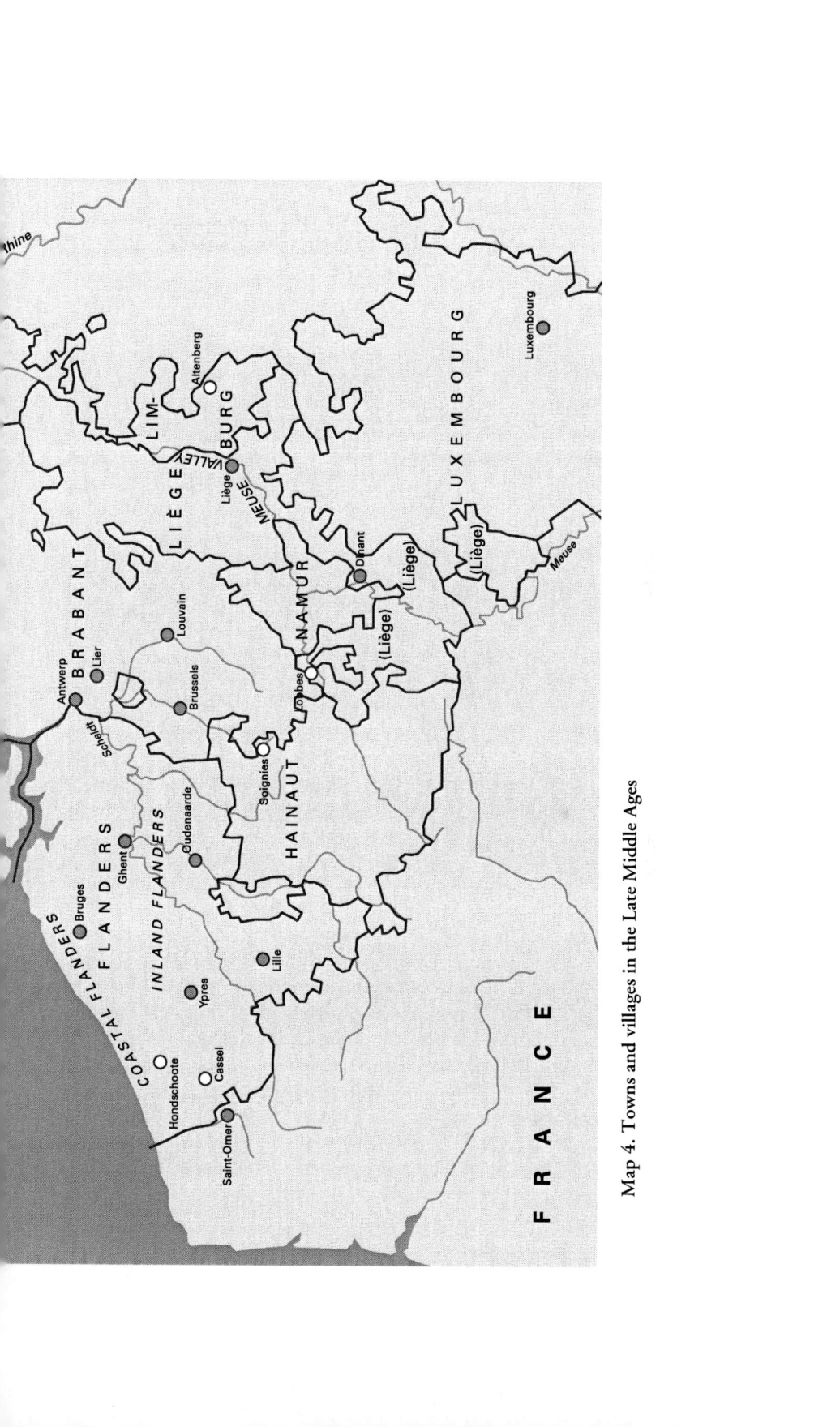

Table 6.1 Five wealth categories, each constituting 20 per cent of the urban population, and their share of total wealth

	Eight towns South LC c.1400	Alkmaar 1500	's-Hertogenbosch 1502	's-Hertogenbosch 1552	Leiden 1498
Poorest 20 %	5 %	1 %	1 %	1 %	0 %
Next 20 %	7 %	3 %	3 %	3 %	1 %
Next 20 %	13 %	8 %	7 %	6 %	2 %
Next 20 %	21 %	21 %	17 %	16 %	12 %
Richest 20 %	54 %	67 %	73 %	74 %	85 %
Gini coefficient			0.68	0.70	

Sources: Van Uytven & Blockmans, 'De noodzaak' (for 8 towns; Soignies, a small town dominated by quarries, is omitted because of its exceptional structure), Van Gelder, 'Een Noord-Hollandse stad', Posthumus, *De geschiedenis van de Leidsche lakenindustrie*, i:386–399, and Blondé, *De sociale structuren*, 61–62, 143, and 188.

of the total population, and sometimes also the nobility and clergy, were exempt from taxation, and thus largely omitted from registration. Wealth was spread fairly evenly among the rest of the population. This can be seen in the medium-sized towns of Mons and Soignies (in Hainaut), Luxembourg, Namur, Ninove and Louvain (Brabant), Oostende, Diksmuide, and Eeklo (Flanders), investigated for the decades around 1400 (Table 6.1 above). Similar percentages apply to the large city of Ghent, although those without property are left out of the registration there.[39] This relatively even distribution of wealth, as well as the fact that the distribution was much more uneven in Kortrijk where guild power was weaker, seems to reflect the success of corporatism in protecting a fairly large middle group of independent craftsmen, small traders, and shopkeepers.

Only in the 16th century did further marked changes in industrial organization in the towns occur. Such changes may have first taken place in the Holland towns, where guild power was weaker than in Flanders or Brabant. The polarizing effect can even be seen in a medium-sized town such as Alkmaar, which still possessed many agrarian traits and was more dominated by middle groups than other Holland towns. Still, the distribution of wealth was more skewed than in towns of similar size in the southern Low Countries, when around 1500, the lower 40 per cent of population had only 4 per cent of the total wealth and the upper 20 per cent had 67 per cent. In Leiden, a major centre of cloth production, where the large drapers in the 15th and 16th centuries began to dominate the sector, this distribution was even more pronounced. In 1498 the poorest 60 per cent of the Leiden population, mainly textile workers, owned only 3 per cent of the total wealth, and most of them owned hardly any property or none at all. In contrast,

[39] Blockmans, 'Peilingen', i: 215–270, iii: 199–210.

the top 3 per cent of the Leiden population, mainly drapers, owned more than half of the wealth.[40] These figures clearly reflect the social polarization in this city, which paralleled the emergence of more capitalist production relations.

In Flanders changes in the organization of production were less fundamental, but when they occurred, it was mainly in the new sectors in developing industrial towns and villages. This applied to tapestry production in and around Oudenaarde, which flourished as an export industry from the early 16th century. The necessary supplies of raw materials and semi-finished products, the risks, high prices, and long production periods made capital an all-important factor in this sector.[41] Often the relatively expensive tools and the costly dyed yarn were advanced or leased out by the tapestry masters to the weavers. The fact that many tapestry workers incurred debts and owed money to an entrepreneur, bound them even more to their employer. Weavers, both in town and countryside, were in all respects subordinated to the entrepreneurs and under the control of the urban guild, which was dominated by the large tapestry masters.[42] In this sector the labour force consisted mainly of wage labourers, not independent producers. Many weavers worked for piece wages, and sometimes the tapestry workers themselves employed others. Although the number of journeymen was limited formally to three per tapestry master, the number of employees was unrestricted, and various forms of subcontracting were used. Thus, hierarchical concentrations emerged, dominated by a few urban entrepreneurs, some of whom employed up to 300 people and sold the output to the big tapestry merchants in Antwerp, the most important market.

Transitions in production relations can be observed even more clearly in the 'new draperies' in Hondschoote in the far south of Flanders. Hondschoote was not an old industrial town with urban rights, but a proto-industrial village focused on the production of serges, a lighter and cheaper cloth made from coarse wool.[43] Its success in international markets caused this village to grow very rapidly to some 15,000 inhabitants around the middle of the 16th century. Corporatism was weak there and there was little regulation of production. Merchants held a clear monopoly in trade, buttressed by the monopoly they held in practice on the process of dyeing. The largest merchants sold some 20,000 to 30,000 lengths of serge cloth per year, which was the total annual output of many thousands of workers. At first, production was undertaken by independent workers, but as a result of competition, the dominance of large merchants and the absence of regulation or protection for small producers, most workers lost ownership of their looms in the course of the 16th century and became proletarianized. The wages they earned were low, especially since many weavers migrated to Hondschoote

---

[40] See also Brand, 'Urban policy', criticizing DuPlessis and Howell, 'Reconsidering the early modern economy'.
[41] Vanwelden, *Het tapijtweversambacht*, 46–47, 82, and 100–101.
[42] Stabel, *De kleine stad*, 190–194.
[43] Coornaert, *La draperie-sayetterie*, 29–31, 338–343, 356–372, and 396–403.

and flooded the labour market, and the workers had no organization. Labourers also had to cope with continual competition from the cheap labour of workers in the surrounding villages, whereas the cost of living in Hondschoote was much higher. To some extent the workers were able to overcome this by working a small plot of land, echoing the proto-industrial background of industries in this area. At the same time this was a further intensification of labour which robbed these people of every spare hour. Child labour was also used to obtain additional income, with children often employed from the age of 6 or 7.

In other textile centres, particularly in Holland, the rise of permanent child labour can also be observed.[44] Earlier, children had been used only for industrial activities within the household or as part of their occupational training, and then only when they were older, but in the 16th century child labour for wages outside the household increased significantly. Orphans and foreign boys, in particular, were hired by textile entrepreneurs, often with municipal authorities or orphanages as intermediaries. From the late 16th century on, such children, sometimes as young as 7, but generally beginning at 9, were almost systematically exploited. This was most pronounced in Leiden, where wages were very low, work heavy, the prospect of a career only faint, and bargaining power almost absent.

In the large older cities there were also some infringements of guild power and small-scale production. In Antwerp, the entrepreneur Gillis van Schoonbeke was the most notable example.[45] Starting as a land speculator and property developer, around 1550 he acquired a dominant position in the building industry and public works in Antwerp, after he was commissioned by the town government to build a new part of the city and the new city ramparts. He developed a building firm which included brick ovens, chalk ovens, and peateries, employing many thousands of wage labourers. Through his vertical organization of production he could undercut all competition, particularly that of small independent masters, driving them out of the market. As soon as he achieved an actual monopoly in public works in Antwerp, backed by the town government which had become increasingly dependent on him, he started to force wages down.

Van Schoonbeke was unusual, however, even in the metropolis of Antwerp. He was successful in such sectors as the building industry, where guild power was weak, but not in sectors with strong corporatism. Also, his industrial organization remained unique; he was not a sign of structural changes in Antwerp economy and society.[46] In general, most industrial sectors did not lend themselves to large-scale production, thus precluding further changes in the organization of production, and the restrictions and regulations enforced by the guilds and small

[44] Posthumus, *Geschiedenis van de Leidsche lakenindustrie*, i:361–362 and iii:575–613.
[45] Soly, *Urbanisme en kapitalisme*, 275–280, 301, and 415–424.
[46] Ibid: *Urbanisme en kapitalisme*, 411–447 and 'Nijverheid en kapitalisme', 331–352. For discussion of resistance to Van Schoonbeke, see below, p. 276.

independent producers were too robust to be completely broken. These groups were sometimes supported by the merchants, who saw the large entrepreneurs as their potential rivals. In the end, even Gillis van Schoonbeke lost out: his position and monopolies were broken because his operations provoked too much resistance. In addition, industrial activities generally were relatively risky, sensitive to business trends and fashion, and as a result most people regarded investing in expensive capital goods as too risky. These factors precluded a development towards large factories in this period.

In 16th-century Holland, the development towards more centralized wage labour proceeded further than in Flanders and Brabant. This was the logical sequel of the late medieval development of Holland's industries, both in town and countryside, which had become increasingly capital intensive and employed mainly wage labourers. The process was driven by the near absence of obstacles and restrictions to capitalist development and the openness and keen competition in markets for goods, land, labour, and capital in Holland. Also, capital was relatively cheap there and labour was expensive, thus stimulating investments in technology and fixed capital goods. Guild restrictions were weak, and did not inhibit the introduction of technology or the centralization of production. Moreover, Holland industries, having few nobles in the region to attract as customers, had always focused on products for the middle classes; these were more uniform and better suited to large-scale production than luxury products.[47] All this resulted in the rise of substantial production units in Holland which worked with expensive capital goods and relatively large numbers of wage labourers, compared with the workshops of craftsmen in Flemish and Brabantine towns. This can be observed from the brick ovens, shipbuilding yards, bleacheries, and breweries, each employing about ten wage labourers or more, and often including a few women and children among them.[48] A similar situation was found in peateries and some textile workshops. In these industries the distance between the labourers and the entrepreneur was increasing, and many owner-entrepreneurs were no longer directly engaged in the organization of production but instead delegated this task to a manager.

Large investments in capital goods and more efficient organization made labour productivity relatively high in the Holland industries. Still, even in Holland this development seems to have halted in the course of the 16th century. Investment in industries, remaining risky compared with property investment, did not increase further. Wealthy burghers invested instead in urban debts and in land. They bought many plots of land from peasants, thus turning small-scale peasant property so characteristic of the medieval Holland countryside into large-scale burgher property. Together with the transition in proto-industries,

---

[47] Van Bavel and Van Zanden, 'The jump-start', 523–528. For industries in Holland, see also Noordegraaf, 'Betriebsformen'.
[48] Unger: *A history of brewing*, 103–104, and *Shipbuilding*.

this resulted in a transformation of rural society in Holland. A new pattern of large land ownership also emerged in the newly reclaimed polders, which came into being mainly through investments by wealthy burghers, as happened in Beijerland, the first polder in Holland, reclaimed in 1559. Around the middle of the 16th century, 35 per cent of the land in Holland was owned by burghers and urban-based institutions, and even more in the southern and central parts, increasing to perhaps 50 per cent by the end of the century.[49] This resulted in the rise of large land ownership, a significant increase in the availability of leased land, the emergence of large tenant farms, and a breakthrough to agrarian capitalism in Holland, which took place in the late 16th and 17th centuries.

This was an exceptional development, as no other part of the Low Countries experienced a comparable rift in the social distribution of landed property during the late medieval or early modern periods. In highly urban Flanders, for example, the process of accumulation of land by wealthy burghers slowed during the 15th and 16th centuries.[50] The exceptional development in 16th-century Holland was due to a host of factors. The urbanization rate was extremely high, higher than anywhere else in Europe, and the burghers' wealth was growing rapidly. The emergence of more absolute rights of property and lease rights to land, the latter taking place in the 16th century, made it attractive to invest in land. This land became available because of the social polarization which was inherent in the specific organization of proto-industrial activities in Holland, and which weakened the economic position of landowning peasants. Their decline was further accelerated by the political-religious disturbances and the related military operations at the end of the 16th century. The peasants with hardly any capital reserves were worst affected and often had to sell their land.

This massive investment in landed property by wealthy burghers was made at the expense of other types of investment, most notably in industries. Even in Holland, with its secure and open markets, investment in industries remained risky compared with real estate investment, and profits were limited compared with those made in trade. Urban annuities were another attractive alternative, balancing risks and profits, and, for those interested, landownership and annuities could enhance one's prestige and political influence. This, together with exhaustion of the scope for further scale-enlargement and technological innovation, limited investment in industries. As a result, from the mid-16th century, the decline of small-scale commodity production in Holland almost came to a standstill, and industrial workshops remained limited in size.

Fully proletarianized labour also remained more expensive than forced or peasant labour. From the mid-14th to the mid-16th centuries, Holland seemed to develop more capitalist production relationships, determined by the market, but in the late 16th century semi-forced labour relationships became more

---

[49] Van Bavel, 'Rural development'. For the polders, see also De Vries, *Dutch rural economy*, 192–196.
[50] Thoen, 'A "commercial survival economy" ', 130–131.

important. Under the circumstances, and particularly with the state of technology at the time, it was impossible to secure greater benefits by further investing in labour-saving technology, either in agriculture or in industries. Coerced labour remained the safest road to high profits, and was deployed from the late 16th century on by Holland, and the Holland-dominated Dutch Republic, most notably in its American and Asian colonies. In addition, cheap foreign peasant labour was increasingly used by Holland entrepreneurs, either in its own region in proto-industries organized by these entrepreneurs or in the form of migrant labour employed in Holland.[51] The peasants worked for wages, but part of their subsistence costs could be shifted to their peasant households, so that wage labour of full proletarians living in Holland itself could not compete with them. Also, from the middle of the 16th century, guilds were founded in large numbers in Holland.[52] Their rise may have protected small-scale independent production for the market and slowed down further scale-enlargement, and formed another element which precluded a possible development towards some type of industrial capitalism in Holland.

The development of larger production units and the centralization of textile industries in manufactories, which took place from the late 16th century in part of the Holland linen, cloth, and silk production,[53] remained an exception. In many sectors large manufactories only emerged when semi-forced labour was used below market costs, as in the bridewells and rasp- and spinning houses, or by employing orphans, and not as a result of capitalist development.[54] It was exactly in Holland that the system of correction houses with coerced labour became most fully developed. Apart from these cases, the growth of wage labour and scale-enlargement in the organization of industrial production came to a standstill after the late 16th century. In the end the large merchants remained dominant in the Holland economy, also because in the political arena the organized craft sector was not able to offer a sufficient counterweight and their interests were well served by the policies of urban and territorial governments.[55] In many Holland towns, and above all in Amsterdam, merchants had a strong political position, which was later extended to the provincial level, and even to the whole of the northern Low Countries, with the Dutch Revolt. In the late 16th century, about 80 per cent of the burgomasters of Amsterdam were directly involved in trade, and these could exercise a powerful hold over the organization of the economy in Amsterdam, in Holland, and indeed in the Republic as a whole.[56] Such developments were reflected in the social distribution of capital

---

[51] Van Zanden, *The rise and decline*, 8–11, 77–79, and 103–109, and Lucassen, *Naar de kusten*, 159–182.

[52] Lourens and Lucassen, 'De oprichting en ontwikkeling', esp. 49–53. See also section III.3, pp. 121–122.

[53] Noordegraaf, 'Tussen ambacht en manufactuur'.   [54] Cf. Spierenburg, 'Early modern prisons'.

[55] Lis and Soly, 'Different paths of development', esp. 230–238.

[56] Lesger, *Handel in Amsterdam*, 140–144. Van Dillen: *Van rijkdom en regenten*, 310–313, and *Amsterdam in 1585*, xxxiv–xxxv.

in Holland. In the period 1500–1650 total capital wealth in Holland increased from 10–12 million guilders to 500–550 million guilders, i.e. more than tripling per capita wealth in real terms.[57] This wealth was mainly concentrated in the cities, in the hands of a small urban elite which had gained its wealth mainly from long-distance trade. Of all the Holland towns, the distribution of wealth was most skewed in Amsterdam, where in 1585 the Gini coefficient of wealth distribution was about 0.74. Of the 391 people who paid the highest taxes, and whose occupation was mentioned, 278 were merchants, compared to 45 industrial entrepreneurs. The merchant predominance was even greater among the highest taxpayers. In 1630 the Gini coefficient had moved further up to about 0.85. At that time, taxed wealth in Amsterdam was 63 million guilders, with the top 1 per cent (all active in long-distance trade) owning one-third.[58]

Although the transformation in Holland had been radical, since it occurred in a society which had originally been dominated by peasant landowners on family holdings, it halted after the late 16th century. The same applied to coastal Flanders, which had witnessed the rise of agrarian capitalism in the 15th and 16th centuries; and later on, to an even greater extent to regions such as coastal Frisia and the Guelders river area, where increasing commercialization, scale-enlargement, and proletarianization left deep marks. These were among the earliest European examples of regions undergoing a transition to a mainly capitalist economy and society. But opportunities for further scale-enlargement became exhausted, because of the state of technology, or unattractive compared with other investment possibilities. This applied not only to agriculture, but also to urban industries, where in highly urbanized Holland further developments should have taken place. Investments in land, debts, and trade, and acquiring instruments of coercion, were safer and more attractive. The situation was different in some proto-industrial regions, such as the Vesdre area, or regions where scope for capital intensification and scale-enlargement was still present, as in the Meuse valley, with its metallurgical and mining activities. These were the regions where the basis for industrial capitalism, and the associated social changes, would be laid. Other regions, sometimes neighbouring ones, remained characterized by independent small-scale producers. Drenthe and Veluwe were among these, with small and medium-sized peasant farms on owned land remaining predominant and hardly any structural change in economy and society. In inland Flanders the late medieval structure of small peasant holdings and small-scale craftsmen dominated by urban merchants underwent some development, but mainly through extreme intensification and fragmentation of units of production. Its location close to coastal Flanders, which underwent a transition to large-scale agrarian capitalism, is illustrative of

---

[57] Van Zanden: 'Economic growth', esp. 13–16 and 21–23, and 'Tracing the beginning'.
[58] Goldsmith, *Premodern financial systems*, 204–206.

the variegated mosaic the late medieval Low Countries formed with respect to social change.

State formation, Fiscality, and Bureaucracy

Alongside the developments in agriculture and industries, social structures were also influenced in the later medieval period by the rise of territorial principalities and the process of state formation, with the parallel rise of fiscality and a bureaucracy. Although this process in the Low Countries was slow and characterized by the emergence of a host of medium-sized principalities and other polities, instead of by a single state, it nevertheless had some social effects, especially where a territorial principality was established relatively early and became well-developed, as in Flanders. The effects were ambivalent. On the one hand, the process undermined existing forms of self-determination and political participation, but on the other hand state formation in the Low Countries stimulated freedom and offered possibilities for representation. Within the state apparatus itself, an ambivalent social development can also be observed. On the one hand, the process offered *homines novi* from the urban middle groups the chance of a career in princely service, but on the other hand it strengthened the position of the upper nobility. We will assess these opposing developments here.

In some cases, the growing authority of territorial lords in the 12th and 13th centuries brought freedom for servile or semi-unfree people, as the princes granted franchises to towns, villages, and even whole areas, as in Namur and Brabant in the first half of the 13th century.[59] Here, in a deliberate policy, the princes undermined the power of feudal lords over the local population, a power which was already on the decline there. The rise of territorial principalities also took place in parallel with the development of new political-legal organizations, or the incorporation of existing ones, such as the rural aldermens' courts in the Guelders river area. Especially in regions where the power of feudal lords had been strong, all this may have reduced the arbitrariness of levies and increased legal security. In other regions, however, the process of state formation resulted in collisions with the population, especially where political self-determination was well developed, feudalism traditionally had been weak, and princely rule began late. This was the case in Friesland and Drenthe, but also in Westfriesland, Kennemerland, and Waterland, the three northern parts of Holland. The rural population there experienced the growing power of the Count of Holland infringing on their practice of self-government and their customary organization of the distribution and levying of local and central taxes. They resisted the growing authority of noblemen and comital representatives, who undermined the power of their village communities, and the erosion of their rights and customs in general.[60] Their revolt came to an end in 1275, as the count decided

---

[59] Steurs, 'Les franchises'; see also section III.3, p. 96.
[60] Van Bavel, 'Rural revolts'; see also sections III.1, p. 74, and III.3, p. 96.

to make concessions in the sphere of self-government in local justice, fiscal matters, water management, and the administration of collective goods, laid down in a charter.[61] In the longer run, however, most of these rural areas lost out to growing princely authority and the noblemen who functioned as the local officers. In regions such as these, which previously had little noble influence, the process of state formation went along with a growing power of the nobility; not as landowners but as office holders. Towns, on the other hand, were mostly able to retain more of their power of self-determination and relatively broad political participation, especially where guilds had acquired a role in town administration in the decades around 1300.

State formation slowly eroded earlier forms of political participation, but the rising importance of taxation and credit operations to territorial lords also offered opportunities for the rise of representative organizations. In the earliest phase of the slow and incomplete process of state formation, territorial lords still depended heavily on their income from landed properties and regalian rights, especially the right to levy tolls. The territorial lords who controlled large rivers, such as the Count of Holland and the Duke of Guelders, profited enormously from the high and growing tolls. Around 1400, as much as a quarter to one-third of their revenues came from river tolls.[62] Taxation, however, was gradually becoming more important as a source of income for the territorial lords. Even in Holland, with its many rivers, by the late 14th century the income from taxes overtook other revenues.[63] Taxes were mainly aids or semi-voluntary contributions to be imposed with the consent of the subjects or their representatives. Initially these aids were only levied on special occasions, such as the marriage of the prince, but they increasingly became more regular and were granted for several years in a row, as in Hainaut, where from 1324 to 1438 no fewer than 38 such aids were levied, and later in the century almost every year.[64] The need to have the consent of the subjects to levy the aids forced the territorial lords to consult a body in which the interests of the subjects were represented, at least in theory. The extent of representation should not be overestimated, since not all subjects were directly represented in the Estates, but only in name, that is, through the clerical elite, nobles, and patricians. This body was later formalized as the Estates. In urban regions such as Flanders and (later) Holland, cities played an important part in these Estates, since the most important fiscal base was located there; by 1400 the cities and their populations in Holland paid more than 40 per cent of the aids, and in Flanders as much as 54 per cent.[65]

---

[61] Hoppenbrouwers, 'Op zoek naar de "kerels"', 228–229. For the revolts, see also below, pp. 271–273.
[62] Weststrate, 'Laat-veertiende-eeuwse Gelderse riviertolrekeningen', esp. pp. 228–229.
[63] Bos-Rops, *Graven op zoek naar geld*, 234–237 and 244.
[64] Piérard, 'Les aides', 200 and 217–225. For the link to representation, see Blockmans, *De Bourgondische Nederlanden*, 21–23.
[65] Blockmans, 'Finances publiques', 79.

In the Low Countries, therefore, fiscal matters were directly linked to the rise of representation and Estates. Some of the subjects, particularly the elite, thus acquired influence in political decision-making. Although the Estates certainly were not fully democratic institutions, representation was broader than in many surrounding areas, and perhaps similar to parts of Germany and Switzerland. In particular, the influence of the burgher elite at the central level of the principalities was exceptional. However, this influence was not an automatic result of the rise of taxation, which can be seen from the various European examples where much less scope existed for burghers to be represented. The balance among social groups probably played a determining role in this difference.[66] The pre-existing tradition of political self-determination and particpation of broad groups, as institutionalized in the high medieval associations and communities, underlay this balance, especially in Flanders, Holland, and other regions where associations were well developed. Perhaps the political fragmentation in the Low Countries was also a principal element, since territorial lords had to compete with one another and had to rely on the support of their subjects. Moreover, since they lacked the means to coerce people, they had to rely on well-developed markets to acquire resources and capital, and therefore had to cooperate with various social groups.[67] In some regions the rural nobility were a relatively powerful counterweight to the princes, whereas in others—as in Flanders and Holland—it was the towns and urban patriciates who had this function, also because they played a main role in providing credit.

In the meantime, in the 15th and 16th centuries, growing princely power further eroded self-determination where it still existed, as in some of the bigger towns with guild influence in political life. These towns and guilds often grimly defended their power and privileges, but mostly lost out to growing Burgundian and Habsburg power, as happened to Liège and to Utrecht, where Charles V in 1528 made an end of the political and military role of the guilds. This process was most clear-cut in Flanders, where central authorities slowly broke the power of the cities, but only after some fierce encounters. Ghent, Flanders' most particularist city, which in the first half of the 14th century under the leadership of Jan van Artevelde had even dreamt of becoming a city-state, fought hard against the process of further centralization under the Burgundians and Habsburgs.[68] A main area of conflict was the administrative autonomy of the city and the attempts of the prince to interfere in appointments of town magistrates, as in 1448–53, when the guilds reaffirmed their grip on local

[66] Dhondt, 'Les origines'.
[67] For borrowing in the capital market, see section V.2 pp. 190–191, and for the social balance among princes, towns, and nobility, see sections III.1, pp. 74–75, and III.3, pp. 111–116. For the early modern period, see Prak and Van Zanden, 'Towards an economic interpretation'.
[68] Blockmans: 'Voracious states' and *De Bourgondische Nederlanden*, 22–24. For Ghent in 1448–53, see Haemers, *De Gentse opstand*, 137–147, and for the struggles between the princes and the towns, see also below, pp. 274–276.

government, some members of the upper middle class became aldermen, and ducal protégés were expelled from the town, and again in 1488–92. In the end, however, after the revolt by Ghent against the central government in 1540, it was Charles V who defeated his native town, humiliated its burghers, and took away the urban privileges and those of the guilds. By replacing the deans of the guilds, reducing the authority of the aldermen, and having them appointed by princely commissioners, the influence of craftsmen in town politics was severely curtailed.[69] But despite the centralizing tendencies, regional power, local and urban privileges, and older representative structures remained important, and in practice the Low Countries did not form one unified legal-political territory. When Alva, the Habsburg governor of the Low Countries around 1570, tried to promote further centralization by instituting a uniform fixed system of taxation, this attempt intensified the recently ignited revolt, which produced the separation of the northern parts of the Low Countries from the Habsburg Empire and a revitalization of particularist tendencies.

The rise of territorial principalities from the 12th and 13th centuries on also brought a redistribution of resources. A large part of state revenues was spent on military and administrative offices, offering new opportunities for nobles to gain access to surpluses in the service of the state. A few people of non-noble background also profited by making a career in the civil service. An early example is Robert of Aire, who became chancellor of the Count of Flanders in the second half of the 12th century, and a very competent one.[70] But most of these opportunities were taken by nobles, especially in principalities where they traditionally held a prominent position, such as in Guelders. Nobles especially enriched themselves when they succeeded in leasing offices, and even more in pawning or buying them, which offered prospects of large revenues, either directly from emoluments, or from withholding part of the revenues, by accepting gifts and bribes—although this was often officially prohibited—and by establishing extra levies, sometimes even by extortion.[71] In this centuries-long formative period, when the nascent state only started to replace older societal structures, civil officers were well placed to act as middlemen or power brokers with local or regional and national networks, and had opportunities to profit through corruption, patronage, and abuse of power.

Because public offices were often leased, pawned, or sold, they could also be amassed by a few successful nobles. Since the number of profitable offices was relatively small, this process led to polarization among the nobility. One minor nobleman who gained in late 14th-century Holland was Bruisten van Herwijnen who accumulated offices, mainly by pawn, a widespread practice in the period. He became castellan of Loevestein, bailiff of Zierikzee, dike reeve

[69] Dambruyne, *Corporatieve middengroepen*, 34–37, 137–139, and 530–536.
[70] Prevenier, 'Officials', 3.   [71] Blockmans, 'Corruptie, patronage', and Kuys, *Drostambt*, 75–78.

of the Grote Waard, steward of Zeeland east of the Scheldt, and steward of the Land of Altena and the Woudrichemmerwaard.[72] At the peak of his financial and political power, however, the count accused him of abuse of power and refusal to render account properly. Bruisten had to flee as the count confiscated all his properties. Both his advance to great wealth and his fall were not unusual in this period. In general, the nobility were very eager to use every opportunity to strengthen their position in state service—at times too eager. This was even more the case since other revenues from jurisdiction, seigniorial rights, and other levies were eroded precisely because of the increasing power of the central state. This process of state formation, however, did not lead to a new social structure, but was a new instrument for the nobility, or at least some of its members, to strengthen or maintain their position and gain new access to the surplus.

This avenue to surpluses became ever more important as state formation and the development of fiscality proceeded intermittently. At first this process in the Low Countries was driven by the dozen medium-sized principalities which had emerged in the high Middle Ages. The revenues of the princes were not yet impressive, but growing: around 1390 the count of Holland and Zeeland collected annually tens of thousands of guilders, the equivalent of about one tonne of fine silver.[73] In the 14th to 16th centuries the Burgundian and Habsburg rulers slowly brought these principalities and enclaves of the Low Countries together through marriage strategies, chance, and conquest. This was a protracted, sometimes painful process, and even after its completion in 1543, the Low Countries remained politically a loosely knit part of Europe, compared with England, for instance, although perhaps more similar to Germany, Switzerland, and northern Italy. The Burgundian and Habsburg rulers tried to consolidate their territories, in part successfully, by building a state apparatus with central councils for the various policy fields, such as the Council of Finances, established in 1531. An earlier step in building a coherent bureaucracy was the establishment of Chambres des Comptes in Lille, Brussels, and the Hague in the decades around 1400. These Chambers, auditing the accounts of financial officers at the local, regional, and national levels, formed the central system of the Burgundian Low Countries.[74] They allowed the government to check and control the financial streams, and created a more widespread and shared administrative culture and terminology, as well as uniformly structured accounts, produced in ever greater numbers. At the same time, fiscal streams became bigger. In 1395 the Burgundian state annually received some 440,000 golden coins, of which 40 per cent was from aids, and in 1445 the total came to about 500,000 pounds, or 16.7 tonnes of

---

[72] Beelaerts van Blokland, 'Een Geldersch edelman'. For the pawning of offices, see Kuys, *Drostambt*, 71–74 and 129–131.
[73] Bos-Rops, *Graven op zoek naar geld*, 74–103 (and for coins/silver: 56–67).
[74] Stein, 'Burgundian bureaucracy'.

fine silver. By 1465 this had further grown to 18.3 tonnes of silver, of which 43 per cent was from aids, which was more than the revenues of the English or Castilian crowns.[75] Fiscal revenues increased hugely from that time, with total revenues in 1531–4 reaching 2,450,000 pounds annually, of which 80 per cent was from aids.

These taxes to a large extent redistributed money from peasants, craftsmen, and other ordinary people to the noblemen and patricians in state service. The distribution of the fiscal burden reflected the limited representation of people in the Estates, since clerics, nobles, and sometimes patricians were partly exempt, or paid lower taxes.[76] Moreover, the urban governments in the Low Countries succeeded in preventing taxation of international trade and commercial capital, thus protecting merchant interests. To aggravate matters for ordinary people, the taxation systems used were often regressive, and had a fairly low level above which all wealth was taxed by the same amount, thus sparing the wealthiest. In practice, ordinary craftsmen and peasants paid most, with taxation being especially hard on them. In the town of Ypres, in the period 1430–1510, central taxes per capita amounted to 4–7 per cent of the yearly wage of a hodman. The countrymen were worst off, since the cities were often represented in the Estates and had at least some protection for their interests. This, too, was reflected in the distribution of the fiscal burden, with the per capita burden in 1445 in rural Namur being about five times higher than in urban Flanders or Brabant. It was not until the 15th and 16th centuries, and particularly under Charles the Bold from 1469 on, that taxation became organized on a somewhat more equal footing. Although the opposition of the Estates delayed and at times even frustrated the process, exemptions were slowly eroded, or taxes became based on direct calculation of a specific sum per hectare or income from wealth, similar to the water management taxes that already existed from the 13th and 14th centuries, where taxes were levied in strict proportion to the area of land owned or used. These changes did not mean that taxes became progressive, but at least they became less regressive.

The acceleration in state formation, and the rising fiscal revenues, provided noblemen with even better opportunities to profit by way of state service. Guy de Brimeu, one of the confidants of Duke Charles the Bold, collected so many offices that in 1473–6, of his annual income of 32,000 pounds, only 5,000 pounds were from his patrimonial goods and most of the rest from his various offices.[77] Those who acquired governorships could build a regional power base, as did the margraves of Baden, who kept the governorship of Luxemburg in the family from 1488. Bernhard of Baden used this position in the 1520s to enrich himself, and also introduced new tolls at the town gates. It was not until 1531, that Charles V

---

[75] Blockmans, 'The Low Countries'.
[76] Blockmans, 'Finances publiques' (the following example from Ypres is on p. 89).
[77] Zmora, *Monarchy, aristocracy*, 32–35, and for the following information: 61–64.

succeeded in regaining control over this office, by paying a heavy indemnity to Bernhard. Noblemen also benefited from their position in state service as they tried to build up estates by consolidating landholdings and combining these with seigniorial rights, often in their area of origin. The prince supported these attempts by remitting conveyance taxes, and granting them confiscated goods and fiefs there. In 15th-century Flanders, half of the top officers held five fiefs or more.[78] The exploitation of these estates could be furthered by using the instruments of state power, as Jean de Glymes, marquis of Bergen-op-Zoom and governor of Hainaut, did around 1550 on his family estates, when sending his troops to intimidate the peasants there. In this way, the link between the princes and the nobility close to them magnified the power and wealth of both. State formation was a motor of inequality, both within the nobility and within society as a whole.

In addition to the nobles, some professionals from middle groups, the *homines novi*, moved up and enriched themselves through their offices. The increasing importance attached to education, and academic education in particular, played an important role in this,[79] since it was relatively easily accessible to middle groups in the Low Countries. Expertise and knowledge became important criteria for becoming a higher official. The urban bourgeoisie in particular used this path to state service, especially in Holland and Flanders. In 15th-century Flanders, no fewer than half of the higher offices came to be held by burghers, a few originating from the crafts elite, but by far the majority from the patriciate.[80] The increasing emphasis on expertise opened even the highest offices under Burgundian and Habsburg rule to them. Viglius van Aytta, the president of the Secret Council and the most powerful state official in the mid-16th-century Low Countries, did not make his career through birth, since he was from a family of Frisian gentlemen farmers, barely meriting designation as lower nobility. His career in state service was gained through academic knowledge and administrative ability, as an educated lawyer and professor of law.[81] Around the middle of the 16th century, Governess Mary of Hungary went furthest in promoting professional civil servants: she wanted to entrust the government to them rather than to the high nobility. People such as Viglius appointed many professionals in administrative positions, and this happened also in the highest ecclesiastical ranks. Under the influence of Viglius and Granvelle, a principal adviser to the Habsburgs in the Low Countries who was also of non-noble background, such positions were entrusted to academic theologians, not to nobles as had earlier been the case, thus provoking bitter resentment among the high aristocracy.

---

[78] Dumolyn, *Staatsvorming*, 113–126 and 235–236. For Jean de Glymes: Zmora, *Monarchy, aristocracy*, 63.
[79] De Ridder-Symoens, 'Possibilités de carrière'; see also section VI.4, pp. 316–319.
[80] Dumolyn: 'Dominante klassen', esp. 87–93, and *Staatsvorming*, 150–172.
[81] Postma, *Viglius van Aytta*, 17–34, 99–102, and 129–137, and Baelde, 'Edellieden en juristen'.

These offices offered burghers a path to upward mobility and the opportunity to become part of the nobility, as often happened in Flanders, for instance. When non-noblemen attained high office in the Low Countries, they often gradually made their way into the nobility by adopting the lifestyle of nobles, buying seigneuries, marrying noblewomen, and through the status of their office, a process which sometimes took several generations.[82] This may have applied to a much lesser extent to Holland, where the nobility had always been weak and the position of burghers and bourgeois culture and lifestyle had been well established for centuries. In the 16th century the small number of nobles there lost most of whatever political power, fiscal exemptions, and military functions they still had, forcing them to cultivate their noble lifestyle at the margins of society, even though its prestige remained.[83]

It is debatable how much this process of state formation brought about a fundamental change to bourgeois dominance. Indeed, only in a few parts of Europe, perhaps including northern Italy, Switzerland, and western Germany, were the bourgeoisie as influential as in the late medieval Low Countries, and this was true even in state service, traditionally the province of the nobility. Alongside some of the nobles, it was urban professionals who as *homines novi* increasingly moved up and enriched themselves through such positions, especially in Holland and Flanders. Also, the growing financial needs of the state opened the way to representation of burghers, or at least the burgher elite, again most clearly in Holland and Flanders, but also in Brabant. However, this was mainly the extension of the burgher influence that had already developed. At the same time, state formation demolished earlier forms of political organization, some of which offered much broader participation. In the 13th and 14th centuries it eroded those in the countryside of regions like Frisia, northern Holland, and coastal Flanders, and in the 15th and 16th centuries those in the guild-dominated towns. State formation also strengthened the power and wealth of the noble elite. On the other hand, in its first phase in the 12th and 13th centuries, it had undermined the feudal power of the nobility where this had threatened princely authority. The ambivalent effects of state formation, therefore, built partly on earlier regional characteristics, but to some extent also evened out regional differences in social organization. The still limited weight of the process brought hardly any fundamental ruptures, however, and when it started to do so, around 1570, the Revolt broke out (see the next section). The developments in industries and agriculture were much more crucial than the process of state formation in bringing about social change, and even more in sharpening regional differences in social organization.

---

[82] Dumolyn, 'Dominante klassen', esp. 81–82, and Dumolyn and Van Tricht, 'Adel en nobiliterings-pro-cessen'.

[83] Van Nierop, *Van ridders tot regenten*, 185–187 and 224–227.

Social Conflicts

Each of these socio-economic and political processes, especially as they accelerated in the late Middle Ages, produced social friction, popular unrest, and sometimes open conflicts, especially in cases where infringements were made upon political or economic self-determination. One phase of massive social conflicts took place in the 13th and early 14th centuries, especially in the regions bordering the North Sea, where self-determination and broad participation were highly developed. In this period several regions experienced fierce resistance to the advance of territorial lords, including Westfriesland, Frisia, and Drenthe, where conflicts occurred in the period 1225–40.[84] The risings by the rural populace were directed especially against extension of princely rule, increasing taxation, abuses in taxation, and attempts at feudalization, and aimed to defend the communal forms of self-determination. The communal character of these revolts is most clearly evident in the rebellion of the rural population of Kennemerland against the Count of Holland in 1274/5. The Kennemers not only defended their communal organization and customary law, but even sought to extend their associative communality over a much wider area, and even over the entire prince-bishopric of Utrecht, as noted in a contemporary chronicle.[85] After the rebels had defeated the noblemen and destroyed several castles in their home region, they marched to the town and episcopal see of Utrecht, some 50 km away. They presented themselves to the townspeople as the free people of Kennemerland, and called upon them to join their struggle, and to banish all noblemen and distribute their properties among the poor. The urban craftsmen followed this exhortation, took control of the town government and expelled the noblemen from the town, and united in friendship with the Kennemer rebels. The goals of rural and urban rebels were similar, but clearly the initiative for this joint action was taken by the rural rebels. Although most of their self-determination was slowly eroded in the long run, this and several other revolts were fairly successful. Even for territorial lords aided by their armies of nobles, it seems to have been difficult to change the socio-political status quo.

Simultaneously in the towns, resentment of the growing wealth and power of the ever smaller group of patricians, and the favouritism and abuses associated with it, provoked increasing social unrest, which became endemic in the late 13th and early 14th centuries. Between 1302 and 1385 Ghent witnessed 11 years of urban revolt, Ypres 12 years, and Bruges 16.[86] Unrest was especially prevalent among the craftsmen in the industrial centres, often supported by the new rich who were denied access to the patriciate. The episcopal city of Liège was one of the cities where revolts were fiercest around the middle of the 13th century, when Henri de Dinant, himself a merchant, fought the patrician

---

[84] Van Bavel, 'Rural revolts'. See also section III.2, pp. 91–92, III.3, p. 96, and above, pp. 263–264.
[85] For a more extensive discussion: Van Bavel, 'Rural revolts'.
[86] Verbruggen, *Geweld*, 18, and Dumolyn & Haemers, 'Patterns of urban rebellion', 374–378.

oligarchy and the clerical elite, and increasingly found himself the leader of a popular movement.[87] In the Flemish towns, too, the craftsmen rose, increasingly organizing themselves through the guilds. These urban uprisings were for the most part bloodily repressed, as in Saint-Omer in 1280, where several weavers who staged a revolt were banished by the town magistrate and others were buried alive. This also happened in Ypres. But sometimes, as in Ghent in 1280, such revolts were successful.[88]

Often, the insurrection was a multi-faceted protest by various groups, sometimes shifting in composition, and focused on current tangible complaints rather than on long-term social changes. The rise of wage labour and new forms of social inequality and economic dependence may have fuelled discontent, although this is hard to ascertain. But more tangible reasons dominated the resentment, such as the increases in excises and taxation, abuses in taxation, monopolization of power by a small, closed patriciate, favouritism, and abuses in town government. To eliminate this, the urban middle groups demanded participation in urban government and control over finances. Gradually these demands evolved into a programme that could be put into operation through the guilds, which extended their influence over economy, society, and politics in many cities, particularly around 1302, and defended the interests of small-scale craft producers. The extent of their success must be qualified, however, since in the end the old elites, now supplemented by the new rich, retained a large part of their economic and political power.[89]

Beginning in 1323 in coastal Flanders, discontent in the towns was combined with a rural revolt in what became the largest and longest revolt in western Europe in the late Middle Ages.[90] The uprising in the Flemish countryside was triggered by resentment of the taxation abuses, the more so since the taxes were destined for indemnity payments to the hated French king. Deeper underlying causes of unrest were perhaps the great changes in the economy and society of coastal Flanders, bigger than anywhere else in the Low Countries at that time, and including the extension of urban land ownership, the introduction of short-term leasing, the mounting debts of peasants, and growing social inequality. Hatred in 1323 at first turned against comital bailiffs and tax collectors, who were taken prisoner by the insurgents. In the second phase of the revolt, demands and actions by the insurgents became much more radical, directly aimed at the nobility and patriciate, at large landowners, and at the levying of tithes, thus almost constituting a social revolution. The core of the revolt was in the countryside, with peasants and proletarianized countrymen led by the large farmers joining forces with the craftsmen and perhaps wage labourers from many

---

[87] Vercauteren, *Luttes sociales à Liège*, 48–59. [88] Boogaart, 'Reflections'.
[89] Van Uytven, 'Plutokratie'. See also section III.3, pp. 118–121.
[90] Sabbe, *Vlaanderen in opstand*, 22–35, 55–62, and 77–85, and TeBrake, *A plague*, 57–60, 71–86, 112–122, and 139–156.

Flemish cities. The rural insurgents used the organizations they had developed in the high Middle Ages, such as village communities and assemblies, and also employed their century-long experience in association, thus building on existing political practices.[91] Village leaders were delegated to regional bodies, giving coherence to the revolt, and captains were chosen to lead the revolt and replace the comital bailiffs. The captains convened courts and collected public taxes and revenues, providing clear organization for the revolt, with public authority in most of Flanders fairly effectively taken over by the insurgents for several years. Nobles and princes throughout western Europe understood the threat the revolt posed, fearing that it would be an example to other regions. They set aside their internal conflicts to jointly fight this threat, supported by the pope, who used the religious weapons of interdict and excommunication. In the final battle near Cassel, more than 3,000 insurgents were killed. Repression was harsh, with horrific execution of the revolt's leaders, the execution of thousands of insurgents (sometimes without trial), confiscation of insurgents' goods, imposition of enormous indemnity payments, and withdrawal of the privileges and bylaws of towns and rural districts. This example was intended to prevent people from ever contemplating revolt again.

After the mid-14th century, social conflicts seem to have lessened, at least in scale. This was partly the result of the demographic decline in this period, and the increase in real wages, improving the situation for most people. However, the improved bargaining power of lower groups cannot automatically be assumed to result in social peace, as is shown by the English example, where the determination of the large noble landowners to keep wages down after the Black Death, restrict the freedom of the working population, and maintain the level of their revenues was one of the main causes of the Peasants' Revolt of 1381. So, in the relatively quiet situation in the Low Countries, the more determining elements were the increased representation of middle groups in urban government, the power of the guilds as representatives of small independent producers, and the development of representative organizations, such as the Estates. It was mainly the middle groups in society, the burghers and master craftsmen, who profited from these developments; they now had too much to lose to risk staging another revolt. After a turbulent but creative period of some three centuries, a new socio-political equilibrium emerged, and the elite formed coalitions with some middle groups in society who had an interest in preserving the status quo. In Ghent, for instance, this happened around 1360, with the master weavers, the patricians, and the small tradesmen forming a coalition which excluded the fullers and labourers from decision-making; the coalition remained in power up to 1540.[92] This contributed to relative stability. Perhaps even more important in the new equilibrium was the increasing and more effective repression by territorial lords. They no longer had to rely on urban militias and feudal armies, but now commanded a reliable armed

---

[91] Van Bavel, 'Rural revolts'.   [92] Verbruggen, *Geweld*, 32–35.

force of mercenaries whom they could use to suppress all unrest immediately, especially since the fiscal resources from ever larger areas could be concentrated against individual cities or regions that rebelled.

In the 14th and 15th centuries hardly any revolts occurred in the countryside, and urban revolts were usually smaller and limited to individual cities, mainly aimed at securing living standards. Risings against the patriciate were instigated by small independent craftsmen and journeymen. The proletariat and the poor played a lesser role, except in food riots and when they were used as shock troops by the middle groups, to be once again abandoned if demands were met or the poor became too radical. In Flanders, from the late 14th century on, the uprisings were often linked to political aims in the guild tradition and resistance by local authorities to the centralizing Burgundian state. Again, craftsmen and their guilds played a key role in this to defend their participation in politics, but now were often allied with some of the urban elite. This was true of the risings in Bruges (1436–8) and Ghent (1449–53). Besides defending urban autonomy and guild power, practical social policies were also implemented, as in Ghent in the second, more radical phase of the revolt, when the lower proletarian groups began to join in.[93] The property of the pro-Burgundian patricians was confiscated and publicly auctioned, money and peat were distributed more frequently, beer was given to the poor, excises were reduced, and direct taxes were introduced. Similar uprisings in Dinant (1465) and Liège (1466–8), primarily directed against the increasing Burgundian influence, were crushed by Duke Charles the Bold. He first destroyed Dinant and later reached a new level of atrocity in the destruction of Liège, killing about a quarter of the (mostly unarmed) population, drowning hundreds in the Meuse river, and setting fire to the city—all to erase this hotbed of rebellion.

In Flanders and in Brabant and Liège, the guilds were well placed to lead the urban revolts, since in addition to their organization and political influence, they had a fairly strong military, sometimes enabling them to win their demands, although their power was increasingly curtailed by the central authority. In Holland, on the other hand, guilds were few and had little formal and political power, so weavers and fullers in the Holland towns used other instruments, such as the strikes and walk-outs favoured by the fullers, the most proletarianized of the urban workers, to put pressure on the town governments to meet their demands. In the period 1370–1480 the Leiden fullers went on strike seven times and attempted to do so five times.[94] Their actions were well organized, mainly through informal contacts and religious brotherhoods, and had a clear set of demands. These did not entail any political issues, since in Holland there was no

---

[93] Dumolyn and Haemers, 'Patterns of urban rebellion', 378–380, Boone & Prak, 'Rulers, patricians and burghers', 106–111, Haemers, *De Gentse opstand*, 137–147 and 239–264. See also above, pp. 265–266.
[94] Boone and Brand, 'Vollersoproeren'.

tradition of guild representation, but concentrated rather on economic demands such as higher wages, prohibition of the truck system, and better working conditions. Although the strikes were occasionally successful, they were mostly suppressed by the magistrate, often in collaboration with the territorial lord, and the leaders were severely punished, either by execution or by lengthy banishment.

The independent craftsmen belonged to a group with shared interests and a common position on production relations, and were well aware of this. Their solidarity was also fostered in their well-developed organizations. Wage labourers did not generally have such a consciousness, although the Leiden fullers may have been an exception. Among the noble elite, class consciousness had always been strong, and this remained the case among the new elite of nobles, patricians, and civil officials. It was nurtured by their association in elite brotherhoods such as the brotherhood of the Holy Blood in Bruges or the brotherhood of the Illustrious Blessed Virgin Mary in 's-Hertogenbosch. The meals of the latter increasingly served as occasions for the nobility and patriciate of the town, the surrounding countryside, and even some neighbouring regions to meet.[95] Other voluntary organizations, such as some of the chambers of rhetoricians and particularly some archery clubs, also enabled the elite to assemble and socialize, fostering the development of common religious, moral, and social values. As a result, the elite groups often closed ranks against a common threat or enemy, and were joined in this by the Burgundian/Habsburg prince, who harshly quelled all unrest.

The other, lower groups in society lacked such coherence, especially as they were confronted with fairly abstract processes, such as scale-enlargement and polarization, with socially divergent effects. This was particularly the case in the regions which witnessed a transition to a capitalist economy and society. Large groups lost out in this transformation because of their loss of economic independence, the decline in real wages, and fall in living standards. This process caused tensions and unrest. An expression of such tensions was the revolt of the Cheese and Bread People in northern Holland in 1491–2, which was fuelled by the severe decline in living standards and by high taxes.[96] Before Duke Albrecht of Saxony and his mercenaries defeated the rising, the insurgents had killed a comital steward, dismembering his corpse, and destroyed burgher titles to land. This points to tangible foci of discontent, but there was no clear social agenda or ideological programme. The same applied to the mounting critique by writers on differences between rich and poor and the treatment of workers by the entrepreneurs. Two examples were the playwright Cornelis Everaert, a fuller and member of the chamber of rhetoricians in early 16th century Bruges, and Jan van Houtte in Leiden.[97] Everaert was very critical of abuses by entrepreneurs and merchants, the vicissitudes of the market, and the uncertainty of market

[95] Van Dijck, *De Bossche optimaten*, 85–87 and 180–187.
[96] Hugenholtz, 'Het Kaas- en Broodvolk'. [97] De Vries, 'Rederijkersspelen'.

dependence, but he did not advocate any type of socialism or call for revolution. Rather, he came up with more corporatist medieval solutions, and in the end submitted to governmental rule.

The 16th century saw many disturbances and minor uprisings in towns, sometimes aimed against scale-enlargement and the growing power of big entrepreneurs. In Antwerp, for instance, there was a rising against the privileges and monopolies of Gilbert van Schoonbeke. Under pressure from thousands of people—craftsmen, the proletariat, and outcasts—the city government was compelled to limit Schoonbeke's position and withdraw his privileges, but Charles V had his German mercenaries put down this Antwerp revolt in 1555.[98] He also curtailed the participation of guilds in urban government. In Utrecht, where the guilds had retained powerful military and political roles, their authority was removed by Charles V in 1528, partly in reaction to their insurrection in 1525, when they had revived all their traditional guild claims, elected a new town magistrate, and demanded a more equal distribution of taxes and excises.[99] Habsburg rule clearly took the side of the urban elite. Also, new means of social cohesion were devised by the authorities, increasingly on a central level, and often associated with strict repression. An example was the reorganization of poor relief, linked to harsh legislation and the prohibition of mendicants and beggars.[100] If necessary, there was outright repression of all disturbances by the central Habsburg authorities, followed by execution of the leaders of revolts, tightening the night watch, the introduction of the obligation to register residence, the withdrawal of privileges granted earlier, and often humiliation of the burghers of a town that staged a revolt.[101] At the same time, the labouring people had no direct economic and social alternative. This was very different from the situation around 1300, when the guilds, with their protection of independent small-scale production, along with their demand for political representation, formulated a clear programme. But now, except for some intellectuals arguing for the abolition of private property, they did not propose any new programme. The focus in the 16th century was on practical problems and abuses, and while there was widespread hatred by the poor of the rich, there was no coherent ideology but rather the clinging on to the ideal of small-scale craft production.

Among the few exceptions were the Anabaptists, the most radical offshoot of the Reformation. They first appeared around 1526, and soon established a strong presence in northern areas of the Low Countries. In addition to their religious beliefs, often mixed with chiliastic expectations, the Anabaptists had clear ideas on economy and society. They disapproved of private ownership of property, believing that it should be used for the benefit of all, and they

---

[98] Soly, *Urbanisme en kapitalisme*, 298–302 and 440–447, and Dumolyn, 'The legal repression'.
[99] Van Kalveen, 'Bijdrage'. [100] Section VI.4, pp. 310–313.
[101] Dumolyn, 'The legal repression'.

strove for voluntary common ownership of goods.[102] Their supporters were mainly the small, often impoverished craftsmen and the proletariat, and they were led by small craftsmen such as the tailor Jan van Leiden and the baker Jan Mathijsz. There were very few members of the elite among the followers, except for a few sympathizers among authorities in Amsterdam. In 1535 the Anabaptists rebelled in many places, such as in Amsterdam, their main centre, and also in Waterland, Leiden, and Friesland. The repression by local and central authorities was often severe, and hundreds of Anabaptists were killed.

The insurrections in Holland and Friesland were not successful, but the Anabaptists did manage to take power in the town of Münster in Westfalia. Thousands of Anabaptists from Holland and Friesland decided to go there. The social and economic revolution that was implemented in Münster in 1533–5 reflects the ideas they held. Common ownership of property was introduced, not voluntarily, but on a compulsory basis by the new authority.[103] Accounts and titles were burned and personal valuables and money were confiscated. The town council was to provide food, clothing, and housing. These revolutionary principles also explain why the repression of this revolt was so harsh, as was the repression of any Anabaptist activity in the Low Countries. Most Protestants executed by the authorities in this period were Anabaptists; in Antwerp they accounted for 89 per cent of all Protestants executed.[104] Although they were sometimes tolerated by local authorities, the harsh repression was often supported by the bourgeoisie, which had become frightened by the revolutionary aspects of the movement, and by Lutherans and Calvinists, who severely attacked the Anabaptists, condemning their ideas. The later revival of Anabaptism under Menno Simons was more spiritual and no longer included revolutionary programmes.

Elements of social discontent but without any clear socio-economic programme can also be found in the iconoclasm of 1566–7 and the Dutch Revolt in the following years. This was clearest in the new industrial centres in south-west Flanders, such as Hondschoote, where iconoclasts attacked not only churches and priests, but also merchants and entrepreneurs. Almost all the convicted iconoclasts and participants in the first phase of the religious troubles there were propertyless. At the beginning of the Dutch Revolt, however, possible socio-economic elements and desires became overshadowed by a complex of religious and political programmes against the Catholic Habsburg regime, which were to a large extent led and guided by patricians and some nobles defending the federal and constitutional model.[105]

---

[102] Klassen, *The economics of Anabaptism*, 28–34. For the following see Zijlstra, *Om de ware gemeente*, 98–111 and 250–260, although with more emphasis on the religious aspects.
[103] Stayer: *Anabaptists*, 236–237 and 256–257, and *The German Peasants' War*.
[104] Marnef, *Antwerpen*, 119–122. See also Zijlstra, *Om de ware gemeente*, 66 and 232–247.
[105] Van Nierop, 'The nobility'.

It is difficult to assess the effects of the late medieval disturbances and risings. Were they part of a long process of bourgeois revolution for which the Low Countries were the European prototype?[106] It would be difficult to argue for this thesis, since the revolts were supported by very heterogeneous and different groups. Moreover, the word 'revolution' does not seem appropriate for the late medieval revolts in the Low Countries. Most of the successful ones were defensive in nature; all were cases of resistance against perceived or real threats to the status quo, as was the case with the rural populations of Frisia and Drenthe. To a large extent, this also applied to the successful struggle of the guilds, since they protected existing small-scale production against the scale-enlargements and growing power of the big entrepreneurs; and also applied to the Dutch Revolt, in which burgher associations, towns, and provinces reacted against the centralizing Habsburg regime. Revolts which in themselves caused fundamental social changes, however, do not seem to have taken place. The apparent impossibility of forcing social change through revolt is one element in the long-term continuity of regional social structures and the absence of a reduction in regional differences over the centuries. Moreover, even these defensive revolts could only succeed if there were conflicts of interest among the elite that prohibited common action, as happened between the urban patricians and the territorial lords around 1300. The increasing power of princes made successful revolts by those outside the elite even more improbable, especially since the princes could employ their enormous financial power to hire mercenaries, which allowed them to crush all local and regional resistance. This growing financial power allowed the central Habsburg state to force some changes, especially from the early 16th century, possibly increasing uniformity of social structures in the Low Countries. Such changes entailed limiting guild power and broad participation in politics, the reduction of noble and urban privileges, the emergence of a group of civil servants, and the introduction of a uniform fiscal system. But just when this programme started to be implemented, the Revolt broke out and to a large extent prevented implementation of the changes.

VI.2. DEMOGRAPHIC CHANGE AND URBANIZATION

Population Numbers and Urbanization

Throughout the Middle Ages, and particularly in the period 900–1300, the Low Countries experienced enormous population growth. Total population numbers were roughly 190,000 around the middle of the 7th century, rising to 300,000 around 800, and 400,000 around 900.[107] Around 1300 the Low Countries

---

[106] Tilly, *European revolutions*, 52–78 and 100–103.   [107] See section II.2, pp. 35–37.

probably had some 2 million inhabitants or more, and the highest population density in Europe outside Italy. This created a growing tension between population and resources. The increasing Malthusian stress was heightened by the ecological problems of the subsidence of peat soils, the sweeping away of coastal areas by the sea, and the increasing drifting of sand, all of which were an unintentional result of intensified land use and economic and social change.[108] Although living standards and real wages in the Low Countries were relatively high compared with other parts of north-western Europe, there was increasing pressure in the decades around 1300. Added to this were growing market competition (the land and lease markets included) and the ensuing polarization which caused poverty and famine on a massive scale. Hunger and plague struck the Low Countries from the early 14th century on, albeit with significant regional differences.

The first catastrophe was the Great Famine, ravaging all of north-western Europe from 1315 to 1322. Bad weather, harvest failures, and rinderpest struck the population, for the most part already hard pressed, leading to malnutrition and disease. The towns, which depended on food trade, were severely hit, with grain prices rising three- to fivefold, and in some cases even 20 to 25 times above the normal level, as in Valenciennes and Mons in 1316, the worst year.[109] Large landowners and farmers profited from the high prices, as did some grain merchants and speculators, but other people were dying in large numbers: in the towns of Flanders probably some 5 to 10 per cent of the population succumbed in 1316, in the countryside probably less. In the industrial town of Ypres alone, 2,794 deaths were listed in the municipal records from May to October 1316, most of them poor people who died in the streets and were carried away to be thrown into common ditches. In Bruges, casualties were fewer, thanks to the intervention of the city magistracy which bought some 20,000 hectolitres (hl) of grain, probably in south-western France, and sold it at or below cost to licensed bakers. This was enough to feed about one-third of the urban population for a whole year.

The Black Death, the biggest disaster to hit medieval Europe, reached the Low Countries in 1348. It is assumed that this epidemic and the subsequent outbreaks of plague reduced the European population by a third. In the Low Countries, too, massive numbers of people died, although regional differences were pronounced. In Artois, from 1300 to the beginning of the 15th century, the population was reduced by more than half.[110] Even in 1469, after a fairly strong recovery over several decades, population numbers were still more than 40 per cent below those of 1300. On the other hand, Flanders, directly to the

---

[108] See section II.2, pp. 44–49.
[109] Jordan, *The great famine*, 116–121, 135, and 143–148. For the estimates of deaths, see below in this chapter, and Van Werveke, 'La famine'.
[110] Bocquet, *Recherches*, 128–129 and 141–143.

north of Artois, was not hard hit at all; in fact, it was difficult to find any evidence of the plague there, and the same applied to Holland.[111] Between 1348 and 1400 population numbers there were probably reduced by only 5 to 10 per cent, and since population growth had still been strong there in the first half of the 14th century, this resulted in a population level in 1400 that was much like that in 1300. This is very exceptional in a European perspective, especially since population densities and pressure on the land were high there, just as in Flanders. We will return to this paradoxical situation later on.

Differences can also be observed between the north and south of the Low Countries after the 14th century. The first extensive set of hard data on population numbers from fiscal records for the Low Countries as a whole is available for the second half of the 15th century.[112] At that point some 2.5 million people lived there, with some 1.5 million in the south (i.e. present-day Belgium plus Luxembourg and Walloon Flanders, but excluding Picardy and Artois). This number increased only slowly: from 1.55 million around 1500 to 1.8 million around 1550 and 1.75 million around 1600. In the north, the area of the present-day Netherlands, after a relatively modest decrease in the second half of the 14th century, the population increased from 0.9–1.0 million around 1500, to 1.2–1.3 million around 1550, to 1.4–1.6 million at the end of the 16th century. At that time some 3.2 million people lived in the Low Countries.

In the course of these centuries an ever greater part of the population of the Low Countries lived in the cities. In the early Middle Ages urban centres were still very small. Dorestad, probably the most important, had no more than 1,000 to 2,000 inhabitants at the height of its prosperity, around the year 800.[113] The other trading centres probably had only a few hundred. Most of the trading centres were very ephemeral; most virtually disappeared in the era of Viking attacks. True urbanization began in the high Middle Ages,[114] as the growth of agrarian surpluses and industrial production, stimulated by growing trade and the purchasing power of the urban elite, and often combined with the non-economic force acquired by the towns, enabled urban growth, especially in the Meuse valley and Flanders. One of the main urban centres of the period and the location for several of the largest religious landowners was Liège, which had some 5,000 to 10,000 inhabitants in the 11th century.[115] A rough estimate for Holland and Zeeland around 1200 is that perhaps 5 per cent of the population

---

[111] De Boer, *Graaf en grafiek*, 29–133. Some evidence was found by Blockmans, 'The social and economic effects'.
[112] Blockmans et al., 'Tussen crisis en welvaart', 43–45. Figures for 1600: Mols, 'Die Bevölkerungsgeschichte', and Van der Woude, 'Demografische ontwikkeling', esp. 128–139.
[113] Clarke and Ambrosiani, *Towns in the Viking Age*, 28–30.
[114] Verhulst, *Rise of cities*, 68–110, and section III.3, pp. 107–110.
[115] Genicot, *Les grandes villes*, 211, and Despy, 'Naissance des villes', I:97–101.

Table 6.2 Estimates of the urbanization rate for various principalities in the Low Countries, by year 1200–1600 (percentage of total population; * = only cities over 5,000 inhabitants)

	1200	1250	1300	1350	1400	1450	1500	1550	1600
Artois			30			25			
Brabant					31		35		
'Belgian' Brabant			27*	32*	39*	41*	47*	41*	
Flanders					36/33*	24*	25*		
Friesland							22		
Hainaut					30		29		
Holland	5	8	13	23	33		45	45	55
Liège						26			
Luxembourg							15		
Namur						28			
Low Countries			c.20			34			

Sources: De Boer, ' "Op weg naar volwassenheid" ', Van Bavel & Van Zanden, 'The jump-start', 505, Blockmans et al., 'Tussen crisis en welvaart', 43–46, Arnould, *Les dénombrements*, 278–284, Bocquet, *Recherches*, 128–129 and 169–170.

lived in cities; in Flanders, Artois, and the Meuse valley the figure must have been substantially greater. (See Table 6.2.)

In the 13th and 14th centuries the extent of urbanization in the Low Countries increased, making this one of the most urban parts of Europe, second only to northern Italy. About 1300 the overall urbanization rate in the Low Countries was roughly 20 per cent. It was highest in Artois and Flanders.[116] There, some really big cities were to be found, such as Bruges, Ypres, and particularly Ghent, with some 60,000 inhabitants, second to Paris, the biggest city north of the Alps. In this period Artois and Walloon Flanders, with cities such as Lille, Arras, Douai, and Saint-Omer, all with 30,000 inhabitants or more, may have been equally urbanized.[117]

Following the Black Death, absolute population numbers in the cities declined, but the urbanization rate rose, most clearly in Holland. The south-west, Artois and Walloon Flanders, was perhaps the only place where the rate stagnated or even declined in the 14th and 15th centuries, as these large cities were reduced to no more than 15,000 inhabitants. Cities in northern Flanders also declined in size, but not as drastically. Elsewhere, the proportion of people living in the towns rose. In the late 15th century the urbanization rate ranged from 15 per cent in Luxembourg to a staggering 45 per cent in Holland, with the average

---

[116] The estimates by Bairoch et al., *La population des villes*, 253–253 and 259–261, however, are far too high, especially for Bruges around 1400 (125,000 inhabitants).
[117] Derville, 'Le nombre d'habitants'.

for the Low Countries being 34 per cent.[118] In this period, when the Low Countries began to surpass Italy in urbanization, the centre of urbanization became firmly located in Holland, where the growth of cities proceeded relatively and absolutely. The core of urbanization thus gradually shifted north, from Artois and southern Flanders in the 12th and 13th centuries, to northern Flanders in the 14th and 15th centuries, to Holland in the 15th and 16th centuries. By then, the Low Countries had become by far the most urbanized part of Europe.

The proportion of people living in large cities in the Low Countries was also the highest in Europe: around 1550, 20 per cent of the population lived in cities of more than 10,000 inhabitants,[119] compared with 6 per cent on average in Europe as a whole. Still, in contrast to the centralized kingdoms of England and France, with their huge capitals, there were no genuinely big cities: instead, the Low Countries had polynuclear systems of numerous medium-sized towns, without any clear hierarchy.[120] Various elements played a role in this, including the political fragmentation and the boundaries between the various principalities, as well as the pronounced functional specialization of cities, and perhaps some cities' use of non-economic force over (their) countryside. Only in the second half of the 16th century, with the rise of Antwerp (about 100,000 inhabitants in 1565) and later Amsterdam, did this begin to change when more pronounced urban hierarchies emerged in the Low Countries.

Regional Differences in Demographic Development

The sharp regional contrasts in population recovery after the lows of the 14th century, which were particularly apparent in the countryside, require further investigation. In the Guelders river area rural population figures showed long-term stagnation, while the size of towns increased only slowly.[121] It was not until the end of the 18th century that the population in the countryside exceeded that in the 14th century. The same applied, perhaps to an even greater degree, to Artois. In inland Flanders, population developments were clearly different. This region was not as hard hit by the 14th-century crisis, and from as early as 1380 rural population numbers recovered and started to rise rapidly. This sharp and prolonged rise was only stopped by the acts of war and the havoc in the countryside during the political and religious troubles at the end of the 16th century. The population losses in this dramatic

[118] Blockmans et al., 'Tussen crisis en welvaart', esp. 44–45 (all cities). See also De Vries, *European urbanization*, 28–43, and Pauly, 'Anfänge der kleineren Städte'.
[119] De Vries, *European urbanization*, 36 and 39.
[120] Stabel, *Dwarfs among giants*, 27–31 and 63–80.
[121] Van Schaïk, *Belasting*, 273–277, and Brusse, *Overleven door ondernemen*, 28–32.

period, however, were made up for in the first half of the 17th century.[122] In Holland, after a slight decline around the middle of the 14th century, the rural population numbers also quickly recovered. Holland even experienced a population explosion during the 15th and 16th centuries. Around 1600 this growth came to a halt in the countryside—first in the south and later also in the north—and this demographic stagnation continued well into the final decades of the 18th century.[123] Urban population numbers kept on rising, especially in the period 1570–1620, when the growth was some 1.5 per cent per year on average.

Population densities were very high, much higher than anywhere else in Europe outside northern Italy, but differences among regions were pronounced. If we look at the combined figures for town and countryside, the most densely populated regions such as inland Flanders, Walloon Flanders, and Holland in the second half of the 15th century had some 70 people per km^2.[124] In the southern half of Brabant the density was 55, in Hainaut 40, and in Artois about 35 people per km^2. The northern half of Brabant, which consisted mainly of the sandy Campine, had 30 people per km^2, the sandy Veluwe no more than 15 people, and the province of Luxembourg, consisting mainly of the infertile Ardennes, only 6 people per km^2. These contrasts may initially seem to be linked to soil quality, which should especially affect rural population densities, but closer examination shows that this was not completely the case. Striking, for instance, are the relatively low population densities in fertile Artois, with only 26 people per km^2 in the countryside in 1469, and in the district of Nijvel, perhaps the most fertile part of Brabant, where rural population densities declined from 49 in 1374, to 33 in 1437, and 27 in 1480. Striking also was the situation in the Guelders river area, with its fertile alluvial clay land. The region was one of the first to be occupied and became one of the most densely populated regions in the early medieval Low Countries. However, in the 15th century the countryside in this region accommodated no more than 25 people per km^2.[125] Compared with the marshy peatlands in Holland located immediately to the west, where there were as many as 50 people per km^2, this is surprisingly few. In the course of the 16th century, when rural Holland experienced significant population growth and densities increased to 60–80 people per km^2, while those in the Guelders river area remained the same, differences among the regions increased even further. Inland Flanders, consisting mainly of loamy soils of mediocre quality, even had 60 to 90 people

---

[122] Thoen, *Landbouwekonomie*, 36–40 and 155–164, and De Brouwer, *Demografische evolutie*, 108–111 and 140–154.
[123] Lesger, *Hoorn als stedelijk knooppunt*, 217–223, and Van Zanden, *The rise and decline*, 23–25 and 35–37. Cf. also below pp. 285–287.
[124] Blockmans et al., 'Tussen crisis en welvaart', 46.
[125] Van Bavel, 'People and land', and for Artois: Bocquet, *Recherches*, 166–170.

per km^2. These pronounced regional differences were not necessarily linked to soil quality.

It is difficult to explain such regional differences using the Malthusian model. In the 14th century several regions showed a dramatic decline in population, but in others the decline was only moderate: in densely populated regions such as Flanders and Holland, with relatively infertile soils, the crisis should have hit hardest, but did not. Differences in development in the 15th and 16th centuries were perhaps even more pronounced. In the relatively sparsely populated Guelders river area with fertile soils, there was stagnation or even further contraction of population numbers which persisted well into the 18th century. The orthodox neo-Malthusian model cannot explain why the demographic recovery took so long to materialize, while the balance between population and potential production had already recovered due to the enormous decline in population. Densely populated inland Flanders and Holland, on the other hand, experienced rapid population growth in the 15th and 16th centuries. This is even more surprising since these two regions were also the most urbanized in the Low Countries, and thus most affected by the excess mortality in the cities, the 'urban graveyard' effect.

Although this was not necessarily true for all cases, excess mortality did exist in most late medieval towns.[126] Mortality rates in the cities were high because of high infant mortality, bad sanitation, and overcrowded quarters, leading to the spread of infectious diseases. In the Flemish cities death rates in ordinary years were indeed very high, and they were even higher in crisis years. Around the middle of the 15th century annual child mortality in Hulst, a smaller town in coastal Flanders, was at least 65–70 per thousand. Total mortality in the cities was between 35 and 45 per thousand, and significantly higher than in the countryside. Moreover, birth rates were clearly lower in the cities because of the surplus of unmarried women there and the relatively high age at first marriage.[127] As a result, there were fewer children per household in the cities than in the countryside. Households in the cities averaged 3.5 to 4.5 people; 3.2 to 4.3 people in late medieval Ypres, and 3.86 people in Leiden (1581), whereas in the countryside the average was 5 or more, and in the Veluwe in 1565 as many as 5.5 to 6 people per household.[128] The combination of low fertility and high mortality meant that urban population numbers could only be maintained with massive immigration from the countryside.

The combined effect of high urbanization, the existing population pressure, and rather infertile soils should have limited population numbers in Holland and inland Flanders, but it did not. Because cities were unable to generate population growth, we have to turn to the countryside to explain the divergences.

---

[126] This is qualified by Van der Woude, 'Population developments'. For the following data, see also Stabel, *Dwarfs among giants*, 115–122.
[127] See also below, p. 291.   [128] Daelemans, 'Leiden 1581', 149.

Apparently, in some regions the countryside functioned as a breeding ground. The main explanation for the strong rural population growth in Holland and inland Flanders seems to lie in social property systems. These were the regions where most of the land was peasant owned. If they desired, the users of the land could divide their farms among their children. Options for dividing holdings were further increased by the fact that customary law in these regions tended to favour partible inheritance rather than monogeniture.[129] Thus, at least potentially, all children in these peasant families, in contrast to children of tenant farmers, for instance, had direct access to a small plot of land. Landownership and inheritance patterns in this region offered to a relatively large group the prospect of owning at least some land, securing their subsistence, and supporting a household, so that they could marry and establish their own families relatively early, that is, compared with children in regions dominated by large land ownership.[130] Moreover, in areas dominated by peasant ownership, the land appears to have been divided relatively evenly among the owners. Thus, many country dwellers in these regions had access to a piece of land large enough to support a family. This gave rise to a demographic pattern characterized by relatively high and early marriage and rapid population growth, combined with subdivision of farms. This tendency was further enhanced by the presence of markets and the possibility of labour-intensive specialization. The fact that real wages in Holland and Flanders were higher than anywhere else in north-western Europe intensified the process and also reduced the urban excess mortality. The combination of high real wages, cities that accommodated people, and a countryside that bred them resulted in high population densities.

In Holland and inland Flanders the structures of tenure and production, dominated by families farming their own land, were mostly unchanged from the high Middle Ages until well into the 16th century (in Holland), or even into the 19th century (in Flanders).[131] Despite high population densities, there was no fundamental break in demographic patterns in either region up to the middle of the 16th century. Thus, in these areas with mediocre soils there was an enormous rural population reservoir which could continually be used to swell the masses of the urban population. Under certain circumstances this reservoir spilled into the towns in large numbers: for example, as a result of the subsidence of peat soils in the Holland countryside in the 13th and 14th centuries. This partly explains the pronounced wave of urbanization in this period.[132] The pattern of urbanization and the size distribution of cities in the later Middle Ages show a multitude of smaller and medium-sized cities without any clear hierarchy and

---

[129] Hoppenbrouwers, 'Doorgifte van erfgoed', 88–98.
[130] This would be in line with Brenner, 'The agrarian roots', esp. 29–31, although more and different elements seem to have played a role in this than those taken into account by Brenner, as shown in Van Bavel, 'People and land'.
[131] For the latter: Thoen & Vanhaute, 'The "Flemish husbandry" '.
[132] De Boer, *Graaf en grafiek*, 333–338. See also section II.2, pp. 44–45.

reflect the fact that urbanization in Holland was to a large extent driven by push factors in the countryside.[133] Because property relationships in the countryside were not affected, the rural population density in Holland was able to recover and reached the highs observed around the mid-16th century to form a new reservoir of people, even despite the fact that most problems with flooding and drainage remained.

On the other hand, in the Guelders river area and some other regions dominated by large land holdings, from the 13th to the late 16th century, a structural rupture occurred in property exploitation, production structures, and land use. The rise of short-term leasing and the emergence of large tenant farms reduced the hold of land users on the land and made it impossible for them to divide the land among their children. Instead, the accumulation of leased land reduced the number of people having access to land. At the same time, the fierce competition for land forced the large farmers to reduce labour input, which was enabled by specialization for the market and investments in capital goods.[134] Not only did the countrymen lose access to their main means of production and their economic independence, but they also had to cope with decreased earnings because of the reduction in employment opportunities in agriculture and the decline in real wages from the mid-15th century on. Nor did they find an alternative in proto-industrial activities, since none developed in the region. This situation led to migration from the countryside to nearby cities, and also to lower marriage rates and later marriages, resulting in a decrease in the average number of children. This transition to a new socio-economic structure in the countryside, which was closely linked to the specific property structures, had a highly negative effect on rural population developments in this region.

The same negative effect occurred later in Holland. It took place in the course of the 16th century as a result of structural changes both in proto-industries and in agriculture which were similar to those that had taken place earlier in the Guelders river area. This resulted in a decrease of rural population densities in large parts of Holland. In this period the area of agricultural land was enlarged considerably as a result of large-scale drainage projects and the reclamation of new polders, but the rural population numbers stagnated or even contracted, resulting in a decrease in average population densities in the Holland countryside.[135] This began around 1570 in the south, where changes in property and production structures happened first, and the north followed around the mid-17th century. The decline seems to have been brought about by changes in marriage patterns, as well as migration to the cities. This led to a decline in rural population and an exodus from the countryside, which partly explains the simultaneous acceleration

---

[133] De Vries and Van der Woude, *The first modern economy*, 19 and 62.
[134] Van Bavel, 'Land, lease'. See also section VI.1, pp. 244–247 (for the absence of proto-industrialization), and VII.1, pp. 335–336.
[135] Van Zanden, *The rise*, 35–40, and De Vries, *Dutch rural economy*, 88–96.

in urban growth and the increase in the urbanization rate in Holland from 1570 on, which grew to no less than 55 per cent in 1622.[136]

The regional diversity within the Low Countries thus illustrates the fact that pre-industrial population developments in the countryside, and to a large extent population developments in general, did not encounter a fixed upper limit or population ceiling. Rather, they reached a limit which to an important extent was determined by property structures, exploitation, and production structures. The limit could shift considerably when changes took place in regional structures. These developments on a macro level were in part mirrored at the micro level of the household.

Over time, especially in the 16th century, various regions in western Europe experienced a strengthening in the long predominance of the nuclear family. These families did not include large numbers of relatives, but only parents and their children. It is difficult to say exactly when this type became dominant in the Low Countries, since data are mainly available only from the late 16th century. At that point, extended families living under one roof were rare in both town and countryside: only 4–8 per cent of households included other relatives, although in the city of Leiden in 1581 the figure was 13 per cent.[137] In the parts of Overijssel where arable farming and proto-industrial activities were important, such as Twente, around the middle of the 18th century this figure was also higher (about 25 per cent), although it is by no means certain whether this was a relic of an older, late medieval situation. But even there, the proportion of kin (mainly grandparents) living in extended families in the total population was no more than 5 per cent.

This situation, and the dominance of the nuclear family, were the result of a general weakening of kinship ties and the importance of the extended family in the later Middle Ages. Kinship influence on marriage, inheritance, and property was reduced, while the influence of the nuclear family and the individual increased. This enabled easier and swifter transactions, and thus formed an element in the rise of market exchange, particularly of land.[138] Kinship influence over orphans also weakened, and from the 14th century the authorities took over their care through orphans' courts and trustees, administering orphans' properties and exercising custody over them, although in the Flemish cities relatives' influence seems to have remained more pronounced.[139] The declining importance of kin can also be observed in the practice of the feud. Avenging a crime by way of self-help, and taking blood revenge on a perpetrator of harm and his relatives, aided by one's own kin, was fairly common in late medieval western Europe,

---

[136] Van der Woude, 'Demografische ontwikkeling', esp. 131–135, and De Vries, *Dutch rural economy*, 84–89.
[137] Daelemans, 'Leiden 1581', esp. 159–161, and Slicher van Bath, *Een samenleving onder spanning*, 109–112.
[138] See section V.1, pp. 165–166. For early medieval nuclear families, see section IV.1, pp. 127–128.
[139] Danneel, *Weduwen en wezen*, 76–78 and 417–422.

although much less so in relatively strong centralized states such as England and Normandy. In the Low Countries the feud was still practised in the later Middle Ages, as in the large Flemish cities in the 14th century.[140] In cities such as Ghent, kinship and client relationships were very important, particularly among patricians who lived in extended family enclaves with large complexes of houses; they practised feuding extensively. Patricians and non-patricians often settled disputes between themselves and used their kin groups, with little interference by public authorities.

The practice of feuding could lead to destruction, but the feud was also bound by rules of fair play and often resulted in reconciliation and indemnification of the victim's family, aspects that the modern administration of justice cannot offer. From the 14th century on, however, feuding slowly disappeared in most parts of the Low Countries. First, it became more embedded in law, with the state demanding that the crime be brought to court to prevent innocent relatives of the perpetrator being hurt, and to regulate any retaliation. Later the feud was prohibited and gradually disappeared. This happened first in regions with strong central power, and later, only in the 16th century, in those with less centralized authority, such as on the Zeeland islands and in Friesland, where territorial lords had always been weak.[141] In Friesland, the corruption of this system can be clearly observed in the late 15th century, when feuding parties started to hire mercenaries in ever larger numbers—often foreign mercenaries, who did not obey the rules of feuding.[142] The mercenaries did not capture people, but killed them, leading to escalating violence and anarchy. The system of feuding degenerated into private wars without rules. In the end, Duke Albrecht of Saxony used the anarchy in Friesland to step in with his mercenary captains and establish his authority as a territorial lord over Friesland.

The rise of the nuclear family and increasing individualization were among the main elements that led to the disappearance of feuding. Beginning in the 14th century, kin members increasingly refused to help a distant relative or pay blood money for him, or they bought off their liability.[143] In the course of the transition of economy and society, and the rise of markets for land, labour, and capital, economic ties became more important than personal or familial ones, and kinship lost its significance. In a way this is exemplified in the hiring of foreign mercenaries instead of looking to kinsmen for help. Increasing mobility and migration also weakened family ties. Another element was the resentment of urban and rural communities against the settling of disputes by way of violence, fearing that this practice would destabilize the community. Moreover, corporative organizations, such as villages, towns, guilds, and fraternities, which arose from

[140] Nicholas, *The domestic life*, 198–206. See also section III.3, p. 118.
[141] Glaudemans, ' "*Om die wrake wille*" ', 12–13 and 55–69, and Noomen, 'De Friese vetemaatschappij'.
[142] Mol, 'Hoofdelingen en huurlingen'.
[143] Hoppenbrouwers, 'Maagschap en vriendschap', 87–90 and 95–96.

the 11th and 12th centuries, gradually attracted people's loyalty, replacing wider family ties. But most relevant were the rise of states and the monopolization of authority and force by the state. This was theoretically the case, since the state was coming to be seen as the sole upholder of peace and justice, as well as practically, since only central states were in a position to bear the rising costs of policing and warfare. The rise and development of the legal system, the professionalization of the administration of justice, and the growth in manpower to trace and apprehend perpetrators were all relevant here, and resulted in the disappearance of feuds.

The growing importance of economic ties over personal ones is also shown in household composition. Resident kin decreased in number, to be replaced by residents with an economic tie to the household. Some households had paying guests (boarders), but much more important were paid servants. In the countryside servants were mainly young men and women who left home at the age of about 15 to work in another household as a wage labourer until they were ready to start their own family. This type of wage labour was part of a life cycle, often a peasant life cycle. Unfortunately, the numerical importance of live-in servants in the later Middle Ages is difficult to assess because they are largely absent from the fiscal sources. However, the figures for the 17th and 18th centuries suggest that servants probably made up 10–15 per cent of the total rural population.[144] Their number was highest on large farms, which needed the most additional labour. The number of servants on the small holdings in inland Flanders was smaller; some 6 to 8 per cent of the rural population there consisted of live-in servants.[145] In the 16th-century cities, servants made up around 10 per cent of the total population, as in Ypres in 1506 and Leiden in 1581, where they were usually older girls and young women.

On average, late medieval households thus contained only a few people, with a small number of children, particularly in the cities. The size of households showed regional differences, associated with differing chronologies for the disappearance of extended households and regional differences in the importance of live-in servants, but they were mainly the result of differences in birth and mortality. Mortality figures were high, from 40 to 70 per 1,000, as established for the 14th- and 15th-century Flemish countryside; mortality in the cities was even higher.[146] These figures imply an average life expectancy at birth of about 20 years, declining to 14 years in a period of crisis, as around 1400, but rising in the later 15th century to 25–30 years. In the third quarter of the 16th century, a period of high food prices, average life expectancy declined again to about 15 years, as shown for the small town of Hulst in coastal Flanders. There, as

---

[144] Slicher van Bath, *Een samenleving onder spanning*, 112–114.
[145] Vandenbroeke, 'Prospektus', esp. 15–21.
[146] Thoen, *Landbouwekonomie*, 74–79 and 94–99, and for the cities: Stabel, *Dwarfs among giants*, 117–119 and *De kleine stad*, 57–59. Cf. also Nicholas, *Medieval Flanders*, 367–368.

elsewhere, high death rates were mainly the result of high child mortality. Those who survived the dangerous childhood years could expect to live to a fairly ripe age. Mortality rates for adults at the time were about 25 to 35 per 1,000 in the Flemish countryside and 35 to 45 per 1,000 in the cities. Differences among the social groups were marked. The buyers of life rents in the city of Oudenaarde, being mainly young adults from relatively wealthy backgrounds, generally died at 50–55 years of age in the late 15th century, and at 55–60 years some decades later.[147] These high ages point to the social differences in life expectancy.

Regional differences are much better documented in the birth statistics. Birth figures are mainly determined by female age at marriage and nuptiality, for which some scattered 15th- and early 16th-century data are available. According to a report on the countryside around Leiden, all women over 40 were married or had been married, and the same was true for almost all women aged 30–39.[148] The people reported on were born between 1490 and 1525 and had generally married young: on average, 23.1 for men and 20.4 for women. This tallies with the 16th-century data on the rural outburghers of Oudenaarde in inland Flanders.[149] The average age at marriage for male outburghers was 20 to 25 years, which is relatively young. In these two regions, dominated by small peasant holdings where small-scale agriculture was combined with proto-industrial activities, people married young and nuptiality was high. The high population densities and the fragmentation of farms that resulted from this are discussed above. Proto-industrialization could strengthen this reproductive pattern. The labour-intensive cottage industries originated as a logical extension of the peasant economy and enabled the peasants to employ the surplus labour of all household members. Proto-industrial families had alternative earnings from their industrial activities which lessened the need to delay marriage until some land had been acquired, for instance, through inheritance. Moreover, the children of these families boosted incomes by carrying out proto-industrial activities within the household.[150] The expansion of such cottage industries, which was aided by growing demand from urban markets, thus intensified the reproductive pattern and led to higher population densities. But apart from any possible direct influence, it is clear that proto-industrial families were widening their opportunities to earn an income by tapping additional resources. Thus, smaller farms became viable and population numbers increased even further, especially in the already densely populated Flemish countryside in the course of the 16th century.

A very different pattern occurred when proto-industrialization resulted in polarization and proletarianization, as was the case in Holland. The results were similar to those in regions where proletarianization occurred in the agricultural

---

[147] Stabel, *Dwarfs among giants*, 117–119. [148] Van Zanden, *The rise*, 26–29.
[149] Thoen, *Landbouwekonomie*, 171–174. For the outburghers, see section III.3, p. 115.
[150] See Medick, 'The proto-industrial family economy', esp. 302–306.

sector, as in the Guelders river area in the 15th and 16th centuries. Indeed, those country dwellers who had no land or hardly any—a group which was steadily growing in both the Guelders river area and later Holland—had significantly fewer children than other rural population groups. The difference could be as much as 1.5 to 2 children per household.[151] Moreover, the nearly landless countrymen had fewer opportunities to earn a living in the countryside as a wage labourer, as a result of reduced employment opportunities, which led to a further adjustment in their marriage pattern, resulting in even fewer children.

In Holland, the demographic regime in the countryside, which had been a peasant regime, changed along these lines in the course of the 16th and 17th centuries, with nuptiality decreasing and age at marriage rising substantially. This was due to changes in the organization of proto-industries and, somewhat later, a transition in agriculture, with the disappearance of peasant ownership, the rise of large holdings, and the shift to a capitalist rural economy. In this period the average marital age in the Holland countryside increased considerably. In the village of Maasland, in the peatlands, the average age at first marriage in the second half of the 17th century was 30 for men and 27 for women.[152] These figures are surprisingly high: about 7 years greater than was the case for the environs of Leiden in 1540. Further, the age of majority in Holland was raised considerably. In the 15th century, girls attained their majority at 13–20 and boys at 12–22. By the end of the 16th century, this had increased to a minimum of 25, which applied both to cities and to rural areas.[153] This contrasted with neighbouring provinces, such as Utrecht and Brabant, where the age of majority was raised only slightly or not at all. The significant increase in Holland may have been partly due to the growing influence of Roman law, which also set majority at 25, but Roman law became more influential everywhere without a similar effect in other regions. Therefore, the simultaneous demographic and economic changes in Holland were probably much more important. The demographic changes in rural Holland are shown by the decline in the number of resident children per household in the Krimpenerwaard from 2.72 in 1622 to 2.08 in 1680.[154] All data thus point to a transformation in demographic patterns in Holland. The change probably took place even earlier in the cities, where low nuptiality and older age at marriage were already the norm in the late Middle Ages. In fact, this can be seen in the advent of the 'European marriage pattern'. This rise was connected to radical changes in property and production structures, which took place early in several cities and regions such as the Guelders river area (*c*.1450–1600), and somewhat later in rural Holland (*c*.1550–1650), and even later in rural inland Flanders.

[151] As demonstrated for inland Flanders in the period 1400–1540: Thoen, *Landbouwekonomie*, 204–210.
[152] Noordam, *Leven in Maasland*, 106–107. See also Van Bavel, 'People and land'.
[153] Ankum, 'Études', esp. 295–299.
[154] Van der Woude, 'Population developments', 55–75, esp. 69 table 4.

The Position of Women

Both within the household and outside it, the position of women in the Low Countries seems to have been strong compared with other parts of western Europe. This applied particularly to the period before the 14th century. Women often provided revenue for the household by working on the farm, engaging in industrial activities, and even participating in business; selling goods or acting as managers, becoming teachers or innkeepers, and their position could be fairly independent. They thus played an active part in economic life, and to some extent also in politics and administration. In the 12th and 13th centuries in Flanders, women from the upper nobility sometimes held high administrative positions, such as castellan, financial receiver, or tax farmer, as widows or on behalf of their husbands, but also in their own right.[155] The position of married women was buttressed by legal security, as well as by the independent material position they enjoyed from marriage settlements and hereditary laws. Feudal properties in theory could only be inherited by the eldest son, or in some regions by the youngest son, and were not divided among the children, certainly not the daughters, but it is noteworthy that the Low Countries were the first area in north-western Europe where feudal succession of women was permitted, beginning as early as the late 11th century.[156]

The fact that feudal and manorial organization were not important in most of the Low Countries further strengthened the position of women. In regions where manorial organization had been strong and lords had been keen on preserving the integrity of the servile holdings, primogeniture (as in the west of Artois and Luxembourg) or ultimogeniture (as around Cambrai and Valenciennes) were predominant, with girls often excluded from inheriting.[157] In regions where feudalism and manorialism had been weak, such as coastal Flanders, inland Flanders, and Holland, and in the Low Countries more generally, women could inherit from their parents just as their brothers could, no matter what their marital status.[158] In addition, they often controlled the properties they brought into the marriage as well as the communal properties, with husbands and wives often serving as each other's heirs. Inheriting from their husbands also strengthened the position of the women who were widowed, offering them better prospects for remarriage. All in all, up to the 13th century, in the western part of the Low Countries and probably elsewhere, women were treated as almost equal to men in legal and economic matters.

This situation did not continue. Changes during the late Middle Ages show a very mixed picture. On the one hand, the rise of the labour market enabled young, unmarried women to look for paid work outside their own family, as a servant, maid, or in another position. Many young women from the countryside

---

[155] Kittell, 'Women in the administration', 487–508. See also section V.3, pp. 207–208.
[156] Ganshof, *Feudalism*, 140–144.   [157] Jacob, *Les époux*, 47–51, 363–367, and 374–380.
[158] Godding, 'La famille', and Kittell, 'Testaments of two cities'.

went to the cities to find jobs there, contributing to the over-representation of women in the population of most north-west European cities in the period, with sex ratios of 110–120 women to 100 men, as in Ypres (1506), or even 130–140 to 100, as in Leiden (1581) and Louvain (1597).[159] Young women could now acquire some property before marriage by performing wage labour, strengthening their position.[160] At the same time, their position in the urban marriage market may have been weakened by their numerical preponderance, although the ratio between the group of women at the age they married and the group of men when they married seems to have been more balanced.

Other developments weakened the position of women. The exercise of political power and public office was increasingly judged as incompatible with womanhood. The role of women in comital administration, as found earlier in Flanders, now disappeared. The formal position of women in the guilds was also affected, especially after 1300, when guilds acquired political power in many towns, and exercising this power was deemed unsuitable for women. In the economic sphere, the rise of extra-household labour and wage labour had a mixed result. On the one hand, it allowed more freedom to unmarried women, but on the other, it probably undermined the role of married women, since their position was often based on their role in the household economy, which now increasingly gave way to market-oriented enterprises in which the family was no longer the main production unit.[161] Women were becoming relegated to simple activities such as scouring and spinning wool. At the same time their legal position deteriorated, particularly in matters of marriage and inheritance. Although there was diversity, with the position of women remaining stronger in the northern Dutch-speaking parts of Flanders, marriage customs started to place more emphasis on the male line of the family, as has been demonstrated for Douai, Lille, and other parts of southern Flanders.[162] In 16th-century Lille, written custom came to deny the rights of women as joint owners of community goods; these were now placed firmly under the control of their husbands. Law and custom could be circumvented by making individual arrangements, such as by drawing up a will, but this option was more expensive and cumbersome.

From around 1400, as in other parts of north-western Europe, new ideas about marriage and the household emerged, with greater emphasis on the separation between the public and private spheres. The woman was clearly relegated to the latter and placed under the authority of her husband. In the house she was only given tasks related to bringing up children and housekeeping, guided by new ideas on good motherhood and domestic life as propagated in humanist literature

---

[159] Daelemans, 'Leiden 1581', 147.
[160] De Moor and Van Zanden: *Vrouwen*, 41–59, and 'Girl power'.
[161] Howell, *Women*, 87–94, and qualified for Leiden by Kloek, *Wie hij zij*, 48–77.
[162] Howell, *The marriage exchange*, 199–208, and Jacob, *Les époux*, 41–43 and 47–64.

and enforced by judicial verdicts.[163] Women were increasingly penalized for not living up to the new standards of motherhood. Older unmarried women and those working as midwife, matchmaker, or hostess were increasingly viewed with suspicion. Such women were also the main victims of witch hunts. As in other parts of western Europe, the first systematic persecution started in the second half of the 15th century, with a massive one taking place in Arras, the Vauderie, starting in 1459–60.[164] The first half of the 16th century saw trials in Luxembourg, Namur, and Douai, mainly in the southern parts of the Low Countries. About four-fifths of the accused in these trials were women, mainly older single women, often poor, and not integrated into local or familial networks.

Despite the late medieval changes, the position of women in the Low Countries still seems to have remained relatively favourable compared to other parts of Europe. Not all discriminatory measures were strictly followed, and often women could continue informally in all kinds of economic positions, such as retailing.[165] In most parts of the Low Countries, women engaging in trade were considered legally capable; in Holland, all unmarried women over 25 were considered so, and were not placed under the guardianship of a man. That the position of women remained relatively firm and independent is confirmed by the reaction of foreign visitors in the Low Countries. In 1517, the Spanish envoy Antonio de Beatis noted in his travel journals how active women were in economic life, for instance, in running excellent inns and handling the administration themselves. His descriptions were echoed by the Italian Guicciardini in 1567, who condemned this typically Low Countries situation. Perhaps the relatively prominent role of women was found mostly in the north, more specifically in Holland. In this respect, it may be significant that the witch hunts were much less fierce there, with the Holland-dominated Dutch Republic in 1605 becoming the first country in Europe where such persecution was stopped and even prohibited. Perhaps this is related to the century-long tradition of nuclear families and women's independence there, and possibly also to the high level of commercialization, specialization, and occupational differentiation. This is a field where much scope for further research exists.

VI.3. COMMERCIALIZATION AND OCCUPATIONAL DIFFERENTIATION

Commercialization greatly increased in the Low Countries, particularly from the 11th to 12th centuries on, as shown by the significant rise in the number of

---

[163] Naessens, 'Judicial authorities' views', and Pleij, *De sneeuwpoppen*, 278–288.
[164] Soly, 'De grote heksenjacht', esp. 112–115.
[165] Stabel, 'Women at the market', and Van Aert, 'Tussen norm en praktijk'.

markets, the growing amount of goods traded, the rise of cities, the abandonment of self-sufficiency by large institutions, and the growth of specialized industries.[166] For the later period more concrete indicators are available which show the high level of commercialization in the Low Countries. One is the volume of international trade: imports around 1550 are estimated at 20–22 million guilders per year (mainly silk from Italy, cloth from England, and grain from the Baltic), and exports at 16 million (mainly linen, serges, cloth, and tapestries).[167] Imports per capita were about four to five times higher than in France and England at the time, pointing to significant involvement in international trade and the extent of commercialization. The latter is even more evident if we assume that regional trade within the Low Countries must have been much more important than international trade, facilitated by the unimportance of boundaries or institutional obstacles, the abundance of transport possibilities, and the strong and growing regional specialization.

But, despite the high general level of commercialization in the Low Countries as a whole, great regional diversity in the extent, causes, and effects of commercialization existed. This can be observed most clearly in the countryside. In peasant-dominated Drenthe, for instance, involvement in trade and specialization remained limited; there was no fundamental change until the 19th century.[168] On their small and medium-sized farms, peasant families concentrated on cultivating bread grains and tending a few livestock, mainly for their own subsistence. Long-term security and the consumption needs of the household were much more central to their production decisions than the market was. In line with this, common lands remained very important, and exploitation of the commons for market purposes was resisted.[169] Non-agricultural side activities were fairly unimportant and did not show proto-industrial dynamism. In general, the peasant structure remained largely intact over the centuries, with little commercialization.

Agricultural commercialization in the Guelders river area, on the other hand, was very pronounced. Livestock breeding became increasingly more labour- and capital-intensive in the course of the 15th and 16th centuries. This applied particularly to the sectors that developed strongly there: horse breeding and the fattening of oxen. Large-scale farmers usually had large capital reserves at their disposal, endeavoured to reduce labour input, and had good contacts with the market. For them such branches of livestock breeding were very suitable. As a result, horse breeding and summer grazing developed in the area, and became incorporated in an international market system extending from Denmark to

---

[166] Section V.4, pp. 219–224, and this section below, pp. 300–301, and section VII.1, pp. 325–327 and VII.2, pp. 343–344.
[167] Brulez, 'The balance of trade'.
[168] Van Zanden, 'From peasant economy', esp. 38–40, although nuanced by Bieleman, 'De verscheidenheid'.
[169] Van Zanden, 'The paradox of the marks'.

northern France.[170] Relatively important was the construction of dovecotes, fishponds, and duck decoys, some of which required large capital investments. The livestock sector there became very market oriented, labour-extensive, and capital intensive. These developments were closely connected with the rise of short-term leasing and large tenant farms. Tenant farmers were probably more inclined than other farmers to focus on the market and specialize, since they needed to do so to compete successfully for leased land. Minimizing risks, in itself a sound strategy under the circumstances, had to give way to profit maximization, with specialization and reduction of labour input forming the main instruments to achieve it. Moreover, the large tenant farmers, in collaboration with their landlords, had the capital needed to make the investments for these often costly specializations.

In inland Flanders, despite the proximity of large cities and extensive markets, commercialization was more limited and different in nature, with the labour-intensive and market-oriented cultivation of cash crops and proto-industrial activities combined with subsistence farming. Intensive grain cultivation to meet household consumption needs remained important. Decisive in this fairly low level of commercialization were the dominance of peasant ownership, in combination with the high degree of non-economic coercion applied by towns and urban merchants in market exchange, which made specialization for the market less attractive to the rural population. The presence of large cities and urban markets, therefore, did not necessarily or automatically lead to significant commercialization of the countryside.

In fact, urban demand was felt almost everywhere in the Low Countries, so this cannot be a determining factor for differences in commercialization and specialization. In some cases urban demand may indeed have accelerated developments, as in the rapid changes in Holland which were close to urban centres, in contrast to the slow development of the rural economy in Drenthe, one of the regions where transport to market was most difficult. But the extent to which farmers reacted to market impulses was largely determined by the social organization of the countryside itself, in which the structures of landownership and land use played a crucial role. If such elements were opening possibilities, creating incentives, or forcing people to commercialize their production, then regions located far from the urban market may also have developed specializations for this market. In the later Middle Ages, and certainly by the 16th century, specializations spanned large areas, in some cases even throughout Europe. This was the case, for instance, with oxen; the consumption of their meat was concentrated in the Low Countries and Italy, but they were raised in parts of Hungary, Poland, northern Germany, and Denmark.[171] The determining factors were the availability of capital and land (the most important production factors)

---

[170] Van Bavel, 'Land, lease and agriculture', 35–39. See also section VII.1, pp. 334–335.
[171] Blanchard, 'The continental European cattle trade', and Gijsbers, *Kapitale ossen*, 42–47.

and trade privileges, all factors associated with the large landownership of the nobility. As a result, rural specializations and their intensity were not radially distributed over Europe around the big urban centres, but formed a patchwork in very specific regions only, and this pattern was related to the social and economic structure of the rural economy rather than to geographical factors. This also applied to growing rye. In Poland and the Baltic, large quantities of rye were produced for the Holland market. This was done on large estates, partly geared towards market-oriented grain production, using large numbers of mainly unfree labourers, clearly integrated in the regional social organization.[172] Even transport costs were greatly influenced by this structure, since they were reduced by using *corvée* labour to transport grain from the estates to the Baltic coast.

These examples show that the presence of market demand itself cannot account for the extent and specific direction of response of the rural economy. Urban demand may have accelerated developments, but it did not necessarily lead to increasing specialization, scale-enlargement, and larger surpluses. It could also sustain or even intensify a situation of small-scale peasant agriculture, leading to further fragmentation and declining labour productivity, as has been demonstrated for inland Flanders, and parts of Holland, or to a lesser extent for Drenthe and Twente. The opposite happened in the Guelders river area. In response to demand from urban and non-urban markets relatively far from the region, agriculture became distinctly more labour-extensive, with larger surpluses but lower physical yields. In regions where the market was near and accessible enough to be sensitive to market demands (which was the case in most parts of the Low Countries) agricultural specialization can be observed in this period, but the degree to which farmers reacted to market demands, and the direction they gave to market specialization, depended greatly on regional production factors and the social distribution of land, capital, and power.

What has been said above applies mainly to agriculture. Non-agricultural activities in the countryside were generally much more commercialized and often aimed at international markets, as in the two regions where proto-industrialization was most obvious, inland Flanders and Holland. The rural woollen industry in inland Flanders was almost completely limited to the preparatory phases: carding, combing, and spinning the wool. These activities were largely organized in a putting-out system,[173] with the rural production dependent on urban entrepreneurs, who often also supplied the raw material. Moorsele near Kortrijk is an example of this, where women from the surrounding countryside came each Saturday to receive wool from Kortrijk drapers to comb and spin, and then delivered the yarn to receive their wage. Equally commercialized was the most important proto-industrial sector in inland Flanders, the linen sector, although it was organized differently, with many intermediate actors in the trade. There were

---

[172] Sundhausen, 'Zur Wechselbeziehung'.
[173] Holbach, *Frühformen von Verlag*, 61 and 151–153.

the itinerant merchants in the countryside, the village markets, the merchants in the regional market towns (as in Oudenaarde), the merchant-bleachers, and the wholesalers and intermediaries in larger cities such as Ghent. Much of the output ended up in the hands of the big, often foreign, merchants who exported the linen, such as the Spanish merchants in Antwerp.[174] Ultimately, Flemish linens were often destined for foreign markets: in France, Italy, England, and to an increasing extent in Spain, or through Spain, in the New World.[175] Nevertheless, the production of Flemish linens remained dominated by independent small-scale producers.

The products of proto-industrial activities in the Holland countryside, too, were to a large extent transported to non-local markets or even exported abroad.[176] The IJssel bricks and paving tiles found markets in England, at least from the late 14th century on, as shown by the cargoes of tens of thousands of bricks brought by Gouda and Rotterdam ships to Newcastle, Great Yarmouth, and Chichester. In addition, large quantities were transported as ballast on ships going to Denmark and the Baltic region, an export which rapidly developed in the 15th century. Peat was mainly sold in the cities of Holland, but it was also exported to Flanders, Brabant, and the saltworks in Zeeland. Notwithstanding incidental attempts by authorities to restrict the export of peat for fear there would be a fuel shortage, exports increased rapidly in the 16th century: in the period 1540–65, 1.5 million tons of turf were exported abroad from Holland annually. Another Holland export popular on international markets was cheese, sold in Germany and in the Antwerp fairs. These characteristic products had little competition and remained successful on international markets.

The importance of proto-industrial production in most cases was not necessarily connected to the proximity of urban markets, since raw materials, semi-finished goods, and finished products could easily be transported over longer distances. In Hessen, and further east in Germany, small-scale peasants started to produce yarn on a massive scale. This was transported to the Wuppertal area in the Rhineland, to be further processed and bleached there, and then transported to Amsterdam to be used in the Holland and Flanders textile industries.[177] In the regions between Hessen/Wuppertal and Holland, a distance of several hundred kilometres which included Cleves and the Guelders river area, there was no such market-oriented specialization, showing that geography alone is not the decisive factor, but rather the social and property structures of a region.

[174] Sabbe, *De Belgische vlasnijverheid*, 273–277, Goris, *Étude sur les colonies marchandes*, 289–315, and Dambruyne, *Mensen en centen*, 253–257.
[175] Boone, 'Les toiles de lin', and Sabbe, *De Belgische vlasnijverheid*, 171–174 and 261–273. See also sections VI.1, pp. 248–249, and VII.2, p. 346.
[176] Van Bavel, 'Early proto-industrialization', 1151 and 1157–1159, Diepeveen, *De vervening*, 46–47, 105–106, and 133–137, and Cornelisse, *Energiemarkten*, 224–234.
[177] Dietz, *Die Wuppertaler Garnnahrung*, 21–34 and 69–82.

Industrial production in the cities was also very commercialized, and aimed at local, regional, or even international markets. Some cities developed clear specializations for the international market, in some cases as early as the high Middle Ages. A good example is the brass and copperware from Dinant, with dinanderies being traded all over western Europe in the 11th and 12th centuries. This export orientation was equally strong in cloth production in the Flemish towns. Cloth from Ypres was traded at markets as far away as Novgorod in the 1130s. In the 14th century, cloth from 10 Flemish towns was found in European markets, and in the 15th century another 10 smaller towns joined the ranks of cloth exporters.[178] At this time Flemish cloth was mainly marketed in Germany, Poland, and Russia, but also in the Mediterranean. The importance of producing for export can also be documented for the brewing industry, where commercialization and export orientation became very pronounced in the course of the 14th and 15th centuries, especially in Holland.[179] In the 14th century Holland was still a net beer importer: in the 1360s some 5.6 million litres were imported annually from Hamburg to Amsterdam. At the time, the three biggest beer-producing towns in Holland (Gouda, Delft, and Haarlem) produced about 11 million litres a year. At the beginning of the 15th century, this production had trebled, and a large proportion was exported; in Haarlem 55 per cent of total output was shipped away, mainly to Flanders and Brabant. In the Brabantine city of Antwerp, only a quarter of the beer consumed was produced by local brewers, and all the rest was imported from Haarlem. The peak of this export was reached around 1514, when the three Holland towns produced annually some 110 million litres of beer, only 7 per cent of which they consumed themselves. The export orientation of the Holland brewing industry ran parallel with scale-enlargement and increasingy capitalist production relations, just as was the case in the metallurgical industry in Liège. These processes were not necessarily linked, however, as shown by the cloth industries in Flanders and Brabant, where small-scale producers also worked for international markets.

Estimating the extent of commercialization is not easy, but it is safe to assume that in the 16th-century Low Countries the Holland economy had the highest degree of market orientation. This region had an extremely high urbanization rate, urban industries and services were almost exclusively aimed at the market, and there was a strong proto-industrial sector, also aimed at the market, and highly commercialized agriculture, specializing in livestock. Of the end-products of agriculture and industries around the year 1500 some 85–90 per cent was destined for the market.[180] Geographical conditions—the virtual impossibility of growing

---

[178] Stabel, *Dwarfs among giants*, 146–148.
[179] Unger, *A history of brewing*, 28–34, 50–59, and 73. See also Van Zanden, 'Holland en de Zuidelijke Nederlanden', esp. 363–365.
[180] Dijkman, 'The development'.

bread grain there, and the easy access to waterways—were responsible to some extent, but other factors such as the flexible, open markets, their favourable institutional organization, and the fundamental changes in the organization of production also played a part.

Increasing commercialization resulted in increasing specialization and occupational differentiation, but the extent of this is difficult to estimate, particularly given the problems of distinguishing full-time occupations from part-time, combined ones. Perhaps the period around 1100 was one of change in the organization of a number of urban industries, as assumed for cloth production in the Flemish cities, as the shift to the broadloom and higher-quality cloth required more skills and promoted division of labour.[181] In the 13th century occupational specialization seems to have been fairly strong in the Holland cities, even if they were still small at the time. The sources for Dordrecht mention 53 different occupations, those for Amsterdam in the 14th century some 50.[182] In the 13th century the rise of professional millers and bakers can be observed in these cities, indicating occupational specialization. Households saved an hour or two a day from time previously spent in hand milling and baking. The rise of guilds in the 13th and 14th centuries, mainly in the Flemish and Brabantine towns, was also an important step. Since certain jobs/tasks were reserved for or even monopolized by guilds, their rise must have resulted in more occupational differentiation in the towns. In the bigger cities there were often many guilds, up to 50 or 60 in Ghent and Bruges, entailing sharp differentiation among them. Moreover, many guilds were divided into several occupational groups. In the 16th century Ghent had about 100 of these, with the craft of woodworking being divided into ebony carvers, loom makers, woodcutters, wood sawyers, wood turners, carriage builders, wood sculptors, coopers, drawer makers, bedstead makers, frame makers, shipbuilders, cabinetmakers, chair makers, and carpenters.[183] Entering these crafts or switching was not always easy, and infringements on occupational monopolies were sometimes hotly contested.

Occupational differentiation also increased in the countryside. A clear example is water management. Initially, construction and maintenance of hydrological projects was mainly carried out by the peasants themselves, with the regular work on the dikes often divided among the owners and users of the neighbouring plots of land. In the later Middle Ages, however, this system increasingly proved to be inadequate. The labour needed for constructing and renovating the ever bigger dikes started to exceed the abilities of those who owned the adjacent lands, and the cost had to be apportioned over larger areas. Moreover, water management increasingly required specialized labourers, who were rewarded with money wages for constructing and maintaining water mills and sluices and other expensive devices. Thus, there was monetarization of water

---

[181] Verhulst, *Rise of cities*, 135–137, and Munro, 'Medieval woollens', 194–197 and 218–222.
[182] Baart, 'De materiële stadscultuur'.   [183] Dambruyne, *Corporatieve middengroepen*, 26–31.

management obligations, with taxes levied in money, and used to hire labourers.[184] In coastal Flanders, this development had begun earliest, in the late 13th century. This early move was further stimulated by the gradual change from peasant land ownership to the leasing out of large land ownership, and from a peasant society to agrarian capitalism. This change affected the functioning of the communal organizations for water management: their administration was increasingly controlled by large landowners. A similar transition took place in Holland in the 15th and 16th centuries. At the beginning of the 16th century, water management obligations in Holland, too, were almost exclusively fulfilled indirectly, that is, by paying a money tax. Only regular work on the smaller dikes was still carried out by the neighbouring landowner or user himself.

Whether the degree of specialization and occupational differentiation in the countryside increased more in general, however, is difficult to determine. In the late Middle Ages the rural population of Holland combined many different activities according to the seasons or even within the same season. Industrial activities were combined with peat digging, groundwork, and some farming on their smallholdings. This does not mean that the Holland countryside of the 15th century was an unspecialized peasant society, however. This combination of activities was seldom aimed at subsistence, but instead at the market, and often performed for wages, with a combination of specializations.[185] As early as the 15th century, the extent of agricultural activities in the countryside in Holland was surpassed by non-agricultural activities, almost completely oriented towards non-local or even non-regional markets. This process further intensified in the course of the 16th century, as the Holland countryside also underwent a transformation in the agricultural sector.[186] Small peasant farms were gradually replaced by large tenant farms, a process which was accompanied by marked specialization and commercialization of agriculture. The latter development, much more than the subsidence of the soil in the 14th century, really swept away the link between non-agricultural activities in the countryside and small farms and subsistence farming. Now the road was open to further occupational differentiation among farmers, wage labourers, various craftsmen, and people operating in the service sector. In other regions, however, such as inland Flanders, this link between subsistence farming and industrial activities remained until well into the 19th century; this was also true of regions such as Twente, Drenthe, and the Campine. In these regions, occupational differentiation, specialization, and market orientation were clearly less pronounced. In Drenthe at the beginning of

---

[184] Soens: 'Explaining deficiencies of water management', and 'De mythe' (for Flanders); and Van Dam, 'Ecological challenges'. See also section II.2, pp. 43–44.
[185] In the debate, the low level of specialization is stressed by De Vries, *Dutch rural economy*, 119–121, but he is criticized by Noordegraaf, 'Het platteland van Holland'. See also De Vries, 'The transition to capitalism', esp. 76–80.
[186] De Vries, *Dutch rural economy*, 119–173. See also above, section VI.1, pp. 259–260.

the 17th century,[187] the number of carpenters, weavers, bricklayers, tailors, and bakers in the countryside was still very small, indicating that such activities were still mostly performed in the peasant households themselves.

Regional differences in specialization and employment opportunities, as well as in population pressure and nominal wages, gave rise to temporary regional migration. Labour migration to Holland was strong in the 16th century, and perhaps even earlier. Holland attracted many temporary labourers from elsewhere because of the high nominal wages, and also because proto-industrial manufactories in Holland were important and these used large numbers of migrant labourers. This was reinforced by the seasonal character of rural economic activities in Holland, with the peak seasons in the various sectors often overlapping. This was true of herring fishing, which had a season starting in July or August and lasting until late October, and of peat digging, which was carried out only from March to July, since the turves had to be dry before the frost set in. Bleaching and brick production also had short production seasons.[188] These overlapped with the busiest period in agriculture, as mowing, haying, and harvesting had to be done mainly in June and July, resulting in a seasonal labour scarcity. This led to migrant workers often being employed alongside local people in all these sectors. In the peat sector, where demand for labour was very high in the short digging season, many temporary migrants were employed, notwithstanding some attempts by local authorities to restrict this practice through stipulations embodied in local bylaws.[189] The temporary migrations often fitted well in the labour cycle of the migrant, who combined different activities through the year, some aimed at the market and others at subsistence, undertaken at home or elsewhere.

The rise of migrant labour in Holland appears to have begun long before the Golden Age and was connected with the rise of proto-industrial sectors from the 14th century on. Subsequently, the number of migrant labourers and the distances they travelled increased, partly because of the disappearance of smallholders in Holland. Particularly from 1570, migrant labourers from within Holland were increasingly replaced by foreign migrant labourers, mainly from peasant regions in the eastern, sandy parts of the Netherlands and Westfalia in present-day Germany.[190] In contrast to inland Flanders, where activities in the countryside involved little seasonal or migrant labour and were mainly performed within the household, a substantial part of the labour input in agriculture in the Guelders river area also came from migrant labour. This was the case particularly in diking, harvesting, pollarding, and planting willows, but also in such labour-intensive tasks as binding hops, transporting dung, and sawing wood. Sometimes

---

[187] Bieleman, *Boeren op het Drentse zand*, 98–112.
[188] Lucassen, *Naar de kusten*, 93, 95, 102, and 107, and Van Bavel, 'Early proto-industrialization?', 1156–1157.
[189] Diepeveen, *De vervening*, 90–91.
[190] Van Zanden, *The rise and decline*, 158–159, dating this shift a little later (*c*.1620).

the migrant workers came from other villages in the region to work in harvesting and diking, but there were also groups from distances of up to 100 km and more, such as the Campine and the Peel, situated south-east of the Guelders river area.[191] These were typical peasant regions where no structural transition of the rural economy had taken place.

Temporary migration thus seems to have originated mainly from peasant regions, whereas permanent migration was probably mostly from regions where proletarization or loss of the means of production took place. Flows of permanent migration were intense in the late Middle Ages; people were very mobile. Most is known about migration of non-paupers from countryside to towns because they had to register in the burgher lists, whereas paupers and those migrating from town to countryside did not. But despite this source problem it is safe to say that the flow of migration was greatest from countryside to town. Sometimes people were pushed out of the countryside because they no longer possessed the means of subsistence. This was most prevalent in Holland in the 13th and 14th centuries when the physical-geographical deterioration made farming less attractive, and in the 16th and 17th centuries as a result of the structural transition in both the proto-industrial and agricultural sectors. Leiden, for instance, received no fewer than 58 new burghers each year in the period 1364–1415; these were mainly poorer people from the surrounding countryside. Including relatives, this comes to about 230 persons immigrating each year, or some 4 per cent of the population, which was not unlike the figures for the nearby city of Gouda.[192] In other instances, pull factors played the main role: higher real wages, labour scarcity because of urban mortality, and the availability of many unskilled jobs. In some cases, push and pull factors both operated to produce an enormous stream of immigration, as with the booming industrial town of Hondschoote in the 16th century: in 1561 alone some 300 apprentices and 34 masters flocked into the town,[193] most of them paupers, looking for work to feed themselves, their women, and children—probably more than a thousand people in total.

The larger the city, the wider was its area of migrant recruitment. Bruges in the 15th century, with its 35,000 inhabitants, received most of its 200 new burghers each year from distances more than 35 km away, whereas the radius for Oudenaarde, with 5,000 inhabitants, was less than 10 km.[194] This links with another general pattern: long-distance migration was mostly from city to city, as with about half the immigrants going to Bruges, whereas countrymen mainly migrated to the nearest city. In addition to these new burghers, who were largely skilled and semi-skilled workers with the means and the motives to acquire citizenship, there were also many unskilled labourers and vagrants. Among them

---

[191] Van Bavel, *Mariënweerd*, 415–416 and 428–429.   [192] De Boer, *Graaf en grafiek*, 135–164.
[193] Coornaert, *La draperie-sayetterie*, 28–29 and 412–414.
[194] Thoen, 'Verhuizen naar Brugge', and Stabel, *De kleine stad*, 31–53.

there must have been a great deal of misery, which is reflected in their high death rates, caused by epidemics, food shortages, and infant mortality. Still, the processes of fragmentation of holdings and proletarianization in the countryside kept on driving these people to the towns in massive numbers.

VI.4. WELFARE

Wages and Standards of Living

Social processes at work in the late medieval Low Countries varied between regions, but most of them entailed polarization. The merchants, entrepreneurs, and state officials were among the winners. Some middle groups also advanced, especially tenant farmers, but also lower civil servants and guild masters who managed to become successful subcontractors. But many more people lost out, including the proto-industrial peasants who saw their holdings become fragmented, the country dwellers who became proletarianized wage labourers, and the craftsmen who lost their means of production.

Proletarianization is often equated with poverty, but it did not have to be intrinsically disastrous, especially if a wage labourer was free of non-economic coercion exercised by employers and could count on reliable, open labour, product, and capital markets. However, these circumstances were unusual, although Holland in the 14th and 15th centuries may have come closest to providing them.[195] Another determinant of the position of proletarianized wage labourers was the level of wages. Real wages are difficult to calculate because of uncertainty about days worked, differences in wages per town, per area, per season, and per job, and fluctuations in prices, but in general real wages and standards of living were high in the late medieval Low Countries compared with other parts of north-western Europe. They were particularly high in Holland, probably as a legacy of the colonization of this frontier area in the 11th to 13th centuries, when labour was scarce, and as a result of the high labour productivity in the Holland economy, connected to the high investments in capital goods.[196] In Flanders and Utrecht wages were lower than in Holland, but still higher than in other parts of north-western Europe. In the second half of the 14th century, wages in many parts of the Low Countries underwent marked changes. First, after the chaos of the Black Death, there was a drastic fall in real wages, and only in the 1390s did they start to increase, as would be expected as a result of the sharp population decline.[197] This led to a short golden age for wage labourers, up to the mid-15th century, with real wages

---

[195] Sections V.2, pp. 191–192, V.3, pp. 207–212, and V.4, pp. 239–240.
[196] Van Bavel and Van Zanden, 'The jump-start', 510–516.
[197] Munro, 'Wage stickiness', 227–228.

often not seeing such levels again until the second half of the 19th century. In Holland, on the other hand, there was only a slight population decline, followed by rapid growth, which prevented a rise in real wages. Wages in the Low Countries thus converged after the Black Death at a relatively high level, but they became severely depressed in the period of population growth in the 16th century.

Besides these long-term trends in real wages, following from demographic developments and the resulting wage–price scissors but also as a consequence of economic trends and structural social changes, there were short-term fluctuations in real wages as a result of crop failures or war, which pushed up prices and cut purchasing power. In the town of Zutphen, for instance, the real daily wage of an unskilled labourer in the period 1420–1500, calculated over the year, oscillated between more than 12.5 litres of wheat and barely 2.5 litres. The latter meant severe hunger for him and his household.[198] The degree of price volatility was a main determinant in the well-being of labourers. If a relatively high standard of living was often interrupted by a sharp decline, this severely affected the worker's household and created a great deal of insecurity. Worst off and most dependent on the vicissitudes of the grain market was the substantial group of people who did not have full employment or a plot of land large enough to sustain a family. It is difficult to measure the size of this group, but the figures on households exempted from paying taxes because they were considered too poor may be the best indicator. In the 15th-century Low Countries, these fiscal poor made up about a quarter of the total population.[199] There were many more of them in the countryside and smaller cities than in the big cities, and from the middle of the 15th century their numbers increased.

The position of the lower groups in society became much worse in the late 15th and 16th centuries, when a clear acceleration occurred in the processes of proletarianization, polarization, and fragmentation. In the late 14th and early 15th centuries those who were fully employed received fairly high real wages, but their position deteriorated later because of the population increase, which pushed food prices up and wages down. Thus, the unfavourable effects of social and demographic developments were combined, ending the golden age of the wage workers. Around 1550 the real wages of unskilled workers in Zutphen, for instance, were about 40 per cent lower than they had been in 1450.[200] An even sharper decline can be observed in the Flemish and Brabantine towns, where the purchasing power of a daily wage for a bricklayer's apprentice declined, in the period from 1500/1505 to 1540/1550, from 14 to 12 litres of wheat (in

---

[198] Kuppers and Van Schaïk, 'Levensstandaard en stedelijke economie', 15–16, and Sosson, 'Corporation et paupérisme'.

[199] Blockmans and Prevenier, 'Armoede in de Nederlanden', also for the measurement of poverty, below.

[200] Kuppers and Van Schaïk, 'Levensstandaard en stedelijke economie', and Blockmans, 'Armenzorg en levensstandaard', 155–157.

Antwerp), from 18 to 10 (in Bruges and Brussels), and from 16 to as low as 8 litres (in Ghent). This decline in real wages benefited large tenant farmers and entrepreneurs, but hurt wage labourers, thus contributing to further polarization. The gap between wealth and poverty was rapidly widening, and more and more people were afflicted by poverty. This can be measured, for instance, in the proportion of the household budget spent on bread, the staple food of ordinary people which provided the cheapest source of calories. If the threshold for poverty was 44 per cent of the budget spent on bread, a mason journeyman in the 16th century fell only occasionally below this threshold, but a mason labourer did so in 40 per cent of those years, and an unskilled labourer in as many as 75 per cent. This threshold is fairly low, since even 60 per cent of the budget spent on bread would leave the household with some funds for housing, heating, and additional required foodstuffs, but it is clear that even a fully employed labourer had difficulties in avoiding poverty in this period. This is confirmed by the registration of poor people on relief or having applied for relief in Louvain in 1546: as many as 60 per cent were craftsmen, mainly weavers and fullers, whereas only 5 per cent were day labourers, and most of the remainder were widows and the handicapped.[201]

The diet of ordinary households consisted of very basic foodstuffs, such as bread, peas, and beer, which took by far the largest share of the budget. Vicente Alvares, a Spanish visitor travelling through the Low Countries in the mid-16th century, noted that people's daily food was very scanty, consisting mainly of salted soup with cheese and black bread, and a stew, washed down with huge quantities of beer.[202] Bread and peas were indeed the cheapest source of calories, and beer, which adults consumed at a rate of over a litre a day, was the cheapest liquid source. Thus, for the majority of the population, there was not much scope for further cutting back, except for a shift from wheat bread—if any was eaten at all—to rye bread, from meat to cheese or peas, and from woollen clothes to linen.[203] If a long-term decline in real wages was accompanied by disastrous events, such as crop failures and resulting price rises, this led to severe crises. Around the middle of the 16th century, there were several years of crisis, which brought serious want, a decline in the standard of living, epidemics, and high mortality, as in 1556–7 and 1565–6, the so-called hunger year.[204] At price peaks, such as those around the middle of the 16th century, this caused severe problems for large sectors of the population, exacerbated by speculation and hoarding by the rich. It was especially the wage labourers who, having become dependent on the market, were hit most severely. It seems, however, that compared with earlier periods of crisis, such as the beginning of the 14th century, the peaks were

[201] Cuvelier, 'Documents', 48–55 and 101–115.
[202] Van der Wee, 'Nutrition and diet', and Van Uytven, 'Beer consumption'.
[203] Unger, 'Prices'.
[204] Kuttner, *Het hongerjaar 1566*, 193–210, and Van Zanden, 'Economic growth'.

mitigated somewhat by increasing market integration. Grain imported from the Baltic, for instance, reduced price fluctuations and made rye relatively cheaper, although risks from possible blockades of the Sound remained. Another positive influence was probably the more determined attempts by town governments to reduce price fluctuations in grain and bread by regulating or even freezing the price of bread, prohibiting speculation, buying and storing grain, and distributing it.[205] This grain policy was in place from the 13th century on, but became more stringent after the crisis of 1437–9, and very systematic and general around the mid-16th century.

In Holland, although there was massive population growth, and most people became poorer, standards of living did not decline as quickly as in other parts of Europe. To a lesser extent this applied also to the Low Countries as a whole.[206] In most other parts of Europe real wages were halved in the period 1500–1800, but the decline in the Low Countries, as well as in most parts of England, was slight. This resulted in a divergence of real wages between north-western Europe and other parts of Europe, especially in the years 1500–1650. Since the Low Countries in this period experienced rapid population growth, perhaps even greater than elsewhere in Europe, but this growth did not result in substantially declining real wages, it is possible to say that although the Malthusian trap may not have been fully sprung, at least it became less tight.[207] At the same time, particularly in those regions undergoing rapid economic development such as Holland, there were many losers. Economic growth was accompanied by growing social inequality. In regions such as peasant-dominated Drenthe or the Campine, polarization was less pronounced and more people could thus fall back on their own smallholdings for subsistence and avoid market dependence, thereby limiting insecurity and preventing part of the 16th-century decline. On the other hand, the process of fragmentation of holdings through population growth, and the more limited prospects of economic growth, caused widespread poverty, even if it may have been more evenly distributed there. Although the nature of the processes in the 16th century could differ, the results were often quite similar: increasing poverty, misery, and hunger for a substantial proportion of the population.

Poor Relief

These developments gradually strained existing forms of poor relief beyond their limits, and were further aggravated by the weakening of kin ties and the growing migration. In the high Middle Ages a very diverse patchwork of poor relief

---

[205] Van Schaïk, 'Prijs- en levensmiddelenpolitiek'.
[206] Noordegraaf, *Hollands welvaren?*, 145–166, Scholliers, 'Le pouvoir d'achat', esp. 305–306, Van Zanden, 'Wages', and Allen, 'The great divergence'.
[207] Allen, 'The great divergence', 413 and 428–435. For the strong population growth there, see section VI.2, pp. 279–280.

had emerged. Probably the most important relief was help provided by kin and neighbours, which formed the main security nets of the period. Institutional poor relief was principally provided by religious and semi-religious institutions, with distributions by monasteries, foundations, and parish funds. In the high Middle Ages, in the general wave of horizontal association and the formation of communities, new charitable organizations emerged, mostly managed by laymen. In the villages and parishes of the countryside, people founded and organized poor boxes, and the formalization of commons and other organizations of communal agriculture often offered the poorest some access to land, either to the common land or the stubble after harvest for pasturing a cow.

In the emerging cities, too, new forms of poor relief developed together with the associations of people in urban communities. Formal organizations for poor relief were developed as a vital element of community building, and were needed even more in the urban context than in the countryside because of the larger proportion of migrants, greater mobility, and higher rates of mortality. The late 12th century in the south-western areas, and the 13th century in the other parts of the Low Countries, were key periods in the emergence of new forms of institutional poor relief in the cities.[208] Together with northern Italy, the Low Countries saw the greatest development of poor tables, also called tables of the Holy Spirit, aimed at distributing aid to the poor. The first mention of a poor table is in Tournai (1167), and in the following decades they multiplied, not only in the towns, but also in the countryside. The tables were organized by parish, but increasingly supervised by laymen. Funding, sometimes amounting to large properties in land and mainly in rents, was assembled by merchants and better-off craftsmen, but many smaller donations came from the middle strata of society. Another new charitable institution which emerged in the same period was the hospital, where the needy could find shelter and food for several nights. Again, the south-west led the way, and hospitals were founded in Tournai (1112), Arras (1179), Ypres (1186), and Bruges (1188). In the north, hospitals did not start to emerge until the second half of the 13th century. It was mainly the patricians or urban magistrates who took the initiative in founding such institutions. The fact that the authorities and laypeople played a large role in these developments is sometimes interpreted as a struggle by laymen and the state for secularization, against the Church, but this seems to be incorrect.[209] There were conflicts of interest and juridical procedures, but on the whole cooperation was more the rule, and laymen and urban communities played an important role from the beginning.

Except for the leper houses, the hospitals were not at first specialized, but cared for all the needy. In the 14th and 15th centuries, however, some began to

---

[208] Marechal, 'Armen- en ziekenzorg', and Tits-Dieuaide, 'Les tables des pauvres'. On poor relief as part of urban community building: Lynch, *Individuals, families*, 5–18 and 103–110.
[209] Bonenfant, 'Hôpitaux et bienfaisance', and Maréchal, *Sociale en politieke gebondenheid*, 55–75.

concentrate on giving shelter to needy travellers or pilgrims, others on looking after the ill, lunatics, the elderly, sufferers from skin diseases, orphans, or the homeless.[210] The hospitals specializing in the care of the ill focused on nursing body and soul, but real medical treatment was limited or non-existent. The staff consisted mostly of lay brothers and sisters, some servants, a manager, and sometimes a few clerics. It was only from the 14th century that the largest hospitals started to hire a permanent surgeon, a practice which spread in the 15th century, although in Liège, for instance, this was still exceptional. Town governments also began to hire surgeons: the city of Utrecht employed four surgeons, and they were expected to treat the wealthy burghers at a fair fee and the poor free of charge, and in the first half of the 16th century the medium-sized Flemish town of Oudenaarde had no fewer than 17 doctors and surgeons, and an equal number of assistants and apprentices.[211] Incidentally, a qualified doctor, who had studied medicine at a university, was also hired by the city. Beginning in the 15th century, cities demanded that practitioners of medicine provide proof of their ability, however basic it might be. In Utrecht and Leiden such tests were introduced around the middle of the 15th century for doctors and surgeons, and later also for barbers and tooth-drawers. From the late 13th century on, professional pharmacists also appeared in the cities, at first in the largest ones, such as Ghent, Ypres, Bruges, and Liège. These apothecaries practised a profession which developed from the less specialized group of grocers, and their prescription books show that their main function was to prepare medicines to treat gastric and intestinal complaints.

In the 15th and 16th centuries, an ever-increasing number of professionals operated in the medical field, but it is not clear what effect this had on the health, labour productivity, and life expectancy of the population. Leprosy was successfully combated, but mainly by isolating lepers and those suspected of having the disease. As a result of strict measures, the number of lepers in Lille and Douai was reduced by two-thirds in the 14th century.[212] Many leper hospitals stood empty and after the 15th century this disease had virtually disappeared from the Low Countries. On the other hand, physicians were powerless against epidemics such as the plague or cholera. In general, data on life expectancy do not show a fundamental rise in this period, so either the increasing number of medical professionals had no effect, or their effect did no more than balance other negative factors.

The later Middle Ages thus saw increased specialization in charitable work and in its organizational structure. In addition to the aid offered by all these organizations, guild members could also count on assistance from the guild, particularly if they were struck by the death of the breadwinner or another family

---

[210] De Spiegeleer, *Les hôpitaux*, 155–168 and 207–208, and Kossmann-Putto, 'Armen- en ziekenzorg'.
[211] Stabel, *Dwarfs among giants*, 180–181. For the pharmacists: De Backer, *Farmacie te Gent*, 18–23.
[212] Clauzel, 'Les maladies', 213–217.

member, or illness or disability. Sometimes the guild members made regular contributions to a common chest to meet such expenses, as a form of mutual insurance. But such support was available only to members of the guild and their families, not to the lowest strata in society. The poor depended on the other forms of relief and on smaller distributions by all kinds of foundations established through wills or by alms given directly. All in all, there was much fragmentation of poor relief, which increased with the rise of new organizations, since the older forms of relief remained. The motivations for providing relief were diverse, and varied with the organization; Christian inspiration and charity played a large part, but so did more mundane aims, including offering mutual aid and insurance, maintaining a labour reserve, and even repression, with poor relief used to stifle potential revolts.[213] These aims, however, were not exclusive and often overlapped.

The fragmentation of charitable institutions offered the poor a variety of recourse, but this does not mean that the total volume of relief was sufficient. Calculations are scarce and often available only for individual institutions.[214] The parish fund of 's-Hertogenbosch, a city that had some 20,000 inhabitants in 1526, distributed 186 kg of bread per head annually to 550 people. In Mechelen, a Brabantine city of comparable size, four parish funds distributed to some 400 people an average of 100 kg of rye bread annually, providing about a quarter of the calorific needs of one adult. Additionally, they distributed some 5 kg of pork meat annually per person and smaller amounts of money, shoes, eggs, and peat. Taking into account its many forms, the total relief could be substantial, but it varied with the town and often was not sufficient, particularly in times of declining real wages and job opportunities, as in the 16th century. The poorer strata of society had to use these forms of poor relief within a more comprehensive survival strategy, which included occasional wage labour, use of some land, cottage industry, family help, and begging, to keep their heads above water. Still, in some years of dearth, this was not sufficient. Even in 's-Hertogenbosch, famous for its generous distributions, the years 1425–6 and 1436 saw people dying of hunger—but this was exceptional. There was no mass starvation in the Low Countries, and the organization of relief apparently worked fairly well.

Around 1500, however, systems of poor relief came under pressure. One reason was the rise of the institution of provisioners; they were often from the middle or higher strata of society and paid a substantial entry fee to the hospital to be lodged there. Their numbers rose from the 14th century onwards, particularly in the north-east, and they took up much of the space available in hospitals,

---

[213] Maréchal, *De sociale en politieke gebondenheid*, 296–297. See also sections V.3, p. 210, and VI.1, p. 276.

[214] Blockmans and Prevenier, 'Armoede in de Nederlanden', esp. 519–527. There is a more comprehensive analysis for Mechelen in Blockmans, 'Armenzorg en levensstandaard te Mechelen'.

which often changed their function to providing a home for the elderly or a boarding house. More significant in the pressure on poor relief, however, were the general changes in economy and society in various parts of the Low Countries that accelerated in the early 16th century. These included social polarization, increased mobility and migration, growth of cities, proletarianization and the rise of wage labour, and the decline of family networks. At first these developments, the growth of poverty, and the dissolution of medieval networks were balanced by the rise and extension of existing institutions for charity, mainly in the cities, but increasingly this system came under stress, particularly where the changes were most pronounced, as in coastal Frisia, the Guelders river area, and later in Holland. The rise in food prices and decline in real wages from the mid-15th century on made the situation even more difficult.

As a consequence of these elements, the earlier, more positive medieval view of poverty and the poor was replaced by a negative one, in a process that had begun in the 13th century, but had now become dominant. Poor people and beggars were increasingly blamed for their own situation, and the poor came to be viewed as a nuisance and a threat to social stability, a view forcefully expressed by Erasmus in 1524.[215] Also, non-resident poor were increasingly excluded. A second, more constructive response, was the growing call for reform of poor relief at the beginning of the 16th century.[216] The plans for reform were most clearly expressed and theoretically underpinned by some humanist writers, most notably Juan Luis Vives. In his book *De subventione pauperum* (1526), dedicated to the magistracy of Bruges, he no longer focused on giving alms and charity, as in the medieval tradition, but proposed effective solutions to poverty and its negative consequences, albeit with no thought of reform of social structure or property redistribution, let alone social revolution. Protestant ideas played no role in his work or in effecting the reforms proposed. At most, the threat of radical Anabaptism around 1525 stimulated reform, but many steps had already been taken before the real penetration of Protestant ideas in the Low Countries. In the second quarter of the 16th century many of the reform ideas were realized, the Low Countries being the part of Europe where poor relief was first and most thoroughly reorganized. To some extent, the reform measures taken can be seen as reorganization and rationalization, with the merger of smaller funds and the introduction of better control and administration, but there were also changes in the aims of poor relief, including clearer exclusion of the non-deserving poor, enforced by strict regulation. Poor relief should prevent people from dying of hunger and offer a safety net, but it was now increasingly used as an instrument to prevent voluntary unemployment and begging, forcing all able-bodied people to work and thus creating a large reservoir of cheap wage labourers.[217] Now a

---

[215] Lis and Soly, *Poverty and capitalism*, 82–87.
[216] Parker, *The reformation of community*, 65–66 and 86–90, and Van der Heijden, 'Vives'.
[217] See also section V.3, p. 210.

clear, direct link was forged between poor relief and the preservation of order, in a coherent system, buttressed by social regulation. At the same time, it became more anonymous, with less direct personal contact between giver and receiver of charity; the religious element became less prominent, and the role of public authorities became larger.

The first attempts to reorganize poor relief along these lines were made by local authorities in the towns of Ypres, Mons, and Leeuwarden in 1525, and then by regional and national ones. The climax of this process was the edict promulgated by Emperor Charles V in 1531, which was directed against vagrants and ordered a full, systematic reform of poor relief. Although legislation was enacted at the national level, there were still large regional differences in implementation. The measures and reorganization of poor relief were first carried out in the coastal areas, including Friesland. The reforms started in the first half of the 16th century, and were more generally and radically implemented in the second half.[218] From the geographical location of the reforms it is clear that urbanization was not the main factor: Friesland, for instance, was not highly urbanized. Instead, they were stimulated by the transition in economy and society. In the Frisian case, this transition related mainly to the rural economy, with the rise of wage labour and sharp social polarization resulting from the emergence of large tenant farms in the coastal areas. Another factor was the comparative lack of influence in Friesland and Holland of the nobility and the church, both often opposed to reforming poor relief.[219] The nobles felt that anonymous charity robbed them of the chance of enhancing their family's prestige, creating bonds of patronage, or practising nepotism. The clergy objected to the prohibition of begging, especially for decent poor and mendicant monks, the loss of ecclesiastical influence in the administration of charity, and the undermining of individual acts of charity, which seemed to weaken the Catholic notion of salvation through works of mercy. The fact that nobles and ecclesiastics had little influence in the northern coastal parts of the Low Countries made it much easier to carry out the reforms there.

The reorganization of poor relief also had another aspect, even more clearly connected to the increased importance of wage labour and the high degree of proletarianization in these regions: namely the harsh measures taken by authorities to increase the supply of labour in the market, prohibiting begging and vagrancy, and discouraging voluntary unemployment. It was in regions where the transition in economy and society was most pronounced that harsh political action first took place.[220] Such measures built on a long tradition, as reflected in the bylaws regulating and restricting begging in Leiden and Utrecht, which had been issued as early as the 14th century, and the practice of banishing beggars

---

[218] Spaans, *Armenzorg in Friesland*, 43–68.
[219] Decavele, *Dageraad van de Reformatie*, 117–136 and 139–151.
[220] See Lis and Soly, *Poverty and capitalism*, 90–96.

from the town. In the 16th century, however, this regulation was made more severe by completely prohibiting begging and appointing officials specifically to apprehend beggars, as happened in Haarlem. The sweep of the measures there, promulgated by a magistracy dominated by the urban elite of wealthy merchants and entrepreneurs, was probably at least partly linked to the early importance of wage labour and the demand for cheap, proletarianized labour.

Beggars were increasingly seen as profiteers. Only disabled people who did not beg but stayed at home were seen as deserving of poor relief. Those able to work should work. Again, this idea was not new, but had appeared in the legislation enacted for Brabant by Philip the Good in 1459 prohibiting vagrancy and ordering that people wandering around without a job—except for the elderly and disabled—should be arrested, put in gaol for two months, and afterwards sent to the galleys as oarsmen.[221] Such forced labour became systematized and was given a theoretical foundation by the Holland writer and humanist Dirk Coornhert, who in 1567 suggested that the idle poor should be educated through forced labour to become useful members of society. These ideas were put into practice by the Amsterdam magistrates, who built a house of correction for men in 1589, soon followed by dozens of workhouses in other towns in the Dutch Republic.[222] This was in accord with a general movement, which began in the 15th century, to incarcerate undesirables such as juvenile delinquents, lunatics, and vagrants. A clear concentration of prison workhouses soon developed in the coastal parts of the north. The idealistic goal of educating the inmates was soon put aside, as reducing the cost of incarcerating criminals and making profitable use of cheap forced labour became paramount. The final result of the 16th-century changes was a combination of harsh repression and well-developed relief. Nevertheless, in this respect the 16th century should not be viewed as a complete break with past practices, but rather as an acceleration, completion, and systematic implementation of developments which had begun much earlier, particularly in the 12th and 13th centuries. This applied to the centralization and rationalization of charity and the role of laymen and state influence, as well as to the measures against the undeserving poor. These developments resulted in a system of poor relief which was able to endure far into the 19th century.[223]

Education and Literacy

The geographical patterns in the rise of formal education are similar to those observed for that of charity. In the early Middle Ages the few centres of formal education and learning were found in the abbeys and cathedrals. Among them

---

[221] Van den Eerenbeemt, 'Bestrijding der bedelarij', esp. 159–161.
[222] Lis and Soly, *Poverty and capitalism*, 118–119, and Spierenburg, 'The sociogenesis', esp. 10–22.
[223] Heerma van Voss, 'The embarrassment of poverty'.

were Echternach, Saint-Hubert, Stavelot, Malmedy, and the espiscopal cities of Liège and Utrecht.[224] They were mainly located in regions identified as early medieval centres of economic development, the Meuse valley in particular. In the 10th and 11th centuries, a few abbeys in southern Flanders and Artois also emerged as intellectual centres, such as St Vaast, St Bertin, and St Amand, again coinciding with the economic rise of these regions. In the high Middle Ages education became increasingly concentrated in the cities, with the chapters in episcopal cities playing an important role. Liège even received the honorary title of 'the Athens of the north', thanks to the flourishing of knowledge and literature, especially under Bishop Notger, around 1000. In the 11th to 13th centuries education, literacy, and the use of written instruments in the Low Countries took a major step forward; this period was critical in laying the foundations of the modern educational system. Increasing demand for education for laymen led to the rise of urban schools, where the curriculum was aimed at practical competence in reading, writing, arithmetic, and basic Latin. Ghent in 1179 was the first city in the Low Countries, and indeed north of the Alps, where burghers could enjoy an institutionalized non-religious education.[225] In other parts of north-western Europe this only occurred in the 13th century at the earliest. In the same century Latin schools at the parish level are mentioned, as in Flemish villages such as Dikkebus (coastal Flanders) mentioned in 1102, and in Roulers (1152).[226] In this period the educational and intellectual centre of the Low Countries shifted to Flanders.

The production of written texts, which had until then been minimal, increased significantly from the 12th century on. Many of them were drawn up in the princely chanceries and administrations, but even more were produced by towns and villages in the form of charters, bylaws, and urban accounts. Bylaws had probably been drafted from the late 11th century in towns in southern Flanders, but in the 12th century written bylaws multiplied, in Saint-Omer (1127, 1128), Arras (1163), and other Flemish and Artois towns, and later in the century they were also drawn up in towns and villages in Zeeland, as in Domburg and Westkapelle.[227] Sometimes bylaws were ratified by the territorial lord, but often they were written down by the urban or village community, or were based on an earlier draft made by the community. Towns also made registers of important documents, as mentioned for Valenciennes in 1114, and registers of new burghers, as in the Flemish suburb Pamele in 1166. Annual urban accounts were kept from the first half of the 13th century, as in Arras in 1241, and later in Mons (1279), Bruges (1280), Ghent (1280), and Dordrecht (1283). Writing and administrative services there did not remain a clerical monopoly. In the late

---

[224] Riché, *Les écoles*, 63, 106–108, 140, and 164–167.
[225] Pirenne, 'L'instruction des marchands'.   [226] Riché, *Les écoles*.
[227] Burgers, 'Vlaamse stadskeuren'. For the urban accounts see section III.3, pp. 118–119, and V.2, p. 186.

12th century laymen started to supplement and even replace the clerics, as in the comital administration in Flanders, where in 1187 eight laymen were employed alongside fifteen clerics, and laymen predominated a few decades later.[228] Most did not specialize in writing, a task entrusted to the *scriptores*, and had only basic schooling: they learned by doing. But by the 13th century, increasing numbers of men employed in administration by towns and by territorial lords had received training in academic law schools in Bologna, Orléans, and Paris.

Growing numbers of written documents were also produced by notaries, who appeared in the Low Countries in the late 13th century and combined the art of writing with some knowledge of law. Here generally they did not hold positions comparable to those in southern Europe, because they had to compete with reliable systems of producing written instruments that were already well established, most notably the aldermen's courts.[229] Civil jurisdiction in these public courts had emerged in the 12th century, and such courts made it possible to obtain simple, clear instruments inexpensively, written by professional scribes. Such courts were used for all kinds of legal matters, inheritances, and transactions, and produced huge quantities of written documents. Some 35,000 charters issued by the Douai aldermen from 1224 onwards have been preserved, and the aldermen of Ypres issued about 7,000 charters in the period 1249–91 alone. The rise of long-distance trade and the increasing number of impersonal transactions in the market also pushed up demand for written texts and commercial administration. The public courts, notaries, and professional scribes hired by the parties themselves met this demand. In the late 13th century, for instance, the brothers Duking, two wealthy wine merchants in Dordrecht, employed their own clerks, but merchants probably also kept written records themselves.[230] To a large extent the penetration of writing in the Low Countries was a process from below, and not imposed from above.

Probably associated with this, from the late 11th century, and certainly by the 12th, writers switched from Latin to the vernacular. This happened first in Artois and southern Flanders, where French was used in some private charters and the administration of the Abbey of St Vaast, as well as in documents in the village of Chièvres in Hainaut (1194) and in the towns of Douai, Cambrai, and Arras. Somewhat later, in the more northern parts, Dutch was introduced, at the beginning of the 13th century in Flanders, and half a century later in Zeeland and later in Holland.[231] Again this trend was driven from below. In Zeeland local bylaws were probably written in Dutch from the late 12th century, but the chancery of the court of Holland and Zeeland only changed to the vernacular from about 1285. It was not necessarily in the larger cities that the vernacular was

---

[228] Prevenier, 'Officials in town', and De Hemptinne and Vandermaesen, 'De ambtenaren'.
[229] Murray, *Notarial instruments*, 20–23.
[230] Dijkhof, 'Goatskin and growing literacy'.
[231] Kadens, 'De invoering van de volkstaal', and Burgers, 'De invoering van het Nederlands'.

first introduced in written texts: it is probably not a coincidence that the oldest preserved charter in Dutch is one issued by the aldermen of the small Flemish village of Bochoute in 1249.

The social and economic consequences of this shift must have been far-reaching. Reading and writing came within reach, and written texts became accessible to a much larger group of people than before, when they had been reserved for a small, mainly clerical elite. This also fitted in with the growing demand of the population in towns to have a firmer grip on the administration of the urban finances by the patriciate, particularly in the late 13th century. Sometimes they even explicitly demanded a change to the vernacular to allow for more control, a practice which had perhaps already existed in the countryside following the rise of the village communities. Moreover, the rise of horizontal associations such as guilds and hospital fraternities probably stimulated the spread of writing, and especially writing in the vernacular to ensure regulation and accountability.[232] Because of this shift, and the increasing use of paper in place of parchment from the late 13th century, the cost of drafting a written document was much lower, and more people (including merchants) were able to write such documents themselves. The increased use of documents offered more security, which was appropriate for a society and economy where impersonal transactions became more important, and where reputation and word of honour were no longer sufficient. These elements also explain why this trend started in the south-west and spread to the north. This was not only in line with the pace of economic development and the rise of market exchange, but was also linked to the emergence of urban and rural communities and horizontal associations, which had occurred early in the south-west.

These changes were also reflected in the development of an education system. In the later Middle Ages education became increasingly diverse. On-the-job training was offered in the guild system, as part of a complex relationship between master and apprentice. There are clear advantages to this system. Guilds offered a system of training and education, often long and fairly thorough, and the system also placed a premium on knowledge and technical skills through its organization and place in society.[233] On the other hand, the guilds jealously guarded knowledge and sometimes monopolized skills, and also allowed master craftsmen to exploit the system of apprenticeship to acquire cheap labour and keep apprentices much longer than needed for training. It is not easy to assess whether the positive economic effects of guild organization outweighed the negative ones. The patterns of regional economic development suggest that in the circumstances of the 13th and 14th centuries it was an efficient organization for vocational training, as evidenced by the growth of industries in the Flemish

---

[232] De Hemptinne, 'De doorbraak van de volkstaal'. For the communities and associations, see section III.3, pp. 120–121.
[233] Van Zanden, 'Common workmen', and Epstein, 'Craft guilds'.

cities where guilds were powerful. In the 15th and 16th centuries, on the other hand, more efficient options had become available, as indicated by the rise of urban industries in Holland, where guilds were weak, and by the relatively low skill premium there.

Probably a more efficient option was formal education, which was more universal and diverse than in other parts of Europe. The basis of the educational hierarchy in the Low Countries was particularly impressive.[234] Towns in the later Middle Ages often had many schools offering basic education, and the larger cities had dozens, where children of 6–8 years old learned to read and write in the vernacular and were taught some mathematics. There were differences between boys and girls and between rich and poor in the attendance at primary schools, but they were not absolute. Girls also had the opportunity to go to a primary school, often taught by a woman. Education for children from poorer families was facilitated by town governments, either by paying the school fees or subsidizing them for private schools, or by appointing a schoolmaster for the poor, as happened in Dordrecht in 1283.

After having acquired basic skills at the primary level, many boys went to a secondary school, where they often stayed about five years, and where Latin had a prominent position in the curriculum. These Latin schools, mainly found in the larger cities, generally had several hundred pupils, from 300 in Gouda and 600 in Alkmaar to 1,000 in Nijmegen and 's-Hertogenbosch in the mid-16th century.[235] Perhaps as many as a quarter of boys in the cities attended these schools. In the countryside, too, a fairly dense network of primary schools existed. It is not clear just when the school system developed in the Low Countries, but in the 13th and 14th centuries numerous schools are mentioned in the sources. Probably there is again a link with the process of association and the formation of village and town communities in the 11th and 12th centuries, as well as with the formation of parishes and charitable organizations, all of which fostered the production and use of written texts. Education and the organization of schools were not the exclusive domain of the church: in the Holland towns in the 14th century half the schoolmasters were laymen, and in the late 15th century the proportion had risen to four-fifths. In the same period, territorial lords and especially town magistrates increasingly extended their control over schoolmasters, their appointment, the school buildings, and the school regluations.[236]

By the late Middle Ages, a great deal of energy was devoted to offering primary education to broad groups of society, with a dense network of all types of schools. In the late 15th and early 16th centuries ideas on education were further developed, buttressed by the Devotio Moderna and humanist writers such as Vives, and a complete system of schools was developed, but these developments

---

[234] De Ridder-Symoens, 'Stad en kennis', esp. 133–134.
[235] Post, *Scholen en onderwijs*, 131–135.
[236] De Ridder-Symoens, 'La secularisation', esp. 722–727.

were built on a century-long tradition in the Low Countries. Besides the Latin schools, various others offered vocational instruction and practical skills. In several towns from the late 15th century, commercial schools emerged (also called French schools), where foreign languages, bookkeeping, and arithmetic were taught, as well as other knowledge useful to a merchant, such as measures and coinage. A system of public schools for poor children was established in the early decades of the century.[237] In Walloon Flanders and Artois, around Lille and Aire, in 1569, 83 out of 91 parishes had a school and the larger villages had more than one.[238] The same was true of Holland, Groningen, and Friesland, and the Frisian provincial court boasted in 1554 that almost all villages had a school with a schoolmaster, and that Friesland had more schoolchildren than any other province. In these regions the ideal of universal education for all—at least for boys—was almost attained, often guaranteed by the local government. In contrast, in Gelderland, parts of Brabant, and strikingly in inland Flanders (which had the edge in education in the 12th and 13th centuries), there were hardly any schools in the countryside. In one part of inland Flanders, around Ninove, in the late 16th century only 3 of 40 rural parishes had a school.[239]

As a result of the dense network of schools, literacy in both town and countryside in the 14th to 16th centuries was widespread.[240] The town of Valenciennes in Hainaut, with 10,000 to 15,000 inhabitants, had some 25 schools, with a total of 145 girls and 371 boys in 1386, and 161 girls and 630 boys in 1497. Assuming that the schooling lasted for three years, from about 7 to 10 years of age, it means that just about all boys went to school, including sons of labourers, and about a quarter of all girls. In Holland, literacy was also high. In 1585, as many as 55 per cent of all bridegrooms in Amsterdam and 32 per cent of all brides were literate, higher than in any other part of western Europe, including England, where about 15 per cent of the population were literate.[241] There were no differences in literacy among men born in Amsterdam, in smaller cities, and in the countryside, which points to the fact that literacy was not solely an urban phenomenon. This is confirmed in Guicciardini's observations in the 1560s: he was surprised that almost everyone in the Low Countries could read and write, including the country dwellers, and that the majority knew formal grammar and many were able to speak French or another foreign language.[242] There is probably gross exaggeration in the claim by the conrector (assistant head) of the local grammar school in 1555 that in the city

---

[237] Decavele, *Dageraad*, 137–139, and for commercial schools, Davids, 'The bookkeeper's tale'.
[238] Derville, 'L'alphabétisation', esp. 763–764; and for Frisia, see Post, *Scholen en onderwijs*, 17–20 and 82–88.
[239] Toussaert, *Le sentiment religieux*, 60–66.
[240] Derville, 'L'alphabétisation', 765–766, and Van Zanden, 'Common workmen'.
[241] Kuijpers, 'Lezen en schrijven', esp. 506–511, and Van Zanden, 'Common workmen', 17–19.
[242] Ciselet and Delcourt, *Belgique 1567*, 29–30, and Van Zanden, 'Common workmen', 10–13.

of Amersfoort ordinary burghers spoke Latin in a manner that could not be corrected by Cicero, and maidservants sang songs in Latin when working,[243] but education at a basic level, or above it, must have been widespread in the Low Countries.

Distances to a university became shorter in 1388, when one was founded in Cologne. In the 15th century more than 40 per cent of the Cologne students were from the Low Countries.[244] Acquiring academic education became even easier when a university was founded in the Brabantine city of Louvain in 1425, and one in Douai in 1559. Access to academic education was helped by the dense network of primary schooling in the Low Countries, and it was affordable even for middling groups in society. Poor students could apply for subsidies from their town, as happened in Ghent, Bruges, and Ypres in the 14th century, and later also in smaller towns. Investing in academic education often paid off, since there was ample employment for graduates, as priests, canons, schoolmasters, clerks, doctors, town officials, and state bureaucrats, and it formed the key to success in acquiring public office.

In the 14th to 16th centuries Holland used its human potential (including women and those living in rural areas) even more than other regions in the Low Countries, as shown by the high level of literacy and the low skill premium there, which was the lowest in western Europe.[245] The reason for this can probably not be found in the high level of urbanization, since all indicators suggest that literacy in the countryside was as high as in the towns. Perhaps religious movements played a role, for the leaders of the Devotio Moderna and intellectuals such as Erasmus—in contrast to Italian humanists—energetically promoted education and reading.[246] But social structure may have been more important, because there was a fairly equal distribution of social and economic resources and power in medieval Holland, and the middle groups played an important role in society. Also, in Holland and in several other parts of the Low Countries, there was a lively tradition of association from the 11th century on, with a large proportion of the population taking responsibility for the administration of semi-public or public organizations, such as poor chests, village communities, and water management boards. The high level of literacy in its turn had several social and economic effects. A fairly broad segment of the population was able to participate in social, cultural, and political life. Also, it made available a broad reservoir of skilled people, especially vital to the rise of a services sector. The widespread use of writing also opened further possibilities for impersonal transactions and long-lasting obligations, stimulating the growth of market exchange, particularly in land, lease, and capital markets.

---

[243] Cited in Bot, *Humanisme en onderwijs*, 43.
[244] De Ridder-Symoens: 'Stad en kennis', and 'Rich and poor men'.
[245] See also section V.3, pp. 212–213, and Van Zanden, 'The skill premium'.
[246] Bot, *Humanisme en onderwijs*, 17–28.

Living Conditions

Just as in poor relief and education, public authorities played a growing role in the later Middle Ages in improving living conditions. This was especially true in cities, where living conditions had become precarious, but at the same time most progress was made by regulation and developing public provision. Many of the problems in the late medieval cities were caused by the fact that space was scarce within the walls, and people were packed together. Smaller cities did not occupy more than about 20 hectares, and the medium-sized cities were about 20 to 40 hectares, meaning that 100–200 people were squeezed into each urban hectare. The biggest city in the Low Countries, Ghent, occupied 644 hectares, which on average housed some 100 people per hectare.[247] Moreover, substantial parts of the space within the walls were taken up by monasteries and by the gardens and orchards of patrician houses, leaving less space for the rest of the population. As a consequence, late medieval cities were often more densely populated than modern cities are. This situation led to pollution by excrement and other waste, and resulted in epidemics, a risk increased by poor sanitation. The industries, including the highly polluting processes of fulling and tanning, made matters worse. Living conditions in the cities must have been appalling, as the high urban mortality rates indicate.

The concentration of wooden thatched houses, combined with heating, cooking, and brewing, often without a proper chimney, produced many fires. Every city in Hainaut in the 14th and 15th centuries experienced a major fire every five years, often destroying hundreds of houses.[248] One of the towns in the Low Countries most severely hit by fire was Breda in Brabant in 1490 and again in 1534, when about 1,000 houses burnt down and the remains of the town were covered with ash and grit for almost a year. Fixed capital, in the form of buildings, workshops, and tools, was hit particularly hard by the fires, a risk which probably reduced investments. In the late Middle Ages the authorities increasingly started to regulate developments in this area. They required all households to have a ladder, bucket, and water,[249] and the inspection of chimneys was organized: in Mons in 1413 night watches were appointed, and holes were made in the ice during frost in order to have access to open water.

Urban authorities also encouraged and later enforced the building of houses in brick or stone, which reduced the risk of fire. In the 13th century almost all houses were still made of wood or thatched walls, with thatched roofs, or finished with wooden planks, but these were increasingly replaced by brick houses with tiles. This process accelerated in the 14th century, when municipal governments started to subsidize, and later enforce, the use of tiles for roofing.[250]

---

[247] Van Uytven, 'Stadsgeschiedenis', 199.
[248] Ryckaert, 'Brandbestrijding', 248.   [249] Ibid.
[250] De Meyer and Van den Elzen, *De verstening van Deventer*, 9–23, and Kolman, 'Verstening van woonhuizen'. See also section VII.2, p. 350.

The use of brick for walls was made compulsory shortly thereafter. The Hansa towns in the north-east, such as Kampen and Deventer, were the first to do this; there, by 1425, all houses were made of brick or stone. In the Holland towns, at this time, such regulations either applied only to the main street, or were applied less strictly elsewhere, and a thatched roof was allowed if it was plastered with loam. A century later, however, the switch to brick or stone was completed there too. In Flanders, Brabant, and Hainaut, despite early legislation on this matter, it was only in the 16th century that real progress was made, and in Maastricht only in the late 17th century. These regional differences were probably related to the availability of cheap bricks, but also to standards of living, the availability of capital, and perhaps the determination of public authorities to combat fires. The measures in their turn must have had positive effects on the economy: by stimulating demand for bricks and other products, thus contributing to industrial development, as well as reducing the risk of fire and thus preventing loss of goods, thereby further stimulating investment in fixed capital goods.

The authorities also provided collective goods by constructing and maintaining public buildings, often taking over this role from the manorial or banal lord in the 12th and 13th centuries, as urban communities grew in strength and independence. In Louvain, for instance, the town acquired control over the town hall, the bread hall, the cloth hall, and the weighing house, and only the corn hall remained in the hands of the lord.[251] The towns invested heavily in these buildings for reasons of prestige, but also to accommodate trade: the impressive 130-metre-wide cloth hall in Ypres, built in the 13th century and offering a sales area of some 2,500 m^2, was the main example. By way of stricter regulation, particularly from the 13th century on, the authorities also combated industrial pollution. Polluting industries such as fulling, for instance, were concentrated downstream, and industries causing smoke and risk of fire, such as chalk ovens, were banned to the countryside. Town governments also enacted restrictions on or even prohibitions against keeping cattle within the city walls, as in Louvain in 1568, and started to organize refuse collection and to dig cesspits. In many cities wells were dug, constructed, and maintained by the town government.[252] In the 14th century, Mons, the capital of Hainaut, built several of these wells, and a fountain, in the marketplace.

The authorities also played a role in urban planning and development, just as they had done in the 11th and 12th centuries in the planning and regular parcelling of reclaimed land in the countryside, most prominently in the Holland peat areas. In the cities similar forms of regular outlays can be found, most clearly in the towns newly founded by territorial lords, such as Nieuwpoort in Flanders (second half of the 12th century) or Elburg in Guelders (14th

---

[251] Van Uytven, 'Stedelijke openbare diensten'.
[252] Piérard, 'Mons', and Van Uytven, 'Stedelijke openbare diensten'.

century), both characterized by a rectangular street pattern.[253] In existing towns local authorities took responsibility for planning and constructing new roads and marketplaces, often paving the main ones. In Mons this was carried out on a fairly large scale in the second half of the 14th century, and the town government compensated the owners of houses demolished to make way for the newly planned streets.[254] Nevertheless, it can also be seen how certain aspects of urban development were left to the market, particularly as capitalist entrepreneurs became more powerful in the 16th century.[255] A clear example was mid-16th-century Antwerp, where private initiatives were dominant, with the big entrepreneur Gilbert van Schoonbeke playing a particularly large role. In the years 1542–53 he built more than 20 streets, buying open land within the city walls, dividing the land into lots, building new houses on them, and selling them to real estate traders. In the years 1547–9 he developed a new weighing house and the surrounding streets, selling the development in lots for 63,000 guilders, making a profit of 73 per cent on his initial investment. This excessive profit was only possible because of his political influence and the bribes he paid to members of the city government. His biggest project was the development of the Antwerp Nieuwstad, the New Town, covering 24 hectares. There and elsewhere he adopted a regular pattern of spacious rectangular squares, often with a central public building, and four wide, straight streets leading to the square, with the land alongside divided into regular plots, built with uniform, functional houses.

Housing construction underwent significant development in the later Middle Ages. In the 14th to 16th centuries, houses acquired many of the features found in modern houses: walls of brick or stone and glass windows were introduced, as were a chimney, gutters, separate kitchens, and cesspits.[256] These novelties were increasingly incorporated in the houses of middle-class burghers, making them similar to the mansions of the elite. At the same time, the social polarization of the period was also expressed in housing. Poor people and polluting industries were found mainly in the suburbs, whereas the wealthier people were concentrated in the town centres, where ceremonies and public life were found. By contrast, the workers in the industrial centre of Hondschoote lived in miserable conditions, often with ten or more people squeezed into scanty back premises or clay huts. Dwellings in the workers' quarters of 16th-century Leiden were very small and generally consisted of only one or two rooms.

In the countryside a similar polarization of living conditions can be observed. On the one hand, a multitude of large and fairly luxurious farmhouses were built of brick or stone, surrounded by outbuildings, stables, and barns. This was most

---

[253] Rutte, *Stedenpolitiek en stadsplanning*, 59–64.   [254] Piérard, 'Mons'.
[255] Soly, *Urbanisme en kapitalisme*, 149–176 and 371–382. For Liège: Hélin, *Le paysage de Liège*. See also section VI.1, pp. 256–260.
[256] Meischke, *Het Nederlandse woonhuis*, 95–100 and 109–123.

visible in the regions where large tenant farmers emerged. In coastal Friesland, the large one-room spaces for household use and livestock gave way in the course of the 15th and 16th centuries to separate living quarters and stalls, often with a separate dairy room and a spacious barn. On the other hand, in the same regions increasing numbers of cottages and huts were found, built by the growing host of day labourers and paupers. In general, however, there was a great deal of progress in rural building, especially in Holland. At the beginning of the 16th century, only a few buildings in the countryside were brick, but by the middle of the century almost all farms were brick, and around 1600 even labourers' dwellings were.[257] In the Campine and in Twente, on the other hand, timber framing with wattle and daub remained dominant up to the 17th century, and was still used occasionally in the 19th century.

There was substantial development in furniture in the late Middle Ages as well. Archaeological finds show how oil lamps, chamber pots, and baking and frying utensils appeared from the 14th century.[258] More complete overviews of household furniture can be obtained from inventories, available in greater numbers from the 15th and 16th centuries on, although these were clearly biased towards the upper end of the social spectrum. An early sample of 37 inventories for typical burgher households in Deventer and Zwolle from the period 1455–1505 shows a wide range of large quantities of furniture.[259] These households, mainly of independent, upper-middle-class craftsmen, each possessed a few seats, 6–10 chairs, a few stools, some 15 chair cushions, a cupboard, and 3 chests. In the kitchen they had many utensils; on average, 10 cooking pots and 6 cauldrons. For coastal Friesland, a highly commercialized region, a larger sample is available for rural households in the second half of the 16th century.[260] Paupers, accounting for perhaps a quarter of the population, are absent from this sample. Still, it is clear that ownership of furniture and tools was widespread among country dwellers. The wealthier third of farming households, all owning more than 10 cows, had a wagon, boat, plough, butter churn, cheese press, and 2 cheese vats. Of the middling group almost half had these fairly expensive items. In household textiles, the wealthier farmers possessed 12 blankets, 6 tablecloths, 4 towels, 40 bed sheets, and 10 cushions; the middling ones had about half that number. The wealthier farmers typically possessed the same amount of furniture as the burghers from Deventer and Zwolle, and the middling households about half that quantity.

Most of the furniture found there was not made within the household, but was increasingly produced by specialized craftsmen, labourers, or proto-industrial workers. Many of these were found in regions such as inland Flanders, the Meuse valley, and particularly Holland, which experienced a process of industrialization

---

[257] Voskuil, *Van vlechtwerk tot baksteen*, 21–38.
[258] Sarfatij, 'Dagelijks leven in Holland'. [259] Dubbe, 'Het huisraad'.
[260] De Vries, 'Peasant demand patterns', and De Vries, *Dutch rural economy*, 214–224.

in the late Middle Ages, both in town and countryside. At the same time, in regions such as coastal Frisia, the Guelders river area, and Artois, agriculture also became more specialized and aimed at the market. Processes like these often went in tandem with accumulation and social polarization, with the relatively small group of winners—large landowners, noble office holders, merchants, entrepreneurs, and large tenant farmers—increasing their purchasing power and exercising greater demand for more luxurious industrial goods and foodstuffs. At the other end of the social spectrum, many lost their land and hence direct access to food, retaining only their labour. They became dependent on the labour market for obtaining income and on the market for products and goods for their food and other needs. Peasant regions such as Drenthe and the Campine, on the other hand, experienced much less change, with production aimed mainly at subsistence and the peasant households remaining the centres of interlinked production and consumption. In the next chapter we will look at the consequences of these different patterns for the actual development of agriculture and industries.

VII

The Economy in the Late Middle Ages: Agriculture and Industries

VII.1. AGRICULTURE

Population Pressure and the Growth of Markets, 1100–1350

In the Low Countries two processes had a profound influence on the agricultural sector in the 12th and 13th centuries. First, there was enormous population growth, which resulted in high population densities and pressure to extend agriculture to ground that had been extensively cultivated. Secondly, there was a growth of trade, markets, and cities, accompanied by the emergence of an institutional and physical infrastructure for exchange and trade. Overall, the result of these processes was intensification and increasing specialization of agriculture, but these developments did not occur everywhere in the Low Countries. In Flanders, there was specialization from an early stage, with sheep, and later cattle, dominant in the coastal parts, industrial crops in the inland part, and cereals in the southernmost part, linking up with neighbouring Hainaut, where as early as the 12th century cereal cultivation had become clearly dominant.[1] The growth of specialization was at least in part associated with the presence of large land ownership; for example, the comital properties in Flanders, which were spread over the three different regions and supplied different products. Because these properties were incorporated in the comital economy as a whole, specialization could be pushed further.

A similar process took place on the granges, the large agricultural units formed in the 12th and 13th centuries mainly by the Cistercian and Premonstratensian orders, as well as other large landowners. Being part of the larger whole of an abbey's economy increased specialization, and allowed to profit from the comparative advantages offered by the region for specific products, as well as providing the financial opportunities to invest and bear the risk inherent in specialization. This can be observed from the increased ownership of sheep in the Premonstratensian granges in the Campine in this period. Around 1200, on the grange of Sterksel

---

[1] Thoen, 'The count and the countryside', 269–276, and Sivéry, *Structures agraires*, 84–85.

in this infertile sandy region, the Abbey of Averbode had some 350 sheep, a few dozen cows, and 15 beehives. Such numbers were probably not uncommon in the granges and estates of this region.[2] In this specialization, and in the flow of goods within the economy of an abbey, the urban mansions formed the main link, and each abbey had several of them in strategically located towns, often close to the granges. Direct links with the urban market developed, and more and more of the produce of the granges was marketed in the cities instead of being transported to the abbey. The produce of the granges in the Campine was sold in the smaller market towns founded in this period at the borders of the region, such as Oisterwijk, Turnhout, and Hoogstraten. This reflected the general development in which the growing cities and the markets exercised a greater influence on agriculture, inducing further specialization. Such specialization, which grew in the 12th and 13th centuries, was mainly found on large estates and close to markets.

The increase in commercialization in this period needs to be qualified, however: most of the agricultural production still took place in almost fully closed units, such as the family farm, manor, or village, and was primarily aimed at self-sufficiency. Even in inland Flanders, increasingly dominated by large cities and growing markets, agricultural specialization for the market was probably less important than the trend towards subsistence-oriented intensification, driven by the needs of a growing rural population to feed itself. In this region, dominated by small peasant-owned holdings, the specialization was labour-intensive, requiring ever-increasing labour input. As a result of population pressure, aided and further strengthened by market demand, agriculture in the second half of the 13th century in Flanders was very progressive in many respects, including the introduction of new techniques, new rotation systems, and new crops.[3] However, the peasants on their smallholdings gave specific direction to the innovations. Their principal goal was to maximize physical output, even at extreme labour inputs. This resulted in intensive cultivation of cereals, with the more extensive cattle grazing pushed aside. Moreover, fixed rotation systems were abandoned to allow for more intensive use of the land. Local bylaws or communal regulations no longer restricted the choice of crops to cultivate in the 13th century, allowing more space for peas, clover, and vetches in the rotation, which often replaced the fallow fields in inland Flanders and Artois.

Other specializations also responded to the intensification of agriculture. In inland Flanders the rise of labour-intensive cultivation of flax, linked to the emergence of proto-industrial processing of the flax and to rural linen production, accelerated in the late 13th century.[4] At the same time, the Haspengouw and the

---

[2] Dekkers, 'De uitbating', esp. 15, and Steurs, *Naissance d'une région*, 380. For the rise of market towns see also sections III.3, pp. 108–110, and V.4, pp. 223–225.

[3] Verhulst, 'L'intensification et la commercialisation', and Thoen, 'The birth'.

[4] Thoen, *Landbouwekonomie*, 980–993, and for woad, Joris, 'Les moulins à guède'.

adjacent part of Namur saw the emergence of woad production, with hundreds of tonnes of this dyestuff produced there each year. The dye was mainly destined for the urban textile industries, and the woad plant offered the additional advantage of being suitable for fodder. The cultivation of these cash crops required extreme care, with heavy fertilizing, weeding, and trenching, often with the spade, which made it very labour-intensive. The land was ploughed as often as 4 or even 6 times a year. All elements of the famous 'Flemish husbandry', with its specialization and intensive land use, were already in place at this early stage.

Other agricultural innovations of the period required more capital, and so were available only to large-scale farmers or on large holdings. Ponds, sometimes with a mill, were built and used for pisciculture. In the area around Brussels in the 12th and 13th centuries dozens of artificial ponds were created,[5] mainly by large landowners. The priory of Sept Fontaines owned 14 fish ponds in the Brussels area. Among the species farmed in these private fishponds were pike and carp. Newly introduced from the Danube area, carp grew rapidly and spawned readily, and were highly valued by the elite as a status symbol. Around 1400 the Duke of Brabant harvested some 13,000 carp annually from his ponds. Farming carp was systematic: a pond was filled with young fish, often spawned by selected brood stock, and harvested as a single age group.[6] Another example of capital-intensive innovation was the introduction of large, heavy ploughs, drawn by large teams of oxen or horses. At the same time, iron was increasingly used in place of wood for plough shares, which helped to make the furrows deeper. This type of agricultural innovation was costly. It stimulated cooperation among villagers, who were forced to pool resources to obtain access to a heavy plough and a team of horses, but on the other hand it favoured the large farmers and could play a role in the breakdown of village solidarity.

In the labour-intensive husbandry in inland Flanders, the physical yields per hectare were increased enormously in the 13th century by reducing the area left fallow, but mainly by more intensive cultivation methods.[7] Yields per hectare around the year 1300 could amount to 18 hectolitres (hl) of wheat, with peaks of up to 30–35 hl/ha, as in the area around Lille, Saint-Omer, and Valenciennes in the south of Flanders, as well as in Hainaut and Artois. In themselves these figures do not tell the whole story, since they need to be viewed in the context of the agrosystem as a whole, including soil quality, the rotation system, and the frequency of cultivation. Nevertheless, they are strikingly high compared with figures elsewhere and in later centuries, which are on average a third lower.[8] At the same time, the surpluses and labour productivity probably decreased owing to the labour-intensive cultivation of scarce land under pressure of mounting population growth.

---

[5] Deligne, *Bruxelles*, 39–40 and 131–149.   [6] Hoffmann, 'Economic development'.

[7] Derville, 'Dîmes'. Cf. Dejongh and Thoen, 'Arable productivity', 37–45, who are more sceptical of the value of figures like these.

[8] Cf. below, pp. 331–332.

On the sandy soils of Drenthe and the Campine, population pressure was more limited, but there were still clear signs of intensification influenced by population growth. A main element was the increase in rye cultivation, which was often sown almost continually on the same fields in response to the growing need for bread cereal. This semi-permanent rye cultivation exhausted the soil and required regular manuring and improvement of the soil. For this purpose sod was used, mainly cut in the heathlands and carried to the fields to be mixed with manure, clay, or sand; in the course of centuries these layers sometimes became 1.5 m thick. The start of this labour-intensive practice of sod-manuring in the sandy soils of north-western Europe, from Denmark to the north of present-day Belgium, can be dated fairly well through radiocarbon dating and pollen analysis. In some regions, such as East Friesland in the north of what is now Germany, as well as in the relatively densely populated Campine, this practice seems to have started on a small scale in the high Middle Ages.[9] In the eastern parts of the Netherlands, such as Drenthe, on the other hand, there were small, isolated instances in the 13th century, but the practice only gained momentum in the 16th and 17th centuries.

This system created an intensively cultivated infield, close to the village, and allowed for further nuclearization of settlement. Around the almost permanently sown infield was the more extensively used arable land, which was less manured and regularly left fallow or used as convertible land for pasturing, and was surrounded by the extensively used wastelands.[10] This infield–outfield system was often applied to less fertile soils. The infield was then permanently cultivated, in contrast to the earlier use. This created arable land at a fixed location and fostered a closer tie between peasant and plots of land, since periodic shifts or redistributions were no longer necessary, thus opening the way to more absolute ownership.[11] Associated with the practice of sod manuring was an increase in sheep grazing in sandy regions such as Drenthe; forests were cut down to meet the need for sod, resulting in an extension of heathlands. The sheep and their wool were the main marketable elements in these regions. Apart from this, self-sufficiency remained dominant. The different chronology of this complex of changes on the sandy soils, and particularly the regional variation in the diffusion of sod manuring, is explained mainly by differences in population pressure. The first phase took place in the 11th to 13th centuries and the second in the 16th to 17th centuries, both being periods of population pressure. The fact that the practice was applied much earlier in the more densely populated Campine than in Drenthe provides further evidence for the importance of this factor.

The development of sod manuring combined with semi-permanent rye cultivation was part of the general, long-term extension of cereal production, which started in the early Middle Ages and was achieved by more intensive

---

[9] For East Friesland: Behre, 'The Plaggenesch', 84–86, and Spek, 'The age of plaggen soils', for critical remarks on this dating. See also Spek, *Het Drentse esdorpenlandschap*, 784–814.
[10] Bieleman, *Boeren op het Drentse zand*, 591–604.   [11] For this development, see section V.1.

cultivation and by the extension of cultivated area. This resulted in higher output, but not necessarily in larger surpluses. In the high Middle Ages, the application of labour-saving techniques indeed helped increase surpluses, at least in some regions, but in the 12th and 13th centuries the land became increasingly scarce, whereas population growth continued, eroding the favourable effects of the new techniques. The rapid and ongoing population growth led to more intensive land use and reclamation of marginal lands, resulting in smaller surpluses. In regions where all land had already been reclaimed, it may have led to marginalization of pastoral farming and a tendency towards grain monoculture.

Population pressure reached its maximum in the first half of the 14th century, when surpluses decreased further and land became even scarcer, driving up sale and leasing prices. Large landowners profited, but those who farmed the land were pressed hard in the face of the declining surpluses. In regions where most peasants held their land at fixed rents or even in full ownership, as in Holland, the increase of charges and burdens was limited, but where land users did not have firm control over their land, lords could drive up prices for rents, fines, or leases. For peasants with smallholdings, whose numbers grew considerably with the ongoing population growth and resulting fragmentation of holdings, the situation was perhaps worst: they had to supplement their agricultural earnings with wage labour (as wages declined) and buy additional food (as food prices rose). Their subsistence levels were becoming more and more depressed in this period.

The most dramatic result was hunger and starvation. Famine was a recurrent phenomenon in the Middle Ages, and in 1124–5 many parts of the Low Countries were severely affected.[12] In Flanders the count took measures to counter the effects, such as distributing bread and prohibiting brewing to save grain, but also making it compulsory to sow peas and beans, since these would ripen earlier and could alleviate some of the distress. Such catastrophes occurred increasingly and with greater severity towards the beginning of the 14th century because of the increasing population pressure and exhaustion of opportunities to wring more output from the land. The worst scarcity, the Great Famine of 1315–22, may have killed as much as 10 per cent of the population, and shortly afterwards, in 1347–8, the Low Countries were hit by the Black Death.[13] The bacillus may be seen as an exogenous element, but it affected a population weakened by scarcity of land and shortages of food. The effect of the plague may have been intensified by agricultural specialization and the shift to more lucrative cash crops, forced by the competitiveness of the newly introduced lease system, thus reducing the production of bread grains. The wide regional differences in population decline, with some regions only mildly affected by the Black Death, suggest that these socio-economic elements were indeed the main causes of its disastrous effect.

---

[12] Van Caenegem & Demyttenaere, *De moord*, 16–17 and 114–116.
[13] Jordan, *The great famine*, 143–148. For the effects of the Black Death, see also section VI.2, pp. 279–281.

Population Decline, Transition, and Specialization, 1350–1600

The population decline of the mid-14th century and the associated fall in demand for grain led to a retreat in arable farming, mainly to the soils most suitable for it, and to a growth in the importance of livestock, stimulated by rising prices for livestock products. In the Guelders river area the proportion of land being sown decreased from 35–50 per cent around the middle of the 14th century to 20–35 per cent a century later.[14] This resulted in the concentration of arable farming on the more favourable soils and made more manure available for the less arable, but yields per area sown did not necessarily increase after the mid-14th century, and they often decreased, as demonstrated for southern Flanders.[15] This was probably caused by the less intensive use of the land, a result of relative land abundance, labour scarcity, and high wages. Indirectly, it shows that population pressure and the high price of grain had indeed been the main factors behind the high yields of the 13th century. In most of the Low Countries, unlike most of England,[16] the relationship between population levels and yields per area sown was positive, probably because most parts of the Low Countries were at the intensive margin of cultivation, thus allowing labour inputs to have a determining effect on physical yields per area.

The reduction in the share of the land devoted to growing crops and the stagnation or decline of output per area sown together often resulted in a sharp decline of total output of grain after the mid-14th century, just like that found in many parts of Germany and France. This was true of the Cambrésis, a region focused on large-scale grain cultivation, just south of Flanders (see Table 7.1).

Elsewhere, however, there was no more than a slight decline in total grain output after the mid-14th century, and in some regions output stabilized at a

Table 7.1 Index of total grain output in the Cambrésis, 1320–1700 (1370 = 100)

Years	Wheat/barley	Oats
1320	145/150	160/170
1370	100	100
1450/60	75	65/70
1520/40	85	80
1610/20	75	50
1700	100	50

Sources: Neveux, *Vie et déclin*, v–vii and 60–66, although criticized by Sivery, *Structures agraires*, 365–367; cf. also the discussion by Morineau, 'Cambrésis et Hainaut'.

---

[14] Van Bavel, 'A valuation', 305–306.
[15] Derville, 'Dîmes', and Tits-Dieuaide, *La formation*, 92–103. See also Table 7.1.
[16] On this contrast, see Campbell, 'Land, labour, livestock', esp. 144–148, placing Norfolk between England and the Low Countries.

fairly high level.[17] This applied particularly to regions where the Black Death had not been so devastating, as in inland Flanders, but it was also true for Brabant and the Haspengouw, where the rising demand from the cities which were growing in importance in this period probably played a role in the minimal decline of total grain output. If the probable increase in livestock production in this period is also taken into account, then it is even more apparent that total land productivity in most of the Low Countries remained relatively stable; a surprising feature considering the high levels attained before the mid-14th century. Moreover, the decline did not last as long in most of the Low Countries as elsewhere in Europe because of the relatively slight effect of the plague and the early demographic recovery there. After population lows for about a century, in most regions population again began to increase in the course of the 15th and 16th centuries, resulting again in rising grain prices and mounting land scarcity. In regions where this development was most pronounced, as in inland Flanders, attempts to increase physical yields often used methods similar to those of the 13th century, which had been the formative period for developing new techniques and methods. Total grain output now increased markedly, as observed for south-west Brabant,[18] an area adjacent and similar to inland Flanders. Output there reached its peak in 1550–60, at a level which was almost 50 per cent higher than it had been at the start of the 15th century.

Small freeholders, who had little land, strove hardest to increase physical yields. They achieved this by turning to intensive agriculture, as shown most clearly in inland Flanders.[19] In practice, this meant increasing cultivation of labour-intensive industrial crops, reducing land left fallow, increasing dominance of arable farming over livestock, and devoting a growing proportion of arable land to bread grains. In the area around Oudenaarde in 1541–50, smallholders devoted 60–80 per cent of the sown area to bread grains, mainly for their own consumption. Despite the reduction in fallow, the growing scarcity of manure and extension of grain cultivation to the more marginal soils in inland Flanders, they succeeded in obtaining very high total yields per hectare. By applying labour-intensive tilling of the soil, often using a spade, smallholders here often harvested as much as 16–20 hl of wheat or rye per sown hectare. In other parts of western Europe, typical wheat yields ranged from 9 to 20 hl/ha, whereas the high yields in inland Flanders were obtained despite the mediocre soil conditions on the sandy-loamy soils. Opportunities to obtain high yields from small farms by increasing labour input apparently were great, although at the expense of labour productivity, and often resulting in a reduction of living standards. Similarly high yields were obtained from specialized farms

[17] Van der Wee, 'Agricultural development', 1–23, and Jansen, 'Tithes'.
[18] Daelemans, 'Tithe revenues'. For a similar rise near Namur cf. Ruwet, 'Pour un indice'.
[19] Slicher van Bath, 'The rise of intensive husbandry', esp. 136–137 and 148–149, and Thoen, *Landbouwekonomie*, 692–733, 812–822, and 839–844.

Table 7.2 Output of wheat in hl/ha of sown land in various parts of the Low Countries, 1325–1600: the Culemborg area in the Guelders river region (1), the Lille area in southern Flanders (2), the Oudenaarde area in inland Flanders (3), the Veurne area in coastal Flanders (4), and Onnaing in Hainaut (5)

Years	(1)	(2)	(3)	(4)	(5)
1325–1350	–	20	–	–	–
1350–1375	–	24	–	–	–
1375–1400	16	–	–	–	–
1400–1425	–	20	18	–	21
1425–1450	12	–	–	–	22
1450–1475	–	22	15	–	17
1475–1500	13	–	–	–	17
1500–1525	–	–	16	–	20
1525–1550	–	20	13	–	21
1550–1575	–	–	14	10	14
1575–1600	13	–	–	10	10

Sources: Dejongh & Thoen, 'Arable productivity', Van Bavel, 'A valuation', Thoen, *Landbouwekonomie*, 813, Morineau, *Les faux semblants*, 97–130.

concentrating on wheat production, as in southern Flanders, but these left ample amounts of land fallow and favoured wheat yields at the expense of total output.[20] (See Table 7.2.)

The figures in Table 7.2 need to be interpreted in the wider context of the agricultural system as a whole, the proportion of fallow land, and the place of a particular crop in the overall rotation system, but they show the great differences in output per hectare and the general stagnation of output in the late 14th and 15th centuries. This stagnation, or even decline, was most pronounced in regions dominated by large tenant farms, such as the Guelders river area, coastal Flanders, and coastal Friesland. The large-scale tenant farmers who operated on a capitalist basis endeavoured to maximize their profits, partly in order to continue to win the competition for leased land. They achieved this through specialization and the reduction of labour inputs, which enabled them to improve the ratio between output and wage costs, by far the main variable cost item. As a result of reduced labour inputs, physical yields of grain in these regions usually showed downward trends, as in the Guelders river area, where output of the main arable crop, oats, went down from 39 hl/ha in the third quarter of the 14th century, to 30 hl/ha around the year 1400, and to 22 hl/ha in the late 15th and the 16th centuries.[21] This took place despite increasing investment in manuring and polder drainage and confining arable farming to the best lands. The large tenant farmers there valued increased labour productivity and growing surpluses over high physical yields. As a result of increased imports of relatively cheap grain from the Baltic

---

[20] Dejongh and Thoen, 'Arable productivity', esp. 40–42.
[21] Van Bavel, 'A valuation', 297–309.

in the 16th century, intensive grain production for the market became even less remunerative in these regions. This is also reflected in the extensive grain cultivation in southern Brabant and the Haspengouw, and perhaps also in parts of Hainaut, as shown by the decline of physical yields in Onnaing (cf. Table 7.2). The start of the 'Little Ice Age', with its colder temperatures and higher rainfall, probably also affected agriculture unfavourably, but its role was not decisive, as is shown by the simultaneous rise in total physical output on the Flemish peasant smallholdings. Population trends, market opportunities, and especially the social distribution of land were far more important in this respect.

If one calculates the urbanization ratio, the proportion of the rural population engaged in non-agricultural production, and the food traded, some idea of labour productivity in agriculture can be indirectly obtained. These calculations show that around 1500 agricultural labour productivity in the Low Countries was by far the highest in Europe, with some 175 mouths fed by 100 people working in agriculture, as against 100 (Poland) to 135 (England, France, Italy) fed in other parts of Europe.[22] In the 16th century, there was a divergence between the northern and southern parts of the Low Countries, with the north showing a further rise to about 200, whereas the south stagnated. This divergence reflects the presence of the many regions in the north where agriculture became capital intensive, as in the Guelders river area, coastal Frisia, and later Holland, whereas in the south the labour-intensive alternative was often chosen, as most clearly in inland Flanders and many parts of Brabant.

This divergence is also reflected in the types of regional specialization. Agriculture became much more specialized in the later Middle Ages, in reaction to growing market demand, and further stimulated by population decline in the second half of the 14th century, which made more land available, reduced the demand for grain, and increased purchasing power for several social groups, thus stimulating the rise of industries and making specialization in industrial crops more feasible. In regions dominated by small peasant holdings, such as Holland and inland Flanders, this specialization was usually labour intensive. Capital available for investment was limited there and peasants were more likely to have used the surplus labour they had available within their own families to produce labour-intensive crops such as flax, hops, and madder in inland Flanders, or hemp, rape, mustard, and hops in Holland.[23] In the area around Oudenaarde in the first half of the 16th century, no less than 8 per cent of the arable land was sown with flax, often processed further within the same household. Not surprisingly, the highest proportions were found on the smallholdings of a half to 4 hectares, which had an average of 15 per cent used for flax cultivation. This

---

[22] Van Zanden, 'The development of agricultural productivity', 368–370. For labour productivity see also below, p. 342.
[23] Bieleman, *Geschiedenis van de landbouw*, 52–56, 65–67, and 73–75, and Thoen, *Landbouwekonomie*, 722–733 and 993–1000. For the link with proto-industralization, see sections VI.1, pp. 248–250, and VII.2, p. 361.

must have been close to the physical maximum because of the soil exhausting effect of this crop.

In Holland other labour-intensive sectors emerged, such as horticulture, fruit growing, and dairy production. Commercial butter and cheese production grew in the 14th and early 15th centuries. By around 1440, some 400,000 kg of butter and 425,000 kg of cheese from the northern part of Holland alone passed the toll at Kampen at the mouth of the IJssel river; this cargo was the total annual output of more than 20,000 cows.[24] At the time, two-thirds to three-quarters of the rural households in Holland were involved in commercial dairy production. In the 15th and 16th centuries, cheese production was particularly high in northern Holland, near Alkmaar and Edam. In the Zeevang, which had about 3,000 hectares of land, 2,000 to 2,500 cows were kept, specifically to produce cheese exported from Edam.[25] This labour-intensive type of agriculture was dominant in Holland up to the 16th century, when a fundamental change in rural social structure took place. With the growth of large landholdings and the rise of large tenant farms, a type of capital-intensive agriculture emerged that resembled that of the Guelders river area, with capital-intensive fattening of oxen becoming important, for instance.

These large tenant farmers aimed to increase labour productivity by opting for labour-extensive crop cultivation and branches of livestock farming, and by using capital investments to further reduce labour input.[26] The combination of large landholders and large tenant farmers that emerged there appears to have had a favourable effect on the level of investment. Within the lease system, large landowners were inclined, or forced, to reinvest a substantial proportion of their lease income. In the Guelders river area they spent about 16 to 20 per cent of their gross income on investments in agricultural holdings, which is a high proportion, at least compared with the large landowners in peasant-dominated areas.[27] These proportions rose during the 16th century, while tenants also spent large sums of money on their holdings: for maintenance and construction of hydraulic works, for maintenance of farm buildings, and to purchase livestock, seed, and implements. From 1569 to 1573, Rienck Hemmema, on the 25-hectare holding he owned and farmed in coastal Frisia, spent 4 per cent of his budget on agricultural implements and more than 10 per cent on repairing and constructing farm buildings, as well as making smaller investments in fruit trees, dike repair, and a boat for transport.[28] Large tenant farmers may have invested even more of their large financial resources because of the fierce competition for leasehold land.

[24] Van Bavel and Gelderblom, 'Land of milk and butter', and De Vries, *Dutch rural economy*, 157–161.
[25] Boschma-Aarnoudse, *Tot verbeteringe*, 122–125, 140, and 253–257.
[26] See also Van Bavel, 'Land, lease and agriculture'.
[27] Van Bavel, *Transitie en continuïteit*, 539–551, compared with Thoen, *Landbouwekonomie*, 596–604. Comparable figures for peasant investment are not available.
[28] Slicher van Bath, 'Een Fries landbouwbedrijf', esp. 126–130.

Regions such as the Guelders river area saw great changes in agriculture, with an increase in capital input and a reduction in labour input. From the 14th century, arable farming there had become relatively insignificant, and an increasing proportion of the arable land was used to grow fodder crops such as beans, rape seed, and especially oats, the most important arable crop in this region.[29] Oats were generally grown using a form of convertible husbandry, which emerged there in the 16th century. In this rather extensive system, farmers were able to produce some grain at low labour inputs, while dairy and meat production could be increased. At the same time, the number of ploughings could be reduced, so that labour productivity rose.

The livestock sector was very market oriented, and had become labour extensive and capital-intensive in the course of the 15th and 16th centuries. This applied particularly to the sectors that were strongly developed there, i.e. horse breeding and cattle grazing on pastures; both were very suitable for large-scale farmers who usually had large capital reserves, endeavoured to reduce labour input, and had good contacts with the market. In the later Middle Ages, these specializations extended over large areas, in some cases even all of Europe, as was most clear for oxen, with the late 15th century seeing the formation of an international network of production and consumption.[30] Many of the oxen consumed in the Low Countries were bred in Denmark and Schleswig-Holstein, with tens of thousands being driven south each year to be fattened during the summer in coastal Frisia, the Guelders river area, and other regions where large farmers had ample land and capital available. In the autumn the fattened oxen were marketed and slaughtered in the cities in Holland, Brabant, and Flanders; by around the middle of the 16th century, each year in October some 3,500 fattened oxen were traded in the weekly oxen market in Lier alone. In the course of this specialization, cattle were bred ever bigger, with the average size of bulls and steers found in Deventer rising from 115 cm in the 13th and 14th centuries to 127 cm in the 15th and 16th centuries,[31] and were slaughtered ever younger.

Labour-intensive commercial crops, however, were of little importance in these regions, in contrast to regions dominated by small family holdings. The rise of large tenant farms thus resulted in a reduction of labour input and a sharp decline in agricultural employment. In two 16th-century examples from large farms in the Guelders river area, only 0.1 man-years of labour per hectare were used. This corresponds with the figures found for large farms in the 18th and 19th centuries,[32] i.e. 0.1 to 0.15 per hectare, whereas on family farms it averaged between 0.25 and 0.5 man-years per hectare, and on small farms up to 1.0 or even 1.2. This combination of capital-intensive with labour-extensive specialization

---

[29] Hoppenbrouwers, 'Agricultural production', esp. 100–101.
[30] Gijsbers, *Kapitale ossen*, 29–39 and 42–47.
[31] IJzereef and Laarman, 'The animal remains', 413–414.
[32] Van Bavel, 'Wage labour, and Vanhaute, 'Agrarian labour', esp. 155.

resulted in large surpluses of oats, barley, oxen, and horses, which were exported mainly to the densely populated (proto-)industrial regions of Holland, Flanders, and Brabant.

Changes were much slower in the sandy regions in the eastern Low Countries, although there too some specialization for the market can be observed.[33] In the 16th century in the Veluwe and the Campine, livestock were very numerous, with the numbers of horses and sheep in the Veluwe surpassing the early 19th-century numbers. The 110,000 sheep kept in this region were concentrated on the large farms: some 10 per cent of farmers there kept more than 80 sheep, benefiting from their ample access to the common heathlands. These sheep were not kept in a communal flock with a village shepherd, as in Drenthe, but the large farmers each hired their own shepherd, who also brought in his own sheep, some 25 on average. This specialization was very extensive, but almost wholly aimed at the market. In Drenthe, a sandy region in the north-east, changes were very slight. Apart from some intensification and minor increases in the degree of commercialization, the peasant structure remained largely intact there, with no structural transformation of the rural economy up to the 19th century.[34] On their small and medium-sized farms, peasant families concentrated on the cultivation of bread grains and tending livestock on a small scale, mainly for subsistence. Long-term security and the consumption needs of the individual household were much more central to production decisions than the market and possible profits to be made. Thus, common lands and collective rules remained very important, and exploitation of the commons for market purposes was resisted.[35] Agriculture was fairly extensive, with large wastelands and low physical yields. Some slow, intermittent rises in yields did take place over the centuries, but these were chiefly the result of population growth and intensification, and did not result in an increase in labour productivity.

In agriculture, three types of regions can be discerned in the late medieval Low Countries. One type, represented by Drenthe, experienced only slight specialization, with agriculture remaining diversified and predominantly subsistence oriented. A second type, as in inland Flanders, had increased market orientation through labour-intensive crops such as flax or other industrial crops, or labour-intensive production of cheese and butter, as in Holland, combined with intensive subsistence farming. And a third type, represented by the Guelders river area, experienced specialization in labour-extensive and capital-intensive sectors, mainly in cattle breeding and fattening, but also in more extensive types of large-scale grain cultivation. To a growing extent, these regions became part, and perhaps even a nodal point, of a process of specialization spanning the whole of western and northern Europe, as observed for wheat (exported from

---

[33] Bieleman, 'De verscheidenheid van de landbouw', and Roessingh, 'De veetelling van 1526', esp. 20–24.
[34] Van Zanden, 'From peasant economy', esp. 38–40.   [35] Van Zanden, 'The paradox'.

southern Flanders, Artois, and Picardy), rye (imported from the Baltic), wine (from the Rhineland), oxen (from Denmark to the Guelders river area and further to Brabant), or butter and cheese (exported from Holland). As a result of this increasing specialization and growing complementarity of regions in the later Middle Ages, and the further development of the physical and institutional framework of markets, huge flows of agricultural goods were generated. To some extent, this even applied to parts of the Low Countries outside the focal point of economic development, such as Luxembourg. There, in the second half of the 15th century, some 6,430 hl of wine were traded in or through the town of Luxembourg each year, and some 8,000 to 11,000 head of cattle were transported annually along the toll at Sierck-sur-Moselle,[36] indicating that this region was at least partly integrated into the market for agricultural goods.

Trade in grain, the staple food of the period, was even greater, particularly in the core regions of inland Flanders, western Brabant, and, increasingly, Holland. The main producers of grain surpluses in the 14th and early 15th centuries were southern Flanders and Artois, which specialized in the production of the bread grain wheat and, to a lesser extent, rye. Grain was transported over land to one of the transit towns on the rivers running north, especially Saint-Omer, Lille, Douai, and Valenciennes, to be shipped to Ghent and further north. Already in 1321–4 some 219,000 hl of bread grain was traded through Saint-Omer alone, enough to feed 70,000 mouths for an entire year, rising to 259,000 hl around 1420.[37] By around 1400 some 723,000 hl were traded annually through Douai, and 81,000 hl through Lille. Including the smaller centres, the total was perhaps 1.5 million hl per year. If a quarter of the land in this region was sown with bread grain, and if the physical output is set at a fairly high 14 hl/ha, then 1 km² produced 350 hl, of which about 150 hl were consumed locally. The amounts exported annually thus formed the total surplus of an area of some 7,500 km², and were enough to feed some 500,000 people in Flanders, Brabant, and Holland.

From about 1470 on, Holland also imported more bread grain from the Baltic area, partly replacing imports from southern Flanders and Artois. In the mid-16th century, some 0.9–1.2 million hl of grain were transported through the Sound, most of which was destined for Amsterdam.[38] The influx of such massive amounts of bread grain made it possible to feed half the population living in Holland towns and enabled the rural population of Holland to specialize in butter, cheese, and proto-industrial activities. The high water tables resulting from the subsidence of the peat soil made cultivation of bread grain in the Holland countryside difficult, and the more lucrative specializations made it less

---

[36] Yante, 'L'approvisionement alimentaire', esp. 348–350.
[37] Derville, 'Le grenier des Pays-Bas'.
[38] Van Tielhof, *De Hollandse graanhandel*, 18–34 and 86–98. For market structures, also in inland Flanders: section V.4, pp. 224–228 and 234–238.

worthwhile to devote energy to grain cultivation, particularly now that grain was available in the market. In inland Flanders, bread grain was also easily available from the 13th century, but the less favourable market structures, both for selling cash crops and proto-industrial products and for buying grain, seem to have induced peasants there to retain more self-sufficiency in grains, thus slowing further commercialization and specialization.

Fishing

Regional specializations can also be observed in fishing. Eel fishing, usually near the many sluices, became important in Holland. In 1500, at the Spaarndam dike alone, annual catches of 160,000 eels, or 10–20 tonnes, were usual.[39] In the major rivers salmon fishing was particularly common, as in the Biesbosch on the Holland–Brabant border, where the rivers ran slowly through shallow channels. Salmon and shad were caught here through *steken*, consisting of some 150 to 200 m of palisades, with fences of plaited twigs, intersected by bag-nets. In the 16th century these *steken* were often placed side by side for many km, with several long rows found in the Biesbosch.[40] In 1563 some 60,000 shad, 16,000 salmon, and 55 sturgeon were caught there by about 150 full-time fishermen.

By far the most important fishing sector for economic development, however, was the herring fishery. This provided employment to many tens of thousands, not only shippers and fishermen, but also shipwrights, freighters, traders, coopers, herring packers, salters, rope makers, and net menders, and its effects radiated through the entire economy. In the 16th century, salted herring had become perhaps the main export product of the northern parts of the Low Countries. Developed as a coastal fishery, the herring fleets ventured ever further over the North Sea in the course of the 13th and 14th centuries, even to the English and Scottish coasts, as far as 400 km from their home ports, aided by the development and adaptation of the buss, a boat well suited to herring fishing and the new practice of gutting and salting herring at sea, which improved the keeping qualities of the fish. A major impetus for Dutch herring fisheries was also provided by exhaustion of the competing herring supplies from Scania and the Baltic around 1400, as a result of the depletion of the shoals and insecurity resulting from acts of war. This increased profit margins and encouraged the Dutch to invest in more ships and equipment.[41] Around the middle of the 15th century, Holland, Zeeland, Flanders, and England were still about equally strong in herring fishing. The port of Dunkirk alone, which had 60 herring busses, in good years boasted catches of 20 million gutted herring and 12 million fresh herring.[42] But in the

[39] Van Dam, *Vissen in veenmeren*, 103–137 and 244–247.
[40] Martens, *De zalmvissers van de Biesbosch*, 114–121 and 142–155.
[41] Unger, 'The Netherlands herring fishery'.
[42] Degryse, 'De laatmiddeleeuwse haringvisserij', and Sicking, *Zeemacht en onmacht*, 73–79.

Table 7.3 Estimated number of busses engaged in herring fishing, 1439–1600

	1439	1477	1562	1600
Holland	100	150	400	500–800
Zeeland	150	150	200	160
Flanders	>150	>150	100	<100?
Total	>400	>450	700	760–1,060

Sources: Van Vliet, 'Zeevarenden op de vissersvloot', De Vries and Van der Woude, *The first modern economy*, 241–250 and 294–295, and, with a much higher estimate for 1600, Van Bochove, 'De Hollandse haringvisserij'

following decades Holland eclipsed all the others as *the* herring nation in the North Sea. At its peak, Holand herring fishers cured more than 200 million herring a year, or about half of the total European production. (See Table 7.3.)

The growth spurt in the rise of herring fishing in Holland from 1450 to 1550, and in northern Holland from 1540 to 1590, had several causes. At the start of this period, it was a proto-industrial activity there, practised by peasants as an adjunct to working their smallholding within a seasonal cycle, thus providing crews for the ships at relatively low wages. The availability of relatively cheap hemp, ropes, sails, and fishing gear is also linked to the proto-industrial structure of the Holland countryside, since this equipment was produced mainly by peasant households, as with hemp cultivation and rope making, which were concentrated in the eastern parts of the Holland peatlands, such as the Krimpenerwaard.[43] The capital-intensive sector of herring fishing also profited greatly from the low cost of credit and the smoothly functioning system of *partenrederij*, the divided ownership of ships. The efficient protection of herring fleets and the well-organized market in Holland also helped the rise of herring fishing, with the public authorities playing a large part from the 14th century. In Holland herring processing and trade were highly regulated, mainly by urban bylaws. In Brielle the bylaws of 1346, greatly extended in the period 1445–60, regulated the location of sale, the quality of the fish, and the material and size of herring tuns. The laws were detailed, extensive, and strictly enforced, and fines were high. Legislation was also increasingly enacted at a provincial or central level, as in 1509 when the government ordered several cities to improve the quality of herring for export so that its position would not be weakened in international markets.[44] The standards applied to quality and packing reduced insecurity and information costs for foreign traders, making Holland herring more competitive in the market. The early and active role of public authorities thus stimulated the rise of this sector.

In the course of the 16th century, Holland herring fishing underwent a fundamental organizational change, giving it a further boost, but at the same

---

[43] Bieleman, *Geschiedenis van de landbouw*, 65–68. For proto-industrialization in Holland, see also section VI.1, pp. 248–250.

[44] De Wit, 'Reders en regels'.

time eroding its successful proto-industrial base and impeding its growth in the long run. Herring fishing became more specialized, large-scale, and increasingly used proletarian wage labourers, thus embodying the general transition of Holland's economy and society. The favourable institutional setting in which this transition took place further stimulated this sector, especially because of the capital that was available for investments in better and bigger ships. By the early 16th century, busses had become large, three-masted vessels with a full deck, and an average size of about 60 tonnes, increasing further in the course of the century to about 140 tonnes.[45] At the same time the sector lost some of its proto-industrial advantages, as proto-industry disappeared from rural Holland, beginning in the south. This led to rising wage and materials costs and a loss of competitive edge, and stagnation beginning in the early 17th century. In the inland fishing sectors in Holland a similar social transformation took place even earlier. In the 14th century patricians from Leiden and Rotterdam leased the larger inland fishing waters and actively participated in the fish trade, and around the middle of the 15th century large, internationally oriented companies emerged in which fish merchants played an important part.[46] The competition for fishing leases and the high capital needs contributed greatly to the profound and early polarization of this sector. Thus, the fishing sectors were representative of the proto-industrial transition in Holland, and perhaps even of the development of Holland economy and society as a whole.

Growth and Sustainability

The more intensive use of land and water in the Low Countries for agriculture and fishing led to ecological problems, but outright disasters were avoided. Perhaps the worst threat was overfishing. The use of trawl nets and net poles and the practice of smothering or catching young fish, were said to have nearly emptied some rivers in Holland, such as the Meuse near Rotterdam, of fish in the first half of the 14th century.[47] Intensive fishing, however, was not the only factor here. As more and more dams, sluices, and water mills were erected from the 11th century, and the felling of trees, erosion, industrial pollution, and human contamination increased, the cool, clear, stable watercourses of the Low Countries became increasingly stagnant, turbid, and warmer. This made aquatic habitats much less suitable for fish like sturgeon, salmon, and trout,[48] and the anadromous sturgeon and salmon were affected especially badly by the artificial blockades in the watercourses, causing these species to decline or almost disappear.

Two centuries later a similar reduction in fish was observed for the brackish water of the large Zuiderzee, where herring and anchovy, as well as eel, smelt,

---

[45] Unger, 'Dutch herring'.
[46] Van Dam, *Vissen in veenmeren*, 171–189. See also section VI.1, pp. 249–250.
[47] Van Dam, *Vissen in veenmeren*, 132–134.   [48] Hoffmann, 'Economic development'.

and flounder were caught by fishermen from Guelders and Holland.[49] Around the middle of the 16th century, fishing grounds in the Zuiderzee seem to have been depleted by overfishing. The culprits were the new 'water ships', big ships provided with a compartment to keep fish alive. Another factor was the increasing use of enormous drift and drag nets used by fleets of 30 to 50 ships, which emptied the sea. The small meshes of the nets also caught undersized young fish, which were used to feed pigs and ducks. According to complaints made in 1555, the Zuiderzee ran the risk of becoming 'wholly infertile and robbed of fish'. The depletion of rivers and then lakes and inland seas stimulated the authorities to take restrictive measures, such as prohibiting the use of nets with small meshes, fishing by torchlight, or the full cordoning off of watercourses. As these were not sufficient to protect the fish stock, from the 12th century on other responses to the growing scarcity of fish were developed, including the construction of artificial fish farms with many hundreds of ponds and duck decoys, as well as introducing and rearing species well suited to such an environment, such as carp. Another response increasingly used was that fishermen went ever further out to sea; for example, herring fleets went as far as the Scottish coast. These developments are reflected in consumption patterns, as witnessed, for instance, by fish remains at a site in the IJssel town of Deventer.[50] There, indigenous freshwater fish were predominant in the high Middle Ages, but remains from the 13th and 14th centuries increasingly yielded farmed carp, and from the 15th and 16th centuries sea fish such as cod and herring.

With respect to the soil, intensive use did not necessarily lead to exhaustion, and sometimes had the opposite effect. Fertilization methods applied to avoid exhaustion could be either capital-or labour-intensive, depending on the nature of the farm and regional structure. In inland Flanders cultivation of the land was so labour-intensive that even the relatively infertile sandy-loamy soils produced high yields. To increase the supply of manure, cattle were kept in stalls throughout the year and fed with fodder crops, often linked to the introduction of vetches and other legumes in the rotation, which in turn increased supplies of nitrogen in the soil. Also, and to an increasing extent, night soil or manure was bought by the farmers. In 1571 the Frisian farmer Rienck Hemmema used 196 wagonloads of manure produced by his own livestock and 163 wagonloads bought in the nearby town of Franeker to fertilize his 8.5 hectares of arable land. On his farm, each hectare was manured once every 6 years with 70 tonnes of manure.[51] In other regions, marling was used to combat the acidity of the soil, as was done in the region around Liège from the beginning of the 13th century.[52] And for sandy soils, sod manuring was used.

---

[49] Ypma, *Geschiedenis van de Zuiderzeevisserij*, 48–71.
[50] IJzereef and Laarman, 'The animal remains'.
[51] De Vries, *Dutch rural economy*, 149–152.   [52] Genicot, *Rural communities*, 42.

The practice of sod manuring, however, had detrimental side-effects on forests, which were also affected by the increasing demand for wood for heating houses, building, and industrial purposes, in some regions leading to deforestation, such as on the Veluwe and the Ardennes. It also led to sand drifting as a result of overstocking of the heathlands. The most acute threat to the agricultural land, however, was the loss of land to the water, which resulted from subsidence of peatlands, erosion of dunes, and neglect of dikes, further aggravated by digging peat and winning salt.[53] The authorities responded by passing legislation restricting the practices, but the construction of dikes, sluices, and wind/watermills, collectively paid for by taxes, was more effective. A private response was investment to create new polders, particularly in times when food prices were high and agriculture was profitable, as later in the 16th century, especially in Holland and Zeeland. So even in such delicate and threatened environments there was never any irreversible deterioration.

It is difficult to determine precisely the extent to which late medieval developments in agriculture resulted in economic growth. Extensive growth as a result of the increase in agricultural land was rare in this period, unlike during the 11th to 13th centuries, when the area had been greatly extended. The later Middle Ages were characterized by stagnation, or an alternation between upward and downward cycles, mainly associated with the profitability of agricultural land, with demographic developments being a main factor. Another development, found mainly in regions dominated by small peasant holdings and further stimulated by market demand for industrial crops, was intensification of agriculture, with both land and rural labour being more intensively used. This intensification, with high and ever-increasing labour input, produced large amounts of raw materials and semi-finished goods at relatively low prices, and these regions also generated cheap and abundant labour. At the same time, the highly intensive character of production often depressed labour productivity. Real economic growth and a rise in labour productivity were found in only a few regions, such as the Guelders river area and coastal Friesland. These were the regions that were becoming dominated by large tenant farms where capital inputs were high, often aimed at introducing labour-saving techniques and specializations. This development, generally at great social cost, resulted in higher labour productivity and large surpluses, although in the late 16th century the ceiling for this development seems to have been reached,[54] when all technological opportunities were used, and further scale-enlargement and higher levels of in-depth investments in agriculture became unprofitable.

---

[53] Sections II.2, pp. 44–46, and VII.2, pp. 357–359.
[54] As can be gathered from 17th- and 18th-century developments in the Guelders river area: Brusse, *Overleven door ondernemen*.

VII.2. INDUSTRIES

Industrial Concentrations in Town and Countryside

In the high Middle Ages industrial activities were generally small-scale, dispersed, and often performed within the household, and they mostly remained so, but some specialization and concentration did occur, associated with improvement in the physical and institutional framework of markets and transport. Some of this took place in the countryside, but it was more characteristic of the cities. Cities often developed clear industrial profiles, stimulated by the protection of city walls, the increased security, institutional advantages, the presence of markets, and the concentration of people. All of these provided demand, as well as scope for specialization and division of labour.[55] The most successful examples of urban-based industrial development were the cities of the Meuse valley and southern Flanders/Artois. In Huy, Dinant, and other towns in the Meuse valley, from the 11th century on, the copper industry flourished, and the copper, brass, and bronze produced there found its way to markets in the Rhineland, France, and later England. But the Flemish towns that concentrated on textile production were even more successful.

In the 11th and 12th centuries Artois, southern Flanders, and Hainaut added growing urban cloth industries to already existing rural production. This took place first in the southernmost cities such as Arras and Saint-Omer, where light *sayetterie* (the manufacture of light woollen cloth) was dominant, but in the 12th century it shifted further north, to Cambrai, Lille, Douai, Tournai, and Valenciennes.[56] In the 13th century Douai, Lille, Tournai, Binche, and Mons also became important as producers of linen,[57] while cities in northern Flanders then became dominant in cloth production: Ghent, Bruges, and Ypres. The focus there was mainly on heavy cloth, some of a very high quality, such as the fine coloured cloth of Ghent and Ypres. In these rapidly growing cities, among the largest in western Europe, with tens of thousands of inhabitants, half or more of the population became employed in textile industries. Their products were exported all over Europe. In the 13th century, the fall in transport costs allowed even the cheaper Flemish cloths to be profitably exported to markets abroad,[58] including Mediterranean ports, where they successfully competed with local products.

In the urban industries, most workshops were small, owned by the craftsmen working with relatively simple tools. Some scale-enlargement took place in the 11th to 13th centuries, and some technological innovations were introduced,

---

[55] Verhulst, *The rise of cities*, 119–148, and sections III.3, pp. 108–114, and IV.2, pp. 156–157.
[56] Van der Wee, 'Structural changes'.   [57] Sabbe, *De Belgische vlasnijverheid*, 49–55.
[58] Chorley, 'The cloth exports'.

such as the broad loom in Flemish cloth production, but the success of urban industries was principally based on a far-reaching division of labour. This division, particularly useful in a complex process such as the production of heavy cloth, allowed for increased labour productivity and integration of large numbers of semi-skilled and unskilled labourers in the production process. It also promoted standardization of mass production, offering major advantages in export, as witnessed by the success of Flemish cloth in international markets. From the late 13th century on, such urban industries were mainly organized in the guilds within a corporative system.[59] The system protected small-scale production by independent craftsmen, and at the same time guaranteed strict regulation and quality control, vital in sectors where production was substantially aimed at export. In the urban cloth sector, particularly in the large Flemish towns, this system was most pronounced. Besides the general advantages of being located in cities rather than the countryside, textile production in Flanders, as well as copper production in the Meuse valley, also benefited from two additional factors more specific to the two regions. Agriculture there began to generate the surpluses needed to feed the growing urban population and give the urban workers security about their subsistence; southern Flanders and Artois, in particular, produced huge amounts of bread grain. Moreover, they had easy access to relatively cheap raw materials and markets for the final products as a result of their favourable institutional frameworks and relatively low and declining transport costs.

The growing influence of markets can also be observed in the countryside, where production was on an even smaller scale, and often performed in an unspecialized way within the household, like brewing and baking, or by small craftsmen. But in addition, some regional specializations can be observed which reflected the growth of markets and trade. A clear early example was pottery production. In the 9th to 13th centuries, pottery production in the Low Countries became mainly concentrated in the rectangle bounded by Namur, Roermond, Cologne, and Bonn. Production in this area was favoured by the old clays found there, allowing firing at high temperatures and producing a strong ceramic. Fuel was available nearby in the form of brown coal. The pottery centres in this region, such as Schinveld, Andenne, Raeren, and Pingsdorf, sometimes consisted of several kilns, producing massive quantities of cooking pots, pipkins, pitchers, and jugs, mainly destined for export. Analysis of archaeological finds shows that from Schinveld, for instance, pottery was exported in the 13th century to Brabant, Utrecht, and Holland.[60]

Production was even more extensive at Andenne, situated on the Meuse south of Liège, where a settlement developed near an important religious community. The specialist potters there produced large quantities of wheel-thrown ceramics from the late 11th century on. The partially glazed yellow jugs typical of Andenne

---

[59] Sections V.3, pp. 205–206, and VI.1, pp. 253–256.
[60] Brongers, 'Ceramological investigations', and Verhoeven, 'Ceramics and economics'.

were exported all over the Low Countries, as far as Frisia in the north. Finds from the mid-12th century show that about a third of all pottery used in the Meuse valley, Brabant, and all the way up to the Guelders river area was produced in the Andenne region.[61] Written sources from before the 14th century hardly mention such large-scale industry there; everything we know is from archaeological finds. The large quantities produced and the quality of the ceramics (the strong material, shape, decorations, and standardization), however, point to the industrial nature of the production and the specialization of the workers.

In the 14th century, particularly from *c*.1350, there was further concentration of pottery production. The fairly sudden decline in production in Schinveld, Brunssum, Andenne, and other older centres is sometimes attributed to political unrest or population decline after the Black Death, but it was probably the rise of trade, increase in surpluses, and growing opportunities for industries that resulted in a further concentration in locations most favourable to production. The new focus was the area of Aachen, Cologne, Raeren, and Siegburg, a small part of the earlier pottery area where large-scale production already existed but now further developed and eclipsed other centres. There was a parallel development in technology. In Siegburg, in the 13th century, attempts to produce harder non-porous pottery succeeded with the production of proto-stoneware, and around 1300 stoneware that was fired to a high temperature of 1050–1200°C was developed. This technique, developed in only a few decades, would remain in use for centuries, until far into the modern period. Siegburg became the pre-eminent centre of stoneware production in all of Europe, and its pottery flooded the Low Countries and drove locally produced pottery out of the market.[62] At some sites, up to half of the excavated pottery was produced in Siegburg.

Rural industries became increasingly specialized and geographically concentrated. The same process can be observed in the linen industry, which developed greatly in the 13th century in the countryside of southern Flanders, Artois, and Hainaut. Such rural specializations, aided by the lower cost of living in the countryside, offered growing competition to the urban industries, certainly when they started to produce for export. Small towns in Flanders and Brabant also came to the fore as industrial exporters, particularly for cloth in the course of the 14th century. The competition probably increased most in international cloth markets, where the English were also coming to the fore. Moreover, in the Mediterranean, where the Flemish cloth producers found a large part of their markets, trade became disrupted by warfare beginning in the 1290s, pushing transaction costs up.[63] The joint effect of these developments hit the big Flemish cities hard.

---

[61] Borremans and Warginaire, *La céramique*, 73–88.
[62] Hurst, Neal, and Van Beuningen, *Pottery*, 176–184 and 194–208. Also Stephan, 'The development'. For regional specialization see also section VI.3, pp. 298–300.
[63] Munro, 'The symbiosis', esp. 20–25.

Different Strategies of Urban Industries: Flanders and Holland

Big cities, particularly the Flemish ones, tried to counter the effect of these threats by pursuing several strategies, both economic and non-economic. The main economic response was diversification and specializing in the high-quality segment of woollen cloth production, i.e. concentrating on luxury products, as the large cities in Flanders did around 1300. Although it made cloth production more dependent on fine foreign wool, especially English wool, which was imported in thousands of tonnes to Flanders in the 14th century, the shift offered various advantages. In such luxury segments towns could profit most from the advantages they possessed: safety and security, a highly skilled labour force, opportunities for division of labour, strict regulation and quality control, and an international reputation resulting from this. Also, transaction costs for marketing the expensive products were relatively low.

Another strategy was the use of non-economic coercion, most clearly in linen and cloth production. Urban governments, particularly when dominated by guilds, as they were in Flanders, tried to prohibit rural industries and strove to acquire and apply urban privileges in trade and production, mainly starting in the 14th century.[64] In the linen sector the endeavours of the towns were mainly aimed at forcing the finishing, bleaching, and marketing of rural products to the towns. This policy, observed in inland Flanders but perhaps even clearer in Hainaut, reserved the highest value-added production stages for the towns and allowed urban merchants control over marketing the product, providing them with an excellent basis for monopsonic exploitation through trade. In the cloth sector, town governments even tried to eliminate all rural production, except for the labour-intensive spinning and other preparatory activities, which were an essential and cheap complement to urban production. In the 13th century, production of woollen cloth was probably still important in the Flemish countryside,[65] but this changed around 1300, as the Flemish cities started to eliminate rural competition in weaving and finishing, using privileges received from the count to justify their actions,[66] and not hesitating to apply force. Ghent and Ypres adopted this policy, as did the smaller city of Oudenaarde. Fines were imposed for possession of looms and shearing tables, and sometimes even more drastic action was taken, such as an armed campaign of urban militias aimed at confiscating or destroying rural looms.

The third type of strategy combined the preceding elements of quality improvement and non-economic force, and was aimed at slowing or prohibiting

---

[64] Sections III.3, pp. 107–108, and V.4, pp. 229–230. See also Sabbe, *De Belgische vlasnijverheid*, 87–103, and Van Bavel, 'Proto-industrialization'.

[65] This is assumed, for instance by Thoen, *Landbouwekonomie*, 1013–1014, although clear evidence is scarce.

[66] Van Uytven, 'Die ländliche Industrie', esp. 65–67, and Nicholas, *Town and countryside*, 99–116 and 188–221.

the mechanization of certain stages of cloth production. The most striking example was the partial disappearance of the fulling mill. Substituting mechanical fulling for foot fulling—a very complex and time-consuming process—could enormously reduce the costs involved in this production stage. Foot fulling required four days' labour for a master fuller and two journeymen per cloth, but mechanical fulling by water-driven hammers took less than a day per cloth and required only one workman.[67] In the 13th and early 14th centuries, some fulling mills were used in towns in Brabant, Namur, and Artois, but shortly afterwards they all but disappeared from urban cloth production, even though the population decline and the associated rise in wages should have made their use more attractive. The main reason for the decline of the fulling mill seems to have been that drapers and merchants refrained from using it, or were opposed to it, fearing that it would harm the reputation of their high-quality urban cloth on international markets, since the assumption was that mechanical fulling could damage the cloth.[68] This was associated with the shift to high-quality cloth production as observed in many towns in Flanders and Brabant around 1300. In addition, the fullers' guilds may have encouraged restrictions on the use of fulling mills to protect the employment of their members. Not surprisingly, therefore, the fulling mill remained in use and was even increasingly used in the small production centres in Artois, such as Aire and Hesdin, and around the Vesdre, where cheap cloth was produced and guilds were weak or absent.[69] In the Vesdre area, even before 1413, four fulling mills operated in the village of Verviers, foreshadowing the later structure and flourishing of cloth production there.

A similar process can be observed in the application of labour-saving iron carders.[70] This instrument, introduced in the 13th century, saved time carding the wool, but produced a slightly rougher quality yarn, and was thus banned by most drapers and cloth merchants, particularly in cities concentrating on luxury cloth, as in 14th-century Flanders and Brabant. Even more time could be saved by using the spinning wheel, introduced in the north-west European woollen sector in the late 13th century; it was well suited to using carded rather than combed wool. This instrument allowed for a reduction of labour input in time-consuming spinning by more than half.[71] This was important, since spinning often caused a bottleneck in cloth production because of the high labour input requirements. But, again, in Flemish cloth production its use was restricted or even banned, particularly for the warp, because of the poorer quality and greater brittleness of the thread it produced, as explicitly stated in the Bruges *Livre des Mestiers* in 1349. These instruments were improved later, with a favourable

---

[67] Munro, 'Industrial entrepreneurship'.
[68] Munro, 'The symbiosis', 45–53. For urban regulation, see also above, sections III.3, and V.3, pp. 205–210.
[69] Van Uytven, 'The fulling mill'. See below, p. 363, for the 16th-century growth in cloth production there.
[70] Munro, 'Medieval woollens', esp. 197–202.   [71] Munro, 'Textile technology', esp. 697–701.

effect on the quality of the products. The 'Saxony spinning wheel', introduced in the second half of the 15th century, made it possible to shape, twist, and wind the yarn simultaneously in one smooth, continuous motion, producing a fine-quality yarn. Although some towns lifted the bans at this time, with Brussels and Louvain doing so in 1467, restrictions on the use of the spinning wheel remained in force in the larger Flemish and Brabantine cloth centres.

The above strategies were not universally adopted by cloth-producing towns in the Low Countries. Holland textile centres such as Haarlem and Leiden, for instance, did not do so. In contrast to the large Flemish towns, they did not concentrate on high-quality production, offered far less resistance to the introduction of labour-saving techniques, and did little to suppress rural activities.[72] The attempts by the Holland cities in the 15th century to suppress weaving and fulling in the countryside were only half-hearted.[73] Moreover, since they had less political weight than their Flemish counterparts, the Holland cities did not have much success. Rural producers were still making cloth, at least the cheaper varieties, using mainly local wool. This was very common throughout the later Middle Ages, until well into the 16th century, even in the immediate surroundings of cloth giant Leiden, which contrasts with the situation around the urban cloth centres in Flanders.

Another difference was in the application of technology. At least periodically there were shortages of unskilled rural labour in Holland. When combined with the generally high level of wages there and the lack of legal instruments to coerce rural labour, this stimulated entrepreneurs to use labour-saving techniques. In the Holland cloth sector, the use of the spinning wheel seems to have been relatively widespread, increasing further in the 15th and 16th centuries; first for weft yarn, but from 1500 also for the warp, even in the larger cloth-producing towns.[74] There is, however, one similarity with Flanders: the absence of fulling mills in town and countryside. The first fulling mill in Holland was built in the city of Haarlem (in 1527),[75] but subsequently the Estates of Holland and the cities restricted the use of such mills, and the entrepreneurs showed no desire to install more of them, at least until the end of the 16th century.

A final difference was the quality of products. The larger Flemish cities concentrated on production of luxuries from 1300, but the absence of a powerful noble elite in Holland and the strength of the urban middle classes there led to a focus on products for the latter, which also found markets elsewhere in north-west Europe. Cloth production in Holland, of various types of quality, started to rise in the 14th and early 15th centuries.[76] In 1400 almost 10,000 pieces of cloth were produced annually in the city of Leiden alone. The other rising industrial sector in

---

[72] Van Bavel, 'Proto-industrialization'.
[73] Posthumus, *Geschiedenis*, i: 102–105 and i: 115–117, and Jansma, 'Het economisch overwicht'.
[74] Posthumus, *Geschiedenis*, i: 57–58.   [75] Kaptein, *De Hollandse textielnijverheid*, 164–165.
[76] Ibid., 42–44, 52–54, and 62–69.

the Holland towns which mainly aimed at middle-class demand was the breweries. Brewing had always been a household activity, but in the 12th and 13th centuries it had become professionalized, and investments had been made in technological improvements. Specialist brewers who eliminated domestic production came to work for an ever-widening market. This process was most pronounced in Holland. Especially from 1325 on, when urban brewers started to replace *gruit* or grut with hops and successfully adopted new brewing techniques, a thriving brewing industry started to develop in Holland cities.[77] These brewers were very successful, both in Holland and abroad. Cities such as Gouda, Haarlem, and Delft soon had dozens or even hundreds of brewers of hop beer, with markets mainly in Brabant and Flanders. Around the middle of the 14th century, production in these three towns reached some 11 million litres in total, increasing dramatically in the following decades to some 30 million litres around 1400.[78]

The differences between the Holland and Flemish industries, which were apparent around 1300, became even more marked from the middle of the 14th century.[79] The population decline and associated changes in purchasing power favoured the middle groups in society and stimulated demand for consumer items for this market. This benefited Holland industries, which already specialized in products that did not require the finest production methods, but competed on the basis of reasonable prices, and which had already adopted many labour-saving techniques, partly because of the high wages and the relatively low cost of capital there. This difference became more crucial when the population decline drove up wages in industries all over Europe. The fact that the population decline in Holland was less pronounced than elsewhere gave Holland industries an additional boost in international competition. Aided by its good location and transport facilities, and by the open institutional framework of exchange, Holland industries were now able to reach consumers internationally, profiting from the growing consumer demand from the middle classes. They marketed massive quantities of brick for those able to build their houses in this material, of peat used for heating purposes, and of relatively high value-added foodstuffs such as herring, cheese, and butter, in addition to middle-range cloth, linen, and beer. On the other hand, Flemish urban industries, having chosen to concentrate on luxury products around 1300, were unfavourably affected by the population decline in this period. Elite consumers, who often obtained their revenues from land or entrepreneurial activities, were hit by declining prices for agricultural products and rising wages, reducing demand for luxury goods. Moreover, in the Flemish cities, there was greater opposition to adopting labour-saving techniques, and this had a detrimental effect in this period of rising wages and must have led to loss in middle-class markets precisely when such techniques became more important.

[77] Unger, 'Technical change'. See also section VI.3, p. 299.
[78] Unger, *History of brewing*, 50–68.
[79] Van Bavel and Van Zanden, 'The jump-start', 526–528.

Technological Innovation

One of the sectors where changes were biggest was building. The 12th and 13th centuries saw a boom in building in stone in the Low Countries. Castles, churches, and houses were built in stone or brick by the thousand, which promoted stone quarrying and brick production. Increasingly, stone was quarried in the Low Countries rather than being imported, as evidenced by the sharp decline *c.*1200 in imports of tuff from the Eifel, formerly a main source of stone. The large-scale quarrying of slate now emerged in the Ardennes, at Fumay and Rimogne, near the present French–Belgian border.[80] Production was organized particularly by abbeys, but in the 13th century private entrepreneurs appeared on the stage, often entering into partnerships to bear the high expenses of acquiring concessions or quarries from the abbeys. Quarrying itself was simple, consisting of opencast mining, using fairly basic tools. At first, the stone was destined mainly for use by the abbeys themselves, but when quarrying became more regular and took place at a larger scale in the 13th century, the market became its destination. The slate was mainly transported downstream via the Meuse and sold in the central Meuse valley, but soon it was also transported further, even up to Holland. The same development can be observed, for instance, with limestone, quarried in the Ardennes and around Tournai, with sandstone quarried on a massive scale in Bentheim, just across the present German border, and with marl, quarried close to the surface in the area around Maastricht, and used for marling land and in building.[81]

In the same period, from the second half of the 12th century, brick production began in the Low Countries. Brick ovens sprang up particularly in regions where natural stone was unavailable, and clay and turf could easily be dug, as in Friesland and Holland.[82] In Holland, along the Oude Rijn near Leiden and along the Hollandse IJssel, increasing numbers of bricks, floor tiles, and roofing tiles were produced. The building of hundreds of castles was a major stimulus for the brick industry, particularly in the 12th and 13th centuries, as was the walling of the ever-growing number of cities, from the 13th century on, requiring tens of millions of bricks. Many brick ovens were operated by the urban governments, and the number of private ovens increased. Growing demand for brick building materials was also a result of the increasing number of brick-built houses in the cities. At first, bricks were only used for the patrician houses, but by the 13th century the wooden and half-timbered houses of ordinary townsmen were being replaced by brick houses roofed with tiles; the process greatly accelerated in the early 14th century,[83] further pushing up demand for bricks and tiles.

---

[80] Fanchamps, 'Les ardoisières des Ardennes'.   [81] Engelen, '2500 jaar winning van kalksteen'.
[82] Hollestelle, *De steenbakkerij in de Nederlanden*, 12–22 and 100–127, and below, pp. 356–360.
[83] Kolman, 'Verstening van woonhuizen'. See also section VI.4, pp. 320–321, and, for the building of castles, section III.1, pp. 64–66.

Demand for building materials was also stimulated by the massive building programmes of churches. In Friesland and Groningen, in the late 12th and 13th centuries, many Romanesque and Romano-Gothic village churches were built of brick; about 30 of these still stand and a further 40 survive in part. In the 13th century many large Gothic churches emerged in the cities, particularly in the south. The construction of these churches and their tall towers, with ever higher vaults and spires, required not only huge amounts of stone, brick, lead, and glass, and ample capital, but also technical skills and advanced knowledge of materials, processing, and construction. Such specialized skills were rare and the few labourers who had these skills were sometimes grouped in lodges, where their skills could be transferred. Their empirical knowledge revolutionized the art of building in the 13th century, and lent maximum light to the churches. Perhaps this process was supported by the growing theoretical knowledge of stereotomy, as practised by architect-engineers such as Villard de Honnecourt, who worked in and around Cambrai between 1225 and 1250.[84] He devised perpetual motion wheels, water-powered saws, and catapults, and became famous as a master architect, using inventions such as flying buttresses.

The early rise of Gothic architecture is a clear indicator of the availability and development of human and physical capital. In the 13th-century Low Countries, two regions stand out in this respect: inland Flanders, where the *Scheldegotiek* found expression in the churches of Ypres, Ghent, Oudenaarde, Kortijk, and nearby Tournai, and slightly later, the Meuse valley, with the *Maasgotiek* in Maastricht, Meerssen, Thorn, Liège, Walcourt, Dinant, and Huy.[85] In the same period, from the early 13th century, civic architecture developed as well, with large town halls, cloth and meat halls, belfries, and impressive infirmaries being built in stone. Again, Flanders led the way, as with the cloth hall of Ypres, with its 130-m façade, and the hospital ward of the Bijloke in Ghent, 16 m wide, 55 m long, and 18 m high, built in 1228/9.

The belfries and some other public buildings were increasingly adorned with modern mechanical clocks. At the end of the 13th century, weight-driven, escapement-controlled clocks were introduced, making it possible to keep track of time precisely. Some decades later, turret clocks with mechanisms which struck every hour appeared as public clocks, first in Italy, but only a decade or so later also in the Low Countries. Public clocks were installed in Valenciennes (1325–44) and Bruges (probably in 1345), and next in Ghent (1376), Tournai (1377), and Kortrijk (1382), in most cases at the initiative of the town government.[86] In this period the centre of public clock construction shifted from Italy to the Low Countries. Technicians from the Low Countries must have had a solid reputation

---

[84] Gimpel, *The medieval machine*, 114–146, and Lalblat, Margueritte, and Martin, 'De la stéréotomie médiévale'.
[85] Van de Walle, *De gotiek in België*, 33–36, 47–54, and 60–64, and Timmers, *De kunst van het Maasland*, ii: 20–39.
[86] Dohrn van Rossum, 'The diffusion of the public clocks'.

in this area: clockmaker Jan van Delft, who worked earlier in Dendermonde with two colleagues from Delft, was hired in London in 1368–77. Associated with the rise of the mechanical clock in the same period, the unequal canonical hours were replaced in the Low Countries by precise, regular hours.[87] All this can be linked to the need to regulate labour and the length of the working day, and thus to the early rise of hired or wage labour in this part of Europe. It was also associated with the need to regulate trade, which was the explicit goal of the public clock installed near the cloth hall in Valenciennes, for instance. In the 15th century both the public clocks and the modern hours had become standard.

In industries, too, the 11th to 13th centuries saw rapid, almost revolutionary, technological innovation. After the older vertical loom had been replaced by the horizontal pedal loom in the high Middle Ages, allowing for higher-quality, more densely woven cloth, the heavy horizontal broad loom was introduced in the 13th century, principally in the Flemish cities. The broad loom, which was operated by two men, was able to produce better quality cloth as well as to raise labour productivity.[88] The 12th and 13th centuries also saw significant improvement in mill technology, with the introduction of the overshot mill, often supplied with a mill race. To store hydraulic energy and ensure a steady supply of water, weirs were sometimes constructed, at the same time fulfilling a role in water management and offering opportunities for pisciculture. The basin of the small river Zenne in the area around Brussels probably had about 45 water mills before 1200, which increased to more than 110 around 1450.[89] Many were supplied with a pond and mill race, in some cases up to a kilometre long, requiring large investments but increasing the number of locations suitable for the construction of a mill. Also, mills, driven by water or wind, were now increasingly adapted and used for industrial production, as in fulling and woad production, as well as for hammering iron, milling oak bark for tanning, grinding metal, and sawing wood. These industrial mills were introduced in the 11th to 13th centuries, but they became very widespread in the 14th century, pushing forward mechanization of industrial production.

Not all innovations were immediately applied on a large scale, and technological change was sometimes slowed by non-economic considerations and restrictions, as with the spinning wheel and fulling mill, and perhaps even more clearly with ordinary grain mills. In the high Middle Ages the strength of banal authority may have been a stimulus to construct mills in the countryside, but in the later Middle Ages it became an obstacle. The wider availability of capital and the lower cost of credit could have made possible the building of more mills by private investors, but privileges and banal rights restricted the number, particularly where banal lords were powerful, as in Namur.[90] This made

---

[87] Prevenier, 'Ouderwets en modern'. See also section V.3, pp. 205–206.
[88] Munro, 'Medieval woollens'. [89] Deligne, *Bruxelles et sa rivière*, 19–23, 36–43, and 263.
[90] Genicot, *L'économie rurale*, iii: 99–102. See also section IV.2, pp. 158–160.

distances to mills longer than necessary, sometimes 6 km or more, and waiting times for milling became long, provoking resistance and evasion by countrymen and causing huge losses of time.

In other areas, however, technological innovations were increasingly applied, particularly in the late 14th and 15th centuries. This happened mainly in rural industries where guild restrictions were absent, but also more generally because of the scarcity of labour and relatively high wages of the period, making investment in labour-saving techniques more attractive. Innovation was particularly extensive in the iron industry. Blast furnaces built of stone, up to 4 of 5 m high, gradually replaced the small wind furnaces from the middle of the 14th century, around Liège and some decades later between Sambre and Meuse.[91] Earlier, from the 12th and 13th centuries, this industry had been relocated to the water courses in order to use water power to power the bellows. These water-powered blast furnaces were not very large, but they were much larger than the ovens used before and allowed for producing larger volumes of iron (and also foundry iron) and better removal of impurities. They employed a relatively large number: some 20 to 25 permanent, specialized labourers, and some 150 temporary ones for carrying, mining, and burning charcoal. In the county of Namur the 14th-century iron industry was no longer organized on estates, as in the area between Sambre and Meuse, where the iron workers were organized in communities and acquired some self-determination. In 1384 five mining and iron-producing villages formed an association and drew up their own statutes, providing a strong counterweight to the local and territorial lords.[92] Forges were mainly operated and owned by associations of iron workers. In the Liège area, on the other hand, the industry had a corporative character and was mainly practised on the large estates of religious institutions and lords, which also supplied the ore and wood. The lords leased out the iron works to professional furnace-masters, who often became entrepreneurs.

The development of this sector was in part associated with the rise of the arms industry in Wallonia. In the later Middle Ages there was an evolution in military techniques linked to the introduction of gunpowder, as well as a dramatic increase in the amounts of money spent on warfare,[93] and the southern Low Countries became a centre of arms production. Cannons, first made of copper or bronze and later of iron, were introduced in the late 13th century and were produced there in large numbers by the early 15th century, including some of the largest cannons of the time, such as the 'Dulle Griet' in Ghent, which weighed more than 16 tonnes, or the 35-tonne cannon in Brussels. Ghent in 1479 had no fewer than 486 cannons and guns, and often ordered many thousands of cannonballs per year.

[91] Bourguignon, 'Le sidérurgie', esp. 86–90.
[92] Sprandel, *Das Eisengewerbe*, 131–132, and Gillard, *L'industrie du fer*, 9–11.
[93] For the following: Contamine, *La guerre au Moyen Age*, 258–275, and for fiscality and centralization: section VI.1, pp. 263–268.

Towns such as Liège, Huy, Dinant, and Maastricht had long been regional centres of arms production, but in the 16th century Liège began to stand out. It gained an international reputation for producing cast-iron cannons, guns, and ammunition, with the casting of iron cannon balls increasing there from the beginning of the 15th century.[94] In the second half of the 16th century, the development of plate hammering using hydraulic tilt hammers in the valley of the Vesdre river near Liège allowed for mechanization of parts of the production of armour. The same area began to produce gunpowder made of saltpetre, sulphur, and charcoal. Demand for this product was huge, since the weight of the gunpowder used was nearly as much as that of the ball fired. Often tens of thousands of pounds of powder were needed for a military campaign. There was also mining and preparation of sulphates and vitriol used in the production of textiles, metal, and mordant, and the production of alum for dyeing textiles. These technologies all emerged in the Liège area in the first quarter of the 16th century and grew in the late 16th century. The distillation and refinement of such products, partly mined in this region, required very expensive factories which cost thousands of guilders and more, as well as enormous amounts of fuel. Here the Liège area had an advantage, with its easy access to coal, and its most successful entrepreneur in the late 16th century, Jean Curtius, began by producing powder and saltpetre in 1576, and linked this to the mining of coal.[95]

The rising demand for cannons and cannonballs, as well as for iron household utensils, cauldrons, cast-iron stoves, and agricultural tools, further stimulated the metallurgical sector, which flourished in Wallonia in the 15th and 16th centuries. At the same time, the rise of capitalist production relationships and the weakening of corporative restrictions, leading to a scale-enlargement of production units, also stimulated investment in labour-saving techniques. In the 16th century improvements were introduced in the iron industry, with ever-bigger blast furnaces, which were rectangular stone-built pyramids, 5 to 10 m high, and producing 100 tonnes of iron per year; the bigger ones could even produce up to 200 tonnes. Several such furnaces were built in the Liège area, for example, around Huy on the Hoyoux river and around Durbuy on the Ourthe river. In 1500 the small area around Durbuy had no fewer than seven iron foundries and six blast furnaces. Some villages in this area owed their existence almost entirely to mining and forging.

Namur and the area between Sambre and Meuse were even larger centres of iron production, although the techniques employed there were probably somewhat less sophisticated than those used in England and the Eifel. Around the middle of the 16th century, when metallurgy was flourishing, this area had 70 forges and 32 blast furnaces. In total, some 10,000 tonnes of iron were

[94] Gaier: *Four centuries of Liège gunmaking*, 18 and 27–29, and *L'industrie et le commerce*, 149–154.
[95] Lejeune, *La formation du capitalisme*, 157–169 and 279–300.

produced annually in Wallonia at the time, or almost 10 per cent of the total production in Europe.[96] After this period, the centre of metallurgy shifted to the Pays Gaumois in Luxembourg, on the northern edge of Lorraine, where in 1574 52 blast furnaces were working, and later on there were even more. In the 17th century the area of the Ardennes and Eifel in total had some 500 blast furnaces.[97] The production of iron required large amounts of charcoal: for each 1,000 kg of foundry iron produced, some 10,000 kg of wood was needed, that is: 1,000 to 2,000 tonnes of wood per oven per year. This shows how devastating the effect of the iron industry on the forests was, although in Namur the forests only came to be depleted in the 18th century. Lead- and ironworking also caused heavy pollution, as is shown by the aerosols deposited in peat bogs in the Hautes Fagnes, indicating that levels of lead and bromine were as high as in the industrialized 20th century, and levels of titanium were as much as two-and-a-half times higher than today.[98]

From 1560 on, the iron industry in the Liège area underwent some transformations, as smelting stagnated when production departed for more southern regions, but the processing of iron rapidly grew in importance. This was helped by the plentiful supply of coal, which could not be used for smelting but was suitable for processing activities. It was helped even more by technological progress in the Liège area, with many capital-intensive investments being made in new techniques, which increased labour productivity and reduced prices.[99] Watermills and windmills were increasingly used for metalworking, for forging, cutting, grinding, and polishing metal. At the beginning of the 15th century, six mechanical forge hammers were operating between Meuse and Sambre, as well as in Hainaut, around what would later be Charleroi. In 1560 the county of Namur had 85 forge hammers, but the largest ironworking area was around Liège, where the production of sheet iron, tools, nails, and all kinds of hardware was concentrated. Around 1500 the slitting mill was introduced, perhaps even invented, in the Liège area.[100] Such mills provided the smiths with slender rods that could easily be converted to nails, often by proto-industrial peasant-smiths. In the late 16th century this mill was further developed into a rolling and slicing mill, producing iron sheets and slicing them into easy-to-process rods. One rolling mill could produce some 200 tonnes of these rods annually. Second to Holland, the Liège area or Meuse valley took the greatest advantage of technological innovations in industries in the late medieval Low Countries, and it had an even greater emphasis on costly fixed-capital goods and high consumption of energy.

[96] Hansotte, 'Contribution à l'histoire'. Estimates for Wallonia collected by Kellenbenz, 'Europäisches Eisen', 439–440, are incomplete and much too low.
[97] Bourguignon, 'Le sidérurgie', esp. 86–90, and Gillard, L'industrie du fer, 47–56.
[98] Frenzel, Görres, and Kempter, 'Die frühe landwirtschaftliche und gewerbliche Tätigheit'.
[99] Gutmann, Toward the modern economy, 61–63.
[100] Hansotte, 'La métallurgie wallonne', esp. 36, and Gale, Iron and steel, 21–22.

Sources of Energy

Energy consumption and extraction of fuels greatly increased in the 12th to 14th centuries. Huge areas of peat were dug in this period, particularly in coastal Flanders and north-western Brabant. After most of the woods in Flanders had been felled, and the remains were protected by comital law, the growing cities had to turn to turf for fuel. In the 12th century, this was acquired mainly from the coastal areas in the west and north of Flanders, but from the middle of the 13th century it became necessary to go further afield, to north-western Brabant. Investors from Bruges and Ghent, some 100–150 km away, bought concessions to dig hundreds of hectares there. In the Zevenbergse Moer alone, in 1306, at least 36 people and institutions from Bruges possessed rights to the peatlands.[101] These concession holders also built the physical infrastructure, which consisted of canals, roads, discharging berths of several hectares, and harbours. In 1325, 100 km of main canals had been dug here, up to 12 m wide and 2 m deep, with dams, sluices, and drains to ensure navigability. Total production in this area in the last quarter of the 13th century was some 650,000 m^3 of raw peat per year, increasing in the first quarter of the 14th century to 1.2 million m^3 per year, dug by some 700 labourers. This was a first but decisive step in the shift from organic to mineral fuel in the Low Countries, and was taken much earlier than in most other parts of Europe. (See Table 7.4.)

The shift to mineral fuel received a further impetus in the 14th to 16th centuries, when coal was increasingly used to generate energy, especially in the area around Liège, where it had been mined earlier but on a smaller scale. Around the middle of the 13th century there were some 45 coal mines in the area around Mons and probably even more around Liège, the oldest coal-mining district in Europe. Mining was financed via joint investments by landowners and entrepreneurs, such as the Abbey of Val Saint-Lambert in Seraing, which in 1313 constructed a major canal north-west of Liège to drain the mine shafts, and which was used further downstream to power some mills and supply water for the fountains

Table 7.4 Amounts of raw peat extracted in the Low Countries, 1200–1599 (raw peat in m^3 millions per year)

Year	Flanders	Holland	NW Brabant	North	Total
1200–1299	0.5	0	0.2	0	0.7
1300–1399	0.5	1.3	0.9	1.3	4.3
1400–1499	0.5	2.7	0.7	2.2	6.0
1500–1549	0.3	3.6	0.7	3.0	7.6
1550–1599	0	9.0	0.6	7.1	16.7

Source: Leenders, *Verdwenen venen*, 257–261 and 268–269.

[101] For background on this discussion see, generally, Leenders, *Verdwenen venen*, 139–155; and for Flanders: Nicholas, *Town and countryside*, 135–136 and 290–293.

in the city of Liège. Next, the abbey contracted with groups of entrepreneurs to organize the actual mining, as in 1356, when four entrepreneurs contracted to mine coal in a 7 hectare plot owned by the abbey for one-fifth of the net yield plus 4 per cent for use of the canal.[102] The coal mines at the time were still fairly small, however. Even in the early 15th century, when mining had grown further in importance, output from a typical mine near Mons was no more than 147 tonnes per year, with some 10 labourers employed per mine.[103] In total about 2,000 workers were employed in coal mining at the time in the Liège area.

The real acceleration occurred in the 16th century, when mining was undertaken on a larger scale and output grew. In the Hainaut coal fields, some 30 labourers were employed in each mine, and in the mines near Liège, on the left bank of the Meuse, often up to 100 were employed.[104] In 1510 some 25,000 tonnes were produced annually around Liège; by 1545 the figure was 48,000 tonnes, and in 1562 it had risen to 90,000 tonnes, of which 40 per cent was exported, probably mostly north along the Meuse. In the second half of the 16th century, there was a rise in the number of consortia of entrepreneurs in mining around Kerkrade and Aachen, and particularly around Liège. Such consortia invested heavily in the mines, making the area the most developed coal-mining district in Europe at the time. Around 1560 many mines were about 100 m deep, and in Liège some even went to 350 m, much more than the 50 m depth common in 17th-century England. Such depths were made possible by improved mining techniques and using adits to carry off the water. The deeper the mineshafts became, the more expensive they were, requiring major investments to acquire the mine, up to tens of thousands of guilders, not to mention wages, wood, iron, and bricks for baskets and hampers to lift the coal; tubs, pumps, and bucket chains to drain water from the mine; and chains, horses, horse harnesses, and ventilation shafts.

Coal was also imported from Newcastle and Sunderland, particularly to areas in the north of the Low Countries. By the late 14th century, at least 1,500 tonnes a year were shipped to Holland. However, although the importance of coal was increasing, even in the 16th century peat was still the main source of energy in the Low Countries. There were various peat areas, with the location of digging constantly shifting, since peat layers became exhausted or impossible to reach because of problems with ground water. In the Holland peat area in particular, where major water problems already existed, large-scale digging of peat undermined hydrologic safety and reduced the amount of agricultural land. The most telling example is the Haarlemmermeer, a group of smaller lakes, which steadily extended into one giant lake of no less than 17,000 hectares. This happened as a direct result of cutting peat and indirectly from the erosion of the

---

[102] Kranz, 'Clergy and coal'.   [103] Van Uytven, 'Die ländliche Industrie', 59–60.
[104] Lejeune, *La formation du capitalisme*, 129–136, and Kranz, *Lütticher Steinkohlenbergbau*.

weakened shores, a process that had begun before the middle of the 15th century and progressed with the intensification of peat-digging.[105]

The authorities took some action to tackle these problems through regulation, but the interests and vested rights of landowners and entrepreneurs made it difficult to change existing practice.[106] Restrictions and maximums were imposed, enforced by fines, but the offenders simply paid the fines. Either it was more lucrative to pay the fine and break the law, or the enforcement of the law was lax because of corruption or the weakness of the authorities when faced with the powerful urban entrepreneurs. Another policy which had more success was to use legislation to influence the method of digging. For instance, it was decided that digging should be done in compartments, with small dikes to protect the affected land, and when the digging was finished, trees were to be planted and the land made suitable for agriculture again. Most effective, however, was investment in technical methods to drain and create new polders, reclaiming the land from the water. In this process the wind- and watermill played a large part; by 1500 some 215 windmills were used for drainage purposes in Holland, with about 50 new ones being established each decade. Installing them required advances in several fields.[107] First, large amounts of capital had to be available, since the mills required major investments. Again, cheap capital and the accessible capital market in Holland facilitated such investments, in combination with the increasing profitability of agriculture in the 16th century that resulted from rising food prices. Moreover, establishing a wind- or watermill required additional investment in water management for building dikes, canals, and reservoirs. Further, institutional and coordination problems had to be solved, since building a mill raised water levels outside the drained polder. Technical improvement in windmills and sluice technology were also needed. One major step was the gradual, pragmatic innovation of the windmill brake, which was required to stop the machines. This was especially pressing because windmills were becoming ever larger in the 14th and 15th centuries, with wing spans up to 20 m, as large as modern windmills. Around 1400 the Flemish brake was developed, which enabled more regular braking that used less pressure on the spur wheel, which led to less wear and tear but required that the carpenter install it with great precision.[108]

The largest windmills could provide from 20 to 150 hp, considerably more than the 5 to 7 hp that could be provided by watermills, which made them important sources of energy, particularly in the coastal areas.[109] In southern Flanders, around Lille and Douai, 96 of the 145 villages investigated had mills

[105] Van Dam, *Vissen in veenmeren*, 58–70. See also section II.2, pp. 45–46.
[106] Van Dam, 'De tanden van de waterwolf', 81–91.
[107] Van Bavel and Van Zanden, 'The jump-start', 520–521.
[108] Coutant and Groen, 'The early history', 1–17.
[109] Davids, 'Innovations in windmill technology', Van Olst & Boekwijt, *Delftse windmolens*, 16–23, and Derville, 'Moulins, cultures industrielles'.

in the mid-16th century, with a total of 194, of which only 23 were watermills. Among them were 130 grain mills, about one for every 120 households, as well as 14 for processing woad, and no fewer than 44, often owned by Lille merchants, for pressing oil. There were even more in Holland, where numerous large windmills were built, particularly in the towns: Delft had 9 post mills within the town and 3 large, fixed brick tower mills on the city walls, which were erected in the 15th century. In the late 16th century the total energy produced by windmills in Holland would otherwise have required tens of thousands of horses. This energy was increasingly used also for industrial purposes, with hundreds of industrial windmills erected in late 16th-century Holland, as technical innovations were implemented and windmills were adapted for sawing, pressing oil, and processing hemp, with Holland in the vanguard of innovation.

Thanks to the wind- and watermills and the favourable economic and institutional setting, the difficulties presented by water in Holland could to a large extent be overcome. The increasing use of windmills to remove the water, combined with the construction of dikes as well as the use of scoops to enable large-scale dredging of peat below the water table from *c.*1530, made possible a new round of large-scale extraction in Holland.[110] In the village of Zegwaard alone the annual output was 35,000 to 40,000 barrels (8 million litres) in 1520–1, which rose to 140,000 to 150,000 barrels in the 1560s.[111] About 200 peat diggers worked there, including 130 from Zegwaard itself. The total peat output in Holland can be roughly estimated. In the period 1540–65, some 1 to 1.5 million barrels of turf were exported yearly from Gouda and Rotterdam.[112] Added to this were exports through other cities (such as Delfshaven); about 500,000 to 800,000 barrels of turf used in the Delft and Gouda breweries; about 500,000 barrels needed in the brick ovens and lime kilns; and the turf used for heating and other purposes. In the Holland peat area, this would amount to a total output of turf of perhaps 4 to 6 million barrels per year around the middle of the 16th century. Alternative calculations based on the number of hectares of peatland and the thickness of the peat layers result in even higher estimates, up to 6 million m^3 of wet peat (or 2.3 million m^3 of dried turf, i.e. some 10 million barrels) annually in the 17th century for all of the Holland–Utrecht peat region.[113] Easy access to large quantities of peat was an advantage for Holland's industries, particularly those requiring thermal power, such as brewing, bleaching, salt refining, and brick making.

The availability of peat did not automatically promote economic development, however.[114] Drenthe, in the north-east of the Low Countries, also had vast

---

[110] Ibelings, 'Het begin van het slagturven'. For the consequent ecological problems, also below, pp. 368–369.
[111] De Vries, *Dutch rural economy*, 65 and 203.
[112] Diepeveen, *De ververing*, 133–136, and Van Bavel, 'Proto-industrialization', 1137–1139.
[113] De Zeeuw, 'Peat and the Dutch Golden Age', whose estimates seem to be confirmed by Cornelisse, *Energiemarkten*, 250–271.
[114] Van Zanden, 'The ecological constraints'.

reservoirs of peat, yet that did not promote economic growth or industrialization there. Rather, these reservoirs were exploited by Amsterdam entrepreneurs in the 17th century, with the peat being exported to Holland; the only activity stimulated in Drenthe was the simple work of poor peat diggers. The export of peat, and later coal, over large distances was very feasible if waterways existed or could be constructed profitably, as in north-western Brabant where peat was exported to Flanders in the 13th century. Still, the presence of peat was favourable for Holland and helped the growth of Holland's industries. In the period 1480–1572, fuel became cheaper in Holland, especially compared with wages and food prices.[115] From *c*.1540 fuel prices rose rapidly in Antwerp and Flanders to a level some 50 per cent higher than in Holland. This situation allowed for higher energy consumption per capita in Holland than elsewhere and gave the Holland industries a clear advantage in energy-intensive industries. The export-oriented Holland breweries consumed more than half of the energy used in industries, but baking, refining industries, brick production, chalk burning, and bleaching were also typical capital- and energy-intensive industries favoured by the low cost of capital and peat in Holland. In the beginning of the 16th century in Holland, probably some 14 gigajoules were used annually per capita, which was as much as Holland used in the 17th century, and almost as much as the 16–25 gigajoules used in energy-hungry England around 1700.[116] In the long run, however, the peat in Holland was exhausted, and increasing amounts had to be imported from the northern part of the Low Countries, as well as coal from Wallonia and England. Moreover, after the technique of dredging was introduced around 1530, peat digging no longer offered scope for technological innovation, but remained a simple activity performed by large numbers of unskilled labourers, in contrast to coal mining, where investments and innovations strongly increased labour productivity. In the long run the contribution of peat to the Holland economy was limited.

Overlooking these developments, it is clear that the 12th and 13th centuries in the Low Countries marked a clear shift in the field of energy. Wood had always been used, along with human power and that of oxen, but now became much scarcer and was superseded by a whole range of other sources of energy: horse power became more prevalent for transport, but inanimate sources of energy, such as water power and peat, became especially significant. Wind from windmills and sails also became much more important from the 12th century. Combined, these sources of energy allowed for a rise in labour productivity in the 12th and 13th centuries. The next phase was driven by the rise of coal. In the late Middle Ages, it came also to be used for domestic heating, which was enabled by an increasing use of stone or brick chimneys beginning in the

---

[115] Cornelisse, *Energiemarkten*, 188–190 and 212–213.
[116] De Zeeuw, 'Peat and the Dutch Golden Age', Van Zanden, 'Werd de Gouden Eeuw uit turf geboren?', and Cornelisse, *Energiemarkten*, 215–228.

14th century, along with the iron stove, from *c.*1500, which channelled the dirty coal smoke away from the living quarters.[117] Still, peat remained by far the most important source of inanimate energy, as shown by reconstructions for the Dutch Republic in the 17th century. Peat provided 1.2×10^{12} kcal of energy per year, followed by coal, supplying some 40 per cent of this amount, wind for propelling ships about 8 per cent of this, and wind from windmills some 4 per cent.[118] In the shift from organic to mineral sources of energy, turf constituted a very important intermediate stage, and in the late medieval Low Countries it was probably the main stage. Within the Low Countries, Holland had the most favourable situation with respect to energy supply, since it had ample peat, and also many windmills, and easy access to English coal. Energy prices were lower—although not spectacularly lower—and in the 15th and 16th centuries energy consumption was higher than elsewhere. In the long run, however, the Liège region, with its easy access to coal, was to prove even more favoured, especially when peat reserves became exhausted and technological innovation enabled digging in deeper coal layers. This became more crucial in a process that had begun in the 12th century, as ever more inanimate energy was required to drive the increased power needs of production.

Rural and Urban Industries in the 16th Century

In the 16th century, not only the extraction of minerals, but also industrial production boomed in the countryside. In inland Flanders the linen industry had become especially important in the the later Middle Ages. In the 14th century the rural population needed to find additional sources of income, confronted with fragmentation of holdings and later with a declining profitability of agriculture, while the urban monopolies closed off the option of rural cloth production. Linen manufacture came to the fore in Flanders and Hainaut as an alternative, aided by the possibility of combining it with the labour-intensive cultivation of flax.[119] After its rise in the last decades of the 14th century, and a period of stagnation in the second half of the 15th century, rural linen manufacture experienced a second phase of expansion and a definitive breakthrough in the first half of the 16th century, particularly in inland Flanders.[120] At the time, in the countryside this industry employed no less than 20 per cent of the labour input there, which was mainly provided by semi-independent peasants combining activities in linen production with a small agricultural holding.

---

[117] Van Dam, 'Het onderaardse bos', esp. 197–201.
[118] Unger, 'Energy sources', and Table 7.4 above, p. 356. Van Zanden, 'Werd de Gouden Eeuw uit turf geboren?', has a much lower figure for coal.
[119] Sabbe, *De Belgische vlasnijverheid*, i: 74–78 and i:134–155, and Thoen, *Landbouwekonomie*, 980–993.
[120] Thoen, *Landbouwekonomie*, 993–1010, and Sabbe, *De Belgische vlasnijverheid*, i: 167–182. See also Vermaut, 'Vijf variaties op het thema', criticizing the figures offered by Sabbe.

The expansion of this sector in the 16th century can be seen from the rise in the number of pieces of linen traded on the Flemish markets: in Ghent, from 5,300 in 1511 to 14,400 in 1561, and in Oudenaarde from a few thousand in the 15th century to 10,000 to 15,000 around 1570–5. At that time, some 100,000 pieces of linen were traded on the urban markets in Flanders. Increasing numbers were exported. In 1553, no fewer than 87,000 pieces of linen were sent from Flanders to Spain, the main outlet and transit area for trade to America, compared with only 10,000 to 15,000 pieces of linen from Hainaut, which at the time was greatly surpassed by Flanders as the centre of linen production.[121] Although cities hosted some linen weavers, it is safe to assume that by far the greatest part of this linen was produced in the countryside.

To an increasing extent the capital intensive process of bleaching was performed outside Flanders: for example, in 's-Hertogenbosch, and from about 1570 also in Holland, especially in the area around Haarlem. Around 1585, Haarlem had at least 40 bleacheries where large quantities of Flemish linen were bleached.[122] This is a clear example of regional specialization that rapidly increased in the 16th century, mainly as a result of market integration. Another example is the import of yarn from Hessen and Wuppertal to Holland, where it was used by the textile industries.[123] Holland industries clearly concentrated on capital-intensive production and avoided the labour-intensive stages, reflecting the low cost of capital and the high cost of labour there. This regional specialization emerging on the basis of different mixes of production factors stimulated an intense inter-regional trade in raw materials and semi-fabricated goods, as in the linen sector where the production of flax, the spinning of yarn, the weaving of cloth, and the bleaching were each concentrated in different regions. Regional specialization can also be seen in the tapestry manufacture, which appeared in the Flemish countryside in the second half of the 15th century: especially from 1540–50 this sector developed significantly in the southern part of the region, and was highly concentrated around Oudenaarde, the emerging centre for tapestry, and in the Land of Aalst, around Geraardsbergen.[124]

At the same time some areas experienced a rise or renaissance of cloth production, particularly in the rural centres and smaller towns of southern Flanders.[125] One of the elements in the rise of these 'new draperies' was the revival of the light cloth production that had long existed, the *sayetterie*, as in Arras, Lille, and Hondschoote in the 16th century. Production was especially strong in Hondschoote, where around 1565 it peaked at no fewer than 80,000 pieces of *sayes* (a type of light woollen cloth) a year, which were mostly transported overland to

---

[121] Sabbe, *De Belgische vlasnijverheid*, i:167–174 and i:261–267.
[122] Regtdoorzee Greup-Roldanus, *Geschiedenis der Haarlemmer bleekerijen*, 24–28 and 102.
[123] See section VI.2.
[124] Vanwelden, *Het tapijtweversambacht*, 12–15 and 98–101, and Stabel, *De kleine stad*, 190–196.
[125] Munro: 'Spanish merino wools' and 'The new draperies', and Chorley, 'The "draperies légères" '.

the Mediterranean. Hondschoote may well have been the largest cloth-producing centre in Europe at that time. Moreover, the secondary Flemish centres such as Kortrijk, Oudenaarde, and Aalst, and villages on the Flanders–Artois border such as Werveke, Armentières, Nieuwkerk, and Poperinge, produced the cheaper imitations of luxury cloths made of Spanish or Scottish wool rather than high-quality but very expensive English wool. In addition, particularly in French Flanders, there was an innovation in the production of worsteds, which were lighter and thinner than *sayes*— 250–300 g/m^2, as opposed to 600 g/m^2 for cloth made in Lille, and no less than 1,028 g/m^2 for the heavy quality cloth from Armentières.[126] These light worsteds were supple and very fashionable, particularly among the middle groups in society who could not afford the more expensive silks. Elsewhere, as in Weert, in the Campine, the long-established production of cheap, coarse cloth experienced a boom when it found access to international markets.

In general, these fabrics—like the wool-worsted blends and serges—were cheaper and lighter than the older types. These new types of cloth, produced in smaller pieces, typically of only 15–30 m^2, brought in a smaller profit margin but were sold in much greater volumes and had a more rapid turnover. This type of production lent itself well to labour-saving tools, and used carded, wheel-spun wool, for both weft and warp, and the fulling mill. Around Verviers on the Vesdre river the more mechanized cloth industry flourished, with 17 fulling mills in operation around 1525.[127] Cloth production there benefited from low wages, low taxation, and an absence of guilds and craft restrictions. Elsewhere the fullers' guilds still tried to resist the fulling mills, as evidenced by the dispute in Louvain in 1559 and the bloody uprisings of fullers in Mechelen and 's-Hertogenbosch. Most opposition to technological innovation emerged from the small craftsmen, as in late 16th-century Liège, where the small weaver-drapers in the town opposed the introduction of improved looms, since they feared that the expenditure necessary to purchase them would cost them their independence and favour the large producers.[128] They succeeded, but the result led to the eclipse of cloth production in Liège, which lost out to competition from nearby Verviers. On the whole, this type of resistance was unable to stop the process of mechanization, but it created some obstacles in the guild-dominated towns, while there was no resistance in the Vesdre area. This area adjacent to the Meuse valley, also favoured with an abundance of water power, saw a boom in cloth production. Elsewhere in the Meuse valley there was the growth of iron industries, chemical industries, and coal mining. These elements, combined with the availability of agrarian surpluses from neighbouring regions, made the Meuse valley the cradle of the industrial revolution in the Low Countries, and indeed on the European continent.

[126] Clauzel and Calonne, 'Artisanat rural'. [127] Van Uytven, 'The fulling mill'.
[128] Lejeune, *La formation du capitalisme*, 214–216.

Whereas industrial production in the countryside became increasingly regionally specialized, focusing on simple or middle-range products, economic activities in the big cities showed a strong diversification, with the focus on services, finishing industries, and the production of luxury goods. In 's-Hertogenbosch, for instance, the traditional cloth industry declined in the 15th and 16th centuries, whereas there was a rise of sectors such as shoemaking, goldsmiths' art, the manufacture of knives and pins, and the production of hats and bonnets.[129] This industrial reconversion was probably painful, but in the end it succeeded, since the city flourished, growing from 10,000 to 12,000 inhabitants around 1450 to 18,000 to 20,000 around 1530. In the large cities in Flanders and southern Brabant, the concentration on luxury products, which had already started with the transformation of Flemish urban industry around 1300, proceeded even further in the 15th and 16th centuries. Around 1550, in Bruges, Mechelen, Brussels, and most especially in the metropolis of Antwerp, embroidery, satin production, painting, fine tapestry weaving, satin and damask production, sculpture and wood carving, the making of mirrors, printing, music composition, jewellery, and fashion flourished. According to Guicciardini, in the mid-16th century Antwerp had 124 goldsmiths, 300 painters, and 594 tailors and hosiers, compared with only 169 bakers, 78 butchers, and 91 fishmongers.[130] Large cities were well placed for such specialization since the home market offered great purchasing power, easy connections to international markets, guarantees of standard quality through corporative production, and the potential of well-trained workers.[131] Such specialization made skilled labour more important than capital or raw materials as a production factor. Mechanization was impossible in these newly dominant sectors, however. In the light of the later rise of factory industrialization, the development of urban industries in Flanders and Brabant would be a dead end, in contrast to Holland and even more to the Walloon iron industries and the textile industries in Vesdre and Peel, where production was ever further mechanized and labour productivity could be increased by capital investments.

Scale-enlargement and Regional Specialization

A clear example of scale-enlargement, capital investment, and rising productivity was the brewing sector in 15th and 16th century Holland. Total output of breweries in the three major beer-producing towns in Holland rose from 30 million litres in 1400 to 100 million litres around 1570. Three-quarters of this was produced by a mere 100 breweries in the city of Delft alone. Indicative of the scale-enlargement and rise in labour productivity in this sector was the fact that in 1514 Holland had 377 breweries in the towns, employing some 10 workers

---

[129] Blondé, *Sociale structuren*, 131–132.
[130] Dubbe and Vroom, 'Patronage and the art market'.
[131] Stabel, *De kleine stad*, 200–204, and Van der Wee, 'Industrial dynamics', esp. 329–341.

each, whereas at the end of the 16th century there were 183 breweries with 16 workers each, producing the same volume or even more.[132] This increase was promoted by gradual technical improvement and large investments, for instance, in ever-larger kettles, allowing the breweries to produce 6,000 litres or more for each brew, which was the average in Holland brewing around 1560. These kettles were now increasingly placed on iron grates with walls around them, allowing the workers to stand over the kettle and stir the wort. Breweries became massive constructions and required large investments in fixed capital, which could be made only by large urban-based brewers with their capital reserves. Quotas and restrictions, initially adopted to protect the small brewers, were increasingly lifted because the political weight of the large brewers in Holland urban governments was overwhelming, as can be seen most clearly in Gouda. The benefits of scale-enlargement, such as lower unit costs and better marketing opportunities,[133] accrued mainly to the large brewers, while small-scale and rural brewing were wiped out.

Another example of scale-enlargement in a regionally concentrated export industry was brick production in Holland. Along the Holland IJssel, where the tide continually brought new deposits of clay, a process was developed to scoop out the material using dredge scoops in the 15th century. Assisted by the high quality of the IJssel bricks, brick production thrived. By around 1500 the area had several dozen ovens, each employing some six labourers.[134] In the 16th century there was another period of significant expansion as this small area came to have 120 brick ovens, employing some 1,000 people.

Holland was heavily industrialized. Reports by government commissioners on economic conditions there in 1514 make it possible to reconstruct the distribution of labour input in the various sectors of the economy.[135] In this reconstruction, in the Holland countryside only 40–45 per cent of the labour input went into agriculture, 20 per cent into fisheries and related industries, 10 per cent into peat digging and groundwork (spading and diking), 10 per cent into shipping, and 10 per cent into textile production, and some in other proto-industries. In the cities, on the basis of detailed accounts for Leiden in 1498 and Dordrecht in 1555, about 3 per cent of the labour force was engaged in agriculture and fisheries, about 6 per cent in groundwork and construction, 59 per cent in industries, and 31 per cent in services. In Holland as a whole, town and countryside, only 25 per cent of labour was engaged in agriculture, supplying less than 20 per cent of GDP. If fishing and peat digging are included, the primary sector still involved no more than 39 per cent of labour, generating only 31 per cent of GDP.[136] Industry accounted for 38 per cent of the labour

---

[132] Unger, *History of brewing*, 104–113.   [133] Ibid., 163–180.
[134] Hollestelle, *De steenbakkerij in de Nederlanden*, 121–124.
[135] Van Zanden, 'Taking the measure', and Van Bavel, 'Proto-industrialization', 1126–1145.
[136] Van Zanden, 'Taking the measure'.

force and 39 per cent of GDP, and services for 22 per cent and 30 per cent, respectively. This is a very exceptional economic structure for late medieval western Europe: before the Industrial Revolution, on average 80 per cent of the European population were engaged in agriculture. The share of GDP earned in industry in early 16th-century Holland, 39 per cent, was at a level not attained elsewhere in Europe until the beginning of the 20th century, even in England and Germany.

In several areas in the 15th- and 16th-centuries Low Countries agriculture was of only minor importance. This was very clearly true for Holland, at 25 per cent of labour input, and for inland Flanders, probably below 50 per cent. Even in Friesland, which was a distinctly rural and agrarian region, in 1511 no more than 70 per cent of its population was employed in agriculture.[137] A similar percentage can be surmised for the Guelders river area, which, however, experienced almost no rise in the importance of non-agricultural sectors in the 13th to 16th centuries. Cities there grew only slowly, and the non-agricultural activities in the countryside, such as small-scale cloth and linen production and some brewing, disappeared,[138] pushed aside by the products of specialized large-scale industries elsewhere. From then on, many more people in the region were engaged in agriculture, either as independent farmers or wage labourers. The region also had many local craftsmen who fulfilled local needs, such as blacksmiths, millers, and carpenters, but there were hardly any proto-industrial workers, giving the region a more agrarian character than it had had centuries earlier. The same was probably true of Friesland, with its similar social and economic structure and development.

This development was part of a larger process in which certain activities disappeared as a result of an increase in trade and specialization in other regions where there were greater comparative advantages. The regional specialization sometimes embraced all of north-western Europe, or even extended further. A clear example, in addition to the examples of ox rearing and yarn production discussed above, was salt production. In the 15th century the cities in Zeeland had several hundred saltworks, including those in Goes and Bergen op Zoom, but the production of salt began to decline in Zeeland when the finest and most easily accessible silty peats became exhausted or covered with sediment, and was replaced in the 15th century by the relatively cheap imports of raw salt from the Bayonne, Oléron, and the Bay of Bourgneuf.[139] There, salt was formed by natural evaporation in salt pans, and did not require artificial heating, which made production much cheaper. This is a clear example of a comparative advantage, which became increasingly important with the further development of market exchange and the reduction of transaction costs. Capital-intensive refining of imported raw salt, however, remained important

---

[137] Faber, *Drie eeuwen Friesland*, i: 93–99 and ii: table III.1.
[138] Van Bavel, 'Proto-industrie'.   [139] Van Dam, 'Middeleeuwse bedrijven', 85–115.

in Holland and Zeeland, showing the advantage these regions had in accessing cheap capital and perhaps resources such as peat. This type of regional specialization in industrial production, which entailed intensive trade in raw materials and semi-finished goods, was very strong in the Low Countries, probably stronger than anywhere else in Europe. It was driven by geographical differences in the availability of raw materials and the marked regional differences in social structure, and facilitated by the high extent of market integration.

The Main Lines of Industrial Development

Industrial production in the course of the high and later Middle Ages became increasingly aimed at the market rather than the individual household. This development is closely related to the emergence of the institutional and physical framework of trade and markets, developing in the Low Countries faster than in most other parts of Europe. In the course of this process, and furthered by market demand and competition, industries began to operate on a larger scale and became more specialized. The 12th century appears to have been particularly crucial, as specialization quickly advanced, concentration of industries occurred both in towns and countryside, and large-scale production of several products emerged. At the same time, and further evolving in the next century, there was an acceleration in generating and using various sources of energy and technological innovations such as the broad loom, improved kilns, windmills, and industrial watermills.

All this had a favourable effect on the quality and price of textiles, glass, pottery, bricks, tools, furniture, and other products. Reduced prices brought products increasingly within the reach of non-elite groups in society, particularly the middle strata (artisans, retailers, civil servants) in the rising cities, but also larger farmers in the countryside.[140] Demand from these groups was strengthened after the mid-14th century, when their purchasing power increased as a result of population decline and social developments. The Holland industries in particular benefited from this process, since they specialized in middle-range and mass consumption articles. Some of these became typical of Holland, including cheese, butter, turf, bricks, and chalk, and to a lesser extent, beer. All were produced more cheaply in Holland than elsewhere because of the plentiful supply of raw materials, the favourable institutional context, and the availability of cheap capital that enabled investments and economies of scale.

The rise and further growth of rural industries aimed at export, which increased in periods of population pressure such as the 13th and 16th centuries, is another main aspect in the development of industries in the late medieval Low Countries. These rural industries, with their clearly regional specializations,

[140] See section VI.4, p. 323.

focused on mass production, using cheap, low-skilled labour. The availability of cheap labour, which was associated with small peasant holdings and the possibility of subsistence farming that such holdings offered, was often essential in the rise of proto-industries. The fact that the countrymen were not organized, and that taxes and excises, as well as prices, were lower in the countryside, further reduced wage costs. If this labour could be successfully connected with merchant capital and finishing industries in the towns, and with non-local markets, the result was massive proto-industrialization, as observed for inland Flanders, Hainaut, and Holland in the 15th century. The location of rising rural industries was sometimes also associated with availability of raw materials, as in iron production in the Liège area, although improving transport made this element less and less important. The rise of rural industries in some cases was further stimulated by the few restrictions and obstacles to mechanization, allowing for labour-saving investments such as the fulling mill. Investments like these were sometimes more difficult to make in cities where guild restrictions were strong.

These rural industries, often specializing in basic mass production, had their urban counterparts in the highly specialized luxury production in the cities. There was increasing demand for luxury and durable consumer goods, such as luxury types of cloth, leather, weapons, art, and furniture. This demand was further stimulated in the 16th century by the growing purchasing power of the elite, which resulted from the accumulation of capital and the wage–price scissors, with its low wages and high food prices favouring the elite. Specialized luxury industries became concentrated almost exclusively in the largest cities, such as Ghent, Bruges, Brussels, and most notably Antwerp. These offered advantages in accessing markets for capital, labour, and goods, as well as the most favourable conditions for developing human skills, specialization, and diversification, which were essential for such highly specialized industries.

All in all, industrial production increased sharply in both town and countryside. The growing industrial production, and the more intense use of natural resources it brought, caused ecological problems in the densely populated Low Countries. The water, particularly in and around towns, became polluted from industrial processes, although measures were taken to regulate discharges and counteract pollution. Many areas also became deforested as a result of the massive amounts of timber used in industry, as in the 16th century with iron production in the Ardennes, and already in the high Middle Ages on the Veluwe. Peat digging, too, caused ecological problems. In Holland, where there were major problems with drainage, digging on a massive scale undermined safety and reduced available agricultural land. Many of the negative effects, however, could be countered through regulation, and particularly by investments in wind- and watermills, sluices, and dikes. A constant tension can thus be observed between short-term gains and long-term protection of the environment and natural resources. The outcome was generally not negative; the late medieval Low Countries were not parasitic on the environment. Industrial production and extraction of natural resources did not erode the basis for further economic growth and sustainability. In this respect the tensions were much as they are today, but the late medieval Low Countries were perhaps more successful in fighting abuses, imposing restrictions, and developing organizations and legislation to protect natural resources. Holland is a case in point. Although the ecological equilibrium was most precarious there, the threats biggest, and the use of natural resources most intense, this region witnessed no irreversible ecological disasters.

Another effect of industrial development in the late medieval Low Countries was that regions became more distinct. Growing integration and interaction, made possible by the relatively open and flexible markets, greatly increased regional specialization and made differences among regions even more pronounced. These regional differences were built on differences in raw materials, but even more on different social and economic structures. In some regions, such as the Guelders river area and coastal Flanders, this process led to the de-industrialization of the countryside and an almost exclusive focus on commercial agriculture. Other regions, such as Holland, witnessed the increasing success of industries in both towns and countryside, which found markets all over western Europe. This industrial development played a large part in the economic rise of Holland. At the beginning of the 16th century, some 40 per cent of its GDP was generated by industries, whereas the large service sector was also to a great extent tied up with the secondary sector. This success in industrial production was mainly based on Holland's social and institutional framework which had emerged in the 11th to 14th centuries. Hence the flourishing of the Holland industries in the Golden Age was not the fruit of a sudden stimulus around 1585, when Flemish and Brabantine entrepreneurs and industrial workers arrived, but rather the result of a more gradual development that had started in the 14th century and was based on the medieval institutional foundation. Industrial development in the Meuse valley around Liège and Verviers also took place slowly, building on a framework established centuries before. There, it was the production of textiles, coal, and steel which developed out of their medieval roots,[141] forming the next step in industrialization and creating the foundation for the Industrial Revolution in the region. This revolution did not suddenly appear in the 18th and 19th centuries, but had a long build-up, during which the 16th century was a crucial stage of acceleration.

Several paths towards industrialization were laid in the late medieval Low Countries. The ever-greater specialization in luxury products in the large towns

---

[141] Further in-depth research into this development is a clear historiographical desideratum.

would ultimately be a dead end. Most places where larger-scale industrialization and mechanization made headway in the 15th and 16th centuries were rural locations or small and medium-sized towns, in Holland and even more in the Meuse valley. In both cases there was a dynamic process in which small peasant producers and craftsmen gave way to wage labour, capital was concentrated, and there were relatively large investments in fixed capital goods, first in Holland and later in the Meuse valley. In both cases the guilds were weak, in contrast to another path towards industrialization, found in textiles in the large towns in the south, such as Ghent, with the industrial entrepreneurs emerging from the ranks of the successful master craftsmen.[142] These types of industrialization of the 15th and 16th centuries can both be seen as intermediate stages between the small-scale craft production for the market in the Flemish, Artois, and Brabantine towns of the 13th to 15th centuries and the large-scale factory production in Wallonia around 1800.

Industrial development in the late medieval Low Countries contributed to economic growth along two main lines. First, there was Smithian growth, generated by intensification and specialization of labour. This type, found fairly generally in late medieval Europe, was also clearly present in the Low Countries. Intensification was most apparent in the proto-industrial households, where highly labour-intensive methods of small-scale agriculture were combined with very intensive non-agricultural activities, such as processing flax and wool, spinning, and simple weaving. This was part of a cycle of activities which allowed the labourer to use all seasons and all hours of the day productively, thus increasing physical output, although often at the expense of labour productivity per hour. Labour productivity did increase through specialization, which was also found in proto-industrial activities but even more for the urban crafts, where the division of labour was sometimes pushed to extreme limits. These developments were probably stronger in the Low Countries than in most of late medieval Europe. Their contribution to a rise in labour productivity and thus to real economic growth, however, was very limited. Instead, in the long run, the increasing intensification reduced labour productivity.

The exceptionality of the Low Countries is found in another type of growth, which can be called Schumpeterian. This was the result of scale-enlargement and major capital investments in new technology, as well as higher inputs of inanimate energy, which not only increased physical output but increased labour productivity even more. This made industrial goods more widely available at relatively lower prices, as shown in the 15th- and 16th-century inventories of goods.[143] Main examples of this type of economic growth were found in Holland in the 14th to 16th centuries, most notably the brewing industry, but even more in the Meuse valley, with its mechanical fulling in the Vesdre area, mining around

[142] Lis and Soly, 'Different paths', 219–224 and 228–230.   [143] See section VI.4, p. 323.

Liège, and blast furnaces there and elsewhere in Wallonia. All this required very large investments in fixed capital goods, raising labour productivity and laying the foundation for the Industrial Revolution, and it is no coincidence that Wallonia, and more particularly the Meuse valley, was the second area in Europe where the Industrial Revolution took place.

VIII

Economic Growth and Social Change in the Very Long Run

VIII.1. INDICATORS OF GROWTH

This chapter will first reconstruct the patterns of economic growth and the shifts in the economic centre of gravity in the medieval Low Countries. In order to uncover these shifts, indicators of extensive growth (population growth and extension of the cultivated area) and of intensive growth (GDP per capita, health and life expectancy, quality of clothing and housing, technological change, trade and specialization, and urbanization) are used. In the next sections, this reconstruction will be linked to the characteristics of the different regions, in order to assess which factors determined the shifts observed in the centres of economic gravity.

Extensive Growth

The extension of the cultivated area cannot be measured precisely, but some outlines are possible. In the 5th century there were only a few small pockets of cultivated land. From the 6th to early 9th centuries there was a clear extension, but it was concentrated in the fertile or easy-to-reclaim soils: the loess of the Haspengouw, the sandy loam of inland Flanders, and somewhat later the fertile river clay of the Guelders river area. In the 11th to 13th centuries the next surge of extension concentrated in the peatlands of Holland and coastal Flanders, where large-scale reclamation projects took place, while regions further inland saw a more piecemeal extension of agricultural land. The coastal areas in Zeeland and around the Zuiderzee, on the other hand, lost land to the sea. By the 16th century, as a new surge in the extension of agricultural land started, the maximum extension of the agricultural area had already been reached in many of the more fertile and suitable parts of the Low Countries, where all of the area was cultivated. Reclamation projects in this period were thus limited to the most infertile areas, such as Drenthe, the Campine, and the Ardennes, where smaller, piecemeal reclamation was carried out, although large wastelands still remained there. The only region where large-scale extension of agricultural land took place in this period was Holland, where polders and the spread of wind-and watermills provided for a massive extension of agricultural land from the mid-16th century on.

These waves of extension largely coincided with the waves of population growth, although demographic growth in the Low Countries was much stronger than the growth in the agricultural area, and the land/people ratio declined with every wave as a result. The first of these demographic waves, a very modest one, started in the 6th century, when the population slowly began to rise again after the severe reductions in the post-Roman era. Habitation in the 6th to 9th centuries concentrated in the few regions suited to reclamation and arable agriculture. The population of the Low Countries can be roughly estimated at 200,000 around the mid-7th century, rising to 410,000 by around 900. After stagnation in the late 9th and 10th centuries, a new, quick rise in the 11th to 13th centuries was concentrated in such recently occupied areas as northern Flanders and Holland. In the period around 1300 the Low Countries as a whole had 2 to 2.5 million people. Population numbers there from the 7th to 13th centuries rose by a factor of 10–12, compared with a factor of 3–4 for Europe as a whole and 6–7 for western Europe. In the 13th century the Low Countries, which had been very sparsely populated six centuries earlier, became the second most densely populated part of Europe.

The famine and Black Death in the 14th century took a massive toll, as they did elsewhere in Europe. However, regional differences within the Low Countries were pronounced, and overall the demographic effects were less dramatic than in most other parts of Europe. Losses were generally smaller, except for hard-hit regions such as Artois, and recovery was more rapid, most pronounced in Holland and inland Flanders. The late 15th and 16th centuries saw relatively strong population growth in the Low Countries compared with other parts of Europe. At the same time, the demographic preponderance shifted to the north, particularly to Holland. While population growth in the south of the Low Countries almost stagnated, population in the north increased by a half from 1500 to 1600. At that time the Low Countries contained about 3.2 million inhabitants, 15–20 times as many as in the mid-7th century.

Intensive Growth

The indicators of extensive growth for the medieval Low Countries are impressive, but intensive growth is another matter. In the pre-industrial era, population growth and the resulting population pressure often went in parallel with increased poverty and scarcity of land and other resources. Therefore, we must also look at the indicators which point to a possible rise or decline in available surpluses. One of these could be technological change as an instrument to increase labour productivity. Especially in the 10th to 12th centuries the diffusion of new techniques in agriculture, often building on older knowledge, gained momentum: these included three-field rotation, the heavy plough, and the construction of fish ponds. The 11th to 13th centuries also saw significant advances in technology for generating energy, with the improvement and enlargement of mills, and a marked rise in their number, and also a rapid expansion of peat digging and the start of coal mining. In the high Middle Ages, after a longer period of virtual stagnation or even regression, technological improvements were also applied in industries. All these advances were concentrated in Flanders, Holland, and the Meuse valley.

In the 15th to 16th centuries, technological advances were even more concentrated in industries, and often associated with scale-enlargement, most conspicuously in brewing (Holland) and metallurgy and coal mining (the Meuse valley). Investments in technology were helped by the declining cost of capital in the market. Interest rates in the Low Countries fell from 10–12 per cent in the 13th century to 6 per cent in the 16th century, and the capital market became accessible to broad groups in society, particularly in Holland. In the high Middle Ages, however, other forms of allocation and exchange of capital outside the market had been efficient as well, as indicated by the advances in this period, well before the emergence of the capital market.

Investments in technology helped to increase physical output, and often also stimulated labour productivity, which was further increased by processes of scale-enlargement and specialization. This type of growth occurred in regions such as Holland and the Meuse valley. It remains difficult, however, to assess whether such gains were temporary and to what extent they were eroded by the effects of population growth. In agriculture, where the scope for Schumpeterian growth was much smaller, they probably were eroded, but in industries perhaps not. This would then be reflected by falling relative prices in textiles, furniture, and particularly products such as iron and beer, produced by industrial sectors where innovation and scale-enlargement were most apparent.

The growth of surpluses and specialization can also be deduced from the increase in trade. In the Low Countries the first strong surge in commercialization was in the 11th to 12th centuries, as evidenced by the significant rise in the number of markets, the growing volumes of goods traded, the rise of cities, the deliberate move away from self-sufficiency by large institutions, the increasing individual and regional specialization and the growth of industries. This process continued, eventually resulting in a very high level of commercialization in the 16th century. The volume of international trade per capita in the Low Countries around 1550 was about 4 to 5 times the rate in France and England, and domestic, regional trade must have been much greater.

The degree of commercialization of the agricultural sector varied: little commercialization in peasant-dominated Drenthe, and a great deal in the Guelders river area, particularly from the 15th century on. Non-agricultural activities in the countryside were generally fully commercialized, and often aimed at international markets. The rise of proto-industrialization, which was most apparent in inland Flanders and Holland in the 14th to 16th centuries, was therefore important in the process of commercialization. Industrial production in the cities was also highly commercialized. Some cities developed clear specializations for the international market, in a few cases starting in the 11th and 12th centuries, as with the towns in the Meuse valley, Artois, and southern Flanders, and later also inland Flanders. From the 14th century on, commercial success in urban industries was also found in Holland, which experienced the greatest extent of commercialization in the 16th-century Low Countries. Not only did Holland have an extremely high urbanization rate, with urban industries and services almost solely aimed at the market, but there was a strong proto-industrial sector to which the same applied, as well as highly commercialized agriculture. In total, probably far more than three-quarters of the total output of the Holland economy was aimed at the market.

Non-agrarian sectors were very important in Holland, where in the early 16th century only about 25 per cent of labour was engaged in agriculture, supplying less than 20 per cent of GDP. Fishing and peat digging generated some 10 per cent of GDP, industry 39 per cent, and services 30 per cent. Elsewhere in the Low Countries, agriculture was more important but still much less so than elsewhere in Europe. In inland Flanders probably less than half of labour input was in agriculture, and even in distinctly agrarian Friesland the proportion was no more than 70 per cent. This economic structure was exceptional for western Europe. The share of GDP earned in industry in early 16th-century Holland, at 39 per cent, was at a level not attained elsewhere in Europe until the beginning of the 20th century, even in England and Germany.

Among the less direct indicators which show the rise of agrarian surpluses and their availability for the developing non-agrarian occupations is the growth of towns and the rise in the urbanization rate. In the 9th to 11th centuries only a few per cent of the total population lived in towns, by the 13th century this had risen to 20-30 per cent in the core regions, Flanders and Artois, and at the beginning of the 14th century the urbanization rate in the Low Countries as a whole had risen to roughly 20 per cent, making this one of the most urbanized parts of Europe, second only to northern Italy. After the Black Death, absolute population numbers in the towns declined, but the urbanization rate in the Low Countries rose, most clearly in Holland, which experienced a steep rise from 14 per cent in 1300 to 33 per cent in 1400. The south-west, Artois and Walloon Flanders, was perhaps the only region where urbanization stagnated and may even have declined in the 14th and 15th centuries. These regions were exceptions, however. In the late 15th century the urbanization rate in the Low Countries had already reached a high of 34 per cent, and in Holland even 45 per cent. In this period, when the Low Countries surpassed Italy in urbanization, the centre of urbanization became firmly located in Holland.

A more indirect indicator of the availability of surpluses is the flourishing of culture. From the 7th century to the 10th, this was found in the Haspengouw, the Meuse valley, and the Guelders river area. In the 11th to 13th centuries these regions were overtaken by Artois and Flanders, and in the 14th to 15th centuries Flanders and later Brabant excelled in cultural achievements, as in architecture and painting. In the 17th century the centre of cultural florescence shifted to Holland. These indicators thus show a geographical pattern similar to the more direct economic indicators, although the cultural development may have occurred somewhat later, perhaps even when the phase of greatest economic growth was over. It is possible that cultural expansion may have been more closely tied to rising inequality than to economic growth. The same applies to the accumulation of capital. In the 13th century capital was accumulated mainly in Artois and southern Flanders, as shown by the dominance of the Arras burghers as creditors. This dominance shifted to Flanders in the 14th century, to Brabant in the 15th to 16th centuries, and to Holland in the 17th century, in each phase going in tandem with rising inequality in the distribution of wealth and stagnation in the economic expansion of the region.

A direct indicator of intensive economic growth is the development of GDP per capita. All estimates of GDP before 1800 are highly speculative, however, and often based on various unproven assumptions.[1] These figures are often derived from the other quantitative indicators, including population growth and urbanization rate, or from qualitative assessments of economic development, all indicators whose effect on GDP per capita is not totally clear. Using these indicators often leads to circular reasoning. Reliable estimates for the Low Countries are available only from the 16th century on, and then mainly for Holland. Based on a detailed complete input–output table, total GDP for this region around 1510 is estimated at some 24 guilders per person, and corrected for inflation this is about one-third lower than the figure for Holland in 1807.[2] For the Netherlands as a whole, GDP per capita around 1500 is estimated at 0.60 of that of Britain in 1820. It remained at that level in 1570, whereas the corresponding figures for Belgium would be 0.55 around 1500 and 0.65 around 1570.[3] The latter figures, which are much more speculative than those calculated for Holland around 1510, would be similar to those for Italy, somewhat higher than the estimates for Spain and Poland, and well above the estimate for England of 0.45 to 0.49. More figures are needed to better reconstruct developments over time, but meanwhile we have to content ourselves with the impression that growth of GDP per capita was limited and often only temporary: in the very long run growth and differences were often eroded again. Nonetheless, some regional cases may show a more fundamental rise, with the gains sustained for several centuries.

Real Wages and Standards of Living

An indicator much closer to most people's material experience than GDP per capita is the development of real wages. Around 1300, when the first data are

[1] Such as those by Maddison, *The world economy*, 245.   [2] Van Zanden, 'Taking the measure'.
[3] Van Zanden, 'Early modern economic growth'.

available, real wages were high in the Low Countries compared with other parts of north-western Europe, and were particularly high in Holland, probably as a legacy of the colonization of this frontier area in the 11th to 13th centuries, when labour was scarce. Another factor was the high labour productivity in the Holland economy, which was connected to the high investments in capital goods. In the second half of the 14th century wages in many parts of the Low Countries increased, as they did in Europe as a whole, as a result of the population decline and the scarcity of labour. The real wages of the late 14th century were not matched again until the second half of the 19th century. In Holland, on the other hand, there was a slight population decline, followed by rapid growth, preventing such a rise in real wages. Wages in the Low Countries thus converged after the Black Death at a relatively high level.

In the late 15th to 16th centuries real wages came under pressure as a result of fierce population growth, which pushed food prices up and wages down. The golden age of the wage labourers (perhaps too grand a term anyway) ended at this time. Still, in Holland, despite very strong population growth, and to a lesser extent in the Low Countries as a whole, real wages did not decline as fast as in other parts of Europe.[4] This relatively slight decline in the Low Countries, and in England, resulted in a divergence in real wages between those areas and the other parts of Europe in the period 1500–1650.[5]

Real wages are only part of the picture, however, especially since most calculations are for fully employed craftsmen working in large cities, and therefore do not capture the experiences of unskilled labourers, employment opportunities, or alternative sources of sustenance. These suffered in the 16th century, as there was a clear acceleration in the processes of proletarianization, social polarization, and fragmentation of holdings. The simultaneous decline in real wages benefited large tenant farmers and entrepreneurs who hired labourers, but it hurt wage labourers. The gap between wealth and poverty rapidly widened. Particularly in the Guelders river area and Frisia, which were undergoing an agrarian transition, and later in Holland, which was experiencing a proto-industrial and later an agrarian transition, polarization was pronounced and a large proportion of the population was afflicted by poverty. Although average GDP per capita and real wages of fully employed, skilled labourers in Holland were high, they do not capture the experience of the many losers of this period.

Closer to the direct experience of people were the state of their health and their age at death. Figures from the late Middle Ages bring out sharp fluctuations and social differences in mortality, but structural changes in life expectancy in the long run did not occur. Leaving aside infant mortality, the average age at death for men and women in the Middle Ages remained at 35–40 years. If the establishment of hospitals and leper houses from the 12th century on, and the

---

[4] Noordegraaf, *Hollands welvaren?*, 145–166, and Schollie rs, 'Le pouvoir d'achat', esp. 305–306.
[5] Allen, 'The great divergence'.

employment of professional surgeons and academically trained doctors from the 14th century had improved the health of the population, this effect must have been eroded by other factors.

The wider mix of factors which determined standards of living, including health, the quantity and quality of food, clothing, housing, the burden imposed by work, and environmental conditions, can be measured best by stature. Over the period as a whole, statures in the Low Countries show a steady, gradual decline.[6] On the basis of a small number of samples it can be estimated that in the Roman era average male stature was 1.76 m, declining in the early Middle Ages to 1.73. In the 13th to 14th centuries it had further decreased to 1.71, and in the 15th to 16th centuries to 1.69, a low which was maintained in the 17th to 18th centuries. In the golden age of the Dutch Republic, notwithstanding the high average GDP per capita, a very large proportion of the population suffered from poor hygiene, bad living conditions, hard and long hours of work, and malnutrition.

These data suggest that heights, and hence standards of living, in the Roman era and early Middle Ages were fairly high but underwent a long-term decrease in the medieval period which continued into the early modern period. Apparently, intensive economic growth was scarce in the Middle Ages, and the growth that took place was mostly eroded by population growth over time. Positive effects of economic growth on standards of living for the majority of the population were even scarcer, since these were cancelled, or even reversed by the rising social inequality, pollution, and overcrowding. This is a surprising result, particularly for a part of Europe where developments in GDP per capita were relatively favourable. It may have been due to the growing importance of market exchange from the 11th century on, which was able to push up or sustain GDP per capita and feed more people, but at the same time resulted in inequality, pollution, and environmental degradation, and undermined social organizations that had been able to reduce inequality, pollution, and social problems, and thus guaranteed social and ecological sustainability.

Phases and Regional Patterns of Growth

We have seen above that there were several growth phases in the Low Countries. In the 6th to 7th centuries there was a hesitant recovery, followed in the 8th to 9th centuries by clear extensive growth. Intensive growth occurred in some regions, particularly in the Guelders river area and the Meuse valley, but in the longer run these advances did not result in substantially higher living standards, because of the erosive effect of population growth. In the 11th to 13th centuries, the next phase of growth included first both extensive and real growth, but later in the period and up to the mid-14th century, extensive growth alone remained, with growing population pressure probably depressing per capita GDP and

---

[6] Maat, 'Two millennia'. Cf. also section IV.1, pp. 143–146.

living conditions. Despite sharp increases in population, however, food supply per capita did not go down drastically. Land productivity rose enormously as the result of the significant extension of cultivated areas, the opening of new regions, and specialization, and the significant technological progress. These developments make the 11th to 13th centuries stand out in the economic history of the Low Countries. Also, the better transport, higher population densities and land productivity, and in particular the more advanced institutional framework of the economy made it possible to accumulate larger surpluses, destined mainly for the elite, and to build a more complex economy and society. The effect was greatest in industry, with increasing specialization and capital investments, resulting in higher quality products which more people could afford to buy.

In the period 1350–1450, the demographic decline caused a windfall gain in food supply per capita and GDP per capita, but this effect was eroded by population growth later in the 15th and 16th centuries. Again, it was in industry that most development took place. In several sectors labour productivity increased, although declining wages and rising population pressure may have promoted intensive production methods and depressed labour productivity to some extent, particularly in labour-intensive branches of industry, such as textiles.

Among the positive developments in the economic performance of the Low Countries in the Middle Ages, the very large increase in population and an almost equally great rise in agricultural output stand out. The rise in industrial output was even greater, and so probably was that in services, exceeding the rise in population. All in all, GDP per capita rose, although very slowly, with the secondary and tertiary sectors being the positive elements. Other noticeable developments were the rapid increase in trade and specialization, the building of an extensive and relatively smoothly functioning physical and institutional infrastructure, and advances in human capital formation.

Food supply per capita remained static and, in some cases, even declined. There were fluctuations over time, but in the long run there was at best some stability in the number of calories consumed per person. In the composition and quality of the diet, the trend was probably negative. The free peasant in the 6th century Campine, with an abundance of land, probably had easier access to food and a more varied diet than the serf in the 9th century on a manor in the Guelders river area, who was better off than the peasant in the crowded countryside of 13th-century inland Flanders or the journeyman in a 15th-century Holland town. People became more dependent on cereals as their source of calories, making the diet more monotonous. Overcrowding, particularly within the city walls, was another problem and there was increasing pollution, as a result of rising population densities and industrial growth. These negative elements were reflected in the stature of the people in the Low Countries, which declined steadily in the course of the Middle Ages, although not as steeply as the massive population growth would suggest.

The latter was perhaps the biggest achievement of the medieval economy in the Low Countries. Despite the enormous population growth, which by pre-industrial standards was extremely rapid, and despite growing scarcity of land, food per capita did not severely decline, living standards did not drastically deteriorate, and GDP per capita was maintained, while an ever more complex, advanced, and diversified economy was built. Malthusian tension was still present, but the population ceiling was raised ever further, faster, and more successfully than elsewhere in Europe, feeding 15 times more people off the land than at the start of the Middle Ages. In view of the fact that the Low Countries in the late 15th and 16th centuries did experience extreme population growth, much greater than elsewhere in Europe, yet avoided substantially declining real wages or starvation, it is almost possible to say it broke through the Malthusian trap.[7] In this respect, however, the socio-institutional arrangements of the high Middle Ages seem to have been at least as successful in the economic exploitation of resources as those of the later Middle Ages.

VIII.2. POSSIBLE CAUSES OF REGIONAL VARIATIONS IN ECONOMIC CHANGE

In each period a few regions stood out in aspects such as growth, urbanization, wages, the importance of non-agricultural sectors and the complexity of economy and society. In the first growth phase, the Frankish period, the lead was taken by the Haspengouw, the Meuse valley, and the Guelders river area. In the 11th to 13th centuries these regions were overtaken by Artois and southern Flanders, later by inland Flanders, and at the end of the Middle Ages by Holland. In the 16th century, however, there were indications of stagnation in Holland, and of the beginning of industrial development in the Meuse valley. In the course of this process, each of the leading regions attained an ever-higher level of economic development, enabling it to build a more complex economy. Which factors determined this growth and development, and the differences in nature and shifts in economic 'leadership'? Apparently, the regions that experienced intensive growth during the relevant period offered the most security, and were best placed for stimulating exchange, specialization, and investment, without eroding the social and ecological basis for such development. But what factors were decisive?

Geography

Geography played only a modest role in the regional variations in economic growth. This most clearly applies to climate. Not all regions benefited from the improvement in climate in the medieval optimum from the late 11th century on,

---

[7] This assessment is more cautious than the much stronger formulation by Allen, 'The great divergence'.

even though the climate was broadly similar in neighbouring regions. Conversely, economic growth often occurred during the later Middle Ages despite the worsening of the climate and the start of the Little Ice Age. Other geographical factors such as the location of regions along major rivers or by the sea played a bigger role. Rivers became more important as transport routes in the early Middle Ages, when land routes fell into disrepair. Both the Guelders river area and the Meuse valley, two leading regions in the period, were indeed located on major rivers. In the late Middle Ages sea trade increased and the larger ships used required deeper water, thus benefiting ports near the coast and favouring coastal areas such as Flanders and Holland. Still, the effect of geographical location should be qualified, since not all regions with similar locations profited to the same extent. Friesland, located on the sea, lost its commercial position after the high Middle Ages. Other clear shifts in trade are equally difficult to explain by geographical factors, such as the move from Bruges to similarly located Antwerp, or within Holland from conveniently located Dordrecht to Amsterdam. The decline of Bruges is often explained geographically by the silting up of the Zwin, but its location was not very different from Antwerp, situated far up the Scheldt. Nor was Antwerp's location unlike that of Dordrecht, Zwolle, or Deventer. If profitability and the right institutional framework for investment were present, geographical disadvantages could largely be overcome by human action.

Another geographical factor was the availability of raw materials. The plentiful supply of peat in Holland and of ore and coal in the Meuse valley became more important in the late Middle Ages, and perhaps contributed to a shift in economic growth, although the effect on the prices and use of these raw materials was not always great, as is shown for energy in Holland, and availability did not always result in successful exploitation, as capital, property rights, and opportunities for exchange were crucial in this. Also, the relatively low and declining costs of transport in the Low Countries made the proximity of raw materials less important in the course of the Middle Ages. This applied to light and relatively costly materials such as wool, which was increasingly imported from England, Scotland, and Spain, but also to heavier bulk goods such as wood, imported from the Rhineland or Scandinavia, or peat, transported in massive amounts over large distances.

Soil quality, and general environmental changes, also exerted some influence on the economic potential, but were not the decisive factor. The sandy-loamy soils in inland Flanders, despite their infertile character, produced the highest grain yields in late medieval Europe. Human influence was more important there than the quality of the soil. Also, environmental changes over time were profound, especially in the Low Countries, with its vulnerable soils and huge influence of the rivers and the sea. Some changes were to some extent the result of natural causes, as with the 'transgression phases' of the sea, but most came about through human action or the interaction of people and nature. This can be seen in the effects of rising water tables and the increasing incidence of storm surges in the 12th to 14th centuries. These effects varied greatly between coastal Flanders, Zeeland, and Holland, depending on the organization of water management, the extent to which the dunes were exploited, the extent of salt burning and peat digging, and the success of the community in regulating these activities.

Although human intervention often had negative ecological effects, in the medieval Low Countries the delicate balance with nature was maintained fairly successfully. This equilibrium was more precarious there than elsewhere because of the continuous threat of flooding, the pronounced dynamics of natural-geographic changes, and the relatively high population densities, with the related intensity of land use. There were some acute problems, such as erosion and sand drifting (in the Veluwe), subsidence of the soil and loss of land to the water (in coastal Flanders, Zeeland, the Zuiderzee area, and parts of peatland Holland) in the high and late Middle Ages. These effects were often intensified by the self-interest of particular social groups, such as entrepreneurs active in peat digging, iron production, and salt production. These ecological problems were tackled through regulation, either by self-regulation or measures imposed by authorities. Existing practices often proved difficult to change, however, because of the vested rights of particular interest groups, which led to conflicts of interest. For example, peat digging was carried out on a massive scale in Holland and brought huge profits, but it also had a detrimental effects on hydrological safety and eroded the agricultural potential of the region.

Socio-institutional arrangements reduced or partly solved these problems. Horizontal associations could play an important part in this, such as village communities, organizations of commoners, and water management boards, as well as urban communities, which restricted pollution of air and water. In the Low Countries in the 12th to 15th centuries, such associations were generally fairly successful in reducing the possible unfavourable ecological effects of the emergence of the market and the drive to maximize profits. Their success in the long run depended not only on institutional arrangements, but also on the social distribution of power and property among the persons and interest groups involved. In coastal Flanders, for instance, water management in the long run failed because of an increasingly skewed social distribution of land, with a small group of non-resident landowners increasing their hold over water management decisions and maximizing short-term profits at the expense of long-term ecological sustainability.

It would be incorrect, however, to focus on physical-geographic degradation alone, since physical conditions in the Low Countries at certain points were also improved. Often, favourable measures were undertaken to improve the quality of the land or to undo the unintended results of human action. Economic circumstances and the profitability of investments could be the motor, as in Holland in the 14th to 17th centuries when drainage canals, ditches, sluices, and wind watermills were constructed, and agricultural land was enlarged by embankment. The availability of capital and the institutional framework offering flexibility and security formed the precondition for such investments, in combination with the opportunities offered by the market for agricultural products. The other main context in which land was improved was when social circumstances stimulated maximization of physical output, as most clearly in inland Flanders in the later Middle Ages. There the combination of small peasant land holdings, population growth, and fragmentation of farms produced labour-intensive cultivation of the land. As a result of the long use, and fertilization, often through very labour-intensive methods, these poor-quality soils became increasingly fertile. Combined with the very intensive cultivation of the soil, this sometimes resulted in enormously high physical yields in the late Middle Ages, perhaps the highest in all of Europe, on what had originally been mediocre soil. The history of the Low Countries shows how tenacious and resourceful people were in coping with natural difficulties, but also that the key to success or failure was mainly located in socio-institutional arrangements. The shifts in the economic core within the Low Countries were only to a very limited extent determined by geography.

Demography and Urbanization

Population developments were not decisive for economic or social change either. Fluctuations—sharp growth from the 11th to 13th centuries, dramatic decline in the 14th century, stagnation in the 15th, followed by another sharp rise in the 16th century—did exert some influence, particularly on wages and prices, thus either benefiting real wages of labourers or pushing up profits for industrial entrepreneurs and large landowners. However, these demographic trends cannot explain regional divergences in economic or social development. The movement of wages and prices did not provoke fundamental changes over the long run because of its scissors-like character, with the effects reversing direction over the centuries. Moreover, similar demographic conditions or changes often had dissimilar effects according to the region. Scarcity of labour, for instance, is sometimes invoked to explain the rise of unfreedom or serfdom, but for Holland it is called upon to explain peasant freedom and the favourable conditions offered to the colonizers. As these opposing explanations show, the low population densities in themselves cannot be the decisive factor. Similarly, the rise of short-term leasing is often explained by a lack of labourers after the Black Death, while in several parts of the Low Countries a rise took place in the decades around 1300, that is, in a period with an abundance of labour. Demographic developments indeed influenced economic and social changes, but the socio-political and institutional context of the region determined the direction of the changes.

Moreover, demography is not an independent variable. There were sharp differences in demographic trends, which can only be explained by this regional context. An example was the diversity in population developments in the period of the Black Death. About 1300 the population rise of the previous centuries had resulted in increasing Malthusian stress, which was worsened by the ecological problems occurring as the unintentional results of intensified land use. However, the Black Death had only a slight effect in densely populated Holland and inland Flanders, contrasting with a dramatic population decline in Artois, for instance. Similarly striking was the rapid recovery and sharp demographic growth in Holland and inland Flanders in the 15th and 16th centuries, as opposed to the absence of recovery in fertile regions such as Artois and the Guelders river area. These differences cannot be explained in neo-Malthusian terms. The relative mildness of the crisis in Holland and Flanders, which were the most densely populated parts of the Low Countries and had rather poor soil conditions, can only be understood by the balanced distribution of property, freedom, and the high degree of self-determination the ordinary population enjoyed, combined with the convenient organization of exchange and the economic opprtunities. Neighbouring regions, such as the Guelders river area, characterized by large land ownership, the rapid rise of short-term leasing, and sharp social polarization, were hit hard and did not experience a recovery of rural population numbers to the pre-1348 level until the 18th century.

Neither was urbanization a determining factor. Despite its early start and the staggering levels attained from the 13th century, its effects should be placed in perspective. The growth of cities was to a large extent a result of economic developments, rather than the other way around. Particularly in the earliest stages, the availability of agricultural surpluses from the surrounding countryside for the urban population was vital in allowing urban growth. Although towns increasingly succeeded in drawing food and other necessities from a wider area, as the Flemish towns did in the 12th to 13th centuries, and later, even more clearly, the Holland towns from the 14th century on, the town's interaction with the region in which it was situated and the general development of this region still co-determined the potential for urban growth. This element to a large extent determined why urbanization in late medieval Flanders started to stagnate, whereas in Holland the proportion of people living in towns reached new heights. Moreover, the effect of urbanization on further economic development also depended on the institutional organization of town-country relationships, as demonstrated by contrasting the situation in inland Flanders with that in Holland.

Urban demand was felt almost everywhere in the Low Countries, and particularly in the western and central, most urbanized parts, but how a region reacted to this demand differed widely in extent and direction. In inland Flanders, for instance, the extent of rural commercialization in the late Middle Ages remained limited, despite the proximity of several large towns. In the Guelders river area, there was increasing commercialization, but it resulted in extensification of agriculture instead of intensification. The social distribution of land ownership and the production structures in a particular region appear to have been decisive in the divergent responses to urban demand. The interaction between urban demand and the rural economy could stimulate economic development, as seen most clearly in Flanders in the 10th to 13th centuries and in Holland in the 14th and 15th centuries, but the effect was neither automatic nor lasting. In highly urbanized inland Flanders the favourable effects disappeared in the later Middle Ages, mainly as a result of institutional sclerosis and social imbalances.

Polities

Political-military events may have had short-term effects, but were not decisive in causing fundamental changes in economy and society. They could, however, speed up these fundamental, long-term changes, as evidenced in the shifts of the centres of trade. The decline of the Frisian centres of trade in the 9th and 10th centuries, for instance, is easily attributed to the Viking attacks. Even after the attacks stopped, however, these centres did not regain their position, but lost out to the emerging towns in Flanders. Apparently, the latter were able to offer a better context for trade, which had been a more fundamental cause in this shift. The same applied to the shift from Antwerp to Amsterdam as the main commercial centre in the 16th century. Amsterdam, and the surrounding Holland region, offered a favourable institutional framework of trade, free of feudal elements, and with little non-economic power of particular interest groups. These elements, which were firmly built on advantages gained earlier, resulted in the town's growing commercial role in the 15th and 16th centuries; the sack of Antwerp in 1585 merely accelerated the shift to Amsterdam.

A second way in which political elements exercised influence was political organization, which was closely related to socio-institutional organization, but did not operate at identical geographical levels. The socio-institutional framework highlighted in this study—and particularly the social property system as its main constituent—operated mainly at a regional level, but the political organization operated either at a higher level (such as the Carolingian Empire, the Burgundian-Habsburg Empire, or the Duchy of Guelders), or at a lower one (such as that of the banal seigneuries). Only in the early Middle Ages did the two areas geographically overlap, since the Carolingian *pagi* in the Low Countries were quite similar to the regions identified in this study. In the other periods there was a clear interaction, with higher-level polities increasingly extending and intensifying their influence in the course of the Middle Ages, in tandem with the process of state formation.

Whether or not the effect of the polities on economic development was favourable, depended not on the size of the polities, or on unification or fragmentation. Political unification was not necessarily good for economic development or fragmentation necessarily bad. Rather, the effect depended on the exact choices and arrangements of laws, fiscality, and other policies. The key question is whether such policies increased or decreased security (physical and legal), reduced information costs, and created an institutional framework that suited exchange, investment, and economic growth. Moreover, their effect was not direct, but could differ with the region, depending on the regional distribution of power and property.

After the chaotic period in the 5th to 6th centuries, the rise of the Frankish Empire increased safety, standardized measures and coins, thus decreasing information costs, and allowed for increasing exchange and interaction of regions and people within the empire. The Viking raids of the 9th century brought some disruption, but caused little permanent damage, and the same applied to the political fragmentation and the disintegration of the Carolingian Empire. Political stability was restored fairly quickly in newly emerging political unities on a small scale: the banal lordships promoted territorialization and indirectly contributed to the formation of territorial horizontal associations which became an important element in the reduction of lordly arbitrariness. If such a social balance emerged, banal lordships could increase security at a local level, while they may also have stimulated investment in mills and other expensive capital goods. At the same time, from the 11th century on, territorial lords and their principalities emerged; they, too, were organized on a territorial basis and in many cases increased security. The favourable effect of these political organizations on economic development can be inferred from the significant extensive growth in the period 1000–1300. In some regions real growth occurred also, particularly where well-developed territorial principalities emerged, as most notably in Flanders.

In the late Middle Ages, too, the relatively small size of political units in the Low Countries did not affect economic development adversely. Political integration of larger areas was apparently not essential for economic development. Rather, in counties such as Holland and Flanders, which were small compared with England or France, it proved relatively easy for merchants, entrepreneurs, towns and village communities to influence politics, for instance, in monetary or fiscal matters. Property rights were relatively well protected and secure. Nor did the political fragmentation stand in the way of inter-regional exchange, as shown by the fairly high levels of market integration reached there in the 13th and 14th centuries. The rise of the large Burgundian and Habsburg empires, with their dynastic interests, was not an automatic advantage for economic development. On the one hand, the standardization of measures, coins, tolls, taxes, and legal systems, and the disappearance of boundaries reduced transaction costs. On the other hand, however, for those wanting to invest and develop economic activities in trade, agriculture, or industries, it became more difficult to influence political decision-making because of the broader power base and geographical scope of these empires. They brought other interests to the fore at the state level which could potentially hurt the economic activities. It was the nature of political power that mattered, not the size.

The divergencies in development within principalities also show that political unification was not decisive for economic and social development. Even if territorial principalities started to span regions, this did not necessarily lead to levelling. In fact, the differences remained very much in force, as can be seen in the county of Flanders (coastal versus inland Flanders) or the county/duchy of Guelders (the Veluwe versus the Guelders river area). Rather, integration within one principality increased the divergence, with the regions becoming more complementary. It was not until the 16th century that uniformizing tendencies made themselves felt to an increasing degree, as a result of the centralizing policies of the Habsburg regime, but this effect still remained limited and only slightly affected the socio-institutional characteristics at the regional level, before it was stopped altogether by the Dutch Revolt.

VIII.3. SOCIO-INSTITUTIONAL FACTORS

Earlier sections suggest that socio-institutional factors are most important in explaining shifts in economic growth and fundamental economic and social changes; they directed the effects of climatic, geographical, demographic, and political changes in divergent directions. This, however, is not reconcilable with the view held by some that institutions are easily adapted according to best practice and are developed, or copied from elsewhere, according to economic or ecological needs.[8] In this case, institutions can hardly be evoked as the explanatory factor for the long-term regional differences in economic development. The same applies to social structures. In case these would be fluid, then growing inter-regional interaction would even them out in the course of time. In that case, socio-institutional organization would become broadly similar in large areas or civilizations. This is, however, not what we observe in the medieval Low Countries. Even over this thousand-year period, and with ever more intense economic and political interaction, socio-institutional differences in the organization of exchange and the social distribution of power and property between regions remained clear. We will look first at this process of path-dependency and next at its effect on economic development.

The Path-dependency of Socio-institutional Arrangements at the Regional Level

At the start of the early Middle Ages, after the disappearance of Roman authority and the drastic population decline, there was a kind of *tabula rasa* in the Low Countries. Unlike areas in southern Europe, where continuity in the post-Roman period was much stronger, almost completely new societies were formed during the early and high Middle Ages. The new socio-institutional arrangements were

---

[8] As espoused particularly by the first generation of the New Institutional Economics.

mainly concentrated at the regional level, with some 20–25 regions in the Low Countries, each developing its own fairly homogeneous features. This regional diversity is related to the diversity in landscapes, at least indirectly. The wide diversity of landscapes was a result of the profound influence of the sea and the major rivers in this delta area, and further increased in the course of the Middle Ages, as more regions were occupied and landscape was shaped under human influence. The regional geographical diversity influenced not only the chronology and method of reclamation, but also, indirectly, the social and economic structure which emerged in the newly occupied region. In each of the regions, it was in the period of occupation that a social structure emerged, founded on a distribution of rights to land and other resources, and with a specific institutional framework which shaped specific flows of surplus. The very different foundations of the social structure formed the basis for the further path-dependent development of economy and society. This can be illustrated by recapitulating long-run developments in some representative regions.

In sandy Drenthe, and to a large extent also in the Veluwe and the Campine, which were easy to reclaim but infertile, the occupation was very gradual, and characterized by small-scale, piecemeal reclamations by peasants. Peasant property, consisting of medium-sized family farms, became dominant there. Population densities were too low, and monitoring costs too high to make the large-scale introduction of manors feasible, even apart from the fact that the peasants already had an entrenched position, while large landowners and royal power were weak. Attempts by the prince-bishop to introduce more princely authority and manorialism in the 13th century were successfully resisted by the Drenthe peasants. Just as in Frisia and later on the Flemish coast, their revolt was aimed at preserving the existing situation and was mainly defensive. These revolts were mainly reactions of small or medium-scale producers who had direct access to the means of production and a fair amount of freedom, but who feared the loss of economic and political independence and successfully staved off this threat.

In Drenthe, just as in the Campine, small peasants remained dominant and controlled the land, and were relatively free of seigneurial duties. There were few changes in the course of the high Middle Ages, although the rules and peasant organizations became more formal, with the formation of village communities and commons taking place in parallel with a process of territorialization of villages. Commons were also formalized in other parts of the Low Countries, but the types of organization differed according to the regional power balance. In some regions the territorial lords had firm control over waste lands and common lands, as in coastal Flanders, and in the Guelders river area the lords held the strongest position, but in Drenthe and the Campine the peasants were mainly in charge, organizing the use of the commons to increase the sustainability of the peasant economy.

In the later Middle Ages, in Drenthe, and even more in the Campine, the population growth resulted in some intensification of agriculture and there was a little specialization for the market. But in general peasant families concentrated on the cultivation of bread grains and maintaining livestock on a small scale, mainly for subsistence. Long-term security and the consumption needs of the individual household were much more central to production decisions than the market and potential profits. Thus, common lands and collective rules remained very important, and exploitation of the commons for market purposes was resisted. In peasant-dominated Drenthe and the Campine, the commodity market was not important and factor markets even much less so. Transfers of land, labour, and capital remained mainly embedded in social relations, or took place through organizations other than the market, and were restricted. The peasant structure remained largely intact there; other than in nearby coastal Frisia, for instance, there was no structural transformation of the rural economy in Drenthe up to the 19th century.

The Guelders river area was occupied much more rapidly, in the early Middle Ages. After the post-Roman demographic low, when the population slowly started to increase again, settlement became concentrated on fertile soils suitable for growing grain, such as the Haspengouw and later the Guelders river area, whereas many other regions remained virtually unpopulated. In these regions, as in the Guelders river area, royal and ecclesiastical properties began to dominate, accompanied by the rise of manorial organization and the lords' increasing power over the rural population. In contrast to neighbouring regions, such as Holland and the Veluwe, large manorial estates became the norm. The developments occurring in the high Middle Ages did not eradicate this regional distinctiveness, including the most drastic change, the dissolution of the manorial system. In the Guelders river area, the numerous lords in the decades around 1300 made a very rapid change from being manorial lords to becoming large landowners with near absolute property rights to the land, which they leased out for short terms. One stimulus was the demand for agricultural goods exercised by the expanding urban markets, which were easy to reach by way of the rivers. Moreover, the proximity of the reclamation areas and growing towns, both of which offered freedom, made it impossible for the manorial lords to prevent change or to bind people to the land any longer. The manorial lords could also gain from the change, which enabled them to acquire full property rights to the land in a period of rising land and food prices.

Even in a dynamic situation, as with the rapid dissolution of manors, there was no change in the social power structure, since the lords remained predominant. Rather, the expression of their power changed, from non-economic power over labour and agricultural produce to economic control over land. The result was that regions formerly dominated by manorial organization, from the 13th century on became dominated by large land holdings which were mainly in the hands of the former manorial lords, as documented for the Guelders river area. These large land holdings were worked by wage labourers or, more commonly, let out on short-term lease. The lords mostly succeeded in consolidating their position and giving it new substance; social relationships essentially remained unchanged.

The plentiful supply of lease land, combined with the competitive lease market, allowed for the rise of large tenant farms, which were fully oriented towards the market and worked mainly with wage labour. In these regions, including the Guelders river area, coastal Flanders, and coastal Frisia, the rise of markets was of major importance. Exchange of land, labour, capital, and goods through the market became dominant there by the 15th and 16th centuries. This resulted in sharp polarization, perhaps even more than in the towns, particularly as the Guelders river area and similar regions were dominated by large land ownership and had a highly skewed distribution of this vital production factor. Social polarization occurred at the level of land use, too, as a result of the rise of large tenant farmers. Social costs were particularly great there because the lack of social balance and counterweights in a region which had traditionally been dominated by large landlords and where rural associations were weak. The resulting social mix of large landowners, big tenant farmers and proletarianized wage labourers was in place by the mid-16th century and would remain for centuries.

In inland Flanders, despite the early rise of towns and markets, such developments did not occur. Manorialism had never been very important, and dissolved early, while peasants held a strong grip on the land. These smallholder peasants formed part of an exceptional social balance developing in high medieval inland Flanders, together with various associations, some noblemen but also the emerging towns and their elites, and the territorial lord. In Flanders, both the territorial lord and the urban communities in this period acquired a firmer position than their counterparts elsewhere in the Low Countries. The counts of Flanders were able to build on the powerful position they already had there in the Carolingian era, and on the opportunities afforded by their claims to the unoccupied lands in the coastal plain. The towns in Flanders also grew gradually, based on several early medieval foundations, including some long-distance trade, but also using their functions in administration and defence, and their growing industries, which were increasingly aimed at export. Moreover, their position was built on the presence of wealthy consumers drawing surpluses from their manors, lands, and other rights in the countryside. Urban communities emerged in the 11th to 12th centuries, building on the existing tradition of association and relative freedom. In Flanders, but also in Brabant and elsewhere, these communities were recognized or even backed by territorial lords, who allied with the towns to counter the power of the feudal lords.

A vital role in the growing importance of non-kin exchange of land, labour, and capital in the high Middle Ages was played by the emerging voluntary associations, especially in Flanders, in town and countryside. The exchange and allocation of land, labour, and capital was increasingly made by village and urban communities, water management boards, parishes, poor relief organizations, and later the guilds. Goods and products were mostly exchanged through the market. The rise of a commodity market led to social polarization, as a direct result of market competition, and the indirect result of the increasing attractiveness of investing in land and capital goods for the older and new elites, resulting in scale-enlargement of production structures. The polarization was found especially in towns where export-oriented production emerged, as in Flanders. This polarization triggered a reaction in the associations, especially the guilds, but also the commons.

In the late 13th and early 14th centuries, the independent craftsmen and their guilds succeeded in safeguarding their position by a series of mainly successful revolts, especially in inland Flanders. The conflict of interests between the urban patricians and the territorial lords, prohibiting common action, helped to ensure the success of the revolts. They were mainly defensive and protected the existing small-scale production against the growing scale-enlargement and power of big entrepreneurs. The position of small-scale, independent producers in the Flemish towns became well-entrenched, and their political power grew, while their guild organization allowed them to reap the benefits of the rising market, enabling specialization and market orientation, but at the same time shielding them from the problems of polarization and proletarianization. Much more than in rural Drenthe, where the associations of commoners were aimed mainly at protecting the viability of independent holdings by limiting market participation, these associations of craftsmen in the Flemish industrial towns focused on reaping the benefits of market participation. Even in Flanders, however, these associations also had a defensive aspect, which would show itself when Flemish urban industries came under pressure from the 14th century onwards.

Confronted with declining market shares, craftsmen and merchants in inland Flanders had a joint interest in using and further developing coercion over the countryside. In the 13th and 14th centuries, building on the existing privileges and military power of the towns, often developed in close collaboration with the emerging territorial lord, and later with newly acquired privileges and the military strength of the guild militias, the towns, urban elites, and guilds started to employ trade privileges and market coercion. They were well placed to do so, since the market for goods in Flanders developed in the high Middle Ages in an urban setting, with the towns and urban merchant elites able to shape the institutional framework of this market to a great extent. This resulted in urban market forces in Flanders having a major role, and the decline of markets and economic activities in the countryside. Hence urban industries and merchants could operate in a monopolistic environment. Further, a forced interlinking of markets developed, as in proto-industries in inland Flanders, where merchants combined their dealings in the markets for goods, labour, and capital to bind the producers, transferring production risks to them and obtaining goods at lower prices. The merchants used their dominance and monopolies in the market as the main instrument in this strategy. Because producers (peasants and craftsmen) were well-entrenched, and also owned most of the land and capital goods, the urban elites of merchants and entrepreneurs had to concentrate on the market as the most promising avenue in which they could skim off surpluses.

In the long run the application of non-economic coercion in inland Flanders had a detrimental effect on the economy as a whole and undermined the competitiveness of various sectors. The power of the urban merchants and the guild elites, with their shared interests, however, made it difficult to change this situation. Also, since towns competed with one another, it would not be wise for one town to abandon this strategy single-handedly. Caught in this Nash equilibrium, each town feared losing market share to those which still retained it, leading to further institutional sclerosis. This situation hindered the rise of specialization and commercialization in the countryside, and it induced peasants in inland Flanders to cling to their land to safeguard their subsistence and retain some economic independence. The result was an equilibrium composed of rural and urban producers mostly owning the means of production, and urban merchants having access to surpluses through their control over markets. This situation remained in place up to the 19th century, and contrasts with that of coastal Flanders, where large land ownership and the power of large lords had always been more important, and short-term leasing developed rapidly. The emergence of large tenant farms and specialized agriculture can be observed there, more similar to developments in the Guelders river area. This contrast with neighbouring inland Flanders shows how the rise of territorial principalities which spanned regions, as in Flanders, did not lead to a levelling of differences, and perhaps even the opposite.

Holland was a region characterized by peat marshes, which remained virtually uninhabited in the early Middle Ages and had very few manors. The Holland peatlands were not reclaimed until the high Middle Ages. Peasants had a strong position from the outset, acquiring personal freedom and clear property rights to the land, offered in order to attract them to this inhospitable frontier region. In the process of occupation the territorial lord played an important role. On the basis of wilderness rights he could build a firm economic and political position, and therefore did not require a great deal of non-economic force, nor did he have much competition from rival feudal authorities. His position became based on taxes and military service, not on manorial properties, personal connections, or arbitrary levies. This laid the basis for a modern-type relationship between prince and people, almost like that between state and citizen, without personal or feudal elements.

Just as in inland Flanders, market exchange became important in Holland, but markets in Holland, including the factor markets, developed a more open organization, with few barriers and hardly any non-economic elements. This is to a large extent understandable in view of the late occupation of Holland and its specific organization, resulting in a free peasantry, the near absence of manorialism and non-economic barriers, and a weak feudal elite. It also allowed for horizontal associations to be formed at all levels, urban and rural. The associations were able to offer a counterweight to potentially more powerful parties in the marketing. Moreover, the late start of urbanization and the emergence of many small and medium-sized towns in Holland also played a role. Holland did not experience a dominance of a few urban centres and their elites, who might have been able to bend the market organization to their interests; instead, there was always competition among many towns. In Holland, the balance formed by the countervailing forces of different urban elites of numerous towns, the rural nobility, associations, and the territorial lord did not allow one social group to acquire a dominant position.

In many parts of the Low Countries, but especially in Holland, the authorities promoted the development and growth of open markets. This was mainly because the social balance did not allow one interest group to use government power as its instrument. Such a balance existed in Holland, both at the regional level and in the towns, at least up to the 16th century, as merchants became predominant. As a result, the authorities in Holland exerted a positive influence on the rise of market exchange, by removing many obstacles to further growth of the market, increasing security, and reducing abuses. They also contributed to the development of more absolute and exclusive property rights, also for fiscal reasons, and stimulated market exchange over other systems of allocation, except for some increase in the allocation by the government itself.

Chronology was also a factor in this. Since markets in Holland developed later and in a freer setting than, for instance, those in inland Flanders, institutions developed that did not require corporate organization, but allowed for individual and impersonal transactions. Moreover, the open markets which emerged reinforced one another through positive interaction. A smoothly functioning and accessible capital market, for instance, increased the opportunities for ordinary people to operate successfully in the land, lease, product, and labour markets. It also reduced risks and helped these people to avoid economic dependency. These elements, combined with the ecological problems which undermined the option of subsistence farming, all helped to promote the swift rise of markets in Holland. This process, and the ensuing market competition, resulted in a transition to a more capitalist economy and society, which not only had economic effects but also profound social consequences.

In Holland the transition started later but was very swift and even more profound than, for instance, in the Guelders river area. Independent, small-scale producers had been dominant from the period of occupation in the high Middle Ages, but they were now pushed aside as a result of keen market competition and the ensuing polarization. The social structure in Holland changed fundamentally. Elsewhere, independent producers may have lost their land more slowly, and their decline was counter-balanced by the rise of new middle groups, such as the large tenant farmers in the Guelders river area, forming perhaps a tenth of the total population. Holland, on the other hand, experienced the biggest change since it developed from a very egalitarian society of free, small-scale producers in the 13th and 14th centuries to the most polarized, capitalist society in the 16th and 17th centuries.

This transition had huge social costs. The market competition and the scale-enlargement of production structures resulted in proletarianization and social polarization. Combined with the declining real wages of the 15th and 16th centuries, the gap between wealth and poverty was widening rapidly. The growing importance of market exchange also eroded the social networks that earlier had prevented the unfavourable social effects of exchange. Market exchange resulted in poverty for large groups of society: up to half of the populace lived at a minimum subsistence level. Poverty and polarization were most acute in regions where the transition was most profound, such as Holland, but also coastal Flanders and the Guelders river area. At first increasing poverty was partly counter-balanced by the rise and extension of institutional charity, mainly in the cities, but this system came under stress and in the early 16th century it was reorganized. In all respects, Holland, with its high medieval foundation of freedom and open markets, was one of the earliest European examples of a region undergoing transition to a capitalist society.

One would expect that late medieval developments such as the emergence of markets, industrialization, and political unification would eradicate regional differences in socio-institutional organization, but this was hardly the case. The extent to which regions responded to growing markets varied according to the social context. Small-scale peasant producers, such as those in Drenthe and also in inland Flanders, were often less inclined to enter the market, whereas tenant farmers in regions dominated by leased large landholdings, including the Guelders river area, were compelled to do so, because they needed to maximize profits to compete in the lease market. The extent of involvement in the market also depended on the availability and viability of alternative systems of exchange, such as associations and families. Both these alternative organizations and the social property systems took their specific shape in the early and high Middle Ages, and were thus a clear link between the earlier and later Middle Ages.

Conversely, market competition affected the social context. Social changes were slightest in regions where the market was not very important or its organization and effects were influenced by associations of small-scale producers. Where associations were strong, as in Drenthe (villages, commons) or inland Flanders (guilds), and property was fairly equally distributed, further market-driven development was slowed, preventing a capitalist transition of economy and society, while at the same time making development more socially sustainable. Geographical distance from the cores of urban demand played a smaller part in this. For example, inland Flanders was situated at the core of market demand but experienced no fundamental changes in social organization until well into the modern period, either in towns or in the countryside. Coastal Flanders, on the other hand, experienced strong social polarization and a swift transition, mainly as a result of the dominance of large land ownership and the easy availability of lease land, and the fact that horizontal associations were fairly weak there. Alternatives to market exchange were less easily available, and independent small-scale producers had fewer opportunities to shield themselves from the negative effects of market competition.

Growing inter-regional trade even sharpened the regional distinctness. This trade integrated regions within one economic market system, and stimulated regional divergence, with each region using its comparative advantages. The evolving complementarity and specialization of regions had divergent effects. Among these were a focus on agriculture or industries, labour-intensification or extensification, different demographic patterns leading to population growth or stagnation, differences in wealth distribution, and differences in long-term growth rates. All these differences came about in the face of growing economic integration.

Neither did revolts level out regional differences. Most revolts were defensive and brought stability rather than change. Successful revolts against a united elite were very rare. Conversely, it was also difficult for rulers to change existing social structures. The political unification process of the later Middle Ages rather strengthened regional divergence, since the growing exchange within the larger entity made the unified regions more complementary. In the long run, however, it also had a homogenizing effect. Especially in the 15th to 16th centuries, when the Burgundian-Habsburg regime was extending its power over all parts of the Low Countries, central authorities increased their influence at regional and local levels through legislation and the administration of justice. This resulted in a growing interaction among political elements operating at the central level, on the one hand, and social and economic elements embedded in a regional framework, on the other. The central authority developed a dynamism of its own, and was increasingly able to build its own basis of property and power apart from the regional social structure, supported by social groups who based their position on state power, such as state officials. Still, even in the Habsburg period, the position of the state was not strong enough to overrule all other interest groups and eradicate regional differences. Although political-dynastic considerations at a wider geographical level, partly even outside the Low Countries, became more important, this did not lead to substantial uniformity. Whether this would have occurred later remains an open question, because the Dutch Revolt in the late 16th century cut off the process of political integration.

The industrial sector began to develop independently of regional structures. Initially it was very much bound to the land and regional social structures for its organization, but as trade and the importance of capital investments grew, so too did flexibility, particularly in urban industries. Nevertheless, it is striking how much industrial development remained a regional phenomenon and specializations assumed a regional character. This can be observed most clearly in the process of proto-industrialization, which was tied in with the formulation and distribution of rights to land, and with the effect of rights to land on household formation and labour supply, and thus directly linked to regional structures.

Some of these late medieval processes resulted in regional divergence, while others brought about increasing similarities within the integrated areas. The trends of divergence and convergence probably balanced one another in the 12th to 15th centuries, but homogenizing elements then grew in strength, leading to some convergence and a reduction of regional differences within the Low Countries. This was a very slow process, however, and it only accelerated in the 19th and 20th centuries. The region is the most relevant geographical unit for investigating and understanding economic and social history, at least up to the 16th and perhaps even into the 19th century. Until the end of the Middle Ages, the regional chain that had begun with the occupation and the original distribution of rights to land and labour among social groups, which was closely related to the geographical and social context of occupation, remained unbroken.

As a result, boundaries between the regions remained very distinct, often into the modern period. The boundary between the Guelders river area, with its predominance of large landowners, and peasant-dominated Holland, remained sharp and rigid up to the 16th century. Even more tenacious was the socio-economic boundary between coastal Flanders and inland Flanders, which was in place up to the 18th and 19th centuries. This is not to say that these societies were frozen; some of their differences acquired a new appearance over time, but the changes were embedded in the existing socio-institutional framework. The different trajectories and responses to new challenges were rooted in the earlier medieval period.

The medieval history of the Low Countries is a clear demonstration of how great the degree of socio-institutional path dependency and long-term continuity in regional structures was. The socio-institutional framework not only changed slowly over time, but also was specific to a region, and not easily transferable. Contributing to this institutional continuity was the process that took place in the high Middle Ages when the personal bonds of the early Middle Ages were largely replaced by territorial ties. Social institutions such as banal lordship and territorial lordship marked the shift from personal ties to territorial ones on a vertical level. This shift was paired with a rise of voluntary horizontal associations in the high Middle Ages, as within village and urban communities, which were also related to specific territories. But more importantly, the regional structures were so persistent because of their social element, and more particularly the social relations with respect to the main production factor, land. Such relations remained fundamentally unchanged, despite changes in the expression or exact formulation of rights to land and the nature of the transfer of surpluses. Whether a region adapted its institutional organization to dynamic forces, such as the rise of the market, depended not only on the strength of these forces, but especially on the balance of social power and the gains or losses to be made by the dominant group or groups. As a result, this institutional framework of exchange was not easy to change, not only because of the high cost, but more because the dominant social groups had a vested interest in the existing framework.

The Effects of Socio-institutional Constellations on Economic Development

This institutional framework in its turn shaped and directed the effects of climatic, geographical, demographic, and political changes, refracting them in divergent directions. It also largely determined how a region would respond to technological innovations or economic change, and the extent to which it was able to reap their benefits. The effect of this framework did not remain the same over time. In the course of centuries the demands the economy made on this framework changed, because of political events or gradual, long-term changes in technology and forces of production, ecological conditions, and the opportunities for exchange. An existing socio-institutional framework was thus likely to be overtaken in due course by a new framework more suited to new circumstances. In the course of this process it was difficult to adjust the earlier framework exactly because of the social embeddedness discussed at length above. While this lack of adaptability, or involution, did not necessarily lead to an absolute economic decline, it did cause loss of the core position. The framework was thus a crucial element in the shifts in economic leadership in the Low Countries.

In the early Middle Ages the most successful regions were the Meuse valley and the Guelders river area, both characterized by strong manorial organization. These regions witnessed most growth, in population and cultivated area, but also in the introduction of new crops, new techniques, and rotation systems, and in more intensive forms of grain cultivation. After the chaotic, insecure situation in the post-Roman period, the manorial organization of large landowners was beneficial. In combination with the power of local/regional or even supra-regional magnates it provided some security, even if order and stability were unilaterally imposed by the rulers. Manorial organization led to some improvement in security of property, especially considering the low levels of the preceding period. Moreover, this system at least partly improved the position of labour. Although manorial organization bound labour and restricted its mobility, it still offered some protection, secure access to the land, and more freedom of action compared with the previous system of slavery, thus stimulating production. Capital investments were probably also promoted by the manorial system. The manorial lords were able to procure more capital, which was also accumulated through the manorial system, allowing the demesnes to produce more surpluses than peasant farms, particularly in the fairly insecure circumstances of the period, as investment would otherwise be unattractive. Examples are the heavy ploughs and mills, whose spread was promoted by the capital power of the lords and their ability to organize and enforce the use and exploitation of the technologies.

Compared with the previous period, the manorial system also increased integration, both locally and between localities, partly because it was linked to the Frankish integration process and the security offered by Frankish rule. It enabled a certain exchange of surpluses within the local setting and offered some solution for the near absence of money and markets. The fact that the manorial system channelled the economic dynamism towards the lords and centralized its benefits, even though it did so partly through coercion, was a relative advantage in this period of few surpluses: by gathering these small surpluses, it enabled trade and specialization both within and among manors. Although manors seemingly were autarkic systems, they paradoxically were relatively conducive to trade in the circumstances of the early Middle Ages. The regions where the manorial system was strongly developed, such as the Guelders river area and the Meuse valley, had the most developed economy and a relative concentration of surpluses, urban centres, cultural growth, and trade.

The towns in this period were few and very small. Some of them were trading centres mostly involved in long-distance trade in luxury products. These centres, such as Dorestad, Tiel, Dinant, or Huy, had merchants as prominent inhabitants, but they were often associated with a powerful feudal lord or the king, who offered protection and privileges, established a mint and estates, and levied tolls; such institutions followed on and profited from the growth of the centres, but at the same time they enabled their rise by providing some protection and a framework for trade. Another type of town was even more clearly linked to power and landed properties. These were the centres of religious and political power, where surpluses from a large area were brought together, mainly through manorial organization and the levying of tithes. Such centres were mainly found in regions where the king, lords, or religious institutions had relatively strong authority. Although these centres drained surpluses from more productive uses and investment, they provided some demand for specialized industrial products and services, which stimulated specialization and technological innovation. Some of these towns were also centres of learning and promoted writing, particularly those with important monasteries and later cathedral schools, mainly found in regions with many large religious estates, as in the Meuse valley. Because they promoted efficient communication and the reduction of information costs, they stimulated exchange and economic growth. The few hesitant steps forward in economic organization were most clearly taken in the regions with large manorialized holdings and a strong royal presence.

After the 10th century a second phase started, consisting of extensive growth in population and area, as was found in many regions in the Low Countries, as well as intensive growth in some regions, most notably in various parts of Flanders. In the course of this process the economic centre in the Low Countries shifted from the Meuse valley and the Guelders river area to Artois and Flanders. In the Flemish countryside agricultural development, intensification, and specialization were pronounced. Particularly there, agricultural changes resulted both in population growth and, at least initially, also in increasing surpluses. Such surpluses facilitated the growth of industries, trade, and towns, with inland Flanders and Walloon Flanders, together with Artois, becoming the most urbanized parts of the Low Countries and centres of export industries.

Apparently, a new social and economic organization had emerged in Flanders which was more favourable to economic growth than those found elsewhere in the Low Countries. This was especially true of the emergence and specific arrangement of territorial lordship, which assumed its most advanced form in Flanders. The supposition that well-developed territorial princely rule was a crucial element is supported by the fact that all three regions in Flanders developed rapidly, although along different and partly complementary lines. The effect of the rise of princely rule can also be deduced from the relative commercial decline in the same period of Zeeland and particularly of Friesland, where territorial lords did not emerge. The favourable influence on economic development exercised by the relatively powerful territorial lords in Flanders, and their well-developed military and bureaucratic administration, was not the result of direct economic policies, since such policies hardly existed in the period, but came about more indirectly, through increased stability, security, and more secure property rights. In general, in the high Middle Ages, the security of property rights was increased, guaranteed by secular authorities and their administrations, and facilitated by the growing emphasis on education and use of written documentation, most clearly in Flanders and Artois. Arbitrariness was reduced, and bylaws and constitutions created a better, more secure framework for trade and investment.

The counterweight to princely power, provided by banal lords, urban elites, and increasingly by town communities and other associations, found in high medieval Flanders, induced or even compelled the territorial lord to promote general interests over his private ones. The freedom of ever larger proportions of the population also proved a positive asset. The successful regions in this period had very few manors, or they saw the dissolution of this system, while those where manorialism remained longer were clearly overtaken by others in the course of the high Middle Ages. The freedom and opportunity to form associations must also be assessed an advantage. These formed an important social counterweight and contributed to a social balance, thus helping to reduce lordly arbitrariness and insecurity, which had a positive effect on exchange and investments. The associations were also able to provide efficient modes of exchange and allocation. Their role was particularly important in the period 1000–1300, when factor markets were only beginning to emerge, and much of the exchange of land, labour, and capital took place through voluntary associations, such as village and urban communities, guilds, water management boards, parishes and poor relief organizations, and particularly through families and kin. In these respects their organization was more successful than the manor, as is apparent from extensive growth in the 11th to 13th centuries, often combined with real, intensive growth, and predominantly found in regions where associations were well developed.

Another element in the rapid rise of inland Flanders, coastal Flanders, Walloon Flanders, and Artois was the emergence of the market exchange of goods and products. Where commodity markets functioned well, they allowed more exchange and a reduction in transaction costs, leading to increased specialization and some productivity gains. Where the influence of urban communities and associations contributed to a balance of power, as in inland Flanders and Holland, institutions of market exchange emerged that indeed made these markets more accessible, fair, and equal. Moreover, associations reduced the unfavourable side-effects of market competition, such as social polarization or ecological degradation. Important for the effects of growing market exchange was also the fact that many free, independent people could enter the market, such as craftsmen and peasants, allowing them a more equal position in the market and a more equal spread in the gains of market exchange over larger proportions of the population. This situation was found in inland Flanders, and to some extent also in coastal Flanders, although there inequality started to grow in the 13th and 14th centuries.

Economic growth in the high Middle Ages was also promoted by the emerging towns, most clearly in southern and inland Flanders. Towns not only grew in size, but—more importantly—offered increasing security in this period. To some extent this security was physical, by protecting capital and capital goods with city walls and urban militias, and to some extent it was institutional, taking the form of charters, by-laws, and privileges, which offered more secure property rights and promoted trade and investment, and most particularly, investments in fixed capital goods. The development of urban administration and the growing literacy were also important, and the concentration of wealthy consumers helped to increase demand. Some of these towns were also successful in forging more intense inter-urban relations for exchange among merchants and among the centres, as through inter-urban arrangements or organizations, most prominently within the Hansa. Such developments promoted security in trade, lowered information costs, and made inter-regional trade more intensive, even in non-luxury products.

All these elements together, including the rise of territorial principalities and commodity markets, jointly resulted in a better integration of town and countryside, and a better integration of the countryside in the wider economy, thus promoting rural specialization. It was not only large landowners who participated in this process, such as the big abbeys with their urban granges, but also smaller independent producers in the countryside. The integration of town and countryside was also directly shaped through the rural property owned by townsmen in the form of land, jurisdictional rights, and tithes. Compared with the older and alternative constellations it promoted economic development, as evidenced in the fact that cities such as Dordrecht and Groningen, and even more so, Ghent and Bruges, grew rapidly. In the course of the 11th to 14th centuries they outstripped the older urban centres in heavily manorialized regions such as Huy, Dinant, Tongeren, Tiel, and Zaltbommel. It can also be seen from the fact that the economy as a whole developed significantly in these regions, even where such growth was subordinated to the interests of the urban elite of merchants, merchant-entrepreneurs, and guild leaders, as was most apparent in Flanders.

The favourable effect attributed to the associations of free, independent people and the social balance between a strong territorial lord, powerful cities, banal lords, and these associations is also demonstrated through its absence in 14th-century French Flanders and Artois. Property in these regions became less equally distributed as a result of, or at least simultaneously with, the rise of the market. At the same time the role of associations was diminished. In towns such as Saint-Omer and Douai communal organization and guild power were crushed around 1300. Patrician power increased and the social balance was eroded. In the 14th century this region and these towns were more severely affected by demographic catastrophe, reduction in urbanization rate, and economic decline than any other region in the Low Countries. This hardly seems coincidental.

In coastal Flanders, too, the social distribution of property became more skewed in the 13th and 14th centuries, when peasants lost ownership of their land, or lost access to it altogether. Associations remained, but they no longer functioned as power balances since members lost their economic independence. In the short run the economic effect of these developments was positive because of scale-enlargement and increasing specialization, which increased surpluses, but in the long run the result was unfavourable, since the ecological and social sustainability of development were affected. In inland Flanders, on the other hand, small independent producers and associations remained strong, but the towns and their elites, merchants, and guild leaders started to apply more non-economic coercion over the countryside. The fact that trade became artificially channelled through such urban centres in the long run hindered the further rise of specialization and commercialization in the countryside and the further growth of trade. The increasing protectionism of local urban industries and particular interest groups in the industrial sector also had unfavourable economic effects. Once developed, this situation was difficult to change, precisely because of the dominance of urban interest groups which led to an institutional lock-in effect.

As a result, these three Flemish regions started to lose their economic edge. Their relative decline became apparent in the following centuries when factor markets started to emerge in the Low Countries, especially from the decades around 1300. In only a few regions the institutional framework of factor markets stimulated their rapid further growth, and acted as an impetus to commercialization, specialization, investment, and productivity increase. The most conspicuous of these regions was Holland. The relatively equal distribution of property, both in town and countryside, and the fairly even spread of power and the near absence of feudal elements allowed for flexible, accessible, and secure markets for capital, labour, land, and goods. In the 15th and 16th centuries the effect can be seen in the high mobility of land in the market, in the low level of interest rates in the capital market, in the near absence of rent differentials between town and countryside or between social groups, and in the strong integration and openness of labour markets. Organized and functioning in this way, markets were apparently more efficient and conducive to economic growth than other mechanisms of exchange, such as associations or manorial organization, since the strongest growth in the later Middle Ages was found in Holland. This region offered the institutional framework that was most favourable to specialization, investment, and growth through its thriving markets.

In inland Flanders developments were markedly different from those in Holland. The non-economic coercion in Flanders made markets less open and flexible, and also imposed restrictions on production. Under insecure circumstances and small trade flows this system had functioned very well, but in the 14th to 15th centuries, as markets became more pervasive and reliable, transport was improved, and security increased, the system became less necessary and even started to hinder further development and growth. Regions such as inland Flanders and particularly Walloon Flanders were overtaken by those offering a more open and flexible framework for production and exchange, such as Holland and the emerging industrial centres in the Campine and the Vesdre area. This threatened Flemish market shares and provoked the increased use of non-economic coercion in production and trade in Flanders, thus further aggravating the problems.

In Holland the urban elites and entrepreneurs generally supported a free economy and open markets, and rarely applied non-economic coercion. They could afford to ignore the possibility of using non-economic force since they could produce relatively cheaply because they had access to cheap capital and ample scope for scale-enlargement, which was made easier by the weakness of guilds and the presence of a large and flexible labour market. This provided ample scope for further economic growth, particularly through scale-enlargement of production structures and investments in fixed capital goods. Although such developments led to polarization and a high social cost, open markets were an advantage to the dominant social group in Holland, the merchant-entrepreneurs, since they had a good chance to profit from competition in the market. The surpluses produced and the low production costs, paired with greater freedom in commodity markets, gave regions such as Holland a competitive edge in international markets. Combined with the low cost of capital, it also increased Holland's role in long-distance trade and transport services.

In the organization of these markets, the authorities played a mainly positive role. Governments and courts of law in many parts of the Low Countries, and especially in Holland, guaranteed and protected property rights, albeit at least partly for fiscal reasons, and developed a proper central administration of property. Moreover, private registration of property increased, aided by growing literacy which was sustained by the educational policies of the authorities. In these ways, the authorities contributed to the development of more exclusive and absolute property rights, while increasing security and lowering transaction costs, thus helping the rise of land, credit, and commodity markets.

Factor markets also swiftly emerged in the Guelders river area, where in the decades around 1300 manorial lords were transformed into large landowners having near absolute property rights to the land and leasing it out for short terms. The joint investments made by large tenant farmers and landowners, which were forced by the competitive lease system and made attractive by the opportunities for marketing, resulted in an increase in agricultural surpluses. The rapid transition temporarily brought economic growth, but only a small proportion of the population profited from it: mainly the few large tenant farmers and to some extent the large landowners, whereas large segments of the population were reduced to poverty. Moreover, economic growth did not lead to urbanization in this region, since agricultural production was mostly aimed at markets elsewhere, while almost all industrial goods were imported. After all gains from specialization and scale-enlargement had been reaped, in the second half of the 16th century economic development and growth came to a standstill, and this remained the case until well into the modern period.

In the 14th to 16th centuries the strongest growth was found in those regions where markets for land, labour, capital, and goods were most accessible, flexible, and secure, and where the least non-economic coercion was applied. The accessibility and advantages, however, also depended on a balanced distribution of property and power, with equal and independent parties entering the market. This combination was more successful than alternative mechanisms of exchange and allocation, also because it allowed for a close integration of town and countryside through the market. An intense interaction between town and countryside was further promoted when the countryside had a socio-institutional framework which offered flexibility and competition, especially in regions where short-term leasing became dominant. This constellation led to a marked rise in local trade in basic products, an increase in inter-regional trade, and the high mobility of labour and capital. All of these acted as an impetus to specialization, investment, and gains in productivity.

As a result of the growing integration and interaction through markets, regional specialization increased and differences among regions became more pronounced. In particular, the nature and extent of specialization differed significantly. In some regions, such as the Guelders river area and coastal Flanders, integration through market exchange led to de-industrialization of the countryside and an almost exclusive focus on commercial agriculture. Other regions, such as Holland and inland Flanders, experienced the increasing success of urban and rural industries. In inland Flanders rural activities were organized mainly by independent small-scale peasant producers, while the urban elites used their privileged position, both economically and non-economically, within the market system. This produced a stable situation, but it did not allow for much economic growth. In Holland, on the other hand, urban entrepreneurs invested heavily in capital-intensive activities in the countryside and relied increasingly on wage labourers. In the resulting dynamics, there was much more social polarization, but in the short run there was more economic growth and a growing dominance of Holland products in the market.

The story does not end with Holland, however, as the logical and perfect fulfilment of all historical development. From the 16th century some non-economic elements were strengthened and the burgher-merchants shifted their investments to land and public debt. Moreover, as a result of fierce market competition there was strong polarization, first in the towns and later, in the 16th and 17th centuries, also in the countryside, which resulted in the loss of social balance and an increasing dominance of urban merchant-entrepreneurs. The social context needed for a favourable institutional organization of market exchange and a positive effect for broad groups in society was eroded. In the long run this process diminished the social sustainability of growth and eventually economic growth itself, as happened in the course of the 17th century. Other regions developed a social-institutional framework that was more suited to the economic needs of the time. More specifically, the dominance of merchants, the investment choices of urban elites and the disappearance of proto-industrial peasants made Holland less conducive to industrial capitalism. This required a different framework such as that found in the Meuse valley and other parts of Wallonia where industrial capitalism unfolded in the modern era.

The arguments set out above show that all phases of regional economic growth lasted for only a few centuries. Since they were often combined with population growth, the net effect of these phases on GDP per capita in the long run was not very impressive. Moreover, the phases of economic growth often hid a growing unevenness in the social distribution of growth. This was particularly true in the late medieval Low Countries, when the societies of several regions during the growth of GDP per capita experienced polarization and proletarization, resulting in an increasing gap between rich and poor, and increasing poverty, most clearly in economically successful Holland. If success is measured in modal living standards rather than by using an abstract indicator such as GDP per capita, the success of the latter regions can be seriously questioned.

The explanation for the contradiction between GDP per capita and living standards can largely be found in the growing importance of market exchange and the related specialization and scale-enlargement from the 11th century on. This process was able to increase or sustain GDP per capita and feed more people, but at the same time created inequality, pollution, and environmental degradation, and undermined social organizations and horizontal associations that might have been able to reduce such problems and thus guarantee social and ecological sustainability. Regional and central governments could in theory have offered a counterweight, but since their role was greatly influenced by dominant social groups, they did not try to protect or restore this balance, particularly in those regions where social polarization was strongest and the influence of those who profited from this most pronounced. The unfavourable effects of market competition thus countered the possible favourable effects of rising GDP per capita on modal living standards. Conversely, in regions where the market remained unimportant and horizontal organizations strong, living standards for an average family were not necessarily lower, as in peasant-dominated Drenthe. The relationship between market exchange, economic growth, and modal standards of living is not unilinear.

The above overview also shows that the identity of the leading regions changed, and changes, constantly and such regions show ever new combinations of social-institutional organization. Some of these sets promoted economic growth, although this was not always associated with social well-being and ecological sustainability in the long run. The key to economic success seems to have been a relatively efficient system of exchange combined with social balance. All regions that underwent rapid economic growth had a fairly even distribution of power and property, such as inland Flanders in the high Middle Ages or Holland in the late Middle Ages. At the same time, not all regions with such a balance experienced strong economic growth, as was true for Drenthe and the Campine. Apparently this balance had to be paired with an efficient system of exchange. The combination of the two was vital, and the absence or loss of either one led to relative decline. If this is true, the question is how did the manorialized regions in the early Middle Ages fit into this picture. The combination of power and property in manorial organization was definitely not equal, although perhaps it may have been less unequal than believed and less unequal than alternative organizations at the time, such as slave-staffed plantations; it may also have formed a system of exchange that offered optimal possibilities in the circumstances of the period.

None of the socio-institutional frameworks of exchange, production and investment discussed above had economic growth or widespread welfare as their main, explicit goal; if such results occurred, they were to a large extent the unintended by-products or secondary goals of the groups involved. The most notable exception was the high medieval organization in which horizontal associations played a large part, since they had the well-being of a relatively large group of people as a direct goal. Later, too, in the system of market exchange, associations could play this positive role, although no longer directly. The state could also play such an indirect role if allowed to do so under the influence of particular interest groups. These organizations having a role in promoting welfare, such as the guilds, village communities, commons, parishes, and the state, all operated at a territorial level. The territorial aspect presumably was a crucial element, because it increased solidarity and coherence. Moreover, positive action was promoted by the fact that the territory was the arena where both action and reaction, or cause and effect of economic activities, were located. This territorial link became eroded by the late Middle Ages, when market exchange and interregional specialization over ever larger distances made the link between cause and effect less visible and tangible. As a result, people may have felt less need to take responsibility for the effects of economic activities, thus undermining social and ecological sustainability. The nation-state of the 19th to 20th centuries largely restored this link within its geographical territory, but now—with the further growth of market exchange and globalization—it has again been lost. In view of the medieval experience, a new socio-institutional complex at the global level, paired with a more even distribution worldwide of property, power, and knowledge would seem to be the key for a development which combines economic growth with social and ecological sustainability.

The Low Countries in European Perspective

This study has focused on comparing regions within the Low Countries. Yet it is impossible not to notice that each of the core regions that took the lead there stood out in Europe as well. This was true of the Meuse valley in the early Middle Ages, when it was the heartland of Carolingian power, of Artois and Flanders in the high Middle Ages, which together with northern Italy formed the summit of urban-based development, and of the Guelders river area in the late Middle Ages, which was probably the first region in Europe that experienced a transition to agrarian capitalism in the 15th to 16th centuries; and of course, it was true of Holland, which developed to a position as centre of the world economy. At a regional level the core constantly shifted in the Low Countries in the course of the Middle Ages, but in this thousand-year period the Low Countries have always been home to the European cores.

Although this study has not attempted to place the Low Countries in a wider European perspective, some quantitative indicators show that the development of this part of Europe was indeed exceptional. One such indicator is the rapid population growth, over almost the entire medieval period. In the period 1000–1300, the population of the Low Countries grew fourfold, to some 2 million people, compared with only a doubling of population in Europe as a whole. In the 14th to 16th centuries there was further growth, and population densities in the Low Countries became the highest in all of Europe, and similar to northern Italy. In urbanization the Low Countries surpassed other parts of Europe even more decisively: in the 13th century, together with northern Italy, it had an urbanization rate of some 20 per cent, but in the 15th and 16th centuries it quickly surpassed Italy, with this rate rising to a staggering 34 per cent.

The level of real wages was high in the late medieval Low Countries compared with the other parts of Europe, and the decline in real wages in the 16th century was not as pronounced as in the rest of Europe, excluding England, which resulted in a divergence of real wages between these two parts of north-western Europe and the rest of Europe. At the same time, many parts of the Low Countries underwent sharp social polarization, which adversely affected modal standards of living. Despite this decline, if we take height as the main indicator of living standards, the Low Countries will compare favourably with other parts of Europe. The figures on male stature show that living standards in the Low Countries must have been relatively high in the high Middle Ages, and they did not decline in the late Middle Ages as sharply as elsewhere. In the late 17th century, the first period for which comparable international figures are available, average male stature in France was only 1.62 m, with annual fluctuations in averages from 1.60 to 1.65, compared with an average of 1.69 in the Dutch Republic.[9] It is also striking that in the late 17th century the tallest men in France were from Artois, French Flanders, and French Hainaut, which are all regions bordering the Low Countries, with men from Hainaut being on average 4 cm taller than those from central France. The main achievement of the Low Countries was that it was able to sustain the biggest population growth and the highest urbanization rate in Europe, without producing Malthusian crises or appalling poverty.

All these findings together suggest that there were special factors operating in parts of the Low Countries, as well as in the Low Countries as a whole, which may have been more pronounced than in other parts of Europe. One such factor that can be excluded is soil fertility. In this respect the Low Countries were not particularly blessed, with their abundance of sandy soils, wetlands, and poor, stony land. The poor sandy loam of inland Flanders or the wet peatlands of Holland can hardly be considered an advantage in the precocious development of these regions.

One favourable factor was the intense interaction among regions in the Low Countries. This intensity was first the result of the fact that these regions with their sharply divergent socio-economic structures were located close to one another. In other parts of western Europe regions were probably larger or less distinct. This was because of the indirect link between such structures and the soil conditions. The enormous density of various geographical-pedological landscapes in the Low Countries, the result of the special genesis of this area, led to a high density of different economic regions. Associated with this, and even increased by the ethnic diversity, each of these regions acquired its specific socio-institutional characteristics with the occupation in the early or high Middle Ages. The close proximity of the distinct regions contributed to an intense interaction and stimulated economic development. Necessary for such interaction, however, was a physical and institutional framework to make it possible. Here the Low Countries benefited especially from its waterways: the sea, estuaries, and inlets, and the many rivers and canals, offering cheap and easy transport possibilities.

[9] Komlos, 'An anthropometric history'.

But even more important was the institutional setting for interaction provided by relatively well-protected property rights, well-developed systems of exchange, and the relative weakness of institutional barriers to trade.

In the later Middle Ages this exchange increasingly took place through the market. In this part of north-western Europe the proximity of different regions, the strong diversity of each region, and the absence of non-economic barriers and extra-economic power resulted in a free, interlinked, and large market. In the Low Countries, markets became open and flexible to a much greater degree than elsewhere in Europe. As observed above, this was largely the result of a social balance, where independent actors and their associations played an important social and economic role, also indirectly through their influence on the authorities. The more intense exchange promoted by such open and favourable markets led to competition among the regions and to regional complementarity and specialization within this integrated area, starting in the early Middle Ages and growing with the intensity of exchange in the high and later Middle Ages. This interaction most benefited those regions in the Low Countries which in the economic circumstances of the period offered the most favourable social and institutional framework for production and for exchange of land, labour, capital, and goods, either through or outside the market, or combined. Whether this relatively favourable organization was found more in the Low Countries, or at least in large parts of the Low Countries, than in most other parts of Europe, is an assumption which needs to be tested in a future comparative investigation for Europe as a whole.

The socio-institutional framework was crucial for long-term economic development, but the favourable effects of a given framework were often limited in time, since in the long run its economic effects eroded the social, institutional, and ecological bases of development. Examples of this are Artois in the 13th to 14th centuries, coastal Flanders in the 14th to 16th centuries, and the Guelders river area and Holland in the late 16th and 17th centuries, where economic development had been pronounced but began to stagnate as a result of this process. Tentatively, it is possible to argue that an optimum may have been reached at those points for the main interest groups, leading to institutional stagnation. As the institutional framework was no longer adapted to changing circumstances this may have then led to economic stagnation. In all these cases the independent producers were 'used up' in the course of economic growth and reduced to economically dependent wage labourers, leading to social imbalance and a further aggravation of institutional and ecological problems. Conversely, positive economic development required continual change and adaptation of the institutional framework, without benefiting one particular group, to keep on adjusting according to new economic, social, and ecological circumstances. This opportunity was, and is, offered by a social balance.

For the medieval Low Countries as a whole it is possible to argue that such a balance was present to a relatively high degree compared with other parts of Europe. This was particularly the result of the large degree of freedom for ordinary people. This was already true in Frisia and many coastal areas in the early Middle Ages; and also in various high medieval reclamation areas, such as Holland and coastal Flanders; there was the strength of free peasant land ownership in several regions, as in Drenthe, Holland, the Campine, and inland Flanders; and the strength of horizontal associations, such as the villages, hansas, commons, and parishes almost everywhere in the Low Countries. The freedom and independence of large social groups in society and the associations they formed promoted a balance in society. Perhaps we can also add that on the micro-level the legal freedom and economic independence of women in the Low Countries further contributed to this balance. Finally, on a macro-level, the proximity of very diverse regions with very different organizations within the Low Countries created social, economic, and political competition and offered alternatives, as well as contributing to a balance conducive to relatively sustainable economic growth. In our time it seems crucial that we develop a similar set of balances of political and economic power which are fairly evenly spread over people and groups—but now perhaps at a global level—to cope with the economic, social, and ecological challenges that lie ahead.

Bibliography

Note: names beginning with 'van' and 'de' are listed under the last name. Thus 'Van Bavel' is listed under 'Bavel', etc.

Aalbers, P. G., *Het einde van de horigheid in Twente en Oost-Gelderland, 1795–1850* (Zutphen, 1979).
—— 'Horigheid in Oost-Nederland', *Gens nostra* 45 (1990), 47–53.
Achilles, W., 'Getreidepreise und Getreidehandelsbeziehungen europäischer Räume im 16. und 17. Jahrhundert', *Zeitschrift für Agrargeschichte und Agrarsoziologie* 7 (1959), 32–55.
Adam, H., *Das Zollwesen im Fränkischen Reich und das spätkarolingische Wirtschaftsleben: Ein Überblick über Zoll, Handel und Verkehr im 9. Jahrhundert* (Stuttgart, 1996).
Aert, L. van, 'Tussen norm en praktijk : een terreinverkenning over het juridische statuut van vrouwen in het zestiende-eeuwse Antwerpen', *Tijdschrift voor sociale en economische geschiedenis* 2.3 (2005), 22–42.
Aerts, E., 'Middeleeuwse bankgeschiedenis volgens professor Raymond de Roover', *Bijdragen tot de geschiedenis* 63 (1980), 49–86.
Akkerman, J. B., 'Het koopmansgilde van Tiel omstreeks het jaar 1000', *Tijdschrift voor Rechtsgeschiedenis* 30 (1962), 409–471.
Alberts, W. J., *De Nederlandse Hanzesteden* (Bussum, 1969).
—— *Het Rijnverkeer anno 1306: De tolrekening van Lobith over het jaar 1306–1307 betreffende invoer en uitvoer van handelsgoederen* (Zutphen, 1986).
—— and Jansen, H. P. H., *Welvaart in wording: Sociaal-economische geschiedenis van Nederland van de vroegste tijden tot het einde van de Middeleeuwen*, 2nd edn ('s-Gravenhage, 1977).
Algra, N. E., *Oudfries recht 800–1256* (Ljouwert, 2000).
Allen, R. C., 'The great divergence in European wages and prices from the Middle Ages to the first world war', *Explorations in economic history* 38 (2001), 411–447.
Ammann, H., 'Huy an der Maas in der mittelalterlichen Wirtschaft', in H. Stoob (ed.), *Altständisches Bürgertum* II (Darmstadt, 1978), 210–248.
Amstel-Horak, M. H. V. van, 'De Rijnlandse morgenboeken. Een unieke bron uit het pré-kadastrale tijdperk', *Holland* 26 (1994), 87–111.
Ankum, H., 'Études sur le statut juridique des enfants mineurs dans l'histoire du droit privé néerlandais à partir du treizième siècle', *Tijdschrift voor rechtsgeschiedenis* 44 (1976), 291–335.
Antunes, C. A. P. and Sicking, L. H. J., 'Ports on the border of the state 1200–1800: An introduction', *International Journal of Maritime History* 20(2) (2007), 273–286.
Apeldoorn, L. J. van, *De kerkelijke goederen in Friesland: Beschrijving van de ontwikkeling van het recht omtrent de kerkelijke goederen in Friesland tot 1795*, 2 vols (Leeuwarden, 1915).
Arnould, M.-A., *Les dénombrements de foyers dans le comté de Hainaut, XIVe–XVIe siècle* (Bruxelles, 1956).

Arrighi, G., *The long twentieth century: Money, power, and the origins of our times* (London, 1996).

Aten, D., *'Als het gewelt comt': Politiek en economie in Holland benoorden het IJ, 1500–1800* (Hilversum, 1995).

Aubin, H., *Die Entstehung der Landeshoheit nach niederrheinischen Quellen: Studien über Grafschaft, Immunität und Vogtei* (Bonn, 1961).

Augustyn, B., *Zeespiegelrijzing, transgressiefasen en stormvloeden in maritiem Vlaanderen tot het einde van de XVIde eeuw: Een landschappelijke, ecologische en klimatologische studie in historisch perspektief*, 2 vols (Brussel, 1992).

—— 'De evolutie van het duinecosysteem', *Historisch Geografisch Tijdschrift* 13 (1995), 9–19.

Avonds, P., *Brabant tijdens de regering van hertog Jan III (1312–1356): Land en instellingen* (Brussel, 1991).

Baars, C., *De geschiedenis van de landbouw in de Beijerlanden*, 2 vols (Wageningen, 1973).

Baart, J. M., 'De materiële stadscultuur', in *De Hollandse stad in de dertiende eeuw* (Zutphen, 1988), 93–112.

Backer, C. M. E. de, *Farmacie te Gent in de late middeleeuwen: Apothekers en receptuur* (Hilversum, 1990).

Bader, K. S., *Dorfgenossenschaft und Dorfsgemeinde*, Studien zur Rechtsgeschichte des mittelalterlichen Dorfes II (Weimar, 1962).

Baelde, M., 'Edellieden en juristen in het centrale bestuur der zestiende-eeuwse Nederlanden', *Tijdschrift voor Geschiedenis* 80 (1967), 39–52.

Baerten, J., *De munten van de graven van Loon, 12de-14de eeuw* (Sint-Truiden, 1981).

—— and Peeters, J. P., *Muntslag en muntcirculatie in de Nederlanden: Noord en Zuid op de weegschaal 7e-16e eeuw* (Brussel, 1983).

Bairoch, P., Batou, J., and Chèvre, P., *La population des villes européennes de 800 à 1850* (Genève, 1988).

Bangs, J. D., 'Holland's civic lijfrente loans (XVth century): Some recurrent problems', *Publications du centre européen d'études Burgondo Médianes* 23 (1983), 75–82.

Bartlett, R. J., *Trial by fire and water: The medieval judicial ordeal* (Oxford, 1990).

Bautier, A.-M., 'Les plus anciennes mentions de moulins hydrauliques industriels et de moulins à vent', *Bulletin philologique et historique (jusqu'à 1610) du comité des travaux historiques et scientifiques* II (1960), 567–626.

Bavel, B. J. P. van, *Goederenverwerving en goederenbeheer van de abdij Mariënweerd (1129–1592)* (Hilversum, 1993).

—— 'Stichtingsplaats, ontginning en goederenverwerving. De economische ontwikkeling van Norbertijner abdijen in de Nederlanden', *Ideaal en werkelijkheid: Verslagen van de contactdag van de werkgroep Norbertijnse geschiedenis in de Nederlanden* 3 (1993), 44–53.

—— *Transitie en continuïteit: De bezitsverhoudingen en de plattelands-economie in het westelijke gedeelte van het Gelderse rivierengebied, ca. 1300–ca. 1570* (Hilversum, 1999).

—— 'A valuation of arable productivity in the central part of the Dutch river area, c.1360–c.1570', in Van Bavel and E. Thoen (eds), *Land productivity and agro-systems in the North Sea area (Middle Ages-20th century): Elements for comparison* (CORN 2) (Turnhout, 1999), 297–307.

Bavel, B. J. P. van, 'Schakels tussen abdij en stad. De stadshoven van de norbertijner abdijen in de Nederlanden (*ca.* 1250–*ca.* 1600)', *Analecta Praemonstratensia* 76 (2000), 133–157.

—— 'Land, lease and agriculture. The transition of the rural economy in the Dutch river area from the fourteenth to the sixteenth century', *Past & Present* 172 (2001), 3–43.

—— 'Elements in the transition of the rural economy: Factors contributing to the emergence of large farms in the Dutch river area (15th–16th centuries)', in P. C. M. Hoppenbrouwers and J. L. van Zanden (eds), *Peasants into farmers? The transformation of rural economy and society in the Low Countries (Middle Ages-19th century) in the light in the Brenner debate* (CORN 4) (Turnhout, 2001), 179–201.

—— 'Proto-industrie tussen de Gelderse rivieren? Een eerste verkenning naar de niet-agrarische, marktgerichte activiteiten op het platteland van het Gelderse rivierengebied, 1300–1600', *Bijdragen en mededelingen Gelre: Historisch Jaarboek voor Gelderland 2003* (2002), 55–78.

—— 'The land market in the North Sea area in a comparative perspective, 13th–18th centuries', in S. Cavaciocchi (ed.), *Il mercato della terra secc. XIII–XVIII: Atti delle 'Settimane di Studi' e altri convegni* 35 (Prato, 2003), 119–145.

—— 'Early proto-industrialization in the Low Countries? The importance & nature of market-oriented non-agricultural activities in the countryside in Flanders and Holland, c. 1250–1570', *Revue Belge de philologie et d'histoire* 81 (2003), 1109–1187.

—— 'Structures of landownership, mobility of land and farm sizes: Diverging developments in the northern parts of the Low Countries, c. 1300–c. 1650', in Van Bavel and P. C. M. Hoppenbrouwers (eds), *Landholding and land transfer in the North Sea area (late Middle Ages-19th century)* (CORN 5) (Turnhout, 2004), 131–148.

—— 'Rural wage labour in the sixteenth-century Low Countries. An assessment of the importance and nature of wage labour in the countryside of Holland, Guelders and Flanders', *Continuity and Change* 21 (2006), 37–72.

—— 'The transition in the Low Countries. Wage labour as an indicator of the rise of capitalism in the countryside, 1300–1700', *Past & Present* 195 (2007), 286–303.

—— 'The emergence and growth of short-term leasing in the Netherlands and other parts of Northwestern Europe (11th–16th centuries): A tentative investigation into its chronology and causes', in van Bavel and P. Schofield (eds), *The development of leasehold in northwestern Europe, c. 1200–1600* (CORN 10) (Turnhout, 2008), 179–213.

—— 'People and land: Rural population developments and property structures in the Low Countries, c. 1300–c. 1600', *Continuity & Change* 17 (2002), 9–37.

—— 'Structures of landownership, mobility of land an farm sizes: Diverging developments in the northern parts of the Low Countries, c. 1300–c. 1650', in Van Bavel and P. C. M. Hoppenbrouwers (eds), *Landholding and land transfer in the North Sea area (late Middle Ages-19th century)* (CORN 5) (Turnhout, 2004), 131–148.

—— 'Markets for land, labour, capital and goods between town and countryside, 13th–16th centuries: Northern Italy and the Low Countries compared', paper for a conference in Vienna (2007).

—— 'Rural revolts and structural change in the Low Countries, 13th–14th centuries', in R. Goddard, J. L. Langdon, and M. Müller (eds), *Survival and discord in medieval society* (Turnhout, 2010).

—— 'Agrarian change and economic development in the late medieval Netherlands', forthcoming in R. Brenner, J. de Vries, and E. Thoen (eds), *Agrarian change and economic development in Europe before the Industrial Revolution* (2010).

—— and Hoppenbrouwers, P. C. M., 'Landholding and land transfer in the North Sea Area (late Middle Ages-19th century)', in idem (eds), *Landholding and land transfer in the North Sea area (late Middle Ages-19th century)* (CORN 5) (Turnhout, 2004), 13–43.

—— and Gelderblom, O., 'Land of milk and butter. The economic origins of cleanliness in the Dutch golden age', forthcoming in *Past and Present* (2010).

—— De Moor, M. & Van Zanden, J. L., 'Introduction: Factor markets in global economic history', *Continuity & Change* 24 (2009), 9–21.

—— and Zanden, J. L. van, 'The jump-start of the Holland economy during the late-medieval crisis, *c*.1350–*c*.1500', *The economic history review* 57 (2004), 503–532.

Beelaerts van Blokland, W. A., 'Een Geldersch edelman in Hollandschen dienst en het beleg van Loevenstein in 1397', *Bijdragen en mededelingen Gelre* 15 (1912), 513–524.

Beets, D. J., and Spek, A. J. F. van der, 'The Holocene evolution of the barrier', *Geologie en mijnbouw* 79 (2000), 3–16.

Behre, K.-E., 'The Plaggenesch of Dunum', in Behre (ed.), *Environment and settlement history in the N: German coastal region* (Wilhelmshaven, 1990), 84–86.

—— 'The history of rye cultivation in Europe', *Vegetation history and archaeobotany* 1 (1992), 141–156.

—— and Jacomet, S., 'The ecological interpretation of archaeobotanical data', in W. van Zeist, K. Wasylikowa & K.-E. Behre (eds), *Progress in old world palaeoethnobotany: A retrospective view on the occasion of 20 years of the International Work Group for Palaeoethnobotany* (Rotterdam, 1991), 81–108.

Berendsen, H. J. A., *De genese van het landschap in het zuiden van de provincie Utrecht, een fysisch-geografische studie* (Utrecht, 1982).

—— *De vorming van het land: Inleiding in de geologie en de geomorfologie* (Assen, 1996).

Berents, D. A., 'Gegoede burgerij in Utrecht in de 15e eeuw', *Jaarboek Oud-Utrecht* (1972), 78–92.

Besteman, J. C., 'Carolingian Medemblik', *Berichten van de Rijksdienst voor Oudheidkundig Bodemonderzoek* 24 (1974), 43–106.

—— 'Frisian salt and the problem of salt-making in North-Holland in the Carolingian period', *Berichten van de Rijksdienst voor het Oudheidkundig Bodemonderzoek* 24 (1974), 171–174.

—— 'Mottes in the Netherlands', *Château Guillard: Études de castellogie médievale* 12 (1984/1985), 211–224.

—— 'North Holland AD 400–1200', in Besteman, J. M. Bos, and H. A. Heidinga (eds), *Medieval archaeology in the Netherlands: Studies presented to H:H: van Regteren Altena* (Assen, 1990), 91–120.

Bichelaer, A. H. P. van den, 'Het notariaat in Stad en Meierij van 's-Hertogenbosch tijdens de Late Middeleeuwen, (1306–1531): Een prosopografisch, diplomatisch en rechtshistorisch onderzoek', PhD thesis (Amsterdam, 1998).

Bieleman, G. J. H., *Boeren op het Drentse zand, 1600–1910: Een nieuwe visie op de 'oude' landbouw* (Wageningen, 1987).

—— 'De verscheidenheid van de landbouw op de Nederlandse zandgronden tijdens de "lange zestiende eeuw" ', *Bijdragen en mededelingen betreffende de geschiedenis der Nederlanden* 105 (1990), 537–552.

—— *Geschiedenis van de landbouw in Nederland 1500–1950: Veranderingen en verscheidenheid* (Meppel, 1992).

Bigwood, G., 'Gand et la circulation des grains en Flandre du XIVe au XVIIIe siècle', *Vierteljahrschrift für Sozial- und Wirtschaftsgeschichte* 4 (1906), 397–460.

—— 'Les financiers d'Arras', *Revue belge de philologie et d'histoire* 3 (1924), 465–508 and 769–819.

Bijsterveld, A. J. A., 'Een zorgelijk bezit. De benedictijnenabdijen Echternach en St. Truiden en het beheer van hun goederen en rechten in Oost-Brabant, 1100–1300', *Noordbrabants historisch jaarboek* 6 (1989), 7–44.

—— ' "Sinte Willibrordus eygen": Het bezit van de abdij Echternach in Texandrië (Nederland en België), circa 700–1300', in G. Kiesel and J. Schroeder (eds), *Willibrord: Apostel der Niederlande, Gründer der Abtei Echternach. Gedenkgabe zum 1250. Todestag des angelsächsischen Missionars* (Luxembourg, 1989), 271–290.

—— *Do ut des: Gift giving, memoria, and conflict management in the medieval Low Countries* (Hilversum, 2007).

—— and Trio, P., 'Van gebedsverbroedering naar broederschap: De evolutie van het fraternitas-begrip in de Zuidelijke Nederlanden in de volle Middeleeuwen', *Jaarboek voor middeleeuwse geschiedenis* 6 (2003), 7–48.

Binding, G., *Deutsche Königspfalzen: Von Karl dem Grossen bis Friedrich II (765–1240)* (Darmstadt, 1996).

Blanchard, I., 'The continental European cattle trade, 1400–1600', *Economic History Review* 39 (1986), 427–460.

Blickle, P., *Deutsche Untertanen: Ein Widerspruch* (München, 1981).

—— (ed.), *Landgemeinde und Stadtgemeinde in Mitteleuropa: Ein struktureller Vergleich* (München, 1991).

Blockmans, F., *Het Gentsche stadspatriciaat tot omstreeks 1302* (Antwerpen, 1938).

Blockmans, W. P., 'Nieuwe gegevens over de gegoede burgerij van Brugge in de 13e en vooral in de 14e eeuw', in Blockmans et al., *Studiën betreffende de sociale strukturen te Brugge, Kortrijk en Gent in de 14e en 15e eeuw*, vol. 1 (Heule, 1971), 133–154.

—— 'Peilingen naar de sociale strukturen te Gent tijdens de late middeleeuwen', in Blockmans et al., *Studiën betreffende de sociale strukturen te Brugge, Kortrijk en Gent in de 14e en 15e eeuw*, part I (Heule, 1971), 215–270, and part II (Heule, 1973), 199–210.

—— 'La participation des sujets flamands à la politique monétaire des ducs de Bourgogne, 1384–1500', *Revue Belge de numismatique* 119 (1973), 103–134.

—— 'Armenzorg en levensstandaard te Mechelen vóór de hervorming van de openbare onderstand (1545)', *Studia Mechliniensia* 79 (1975), 141–173.

—— 'The social and economic effects of plague in the Low Countries, 1349–1500', *Revue belge de philologie et d'histoire* 58 (1980), 833–863.

—— 'Corruptie, patronage, makelaardij en venaliteit als symptomen van een ontluikende staatsvorming in de Bourgondisch-Habsburgse Nederlanden', *Tijdschrift voor sociale geschiedenis* 11 (1985), 231–247.

—— *Een middeleeuwse vendetta: Gent 1300* (Houten, 1987).

—— 'Finances publiques et inégalité sociale dans les Pays-Bas aux XIVe–XVIe siècles', in J. P. Genet and M. le Mené (eds), *Genèse de l'état moderne: Prélèvement et redistribution: Actes du colloque de Fontevraud, 1984* (Paris, 1987), 77–90.

—— 'Voracious states and obstructing cities', *Theory and society* 18 (1989), 733–755.

—— 'Formale und informelle soziale Strukturen in und zwischen den großen flämischen Städten im Spätmittelalter', in P. Johanek (ed.), *Einungen und Bruderschaften in der spätmittelalterlichen Stadt* (Köln, 1993), 1–15.

—— 'The impact of cities on state formation: Three contrasting territories in the Low Countries, 1300–1500', in P. Blickle (ed.), *Resistance, representation, and community* (Oxford, 1997), 256–271.

—— 'The Low Countries in the Middle Ages', in R. Bonney (ed.), *The rise of the fiscal state in Europe, c.1200–1815* (Oxford, 1999), 281–308.

—— 'Van private naar publieke macht in de vijftiende en zestiende eeuw', in J. A. Frieswijk et al. (eds), *Fryslân, staat en macht 1450–1650: Bijdragen aan het historisch congres te Leeuwarden van 3 tot 5 juni 1998* (Hilversum/Leeuwarden, 1999), 11–25.

—— 'Regionale Vielfalt im Zunftwesen in den Niederlanden vom 13.bis zum 16. Jahrhundert', in K. Schultz (ed.), *Handwerk in Europa: Vom Spätmittelalter bis zur Frühen Neuzeit* (1999), 51–63.

—— and Prevenier, W., 'Armoede in de Nederlanden van de 14e tot het midden van de 16e eeuw: Bronnen problemen', *Tijdschrift voor geschiedenis* 88 (1975), 501–538.

——, Pieters, G., & Prevenier, W., 'Het sociaal-economische leven 1300–1482: Tussen crisis en welvaart: Sociale veranderingen 1300–1500', in D. P. Blok, W. Prevenier, and D. J. Roorda (eds), *Algemene Geschiedenis der Nederlanden* IV (Haarlem, 1982), 42–86.

Blok, D. P., 'De enken', *Driemaandelijkse bladen* 10 (1958), 1–16.

—— 'Holland und Westfriesland', *Frühmittelalterliche Studien* 3 (Berlin, 1969), 347–361.

—— *De Franken in Nederland* (Bussum, 1974).

—— 'Hoofdlijnen van de bewoningsgeschiedenis', *Algemene geschiedenis der Nederlanden* 1 (1982), 143–152.

Blondé, B., *De sociale structuren en economische dynamiek van 's-Hertogenbosch, 1500–1550* (Tilburg, 1987).

—— and Vanhaute, E. (eds), *Labour and labour markets between town and countryside (Middle Ages-19th century)* (CORN 6) (Turnhout, 2001).

—— and Uytven, R. van, 'Langs land- en waterwegen. in de Zuidelijke Nederlanden. Lopend onderzoek naar het pre-industriele transport', *Bijdragen tot de geschiedenis* 82 (1999), 135–158.

Bochove, C. van, 'De Hollandse haringvisserij tijdens de vroegmoderne tijd', *Tijdschrift voor sociale en economische geschiedenis* 1 (2004), 3–17.

Bocquet, A., *Recherches sur la population rurale de l'Artois et du Boulonnais pendant la periode bourguignonne (1384–1477)* (Arras, 1969).

Bodson, M. J., 'L'évolution d'un paysage rural au moyen âge: Thisnes en Hesbaye', *Bulletin de la société Belge d'études géographiques* 34 (1965), 117–158.

Boer, D. E. H. de, 'Graaf en grafiek: Sociale en economische ontwikkelingen in het middeleeuwse "Noordholland" tussen plusminus 1345 en plusminus 1415', PhD thesis (Leiden, 1978).

—— 'Florerend vanuit de delta: De handelsbetrekkingen van Holland en Zeeland in de tweede helft van de dertiende eeuw', in Boer, E. H. P. Cordfunke, & H. Sarfatij (eds), *Wi Florens... De Hollandse graaf Floris V in de samenleving van de dertiende eeuw* (Utrecht, 1996), 126–152.

Boer, D. E. H. de, ' "Op weg naar volwassenheid": De ontwikkeling van produktie en consumptie in de Hollandse en Zeeuwse steden in de dertiende eeuw', in J. M. Baart et al. (eds), *De Hollandse stad in de dertiende eeuw* (Zutphen, 1988), 28–43.

Bonenfant, P.-P., 'L'origine des villes brabançonnes et la "route" de Bruges à Cologne', *Revue belge de philologie et d'histoire* 31 (1953), 399–447.

—— 'Hôpitaux et bienfaisance publique dans les anciens Pays-Bas des origines à la fin du XVIIIe siècle', *Annales de la société Belge d'histoire des hôpitaux* 3 (1965), 115–147.

—— *Des premiers cultivateurs aux premières villes: Civilisations préhistoriques en Wallonie* (Bruxelles, 1970).

Bonnassie, P., 'The survival and extinction of the slave system in the early medieval West (fourth to eleventh centuries)', in Bonnassie, *From slavery to feudalism in south-western Europe* (Cambridge, 1991), 1–59.

Boogaart, T. A., 'Reflections on the Moerlemaye. Revolt and reform in late medieval Bruges', *Revue belge de philologie et d'histoire* 79 (2001), 1133–1157.

Boone, I., Cupere, B. de, & Neer, W. van, 'Social status as reflected in the food refuse from late medieval sites in Namur (Belgium)', *Revue belge de philologie et d'histoire* 80 (2002), 1391–1394.

Boone, M. H., 'Geldhandel en pandbedrijf in Gent tijdens de Bourgondische periode: Politieke, fiscale en sociale aspecten', *Revue belge de philologie et d'histoire* 66 (1988), 767–791.

—— *Geld en macht: De Gentse stadsfinanciën en de Bourgondische staatsvorming, 1384–1453* (Gent, 1990).

—— 'Plus deuil que joie: Les ventes de rentes par la ville de Gand pendant la période bourguignonne: Entre intérêts privés et finances publiques', *Bulletin trimestriel du Credit Communal de Belgique* 176 (1991/1992), 3–24.

—— and Brand, A. J., 'Vollersoproeren en collectieve actie in Gent en Leiden in de 14de-15de eeuw', *Tijdschrift voor Sociale Geschiedenis* 19 (1993), 168–192.

—— —— and Prevenier, W., 'Revendications salariales et conjoncture economique: Les salaires de foulons à Gand et à Leyde au XVe siècle', in E. Aerts et al. (eds), *Studia Historia Oeconomica. Liber amicorum Van der Wee* (Leuven, 1993), 59–74.

—— and Prak, M., 'Rulers, patricians and burghers: The great and little traditions of urban revolt in the Low Countries', in C. A. Davids and J. M. W. G. Lucassen (eds), *A miracle mirrored: The Dutch Republic in European perspective* (Cambridge, 1995), 99–134.

Borger, G. J., 'De ouderdom van onze dijken: Een nieuwe discussie over een oud vraagstuk', *Historisch Geografisch Tijdschrift* 3 (1985), 76–80.

—— Haartsen, A. J., & Vesters, P., *Het Groene Hart: Een Hollands cultuurlandschap* (Utrecht, 1997).

Borremans, R., and Warginaire, R., *La ceramique d'Andenne: Recherches de 1956–1965* (Rotterdam, 1966).

Bos, J. M., 'The bog area of North Holland', in Bos, J. C. Besteman, & H. A. Heidinga (eds), *Medieval archaeology in the Netherlands: Studies presented to H. H. van Regteren Altena* (Assen, 1990), 121–132.

Bos, P. G., *Het Groningsche gild- en stapelrecht tot de Reductie in 1594* (Groningen, 1904).

Boschma-Aarnoudse, C., *Tot verbeteringe van de neeringe deser stede: Edam en de Zeevang in de late Middeleeuwen en de 16de eeuw* (Hilversum, 2003).

Boshof, E., 'Königtum und adelige Herrschaftsbilding', in K. Flink & W. Janssen (eds), *Königtum und Reichsgewalt am Niederrhein: Referate der 2. Niederrhein-tagung des Arbeitskreises niederrheinischer Kommunalarchivare (12.–13. März 1982 in Nimwegen)* (Kleve, 1983), 9–40.

Bos-Rops, J. A. M. Y., *Graven op zoek naar geld: De inkomsten van de graven van Holland en Zeeland, 1389–1433* (Hilversum, 1993).

Bot, P. N. M., *Humanisme en onderwijs in Nederland* (Utrecht, 1955).

Boulvain, F., & Pingot, J.-L., *Une introduction à la geologie de la Wallonie* (Liège, 2002).

Bourguignon, M., 'La sidérurgie. Industrie commune des pays d'entre Meuse et Rhin', *Standen en landen* 28 (1967), 83–120.

Braams, B. W., *Weyden en zeyden in het broek: Middeleeuwse ontginning en exploitatie van de kommen in het Land van Heusden en Altena* (Wageningen, 1995).

Brabant, H., 'Observations sur l'évolution de la denture permanente humaine en Europe occidentale', *Bulletin du groupement international pour la recherche scientifique en stomatologie* 6 (1963), 169–297.

——, & Twiesselmann, F., 'Étude de la denture de 159 squelettes provenant d'une cimetière du 11e siècle à Renaix', *Revue Belge de Science Dentaire* 15 (1960), 561–588.

Brand, A. J. H., *Over macht en overwicht: Stedelijke elites in Leiden (1420–1510)* (Leuven, 1996).

—— 'Urban policy or personal government: The involvement of the urban elite in the economy of Leiden at the end of the Middle Ages', in H. A. Diederiks, P. M. Hohenberg, and M. F. Wagenaar (eds), *Economic policy in Europe since the late Middle Ages: The visible hand and the fortune of cities* (Leicester/New York, 1992), 17–34.

Brenner, R. P., 'The agrarian roots of European capitalism', *Past & Present* 97 (1982), 16–113.

—— 'The Low Countries in the transition to capitalism', in P. C. M. Hoppenbrouwers and J. L. van Zanden (eds), *Peasants into farmers? The transformation of rural economy and society in the Low Countries (Middle Ages-19th century) in light of the Brenner debate* (CORN 4) (Turnhout, 2001), 275–338.

Britnell, R. H., *The commercialisation of English society, 1000–1500* (Cambridge, 1993).

—— 'Commercialisation and economic development in England, 1000–1300', in Britnell and B. M. S. Campbell (eds), *A commercialising economy: England 1086 to c.1300* (Manchester/New York, 1995), 7–26.

Broek, J. van den, *Groningen, een stad apart: Over het verleden van een eigenzinnige stad (1000–1600)* (Assen, 2007).

Broer, C. J. C., & Bruijn, M. W. J. de, *Volc te Voet: Gevolgen van de Guldensporenslag voor de opkomst van de burgerij in de Noordelijke Nederlanden* (Utrecht, 2002).

Brongers, J. A., 'Ceramological investigations into medieval pottery produced at Schinveld', *Berichten van de Rijksdienst voor het Oudheidkundig Bodemonderzoek* 33 (1983), 375–418.

Brouwer, J. de, *Demografische evolutie van het Land van Aalst, 1570–1800* (Historische uitgaven Pro Civitate 18) (Brussel, 1968).

Brulez, W., 'The balance of trade of the Netherlands in the middle of the 16th century', *Acta historiae Neerlandicae: Studies on the history of the Netherlands* 4 (1970), 20–48.

Brunel, G., 'Leasehold in northern France in the twelfth and thirteenth centuries: Economic functions and social impact', in B. J. P. van Bavel & P. Schofield (eds), *The development of leasehold in northwestern Europe, c.1200–1600* (CORN 10) (Turnhout, 2008), 81–98.

Brusse, P., *Overleven door ondernemen: De agrarische geschiedenis van de Over-Betuwe, 1650–1850* (Afdeling Agrarische Geschiedenis Bijdragen 38) (Arnhem, 1999).

Buchet, L., 'La recherche des structures sociales et des conditions de vie par l'étude des squelettes', *Les dossiers d'archéologie* 208 (1995), 60–67.

Buis, J., *Historia forestis: Nederlandse bosgeschiedenis*, 2 vols (Utrecht, 1985).

Buisman, J., and Engelen, A. F. V. van, *Duizend jaar weer, wind en water in de Lage Landen*, 5 vols (Franeker, 1995).

Buitelaar, A. L. P., *De Stichtse ministerialiteit en de ontginningen in de Utrechtse Vechtstreek* (Hilversum, 1993).

Bult, E. J., and Hallewas, D. P., 'Archaeological evidence for the early-medieval settlement around the Meuse and Rhine deltas up to ca. AD 1000', in J. C. Besteman, J. M. Bos, and H. A. Heidinga (eds), *Medieval archaeology in the Netherlands: Studies presented to H. H. van Regteren Altena* (Assen, 1990), 71–90.

Burgers, J. W. J., 'De invoering van het Nederlands in de dertiende-eeuwse documentaire bronnen in Holland en Zeeland', *Tijdschrift voor Nederlandse taal- en letterkunde* 112 (1996), 129–150.

—— 'Het ontstaan van de twaalfde-eeuwse Vlaamse stadskeuren', *Handelingen van de Koninklijke Zuid-Nederlandse Maatschappij voor taal- en letterkunde* 53 (1999), 81–99.

—— and Dijkhof, E. C., *De oudste stadsrekeningen van Dordrecht, 1283–1287* (Hilversum, 1995).

Caenegem, R. van, and Demyttenaere, A., *De moord op Karel de Goede*, orig. by Galbertus Brugensis (Leuven, 2000).

Callebaut, D., 'De topografische groei van Aalst of hoe een zelhof een gebastioneerde stad werd', *Miscellanea archaeologica in honorem H. Roosens*, Archaeologia Belgica 255 (1983), 227–249.

Campbell, B. M. S., 'Commonfield origins: The regional dimension', in T. Rowley (ed.), *The origins of open-field agriculture* (London, 1981), 112–129.

—— 'Land, labour, livestock and productivity trends in English seignorial agriculture, 1208–1450', in Campbell & M. Overton (eds), *Land, labour and livestock: Historical studies in European agricultural productivity* (Manchester, 1991), 144–182.

—— 'Factor markets in England before the Black Death', *Continuity & Change* 24 (2009), 79–106.

Chapelot, J., 'Le fond de cabane dans l'habitat rural Ouest-Européen: État des questions', *Archéologie médiévale* 10 (1980), 5–57.

—— Galinié, H., and Pilet-Limière, J. (eds), *La céramique (V^e–XIXe s.): Fabrication, commercialisation, utilisation: Actes du premier congrès internationale d'archéologie mediévale* (Caen, 1987).

Charles, J. L., *La ville de Saint-trond au Moyen Âge: Des origines à la fin du XIVe siècle* (Paris, 1965).

Chorley, P., 'The cloth exports of Flanders and northern France during the thirteenth century: A luxury trade?', *Economic history review* 40 (1987), 349–379.

—— 'The "Draperies Légères" of Lille, Arras, Tournai, Valenciennes: New materials for new markets?', in M. H. Boone and W. Prevenier (eds), *La draperie ancienne des Pays-Bas: Débouchés et stratégies de survie (14e–16e siècles): Actes du colloque tenu à Gand le 28 avril 1992* (Leuven, 1993), 151–166.

Christians, C., 'Belgium's geographical mosaic', in Christians and L. Daels (eds), *Belgium: A geographical introduction to its regional diversity and its human richness* (Liège, 1988), 19–50.
Ciselet, P., and Delcourt, M., *Belgique 1567: La description de tout le Pays-Bas*, orig. by L. Guicciardini (Bruxelles, 1943).
Clark, G., 'The cost of capital and Medieval Agricultural Technique', *Explorations in economic history* 25 (1988), 265–294.
—— 'The long march of history: Farm wages, population, and economic growth, England 1209–1869', *Economic history review* 60 (2007), 97–135.
Clarke, H., and Ambrosiani, B., *Towns in the Viking age* (Leicester, 1991).
Clason, A. T., *Animal and man in Holland's past: An investigation of the animal world surrounding man in prehistoric and early historical times in the provinces of North and South Holland*, 2 parts (Groningen, 1967).
Claude, D., 'Aspekte des Binnenhandels im Merowingerreich auf Grund der Schriftquellen', in K. Düwel et al. (eds), *Untersuchungen zu Handel und Verkehr der vor- und frühgeschichtlichen Zeit in Mittel- und Nordeuropa*, part III (1985), 9–99.
Clauzel, D., 'Les maladies dans le Nord de La France au XIVe siècle', *Les Pays-Bas Français* 14 (1989), 208–224.
—— and Calonne, S., 'Artisanat rural et marché urbain: La draperie à Lille et dans ses campagnes à la fin du Moyen Age', *Revue du Nord* 72 (1990), 531–573.
Cleveringa, P., Hendriks, J. P. C. A., et al., ' "So grot overvlot der watere. . . ": Een bijdrage in het moderne multidisciplinaire onderzoek naar de St. Elisabethsvloed en de periode die daaraan vooraf ging', *Holland* 36 (2004), 162–180.
Cluse, C., *Studien zur Geschichte der Juden in den mittelalterlichen Niederlanden* (Hannover, 2000).
Cockshaw, P., 'A propos de la circulation monétaire entre la Flandre et le Brabant de 1384 à 1390', *Contributions à l'histoire économique et sociale* 6 (1970/1), 105–141
Collon-Gevaert, S., Lejeune, J., and Stiennon, J., *A treasury of Romanesque art: Metalwork, illuminations and sculpture from the valley of the Meuse* (New York, 1972).
Comet, G., 'Technology and agricultural expansion in the Middle Ages: The example of France north of the Loire', in G. Astill and J. Langdon (eds), *Medieval farming and technology: The impact of agricultural change in Northwest Europe* (Leiden, 1997), 11–39.
Contamine, P., *La guerre au Moyen Age*, 3rd edn (Paris, 1992).
Coopmans, J. P. A., 'De jaarmarkten van Antwerpen en Bergen op Zoom als centra van rechtsverkeer en rechtsvorming', in M. J. G. C. Raaijmakers, H. C. F. Schoordijk, and B. Wachter (eds), *Handelsrecht tussen 'koophandel' en Nieuw BW* (Deventer, 1988), 1–24.
Coornaert, E., *La draperie-sayetterie d'Hondschoote (XIVe–XVIIIe siècles): Un centre industriel d'autrefois* (Rennes, 1930).
Cornelisse, C., *Energiemarkten en energiehandel in Holland in de late Middeleeuwen* (Hilversum, 2007).
Costambeys, M., 'An aristocratic community on the northern Frankish frontier, 690–726', *Early medieval Europe* 3 (1994), 39–62.
Coupland, S., 'Dorestad in the ninth century: The numismatic evidence', *Jaarboek voor munt- en penningkunde* 75 (1988), 5–26.

Coutant, Y., and Groen, P., 'The early history of the windmill brake', *History of technology* 19 (1997), 1–18.

Couteaux, M., *Recherches palynologiques en Gaume, au Pays d'Arlon, en Ardenne méridionale (Luxembourg Belge) et au Gutland (Grand-Duché de Luxembourg)* (Louvain, 1969).

Craecker-Dussart, C. de, 'Une grande route transversale lotharingienne au moyen âge: Tonlieux, foires at marchés avant 1300 en Lotharingie: Actes des 4e Journées lotharingiennes', *Publications de la section historique de l'institute Grand-Ducal de Luxembourg* 104 (1988), 89–102.

Cuvelier, J., 'Documents concernant la réforme de la bienfaisance à Louvain au XVIe siècle', *Bulletin de la commission royale d'histoire de Belgique* 105 (1940), 37–116.

Daelemans, F., 'Leiden 1581, Een socio-demografisch onderzoek', *Afdeling Agrarische Geschiedenis Bijdragen* 19 (1975), 137–215.

—— 'Tithe revenues in rural south-western Brabant', in H. van der Wee and E. van Cauwenberghe (eds), *Productivity of land and agricultural innovation in the Low Countries (1250–1800)* (Leuven, 1978), 25–41.

Dam, P. J. E. M. van, 'De tanden van de waterwolf', *Tijdschrift voor Waterstaatsgeschiedenis* 5 (1996), 81–91.

—— *Vissen in veenmeren: De sluisvisserij op aal tussen Haarlem en Amsterdam en de ecologische transformatie in Rijnland 1440–1530* (Haarlem, 1998).

—— 'Ecological challenges, technological innovations: The modernization of sluice building in Holland, 1300–1600', *Technology and culture* 43 (2002), 500–520.

—— 'Het onderaardse bos: Chronologische afbakeningen in de ecologische geschiedenis', *Tijdschrift voor sociale geschiedenis* 28 (2002), 175–202.

—— 'Middeleeuwse bedrijven in zout en zel in Zuidwest-Nederland: Een analyse op basis van de moerneringsrekening van Puttermoer van 1386', *Jaarboek voor middeleeuwse geschiedenis* 9 (2006), 85–115.

Dambruyne, J., *Mensen en centen: het 16de-eeuwse Gent in demografisch en economisch perspectief* (Gent, 2001).

—— *Corporatieve middengroepen: Aspiraties, relaties en transformaties in de 16de-eeuwse Gentse ambachtswereld* (Gent, 2002).

Danneel, M., *Weduwen en wezen in het laat-middeleeuwse Gent* (Leuven/Apeldoorn, 1995).

Davids, C. A., 'Zekerheidsregelingen in de scheepvaart en het landtransport, 1500–1800', in J. van Gerwen and M. H. D. van Leeuwen (eds), *Studies over zekerheidsarrangementen: Risico's, risicobestrijding en verzekeringen in Nederland vanaf de Middeleeuwen* (Amsterdam, 1998), 183–202.

—— and Noordegraaf, L. (eds), *The Dutch economy in the Golden Age: Nine studies* (Amsterdam, 1993).

—— 'The bookkeeper's tale: Learning merchant skills in the Northern Netherlands in the sixteenth century', in *Education and learning in the Netherlands, 1400–1600: Essays in honour of Hilde de Ridder-Symoens* (Leiden, 2004), 235–251.

Davids, K., 'Innovations in windmill technology in Europe, c.1500–1800: The state of research and future directions of inquiry', *Nederlands Economisch-Historisch Archief jaarboek* 66 (2003), 43–63.

Davies, W., and Fouracre, P., 'Conclusion', in *idem* (eds), *Property and power in the early Middle Ages* (Cambridge, 1995), 245–271.

Day, 'The great bullion famine of the fifteenth century', *Past and Present* 79 (1978), 3–54.
De: see under the last name.
Decavele, J., *De dageraad van de reformatie in Vlaanderen, 1520–1565*, 2 vols (Brussel, 1975).
Deceulaer, H., 'Institutional and cultural change in wage formation: Port labour in Antwerp (sixteenth–eighteenth centuries)', in P. Scholliers and L. Schwarz (eds), *Experiencing wages: Social and cultural aspects of wage forms in Europe since 1500* (New York, 2003), 27–52.
Dechesne, L., *Industrie drapière de la Vesdre avant 1800* (Paris, 1926).
Declerq, G., 'Originals and cartularies: The organisation of archival memory (ninth–eleventh centuries)', in K. Heidecker (ed.), *Charters and the use of the written word in Medieval Society* (Turnhout, 2000), 147–170.
Degryse, R., 'De laatmiddeleeuwse haringvisserij', *Bijdragen voor de geschiedenis der Nederlanden* 21 (1966/1967), 82–121.
—— 'De oudste houten kranen in de Vlaamse en andere havens (13de–16de eeuw)', *Handelingen van het Genootschap voor Geschiedenis* 128 (1991), 5–46.
Dejongh, G., and Thoen, E., 'Arable productivity in Flanders and the former territory of Belgium in a long-term perspective (from the Middle Ages to the end of the Ancien Régime)', in B. J. P. van Bavel and E. Thoen (eds), *Land Productivity and Agro-systems in the North Sea Area (Middle Ages–20th century): Elements for Comparison* (CORN 2) (Turnhout, 1999), 37–45.
Dekker, C., 'De dam bij Wijk', in C. van de Kieft et al. (eds), *Scrinium et scriptura* (Groningen, 1980), 248–266.
—— *Zuid-Beveland: De historische geografie en de instellingen van een Zeeuws eiland in de Middeleeuwen* (Assen, 1971).
—— *Het Kromme Rijngebied in de Middeleeuwen: Een institutioneel-geografische studie* (Zutphen, 1983).
Dekkers, P. J. V., 'De uitbating van de kloosterhof Sterksel door de abdij van Averbode van de veertiende tot de zeventiende eeuw', *Noordbrabants historisch jaarboek* 15 (1998), 13–80.
Deligne, C., *Bruxelles et sa rivière: Genèse d'un territoire urbain (12e–18e siècle)* (Turnhout, 2003).
Delmaire, B., 'A l'origine du bail à ferme dans le nord de la France: Le rôle des chanoines séculiers (fin du XIIe–début du XIIIe siècle)', in J.-M. Duvosquel and E. Thoen (eds), *Peasants and townsmen in medieval Europe: Studia in honorem Adriaan Verhulst* (Gent, 1995), 529–539.
Demolon, P., *Le village Mérovingien de Brebières, VIe–VIIe siècles* (Arras, 1972).
—— 'L'habitat du haut Moyen Age dans le Nord de la France: Réflexions socio-économiques', *Revue du Nord* 71 (1989), 165–179.
—— Galinié, H., and Verhaeghe, F. (eds), *Archéologie des villes dans le Nord-ouest de l'Europe (VIIe–XIIIe siècle)* (Douai, 1994).
Derville, A., 'Les draperies flamandes et artésiennes vers 1250–1350', *Revue du Nord* 54 (1972), 353–370.
—— *Histoire de Saint-Omer* (Lille, 1981).
—— 'Le nombre d'habitants des villes de l'Artois et de la Flandre Wallonne (1300–1450)', *Revue du Nord* 65 (1983), 277–300.

Derville, A., 'L'alphabétisation du peuple à la fin du Moyen Age', *Revue du Nord* 66 (1984), 759–776.

—— 'Dîmes, rendements du blé et "révoluton agricole" dans le Nord de la France au Moyen Age', *Annales: Économies, sociétés, civilisations* 42 (1987), 1411–1432.

—— 'Le grenier des Pays-Bas médiévaux', *Revue du Nord* 69 (1987), 267–280.

—— 'L'assolement triennal dans la France du Nord au Moyen Âge', *Revue historique* 280 (1988), 337–376.

—— 'Rivières et canaux du Nord: Pas-de-calais aux époques médiévale et moderne', *Revue du Nord* 72 (1990), 5–22.

—— 'Moulins, cultures industrielles et marchands dans les campagnes artésiennes et flamandes', *Revue du Nord* 72 (1990), 575–592.

—— 'La finance Arragoise: Usure et banque', in M.-M. Castellini and J.-P. Martin (eds), *Arras au Moyen Âge: Histoire et littérature* (Paris, 1994), 37–52.

—— *Douze études d'histoire rurale: Flandre, Artois et Cambrésis au Moyen Âge: Recueil offert à l'auteur* (Villeneuve-d'Ascq, 1996).

Derycke, L., 'The Public annuity market in Bruges at the End of the 15th Century', in M. H. Boone, C. A. Davids, and P. Janssens (eds), *Urban public debts: Urban government and the market for annuities in Western Europe (14th–18th centuries)* (Turnhout, 2003), 165–182.

Despy, G., 'Villes et campagnes aux IXe et Xe siècles: L'exemple du Pays Mosan', *Revue du Nord* 50 (1968), 145–168.

—— 'Les richesses de la terre: Cîteaux et Prémontré devant l'économie de profit aux XIIe et XIIIe siècles', *Problèmes d'histoire du Christianisme* 5 (1975), 58–80.

—— 'L'exploitation des "curtes" en Brabant du IXe siècle aux environs de 1300', in W. Janssen and D. Lohrmann, *Villa, curtis, grangia: Landwirtschaft zwischen Loire und Rhein von der Römerzeit zum Hochmittelalter* (München, 1983), 185–204.

—— 'Naissance des villes et de bourgades', in H. Hasquin (ed.), *La Wallonie: Le pays et les hommes*, part I (Bruxelles, 1975), 93–121.

Devroey, J.-P., 'Réflexions sur l'économie des premiers Carolingiens (768–877): Grands domains et action politique entre Seine et Rhin', *Francia* 13 (1985), 475–488.

—— 'Les premiers polyptyques rémois. VIe–IXe siècles', in A. E. Verhulst (ed.), *Le grand domaine aux époques mérovingienne et carolingienne* (1985), 73–97.

—— *Le polyptyque et les listes de biens de l'abbaye Saint-Pierre de Lobbes (IXe–XIe siècles)* (Bruxelles, 1986).

—— 'Réflexions sur l'économie des premiers temps carolingiens', *Francia* 13 (1986), 475–488.

—— 'La cerealiculture dans le monde franc', in *Etudes sur le grand domaine carolingien*, chapter VI (Aldershot, 1993).

—— 'Histoire économique et sociale du haut Moyen Âge', in J. Hamesse (ed.), *Bilan et perspectives des études médiévales en Europe* (Louvain-la-Neuve, 1995), 181–216.

—— 'Juifs et Syriens: À propos de la géographie économique de la Gaule au haut Moyen Âge', in J.-M. Duvosquel and E. Thoen (eds), *Peasants and townsmen in medieval Europe: Studia in honorem Adriaan Verhulst* (Gent, 1995), 51–72.

—— 'L'espace des échanges économiques: Commerce, marché, communications et logistique dans le monde franc au IXe siècle', *Settimane di Studio del Centro Italiano di Studi sull'Alto Medioevo* 50 (2003), 347–392.

—— 'Units of measurement in the early medieval economy: The example of Carolingian food rations', *French history* 1 (1987), 68–92.

—— and Devroey–Zoller, C., 'Villes, campagnes, croissance agraire dans le pays mosan avant l'an mil. Vingt ans après', in J.-M. Duvosquel and A. Dierkens (eds), *Villes et campagnes au moyen âge: Mélanges Georges Despy* (Liège, 1991), 223–260.

D'Haenens, A., *Les invasions normandes en Belgique au IXe siècle: Le phénomène et sa répercussion dans l'historiographie médiévale* (Louvain, 1967).

Dhondt, J., 'L'essor urbain entre Meuse et Mer du Nord à l'époque mérovingienne', *Studi in onore di Armando Sapori* 1 (1957), 55–78.

—— 'Les solidarités médiévales: Une société en transition, la Flandre en 1127–1128', *Annales: Économies, sociétés, civilisations* 12 (1957), 529–560

Dhondt, 'Les origines des États de Flandre', *Standen en landen* 69 (1977), 55–104.

Diepeveen, W. J., *De verveening in Delfland en Schieland tot het einde der zestiende eeuw* (Leiden, 1950).

Dierkens, A., *Abbayes et chapitres entre Sambre et Meuse (VIIe–XIe siècles): Contributions à l'histoire religieuse des campagnes du Haut Moyen Âge* (Beihefte der Francia 14) (Sigmaringen, 1985).

—— and Périn, P., 'The 5th-century advance of the Franks', in E. Taayke, J. H. Looijenga, O. H. Harsema, et al. (eds), *Essays on the early Franks* (Groningen, 2003),165–193.

Dietz, W., *Die Wuppertaler Garnnahrung: Geschichte der Industrie und des Handels von Elberfeld und Barmen 1400 bis 1800* (Neustadt an der Aisch, 1957).

Dijck, G. C. M. van, *De Bossche optimaten: Geschiedenis van de Illustere Lieve Vrouwebroederschap te 's-Hertogenbosch, 1318–1973* (Tilburg, 1973).

Dijkhof, E. C., 'De economische en fiscale politiek van de graven van Holland in de dertiende eeuw', *Bijdragen en mededelingen betreffende de geschiedenis der Nederlanden* 108 (1993), 3–12.

—— 'Goatskin and growing literacy: The penetration of writing in the former counties of Holland and Zeeland in the thirteenth century in relation to the changes of the internal and external features of the charters issued', in K. J. Heidecker (ed.), *Charters and the use of the written word in medieval society* (Turnhout, 2000), 101–112.

Dijkman, J., 'The development and organization of commodity markets in late medieval Holland', MS, Utrecht University, 2009.

Dillen, J. G. van, *Van rijkdom en regenten: Handboek tot de economische en sociale geschiedenis van Nederland tijdens de Republiek* ('s-Gravenhage, 1970).

—— *Amsterdam in 1585: Het kohier der capitale impositie van 1585* (Amsterdam, 1941).

Dockès, P., *Medieval slavery and liberation*, tr. A. Goldhammer (Chicago, 1982).

Dohrn van Rossum, G., 'The diffusion of the public clocks in the cities of late medieval Europe, 1300–1500', in B. Lepetit and J. Hoock (eds), *La ville et l'innovation en Europe* (Paris, 1987), 29–43.

Dokkum, H. W., & Dijkhof, E. C., 'Oude Dordtse lijfrenten', in L. M. VerLoren van Themaat (ed.), *Oude Dordtse lijfrenten: Stedelijke financiering in de vijftiende eeuw* (Amsterdam, 1983), 37–90.

Domar, E., 'The causes of slavery or serfdom: A hypothesis', *Journal of economic history* 1 (1970), 18–32.

Droege, G., 'Fränkische Siedlung in Westfalen', *Frühmittelalterliche Studien* 4 (1970), 271–288.

Dubbe, B., 'Het huisraad in het Oostnederlandse burgerwoonhuis in de late Middeleeuwen', in J. W. M. de Jong (ed.), *Thuis in de late middeleeuwen: Het Nederlands burgerinterieur 1400–1535* (Zwolle, 1980), 21–86.

——and Vroom, W. H., 'Patronage and the art market in the Netherlands during the sixteenth century', in J. P. Filedt Kok, W. Halsema-Kubes, and W. T. Kloek (eds), *Kunst voor de beeldenstorm: Noordnederlandse kunst, 1525–1580* ('s-Gravenhage, 1986), 29–37.

Duby, G., *Rural economy and country life in the medieval West* (Columbia, 1968).

——*Guerriers et paysans, VII–XIIe siècle: Premier essor de l'économie européenne* (Paris, 1973).

Dumolyn, J., 'The legal repression of revolts in late medieval Flanders', *Tijdschrift voor rechtsgeschiedenis* 68 (2000), 479–521.

——'Dominante klassen en elites in verandering in het laatmiddeleeuwse Vlaanderen', *Jaarboek voor middeleeuwse geschiedenis* 5 (2002), 69–107.

——*Staatsvorming en vorstelijke ambtenaren in het graafschap Vlaanderen (1419–1477)* (Antwerpen, 2003).

——and Haemers, J., 'Patterns of urban rebellion in medieval Flanders', *Journal of medieval history* 31 (2005), 369–393.

——and Tricht, F. van, 'Adel en nobiliteringsprocessen in het laatmiddeleeuwse Vlaanderen: Een status quaestionis', *Bijdragen en mededelingen betreffende de geschiedenis der Nederlanden* 115 (2000), 197–222.

Dumon Tak, A.M., & Van de Velde, A. P. E., 'Beschouwing over de schedelvorm', *Westerheem* 27 (1978), 155–167.

DuPlessis, R. S., *Transitions to capitalism in early modern Europe* (Cambridge, 1997).

——and Howell, M. C., 'Reconsidering the early modern economy: The cases of Leiden and Lille', *Past & Present* 94 (1982), 49–84.

Dupont, J. A., 'Les pratiques agraires dans le Hainaut belge. La diffusion de l'assolement triennal', in J.-M. Cauchies & J.-M. Duvosquel (eds), *Recueil d'études d'histoire Hainuyere: Offertes à Maurice A: Arnould* 1 (Mons, 1983), 403–422.

Durme, L. van, 'Genesis and evolution of the Romance–Germanic language border in Europe', *Journal of Multilingual and Multicultural Development* 23 (2002), 9–21.

Dygo, M., 'Capitulare de villis and the Bible: On the economic programme of Charlemagne', *Acta Poloniae historica* 80 (1999), 5–14.

Edelman, C. H., 'Enige ongewone aspecten van de bodemkunde', in Stichting voor bodemkartering, *Boor en spade: verspreide bijdragen tot de kennis van de bodem van Nederland* 5 (1952), 184–193.

Eerenbeemt, H. F. J. M. van den, 'Sociale spanningen en overheidsbeleid: Bestrijding der bedelarij in het Noorden van Brabant in de vijftiende en zestiende eeuw', *Varia historica Brabantica* 1 (1962), 145–192.

Egberts, H., *De bodemgesteldheid van de Betuwe* ('s-Gravenhage, 1950).

Egmond, F., 'De strijd om het dagelijks bier. Brouwerijen, groothandel in bier en economische politiek in de Noordelijke Nederlanden tijdens de zestiende eeuw', in C. M. Lesger and L. Noordegraaf (eds), *Ondernemers & bestuurders: Economie en politiek in de Noordelijke Nederlanden in de late Middeleeuwen en vroegmoderne tijd* (Amsterdam, 1999), 153–193.

Egmond, W. van, 'Radbod van de Friezen, een aristocraat in de periferie', *Millennium: Tijdschrift voor middeleeuwse geschiedenis* 19 (2005), 24–44.

Ehbrecht, W., 'Gemeinschaft, Land und Bund im Friesland des 12. bis 14. Jahrhunderts', in H. van Lengen (ed.), *Die Friesische Freiheit des Mittelalters : Leben und Legende* (Aurich, 2003), 135–193.

Eickhoff, E., 'Maritime defence of the Carolingian empire', in R. Simek and U. Engel (eds), *Vikings on the Rhine: Recent research on early medieval relations between the Rhinelands and Scandinavia* (Wien, 2004), 50–64.

Ellmers, D., *Frühmittelalterliche Handelsschiffahrt in Mittel- und Nordeuropa*, 2nd edn (Neumünster, 1984).

—— and Schnall, U., 'Schiffbau und Schiffstypen im mittelalterlichen Europa', in U. Lindgren (ed.), *Europäische Technik im Mittelalter, 800 bis 1400: Tradition und Innovation: Ein Handbuch* (Berlin, 1990), 353–370.

Endrei, W., 'Ein Dutzend mittelalterlicher Webgeräte', in: S. Bangels & L. Smets (eds), *Mittelalterliche Textilien, im besonderen in der Euregio Maas-Rhein* (Sint-Truiden, 1989), 242–248.

Engelen, F. H. G., '2500 jaar winning van kalksteen in zuid-Limburg: Een historisch overzicht', *Grondboor en hamer: Tijdschrift van de Nederlandse Geologische Vereniging* 29 (1975), 38–64.

—— 'Delfstoffen en hun invloed op politieke beslissingen: Het ontstaan van het neutrale gebied Moresnet en de geschiedenis van de mijnbouw in dit gebied', *Grondboor en hamer: Tijdschrift van de Nederlandse Geologische Vereniging* 30 (1976), 20–31.

Epperlein, S., *Bauernbedrückung und Bauernwiderstand im hohen Mittelalter: Zur Erforschung der Ursachen bäuerlicher Abwanderung nach Osten im 12. und 13. Jahrhundert, vorwiegend nach den Urkunden geistlicher Grundherrschaften* (Berlin, 1960).

—— 'Sachsen im frühen Mittelalter. Ein Diskussionsbeitrag zur Sozialstruktur Sachsens im 9. Jahrhundert und seiner politischen Stellung im frühen Mittelalter', *Jahrbuch für Wirtschaftsgeschichte* 1966/1 (1966), 189–212.

Epstein, S. R., 'Cities, regions and the late medieval crisis: Sicily and Tuscany compared', *Past & Present* 130 (1991), 3–50.

—— 'Regional fairs, institutional innovation, and economic growth in late medieval Europe', *Economic history review* 47 (1994), 459–483.

—— 'Craft guilds, apprenticeship, and technological change in preindustrial Europe', *Journal of economic history* 58 (1998), 684–713.

—— *Freedom and growth: The rise of states and markets in Europe, 1300–1750* (London, 2000).

Ervynck, A., and Neer, W. van, 'Dierenresten uit een waterput op de Nieuwe Beestenmarkt: Een blik op de voedselvoorziening van een vroeg-middeleeuws Gent', *Stadsarcheologie: Bodem en Monument in Gent* 23 (1999), 5–13.

Es, W. A. van, 'Dorestad centred', in J. C. Besteman, J. M. Bos, and H. A. Heidinga (eds), *Medieval archaeology in the Netherlands: Studies presented to H. H. van Regteren Altena* (Assen, 1990), 151–182

—— 'Volksverhuizingen en continuïteit', in Es; and W. A. M. Hessing (eds), *Romeinen, Friezen en Franken in het hart van Nederland: Van Traiectum tot Dorestad 50 v.C.–900 n.C*, 2nd edn (Utrecht, 1994), 66–69.

—— 'Friezen, Franken en Vikingen', in Es, and W. A. M. Hessing (eds), *Romeinen, Friezen en Franken in het hart van Nederland: Van Traiectum tot Dorestad 50 v.C.–900 n.C.*, 2nd edn (Utrecht, 1994), 90–92.

—— and Hulst, R. S., *Das Merowingische Gräberfeld von Lent* (Amersfoort, 1991).

Ewig, E., *Spätantikes und fränkisches Gallien: Gesammelte Schriften (1952–1973)*, ed. by H. Atsma, 2 vols (München, 1976).
Faber, J. A., *Drie eeuwen Friesland: Economische en sociale ontwikkelingen van 1500 tot 1800*, 2 parts (Wageningen, 1972).
Fanchamps, M.-L., 'Etude sur les tonlieux de la Meuse moyenne du VIIIe au milieu du XIVe siècle', *Le Moyen-Âge: Bulletin d'histoire et de philologie* 70 (1964), 205–264.
—— 'Les ardoisières des Ardennes et le transport des ardoises sur la Meuse (XIIe–XVIe siècles)', *Le Moyen-Âge: Bulletin d'histoire et de philologie* 78 (1972), 229–266.
Farr, J. T., 'On the shop floor: Guilds, artisans, and the European market economy, 1350–1750', *Journal of early modern history* 1 (1997), 24–54.
—— *Artisans in Europe, 1350–1914* (Cambridge, 2002).
Federico, G., and Malanima, P., 'Progress, decline, growth: Product and productivity in Italian agriculture, 1000–2000', *The economic history review* 57 (2004), 437–464.
Feenstra, R., 'Les foires aux Pays-Bas septentrionaux', *La foire: Recueils de la Société Jean Bodin pour l'histoire comparative des institutions* 5 (1953), 209–23.
Fischer, D. H., *The great wave: Price revolutions and the rhythm of history* (New York, 1996).
Fockema Andreae, S. J., *Studiën over waterschapsgeschiedenis*, 8 vols (1950–1952).
Formsma, W. J., 'Beklemrecht en landbouw: Een agronomisch-historische studie over het beklemrecht in Groningen, in vergelijking met ontwikkelingen elders', *Historia agriculturae* 13 (1981), 7–135.
Fouracre, P., *The age of Charles Martel* (Harlow, 2000).
Freedman, P., *The origins of peasant servitude in medieval Catalonia* (Cambridge, 2004).
—— and Bourin, M. (eds), *Forms of servitude in Northern and Central Europe: Decline, resistance, and expansion* (Turnhout, 2005).
Frenzel, B., Görres, M., and Kempter, H., 'Die frühe landwirtschaftliche und gewerbliche Tätigkeit des Menschen im Spiegel einer ehemaligen Aerosolbelastung der Atmosphäre', in A. Jöckenhövel (ed.), *Bergbau, Verhüttung und Waldnutzung im Mittelalter: Auswirkungen auf Mensch und Umwelt* (Stuttgart, 1996), 213–229.
Fryde, E. B., and Fryde, M. M., 'Public credit, with special reference to north-western Europe', in M. M. Postan, E. E. Rich, and E. Miller (eds), *The Cambridge economic history of Europe* III (Cambridge, 1963), 430–553.
Fuchs, J. M., *Beurt- en wagenveren* (Den Haag, 1946).
Gaier, C., *Four centuries of Liège gunmaking* (Liège, 1976).
—— *L'industrie et le commerce des armes dans les anciennes principautés belges du XIIIme à la fin du XVme siècle* (Paris, 1983).
Gale, W. K. V., *Iron and Steel* (Harlow, 1969).
Ganshof, F. L., 'Manorial organization in the Low Countries in the seventh, eighth and ninth centuries', *Transactions of the Royal Historical Society*, 4th ser. 31 (1949), 29–59.
—— *Feudalism*, (London, 1952).
—— *Le polyptyque de l'abbaye de Saint-Bertin, 844–859* (Paris, 1975).
—— and Berings, G., 'Instellingen Merowingische en Karolingische tijd: De staatsinstellingen in de Karolingische tijd', in D. P. Blok, W. Prevenier, and D. J. Roorda (eds), *Algemene Geschiedenis der Nederlanden* I (Haarlem, 1981), 243–263.
Geary, P. J., *The myth of nations: The Medieval origins of Europe* (Princeton, 2002).
Geel, B. van, et al., 'Holocene raised bog deposits in the Netherlands as geochemical archives of prehistoric aerosols', *Acta botanica Neerlandica* 38 (1989), 467–476.

Gelder, H. E. van, 'Een Noord-Hollandse stad, 1500–1540', *Alkmaarse opstellen* (Alkmaar, 1960), 29–41.

—— and Boersma, J. S., *Munten in muntvondsten* (Bussum, 1967).

Gelderblom, O. C., 'From Antwerp to Amsterdam: The contribution of merchants from the Southern Netherlands to the commercial expansion of Amsterdam (*c*.1540–1609)', *Review* 26 (2003), 247–282.

—— 'The decline of fairs and merchant guilds in the Low Countries, 1250–1650', *Jaarboek voor middeleeuwse geschiedenis* 7 (2004), 199–238.

—— and Jonker, J., 'Completing a financial revolution: The finance of the Dutch East India trade and the rise of the Amsterdam capital market, 1595–1612', *Journal of economic history* 64 (2004), 641–672.

Genicot, L., *L'économie rurale namuroise au bas moyen âge, 1199–1429*, 3 vols (Louvain, 1943–1982).

—— 'Les grandes villes de l'Occident en 1300', in *Économies et sociétés au Moyen Âge: Mélanges offerts à Edouard Perroy* (Paris, 1973).

—— 'Sur le domaine de St-Bertin à l 'époque carolingienne', *Revue d'histoire ecclesiastique* 71 (1976), 69–78.

—— *Rural communities in the medieval West* (Baltimore, 1990).

Gerberding, R. A., *The rise of the Carolingians and the Liber Historiae Francorum* (Oxford, 1987).

Gies, F., and Gies, J., *Cathedral, forge, and waterwheel: Technology and invention in the Middle Ages* (New York, 1994).

Gijsbers, W. M., *Kapitale ossen: De internationale handel in slachtvee in Noordwest-Europa (1300–1750)* (Hilversum, 1999).

Gijswijt-Hofstra, M., *Wijkplaatsen voor vervolgden. Asielverlening in Culemborg, Vianen, Buren, Leerdam en IJsselstein van de 16de tot eind 18de eeuw* (Dieren, 1984).

Gillard, A., *L'industrie du fer dans les localités du comté de Namur et de l'Entre-sambre-et-meuse de 1345 à 1600* (Bruxelles, 1971).

Gimpel, J., *The medieval machine: The industrial revolution of the Middle Ages* (London, 1977).

Glaudemans, C. N. W. M., '*Om die wrake wille*' : *Eigenrichting, veten en verzoening in laat-middeleeuws Holland en Zeeland (ca. 1350–ca. 1550)* (den Haag, 2003).

Godding, P., *Le droit foncier à Bruxelles au moyen âge* (Bruxelles, 1960).

—— and Pycke, J., 'La paix de Valenciennes de 1114', *Bulletin de la commission royale pour la publication des anciennes lois et ordonnances de Belgique* 29 (1979), 1–142.

—— P., 'La famille dans le droit urbain de l'Europe du Nord-ouest au Moyen-Âge', in M. Carlier & T. Soens (eds), *The household in late medieval cities: Italy and Northwestern Europe compared* (Apeldoorn/Leuven, 2001) 25–36.

Goetz, H.-W., 'Serfdom and the beginnings of a "seigneurial system" in the Carolingian period, and survey of evidence', *Early medieval Europe* 2 (1993), 29–51.

Goff, J. le, 'Le temps du travail dans la "crise du XIVe siècle": Du temps médiéval au temps moderne', *Le Moyen Age* 69 (1963), 597–613.

Goldberg, E. J., 'Popular revolt, dynastic politics, and aristocratic factionalism in the early Middle Ages: The Saxon "Stellinga" reconsidered', *Speculum* 70 (1995), 467–501.

Goldsmith, R. W., *Premodern financial systems: A historical comparative study* (Cambridge, 1987).

Goris, J. A., *Étude sur les colonies marchandes méridionales (portugais, espagnols, italiens) à Anvers de 1488 à 1567: contribution à l'histoire des débuts du capitalisme moderne* (Louvain, 1925).

Gottschalk, M. K. E., *Historische geografie van westelijk Zeeuws-Vlaanderen*, 2 vols (Assen, 1955).

—— *Stormvloeden en rivieroverstromingen in Nederland*, 3 vols (Assen, 1971–1977).

—— 'Subatlantische transgressiefasen en stormvloeden', in A. Verhulst and M. K. E. Gottschalk (eds), *Transgressies en occupatiegeschiedenis in de kustgebieden van Nederland en België* (Gent, 1980), 21–27.

Greve, A., 'Die Bedeutung der Brügger Hosteliers für hansische Kaufleute im 14. und 15. Jahrhundert', *Jaarboek voor middeleeuwse geschiedenis* 4 (2001), 259–296.

Grierson, P., 'The gold solidus of Louis the Pious and its imitations', *Jaarboek van het Koninklijk Nederlandsch Genootschap voor Munt- en Penningkunde* 38 (1951), 1–41.

—— and Blackburn, M., *Medieval European coinage, with a catalogue of the coins in the Fitzwilliam Museum, Cambridge*, part I (Cambridge, 1986).

Groenendijk, H. A., *Op zoek naar de horizon: Het landschap van Oost-Groningen en zijn bewoners tussen 8000 voor Chr. en 1000 na Chr.* (Groningen, 1997).

Groote, H. L. V. de, *De zeeassurantie te Antwerpen en te Brugge in de zestiende eeuw* (Antwerpen, 1975).

Grove, J. M., *Little Ice Ages: Ancient and modern*, 2nd edn (London/New York, 2004).

Gutmann, M. P., *Toward the modern economy: Early industry in Europe, 1500–1800* (Philadelphia, 1988).

Haagen, ' "Uitbuiting–door-handel" als verklaringsfaktor voor de vertraagde industrialisering van de linnennijverheid in Vlaanderen', *Handelingen der maatschappij voor geschiedenis en oudheidkunde te Gent* 37 (1983), 215–243.

Haemers, J., *Gentse opstand (1449–1453): De strijd tussen rivaliserende netwerken om het stedelijke kapitaal* (Heule, 2004).

Hagemann, A., 'Die Stände der Sachsen. Mit besonderer Berücksichtigung Westfalens', in W. Lammers (ed.), *Entstehung und Verfassung des Sachsenstammes* (Darmstadt, 1967), 402–445.

Hägermann, D., 'Grundherrschaft und städtischer Besitz in urbanialen Quellen des 9. Jahrhunderts (Saint-Maur-des-Fossés, Saint Rémi de Reims und Saint-Amand-les-Eaux)', in J.-M. Duvosquel and A. Dierkens (eds), *Villes et campagnes au moyen âge: Mélanges Georges Despy* (Liège, 1991), 335–365.

—— and Schneider, H., *Landbau und Handwerk: 750 v. Chr. bis 1000 n. Chr.* (Propyläen Technikgeschichte 1) (Berlin, 1991).

Halbertsma, H., 'The Frisian Kingdom', *Berichten van de Rijksdienst voor het Oudheidkundig Bodemonderzoek* 15/16 (1965/1966), 69–109.

—— *Frieslands oudheid: Het rijk van de Friese koningen, opkomst en ondergang* (Utrecht, 2002).

Hamerow, H., *Early Medieval Settlements: The medieval archaeology of rural communities in north-west Europe 400–900* (Oxford, 2002).

Hansotte, G., 'Contribution à l'histoire de la métallurgie dans le bassin du Hoyoux aux Temps Modernes. Evolution du paysage industriel: Les usines', *Bulletin de l'Institut Archéologique Liégois* 80 (1967), 59–90.

—— 'La métallurgie wallonne au XVIème et dans la première moitié du XVIIème siècle: Essai de synthèse', *Bulletin de l'Institut archéologique liègois* 84 (1972), 21–42.

Hanus, J., *Tussen stad en eigen gewin: Stadsfinanciën, renteniers en kredietmarkten in 's-Hertogenbosch (begin zestiende eeuw)* (Amsterdam, 2007).
Hardt, M., 'Hesse, Elbe, Saale', in W. Pohl, I. N. Wood, and H. Reimitz (eds), *The transformation of frontiers: From late antiquity to the Carolingians* (Leiden, 2001), 219–232.
Harreld, D. J., *High Germans in the Low Countries: German merchants and commerce in golden age Antwerp* (Leiden, 2004).
Hart, S., 'Rederij', in G. Asaert, P. H. Bosscher, J. R. Bruijn, et al. (eds), *Maritieme geschiedenis der Nederlanden II, Zeventiende eeuw, van 1585 tot ca. 1680* (Bussum, 1977), 106–125.
Harten, J. D. H., 'Stroomrug- en komontginning', *Historisch-geografisch tijdschrift* 6 (1988), 20–22.
Hartgerink-Koomans, M., 'Levering van onroerend goed in de Ommelanden', *Tijdschrift voor rechtsgeschiedenis* 15 (1937), 236–268.
Hassan, F. A., *Demographic archaeology* (New York, 1981).
Head, T., & Landes, R. (eds), *The peace of God: Social violence and religious response around the year 1000* (Ithaca, 1992).
Heege, A., 'Rheinische Keramik des Mittelalters: Stand der Forschung unter Berücksichtigung der Funde von Hambach 500', PhD thesis (Göttingen,1992).
Heerma van Voss, L., 'The embarrassment of poverty: Why do the proverbial welfare states border on the North Sea?', in A. Knotter (ed.), *Labour, social policy, and the welfare state* (Amsterdam, 1997), 17–33.
Heidinga, H. A., 'De Veluwe in de vroege Middeleeuwen: Aspecten van de nederzettingsarcheologie van Kootwijk en zijn buren', PhD thesis (Amsterdam, 1984).
—— *Medieval settlement and economy north of the lower Rhine: Archeology and history of Kootwijk and the Veluwe (the Netherlands)* (Assen, 1987).
—— and Offenberg, G. A. M., *Op zoek naar de vijfde eeuw: De Franken tussen Rijn en Maas* (Amsterdam, 1992).
Heijden, M. P. C. van der, *Geldschieters van de stad: Financiële relaties tussen burgers, stad en overheden 1550–1650* (Amsterdam, 2006).
—— 'Juan Luis Vives: Icoon van de vroegmoderne armenzorg', in J. van Eijnatten, F. A. van Lienburg, and H. de Waardt (eds), *Heiligen of helden: Opstellen voor Willem Frijhoff* (Amsterdam, 2007), 61–71.
Hélin, E., *Le paysage urbain de Liège avant la révolution industrielle* (Liège, 1963).
Hemptinne, T. de, 'De doorbraak van de volkstaal als geschreven taal in de documentaire bronnen: Op zoek naar verklaringen in de context van de graafschappen Vlaanderen en Henegouwen in de dertiende eeuw', *Handelingen van de Koninklijke zuid-Nederlandse maatschappij voor Taal- en Letterkunde en Geschiedenis* 53 (1999), 7–21.
—— and Vandermaesen, M., 'De ambtenaren van de centrale administratie van het graafschap Vlaanderen van de 12e tot de 14e eeuw', *Tijdschrift voor geschiedenis* 92 (1980), 177–209.
Henderikx, P. A., *De beneden-delta van Rijn en Maas: Landschap en bewoning van de Romeinse tijd tot ca. 1000*, 2 vols (Hilversum, 1987).
—— 'Die mittelalterliche Kultivierung der Moore im Rhein-maas-Delta (10.–13. Jahrhundert)', *Siedlungsforschung: Archäologie-Geschichte-Geographie* 7 (1989), 67–87.
—— 'De ringburgwallen in het mondingsgebied van de Schelde in historisch perspectief', in *Vroeg-middeleeuwse ringwalburgen in Zeeland* (Goes, 1995), 71–112.

Henderikx, P. A., 'De Lek en de Hollandse IJsel in de vroege middeleeuwen', in Henderikx, *Land, water en bewoning: Waterstaats- en nederzettingsgeschiedenis in de Zeeuwse en Hollandse delta in de Middeleeuwen* (Hilversum, 2001), 163–180.

—— 'De zorg voor de dijken in het baljuwschap Zuid-Holland en in de grensgebieden ten oosten daarvan tot het einde van de 13e eeuw', in Henderikx, *Land, water en bewoning: Waterstaats- en nederzettingsgeschiedenis in de Zeeuwse en Hollandse delta in de Middeleeuwen* (Hilversum, 2001), 181–212.

Henstra, D. J., 'The evolution of the money standard in medieval Frisia: A treatise on the history of the systems of money of account in the former Frisia ($c.600-c.1500$)', PhD thesis (Groningen, 2000).

Herbillon, J., and Joris, A., 'Les moulins à guède en Hesbaye au Moyen Âge', *Revue belge de philologie et d'histoire* 42 (1964), 495–515.

Heringa, J., *De buurschap en haar marke* (Assen, 1982).

Herlihy, D., 'The Carolingian mansus', *The economic history review* 13 (1960), 79–89.

Hildebrandt, H., 'Historische Feldsysteme in Mitteleuropa: Zur Struktur und Genese der Anbauformen in der Zeit vom 9. bis zum 11. Jahrhundert', in *Das Dorf am Mittelrhein: Fünftes Alzeyer Kolloquium, Mainz, 9. bis 11. Oktober 1986* (Stuttgart, 1989), 103–143.

Hillebrand, W., 'Der Goslarer Metallhandel im Mittelalter', *Hansische Geschichtsblätter* 87 (1969), 31–57.

Hocker, F., 'Cogge en coggeschip: Late trends in cog development', in R. Reinders (ed.), *Bouwtraditie en scheepstype* (Groningen, 1991), 25–32.

Hodges, R., *Dark age economics: The origins of towns and trade, AD 600–1000* (New York, 1982).

—— *Towns and trade in the age of Charlemagne* (London, 2000).

Hoffman, Ph. T., Postel-Vinay, G., & Rosenthal, J. T., 'Information and economic history. How the credit market in old regime Paris forces us to rethink', *American historical review* 104 (1999), 69–94.

Hoffmann, R. C., 'Medieval origins of the common fields', in W. N. Parker and E. L. Jones (eds), *European peasants and their markets: Essays in agrarian economic history* (Princeton, 1975), 23–71.

—— 'Economic development and aquatic ecosystems in medieval Europe', *American Historical Review* 101 (1996), 631–669.

Holbach, R., *Frühformen von Verlag und Grossbetrieb in der gewerblichen Produktion (13.–16. Jahrhundert)* (Stuttgart, 1994).

Hollestelle, J., *De steenbakkerij in de Nederlanden tot omstreeks 1560* (Assen, 1961).

Hömberg, A. K., *Westfälische Landesgeschichte* (Münster, 1967).

Hoppenbrouwers, P. C. M., 'Agricultural production and technology in the Netherlands, ca. 1000–1500', in G. Astill and J. Langdon (eds), *Medieval farming and technology: The impact of agricultural change in Northwest Europe* (Leiden, 1997), 89–114.

—— 'Maagschap en vriendschap: Een beschouwing over de structuur en functies van verwantschapsbetrekkingen in het laat-middeleeuwse Holland', *Holland* 17 (1985), 69–108.

—— 'Een middeleeuwse samenleving: Het Land van Heusden' (ca. 1360–ca. 1515)', *AAG Bijdragen* 32 (1992).

—— 'Doorgifte van erfgoed op het laat-middeleeuwse platteland', *Madoc. Nieuwsbrief van Firapeel, vereniging voor mediëvistiek en de Vrije Studierichting Mediëvistiek te Utrecht* 8 (1994), 88–98.

—— 'Op zoek naar de "kerels": De dorpsgemeente in de dagen van graaf Floris V', in D. E. H. de Boer, E. H. P. Cordfunke & H. Sarfatij (eds), *Wi Florens... De Hollandse graaf Floris V in de samenleving van de dertiende eeuw* (Utrecht, 1996), 224–242.

—— 'Town and country in Holland, 1300–1550', in S. R. Epstein (ed.), *Town and country in Europe, 1300–1800* (Cambridge, 2001), 54–79.

—— 'The use and management of commons in the Netherlands: An overview', in M. de Moor, L. Shaw-Taylor & P. Warde (eds), *The management of common land in north west Europe, c.1500–1850* (CORN 8) (Turnhout, 2002), 87–112.

Houtte, J. A. van, 'Les foires dans la Belgique ancienne', *La foire: Recueils de la Société Jean Bodin pour l'histoire comparative des institutions* 5 (1953), 175–207.

—— *An economic history of the Low Countries, 800–1800* (London, 1977).

—— and Uytven, R. van, 'Witschaftspolitik und Arbeitsmarkt in den Niederlanden vom Spätmittelalter bis zur Schwelle des Industriezeitalters', in H. Kellenbenz (ed.), *Witschaftspolitik und Arbeitsmarkt* (München, 1974), 47–68.

Houtzager, D., *Hollands lijf- en losrenteleningen vóór 1672* (Schiedam, 1950).

Howell, M. C., *Women, production, and patriarchy in late medieval cities* (Chicago, 1986).

—— 'Women, the family economy, and the structures of market production in cities of northern Europe during the late Middle Ages', in B. A. Hanawalt (ed.), *Women and work in preindustrial Europe* (Bloomington, 1986), 198–222.

—— *The marriage exchange: Property, social place, and gender in cities of the Low Countries, 1300–1550* (Chicago, 1998).

Hoyois, G., *L'Ardenne et l'Ardennais: L'évolution économique et sociale d'une région* (Bruxelles, 1981).

Hudson, P., 'The regional perspective', in Hudson (ed.), *Regions and industries: A perspective on the industrial revolution in Britain* (Cambridge, 1989), 5–38.

Hugenholtz, F. W. N., 'Het Kaas- en Broodvolk', *Bijdragen en mededelingen van het Historisch Genootschap* 81 (1967), 14–33.

Huiting, J. H., 'Middeleeuws grootgrondbezit in Vleuten en Haarzuilens: Een perceelsgewijze reconstructie', *Historisch-geografisch tijdschrift* 13 (1995), 62–77.

Hurst, J. G., Neal, D. S., and Beuningen, H. J. E. van (eds), *Pottery produced and traded in north-west Europe 1350–1650* (Rotterdam, 1986).

Ibelings, B., 'Het begin van het slagturven in Nederland', *Historisch Geografisch Tijdschrift* 1 (1983), 6–7.

IJzereef, G. F., 'The animal remains', in W. Groenman-van Waateringe and L. H. van Wijngaarden-Bakker (eds), *Farm life in a Carolingian village: A model based on botanical and zoological data from an excavated site* (Assen, 1987), 39–51.

—— and Laarman, F. J., 'The animal remains from Deventer (8th–19th centuries AD)', *Berichten van de Rijksdienst voor het Oudheidkundig Bodemonderzoek* 36 (1986), 405–443.

Immink, P. W. A., ' "Eigendom" en "heerlijkheid": Exponenten van tweeërlei maatschappelijke structuur', in *Tijdschrift voor Rechtsgeschiedenis* 27 (1959), 36–74.

Irsigler, F., 'Die Auflösung der Villikationsverfassung und der Übergang zum Zeitpachtsystem im Nahbereich niederrheinischer Städte während des 13./14. Jahrhunderts', in H. Patze (ed.), *Die Grundherrschaft im späten Mittelalter* (Sigmaringen, 1983), 295–311.

—— 'Grundherrschaft, Handel und Märkte', in K. Flink and W. Janssen (eds), *Grundherrschaft und Stadtentstehung am Niederrhein: Referate der 6. Niederrhein-tagung des Arbeitskreises niederrheinischer Kommunalarchivare für Regionalgeschichte (24.–25. Februar 1989 in Kleve)* (Kleve, 1989), 52–78.

Israel, J. I., *The Dutch Republic: Its rise, greatness, and fall, 1477–1806* (Oxford, 1995).

Jacob, R., *Les époux, le seigneur, et la cité: Coutume et pratiques matrimoniales des bourgeois et paysans de France du Nord au moyen âge* (Bruxelles, 1990).

Janse, A., *Grenzen aan de macht: De Friese oorlog van de graven van Holland omstreeks 1400* (Den Haag, 1993).

Jansen, H. P. H., *Landbouwpacht in Brabant in de veertiende en vijftiende eeuw* (Assen, 1955).

—— and Hoppenbrouwers, P. C. M., 'Military obligation in mediaeval Holland: The burden of the host', *Acta historiae Neerlandicae* 13 (1980), 1–24.

—— 'Sociaal-economische geschiedenis', in *Historie van Groningen* (Groningen, 1981), 123–146.

—— 'Een economisch contrast in de Nederlanden: Noord en Zuid in de twaalfde eeuw', *Bijdragen en mededelingen betreffende de geschiedenis der Nederlanden* 98 (1983), 3–18.

—— and Janse, A. (eds), *Kroniek van het klooster Bloemhof te Wittewierum* (Hilversum, 1991).

Jansen, J. C. G. M., 'Tithes and the productivity of land in the south of Limburg, 1348–1790', in H. van der Wee and E. van Cauwenberghe (eds), *Productivity of land and agricultural innovation in the Low Countries (1250–1800)* (Leuven, 1978), 77–95.

Jansma, T. S., 'Het economisch overwicht van de laat-middeleeuwse stad ten aanzien van haar agrarisch ommeland, in het bijzonder toegelicht met de verhouding tussen Leiden en Rijnland', in H. F. J. M. van den Eerenbeemt (ed.), *Tekst en uitleg: Historische opstellen aangeboden aan de schrijver bijzijn aftreden als hoogleraar aan de Universiteit van Amsterdam* (Den Haag, 1974), 35–54.

Janssen, H. L., 'The castles of the bishop of Utrecht and their function in the publical and administrative development of the bisphoric', *Château Gaillard* 7 (1977), 135–157.

—— 'Tussen woning en versterking. Het kasteel in de middeleeuwen', in Janssen, J. M. M. Kylstra-Wielinga, & B. Olde Meierink (eds), *1000 jaar kastelen in Nederland: Functie en vorm door de eeuwen heen* (Utrecht, 1996), 15–111.

Janssen, W., 'Niederrheinische Territorialbildung, Voraussetzungen, Wege, Probleme', in E. Ennen and K. Flink (eds), *Soziale und wirtschaftliche Bindungen* (Kleve, 1981), 95–113.

—— 'Gewerbliche Produktion des Mittelalters als Wirtschaftsfaktor im ländlichen Raum', in H. Jankuhn, W. Janssen, R. Schmidt-Wiegand, et al. (eds), *Das Handwerk in vor- und frühgeschichtlicher Zeit: Bericht über die Kolloquien der Kommission für die Altertumskunde Mittel- und Nordeuropas in den Jahren 1977 bis 1980* I (Göttingen, 1981), 317–394.

—— 'Die Bedeutung der mittelalterlichen Burg', in H. Jankuhn, W. Janssen, R. Schmidt-Wiegand, et al. (eds), *Das Handwerk in vor- und frühgeschichtlicher Zeit: Bericht über die Kolloquien der Kommission für die Altertumskunde Mittel- und Nordeuropas in den Jahren 1977 bis 1980* II (Göttingen, 1983), 261–316.

—— 'Landerschliessung', in Janssen and D. Lohrmann, *Villa, curtis, grangia: Landwirtschaft zwischen Loire und Rhein von der Römerzeit zum Hochmittelalter* (München, 1983), 81–122.

—— ' "Landnahme" and "Landesausbau" ', in B. Frenzel (ed.), *Evaluation of land surfaces cleared from forests by prehistoric man in early Neolithic times and the time of migrating Germanic tribes* (Stuttgart, 1992), 181–190.

Jelgersma, S., et al., 'The coastal dunes', *Mededelingen Rijks Geologische Dienst* 21 (1970), 94–166.

Joosten, I., 'Technology of early historical iron production in the Netherlands', PhD thesis (Amsterdam, 2004).

——, & Nie, M. van, 'Vroeg-middeleeuwse ijzerproductie op de Veluwe', *Madoc. Nieuwsbrief van Firapeel, vereniging voor mediëvistiek en de Vrije Studierichting Mediëvistiek te Utrecht* 9 (1995), 203–212

Jordan, W. C., *The great famine: Northern Europe in the early fourteenth century* (Princeton, 1996).

Joris, A., *La ville de Huy au Moyen Âge: Des origines à la fin du XIVe siècle* (Paris, 1959).

—— 'Les moulins à guède dans le comté de Namur pendant la seconde moitié du XIIIe siècle', *Le Moyen-Âge: Bulletin d'histoire et de philologie* 14 (1959), 253–278.

—— 'Probleme der mittelalterlichen Metallindustrie im Maasgebiet', *Hansische Geschichtsblätter* 87 (1969), 58–76.

Josse, M., *Le domaine de Jupille des origines à 1297* (Bruxelles, 1966).

Kadens, E., 'De invoering van de volkstaal in ambtelijke teksten in Vlaanderen: Een status quaestionis', *Millennium: Tijdschrift voor Middeleeuwse studies* 4 (2000), 22–41.

Kalifa, S., 'Note sur la nature de la cojuration dans la Frise du Moyen Age: A propos d'ouvrages récents', *L'année sociologique* 9 (1957/1958), 417–426.

—— 'Ébauche d'un tableau des preuves dans le droit frisons du Moyen Âge', in *La preuve* III: *Moyen âge et temps modernes—Recueils de la Société Jean Bodin pour l'histoire comparative des institutions* 17 (1965), 481–506.

Kalveen, C. A. van, 'Bijdrage tot de geschiedenis der gildenbewegingen te Utrecht, mei–augustus 1525', *Jaarboek Oud-Utrecht* (1979), 54–86.

Kan, F. J. W. van, *Sleutels tot de macht: De ontwikkeling van het Leidse patriciaat tot 1420* (Hilversum, 1988).

Kaptein, H., *De Hollandse textielnijverheid 1350–1600: Conjunctuur & continuïteit* (Hilversum, 1998).

Kars, H., & Wevers, J. M. A. R., 'Early-medieval Dorestad, an archaeo-petrological study, Part VII: Amber', *Berichten van de Rijksdienst voor het Oudheidkundig Bodemonderzoek* 33 (1983), 61–81.

Kaspers, H., *Comitatus nemoris: Die Waldgrafschaft zwischen Maas und Rhein: Untersuchungen zur Rechtsgeschichte der Forstgebiete des Aachen-Dürener Landes einschliesslich der Bürge und Ville* (Beiträge zur Geschichte des Dürener Landes 7) (Düren, 1957).

Kellenbenz, H., 'Europäisches Eisen: Produktion, Verarbeitung, Handel: Vom Ende des Mittelalters bis ins 18. Jahrhundert', in Kellenbenz (ed.), *Schwerpunkte der Eisengewinnung und Eisenverarbeitung in Europa, 1500–1650* (Köln, 1974), 397–452.

Kerridge, E., *The farmers of old England* (London, 1973).

Kittell, E. E., 'Women in the administration of the count of Flanders, in *Frau und spätmittelalterlichen Alltag* (1999), 487–508.

—— Testaments of two cities: A comparative analysis of the wills of medieval Genoa and Douai, *European review of history* 5 (1998), 47–82.

Klassen, P. J., *The economics of Anabaptism, 1525–1560* (The Hague, 1964).

Kloek, E., *Wie hij zij, man of wijf: Vrouwengeschiedenis en de vroegmoderne tijd: Drie Leidse studies* (Hilversum, 1990).

Kloek, F. M., 'De arbeidsdeling naar sekse in de oude draperie', in J. K. S. Moes and B. M. A. de Vries (eds), *Stof uit het Leidse verleden: Zeven eeuwen textielnijverheid* (Utrecht, 1991), 66–75.

Knichel, M., *Geschichte des Fernbesitzes der Abtei Prüm in den heutigen Niederlanden, in der Picardie, in Revin, Fumay und Fépin sowie in Awans und Loncin* (Mainz, 1987).

Knol, E., *De Noordnederlandse kustlanden in de Vroege Middeleeuwen* (Groningen, 1993).

—— et al., 'The early medieval cemetary of Oosterbeintum (Friesland)', *Palaeohistoria* 37/38 (1995/1996), 245–416.

Koch, A. C. F., *De rechterlijke organisatie van het graafschap Vlaanderen tot in de 13de eeuw* (Antwerpen, 1960).

—— 'Die flandrischen Burggrafschaften', in Koch, *Tussen Vlaanderen en Saksen: Uit de verspreide geschiedkundige geschriften van A. C. F. Koch (1923–1990)* (Hilversum, 1992), 65–79.

Kolman, C. J., ' "Van Tymmern een steenhuis" Verstening van woonhuizen in Kampen vóór 1350', *Overijsselse historische bijdragen* 100 (1985), 53–82 and 143–146.

Komlos, J., 'An anthropometric history of early-modern France', *European review of economc history* 7 (2003), 159–189.

Können, G. P. (ed.), *Het weer in Nederland: wisselend bewolkt: Een overzicht van ons weer door het KNMI* (Zutphen, 1983).

—— *De toestand van het klimaat in Nederland* (De Bilt, 1999).

Kooistra, L. I., *Borderland farming: Possibilities and limitations of farming in the Roman period and early Middle Ages between the Rhine and Meuse* (Assen, 1996).

Köppen, W., and Geiger, R., *Das Klima derbodennahe Luftschicht* (Braunschweig, 1961).

Kos, H. A., 'Machtsstrijd in Hamaland: De politieke ambities van Balderik and Adela, circa 973–1016', *Jaarboek voor middeleeuwse geschiedenis* 5 (2002), 27–68.

Kossmann-Putto, J. A., 'Armen- en ziekenzorg in de Noordelijke Nederlanden', in D. P. Blok, W. Prevenier, and D. J. Roorda (eds), *Algemene Geschiedenis der Nederlanden* II (Haarlem, 1982), 254–267.

Koster, E. A., *De stuifzanden van de Veluwe: Een fysisch-geografische studie* (Amsterdam, 1978).

—— (ed.), *The physical geography of western Europe* (Oxford, 2005).

Kozial, G. G., 'Monks, feuds, and the making of peace in eleventh-century Flanders', in T. Head and R. Landes (eds), *The peace of God: Social violence and religious response around the year 1000* (Ithaca, 1992), 239–258.

Kraker, A. M. J. de, *Landschap uit balans: De invloed van de natuur, de economie en de politiek op de ontwikkeling van het landschap in de Vier Ambachten en het Land van Saeftinghe tussen 1488 en 1609* (Utrecht, 1997).

—— 'A method to assess the impact of high tides', in C. Pfister et al. (eds), *Climatic variability in sixteenth-century Europe and its social dimensions* (Climatic change 43.1) (Dordrecht, 1999), 287–302.

Kram, G. H. A., 'Boden en wegen van middeleeuwse kooplieden: Enkele Overijsselsche facetten, c.1200–1550', *Vereniging tot beoefening van Overijsselsch recht en geschiedenis* 78 (1963), 15–29.

Kramer, E., 'Onderzoek naar stinswieren', in M. Bierman (ed.), *Terpen en wierden in het Fries-Groningse kustgebied* (Groningen, 1988), 214–225.

Kranenburg, H. A. H., *De Zeevisscherij van Holland in den Tijd der Republiek* (Amsterdam, 1946).

Kranz, H., 'Clergy and coal, a Liege coal mining contract of 1356', *Vierteljahrschrift für Sozial- und Wirtschaftsgeschichte* 85 (1998), 461–476.

—— *Lütticher Steinkohlenbergbau im Mittelalter*, 2 vols (Aachen, 2000).

Kriedte, P., 'Spätmittelalterliche Agrarkrise oder Krise des Feudalimus', *Geschichte und Geselschaft* 7 (1981), 42–68.

Kuchenbuch, L., *Bäuerliche Gesellschaft und Klosterherrschaft im 9. Jahrhundert: Studien zur Sozialstruktur der Familia der Abtei Prüm* (Wiesbaden, 1978).

—— *Grundherrschaft im früheren Mittelalter* (Idstein, 1991).

—— ' "Opus feminile"—Das Geschlechterverhältnis im Spiegel von Frauenarbeiten im früheren Mittelalter', in H.-W. Goetz (ed.), *Weibliche Lebensgestaltung im frühen Mittelalter* (Köln, 1991), 139–175.

Kuijpers, E., 'Lezen en schrijven: Onderzoek naar het alfabetiseringsniveau in de zeventiende-eeuws Amsterdam', *Tijdschrift voor sociale geschiedenis* 23 (1997), 490–522.

—— 'Who digs the town moat? The emergence of a market for labour in late medieval Holland', unpublished paper, Utrecht University, 2008.

Kula, W., *Measures and men* (Princeton, 1986).

Künzel, R. E., *Beelden en zelfbeelden van middeleeuwse mensen: Historisch-antropologische studies over groepsculturen in de Nederlanden, 7de–13de eeuw* (Nijmegen, 1997).

—— 'Op weg naar de mentaliteitsgeschiedenis: Over het vroege werk van Le Goff', *Jaarboek middeleeuwse geschiedenis* 8 (2005), 47–100.

Kuppers, W., and Schaïk, R. W. M. van, 'Levensstandaard en stedelijke economie te Zutphen in de 15de en 16de eeuw', *bijdragen en mededelingen Gelre* 72 (1981) 1–45.

Kuttner, E., *Het hongerjaar 1566* (Amsterdam, 1974).

Kuys, J. A. E., *Drostambt en schoutambt: De Gelderse ambtsorganisatie in het kwartier van Zutphen (ca. 1200–1543)* (Hilversum, 1994).

—— and Schoenmakers, J. T., *Landpachten in Holland, 1500–1650* (Amsterdam, 1981).

Lalblat, C., Margueritte, G., & Martin, J., 'De la stéréotomie médiévale: La coupe des pierres chez Villard de Honnecourt', *Bulletin monumental* 145 (1987), 387–406 and 147 (1989), 11–34.

Laleman, M. C., and Raveschot, P., *Inleiding tot de studie van de woonhuizen in Gent, periode 1100–1300: de kelders* (Brussel, 1991).

Lamb, H. H., *Climate, history and the modern world*, 2nd edn (London/New York, 1995).

Lambrecht, T., 'Reciprocal exchange, credit and cash: Agricultural labour markets and local economies in the southern Low Countries during the eighteenth century', *Continuity & Change* 18 (2003), 237–262.

Landes, D. S., *The wealth and poverty of nations: Why some are so rich and some so poor* (London, 1998).

Langdon, J., 'Horse hauling: A revolution in vehicle transport in twelfth- and thirteenth-century England?', *Past & Present* 103 (1984), 37–66.

Langdon, J., *Horses, oxen and technological innovation: The use of draught animals in English farming from 1066 to 1500* (Cambridge, 1986).

Langen, G. J. de, *Middeleeuws Friesland: De economische ontwikkeling van het gewest Oostergo in de vroege en volle Middeleeuwen* (Groningen, 1992).

Laurent, H., 'Nouvelles recherches sur la Hanse des XVII villes', *Le Moyen Age* 45 (1935), 81–94.

Lebecq, S., 'De la protohistoire au haut moyen Age: Le paysage des "terpen" le long des côtes de la mer du Nord, spécialement dans l'ancienne Frise', *Revue du Nord* 62 (1980), 125–154.

—— *Marchands et navigateurs frisons du haut Moyen Age* (Lille, 1983).

—— 'The role of monasteries in the system of production and exchange of the Frankish World between the seventh and the ninth centuries', in I. Hansen & C. Wickham (eds), *The long eighth century: Production, distribution and demand* (Leiden, 2000), 121–148.

—— 'The northern seas (fifth to eighth centuries)', in P. Fouracre (ed.), *New Cambridge medieval history of Europe*, part I (Manchester, 2005), 639–659.

—— and Costambeys, M., 'The role of monasteries in the system of production and exchange', in I. Hansen and C. Wickham (eds), *The long eighth century: Production, distribution and demand* (2000)

Leenders, K. A. H. W., *Verdwenen venen: Een onderzoek naar de ligging en exploitatie van thans verdwenen venen in het gebied tussen Antwerpen, Turnhout, Geertruidenberg en Willemstad (1250–1750)* (Wageningen, 1989).

—— *Van Turnhoutervoorde tot Strienemonde: Ontginnings- en nederzettingsgeschiedenis van het noordwesten van het Maas-schelde-Demergebied (400–1350): Een poging tot synthese* (Zutphen, 1996).

—— 'The start of peat digging for salt production in the Zeeland region', in M. Lodewijckx (ed.), *Bruc ealles well: Archaeological essays concerning the peoples of north-west Europe in the first millennium* AD (Leuven, 2004), 107–110.

Leeuwen, M. H. D. van, *De rijke Republiek: Gilden, assuradeurs en armenzorg 1500–1800, Zoeken naar zekerheid. Risico's, preventie, verzekeringen en andere zekerheidsregelingen in Nederland 1500–2000* (Den Haag/Amsterdam, 2000).

Lejeune, J., *La formation du capitalisme moderne dans la principauté de Liège au XVIe siècle* (Liège, 1939).

Lesger, C. M., *Hoorn als stedelijk knooppunt: Stedensystemen tijdens de late middeleeuwen en vroegmoderne tijd* (Hilversum, 1990).

—— *Handel in Amsterdam ten tijde van de Opstand: Kooplieden, commerciële expansie en verandering in de ruimtelijke economie van de Nederlanden ca. 1550–ca. 1630* (Hilversum, 2001).

Leupen, P. H. D., 'De Karolingische villa Beek en de stamvader van de Bosoniden', *Bijdragen en mededelingen betreffende de geschiedenis der Nederlanden* 92 (1977), 373–393.

—— *Philip of Leyden: A fourteenth century jurist: A study of his life and treatise 'De cura reipublicae et sorte principantis'*, 2 vols (The Hague/Leiden, 1981).

Limberger, M., ' "No town in the world provides more advantages": Economies of agglomeration and the golden age of Antwerp', in P. O'Brien, et al. (eds), *Urban achievement in early modern Europe* (Cambridge, 2001), 39–62.

—— 'Merchant capitalism and the countryside: Antwerp and the west of the duchy of Brabant (XVth–XVIth centuries)', in P. Hoppenbrouwers & J.L. van Zanden (eds), *Peasants into farmers? The transformation of rural economy and society in the Low Countries (Middle Ages–19th century) in the light of the Brenner debate* (CORN 4) (Turnhout, 2001), 158–178.

Linden, H. van der, *De cope: Bijdrage tot de rechtsgeschiedenis van de openlegging der Hollands–Utrechtse laagvlakte*, (Assen, 1956).

—— *Recht en territoir: Een rechtshistorisch-sociografische verkenning* (Assen, 1972).

—— 'Het platteland in het Noordwesten met nadruk op de occupatie circa 1000–1300', in D. P. Blok, W. Prevenier, and D. J. Roorda (eds), *Algemene Geschiedenis der Nederlanden* II (Haarlem, 1982), 48–82.

Lis, C., and Soly, H., *Poverty and capitalism in pre-industrial Europe* (Brighton, 1982).

—— —— 'Policing the early modern proletariat, 1450–1850', in D. Levine (ed.), *Proletarianization and family history* (Orlando, 1984), 163–228

—— —— 'Corporatisme, onderaanneming en deregulering van de arbeidsmarkt in Westeuropese steden (veertiende-achttiende eeuw)', *Tijdschrift voor Sociale Geschiedenis* 20 (1994), 365–390.

—— —— 'Different paths of development: Capitalism in the northern and southern Netherlands during the late Middle Ages and the early modern period', *Review* 20 (1997), 211–242.

Lodewijckx, M., 'On the issue of continuity and discontinuity applied to the northern Hesbaye region (Central Belgium)', in Lodewijckx (ed.), *Archaeological and historical aspects of west-European societies* (Acta Archaeologica Lovaniensia Monographiae 8) (Leuven, 1996), 207–220.

Lohrmann, D., *Kirchengut im nördlichen Frankreich: Besitz, Verfassung und Wirtschaft im Spiegel der Papstprivilegien des 11.–12. Jahrhunderts* (Bonn, 1983).

—— 'Entre Arras et Douai. Les moulins de la Scarpe au XIe siècle et les détournements de la "Satis" ', *Revue du Nord* 66 (1984), 1023–1050.

—— 'Le moulin à eau dans le cadre de l'économie rurale de la Neustrie (VIIe–IXe siècles)', in H. Atsma (ed.), *La Neustrie: Les Pays au nord de la Loire de 650 à 850* I (Sigmaringen, 1989), 367–404.

—— 'Antrieb von Getreidemühlen', in U. Lindgren (ed.), *Europäische Technik im Mittelalter, 800 bis 1400: Tradition und Innovation: Ein Handbuch* (Berlin, 1990), 221–232.

—— 'Frühe Gezeitenmühlen besonders im flandrischen Amt Hulst', in J.-M. Duvosquel and E. Thoen (eds), *Peasants and townsmen in medieval Europe: Studia in honorem Adriaan Verhulst* (Gent, 1995), 517–528.

Lourens, P., and Lucassen, J. M. W. G., 'De oprichting en ontwikkeling van ambachtsgilden in Nederland (13e–19de eeuw)', in C. Lis & H. Soly (eds), *Werelden van verschil: Ambachtsgilden in de Lage Landen* (Brussel, 1997), 43–77.

Lucassen, J., 'Wage payment and currency circulation in the Netherlands from 1200 to 2000', in Lucassen (ed.), *Wages and Currency: Global Comparisons from Antiquity to the Twentieth Century* (Bern, 2007), 221–263.

Lucassen, J. M. W. G., *Naar de kusten van de Noordzee: Trekarbeid in Europees perspektief, 1600–1900* (Gouda, 1984).

Lyon, B., 'Medieval real estate developments and freedom', *American historical review* 63 (1957), 47–61.

Lynch, K. A., *Individuals, families, and communities in Europe, 1200–1800: The urban foundations of Western society* (Cambridge, 2003).
Maat, G. J. R., 'Two millennia of male stature development and population health and wealth in the Low Countries', *International Journal of Osteoarchaeology* 15 (2005), 276–290.
Maclean, S., *Kingship and politics in the late ninth century: Charles the Fat and the end of the Carolingian Empire* (Cambridge, 2003).
Maddison, A., *The world economy: A millennial perspective* (Paris, 2001).
Malanima, P., 'Urbanisation and the Italian economy during the last millennium', *European review of economic history* 9 (2005), 97–122.
—— 'Wages, productivity and working time in Italy 1300–1913', *Journal of European Economic History* (2007), 121–171.
—— 'Energy systems in agrarian societies: The European deviation', in S. Cavaciocchi (ed.), *Economia ed energia: Secc. XIII–XVIII: Prato, 15–19 aprile 2002* (Firenze, 2003), 61–99.
Maréchal, G., 'Armen- en ziekenzorg in de Zuidelijke Nederlanden', in D. P. Blok, W. Prevenier, and D. J. Roorda (eds), *Algemene Geschiedenis der Nederlanden* II (Haarlem, 1982), 268–280.
—— *Sociale en politieke gebondenheid van het Brugse hospitaalwezen in de middeleeuwen* (Kortrijk,1978).
Marnef, G., *Antwerpen in de tijd van de Reformatie: Ondergronds protestantisme in een handelsmetropool 1550–1577* (Amsterdam, 1996).
Marshall, S., *The Dutch gentry, 1500–1650: Family, faith, and fortune* (New York, 1987).
Marsilje, J. W., *Het financiële beleid van Leiden in de laat-Beierse en Bourgondische periode, ±1390–1477* (Hilversum, 1985).
—— 'Het economische leven', *Leiden: De geschiedenis van een Hollandse stad*, part 2 (2002), 95–103.
Martens, P. J. M., *De zalmvissers van de Biesbosch: Een onderzoek naar de visserij op het Bergse Veld, 1421–1869* (Tilburg, 1992).
Mathieu, J., *Histoire sociale de l'industrie textile de Verviers* (Dison, 1946).
Mayer, T., 'Zur Geschichte der Vogteipolitik in Frankreich und Deutschland', in Mayer, *Fürsten und Staat: Studien zur Verfassungsgeschichte des deutschen Mittelalters* (Weimar, 1950), 185–214.
Mayhew, N. J., 'The circulation and imitation of sterlings in the Low Countries', in Mayhew (ed.), *Coinage in the Low Countries* (Oxford, 1979), 54–69.
McCloskey, D. N., 'The enclosure of open fields: Preface to a study of its impact on the efficiency of English agriculture in the eighteenth century, *Journal of economic history* 32 (1972), 15–35.
—— 'The persistence of English common fields', in W. N. Parker & E. L. Jones (eds), *European peasants and their markets: Essays in agrarian economic history* (Princeton, 1975), 73–119.
McCormick, M., *Origins of the European economy: Communications and commerce, AD 300–900* (New York, 2002).
Medick, H., 'The proto-industrial family economy: The structural function of household and family during the transition from peasant society to industrial capitalism', *Social History* 3 (1976), 291–315.

Melles, J., *Bisschoppen en bankiers : de eerste lombardiers in de lage landen ±1260* (Rotterdam, 1962).
Meischke, R., *Het Nederlandse woonhuis van 1300–1800: Vijftig jaar vereniging "Hendrick de Keyser"* (Haarlem, 1969).
Mendels, F. F., 'Proto-industrialization: The first phase of the industrialization process', *The journal of economic history* 32 (1972), 241–261
Mertens, J., 'Een niet bewaard XVIde-eeuws handboekje voor maten', *Archief- en bibliotheekwezen in België* 50 (1979), 390–394.
Meyer, G. M. de, & Elzen, E. W. F. van den, *De verstening van Deventer: Huizen en mensen in de 14e eeuw* (Groningen, 1982).
Mitterauer, M., *Warum Europa? Mittelalterliche Grundlagen eines Sonderwegs*, 4th edn (München, 2004).
Moerman, J. D., 'Oude smeedijzerindustrie III: Beschrijving der overblijfselen', *bijdragen en mededelingen Gelre* 63 (1968/1969), 1–30, and 64 (1970), 1–41.
Mokyr, J., *The lever of riches: Technological creativity and economic progress* (New York, 1990).
Mol, H., 'Grootgrondbezit van de Friese kloosters', thesis VU (Amstelveen, 1979).
—— 'Friesische Freiheit in Kirchspiel und Kloster', in H. van Lengen (ed.), *Die friesische Freiheit des Mittelalters* (Aurich, 2003), 194–245.
—— 'Middeleeuwse kloosters en dijkbouw in Friesland', in J. J. J. M. Beenakker and H. S. Danner (eds), *Strijd tegen het water: Het beheer van land en water in het Zuiderzeegebied* (Zutphen, 1992), 21–34.
—— 'Hoofdelingen en huurlingen: Militaire innovatie en de aanloop tot 1498', in J. A. Frieswijk, et al. (eds), *Fryslân, staat en macht 1450–1650: Bijdragen aan het historisch congres te Leeuwarden van 3 tot 5 juni 1998* (Hilversum/Leeuwarden, 1999), 65–84.
Mols, R., 'Die Bevölkerungsgeschichte Belgiens im Lichte der heutigen Forschung', *Vierteljahrschrift für Sozial- und Wirtschaftsgeschichte* 46 (1959), 491–511.
Moor, M. de, 'Common land and common rights in Flanders', in De Moor, L. Shaw-Taylor, & P. Warde (eds), *The management of common land in north-west Europe, c.1500–1850* (Turnhout, 2002), 113–141.
—— and Zanden, J. L. van, *Vrouwen en de geboorte van het kapitalisme in West-Europa* (Amsterdam, 2006).
—— —— 'Girl power, the european marriage pattern (EMP) and labour markets in the north sea region in the late medieval and early modern period', working paper, version January 2006, http://home.versatel.be/hanstine/tine/Girlpower%20De%20Moor van%20Zanden.PDF
—— 'The silent revolution: A new perspective on the emergence of commons, guilds, and other forms of corporate collective action in western Europe', *The International Review of Social History* 53, suppl. 16 (2008), 175-208.
Moore, R. I., *The first European revolution, c.970–1215* (Oxford, 2000).
Moorman van Kappen, O., *Met open buydel ende in baren gelde: Enkele beschouwingen over het oud-vaderlandse familienaastingsrecht* (Deventer, 1973).
—— 'De historische ontwikkeling van het waterschapswezen, dijk- en waterschapsrecht in de Tieler- en Bommelerwaarden tot het begin der negentiende eeuw', *Tieler- en Bommelerwaarden 1327–1977: Grepen uit de geschiedenis van 650 jaar waterstaatszorg in de Tielerwaard en de Bommelerwaard* (Tiel/Zaltbommel, 1977), 1–233.

Moortel, A. van de, 'Shipbuilding and navigation in the Rhine delta during the late Viking age', in R. Simek & U. Engel (eds), *Vikings in the Rhineland* (Wien, 2004), 39–50.

Morimoto, Y., 'Essai d'une analyse du polyptyque de l'abbaye de St. Bertin (milieu du 9 siècle): Une contribution a l'étude du regime domanial', *Annuario Istituto giapponese* (1970/1), 31–53.

—— 'Autour du grand domaine carolingien: Aperçu critique des recherches récentes sur l'histoire rurale du haut Moyen Age', in A. E. Verhulst and Y. Morimoto, *Economie rurale et economie urbaine au Moyen Age* (Gent/Fukuoka, 1994), 25–79.

Morineau, M., *Les faux-semblants d'un démarrage économique: Agriculture et démographie en France au XVIII*^{e} *siècle* (Paris, 1971).

—— 'Cambrésis et Hainaut: Des frères ennemis?', *Revue historique* 257 (1977), 323–343

Mostert, M., 'Lezen, schrijven en geletterdheid: Communicatie, verschriftelijking en de sociale geschiedenis van de Middeleeuwen', *Tijdschrift voor sociale geschiedenis* 28 (2002), 203–221.

Müller-Kehlen, H., *Die Ardennen im Frühmittelalter: Untersuchungen zum Königsgut in einem karolingischen Kernland* (Göttingen, 1973).

Munro, J. H., 'Mint policies, ratios and outputs in the Low Countries and England, 1355–1420: Some reflections on new data', *The numismatic chronicle* 141 (1981), 71–116.

—— 'Bullion flows and monetary contraction in late-medieval England and the Low Countries', in J. F. Richards (ed.), *Precious metals in the later medieval and early modern worlds* (Durham, 1983), 97–158.

—— 'Textile technology', in J. R. Strayer (ed.), *Dictionary of the Middle Ages* XI (New York, 1988), 693–701.

—— 'Petty coinage in the economy of late-medieval Flanders: Some social considerations of public minting', in E. H. G. van Cauwenberghe (ed.), *Precious metals, coinage and the changes of monetary structures* (Leuven, 1989), 25–56.

—— 'Industrial entrepreneurship in the late-medieval Low Countries: Urban draperies, fullers, and the art of survival', in P. Klep and C. van Cauwenberghe (eds), *Entrepreneurship and the Transformation of the Economy (10th–20th Centuries): Essays in honour of Herman van der Wee* (Leuven, 1994), 377–388.

—— 'The origins of the English "new draperies": The resurrection of an old Flemish industry, 1270–1570', in N. B. Harte (ed.), *The new draperies in the Low Countries and England, 1300–1800* (New York, 1997), 35–127.

—— 'The symbiosis of towns and textiles: Urban institutions and the changing fortunes of cloth manufacturing in the Low Countries and England, 1270–1570', *Journal of early modern history* 3 (1999), 1–74.

—— 'The medieval origins of the Financial Revolution: Usury, rentes, and negotiability', *International history review* 25 (2003), 505–562.

—— 'Medieval woollens. Textiles, textile technology, and industrial organisation, c.800–1500', in D. Jenkins (ed.), The *Cambridge history of Western textiles* I (Cambridge/New York, 2003), 181–227.

—— 'Wage-stickiness, monetary changes, and real incomes in late-medieval England and the Low Countries, 1300–1450: Did money really matter?', *Research in Economic History* 21 (2003), 185–297.

—— 'Spanish "merino" wools and the "nouvelles draperies": An industrial transformation in the late medieval Low Countries', *The economic history review* 58 (2005), 431–484.

Murray, J. M., 'Family, marriage and moneychanging in medieval Bruges', *Journal of Medieval History* 14 (1988), 115–125.

—— *Notarial instruments in Flanders between 1280 and 1452* (Brussells, 1995).

—— 'Of nodes and networks: Bruges and the infrastructure of trade in fourteenth-century Europe', in P. Stabel, B. Blondé, and A. Greve (eds), *International trade in the Low Countries (14th–16th centuries): Merchants, organisation, infrastructure* (Leuven, 2000), 1–14.

—— *Bruges, cradle of capitalism, 1280–1390* (Cambridge, 2005).

Naessens, M., 'Judicial authorities' views of women's role in late medieval Flanders', in E. E. Kittell and M. A. Suydam (eds), *The texture of society: Medieval women in the southern Low Countries* (New York, 2004), 51–77.

Nazet, J., 'La condition des serfs dans les chartes-lois du comté de Hainaut (XIIe–XIVe siècles), *Contributions á l'histoire économique et sociale* 6 (1970/1971), 83–103.

Nederveen Meerkerk, E. van, *De draad in eigen handen: Vrouwen en loonarbeid in de Nederlandse textielnijverheid, 1581–1810* (Amsterdam, 2007).

Nemery, E., *La Famenne: Histoire d'une region naturelle* (Gembloux, 1975).

Nève, P. L., 'De overdracht van onroerend goed in de middeleeuwen', in J. J. de Groot (ed.), *De levering van onroerend goed: Vijf opstellen over de overdracht van onroerend goed vanaf het Romeinse Recht tot het Nieuw Burgerlijk Wetboek* (Deventer, 1985), 23–38.

Neveux, H., *Les grains du Cambrésis (fin du XIVe, début du XVIIe siècle): Vie et déclin d'une structure économique* (Lille, 1974).

Nicholas, D., *Town and countryside: Social, economic and political tensions in fourteenth-century Flandres* (Brugge, 1971).

—— *The domestic life of a medieval city: women, children and the family in fourteenth-century Ghent* (Licoln/London, 1985).

—— 'Of poverty and primacy: Demand, liquidity, and the Flemish economic miracle, 1050–1200', *American historical review* 96 (1994), 17–41.

—— *Medieval Flanders* (London, 2002).

—— 'Commercial credit and central place functions in thirteenth-century Ypres', in *Money, markets and trade in late medieval Europe: Essays in honour of John H. A. Munro* (Leiden, 2007), 310–348.

Niermeyer, J. F., 'Het midden-nederlandse rivierengebied in de frankische tijd op grond van de Ewa quae se ad Anorem habet', *Tijdschrift voor de geschiedenis* 66 (1953), 145–169.

Nierop, H. F. K. van, *Van ridders tot regenten: De Hollandse adel in de zestiende en de eerste helft van de zeventiende eeuw* (Dieren, 1984).

—— 'The nobility and the revolt of the Netherlands: Between church and king, and protestantism and privileges', in P. Benedict (ed.), *Reformation, Revolt and civil war in France and the Netherlands, 1555–1585* (Amsterdam, 1999), 83–98.

Nijsten, G., 'De ontwikkeling van residenties in het hertogdom Gelre ten tijde van de vorsten uit het huis Gulik en Egmond', in K. Flink & W. Janssen (eds), *Territorium und Residenz am Niederrhein* (Kleve, 1993), 119–149.

Noël, R., 'Deux grandes forêts du nord de la Gaule franque: La "Silua Arduenna" et la "Carbonaria" ', in M. Rouche (ed.), *Clovis, histoire et mémoire*, part I (1997), 631–669.

Nonn, U., *Pagus und Comitatus in Niederlothringen: Untersuchungen zur politischen Raumgliederung im früheren Mittelalter* (Bonn, 1983).

Noomen, P. M., 'Koningsgoed in Groningen. Het domaniale verleden van de stad', in J. W. Boersma, J. F. J. van den Broek, and G. J. D. Offerman (eds), *Groningen 1040: Archeologie en oudste geschiedenis van de stad Groningen* (Bedum, 1990), 97–144.

—— 'De Friese vetemaatschappij: Sociale structuur en machtsbases', in J. A. Frieswijk, et al. (eds), *Fryslân, staat en macht 1450–1650: Bijdragen aan het historisch congres te Leeuwarden van 3 tot 5 juni 1998* (Hilversum/Leeuwarden, 1999), 43–64.

Noordam, D. J., *Leven in Maasland: Een hoogontwikkelde plattelandssamenleving in de achttiende en het begin van de negentiende eeuw* (Hilversum, 1986)

Noordegraaf, L., 'Betriebsformen und Arbeitsorganisation im Gewerbe der nördichen Niederlande 1400–1800', *Hansische Studien* 4 (1979), 54–64.

—— 'Tussen ambacht en manufactuur: Vroegkapitalistische productie- en klassenverhoudingen in de Alkmaarse textielnijverheid, 1500–1800', *Economisch- en sociaal-historisch jaarboek* 44 (1982), 125–135.

—— 'Het platteland van Holland in de zestiende eeuw: Anachronismen, modelgebruik en traditionele bronnenkritiek', *Economisch en sociaal-historisch jaarboek* 48 (1985), 8–18.

—— *Hollands welvaren? Levensstandaard in Holland 1450–1650* (Bergen, 1985).

—— 'De waag: Schakel in de pre-industriële economie', in C. H. Slechte and N. Herweijer (eds), *Het waagstuk: De geschiedenis van waaggebouwen en wegen in Nederland* (Amsterdam, 1990), 11–26.

—— 'Internal trade and internal trade conflicts in the Northern Netherlands: Autonomy, centralism, and state formation in the pre-industrial era', in S. Groenveld and M. J. Wintle (eds), *State and trade: Government and the economy in Britain and the Netherlands since the Middle Ages* (Zutphen, 1992), 12–27.

—— and Schoenmakers, J. T., *Daglonen in Holland, 1450–1600* (Amsterdam, 1984).

North, D. C., *Institutions, institutional change and economic performance* (Cambridge, 1991).

—— and Thomas, R. P., *The rise of the Western world: A new economic history* (Cambridge, 1973).

Oexle, O. G., 'Gilden als soziale Gruppen in der Karolingerzeit', in H. Jankuhn, W. Janssen, R. Schmidt-Wiegand, et al. (eds), *Das Handwerk in vor- und frühgeschichtlicher Zeit: Bericht über die Kolloquien der Kommission für die Altertumskunde Mittel- und Nordeuropas in den Jahren 1977 bis 1980* I (1981), 284–354.

—— 'Die mittelalterlichen Gilden. Ihre Selbstdeutung und ihr Beitrag zur Formung sozialer Strukturen', in A. Zimmermann (ed.), *Soziale Ordnungen im Selbstverständnis des Mittelalters*, 2 vols (Berlin, 1979), 203–226.

Olst, E. L. van, and Boekwijt, H. W., *Delftse windmolens: Van de 13e eeuw tot heden* (Amsterdam, 1978).

Oosterbosch, M., ' "Van groote abuysen ende ongeregeltheden" ': Overheidsbemoeiingen met het Antwerpse notariaat tijdens de XVIde eeuw', *Tijdschrift voor rechtsgeschiedenis* 63 (1995), 83–102.

Opsommer, R., 'Omme dat leengoed es thoochste dinc van der weerelt': Het leenrecht in Vlaanderen in de 14de en 15de eeuw, 2 vols (Brussels, 1995).

Orban, R., 'Longueurs et indices de robustesse des os longs de la population d'âge franc de Coxyde (Belgique)', *Bulletin de la Société Royale Belge d'Anthropologie et de Préhistoire* 81 (1970), 157–173.

Overvoorde, C. J., 'De Leidsche ambachtsbroederschappen', in S. J. Fockema Andreae and R. Fruin (eds), *Rechtshistorische opstellen, aangeboden aan Mr. S. J. Fockema Andreae, hoogleeraar aan de Rijksuniversiteit te Leiden* (Haarlem, 1914), 334–375.

Palmboom, E. N., *Het kapittel van Sint Jan te Utrecht: Een onderzoek naar verwerving, beheer en administratie van het oudste goederenbezit (elfde-veertiende eeuw)* (Hilversum, 1995).

Panhuysen, B. S., 'Maatwerk. Kleermakers, naaisters, oudkleerkopers en de gilden (1500–1800)', PhD thesis (Utrecht, 2000).

Panhuysen, R., *Demography and health in early medieval Mastricht: Prosopographical observations on two cemeteries* (Maastricht, 2005).

Parker, C. H., *The reformation of community: Social welfare and Calvinist charity in Holland, 1572–1620* (Cambridge, 1998).

Paulissen, E., 'De geomorfologie van de Limburgse Kempen', *De aardrijkskunde* 3 (1970), 167–212.

Pauly, M., 'Die Anfänge der kleineren Städte im früheren Herzogtum Luxemburg vor 1500', *Siedlungsforschung: Archäologie–Geschichte–Geographie* 11 (1993), 123–165.

Perizonius, W. R. K., and Pot, T., 'Diachronic dental research on human skeletal remains excavated in the Netherlands, 1: Dorestad's cemetry on the Heul', *Berichten van de Rijksdienst voor het Oudheidkundig Bodemonderzoek* 31 (1981), 369–413.

Perroy, E., 'Le commerce anglo-flamand au XIIIe siècle: La Hanse flamande de Londres', *Revue historique* 252 (1974), 3–18.

Persson, K. G., *Grain markets in Europe, 1500–1900: Integration and deregulation* (Cambridge, 1999).

—— *Pre-industrial economic growth: Social organization and technological progress in Europe* (Oxford, 1988).

Pertz, G. H. (ed.), *Monumenta Germaniae Historica: Legum* III (1863), 698–700.

Petri, F., 'Die Anfänge des mittelalterlichen Städtewesens in den Niederlanden und dem angrenzenden Frankreich', *Studien zu den Anfängen des europäischen Städtewesens: Reichenau-Vorträge, 1955–1956*, (Vorträge und Forschungen) 4 (1958), 227–295.

—— 'Entstehung und Verbreitung der niederländischen Marschenkolonisation in Europa', in W. Schlesinger (ed.), *Die deutsche Ostsiedlung* (1970/1972), 695–754.

Piérard, C., 'Les fortifications médiévales des villes du Hainaut', in *Recueil d'études d'histoire hainuyère offertes à Maurice A. Arnould* I (Mons, 1983), 199–229.

—— 'Les aides levées par les comtes de Hainaut et leur incidences sur les finances urbaines: Un exemple: Mons avant 1433', *Standen en landen* 70 (1977), 183–247.

—— 'Mons: Initiative communale en fait de travaux publics aux XIIIe et XIVe siècles', *L'initiative publique des communes en Belgique: Fondements historiques (Ancien Régime): 11e colloque international [d'histoire], Spa, 1–4 sept. 1982. Actes* (Bruxelles, 1984), 401–417.

Pirenne, H., 'L'instruction des marchands au Moyen Âge', *Annales d'histoire économique et sociale* 1 (1929), 13–28.

Platelle, H., 'La violence et ses remèdes en Flandre au XIe siècle', *Sacris Erudiri* 20 (1971), 101–173.

Pleij, H., *De sneeuwpoppen van 1511: literatuur en stadscultuur tussen middeleeuwen en moderne tijd* (Amsterdam/Leuven, 1988).

Pleijter, G., and Vervloet, J. A. J., 'Kromakkers en bol liggende percelen in de ruilverkaveling Schalkwijk, in het bijzonder bij Tull en 't Waal en bij Honswijk', *Historisch-geografisch tijdschrift* 4 (1986), 13–21.

Pol, A., 'De verspreidingsgebieden van in Nederland geslagen Merovingische gouden munten der 7e eeuw', *Westerheem* 27 (1978), 145–155.

Polet, C., & Orban, R., *Les dents et les ossements humains: Que mangeait-on au moyen âge?* (Turnhout, 2001).

——Leguebe, A., Orban, R., et al., 'Estimation de la stature de la population mérovingienne de Torgny', *Anthropologie et préhistoire* 102 (1991), 111–123.

Pollard, S., *Marginal Europe: The contribution of the marginal lands since the Middle Ages* (Oxford, 1997).

Pons, L. J., 'Holocene peat formation', in J. T. A. Verhoeven (ed.), *Fens and bogs: Vegetation, history, nutrient dynamics and conservation*, (Dordrecht, 1992), 7–79.

Portet, P., 'Remarques sur les systèmes métrologiques Carolingiens', *le Moyen Âge* 97 (1991), 5–24.

Post, R. R., *Scholen en onderwijs in Nederland gedurende de Middeleeuwen* (Utrecht, 1954).

Postan, M. M., *The medieval economy and society: An economic history of Britain, 1100–1500* (Berkeley, 1972).

Posthumus, N. W., *De geschiedenis van de Leidsche lakenindustrie*, 2 parts ('s-Gravenhage, 1908–1939).

Postma, F., *Viglius van Aytta: De jaren met Granvelle, 1549–1564* (Zutphen, 2000).

Postma, O., *De Friesche kleihoeve: Bijdrage tot de geschiedenis van den cultuurgrond vooral in Friesland en Groningen* (Leeuwarden, 1934).

Pouls, H. C., *De landmeter: Inleiding in de geschiedenis van de Nederlandse landmeetkunde van de Romeinse tot de Franse tijd* (Alphen aan de Rijn, 1997).

Power, E., *The wool trade in English medieval history, being the Ford lectures* (London, 1969).

Prak, M. R., 'Politik, Kultur, und politische Kultur: Die Zünfte in den nördlichen Niederlanden', in W. Reininghaus (ed.), *Zunftlandschaften in Deutschland und den Niederlanden im Vergleich* (Münster, 2000), 71–83.

——and Zanden, J. L. van, 'Towards an economic interpretation of citizenship: The Dutch Republic between medieval communes and modern nation-states', *European Review of Economic History* 10 (2006), 111–146.

Prevenier, W., 'Officials in town and countryside in the Low Countries: Social and professional developments from the fourteenth to the sixteenth century', *Acta historiae Neerlandicae* 7 (1974), 1–17.

——*De Leden en de Staten van Vlaanderen, 1384–1405* (Brussel, 1961).

——'La bourgeoisie en Flandre au XIIIe siècle', *Revue de l'université de Bruxelles* (1978), 407–428.

——'Ouderwets en modern bij uuraanduiding in de Nederlanden (14e–15e eeuw)', in D. P. Blok (ed.), *Datum et actum: Opstellen aangeboden aan Jaap Kruisheer ter gelegenheid van zijn vijfenzestigste verjaardag* (Amsterdam, 1998), 347–355.

Prummel, W., *Early medieval Dorestad: An archaeozooligical study* (Excavations at Dorestad 2) (1983), 152–159 (cattle) and 202–213 (pigs).
Quast, J., 'Vrouwen in gilden in Den Bosch, Utrecht en Leiden van de 14e tot en met de 16e eeuw', in W. Fritschy (ed.), *Fragmenten vrouwengeschiedenis*, volume I (1980), 26–37.
Regtdoorzee Greup-Roldanus, S. C., *Geschiedenis der Haarlemmer bleekerijen* ('s-Gravenhage, 1936).
Reichert, W., 'Lombarden zwischen Rhein und Maas: Versuch einer Zwischenbelanz', *Rheinische Vierteljahrsblätter* 51 (1987), 188–223.
Reinicke, C., *Agrarkonjunktur und technisch-organisatorische Innovationen auf dem Agrarsektor im Spiegel niederrheinischer Pachtverträge, 1200–1600* (Rheinisches Archiv 123) (Köln/Wien,1989).
Renard, E., 'La gestion des domaines d'abbaye aux VIIIe –IXe siècles: Notions de base et conseils pour une meilleure compréhension des sources écrites', *De la Meuse à l'Ardennes* 29 (1999), 115–150.
Renes, J., *De geschiedenis van het Zuidlimburgse cultuurlandschap* (Assen,1988).
Rey, M. van, 'Der deutsche Fernbesitz der Klöster und Stifte der alten Diözese Lüttich, vornehmlich an Rhein, Mosel, Ahr und Rheinhessen', *Annalen des Historischen Vereins für den Niederrhein, insbesondere die alte Erzdiöcese Köln* 186 (1983), 19–80 and 187 (1984), 30–89.
Reynolds, S., *Fiefs and vassals: The medieval evidence reinterpreted* (Oxford, 1994).
Reynolds, T. S., *Stronger than a hundred men: A history of the vertical water wheel* (Baltimore, 2002).
Riché, P., *Les écoles et l'enseignement dans l'Occident chrétien de la fin du Ve siècle au milieu du XIe siècle* (Paris, 1979).
Ridder-Symoens, H. de, 'Rich and poor men. Social stratification at the university', in W. Blockmans and A. Janse (eds), *Showing status: Representation of social positions in the late Middle Ages* (Turnhout, 1999), 159–176.
—— 'Possibilités de carrière et de mobilité sociale des intellectuels-universitaires au moyen âge', in N. Bulst & J.-P. Genet (eds), *Medieval lives and the historian: Studies in medieval prosopography: Proceedings of the first international interdisciplinary conference on medieval prosopography, University of Bielefeld, 3–5 December 1982* (Kalamazoo, 1986), 343–357.
—— 'La sécularisation de l'enseignement aux anciens Pays-Bas au Moyen Âge et à la Renaissance', in J.-M. Duvosquel & E. Thoen (eds), *Peasants and townsmen in medieval Europe: Studia in honorem Adriaan Verhulst* (Gent, 1995), 721–737.
—— 'Stad en kennis', in M. Carlier, A. Greven, W. Prevenier, et al. (eds), *Hart en marge in de laat-middeleeuwse stedelijke maatschappij* (Leuven/Apeldoorn, 1997), 131–151.
Riksen, M., Ketner-Oostra, R., Turnhout, C. van, et al., 'Will we lose the last active inland drift sands of western Europe? The origin and development of the inland drift-sand ecotype in the Netherlands', *Landscape ecology* 21 (2006), 431–447.
Rivals, C., *Le moulin à vent et le meunier dans la société traditionelle française* (Ivry, 1976).
Roes, J. S. L. A. W. B., 'De waldgraaf van het (Neder)Rijkswald, 1405–1543', *Bijdragen en mededelingen Gelre* 87 (1996), 6–31.
Roessingh, H. K., 'Garfpacht, zaadpacht en geldpacht in Gelderland in de 17e en 18e eeuw', *Bijdragen en mededelingen Gelre* 63 (1968/1969), 72–97.

Roessingh, H. K., 'De veetelling van 1526 in het kwartier van Veluwe', *Afdeling Agrarische Geschiedenis Bijdragen* 22 (1979), 3–57.

Roover, R. de, 'Aux origines d'une technique intellectuelle: La formation et l'expansion de la comptabilité à partie double', *Annales d'histoire économique et sociale* 9 (1937), 171–193 and 270–293.

—— *Money, banking and credit in mediaeval Bruges: Italian merchant-bankers, lombards and money-changers: A study in the origins of banking* (Cambridge, 1948).

—— 'The concept of the just price: Theory and economic policy', *Journal of economic history* 18 (1958), 418–434.

Rösener, W., Zur Wirtschaftstätigkeit der Zisterzienser im Hochmittelalter, *Zeitschrift für Agrargeschichte und Agrarsoziologie* 30 (1982), 117–148.

—— 'Zur Struktur und Entwicklung der Grundherrschaft in Sachsen in karolingischer und ottonischer Zeit', in A. E. Verhulst (ed.), *Le grand domaine aux époques mérovingienne et carolingienne: Actes du colloque international, Gand, 8–10 septembre 1983* (Gent, 1985), 173–207.

Rosenwein, B. H., *To be the neighbor of Saint Peter: The social meaning of Cluny's property, 909–1049* (Ithaca, 1989).

Rothoff, G., *Studien zur Geschichte des Reichsgutes in Niederlothringen und Friesland während der sächsisch-salischen Kaiserzeit* (Rheinisches Archiv 44) (Bonn, 1953).

Roy Ladurie, E. le, 'L'histoire immobile', *Annales:: Économies, sociétés, civilisations* 29 (1974), 673–692.

Roymans, N. G. A. M., 'The South Netherlands project: Changing perspectives on landscape and culture', *Archaeological dialogues* 3 (1996), 231–244.

Russell, J. C., 'Population in Europe, 500–1500', in C. M. Cipolla (ed.), *The Fontana economic history* I (1976), 36–41.

Rutte, R., *Stedenpolitiek en stadsplanning in de Lage Landen (12de–13de eeuw)* (Zutphen, 2002).

Ruwet, J., 'Pour un indice de la production céréalière à l'époque moderne: La région de Namur', in J. Goy and E. le Roy Ladurie (eds), *Les fluctuations du produit de la dîme: Conjoncture décimale et domaniale de la fin du Moyen-Âge au XVIIIe siècle* (Paris, 1972), 67–82.

Ryckaert, M., 'Brandbestrijding en overheidsmaatregelen tegen brandgevaar tijdens het Ancien Régime', *L'initiative publique des communes en Belgique: Fondements historiques (Ancien Régime): 11e colloque international [d'histoire], Spa, 1–4 sept. 1982. Actes* (Bruxelles, 1984), 247–256.

Sabbe, E., *De Belgische vlasnijverheid*, 2 parts (Kortrijk, 1975).

Sabbe, J., *Vlaanderen in opstand 1323–1328: Nikolaas Zannekin, Zeger Janszone en Willem de Deken* (Brugge, 1992).

Sarfatij, H., 'Dagelijks leven in Holland omstreeks 1300: Vijftien archeologische benaderingen', in H. F. J. Duindam, H. Schoorl, et al. (eds), *Holland in de dertiende eeuw: Leven, wonen en werken in Holland* ('s-Gravenhage, 1982), 22–40.

Schaïk, R. W. M. van, 'De bevolking van Nijmegen in het eerste kwart van de 15de eeuw: Een kritisch onderzoek naar de waarde van de fiskale bronnen', *Bijdragen en mededelingen Gelre* 69 (1976/1977), 7–32.

—— 'Prijs- en levensmiddelenpolitiek in de Noordelijke Nederlanden van de 14e tot de 17e eeuw. Bronnen en problemen', *Tijdschrift voor geschiedenis* 91 (1978), 214–255.

—— *Belasting, bevolking en bezit in Gelre en Zutphen (1350–1550)* (Hilversum, 1987).

—— 'Marktbeheersing. Overheidsbemoeienis met de levensmiddelenvoorziening in de Nederlanden (14de–19de eeuw)', in C. M. Lesger and L. Noordegraaf (eds), *Ondernemers & bestuurders: Economie en politiek in de Noordelijke Nederlanden in de late Middeleeuwen en vroegmoderne tijd* (Amsterdam, 1999), 465–489.

—— 'On the social position of Jews and Lombards in the towns of the Low Countries and neighbouring German territories in the late Middle Ages', in M. Carlier et al. (eds), *Core and periphery in late medieval urban society: Proceedings of the colloquium at Ghent (22–23 August 1996)* (Leuven/Apeldoorn, 1997) 165–191.

Schepper, H. C. C. de, 'Die Einheit der Niederlanden unter Karl V. Mythos oder Wirklichkeit?', in A. Kohler, B. Haider, M. Fuchs, et al. (eds), *Karl V, 1500–1558: Neue Perspektiven seiner Herrschaft in Europa und Übersee* (Wien, 2002), 461–488.

Scherft, P., 'Het stedelijk ijkwezen te Breda, I: Het ijkwezen tot het midden van de 16de eeuw', *Jaarboek van de Geschied- en Oudheidkundige Kring van Stad en Land van Breda 'De Oranjeboom'* 3 (1950), 121–160.

Schlesinger, W., 'Beobachtungen zur Geschicte und Gestalt der Aachener Pflaz in der Zeit Karls des Grossen', in M. Claus et al., *Studien zur europäischen Vor- und Frühgeschichte* (Neumünster, 1968).

—— 'Flemmingen und Kühren: Zur Siedlungsform niederländischer Siedlungen des 12. Jahrhunderts im mitteldeutschen Osten', in Schlesinger (ed.), *Die deutsche Ostsiedlung des Mittelalters als Problem der europäischen Geschichte: Reichenau-Vorträge, 1970–1972* (Sigmaringen, 1975), 263–309.

Schlumbohm, J., 'Produktionsverhältnisse-Produktivkräfte-Krisen in der Proto-Industrialisierung', in P. Kriedte, H. Medick and J. Schlumbohm (eds), *Industrialisierung vor der Industrialisierung: Gewerbliche Warenproduktion auf dem Land in der Formationsperiode des Kapitalismus* (Göttingen, 1978), 194–257.

Schmidt, H., 'Hochmittelalterliche "Bauernaufstände" im südlichen Nordseeküstengebiet', in W. Rösener (ed.), *Grundherrschaft und bäuerliche Gesellschaft im Hochmittelalter* (Veröffentlichungen des Max-Planck-Instituts für Geschichte 115) (Göttingen, 1995), 413–442.

Schmitt, J., *Untersuchungen zu den Liberi Homines der Karolingerzeit* (Frankfurt am Main, 1977)

Scholliers, E., 'Prijzen en lonen te Antwerpen (15de en 16de eeuw)', in C. Verlinden et al. (eds), *Dokumenten voor de geschiedenis van prijzen en lonen in Vlaanderen en Brabant* (Brugge, 1959), 848–940.

—— 'Le pouvoir d'achat dans les Pays-Bas au XVIe siècle', *Album aangeboden aan Charles Verlinden ter gelegenheid van zijn dertig jaar professoraat* (Gent, 1975), 305–330.

—— and Daelemans, F., *De conjunctuur van een domein: Herzele 1444–1752* (Brussel, 1981).

Schulze, H. K., *Grundstrukturen der Verfassung im Mittelalter*, 2 vols (Stuttgart, 1985/1986).

Schuur, J. R. G., 'Late sporen van onvrijheid in noordelijk Nederland', *Tijdschrift voor rechtsgeschiedenis* 65 (1997), 85–105.

Schwarz, G. M., 'Village populations according to the polyptyque of the abbey of St. Bertin', *Journal of medieval history* 11 (1985), 31–42.

Schwind, F., 'Zu karolingerzeitlichen Klöstern als Wirtschaftsorganismen und Stätten handwerklicher Tätigkeit', in L. Fenske, W. Rösener & T. L. Zotz (eds), *Institutionen,*

Kultur und Gesellschaft im Mittelalter: Festschrift für Josef Fleckenstein zu seinen 65: Geburtstag (Sigmaringen, 1984), 101–123.

Segers, J., *Haspengouwse nederzettingsnamen: Een inleiding* (Hasselt, 1994).

Seifert, D., *Kompagnons und Konkurrenten: Holland und die Hanse im späten Mittelalter* (Köln, 1997).

Semmler, J., 'Zehntgebot und Pfarrtermination in karolinger Zeit', in F. Kempf and H. Mordek (eds), *Aus Kirche und Reich: Studien zu Theologie, Politik und Recht im Mittelalter* (1983), 33–44.

Sicking, L. H. J., *Zeemacht en onmacht: Maritieme politiek in de Nederlanden, 1488–1558* (Amsterdam, 1998).

—— 'Die offensive Lösung: Militärische Aspekte des holländischen Ostseehandels im 15. und 16. Jahrhundert', *Hansische Geschichtsblätter* 117 (1999), 39–52.

—— *Neptune and the Netherlands: State, economy, and war at sea in the Renaissance* (Leiden, 2004).

Sivéry, G., *Structures agraires et vie rurale dans le Hainaut à la fin du Moyen-âge*, 2 parts (Villeneuve-d'Ascq, 1977).

Slicher van Bath, B. H., *Mensch en land in de Middeleeuwen: Bijdrage tot een geschiedenis der nederzettingen in Oostelijk Nederland*, 2 vols (Assen, 1944).

—— 'Drenthe's vrijheid', *Bijdragen voor de geschiedenis der Nederlanden* 1 (1946), 161–196.

—— *Een samenleving onder spanning: Geschiedenis van het platteland in Overijssel* (Assen, 1957).

—— *Een Fries landbouwbedrijf in de tweede helft van de zestiende eeuw* (Wageningen, 1958).

—— 'The rise of intensive husbandry in the Low Countries', *Britain and the Netherlands* 1 (1960), 130–153.

—— 'The economic and social conditions in the Frisian districts from 900–1500', *AAG Bijdragen* 13 (1965), 97–133.

—— *De agrarische geschiedenis van West-Europa 500–1850* (Utrecht, 1976).

Slofstra, J., Regteren Altena, H. H. van, Roymans, N., et al., *Het Kempenprojekt: Een regionaal-historisch onderzoeksprogramma* (Waalre,1982).

Slootmans, C. J. F., *Paas- en koudemarkten te Bergen op Zoom 1365–1565*, 3 vols (Tilburg, 1985).

Slotboom, R. T., 'Comparative geomorphological and palynological investigation of the Pingos (Viviers) in the Hautes Fagnes (Belgium) and the Mardellen in the Gutland (Luxemburg)', PhD thesis (Amsterdam, 1963).

Smidt, J. T. de, *Rechtsgewoonten: De gebruiken en plaatselijke gebruiken waarnaar het Burgerlijk Wetboek verwijst* (Amsterdam, 1954).

Snoep, D. P., *Het Utrechtse schip* (Utrecht, 1980).

Soens, T., 'Het waterschap en de mythe van democratie in het Ancien Régime: Het voorbeeld van de Vlaamse kustvlakte in de Late Middeleeuwen', *Jaarboek voor ecologische geschiedenis* (2003), 39–55.

—— '1404 in Vlaanderen: De eerste Sint-Elisabethsvloed in het licht van de waterstaatsgeschiedenis van de Vlaamse kustvlakte', *Tijdschrift voor waterstaatsgeschiedenis* 14 (2005), 79–89.

—— 'Explaining deficiencies of water management in the late medieval Flemish coastal plain, 13th–16th centuries', in H. Greefs, and M.'t Hart (eds), *Water management, communities, and environment: The Low Countries in comparative perspective, c.1000–c.1800: Jaarboek voor ecologische geschiedenis 2005/6* (2006), 35–61.

—— 'Polders zonder poldermodel? Een onderzoek naar de rol van inspraak en overleg in de waterstaat van de laatmiddeleeuwse Vlaamse kustvlakte (1250–1600)', *Tijdschrift voor sociale en economische geschiedenis* 3 (2006), 3–36.

—— and Thoen, E., 'The origins of leasehold in the former county of Flanders', in B. J. P. van Bavel & P. Schofield (eds), *The development of leasehold in northwestern Europe, c.1200–1600* (CORN 10) (Turnhout, 2008), 31–55.

Soetaert, P., *De bergen van Barmhartigheid in de Spaanse, de Oostenrijkse en de Franse Nederlanden (1618–1795)* (Brussels, 1986).

Soly, H., 'Fortificaties, belastingen en corruptie te Antwerpen in het midden der 16e eeuw', in *Bijdragen tot de geschiedenis* 53 (1970) 191–210.

—— 'Het "verraad" der 16de-eeuwse burgerij: een mythe? Enkele beschouwingen betreffende het gedragspatroon der 16de-eeuwse Antwerpse ondernemers', *Tijdschrift voor geschiedenis* 86 (1973), 262–280.

—— 'Nijverheid en kapitalisme te Antwerpen in de 16e eeuw', *Album aangeboden aan Charles Verlinden ter gelegenheid van zijn dertig jaar professoraat* (Gent, 1975), 332–352.

—— *Urbanisme en kapitalisme te Antwerpen in de 16e eeuw: De stedebouwkundige en industriële ondernemingen van Gilbert van Schoonbeke* (Brussel, 1977).

—— 'De grote heksenjacht in West-Europa, 1560–1650: Een voorlopige balans', *Volkskunde* 82 (1981), 103–127.

Somers, J., 'Het laatmiddeleeuws pandbedrijf in de Nederlanden', *Handelingen der Koninklijke Zuidnederlandse Maatschappij voor Taal- en Letterkunde en Geschiedenis* 36 (1982), 169–194.

Sommé, M., 'Réglements, délits et organisation des ventes dans la forêt de Nieppe (début XIVe–début XVIe siècle) in Hommage à Guy Fourquin. Histoire des campagnes au Moyen Age', *Revue du Nord* 72 (1990), 511–528.

Sosson, J.-P., *Les travaux publics de la ville de Bruges, XIVe–XVe siècles: Les matériaux, les hommes* (Bruxelles, 1977).

—— 'Corporation et paupérisme aux XIVe et XVe siècles: Le salariat du bâtiment en Flandre et en Brabant, et notamment à Bruges', *Tijdschrift voor Geschiedenis* 92 (1979), 557–575.

—— 'Les Metiers, Norme et realité: L'exemple des anciens Pays-Bas meridionaux aux XIVe et XVe siècles', in J. Hamesse and C. Muraille (eds), *Le Travail au Moyen Âge* (Louvain-la-Neuve, 1990), 339–348.

—— 'Finances communales et dette publique: Le cas de Bruges à la fin du XIIIe siècle', in J.-M. Duvosquel & E. Thoen (eds), *Peasants and townsmen in medieval Europe: Studia in honorem Adriaan Verhulst* (Gent, 1995), 239–258.

—— 'Le "petit people" des villes: Indispensables mesures et mesures impossibles? Quelques réflexions à propos des anciens Pays-Bas méridionaux (XIIIe–XVe siècles)', in P. Boglioni, R. Delort, and C. Gauvard (eds), *Le petit peuple dans l'Occident médiéval: Terminologies, perceptions, réalités* (Parijs, 2002) 191–211.

Spaans, J., *Armenzorg in Friesland 1500–1800: Publieke zorg en particuliere liefdadigheid in zes Friese steden: Leeuwarden, Bolsward, Franeker, Sneek, Dokkum en Harlingen* (Hilversum, 1997).
Speet, B. M. J., 'Joden in het hertogdom Gelre', in J. Stinner, K.-H. Tekath, and D. M. Oudesluijs (eds), *Gelre, Geldern, Gelderland, geschiedenis en cultuur van het hertogdom Gelre* (Utrecht, 2001), 337–342.
Spek, T., 'The age of plaggen soils: An evaluation of dating methods for plaggen soils in the Netherlands and northern Germany', in A. Verhoeve and J. A. J. Vervloet (eds), *The transformation of the European rural landscape: Methodological issues and agrarian change 1770–1914: Papers from the 1990 meeting of the Standing European Conference for the Study of the Rural Landscape* (Heverlee, 1992), 72–91.
—— *Het Drentse esdorpenlandschap: Een historisch-geografische studie*, 2 vols (Utrecht, 2004).
Spiegeler, P. de, *Les hôpitaux et l'assistance à Liège (X^e–XVe siècles): Aspects institutionnels et sociaux* (Paris, 1987).
Spierenburg, P. C., 'The sociogenesis of confinement and its development in early modern Europe', in Spierenberg (ed.), *The emergence of carceral institutions: Prisons, galleys and lunatic asylums, 1550–1900* (Rotterdam, 1984), 9–77.
—— 'Early modern prisons and the dye trade: The fate of convict rasping as proof for the insufficiency of the economic approach to prison history', *Economic and social history in the Netherlands* 3 (1991), 1–17.
Spiess, K.-H., 'Zur Landflucht im Mittelalter', in H. Patze (ed.), *Die Grundherrschaft im späten Mittelalter* part I (Sigmaringen,1983), 157–204.
—— 'Herrschaftliche Jagd und bäuerliche Bevölkerung im Mittelalter', in W. Rösener (ed.), *Jagd und höfische Kultur* (Göttingen, 1997), 231–254.
Sprandel, R., *Das Eisengewerbe im Mittelalter* (Stuttgart, 1968).
Sproemberg, H., 'Die Seepolitik Karls des Grossen', in Sproemberg, *Beiträge zur belgisch-niederländerische Geschichte* (Berlin, 1959), 1–29.
Spufford, P., 'Coinage, taxation and the Estates General of Burgundian Netherlands', *Standen en landen* 40 (1966), 63–89.
—— *Monetary problems and policies in the Burgundian Netherlands, 1433–1496* (Leiden, 1970).
—— *Money and its use in medieval Europe* (Cambridge, 1988).
Staab, F., 'Die Gesellschaft des Merowingerreichs', in *Die Franken*, pp. 479–484.
Stabel, P., *De kleine stad in Vlaanderen: Bevolkingsdynamiek en economische functies van de kleine en secundaire stedelijke centra in het Gentse kwartier (14de–16de eeuw)* (Brussel, 1995).
—— *Dwarfs among giants: The Flemish urban network in the late Middle Ages* (Leuven, 1997).
—— 'Women at the market: Gender and retail in the towns of medieval Flanders', in M. Boone, T. de Hemptinne, and W. M. Blockmans (eds), *Secretum Scriptorum: liber alumnorum Walter Prevenier* (Leuven,1999) 259–276.
Stabel, S., 'Marketing cloth in the Low Countries: Foreign merchants, local businessmen and urban entrepreneurs: Markets, transport and transaction costs (14th–16th century)', in Stabel (ed.), *International trade in the Low Countries (14th–16th centuries): Merchants, organisation, infrastructure: Proceedings of the international conference, Ghent–Antwerp, 12–13 December 1997* (Leuven, 2000), 15–36.

Stabel, P., 'Urban markets, rural industries and the organisation of labour in late medieval Flanders: The constraints of guild regulations and the requirements of export oriented production', in B. Blondé, E. Hanhaute, and M. Galand (eds), *Labour and labour markets between town and countryside (Middle Ages–19th century)* (CORN 6) (2001), 140–157.

Stayer, J. M., *Anabaptists and the sword*, 2nd edn (Lawrence, 1976).

—— *The German Peasants' War and anabaptist community of goods* (Montreal, 1994).

Steckel, R. H., 'Strategic ideas in the rise of the new anthropometric history and their implications for interdisciplinary research', *Journal of economic history* 58 (1998), 803–821.

Stein, R., 'Burgundian bureaucracy as a model for the Low Countries? The Chambres des Comptes and the creation of an administrative unity', in R. Stein (ed.), *Powerbrokers in the late Middle Ages: The Burgundian low countries in a European context* (Turnhout, 2001), 3–25.

Stephan, H.-G., 'The development and production of medieval stoneware in Germany', in P. Davey and R. Hodges (eds), *Ceramics and trade: The production and distribution of later medieval pottery in north-west Europe* (Sheffield, 1983), 95–120.

Stephenson, C., 'The origin and nature of the taille', *Revue belge de philologie et d'histoire* 5 (1926), 801–870.

Steurs, W., *Naissance d'une region: Aux origines de la Mairie de Bois-le-Duc: Recherches sur le Brabant septentrional aux 12ᵉ et 13ᵉ siècles* (Bruxelles, 1993).

—— 'Les franchises du duché de Brabant au Moyen Age', *Bulletin de la Commission Royale des Anciennes Lois et Ordonnances de Belgique* 25 (1973), 139–295.

Stouthamer, E., *Holocene avulsions in the Rhine–Meuse delta, the Netherlands* (Utrecht, 2001).

Sundhausen, H., 'Zur Wechselbeziehung zwischen frühneuzeitlichem Aussenhandel und ökonomischer Rückständigkeit in Osteuropa: Eine Auseinandersetzung mit der "Kolonialthese" ', *Geschichte und Gesellschaft* 9 (1983), 544–563.

Suttor, M., 'Le contrôle du trafic fluvial: La Meuse, des origines à 1600', *Revue du Nord* 76 (1994), 7–23.

Taffein, C. & Decleer, M., *Das Hohe Venn: Bedrohter Zauber wilder Natur* (Eupen, 1997).

Taylor, C., 'The year 1000 and "those who laboured" ', in M. Frassetto (ed.), *The year 1000: Religious and social response to the turning of the first millennium* (Basingstoke, 2002), 187–236.

TeBrake, W. H., *The making of a humanized landscape in the Dutch Rijnland, 950–1350: Biological change in a coastal lowland* (Austin, 1975).

—— *A plague of insurrection: Popular politics and peasant revolt in Flanders, 1323–1328* (Philadelphia, 1993).

Teunis, H., 'De ketterij van Tanchelm. Een misverstand tussen twee werelden', in R. E. V. Stuip & C. Vellekoop (eds), *Utrecht tussen kerk en staat* (Hilversum, 1991), 153–167.

Teunissen, D., 'Enkele gebeurtenissen uit het leven van de Romeinse veldheer Drusus', *Westerheem* 29 (1980), 321–334.

—— *Palynologisch onderzoek in het oostelijk rivierengebied, een overzicht* (Nijmegen, 1990).

Theuws, *De archeologie van de periferie: Studies naar de ontwikkeling van bewoning en samenleving in het Maas-Demer-Schelde gebied in de vroege middeleeuwen* (Amsterdam, 1988).

Theuws, F. C. W. J., 'Centre and periphery in Northern Austrasia (6th–8th centuries): An archaeological perspective', in J. C. Besteman, J. M. Bos, & H. A. Heidinga (eds), *Medieval archaeology in the Netherlands: Studies presented to H. H. van Regteren Altena* (Assen, 1990), 41–69.

—— 'Landed property and manorial organisation in Northern Austrasia: Some considerations and a case study', in Theuws & N. G. A. M. Roymans (eds), *Images of the past: Studies on ancient societies in northwestern Europe* (Amsterdam, 1991), 299–407.

—— 'Maastricht as a centre of power in the early Middle Ages', in M. B. de Jong, F. C. W. J. Theuws & A. C. van Rhijn (eds), *Topographies of power in the early Middle Ages* (2001), 155–216.

—— 'Proloog van Brabant. Verleden landschappen van Romeinen en Franken', in R. van Uytven et al. (eds), *Geschiedenis van Brabant: Van het hertogdom tot heden* (Zwolle/Leuven, 2004), 17–39.

—— and Roymans, N. G. A. M. (eds), *Images of the past: Studies on ancient societies in northwestern Europe* (Amsterdam, 1991).

Thirsk, J., *Agricultural regions and agrarian history in England, 1500–1750* (Basingstoke, 1987).

Thoen, E., 'Rechten en plichten van plattelanders als instrumenten van machtspolitieke stijd tussen adel, stedelijke burgerij en grafelijk gezag in het laat-middeleeuwse Vlaanderen, buitenpoorterij en mortemain-rechten ten persoonlijken titel in de kasselrijen van Aalst en Oudenaarde, vooral toegepast op de periode rond 1400', in *Machtsstructuren in de plattelandsgemeenschappen in België en aangrenzende gebieden (12e–19e eeuw)* (1988), 469–490.

—— *Landbouwekonomie en bevolking in Vlaanderen gedurende de late middeleeuwen en het begin van de moderne tijden: Testregio: de kasselrijen van Oudenaarde en Aalst, eind 13de–eerste helft van de 16de eeuw* (Gent, 1988).

—— 'The count, the countryside and the economic development of the towns in Flanders from the eleventh to the thirteenth century: Some provisional remarks and hypotheses', in E. Aerts et al. (eds), *Studia Historia Oeconomica. Liber amicorum Van der Wee* (Leuven, 1993), 259–278.

—— 'Verhuizen naar Brugge in de late Middeleeuwen: De rol van de immigratie van de poorters in de aanpassing van het beleid van de stad Brugge aan de wijzigende economische omstandigheden (14e–16e eeuw)', in H. Soly and R. Vermeir (eds), *Beleid en bestuur in de Oude Nederlanden: Liber Amicorum Prof. Dr. M. Baelde* (Ghent, 1993), 329–349.

—— 'Le démarrage économique de la Flandre au Moyen Age. Le rôle de la campagne et des structures politiques (XIe–XIIIe siècles): Hypothèses et voies de recherches', in A. E. Verhulst & Y. Morimoto, *Economie rurale et economie urbaine au Moyen Age* (Gent, 1994), 165–184.

—— 'The birth of the "Flemish Husbandry": Agricultural technology in medieval Flanders', in G. Astill and J. Langdon (eds), *Medieval farming and technology: The impact of agricultural change in Northwest Europe* (Leiden, 1997), 69–88.

—— 'A "commercial survival economy" in evolution: The Flemish countryside and the transition to capitalism (Middle Age–19th century)', in J. L. van Zanden and P. C. M. Hoppenbrouwers (eds), *Peasants into farmers? The transformation of rural economy and society in the Low Countries (Middle Ages–19th century) in light of the Brenner debate* (CORN 4) (Turnhout, 2001), 102–149.

—— 'Transitie en economische ontwikkeling', *Tijdschrift voor sociale geschiedenis* 28 (2002), 147–174.

—— ' "Social agrosystems" as an economic concept to explain regional differences: An essay taking the former county of Flanders as an example', in B. J. P. van Bavel and P. C. M. Hoppenbrouwers (eds), *Landholding and land transfer in the North Sea area (late Middle Ages–19th century)* (CORN 5) (Turnhout, 2004), 47–66.

—— and Soens, T., 'Appauvrissement et endettement dans le monde rural: Etude comparative du crédit dans les différents systèmes agraires en Flandre au bas Moyen Age et au début de l'Epoque Moderne', in *Il mercato della Terra secc. XIII–XVIII: Atti della Trentacinquesima Settimana di Studi 5–9 maggio 2003* (Prato 2004), 703–720.

—— and Vanhaute, E., 'The "Flemish husbandry" at the edge of the farming system on small-holdings in the middle of the 19th century', in B. J. P. van Bavel and E. Thoen (eds), *Land productivity and agro-systems in the North Sea area (Middle Age–20th century): Elements for Comparison* (CORN 2) (Turnhout, 1999), 271–296.

Thurkow, A. J., et al., *Atlas van Nederland*, part 2 ('s-Gravenhage, 1984).

Tielhof, M. van, *De Hollandse graanhandel, 1470–1570: Koren op de Amsterdamse molen* (Den Haag, 1995).

Tihon, C., 'Aperçus sur l'établissement des Lombards dans les Pays-Bas aux XIIIe et XIVe siècles', *Revue belge de philologie et d'histoire* 39 (1961), 334–364.

Tilly, C., *European revolutions, 1492–1992* (Oxford, 1992).

Timmer, R., 'Restanten van Oud-Germaans recht in de Lex Frisionum', *Pro memorie: Bijdragen tot de rechtsgeschiedenis der Nederlanden* 2 (2000), 17–45.

Timmers, J. J. M., *De kunst van het Maasland*, 2 parts (Assen, 1971–1980).

Tits-Dieuaide, M.-J., *La formation des prix céréaliers en Brabant et en Flandre au XVe siècle* (Bruxelles, 1975).

—— 'Les tables des pauvres dans les anciennes principautés belges au moyen âge', *Tijdschrift voor geschiedenis* 88 (1975), 562–583.

Toepfer, B., 'Die Rolle von Städtebünden bei den Ausbildung der Ständeverfassung in den Fürstentümern Lüttich und Brabant', in Toepfer (ed.), *Städte und Ständestaat* (Berlin, 1980), 113–154.

Toussaert, J., *Le sentiment religieux, la vie et la pratique religieuse des laïcs en Flandre Maritime et au 'West-hoeck' de langue flamande au XIVe, XVe et début de XVIe siècle* (Paris, 1963).

Törnqvist, T. E., *Fluvial sedimentary geology and chronology of the Holocene Rhine-meuse delta, the Netherlands* (Utrecht, 1993).

Toch, M., 'Lords and peasants: A reappraisal of medieval economic relationships', *Journal of European Economic History* 15 (1986), 163–182.

Tracy, J. D., *A financial revolution in the Habsburg Netherlands: Renten and renteniers in the county of Holland, 1515–1565* (Berkeley, 1985).

—— 'Herring wars: The Habsburg Netherlands and the struggle for control of the North Sea, ca. 1520–1560', *The sixteenth century journal* 24 (1993), 249–272.

Tracy, J. D., 'On the dual origins of long-term debt in Medieval Europe', in M. H. Boone, C. A. Davids, and P. Janssens (eds), *Urban public debts: Urban government and the market for annuities in Western Europe (14th–18th centuries)* (Turnhout, 2003), 13–24.

Trauffler, H., 'Klostergrundherrschaft und Stadt: Vergleichende Untersuchungen zu den Abteistädten zwischen Maas und Rhein im Hochmittelalter', in A. Haverkamp and F. G. Hirschmann (eds), *Grundherrschaft, Kirche, Stadt zwischen Maas und Rhein während des hohen Mittelalters* (1997), 219–238.

Trimpe Burger, J. A., 'Onderzoekingen in vluchtbergen, Zeeland', *Berichten van de Rijksdienst voor het Oudheidkundig Bodemonderzoek te Amersfoort* 8 (1957/1958), 114–155.

Tys, D., 'Domeinvorming in de "wildernis" en de ontwikkeling van vorstelijke macht. Het voorbeeld van het bezit van de graven van Vlaanderen in het IJzerestuarium tussen 900 en 1200', *Jaarboek voor middeleeuwse geschiedenis* 7 (2004), 31–83.

Unger, R. W., 'The Netherlands herring fishery in the late middle ages: The false legend of Willem Beukels of Biervliet', *Viator: Medieval and renaissance studies* 9 (1978), 335–356.

―― 'Dutch herring, technology, and international trade in the seventeenth century', *Journal of economic history* 40 (1980), 253–279.

―― *The ship in the medieval economy, 600–1600* (London, 1980).

―― *Dutch shipbuilding before 1800: Ships and guilds* (Assen, 1978).

―― 'Energy sources for the Dutch Golden Age: Peat, wind and coal', *Research in economic history* 9 (1984), 221–253.

―― 'Technical change in the brewing industry in Germany, the Low Countries and England in the late Middle Ages', *Journal of European economic history* 21 (1992), 281–313.

―― 'Feeding Low Countries towns: The grain trade in the fifteenth century', *Revue belge de philologie et d'histoire* 77 (1999), 329–358.

―― *A history of brewing in Holland, 900–1900: Economy, technology and the state* (Leiden, 2001).

―― 'Integration of grain markets', paper (2002).

―― 'Prices, consumption patterns and consumer welfare in the Low Countries at the end of the Middle Ages', *Jaarboek voor middeleeuwse geschiedenis* 8 (2005), 252–282.

Uytven, R. van, *Stadsfinanciën en stadsekonomie te Leuven van de XIIe tot het einde der XVIe eeuw*, Verhandelingen van de Koninklijke Vlaamse Academie voor Wetenschappen, Letteren en Schone Kunsten van België (Klasse der Letteren 44) (Brussel, 1961).

―― 'Plutokratie in de "oude demokratieën der Nederlanden" ', *Koninklijke Zuidnederlandse Maatschappij voor Taal- en Letterkunde en Geschiedenis* 16 (1962), 373–409.

―― 'The fulling mill: Dynamic of the revolution in industrial attitudes', *Acta historiae Neerlandicae: Studies on the history of the Netherlands* 5 (1971), 1–14.

―― 'Die ländliche Industrie während des Spätmittelalters in den südlichen Niederlanden', in H. Kellenbenz (ed.), *Agrarisches Nebengewerbe und Formen der Reagrarisierung im Spätmittelalter und im 19./20. Jahrhundert. Bericht über die 5. Arbeitstagung der Gesellschaft für Sozial- und Wirtschaftsgeschichte* (Sigmaringen, 1975), 57–78.

―― 'Imperialisme of zelfverdediging: de extra-stedelijke rechtsmacht van Leuven', *Bijdragen tot de geschiedenis* 58 (1975), 7–72.

―― 'Stadsgeschiedenis in het Noorden en Zuiden', in D. P. Blok, W. Prevenier, and D. J. Roorda (eds), *Algemene Geschiedenis der Nederlanden* II (Haarlem, 1982), 188–263.

―― 'Stedelijke openbare diensten te Leuven tijdens het Ancien Régime', *L'initiative publique des communes en Belgique: Fondements historiques (Ancien Régime): 11ᵉ colloque international [d'histoire], Spa, 1–4 sept. 1982. Actes* (Bruxelles, 1984), 21–43.

―― 'Geldhandelaars en wisselaars in het middeleeuwse Brabant', in H. F. J. M. van den Eerenbeemt (ed.), *Bankieren in Brabant in de loop der eeuwen* (Tilburg, 1987), 1–20.

―― 'De Lombarden in Brabant in de middeleeuwen', in H. F. J. M. van den Eerenbeemt (ed.), *Bankieren in Brabant in de loop der eeuwen* (Tilburg, 1987), 21–36.

―― 'Stages of economic decline: late medieval Bruges', in J.-M. Duvosquel & E. Thoen (eds), *Peasants and townsmen in medieval Europe: Studia in honorem Adriaan Verhulst* (Gent, 1995), 259–269.

―― 'Beer consumption and the socio-economic situation in the Franc of Bruges in the sixteenth century', in Uytven, *Production and consumption in the Low Countries, 13th–16th centuries* (Aldershot, 2001), section XII, 1–24.

―― and Blockmans, W. P., 'De noodzaak van een geïntegreerde sociale geschiedenis: Het voorbeeld van de Zuidnederlandse steden in de late middeleeuwen', *Tijdschrift voor geschiedenis* 86 (1971), 276–290.

Valentin, F., 'Les hommes du Moyen Age: Les découvertes de la paléo-anthropologie', *Les dossiers d'archéologie* 208 (1995), 22–33.

Van: *see under the last name.*

Vandenbroeke, C., 'Prospektus van het historisch-demografisch onderzoek in Vlaanderen', *Handelingen van het genootschap voor geschiedenis gesticht onder de benaming 'Société d'Émulation' te Brugge* 113 (1976) 1–85.

Vanderputten, S., 'Transformations in charter production and preservation during the "Iron Age" (tenth–early eleventh centuries): Some evidence from Northern France and the southern Low Countries', *Jaarboek voor middeleeuwse geschiedenis* 7 (2004), 7–30.

Vandewalle, A., 'Vreemde naties in Brugge', in Vandewalle (ed.), *Hanzekooplui en Medicibankiers: Brugge, wisselmarkt van Europese culturen* (2002), 27–42.

Vanhaute, B., 'Agrarian labour and food production in a peripheral region: Agricultural dynamics in the Antwerp Campine in the "long" nineteenth century', *Histoire et mesure* 12 (1997), 143–164.

Vanwelden, M., *Het tapijtweversambacht te Oudenaarde 1441–1772* (Oudenaarde, 1979).

Velde, H. M. van de, Roode, F. de, and Wiepking, C. G., 'A Merovingian settlement in Zelhem (province of Gelderland)', in E. Taayke, J. H. Looijenga, O. H. Harsema, et al. (eds), *Essays on the early Franks* (Groningen, 2003), 194–211.

Ven, G. P. van de, *Leefbaar laagland: Geschiedenis van de waterbeheersing en landaanwinning in Nederland* (Utrecht, 1993).

Verbeemen, J., 'De buitenpoorterij in de Nederlanden', *Bijdragen voor de Geschiedenis der Nederlanden* 12 (1957), 81–99 and 191–217.

Verbruggen, R., *Geweld in Vlaanderen: Macht en onderdrukking in de Vlaamse steden tijdens de veertiende eeuw* (Brugge, 2005).

Vercauteren, F., *Luttes sociales à Liége (13ᵐᵉ et 14ᵐᵉ siècles)*, 2nd ed. (Bruxelles, 1946).

―― 'Note sur l'origine et l'évolution du contrat de mort-gage en Lotharingie du XIᵉ au XIIIᵉ siècle', in *Miscellanea historica in honorem Leonis van der Essen Universitatis Catholicae in oppido Lovaniensi iam annos XXXV professoris* (Bruxelles, 1947), 217–227.

Verhoeven, A. A. A., 'Ceramics and economics in the Low Countries AD 1000–1300', in J. C. Besteman., J. M. Bos, and H. A. Heidinga (eds), *Medieval archaeology in the Netherlands: Studies presented to H. H. van Regteren Altena* (Assen, 1990), 265–281.

Verhulst, A. E., 'Karolingische Agrarpolitik: Das Capitulare de Villis und die Hungersnöte von 792/93 und 805/06', *Zeitschrift für Agrargeschichte und Agrarsoziologie* 13 (1965), 175–189.

—— 'Das Besitzverzeichnis der Genter Sankt-Bavo-Abtei von ca. 800 (Clm 6333)', *Frühmittelalterliche Studien* 5 (1971), 193–234.

—— 'La laine indigène dans les anciens Pays-Bas entre le XIIe et le XVIIe siècle: Mise en oeuvre industrielle, production et commerce', *Revue historique* 247 (1972), 281–322.

—— 'Der frühmittelalterliche Handel der Niederlande und der Friesenhandel', in K. Düwel et al. (eds), *Untersuchungen zu Handel und Verkehr der vor- und frühgeschichtlichen Zeit in Mittel- und Nordeuropa*, part III (1985), 381–391.

—— 'L'intensification et la commercialisation de l'agriculture dans les Pays-Bas méridionaux au XIIIe siècle', in *La Belgique rurale du Moyen Age à nos jours: mélanges offerts à Jean-Jacques Hoebanx* (Bruxelles, 1985), 89–100,

—— 'La diversité du régime domanial entre Loire et Rhin à l'époque carolingienne: Bilan de quinze années de recherche', in W. Janssen and D. Lohrmann, *Villa, curtis, grangia: Landwirtschaft zwischen Loire und Rhein von der Römerzeit zum Hochmittelalter* (München, 1983), 133–148.

—— 'The origins of towns in the Low Countries and the Pirenne-thesis', *Past & Present* 122 (1984) pp. 3–35

—— 'Der frühmittelalterliche Handel der Niederlande und der Friesenhandel', in K. Düwel (ed.), *Untersuchungen zu Handel und Verkehr der vor- und frühgeschichtlichen Zeit in Mittel- und Nordeuropa* III (Göttingen, 1985), 381–391.

—— 'Die Grundherrschaftsentwicklung im ostfränkischen Raum vom 8. bis 10. Jahrhundert. Grundzüge und Fragen aus westfränkischer Sicht', in W. Rösener (ed.), *Strukturen der Grundherrschaft im frühen Mittelalter* (Göttingen, 1989), 29–46.

—— 'The decline of slavery and the economic expansion of the early Middle Ages', *Past & Present* 133 (1991), 195–203.

—— 'Aspekte der Grundherrschaftsentwicklung des Hochmittelalters aus westeuropäischer Perspektive', in W. Rösener (ed.), *Grundherrschaft und bäuerliche Gesellschaft im Hochmittelalter* (Veröffentlichungen des Max-Planck-Instituts für Geschichte 115) (Göttingen, 1995), 16–30.

—— *Landschap en landbouw in middeleeuws Vlaanderen* (Brussel, 1995).

—— *The rise of cities in north-west Europe* (Cambridge, 1999).

—— 'On the preconditions for the transition from rural to urban industrial activities (9th–11th centuries)', in B. Blondé and E. Vanhaute (eds), *Labour and labour markets between town and countryside (Middle Ages–19th century)* (CORN 6) (Turnhout, 2001), 33–41.

—— *The Carolingian economy* (Cambridge, 2002).

—— and Blok, D. P., 'Landschap en bewoning tot circa 1000: De agrarische nederzettingen', in D. P. Blok, W. Prevenier, & D. J. Roorda (eds), *Algemene Geschiedenis der Nederlanden* I (Haarlem, 1981), 152–164.

—— and Bock-Doehaerd, R. de, 'Het sociaal-economisch leven tot circa 1000', in D. P. Blok, W. Prevenier, and D. J. Roorda (eds), *Algemene Geschiedenis der Nederlanden* I (Haarlem, 1981), 183–215.

―― and Hemptinne, T. de, 'Le chancelier de Flandre sous les comtes de la maison d'Alsace, 1128–1191', *Bulletin de la Commission Royale d'Histoire* 141 (1975), 267–311.

Verkerk, C. L., 'Les tonlieux carolingiens et ottoniens aux Pays-Bas septentrionaux, aux bouches des grandes rivières', *Publications de la section historique de l'institute Grand-Ducal de Luxembourg* 104 (1988), 161–180.

―― *Coulissen van de macht: Een sociaal-institutionele studie betreffende de samenstelling van het bestuur van Arnhem in de middeleeuwen en een bijdrage tot de studie van stedelijke elitevorming* (Hilversum, 1992).

―― 'Tollen en waterwegen in Holland en Zeeland tot in de vijftiende eeuw', in J. J. J. M. Beenakker et al., *Holland en het water in de middeleeuwen: Strijd tegen het water en beheersing en gebruik van het water* (Hilversum, 1997), 97–114.

Verlinden, C., 'Le balfart: Corvée-revenu pour l'entretien des fortifications', *Tijdschrift voor rechtsgeschiedenis* 12 (1933), 107–130.

―― and Craeybeckx, J., *Prijzen- en lonenpolitiek in de Nederlanden in 1561 en 1588–1589: Onuitgegeven adviezen, ontwerpen en ordonnanties* (Bruxelles, 1962).

Vermaut, J., 'Vijf variaties op het thema "De Belgische vlasnijverheid" ', *Handelingen van het genootschap voor geschiedenis te Brugge* 113 (1976), 183–227.

Verriest, L., 'La charité Saint-christophe et ses comptes du XIIIe siècle: Contribution à l'étude des institutions finacières de Tournai au moyen age', *Bulletin de la commission royale d'histoire de Belgique* 73 (1904), 144–267.

―― *Les luttes sociales et le contrat d'apprentissage à tournai jusqu'en 1424* (Bruxelles, 1912).

Vliet, A. P. van, 'Zeevarenden op de vissersvloot, 1580–1650', *Tijdschrift voor sociale geschiedenis* 22 (1996), 241–259.

Vliet, K. van, *In kringen van kanunniken: Munsters en kapittels in het bisdom Utrecht 695–1227* (Zutphen, 2002).

Vos, P. C. and Heeringen, R. M. van, 'Holocene geology and occupation history of the province of Zeeland', in M. M. Fischer, *Holocene evolution of Zeeland (SW Netherlands)* (Delft, 1997), 5–109.

Voskuil, J. J., *Van vlechtwerk tot baksteen: Geschiedenis van de wanden van het boerenhuis in Nederland* (Arnhem, 1979).

Vries, J. de, *The Dutch rural economy in the Golden Age, 1500–1700* (New Haven, 1974).

―― 'Peasant demand patterns and economic development: Friesland 1550–1750', in W. N. Parker and E. L. Jones (eds), *European peasants and their markets: Essays in agrarian economic history* (Princeton, 1975), 205–266.

―― *Barges and capitalism: Passenger transportation in the Dutch economy, 1632–1839* (Utrecht, 1981).

―― *European urbanization, 1500–1800* (London, 1984).

―― 'The labour market', in K. Davids & L. Noordegraaf (eds), *The Dutch economy in the golden age: Nine studies* (Amsterdam, 1993), 55–78.

―― 'An employer's guide to wages and working conditions in the Netherlands, 1450–1850', in C. S. Leonard and B. N. Mironov (eds), *Hours of work and the means of payment: The evolution of conventions in pre-industrial Europe*, Proceedings of the eleventh International Economic History Congress, Sept. 1994 (Milan, 1994), 47–64.

Vries, J. de, 'The transition to capitalism in a land without feudalism', in P. C. M. Hoppenbrouwers and J. L. van Zanden (eds), *Peasants into farmers? The transformation of rural economy and society in the Low Countries (Middle Ages–19th century) in light of the Brenner debate* (CORN 4) (Turnhout, 2001), 67–84.

—— and Woude, A. M. van der, *The first modern economy: Success, failure, and perseverance of the Dutch economy, 1500–1815* (Cambridge, 1997).

Vries, O., *Het Heilige Roomse Rijk en de Friese vrijheid* (Leeuwarden, 1986).

—— 'Staatsvorming in Zwitserland en Friesland in de late middeleeuwen: Een vergelijking', in J. A. Frieswijk (ed.), *Fryslân, staat en macht 1450–1650: Bijdragen aan het historisch congres te Leeuwarden van 3 tot 5 juni 1998* (Hilversum/Leeuwarden, 1999), 26–42.

Vries, S. de, 'Rederijkersspelen als historische dokumenten', *Tijdschrift voor geschiedenis* 57 (1942), 185–198.

Waha, M. De, *Recherches sur la vie rurale à Anderlecht au moyen âge* (Bruxelles, 1979).

Walle, A. L. J. van de, *De gotiek in België: Architectuur, monumentale kunst* (Brussel, 1972).

Wampach, C., *Geschichte der Grundherrschaft Echternach im Frühmittelalter: Untersuchungen über die Person des Gründers, über die Kloster- und Wirtschaftsgeschichte auf Grund des liber aureus Epternacensis (698–1222)*, 2 vols (Luxemburg, 1929/1930).

Warde, P., 'Fear of wood shortage and the reality of the woodland in Europe, c.1450–1850', *History Workshop Journal* 62 (2006) 29–57.

Warlop, E., *De Vlaamse adel voor 1300*, 2 parts, 3 vols (Handzame, 1968).

Wartena, R., 'Vier eeuwen bosbeheer in Gelderland, 1400–1800', *Tijdschrift der Koninklijke Nederlandsche Heidemaatschappij* (1968), 33–40, 94–100, 182–191, and 256–269.

Waterbolk, H. T., 'Mobilität von Dorf, Ackerflur und Gräberfeld in Drenthe seit der Latènezeit: Archäologische Siedlungsforschungen auf der Nordniederländischen Geest', *Offa* 39 (1982), 97–137.

Watson, A. M., 'Toward denser and more continuous settlement: New crops and farming techniques in the early Middle Ages', in J. A. Raftis (ed.), *Pathways to medieval peasants* (Toronto, 1981), 65–82.

Wee, H. van der, *The growth of the Antwerp market and the European economy (fourteenth–sixteenth centuries)*, 3 vols (The Hague, 1963).

—— 'Die Wirtschaft der Stadt Lier zu Beginn des 15. Jahrhunderts: Analyse eines Zollbuches und eines Wollinspektionsregisters', in H. Aubin, E. Ennen, H. Kellenbenz, et al. (eds), *Beiträge zur Wirtschafts- und Stadtgeschichte: Festschrift für Hektor Ammann* (Wiesbaden, 1965), 144–165.

—— 'Structural changes and specialization in the industry of the southern Netherlands, 1100–1600', *Economic history review* 28 (1975), 203–221.

—— 'Monetary, credit, and banking systems', in E. E. Rich and C. Wilson (eds), *The economic organization of early modern Europe* (Cambridge Economic History of Europe 5) (Cambridge, 1977), 290–393.

—— 'Introduction: The agricultural development of the Low Countries as revealed by the tithe and rent statistics, 1250–1800', in Van der Wee & E. van Cauwenberghe (eds), *Productivity of land and agricultural innovation in the Low Countries (1250–1800)* (Leuven, 1978), 1–23.

—— 'Industrial dynamics and the process of urbanization and de-urbanization in the Low Countries from the late middle ages to the eighteenth century: A synthesis', in Wee (ed.), *The rise and decline of urban industries in Italy and the Low Countries (late Middle Ages–early Modern Times)* (Leuven, 1988), 307–381.

—— 'Antwerp and the new financial methods', in Wee, *The Low Countries in the early modern world* (London, 1993), 145–166.

—— 'Nutrition and diet in the Ancien Régime', in Wee, *The Low Countries in the early modern world*, tr. by Lizabeth Fackelman (Cambridge/New York, 1993), 279–287.

—— 'Continuïteit en discontinuïteit in de economische ontwikkeling van Nederland', *Tijdschrift voor sociale geschiedenis* 21 (1995), 273–280.

—— and Haeseleer, P. d', 'Ville et campagne dans l'industrie linière à Alost en dans ses environs (fin du Moyen Âge–Temps modernes)', in A. E. Verhulst, J.-M. Duvosquel, & E. Thoen (eds), *Peasants & townsmen in Medieval Europe: Studia in honorem Adriaan Verhulst* (Gent, 1995), 753–767.

Wenskus, R., *Stammesbildung und Verfassung: Das Werden der frühmittelalterlichen gentes* (Köln, 1961).

Werner, M., *Der lütticher Raum in frühkarolingischer Zeit: Untersuchungen zur Geschichte einer karolingischen Stammlandschaft* (Göttingen, 1980).

Werveke, H. van, 'De bevolkingsdichtheid in de IXe eeuw: Poging tot schatting', *Jaarboek oudheid- en geschiedkundig verbond van België* 30 (1935/6), 107–116.

—— 'Currency Manipulation in the Middle Ages: The case of Louis de Male, Count of Flanders', *Transactions of the royal historical society* 4th ser. 31 (1949), 115–127.

—— 'La famine de l'an 1316 en Flandre et dans les régions voisines', *Revue du Nord* 41 (1959), 5–14.

Weststrate, J. A., 'Laat-veertiende-eeuwse Gelderse riviertolrekeningen als bron voor economisch-historisch onderzoek', *Jaarboek voor middeleeuwse geschiedenis* 4 (2001) 222–258.

—— 'Abgrenzung durch Aufnahme: Zur Eingliederung der Süderseeischen Städte in die Hanse, ca. 1360–1450', *Hansische Geschichtsblätter* 121 (2003), 13–40.

White, L., *Medieval technology and social change* (Oxford, 1962).

Wickham, C. J., *Land and power: Studies in Italian and European social history, 400–1200* (London, 1994).

—— 'The feudal revolution', *Past & Present* 155 (1997), 196–209.

—— *Framing the early Middle Ages: Europe and the Mediterranean, 400–800* (Oxford, 2005).

Wieger, A., 'Das Siedlungs- und Agrargefüge des Condroz und der Famenne in seiner historischen Entwicklung und in der Gegenwart', PhD thesis (Aachen, 1976).

Willems, W. J. H., 'Romans and Batavians: A regional study in the Dutch Eastern River Area', *Berichten van de Rijksdienst voor het Oudheidkundig Bodemonderzoek te Amersfoort* 31 (1988), 7–217.

—— 'Das Rhein-maas-Delta', *Siedlungsforschung, Archäologie, Geschichte, Geographie* 7 (1989), 31–49.

Winter, J. M. van, *Ministerialiteit en ridderschap in Gelre en Zutphen*, 2 vols (Arnhem, 1962).

—— 'Homines Franci, edelen of koningsvrijen?', *Tijdschrift voor geschiedenis* 83 (1970), 346–351.

Winter, J. M. van, 'Die Hamalander Grafen als Angehörige der Reichsaristokratie im 10. Jahrhundert', *Rheinische Vierteljahrsblätter* 44 (1980), 16–46.

——'Das Herkunftsland der Ostsiedler und die Urbarmachung Hollands in der niederländischen Historiographie', in J. M. Piskorski (ed.), *Historiographical approaches to medieval colonization of East Central Europe: A comparative analysis against the background of other European inter-ethnic colonization processes in the Middle Ages* (Boulder, 2002), 281–302.

Wit, J. M. de, 'Reders en regels: Visserij, overheid en ondernemerschap in het zeventiende-eeuwse Maasmondgebied', in C. M. Lesger & L. Noordegraaf (eds), *Ondernemers & bestuurders: Economie en politiek in de Noordelijke Nederlanden in de late Middeleeuwen en vroegmoderne tijd* (Amsterdam, 1999), 633–648.

Wood, D., *Medieval economic thought* (Cambridge, 2002).

Wood, I. N., *The Merovingian kingdoms 450–751* (London, 1993).

——'Political and social structures of the Saxons in the early Carolingian period', in D. H. Green and F. Siegmund (eds), *The continental Saxons from the migration period to the tenth century: An ethnographic perspective* (Woodbridge, 2003), 271–290.

Woude, A. M. van der, 'Het sociaal-economische leven, geografie en demografie 1500–1800: Demografische ontwikkeling van de Noordelijke Nederlanden 1500–1800', in D. P. Blok, W. Prevenier, and D. J. Roorda (eds), *Algemene Geschiedenis der Nederlanden* V (Haarlem, 1979), 102–168.

——'Large estates and small holdings: Lords and peasants in the Netherlands during the late Middle Ages and the Early Modern Times', in P. Gunst and T. Hoffman, *Grand domaine et petites exploitations* (Budapest, 1982), 193–207.

——'Population developments in the northern Netherlands (1500–1800) and the validity of the "urban graveyard" effect', *Annales de démographie historique: études et chronique* (1982), 55–75.

Wouters, W., Cooremans, B., Desender, K., et al., 'Archeologisch en ecologisch onderzoek van een vroegmiddeleeuwse waterput te Kasterlee (prov. Antwerpen)', *Archeologie in Vlaanderen* 5 (1996), 97–109.

Wunder, *Die bäuerliche Gemeinde in Deutschland* (Göttingen, 1986)

Wüstehube, V., 'Das Grubenhaus in Deutschland, Dänemark und den Niederlanden: Seine Entwicklung vom Neolithikum bis zur Merowingerzeit', PhD thesis (Frankfurt am Main, 1996).

Wyffels, C., *De oorsprong der ambachten in Vlaanderen en Brabant* (Brussel, 1951).

——'Contribution à l'histoire monétaire de Flandre au XIIIe siècle', *Revue belge de philologie et d'histoire* 45 (1967), 1113–1141.

——'De kerfstok in onze gewesten', *Mededelingen van de Koninklijke Academie voor Wetenschappen, Letteren en Schone Kunsten van België, Klasse der Letteren* 50 (1988), 19–39.

——'L'usure en Flandre au XIIIe siècle', *Revue belge de philologie et d'histoire* 69 (1991), 853–871.

Yamada, M., 'Le mouvement des foires en Flandre avant 1200', in J.-M. Duvosquel and A. Dierkens (eds), *Villes et campagnes au moyen âge: Mélanges Georges Despy* (Liège, 1991), 773–789.

Yante, J.-M., *Trafic routier en Ardenne, Gaume et Famenne, 1599–1600* (Louvain-la-Neuve, 1986).

—— 'L'approvisionnement alimentaire urbain et rural: Jalons pour une reconstitution des réseaux (Liège, Namur, Luxembourg. XIIIe–XVe siècles)', in E. Rassart-Eeckhout, J.-P. Sosson, C. Thiry, et al. (eds), *La vie matérielle au Moyen Âge: L'apport des sources littéraires, normatives et de la pratique: Actes du Colloque international de Louvain-la-Neuve, 3–5 octobre 1996* (Louvain-la-Neuve, 1997), 335–352.

Ypma, Y. N., *Geschiedenis van de Zuiderzeevisserij* (Haarlem, 1962).

Zagwijn, W. H., Beets, D. J., Berg, M. van den, Montfrans, H. M. van, and Rooyen, P. van, *Atlas van Nederland*, part 13 ('s-Gravenhage, 1985).

Zanden, J. L. van, 'Op zoek naar de "missing link": Hypothesen over de opkomst van Holland in de late Middeleeuwen en de vroeg-moderne tijd', *Tijdschrift voor geschiedenis* 14 (1988), 359–386.

—— 'From peasant economy to modern market-oriented agriculture: The transformation of the rural economy of the Eastern Netherlands 1800–1914', *Economic and social history in the Netherlands* 3 (1991), 37–59.

—— *The rise and decline of Holland's economy: Merchant capitalism and the labour market* (Manchester, 1993).

—— 'Economic growth in the Golden Age: The development of the economy of Holland, 1500–1650', in C. A. Davids and L. Noordegraaf (eds), *The Dutch Economy in the Golden Age: Nine studies* (Amsterdam, 1993), 5–26.

—— 'Holland en de Zuidelijke Nederlanden in de periode 1500–1570: Divergerende ontwikkelingen of voortgaande economische integratie', in *Studia historica conomica* (Leuven, 1993), 357–367.

—— 'Tracing the beginning of the Kuznets curve: Western Europe during the early modern period', *Economic History Review* 48 (1995), 643–664.

—— 'Werd de Gouden Eeuw uit turf geboren? Over het energieverbruik in de Republiek in de zeventiende en achttiende eeuw', *Tijdschrift voor geschiedenis* 110 (1997), 484–499.

—— 'The development of agricultural productivity in Europe', in B. J. P. van Bavel and E. Thoen (eds), *Land Productivity and Agro-systems in the North Sea Area (Middle Ages–20th century): Elements for Comparison* (CORN 2) (Turnhout, 1999), 357–377.

—— 'The paradox of the Marks: The exploitation of commons in the eastern Netherlands, 1250–1850', *Agricultural history review* 47 (1999), 125–144.

—— 'Wages and the standard of living in Europe, 1500–1800', *European review of economic history* 3 (1999), 175–198.

—— 'Early modern economic growth', in M. Prak (ed.), *Early modern capitalism: Economic and social change in Europe, 1400–1800* (London, 2001).

—— 'Taking the measure of the early modern economy: Historical national accounts for Holland in 1510/1514', *European review of economic history* 6 (2002), 131–163.

—— 'The ecological constraints of an Early Modern economy: The case of Holland 1350–1800', *Nederlands Economisch-Historisch Archief Jaarboek* 66 (2003), 85–102.

—— 'Common workmen, philosophers and the birth of the European knowledge economy', paper (Utrecht, 2004).

—— 'The skill premium and the "Great Divergence"', paper (Utrecht, 2004).

—— 'Monasteries, manuscripts', paper (Utrecht, 2006).

Zeeuw, J. W. de, 'Peat and the Dutch Golden Age: The historical meaning of energy-attainability', *Afdeling Agrarische Geschiedenis Bijdragen* 21 (1978), 3–31.

Zijlstra, S., *Om de ware gemeente en de oude gronden: Geschiedenis van de Dopersen in de Nederlanden, 1531–1675* (Hilversum, 2000).

Zimmermann, W. H., 'Archäologische Befunde frühmittelalterlicher Webhäuser: Ein Beitrag zum Gewichtswebstuhl', *Jahrbuch der Männer vom Morgenstern* 61 (1982), 111–144.

Zmora, H., *Monarchy, aristocracy, and the state in Europe, 1300–1800* (London, 2001).

Zuijderduijn, J., *Medieval capital markets? The creation of public debt by Holland cities (13th–16th centuries)* (paper for the second Low Countries Conference, Antwerp 2006): http://www.lowcountries.nl/2006-2_zuijderduijn.pdf.

—— *Medieval capital markets: Markets for rent, state formation and private investment in Holland (1300–1550)* (Leiden, 2009).

Zylbergeld, L., 'Les régulations du marché du pain au XIIe siècle en occident et l' "assize of bread" de 1266–1267 pour l'Angleterre', in J.-M. Duvosquel and A. Dierkens (eds), *Villes et campagnes au moyen âge: Mélanges Georges Despy* (Liège, 1991), 791–814.

Index

Aachen, 53, 56, 62, 64, 193, 221
Aalst, 102
Abbey of Averbode, 326
Abbey of Echternach, 62, 105, 314
Abbey of Lobbes, 53, 102, 201
Abbey of Lorsch, 149–51
Abbey of Mariënweerd, 86
Abbey of Prüm, 128
Abbey of St. Bertin, 61
Abbey of Saint-Hubert, 157
Abbey of St. Peter, 63
Abbey of Werden, 57
abbeys
   familia of, 105
   hydrological projects and, 43
   industries and, 152
   occupational data and, 147
   property rights and, 61–63
   royal properties and, 52–53
   territorial lords and, 71
   town growth around, 103–4
Abdinghof, 62
Achterhoek, 22, 87, 135
advocacy, 71–72
aerosol analysis, 28
agriculture, 1–2, 13, 33, 366
   backlands and, 39–40
   Black Death and, 329–31
   Carolingian period and, 125, 127–34, 140
   cereal culture and, 129–33, 136–37
   changing social structures and, 242–74
   climate and, 15, 18, 38
   commercialization and, 295–98, 326
   communal customs and, 136–40
   communal hay and, 129
   concentrated habitation and, 128–29
   crop failures and, 142–43
   deforestation and, 328
   diversity of Roman, 32–33
   ecological issues and, 47–48
   economic growth and, 372–75, 379–89, 392, 395, 398–99, 403
   erosion and, 19, 44, 47, 340, 342, 357–58, 382
   family farms and, 127–28
   famine and, 50, 109, 127, 142–43, 198, 203, 217, 219, 230, 279, 329, 373
   farm buildings and, 135–36
   farm size and, 246–49
   granges and, 43, 91, 140, 146, 159, 201, 223–24, 325–26, 400
   group solidarity and, 141
   growth of markets and, 324–29
   high status of, 125
   increased implements for, 142
   intensive, 246–47, 328
   lack of information on, 124
   land-labour ratio and, 178
   land reclamation and, 32–50
   land scarcity and, 139–40
   life expectancy and, 143
   Little Ice Age and, 18
   livestock and, 45, 65, 125, 130, 295–99, 323, 330–36, 341, 389
   living standards and, 140–46
   local bylaws and, 326
   manorial organization and, 80–81
   mansus and, 127–28
   market demand and, 132–33
   migrant labour and, 302–3
   miniature open fields and, 138–39
   occupational choices and, 32–33
   open-field farming and, 98, 138–40
   organization of early medieval, 126–29
   output growth and, 141
   pastoral farming and, 125–26, 129
   place names and, 34
   ploughs and, 77, 84, 126–27, 131–34, 142, 323, 327, 335, 373, 397
   ploughhorses and, 134, 136
   pollen analysis and, 38
   pooling capital and, 127
   population growth and, 25–26, 324–38
   production records of, 127
   property rights and, 51–52 (*see also* property rights)
   rainfall and, 15, 24
   religious institutions and, 325–26
   rising prices for, 45–46
   rotation system and, 133
   sharecropping and, 177
   sod manuring and, 328–29, 341–42
   soil and, 7, 23–24, 32, 134 (*see also* soil)
   specialization and, 109, 132–33, 141–42, 325–42
   standardization of holdings and, 128
   stream ridges and, 32
   sustainability and, 340–42

agriculture, (cont.)
  technology and, 77, 84, 126–27, 131–36, 141, 323, 327, 335, 373, 397
  tenant farmers and, 176, 181, 189, 201, 244–47, 252, 260, 285–86, 296, 301, 304, 306, 312, 323–24, 332–35, 342, 377, 390–94, 403
  tenant rights and, 176
  three-field rotation and, 133–34, 137, 138
  village communities and, 94, 98–99
  yield data for, 327, 331–33
  yield ratio and, 131–32
akkers, 34, 129
Albrecht of Saxony, 275
Aldegisl, 30
Alkmaar, 235, 256, 317, 334
allodium, 61
almsgiving, 219
Alpine people, 30
Alva, 266
Alvares, Vicente, 306
amber, 151
Amsterdam, 226, 235–40, 261
Anabaptists, 276–77
Anglo-Normans, 73
annuities, 187–92
anti-Semitism, 183–84
Antwerp, 20, 58–59, 258, 276
  bookkeeping and, 200
  capital market and, 189, 190–91
  commercialization and, 298
  Exchange of, 227
  fashion and, 364
  labour market and, 207, 212
  land market and, 178–180
  location of, 381
  trade and, 226–28, 238–40
Aquitaine, 69
archbishops, 40–41, 53–54
architecture, 351, 376
Ardennes, 344
  ceramics and, 152
  iron production and, 355
  land use and, 18, 24–28, 34
  population growth and, 37
  royal properties and, 53, 56
  soil of, 24
Ardennes Massif, 15
Aretio family, 184
Arkel, 74
arms industry, 353–54
Arnhem, 87, 118, 235
Arras, 70, 107, 115, 120, 185–87, 200, 214, 308
artificial hills, 41–42
Artois, 13, 23–24, 70, 138, 185, 195–96, 236, 279, 281, 343

Asti, 184
auctions, 172
Augustus, 21
Austrasia, 53
Austria, 12
Averbode, 38

Baldwin IV, 69
Baltic Sea, 113, 149, 234
banal lords
  capital market and, 182
  economic growth and, 386, 396, 399, 401
  industries and, 149, 154, 352–53
  land use and, 65–68
  manorial organization and, 88
  welfare and, 321
banks, 184–85, 196–200
bannum, 66, 95
barley, 45, 126–33, 147, 330, 336
Batavian, 29–31
Bauernschutzpolitik, 167
Bavai, 222
Bavai-Tongeren-Cologne road, 29
beans, 126, 329, 335
bearer rights, 189
beer, 119
  agriculture and, 132, 142
  commercialization and, 299
  economic growth and, 374
  industrial issues and, 146–49, 344, 349, 364–67, 370
  standards of living and, 306
  trade and, 231, 236
beggars, 276, 311–13
belfries, 351
Belgae, 28
Belgium, 1, 23, 25, 28
Bergen op Zoom, 72–74, 366
Bernhard of Baden, 268–69
Bishop of Cambrai 111
Bishop of Liège, 74, 111, 194
Bishop of Utrecht, 57, 63, 71–72, 74, 82, 116
  death of, 91–92
  landholders and, 72, 74
  power of, 91–92
  serfdom and, 91
  trade and, 222
Black Death, 37
  agriculture and, 329–31
  capital market and, 192
  changing social structures and, 273–74
  economic growth and, 373–77, 383–84
  industries and, 345
  labour and, 173
  land market and, 173, 177
  leasing and, 173, 177

manorial organization and, 86–87
population decline from, 86–87, 279–81, 304–5
urbanization and, 279–81
welfare and, 304–5
blacksmiths, 147, 366
blast furnaces, 354–55
bleaching, 362
Bonn, 344
bonnetmakers, 207
bookkeeping, 200
Bordeaux, 238
Brabant, 12, 57
agriculture in, 138–39, 327, 331–38
capital market and, 183, 187
changing social structures and, 246, 256, 259, 263, 268, 270, 274
coins and, 196–97
commercialization and, 298–300
economic growth and, 376, 390
elites and, 119
Hansa and, 114
industries and, 344–49, 356, 360, 364, 369–70
labour market and, 201–3, 206–7
land market and, 168, 180
land reclamation and, 28
Lombards and, 184
manorial organization and, 88–89
monetary instability of, 195
public works and, 203
soil of, 23–24
trade and, 229, 233, 236, 238
urban charters and, 112
urbanization and, 279, 283, 291
welfare and, 305, 310, 313, 318–21
brass, 156, 299, 343
Bremen, 41, 60
Brenner, Robert, 6, 8
Brevia Exempla, 63, 125
brewing, 250
commercialization and, 299
economic growth and, 374
industrial issues and, 146–49, 157, 344, 349, 364–67, 370
labour market and, 207
living conditions and, 320, 329
trade and, 231
bricks, 72, 236, 250–51, 258–59, 298, 305
chimneys and, 360–61
commercialization and, 302
housing and, 320–23
industries and, 349–51, 357–60, 365, 367
labour market and, 204, 207, 209
broad loom, 344, 352, 367
bronze, 156, 343, 353

Bronze Age, 28
brotherhoods, 275
Bruges, 1, 42, 108, 110, 196, 200, 309
changing social structures and, 255
cloth industry and, 343
education and, 318–19
elites and, 117–23
labour market and, 211
land market and, 179
migrant labour and, 303–4
money changers and, 196–97
public works and, 203
social conflict and, 271
socio-institutional factors and, 400–1
trade and, 221–29, 234
urbanization and, 281
welfare and, 308, 311
Brussels, 90, 107, 189, 198, 327, 267
bureaucracy, 263–71
burghers
capital market and, 185–86, 190–91
economic growth and, 376
entry levies and, 119
Ghent and, 115
industries and, 157
labour market and, 202, 228–31
land market and, 166–67, 173–75
leasing and, 172–75
manorial organization and, 85
migrant labour and, 303
semi-voluntary loans and, 190
social change and, 243, 251, 259–60, 265–78, 290, 303, 309, 314, 319, 322–23
state formation and, 263–71
towns and, 101
urban communities and, 108–15, 119, 121
usury and, 184–85
Burgundy, 69
dukes of Burgundy, 12, 116–17, 233–34, 269, 274–75, 385–86, 395
butchers, 134, 147, 189, 206, 364
butter, 126, 132, 142, 226, 238, 323, 334–37, 349, 367

Calais, 229
calamine, 151
Cambrai, 70, 111
Cambrésis, 140, 173
Campine, 13, 103
abbeys and, 38–39
agriculture and, 126, 137, 138, 325–26, 328, 336
commercialization and, 301, 303
ecological issues and, 48

Campine, (cont.)
  economic growth and, 372, 379, 388–89,
    402, 405, 409
  homines franci and, 57–59
  industries and, 363
  land market and, 164–65
  land reclamation and, 28, 38, 86
  leasing and, 170–78
  manorial organization and, 76, 81
  population numbers in, 35
  religious properties and, 62
  river clay and, 22–23
  soil of, 25
  trade and, 226
  urbanization and, 283
  village communities and, 99
  welfare and, 307, 323–24
cannons, 353–54
capital market, 166, 248
  accessibility and, 182–83, 188–89
  annuities and, 185–90
  bankers and, 184–85, 196–200
  bearer rights and, 188
  Catholic condemnation of interest and, 182
  changing social structures and, 251
  coin production and, 193–200
  collateral and, 181–82, 187–88
  compulsory redemption and, 187
  Council of Tours and, 183
  craftsmen and, 188–89
  debt data and, 185
  double-entry bookkeeping and, 200
  elites and, 183–84
  emergence of, 182–87
  formal credit and, 189
  increased debtor freedom and, 187
  increased security and, 187–88
  industries and, 249 (*see also* industries)
  institutional improvements in, 187–93
  interest and, 182–199, 212
  IOUs and, 189
  Jews and, 183–84, 187–88
  land ownership and, 181–82, 188
  large investment in, 259–60
  leasing and, 182, 190
  legal issues and, 188–90
  life annuities and, 185–87, 190
  loan tables and, 189–90
  local involvement in, 185
  Lombards and, 183–85, 187–90
  money changers and, 196–97, 200, 225
  mortgages and, 182–83
  pawnshops and, 189
  payment forms and, 194–95
  pledges and, 183
  registering sales and, 187–88
  religious institutions and, 182–83
  retailers and, 188–89
  semi-voluntary loans and, 190
  share shipping companies and, 237–38
  social conflict and, 275–76
  taxes and, 187
  tenants and, 189
  time preference and, 186
  trade and, 224 (*see also* trade)
  urbanization and, 188
  usury laws and, 182–86
  women and, 208
Capitulary of Herstal, 218–19
carbon dating, 21
Carloman, 217
Carolingians, 34, 39, 53, 56, 59
  agriculture and, 127, 129–33, 135–36, 140
  ceramics and, 152
  coins and, 193–94
  counts and, 71
  economic growth and, 385
  lords and, 63–64
  manorial organization and, 76
  technology and, 158
  territorial lords and, 69–70
  towns and, 102
  trade and, 213–20
  Vikings and, 202
  water management and, 97–98
carpenters, 147
cartels, 232
carters, 206
cartulary, 63
Cassel, 273
castellans, 57, 73, 102, 107–8, 266, 292
Catholicism, 30, 182
cattle, 45, 321, 323, 389
  agriculture and, 124–37, 138, 140,
    325–26, 330–37, 341
  commercialization and, 295–99
  community structures and, 98
  industries and, 153, 155
  landholders and, 62, 65
  land market and, 176–77
  trade and, 238
Celts, 28, 31, 33
ceramics, 152, 156, 344–45
cerealization, 129–37
Chamaves, 29, 57–58
Chambres des Comptes, 267
Champagne fairs, 113, 222
Charité de Tournai, 199
charity, 307–13
Charlemagne, 31, 56, 106, 153
  account system for money by, 193
  Brevia Exempla and, 63
  Christianity and, 62
  fortification inspections of, 65

Lex Saxonum and, 60
  weights and measures standards and, 216
Charles the Bold, 71, 268, 274
Charles V, 12–13
  capital market and, 187–88
  changing social structures and, 265, 268–69, 276
  community structures and, 115, 117
  labour market and, 206
  state formation and, 265–66
  welfare and, 312
cheese, 126, 132, 142, 226, 298, 306, 323, 334–37, 349, 367
Cheese and Bread People, 275
Chèvremont, 53
Chieri, 184
Childeric, 29–30
Christallerian model, 3
Christianity, 62, 77, 80–81
Cistercians, 38–39, 43, 91, 201, 223, 325
civitates, 70, 102
Clermont-sur-Meuse, 153
Cleves, 88–89, 171, 298
climate, 3, 14
  economic growth and, 380–81
  land use and, 15, 18–19, 23, 25, 27
  Little Ice Age and, 18, 333, 381
clocks, 351–52
cloth production, 361–63. *See also* textile industry
  changing social structures and, 252, 256
  commercialization and, 299–300
  dyes and, 153–57, 255, 327, 354
  Flemish cloth and, 299, 343–47
  Frisian cloth and, 153–54, 216
Clovis, 30
coal, 24, 153–55, 156, 252, 273, 344, 353–63, 369, 374, 381
Coevorden, 58
coins
  account system for, 193
  debasements and, 195
  English noble, 197
  as expression of value, 195
  French écu, 197
  gold, 193–94, 197–198, 214, 216
  growing availability of, 198
  hoarded precious metals and, 193–95
  labour market and, 209
  minting of, 193–200
  monetary unions and, 197
  money changers and, 196–98, 200, 225
  pennies, 193
  pounds, 193
  quality of, 193
  Rhine guilder, 197
  scarcity of, 193–95, 198–9

shillings, 194
silver, 198, 209
territorial lords and, 195–200
total circulation of, 194
trade and, 214
transfer of capital and, 198–9
uniformity and, 194
Cologne, 13, 53, 64, 156, 171, 221, 235, 344
coloni, 172
commercialization
  agriculture and, 295–98, 326, 335
  economic growth and, 374–75
  fairs and, 298
  geographical conditions and, 299–300
  labour effects and, 295–97, 300–2
  occupational differentiation and, 294–304
  raw materials and, 298
  shipping and, 298
  specialization and, 295–97, 300–2
  water management and, 300–1
commoners
  community charters and, 99
  land and, 48–49, 52, 163–64
  lords and, 99 (*see also* territorial lords)
  organizations of, 382, 391
  rights of, 99–100
communes, 111–12
compurgation, 220
Condroz, 26, 37
coniurationes, 111
consortia, 184
Coornhert, Dirk, 313
copper, 153–55, 156, 299, 343–44, 353
coqs du village, 244
cornmongers, 207
corporatism, 253–58
Council of Finances, 267
Council of Tours, 183
Count of Flanders, 72–74, 97–98, 108, 132, 194–195, 198, 219
Count of Guelders, 86–87, 88–89
Count of Holland, 44, 72, 74, 83, 97, 121, 191, 195, 228, 231, 263, 267, 271
Count of Luxembourg, 233
counts, 108
  territorial lords and, 70–74
  towns and, 108–9
  water management and, 97–98
cranes, 227
credit. *See* capital market
Crespin family, 185
Culemborg, 72–74

Dalen, 130
Damme, 42, 222, 225, 227
dams, 42
Danube, 327

Danzig, 238
death rates, 145–47, 284, 290, 304
debasements, 195
deforestation, 48–49, 328
Delft, 299, 349, 359, 364
Demer, 35
democracy, 121
demography, 282–291
  economic growth and, 383–85
  labour and, 285–93
Dender, 34
Denmark, 25, 142–43, 295–96
dental analysis, 143–45
desertification, 48
Deventer, 58, 113–114, 228, 321–323, 335, 341, 381
Devotio Moderna, 317, 319
Dijle Valley, 24
dikes, 22, 40–48, 84, 150, 300–1, 334, 338, 342, 358–59, 368
Diksmuide, 256
Dinant, 119–120, 152, 156, 193, 214, 222, 229, 274, 299, 343, 351, 354, 398, 401
Admonitio generalis, 216
Dordrecht, 108, 115
  capital market and, 186–87, 190–91, 200
  elites and, 120, 122
  geography and, 381
  socio-institutional factors and, 400–1
  trade and, 228–31, 235, 239
Dorestad, 30, 56, 81, 125, 151
  coins and, 195
  royal tolls and, 106
  trade and, 106–7, 215, 218, 219
Douai, 109, 115, 119, 121, 135, 155, 185, 337, 401
drapers
  changing social structures and, 254–57
  commercialization and, 297, 303
  industrial issues and, 156, 347, 362–63
  labour market and, 205, 207, 210
Drenthe, 2, 4, 13, 22, 61
  agriculture in, 126, 136–37, 138
  cereal culture in, 130
  concentrated habitation and, 128–29
  essen and, 38
  land market and, 165–66
  land reclamation and, 28, 40, 86
  laws of the commons and, 99, 102
  leasing and, 170–78
  manorial organization and, 78, 82, 88, 91
  peat and, 24
  population growth and, 35, 37
  rural social change and, 242–45
  rye, 126
  soil of, 25

  territorial lords and, 72–74
  three-field rotation system and, 133
  village communities and, 98
Drents, 91
dries, 129
Drongen, 224
Duchy of Guelders, 184
duels, 220
Duisburg, 221, 235
Duke of Brabant, 71, 88, 327
Duke of Guelders, 48, 69, 117, 231, 264
Duke of Normandy, 73
Dunkirk, 338–39
Dunkirk II transgressive phase, 21
Dutch Republic, 12, 170
Dutch Revolt, 12–13, 261, 277–78, 387, 397
dux, 31
dyes, 153–57, 257, 327, 354

Echternach, 103, 314
economic growth
  agriculture and, 372–75, 379–89, 392, 395, 398–99, 403
  Black Death and, 373–77, 383–84
  cereal culture and, 129–33
  communal organizations and, 136–42
  currency instability and, 195
  customs and, 136–42
  demography and, 383–85
  explanations for, 3–8
  extensive 372–73
  flourishing culture and, 375–76
  geography and, 380–83
  gross domestic product (GDP) and, 365–66, 369, 372, 375–80, 404–5
  indicators of, 372–80
  Industrial Revolution and, 8
  industries and, 373–80, 383, 386, 390–95, 398–404
  intensive, 373–76
  labour and, 200–13, 373–79, 383, 389–99, 402–4, 408
  land reclamation and, 38–50
  markets and, 234–41 (*see also* markets)
  modern, 8
  neo-Malthusian approach and, 3
  ownership and, 384, 390, 392, 395, 401, 409
  path dependency and, 387–97
  peatlands and, 372–75, 381–82, 392, 407
  politics and, 385–87
  population pressure and, 325–38
  pre-industrial, 1–8
  productivity and, 2 (*see also* productivity)
  property rights and, 381, 386

real wages and, 376–80
regional diversity and, 380–87
research approach to, 8–14
Roman era and, 373
Schumpterian, 370
socio-institutional factors and, 387–409
soil conditions and, 372, 381–84, 389, 407
specialization and, 372–80, 389–92, 395–408
standard of living and, 140–46, 376–80
sustainability and, 340–42
technology and, 373–74
territorial lords and, 386
towns and, 103–10
trade and, 224–28, 234–41
urbanization and, 383–85
Vikings and, 385
villages and, 93–102
economic issues, 1
agricultural prices and, 45–46, 140–46
annuities and, 185–90
Antwerp toll and, 58–59
attracting settlers and, 40–41
banal duties and, 66–68
banks and, 184–85, 196–200
bannum and, 66
capital market and, 181–200
coin production and, 56, 193–200
commercialization and, 294–304
corporatism and, 255–58
double-entry bookkeeping and, 200
fairs and, 298
fiscality and, 263–71
fixed rents and, 174
gift exchange and, 162–63
heriot and, 66–67
industries and, 146–61
land mobility and, 178–81
land ownership and, 242–43
land reclamation and, 32–50, 84
leasing and, 172–78
legal issues and, 170–78
malae consuetudines and, 66
manorial organization and, 75–93
mill construction and, 148–49
money changers and, 196–97, 200, 225
New Institutional Economics and, 4–6
polarization of society and, 2
protectionism and, 231
public auction and, 170
regional diversity and, 2–4 (*see also* regional diversity)
research approach to, 8–14
rising prices and, 174
royal tolls and, 106
slavery and, 77

three-field rotation system and, 133–34
tithes and, 62–63
écu, 197
Edam, 191, 334
education
developing system for, 316–19
formal, 317
Latin schools and, 318–19
politics and, 316
primary, 317–18
religious institutions and, 313–14
secondary schools and, 317
written texts and, 314–16
Eeklo, 109
Eifel, 24, 149, 350, 354–55
Elbe, 29, 50, 94
elites
brotherhoods and, 275
capital market and, 183–84
copper artisans and, 156
homines franci and, 119
hunting and, 124–25
land ownership and, 117–23
land transfer and, 163–67
taxes and, 118–21
urban communities and, 110–11, 117–23
Elten, 87
energy consumption
coal and, 356–58, 360–61
legal issues and, 358
peat and, 359–60
windmills and, 357–59
wood and, 360–61
engen, 129
England, 7–8, 26, 267–68
commercialization and, 295
deforestation and, 49
education and, 318
Industrial Revolution and, 8
iron production and, 354–55
land market and, 167
manorial organization and, 87
mining and, 151
soil of, 25
textile industry and, 363
trade and, 215–16, 219, 225–26, 229–30
wool and, 113 (*see also* wool)
entrepreneurs, 2
changing social structures and, 247–62, 275–78
commercialization and, 297
community structures and, 119, 122
economic growth and, 377, 386, 391–92, 401–4
industries and, 160, 347–60
land use and, 46, 49
manorial organization and, 83

entrepreneurs, (cont.)
  market issues and, 172, 178, 193–96, 203, 207–11, 231, 234
  welfare and, 304, 306, 313, 322, 324
erosion, 19, 44, 47, 340, 342, 357–58, 382
essen, 38, 129
Estates of Holland, 232
esterling, 198
ethnicity, 28–32
Everaert, Cornelis, 275–76

fairs, 196, 221–23, 298
Famenne, 26, 37
families
  average size of, 289–91
  feuding and, 288–89
  kin and, 163–66, 287–89, 307–8, 390, 399–400
  land inheritance customs and, 163–64
  leasing and, 170–78
  living conditions and, 320–24
  trade and, 217
famine, 50, 373
  agriculture and, 127, 142–43, 329
  capital market and, 198
  labour market and, 203
  towns and, 109
  trade and, 217, 219, 230
  urbanization and, 279
farm buildings, 135–36
fenlands, 23, 37, 40
feudal system
  changes in social structures and, 242, 263, 270–73
  economic growth and, 385, 390, 392, 398, 402
  landholders and, 57–58, 65, 68–71, 73
  land market and, 162–68
  leasing and, 171
  manorial organization and, 78–79, 84–85, 90–92
  property taxes and, 167–69
  territorial lords and, 68–69
  urban communities and, 111, 116, 292
  village communities and, 93–96
fiefs, 52, 68, 73, 164, 171, 269
fiscality, 263–71
fishing, 248, 338–40
  commercialization and, 302, 365
  sustainability and, 340–42
  trade and, 240
  yield data for, 338–39
fishmongers, 206, 364
Flanders, 1, 12, 70, 93, 107, 351
  agriculture and, 132–33, 138–39, 141, 325–41
  banal duties and, 66–68
  capital market and, 182–87
  cereal cultivation and, 132–33
  changing social structures and, 242–77
  cloth production and, 153
  coins and, 194–99
  commercialization and, 296–302
  deforestation and, 49
  ecological effects and, 47–49
  economic growth and, 372–76, 379–409
  elites and, 119–23
  feudal system and, 68
  fortification in, 109
  geographical diversity and, 18–19
  hydrological projects and, 41–44
  industries and, 343–51, 356–69
  labour market and, 202–7, 210–11
  land market and, 168
  land reclamation and, 40, 85–86
  leasing and, 172–75
  living standards and, 140–41
  lords and, 64
  manorial organization and, 79, 87–89
  mills and, 157, 159
  Norman invasions and, 65
  place names and, 34
  population growth and, 36
  reclamation and, 34
  regional diversity and, 2, 4, 7
  religious properties and, 63
  sea clay and, 20
  soil of, 23–24, 32
  territorial lords and, 72–74, 108–11, 115–16
  textiles and, 146–47, 248
  trade and, 214, 216, 219, 222, 224–25, 236–39
  urban charters and, 112
  urbanization and, 13, 112, 279–93
  village communities and, 95, 102
  water management and, 97–98
  welfare and, 304, 314–15, 318, 321–24
flax, 126, 147, 214, 247, 249, 326, 333, 336, 361–62, 370
Flemish cloth, 249, 299, 343–47
Flevo lake, 22
Florennes, 151
Floris V, 72
food
  beer, 119, 132, 142, 146–49, 231, 236, 274, 299, 306, 349, 364, 367, 374
  butter, 126, 132, 142, 226, 236, 323, 334–37, 349, 367
  cereal culture and, 129–33
  cheese and, 126, 132, 142, 226, 298, 306, 323, 334–37, 349, 367
  famine and, 50, 109, 127, 142–43, 198, 203, 217, 219, 230, 279, 329, 373

hunting and, 124–25
  meat and, 124–25, 129, 142
  military and, 130
  mills and, 147–49
  percentage of income spent on, 306
  poor tables and, 308
  real wages and, 379–80
  sources of, 124–25
  trade and, 216, 234
  welfare and, 305–7
foot fulling, 347
forestarii, 56
forest county, 25
fortifications, 31, 53, 64–66, 107, 109, 127, 152, 190, 202–3
four-wheeled carts, 222–23
France, 13, 26, 225
  commercialization and, 295–96
  deforestation and, 49
  fortification in, 109
  Industrial Revolution and, 8
  land market and, 167, 181
  leasing and, 176
  linguistics and, 29
  lords and, 64
  religious properties and, 62
  slavery and, 76–77
  soil of, 24
Franks, 28–30
  Antwerp toll and, 58–59
  cereal culture and, 129–33
  Christianity and, 62–63
  coins and, 193
  concentrated habitation and, 128–29
  homines franci and, 33, 57–61
  hunting and, 124–25
  influence of, 32–34
  Kings of, 53
  Lex Frisionum and, 60–61
  Lex Salica and, 60
  manorial organization and, 78–81, 82
  Niederrhein region and, 33
  nobility of, 53
  Normans and, 65
  oral law and, 59
  place names of, 33–34
  population growth and, 32
  royal properties and, 53–57
  royal tolls and, 106
  Saxons and, 31
  soil cultivation and, 32–33
  trade and, 215
  weakening of royal power, 65
freedom, 31,
  capital market and, 187
  changing social structures and, 263, 273

economic growth and, 383–84, 388–94, 397, 399, 402, 409
  elites and, 117, 122
  homines franci and, 58–61
  labour market and, 201, 206, 211
  land markets and, 168, 175
  land reclamation and, 83–86
  manorial organization and, 75–93
  territorial lords and, 67, 74, 87–88
  trade and, 217–18, 232
  urban communities and, 111–12, 116–17, 122, 293
freemen
  Franks and, 58, 60
  Lex Frisionum and, 60–61
  Lex Saxonum and, 60
  regional frameworks and, 31, 58–61, 88
French Revolution, 101
Frethebold, 78
Friesland, 2, 27 (see also Frisia)
  disintegration of central rule and, 65
  ecological effects and, 47
  hydrological projects and, 41
  leasing and, 176
  manorial organization and, 79
  population growth and, 36
  rural social change and, 245
  salt production and, 149–50
  trade and, 214
Frisia, 28, 30–31, 57
  agriculture and, 139, 333–35, 341
  Antwerp toll and, 58–59
  cereal cultivation and, 132–33
  changing social structures and, 242, 244, 262, 269–71
  coins and, 193
  economic growth and, 377, 385, 388–90, 409
  hydrological projects and, 42
  industries and, 345
  labour market and, 203, 209
  land market and, 167
  Lex Frisionum and, 60–61
  living standards and, 140
  manorial organization and, 81, 88–89
  slavery and, 77
  territorial lords and, 64, 72–74
  trade and, 106, 214–20
  urbanization and, 278
Frisia, (cont.)
  village communities and, 96
  welfare and, 311–12, 318, 324
Frisian cloth, 153–54, 216
fuel. *See also* peat
  coal, 356–58, 360–61
  legal issues and, 358
  wood, 360–61

fullers, 147, 209–10, 273–75, 306, 347, 363, 368
furniture, 146, 323, 367–68, 374

Gallo-Roman population, 28
Gaul, 21, 30, 53, 56
Gelderse IJssel, 30
Gembloux, 105
gemeenten, 98
gemeynte-brieven, 99
Genoa, 238
geography. *See also* land
  agriculture and, 140 (*see also* agriculture)
  economic growth and, 380–83
  Low Countries diversity and, 15–27
  Settlement and, 32
Germany, 26, 30, 50
  capital market and, 186
  cereal culture of, 131
  commercialization and, 298–99
  concentrated habitation and, 129
  deforestation and, 49
  Holy Roman Empire and, 75
  Jews and, 184
  land market and, 169
  land reclamation and, 85
  linguistics and, 29
  migrant labour and, 302–3
  Niederrhein region and, 33
  peat and, 24
  religious properties and, 62
  three-field rotation system and, 133
  trade and, 218–19, 225–26, 234
  village communities and, 93–94
Ghent, 1, 63, 70, 202, 351
  burghers and, 115
  capital market and, 185–86
  Charles V and, 115, 117, 266
  cloth industry and, 343
  education and, 318–19
  elites and, 118–19
  fortification of, 109
  grain in, 337
  labour market and, 206
  land market and, 179
  social conflict and, 271, 273–74
  socio-institutional factors and, 401
  state formation and, 265–66
  territorial lords and, 110
  town structures and, 107–8, 154–55
  trade and, 229
  urban communities and, 115
  urbanization and, 281
  welfare and, 309
gift exchange, 162–63
Gimnée, 151

glass, 146, 151, 214–15, 322, 351, 367
Glymes de Jean, 269
God, 81, 210
Godfried of Bouillon, 194
Goes, 366
gold, 152, 153, 193–94, 197–198, 214, 216–17, 226, 233, 267, 364
Golden Age, 8, 211, 236, 302–5, 369, 377–78
Gothic architecture, 351
Gouda, 231–232, 236, 298–299, 303, 317, 349, 359, 365
gouwen, 69–70
granges, 43, 91, 140, 146, 159, 201, 223–24, 325–26, 400
Granvelle, 269
Gravelines, 112
Great Famine, 279, 329
Groningen, 2, 28, 31, 108, 118
  elites and, 122
  Hansa and, 114
  hydrological projects and, 41
  labour market and, 203
  land market and, 169
  leasing and, 176
  population growth and, 37
  socio-institutional factors and, 400–1
  territorial lords and, 74
  trade and, 214, 218
  urban communities and, 116
gross domestic product (GDP)
  measurement, 365–66, 369, 372, 375–80, 404–5
Grote Raad, 231
Guelders river area, 2, 4, 7, 12–13, 21
  agriculture and, 126, 134, 140, 142, 328, 330–37, 341–42
  capital market and, 187–89, 188
  changing social structures and, 247, 251, 262–66, 271
  coins and, 195
  commercialization and, 295–303
  concentrated habitation and, 129
  economic growth and, 372–81, 384–98, 403–9
  essen and, 38
  feudal system and, 68
  homines franci and, 57–61
  hydrological projects and, 43
  industries and, 345, 359–60, 366, 369
  labour market and, 203–4, 209–11
  land market and, 169–70, 181
  land reclamation and, 27–28, 40, 85–86
  leasing and, 171, 173, 175–76
  living standards and, 140
  manorial organization and, 78–79, 82, 85–92

Index

place names and, 34
population growth and, 35–36
proletariat and, 246
religious properties and, 62
resettlement of, 33
royal properties and, 53, 56–57
rural social changes and, 242–45
soil of, 25, 33
territorial lords and, 64–65, 70, 72
trade and, 231
urbanization and, 278, 282–86, 291
village communities and, 95, 97, 99–100
welfare and, 307, 311, 321, 324
Guicciardini, 318, 364
guilds, 2,
   access to, 206
   changing social structures and, 249, 253–78
   commercialization and, 295, 300
   economic growth and, 376, 390–94, 399–405
   elites and, 119–23
   entry fees into, 206
   fixed wages and, 206
   Kaufsystem and, 249
   industries and, 258–59, 344–47, 353–54, 357, 363, 368, 370
   labour market and, 203–08, 211, 213
   length of workday and, 206
   merchant organizations and, 218–19, 227
   as monopolies, 206
   Netherlands and, 121–22, 206–7
   number of holidays and, 206
   power of, 205–08, 211, 213
   professional mobility and, 206
   socio-institutional factors and, 390–94, 399–405
   state formation and, 265–66
   technology and, 353
   town hall and, 219–20
   trade and, 218–19, 226, 229, 239
   urban communities and, 111, 113–14, 117–23, 288, 293
   weak, 206–8
   welfare and, 304, 309–10, 316–17, 322
guns, 353–54

Haarlem, 191, 299, 313, 348–349, 362
Haarlemmermeer, 46, 357
Habsburgs, 11, 13
   capital market and, 198
   changing social structures and, 265–69, 275–78
   economic growth and, 385–87, 395
   trade and, 233, 234
   urban communities and, 116–17

Hagestein stream ridge, 21
Hague, 267
Hainaut, 171, 256, 269
   agriculture and, 135, 138–39, 325, 327, 330–33
   capital market and, 182–83, 185
   economic growth and, 325, 327, 407
   education and, 318
   industries and, 343–46, 355, 357, 361–62, 368
   Jews in, 183
   labour market and, 201
   landholders and, 63, 72–74
   manorial organization and, 88
   state formation and, 264
   urban communities and, 111
   village communities and, 94–95
haistaldi, 23
Hamaland counts, 70–71
Hanseatic region, 13
   living conditions and, 321
   trade and, 225–26
   urban communities and, 113–14
Harald, 64
Harz, 195
Haspengouw, 32, 70
   agriculture and, 135, 138–39, 326–27
   economic growth and, 372
   land use and, 23, 27–30
   leasing and, 173
   manorial organization and, 76, 79
   population growth and, 36–37
   royal properties and, 53
   soil of, 39
Hasselt, 198
Hautes Fagnes, 24
heavy plough, 127, 134, 141
Heerewaarden, 56
heervaart, 202
Heerwaarden, 58
Hemmema, Rienck, 209–10
Henri de Dinant, 271–72
Henry of Ghent, 185–86
heriot, 66–67
Herstal, 53, 56
Herwen, 58
Herwijnen, 58
Herzele, 180
Holocene, 21, 25
Holy Roman Empire, 75
homicide, 60
homines franci, 33
   elites and, 119
   landholders and, 57–61
   land reclamation and, 59
   Lex Salica and, 60
   manorial organization and, 80

homines novi, 269
Hondschoote, 257–58, 277, 303, 322, 362–63
Honnecourt de Vilard, 351
honey, 129, 215
Hoogstraten, 326
Hoorn, 235
horse collars, 222–23
horses, 134, 136, 222–23
horse shoe, 222–23
hospitals, 142, 222, 308–10, 316, 351, 377–78
household. *See* families
housing, 320–24
Hoverberg, 152
huiskampen, 38
Hulst, 109, 289–90
Hungary, 195
hunting, 25, 49, 56, 124–25, 129, 208
Huy de Renier, 156
Huy, 156, 193, 343
   arms production and, 354
   socio-institutional factors and, 401
   trade and, 214, 222, 229
   urbanization and, 119–20
hydrological projects, 41–48

Ice Ages, 15, 18, 333, 381
IJssel, 12, 21–23, 30, 56, 113, 298, 334, 341, 350, 365
IJsselstein, 56, 71
IJzer, 42
Industrial Revolution, 8
industries, 1. *See also* specific industry
   advances in technology for, 157–61
   Black Death and, 345
   burghers and, 157
   castles and, 154–7
   changing social structures and, 242–76
   commercialization and, 294–304
   corporatism and, 255–58
   ecological problems from, 368–69
   economic growth and, 373–80, 383, 386, 390–95, 398–404
   energy sources and, 356–61
   Flanders' strategy and, 346–49
   fuel and, 356–61
   guilds and, 258–59, 344–47, 353–54, 357, 363, 368, 370
   Holland's strategy and, 346–49
   large investment in, 259–60
   living conditions and, 321–22
   main developmental lines of, 367–71
   manorial organization and, 146–49
   military and, 150
   pollution and, 321–22
   population growth and, 290–91
   productivity and, 146, 155, 344, 352, 355, 360, 364, 370–71
   proto-industrialization and, 2, 204–09, 247–52, 255, 262, 286–304, 326, 337–40, 355, 365–70, 374–77, 391, 395, 404
   putting-out system and, 249
   quality control and, 346–49
   raw materials and, 153, 156–57
   Roman era and, 152, 155
   rural, 152–55, 343–45, 361–64, 367–68
   scale-enlargement and, 364–67
   slaves and, 154
   social organization and, 160–61
   socio-institutional factors and, 395–96, 403–4
   specialization and, 150–53, 160–61, 364–67
   taxes and, 363, 368
   technology and, 157–61, 347–55
   towns and, 152–57
   urban, 343–49, 361–64
   workshops conditions and, 343–44
interest rates
   capital market and, 182–93, 196–209, 212
   Catholic condemnation of, 182
   Council of Tours and, 183
   rapid decline in, 192
   regional diversity and, 191–93
   social problems from, 184–85
   usury laws and, 182–83
Iron Age, 28, 41
iron industry, 149–51, 353–55, 363–64
Italy, 1, 7, 267
   commercialization and, 295
   slavery and, 77
   trade and, 225–26
   welfare and, 308
iurati, 111
ius eremi, 56

jewelry, 364
Jews
   capital market and, 183–84, 187–88
   massacres of, 183–84
   trade and, 214
judicial duels, 220
Jülich, 64
Jupille, 53, 79
jurisdictional rights, 68–69

justum pretium, 217
Jutland, 216

Kaufsystem, 249
Kemzeke, 224
Kennemerland, 263, 271
Ketelwoud, 48
kin, 163–66, 287–89, 307–8, 390, 399–400
kings
   Aachen and, 56
   Christianity and, 62–63
   religious properties and, 61–63
   royal properties and, 52–57
   state formation and, 263–71
   as successors to Roman emperors, 53
   trade and, 217–19
Kluizen, 224
Knokke, 42
Kootwijk, 135, 154
Kortrijk, 70, 110, 115, 224, 297–98, 351, 363
kouters, 34, 141
Kromme Rijn, 56, 222
Kromme Rijngebied, 201

labour
   agriculture and, 45, 124–28, 244, 333–34 (*see also* agriculture)
   bargaining power and, 87
   Black Death and, 173
   brotherhoods and, 275
   burghers and, 202, 228–31
   capital goods and, 202
   centralization of, 259
   changing social structures and, 242–76
   child, 258, 290
   commercialization and, 294–304
   corporatism and, 253–58
   demographic change and, 285–93
   entrepreneurs and, 2 (*see also* entrepreneurs)
   foot fulling and, 347
   fortifications building and, 202
   growing demand for, 201
   guilds and, 2, 205 (*see also* guilds)
   haistaldi and, 201
   heervaart and, 202
   horizontal loom and, 155–56
   industries and, 146–61, 344–57, 360–71 (*see also* industries)
   iron production and, 150–51
   land reclamation and, 83–86 (*see also* land)
   leasing and, 170–78
   livestock and, 45, 65, 125, 130, 295–99, 323, 330–36, 341, 389
   living conditions and, 320–24
   long run growth and, 373–79, 383, 389–99, 402–4, 408
   manorial organization and, 75–93, 202–5
   mercenarii and, 201–2
   migrant, 209–12, 259, 302–4
   military and, 202
   mills and, 147–49
   mining and, 151–52
   monetary value for, 200–1
   nature of wage labour and, 205–10
   nobility and, 202
   occupational data and, 148
   occupational differentiation and, 294–304
   organization of, 205–10
   peat digging and, 19, 45, 204, 208, 248–49, 301–2, 358–60, 365, 368, 374–75, 382
   production levels and, 146–49
   productivity and, 2 (*see also* productivity)
   proletariat and, 2 (*see also* proletariat)
   quantitative indicators for, 211–13
   real wages and, 376–80
   reciprocal exchange and, 201–2
   registry data for, 201
   rights to, 51
   salt production and, 19, 147–50, 366–67, 382
   seasonal, 203, 208–09, 212, 244, 302, 339
   seigneurial lords and, 204
   serfs and, 51–52, 59, 62, 75–80, 86–94, 126, 147–49, 154–55, 170–71, 175, 217, 379, 383
   services owed and, 202
   sessi and, 201
   sideline activities and, 146
   slaves and, 76–77 (*see also* slaves)
   social conflicts and, 272–76
   socio-institutional factors and, 387–409
   specialization and, 132–33 (*see also* specialization)
   standard of living and, 140–46, 304–7, 376–80
   technology and, 157–61, 208, 245–46
   territorial lords and, 90–91, 202
   urban social structures and, 252–61
   welfare and, 304–24
   women and, 292–93
labour market, 166
   emergence of, 200–13
   factories and, 204
   fixed wages and, 206, 210
   full-time proletariat and, 208
   guilds and, 203–08, 211, 213
   harvest time and, 204
   length of workday and, 206
   manorial organization and, 205
   mobility and, 209–10
   nature of, 205–10

labour market, (cont.)
    number of holidays and, 206
    organization of, 205–11
    ownership and, 202–3
    professional mobility and, 206
    public works and, 202–3
    quantitative indicators and, 211–13
    regulation of, 205–11
    restrictions in, 205–6
    rural areas and, 203–4, 209
    silver coins and, 209
    skill premium and, 211–13
    supply and demand for, 203–4
    territorial lords and, 206–7
    urban communities and, 202–3, 208
    wage relationship and, 208–10
    women and, 207–11
land
    abbeys and, 38–39
    agriculture and, 129–33, 139–40, 327 (see also agriculture)
    artificial hills and, 41–42
    backlands and, 39–40, 46
    cattle and, 62, 98, 125–40, 153, 155, 176–77, 236, 321, 325–26, 335–37, 341
    cereal cultivation and, 129–33
    changing social structures and, 240–51, 256–70, 273
    climate and, 15, 18–19, 23, 25, 27
    as collateral, 181–82
    commercialization and, 296–301
    common, 52, 163–65
    commoners and, 48–49, 52, 163–64
    deforestation and, 48–49
    desertifaction and, 48
    direct taxation of, 167–68
    ecological effects and, 44–50
    economic growth and, 372–73, 379–84, 388–404, 407–9
    elites and, 117–23
    erosion and, 19, 44, 47, 340, 342, 357–58, 382
    farm size and, 244–47
    fenlands and, 23, 37, 40
    feudal system and, 68–69
    forests and, 24–25
    geographical diversity of Low Countries and, 15–27
    granges and, 43, 91, 140, 146, 159, 201, 223–24, 325–26, 400
    homines franci and, 57–61
    human effects upon, 44–50
    hunting grounds and, 56
    hydrological projects and, 41–44, 46–47
    identity from, 179
    industries and, 349–50, 357–58, 362, 368–69
    jurisdictional rights and, 68
    laws of the commons and, 99, 102
    leasing and, 243–44 (see also leasing)
    Little Ice Age and, 18
    manorial organization and, 75–93
    military and, 57–58, 65–73
    mobility of, 179–81
    ownership and, 83–86, 178–79 (see also ownership)
    patterns of parceling, 40–41
    permanent desertion of, 178
    place names and, 33–34
    pollen analysis and, 18, 28, 38, 42, 124, 133, 328
    population growth and, 25–26
    property rights and, 31, 39, 49, 51 (see also property rights)
    reclamation and, 19, 38–50, 59, 83–86, 88, 91, 242, 388
    rewards of, 68
    river clays and, 20–23
    royal properties and, 52–57
    rural social changes and, 242–43
    salt marshes and, 20
    sand dunes and, 19
    sea clays and, 20
    serfs and, 51–52, 59, 62, 75–80, 86–94, 126, 147–49, 154–55, 170–71, 175, 217, 379, 383
    social change and, 242–43
    socio-institutional factors and, 387–409
    strategic border areas and, 58–59
    stream ridges and, 21–22, 32–33
    surveyors and, 169
    tenant farmers and, 181, 188, 201, 244–47, 251, 260, 285–86, 296, 301, 304, 306, 312, 323–24, 332–35, 342, 377, 390–94, 403
    territorial lords and, 63–75
    urbanization and, 279–91
    voting rights and, 179
    water and, 20–22, 41–47, 97–98
    welfare and, 305, 308, 310, 319, 321–24
Landes, D.S, 7
land-labour ratio, 178
landlords, 59
    changing social structures and, 246–47
    commercialization and, 296
    economic growth and, 390
    homines franci and, 59
    land market and, 167, 170, 177–78, 181
    manorial organization and, 80
    sub rosa arrangements and, 170
    territorial lords and, 72 (see also territorial lords)

land market
    common lands and, 163–65
    compulsory seizure and, 169
    credit and, 180–82 (*see also* capital market)
    emergence of leasing and, 170–78
    exploitation of ownership and, 170–78
    family claims and, 163–64
    feudal system and, 162–66
    fixed rents and, 174
    inheritance customs and, 163–63
    kin control and, 163–66
    land-labour ratio and, 178
    land transfer and, 162–68
    manorial organization and, 164–65
    mobility issues and, 178–81
    notaries and, 168
    overlapping claims and, 163–64
    population growth and, 166
    precaria and, 171
    prevention of, 163
    price movements and, 176–81
    property rights and, 162–67
    property taxes and, 167–69
    public auction and, 170
    public authorities and, 167–70
    regional diversity and, 179–81
    religious institutions and, 166–67
    rent transactions and, 168
    rising prices and, 174
    soil conditions and, 177–78
    sub rosa arrangements and, 170
    supply and demand for, 178
    transaction costs and, 168–70
land mobility, 178–81
Land of Altena, 267
Land of Culemborg, 40
Land of Heusden, 95, 166, 202
land transport, 222–23, 233–36
lating, 177
Latin schools, 318–19
lead, 151, 154, 351, 355
leasing, 2, 332, 340, 390
    Black Death and, 173, 177
    burghers and, 172–75
    capital market and, 181, 190
    changing social structure and, 243–46, 251, 257, 260, 266
    coloni and, 171
    commercialization and, 296
    competition for, 245–46
    economic growth and, 389, 394
    fixed sum, 177
    industries and, 353
    land market and, 160, 170–78
    land mobility and, 178–81
    lating and, 177

manorial organization and, 172, 173–75
of mills, 171
nobility and, 172–73
organization of short-term, 245
orphans and, 172
peasant fiefs and, 171
power and, 175–77
precaria and, 171
regional diversity in, 172
religious institutions and, 172–73
rising prices and, 174, 178
rural social structures and, 244–47
sharecropping and, 177
soil conditions and, 177–78
tenant farmers and, 182, 188, 201 (*see also* tenant farmers)
territorial lords and, 172–73
of tools, 171
towns and, 172
trade and, 223
urbanization and, 286
widows and, 172
Leeuwarden, 132, 232, 312
legal issues
    bans on Lombards and, 189–90
    Brevia Exempla and, 63
    capital market and, 188–90
    community charters and, 99
    compulsory seizure and, 169
    Frankish oral law and, 59
    fuel and, 358
    homicide and, 60
    judicial duel and, 220
    jurisdictional rights and, 68–69
    land contracts and, 166–69
    laws of the commons and, 99, 102
    Lex Frisionum and, 60–61
    Lex Salica and, 60
    Lex Saxonum and, 60
    local bylaws and, 326
    marriage and, 291
    options for, 170–71
    oral law and, 59
    Roman law and, 168
    temporary grants and, 171
    tenant rights and, 176
    tithes and, 62–63
    trial by ordeal and, 220
    urban charters and, 112
    usury laws and, 182–86
    village bylaws and, 96
    water management and, 97–98
Leiden, 121, 209, 249, 256, 258, 275, 312, 348
Leie river, 27, 32, 109, 235
Lek river, 21, 56

lepers, 308–9, 377
Lessines de Gilles, 185–86
levies, 9–10
 capital market and, 189
 changing social structures and, 263, 266–67
 community structures and, 96, 112
 economic growth and, 392
 elites and, 119, 126, 128
 industries and, 146–47, 160, 166
 land reclamation and, 39–40
 manorial organization and, 75, 81, 89–90
 royal properties and, 56
 territorial lords and, 66–67
 trade and, 223, 231
Lex Frisionum, 60–61
Lex Salica and, 60
Lex Saxonum, 60
Liège, 108
 arms production and, 354
 changing social structures and, 247
 education and, 314
 elites and, 119–20
 industries and, 156, 344, 354, 356, 371
 landholders and, 53, 61, 72–74
 land market and, 168
 social conflict and, 271–72, 274
 trade and, 231
 urban communities and, 111
 welfare and, 309
life annuities, 185–90
life expectancy, 143–45, 289–90, 309, 372, 377
Lille, 73, 108, 115, 221, 281, 293, 337, 362
Limburg, 48, 65, 76
limes, 30, 53
linen, 146–47, 153, 249, 261, 295–98, 306, 326, 343–46, 349, 361–62, 366
linguistics, 29, 33–34
literacy, 313–19
Little Ice Age, 18, 333, 381
living conditions, 320–24
loans. *See* capital market
Lobbes, 61, 63, 102, 203
loess soil, 15, 23, 25, 30, 32, 39, 76, 82, 131, 134, 141, 372
Loevestein, 266
Lombards, 183–85, 187–90
looms, 155–59, 208, 253, 257, 300, 344, 346, 352, 363, 367
lords. *See also* feudal system
 banal, 63–75
 Carolingian, 63–64
 feuding amongst, 107
 hydrological projects and, 43–44
 land market and, 164
 Middle Kingdom and, 64
 seigneurial, 93, 95–96, 111, 160, 202, 388
 territorial, 63–75 (*see also* territorial lords)
 urban communities and, 110–23
Lorsch, 62
Lothar, 64
Lothar II, 64
Louis the Pious, 62
Louvain, 103, 105, 107, 110, 198, 293, 306, 319, 321, 348, 363
Low Countries. *See also* specific principality
 Black Death and, 86–87
 changes in social structures and, 242–78
 climate of, 15, 18
 decline of central power and, 36–37
 economic growth and, 372–409 (*see also* economic growth)
 ethnic composition after Roman era, 28–32
 geography of, 15–27
 jurisdictional rights and, 68
 land reclamation and, 32–50
 landscape and, 15–27
 location of, 15
 in perspective, 406–9
 regional diversity and, 2–8 (*see also* regional diversity)
 research approach to, 8–14
 town arrangements and, 103–10
 urbanization ratio and, 1
 village communities and, 93–103
Luxembourg, 103, 183–86, 256, 281, 283, 337

Maaseik, 189
Maasland, 291
Maastricht, 53, 61
 arms production and, 354
 Lombards and, 195–200
 manorial organization and, 76
 territorial lords and, 64
 trade and, 214
Magdeburg, 50
Mainz, 215
malae consuetudines, 66
Malmedy, 314
Malthusian stress, 279
Mannaricium, 33
manorial organization, 61, 389–90
 agriculture and, 80–81, 126–29
 Black Death and, 86–87
 decline of, 174–75
 dissolution of, 86–93
 exploitative nature of, 75–76, 81
 Franks and, 82
 freedom and, 75–93
 increased integration from, 398
 industries and, 146–49

inventory data and, 127
iron production and, 150–51
labour and, 75–93, 201–5
land-labour ratio and, 80
land market and, 164
land reclamation and, 83–86, 88, 91
land transfers and, 168
leasing and, 173–75
market proximity and, 81
medieval production levels and, 146–49
military and, 85
mills and, 147–49
ownership and, 83–86, 90–92
pooling capital and, 127
position of women and, 292
production levels of, 146–49
property rights and, 75–93
remaining traces of, 90
rise of, 76–82
Roman villas and, 76
seigneurial lords and, 202
serfs and, 51–52, 59, 62, 75–80, 86–94, 126, 147–49, 154–55, 170–71, 175, 220, 379, 383
structure of, 76–82
territorial lords and, 87–88
urban elites and, 117
mansus, 127–28
marca regni, 58–59
Mare Flevo, 20
marken, 98
markets, 1
building materials and, 350–51
burghers and, 166–67, 172–75
capital, 181–200
cereals and, 132–33
changing social structures and, 242–76
commercialization and, 294–304
fairs and, 194
guilds and, 2 (*see also* guilds)
industries and, 344 (*see also* industries)
labour, 200–13
land, 162–81
medieval production levels and, 146–49
New Institutional Economics and, 4–6
population pressure and, 325–29
property rights and, 163, 166–70, 173, 175
socio-institutional factors and, 387–409
specialization and, 330–40 (*see also* specialization)
trade, 105–6, 213–41
transport routes and, 32
Vikings and, 202, 218, 280
Marklo, 31, 60
marriage
average age for, 291
changing social structure and, 246, 264, 267

demographic development and, 284–87, 290–93
land and, 165, 176
labour market and, 208
Roman era and, 291
territorial lords and, 66
Marsdiep, 20
Martel, Charles, 31
Mary of Hungary, 269
Mathijsz, Jan, 277
Maurik, 33
Mayen, 149
meat, 124–25, 129, 142
Medemblik, 106
medieval optimum, 18
Mediterranean, 299
Meer Castle, 154
Menapii, 28
mercenarii, 201–2
Merchant Adventurers of London, 226
Merovingians, 30, 33–34, 70, 143
agriculture and, 133, 135–36
coins and, 193
technology and, 158
towns and, 102
Mesen, 221
metal mining, 151–52
Meuse, 11–15, 20, 27
Meuse Valley, 160–61
capital market and, 183
coins and, 193
elites and, 119
homines franci and, 58
hunting in, 124–25
land dynamism of, 21–22
living standards and, 140
mining and, 151
population growth and, 35–36
religious properties and, 62
royal properties and, 53
social conflict and, 274
socio-institutional factors and, 398–99
soil of, 24
trade and, 106, 214, 228
Middle Ages
famine and, 50, 109, 127, 142–43, 198, 203, 217, 219, 230, 279, 329, 373
Golden Age and, 209
landscape and, 15–27
Little Ice Age and, 18, 333, 381
New Institutional Economics and, 4–6
research approach to, 7–14
social change in, 240–324 (*see also* social change)
Middelburg, 229
Middle Kingdom, 64
migrant labour, 209–12, 261, 302–4

military
  agriculture and, 128
  capital market and, 184, 186
  collective conscription and, 202
  conscription and, 202
  Dorestad and, 106–7
  fleets and, 59
  food and, 130
  fortification building and, 64–65
  heervaart and, 202
  homines franci and, 57–58
  industries and, 150, 353–54
  labour market and, 202
  land and, 57–58, 65–73
  manorial organization and, 85
  mounds and, 41
  polities and, 385
  Roman era and, 21
  royal properties and, 53, 56
  social change and, 260, 265–66, 270, 274, 276
  socio-institutional factors and, 391–92, 399
  soldier's pay tax and, 202
  strategic border areas and, 58–59
  territorial lords and, 66
  towns and, 95, 106–8, 110, 391
  trade and, 218, 229, 234
  urban communities and, 115, 121
  villages and, 95, 106–8
mills
  advances in technology for, 158–60
  economic growth and, 397
  enlargement of, 158–59
  fuel and, 356–57
  industrial issues and, 147–49, 156–57, 352–53
  leasing and, 170–71
  watermills and, 358–59
mineral fuels, 356–57
mining, 151–52, 356–58
mints
  account system for, 193
  centralization of, 194
  coin production and, 193–200
  fragmentation of, 196–97
  gold and, 214
  labour market and, 209
  Lombards and, 184
  private entrepreneurs and, 193
mirrors, 364
monasteries, 53–54, 61–64, 107
money changers, 196–97, 200, 229
monopolies
  capital market and, 185–90, 197
  changing social structures and, 243–44, 252, 259, 272, 276

  commercialization and, 300
  community structures and, 107, 118–19
  economic growth and, 391
  education and, 314–16
  industries and, 156, 361
  labour market and, 206
  landholders and, 60
  trade and, 217, 220, 230–32
  urbanization and, 289
Mons, 200, 256, 279, 312
Moorsele, 297–98
mortgages, 182–83
mounds, 41–42
Münster, 277
music composition, 364

Namur, 108, 256, 344
  capital market and, 193, 198
  industries and, 156, 354–55
  iron production and, 354–55
  land market and, 181
  leasing and, 171
  manorial organization and, 86
  religious properties and, 61
  territorial lords and, 66
  trade and, 214, 229, 231
  urban communities and, 112
Nedersticht, 78, 97
neo-Malthusian approach, 3
Nervii, 28
Netherlands, 1–8, 31, 235
  agriculture and, 128, 139, 329, 333–42 (*see also* agriculture)
  banal duties and, 67
  capital market and, 186–91
  changing social structures and, 242–50, 256–77
  coins and, 198–99
  commercialization and, 294–303
  deforestation and, 48–49
  Dutch Revolt and, 12–13, 261, 277–78, 387, 397
  economic growth and, 372–96, 400–9
  geographical diversity and, 18–19
  guilds and, 121–22, 206–7
  Hansa and, 114
  homines franci and, 58
  hydrological projects and, 41–42, 46
  increased wealth in, 261–62
  industries and, 344–50, 355–71
  labour market and, 202–12
  land market and, 164–65, 168–70
  land reclamation and, 28, 34, 40, 84, 244
  leasing and, 172, 175–76, 178
  linguistics and, 29
  manorial organization and, 81–84

migrant labour and, 302–3
mills and, 159
Norman invasions and, 65
peat and, 45
property rights and, 166
public auction and, 170
salt production and, 150
sea clays and, 20
surveyors and, 169
tenant rights and, 176
territorial lords and, 67, 72, 115–16
towns and, 101–2
trade and, 226–41
urbanization and, 13, 280–94
village communities and, 94–99, 102
water boards and, 43–44
welfare and, 304–7, 311–23
Neufchâteau, 34
Neuss, 154
Neustria, 53
New Institutional Economics, 4–6
New World, 298
Niederrhein, 33, 41, 65, 70–71, 94, 169
Nieppe, 49
Nieuwpoort, 112, 321
Nijmegen, 48, 53, 56, 102–3, 193, 212, 235
Ninove, 256
Nivelles, 53, 196
nobility
  Brevia Exempla and, 63
  elites and, 110–11, 117–23
  feudal system and, 68–69
  homines franci and, 59
  hunting grounds and, 56
  labour and, 202
  leasing and, 172–73
  levies and, 66–67
  Lex Frisionum and, 60–61
  Lex Salica and, 60
  Lex Saxonum and, 60
  lords and, 63–75
  monasteries and, 53–54
  Peace of God movement and, 69
  politics and, 266–67 (*see also* politics)
  prestige from owning land and, 178–79
  property rights and, 167
  religious properties and, 61–63
  royal properties and, 52–57
  state formation and, 263–71
  territorial lords and, 73 (*see also* territorial lords)
  trade and, 214, 217–19, 231
  upward mobility and, 269–70
Noordbarge, 130
Normans, 65, 70
Norsemen. *See* Vikings
North, Douglass, 4

North Sea, 15, 20, 158, 214, 216, 234, 271, 338–39

occupation, 51
  abbeys and, 38–39
  after Roman era, 28–32
  artificial hills and, 41–42
  decline of central power and, 36–37
  deforestation and, 48–49
  desertifaction and, 48
  early medieval population numbers and, 35–38
  ecological effects and, 44–50
  effects of civilization and, 44–50
  essen and, 38
  Franks and, 32–34
  geographic factors and, 32
  high Middle Ages and, 38–41
  hydrological projects and, 41–44
  land reclamation and, 38–50
  landscape and, 15–27, 44–50
  peace and security for, 32
  place names and, 33–34
  power and, 32–33, 36, 39–43, 46
  religion and, 38–39
  soil conditions and, 15–27, 32–50
  stream ridges and, 32–33
  transport routs and, 32
  Vikings and, 37
Offa of Mercia, 106
Oisterwijk, 326
Oostende, 256
Oostergo, 36
Ootmarsum, 58
Opgooi, 56
oral law, 59
Oresme, Nicolas, 196
orphans, 174
Oudenaarde, 257, 290, 303, 309, 331, 346, 351, 362
Overijssel, 13, 31, 176, 287
ownership, 9. *See also* property rights
  agriculture and, 128, 132, 325, 328–29, 339
  burghers and, 174–75
  capital market and, 188
  changing social structures and, 242–77, 285, 291, 296–97, 301, 323
  economic growth and, 384, 390, 392, 395, 401, 409
  identity and, 179
  labour market and, 202–3
  land market and, 166–67, 170
  land mobility and, 178–81
  leasing and, 171–78, 243 (*see also* leasing)
  manorial organization and, 83–86, 90–92

ownership, (*cont.*)
  nobility and, 51, 57–61
  population growth and, 285
  prestige from, 178–79
  regional frameworks and, 33, 44
  rural social structures and, 243
  tenant rights and, 176
  trade and, 237–38
  villages and, 102
  voting rights and, 179
oxen, 125, 127, 134, 136, 222, 295–96, 327, 334–37, 360

Paderborn Abbey, 62
pagi, 31, 69–70, 73, 102
palisades, 41
palynological research, 19, 22, 27, 34–35, 130
partenrederij, 237–38
pawnshops, 189
Pays de Herve, 247
Peace of God movement, 69
peasants, 13
  agriculture and, 2, 128 (*see also* agriculture)
  associations of, 64
  Bishop of Utrecht and, 91–92
  capital market and, 182, 189
  changing social structures and, 242–51, 259–62, 268–73, 277
  coloni and, 173
  commercialization and, 295–303
  community structures and, 94, 97–98, 102, 105, 109
  economic growth and, 374, 379, 383, 388–97, 400–5, 409
  free, 68
  homines franci and, 59
  industries and, 146–48, 155, 160, 355, 361, 368, 370
  labour market and, 202–5, 208–09
  land market and, 163–67, 170–80
  land ownership and, 61, 167
  land reclamation and, 38–39, 44–45
  leasing and, 170–78
  levies upon, 66–67
  living conditions and, 320–24
  manorial organization and, 75, 80–92
  peatland and, 7
  tenant rights and, 176
  territorial lords and, 10, 66–67 (*see also* territorial lords)
  tithes and, 62–63
  trade and, 213
  urbanization and, 285, 289–91
  welfare and, 304, 307, 309, 323–24

Peasants' Revolt of 1381, 273
peat, 4, 7, 223
  agriculture and, 139
  Ardennes and, 24
  availability of, 359–60
  capital market and, 194
  development of, 15
  digging of, 19, 45, 204, 208, 248–49, 301–2, 358–60, 365, 368, 374–75, 382
  Drenthe and, 24
  ecological problems from digging, 368
  economic growth and, 372–75, 381–82, 392, 407
  energy consumption and, 359–60
  growing importance of, 45–46
  homines franci and, 57
  industries and, 149–50, 349, 355–61, 365–68
  labour market and, 204, 208–09
  land market and, 172
  land reclamation and, 19, 33–34, 40, 44–46, 84
  leasing and, 172
  manorial organization and, 78–85, 88–91
  oxidation and, 19, 45
  palynological research and, 19
  protection of, 45
  salt production and, 149–50
  sea clay areas and, 20
  social changes and, 248–49, 256–57, 274, 279, 283, 285, 291, 298, 301, 310, 321
  soil conditions and, 24–26, 131, 134–37, 138–41, 337, 339, 342
  territorial lords and, 72
  trade and, 223, 236
  village communities and, 95, 97, 102
  water table and, 19
  Zuiderzee and, 23
Peel, 303, 364
Peelo, 130
pennies, 193
Pepin, 193
Philip of Leyden, 195
Philip the Bold, 195
Philip the Good, 115, 210, 313
Picardy, 13, 147, 185, 238
pigs, 56, 75, 125, 236, 341
Pipin II, 57, 62
Pipin III, 62
Pippinids, 53
place names, 33–34
pledges, 183
Pleistocene, 25
ploughs, 77, 84, 126–27, 131–34, 141, 323, 327, 335, 373, 397

pogroms, 183–84
Poland, 25, 297, 299
politics, 12–13
　aldermen and, 103
　assassination and, 113
　bureaucracy and, 263–71
　coin production and, 194
　corruption and, 266–67
　decline of central power and, 36–37, 64–75
　economic growth and, 385–87
　education and, 316
　Franks and, 29–34
　Frisians and, 30
　gift exchange and, 162
　guilds and, 206
　Hansa and, 113–14
　Merovingians and, 30–31
　occupational choices and, 32–33
　position of women and, 292–94
　principalities and, 266–67
　proletariat and, 246
　royal hunting and, 25
　Saxons and, 29–31
　social conflicts and, 271–78
　socio-institutional factors and, 387–409
　state formation and, 263–71
　territorial lords and, 64–75 (see also territorial lords)
　trade and, 228–34
　upward mobility and, 269–70
　urban communities and, 111–13
　Vikings and, 385–86
　village communities and, 93–103
pollen analysis, 18, 28, 34–35, 38, 42, 124, 133, 328
Poor relief, 307–13
population growth, 1, 26
　agriculture and, 325–29, 325–38
　average life expectancy and, 143, 289–90, 309, 372, 377
　birth statistics and, 290–91
　Black Death and, 86–87, 279–81, 304–5
　child mortality and, 284
　communal organizations and, 136–40
　customs and, 136–40
　decline of, 330–38
　early medieval numbers and, 35–38
　economic growth and, 325–38, 383–85
　farm size and, 246
　feuding and, 288–89
　Frankish power and, 32
　Great Famine and, 279
　land market and, 166
　land reclamation and, 32–50
　living standards and, 140–46, 279

　Malthusian stress and, 279
　market effects and, 325–29
　mortality rates and, 289–90
　regional diversity and, 282–91
　rural, 285
　socio-institutional factors and, 387–409
　soil conditions and, 25, 284
　sustainability and, 340–42
　urbanization and, 278–94
　Viking attacks and, 280–81
　village communities and, 93–103
Portugal, 225–26
portus, 214
Postel, 38
pottery, 146, 149, 152, 156, 158, 215, 344–45, 367
power
　Bishop of Utrecht and, 91–92
　castellans and, 57, 73, 102, 107–8, 266, 292
　Charlemagne and, 60
　coin production and, 193–200
　counts and, 70–71
　elites and, 117–23
　feudal system and, 68–69
　fiefs and, 52, 68, 73, 164, 171, 269
　fortification building and, 64–65
　guilds and, 205–08, 211, 213
　Hansa and, 113–14
　hereditary, 70–72
　kin control and, 163–66, 287–89, 390, 399–400
　leasing and, 175–77
　manorial organization and, 75–93
　monopolies and, 60, 107 (see also monopolies)
　nobility and, 60
　occupation and, 32–33, 36, 39–43, 46
　property rights and, 51–53, 57–60, 63, 67–73
　public authorities and, 169–72
　serfs and, 51–52, 59, 62, 75–80, 86–94, 126, 147–49, 154–55, 170–71, 175, 217, 379, 383
　social power, 10, 92, 389, 396–97
　social structures and, 242–78
　socio-institutional factors and, 387–409
　territorial lords and, 64–75, 87–88, 110–17
　trade and, 228–34
　urban communities and, 110–23
　village communities and, 102–3
precaria, 173
Premonstratensians, 38–39, 43, 71, 223, 325
principalities, 71–74, 266–67

printing, 364
productivity, 2
  agriculture and, 131, 136, 140–42, 327, 331–36, 342
  changing social structures and, 259
  commercialization and, 297
  economic growth and, 372–74, 377, 379, 400–3
  industries and, 146, 155, 344, 352, 355, 360, 364, 370–71
  land market and, 178
  manorial organization and, 87
  welfare and, 304, 309
proletariat, 2, 100, 340
  changing social structures and, 246, 250, 255, 258–60, 270–75
  economic growth and, 377, 390–91, 394, 404
  labour market and, 202, 205, 208–10
  occupational differentiation and, 303–4
  urbanization and, 290
  welfare and, 304–5, 311–13
property rights
  absolute, 2
  allodium and, 61
  capital market and, 188
  commoners and, 52
  distribution of, 9, 163
  economic growth and, 381, 386
  feudal system and, 164
  gift exchange and, 162–63
  land and, 31, 39, 49–53, 57–60, 63, 66–73, 162–67
  leasing and, 170–78
  legal contracts and, 166–67
  long-term security and, 163
  manorial organization and, 51–52, 85, 89–92
  market institutions and, 163, 166–70, 173, 175
  nobility and, 167
  overlapping claims and, 51, 163–64
  public authorities and, 167–70
  recording of, 166–67
  religious institutions and, 61–63, 166–67
  serfs and, 51–52
  socio-institutional factors and, 389–93, 399–403, 408
  taxes and, 169–71
  territorial lords and, 169
  variety of, 165
  villages and, 98, 103
protectionism, 233
Prüm, 62, 87, 128, 146–47
public auction, 170
public authorities
  bureaucracy and, 263–71
  labour market and, 205–11
  land market and, 167–70
  services owed and, 202
Pussabini, Jan, 190
Pussabini, Pieter, 190
putting-out system, 249

Quarters, 225
quays, 227
quern stones, 215

Radbod, 30
rainfall, 15, 24
rape seed, 126, 335
real wages, 376–80
Reformation, 276–277
Reginar I, 70
regional diversity, 2–6
  changing social structures and, 242–78
  commercialization and, 294–304
  growth mechanisms and, 3–8
  interest rates and, 191–93
  labour market and, 200–13
  land market and, 179–81
  leasing and, 172
  origins of, 7
  population growth and, 25–26
  research approach to, 8–14
  socio-institutional factors and, 387–409
  soil conditions and, 7, 15–27
  specialization and, 364–67 (*see also* specialization)
  urbanization and, 282–91
regional frameworks
  castellans and, 57, 73, 102, 107–8, 266, 292
  fiefs and, 52, 68, 73, 164, 171, 269
  fortification building and, 64–65
  freemen and, 31, 58–61, 88
  German Hansa and, 113–14
  homines franci and, 33, 57–61
  land reclamation and, 27–50
  Lex Frisionum and, 60–61
  Lex Salica and, 60
  Lex Saxonum and, 60
  lords and, 63–75
  manorial organization and, 75–93
  religious properties and, 61–63
  royal properties and, 52–57
  serfs and, 51–52, 59, 62, 75–80, 86–94, 126, 147–49, 154–55, 170–71, 175, 217, 379, 383
  slavery and, 59–61, 76–80, 84
  towns and, 103–10
  urban communities and, 110–23

Viking raids and, 37, 64, 70–72, 107, 202, 218, 280, 385–86
village communities and, 93–103
religious institutions
  abbeys and, 38–39 (*see also* abbeys)
  agriculture and, 325–26
  Anabaptists and, 276–77
  attracting settlers and, 40–41
  belfries and, 351
  Brevia Exempla and, 63
  capital market and, 182–83
  Catholic condemnation of interest, 182
  Christianity and, 62–63
  economic growth and, 373
  education and, 313–14
  fuel and, 356–57
  gift exchange and, 162
  judicial battle and, 220
  leasing and, 172–73
  levies and, 66–67
  Peace of God movement and, 69
  pledges and, 183
  poor relief and, 307–8
  property rights and, 61–63, 166–67
  Reformation and, 277
  royal properties and, 53–54, 57
  serfdom and, 91
  slavery and, 77, 80–81
  tithes and, 62–63
  trade and, 214, 222–23
  usury laws and, 182–86
  village communities and, 97
  witch hunts and, 294
Rheims, 53
Rhine, 11, 13, 15, 235
  commercialization and, 298
  Franks and, 29
  homines franci and, 58
  land dynamism of, 21–22
  manorial organization and, 75
  royal properties and, 53
  Saxons and, 31
  technology and, 157–58
  trade and, 214–15, 221, 228
  tributaries of, 21–22
rights
  Lex Frisionum and, 60–61
  Lex Salica and, 60
  Lex Saxonum and, 60
  manorial organization and, 75–93
  mansus and, 127–28
  property, 2 (*see also* property rights)
  towns and, 107–8
Rijkswoud, 49, 53
rinderpest, 279

river clays
  fertile, 134–35
  royal properties and, 56–57
  soil quality and, 20–23, 32, 46, 134–35
Roermond, 344
Roman Army, 21–22
Roman era, 12
  civitates and, 70, 102
  ethnic composition after, 28–32
  forests and, 24
  Frankish succession and, 53
  industries and, 152, 155
  land use and, 18–21, 24, 32–34
  limes and, 30
  linguistics and, 29
  marriage and, 291
  mills and, 147–48
  population decline after, 27
  property rights and, 168
  roadways of, 216, 227
  shipbuilding and, 158
  socio-institutional factors and, 387
  soil cultivation and, 32–33
  towns and, 102–3
  trade and, 213, 217–18
  villas and, 33, 76
Romanesque art, 156
Rorik, 64
royal mint, 56
royal properties
  Aachen and, 56
  Ardennes and, 53, 56
  Franks and, 52–57
  Guelders river area and, 56–57
  regional frameworks and, 52–57
  religious institutions and, 52–53, 57
  strategic border areas and, 58–59
  Utrecht and, 56–57
Ruhr area, 24
Rulles, 34
Russia, 25, 299
rye, 38, 99, 126–33, 148, 236, 238, 297, 306–7, 310, 328, 331, 337

Saale, 15, 50
St. Adelbert, 62
St. Amand, 314
St. Bavo, 107
St. Bertin, 36, 63, 146–48, 314
Saint-Hubert, 105, 217, 314
Saint-Omer, 63, 111, 121, 186, 219–20, 222, 229, 272, 337, 401
St. Pieter, 63
Saint-Quentin, 185
St. Riquier, 147

St. Servaas, 53
St. Vaast, 217, 314
Salian Franks, 29
Salland, 4, 20–21
  essen and, 38
  labour market and, 203
  rural social changes and, 243, 245
salt production, 19–20, 147–50, 214–15, 366–67, 382
Sambre, 24, 151
sand deposition, 15, 19
sand dunes, 19
Saxo, Everhard, 70
Saxons, 28–31, 60
Saxony spinning wheel, 348
sayetterie, 362–63
Scania, 338
Scheldt, 15, 20
  fleet of, 59
  land dynamism of, 21–22
  place names and, 34
  population numbers and, 31, 35
  soil of, 32
  staple at, 109
  tide mills in, 159
  trade and, 230, 240, 242
  trading posts and, 106, 110
Schleswig-Holstein, 29, 30
schout, 95
Schumpeterian growth, 370
Scotland, 49
scratch plough, 134
sea clays, 7, 15, 20, 36, 47, 128, 172, 244–45
seasonal labour, 203, 208–09, 212, 244, 302, 339
Secret Council, 269
seignorage, 195
serfs
  agriculture and, 126
  economic growth and, 379, 383
  industries and, 147–49, 154–55
  landholders and, 52, 59–62
  land market and, 170–71, 175
  leasing and, 170–78
  Lex Frisionum and, 60–61
  Lex Salica and, 60
  Lex Saxonum and, 60
  main obligation of, 75
  manorial organization and, 75–94
  migration of, 88–89
  property rights and, 51–52
  trade and, 219
  wages for, 75
sessi, 203
sharecropping, 177
share shipping companies, 237–38

's-Hertogenbosch, 190–91, 224, 256, 275, 310, 317, 362–364
shipbuilding, 158
shipping, 77, 158, 234, 237–39, 248, 298, 365
Siegburg, 152, 345
silk, 214, 226, 261, 295, 363
silt, 19–22, 149, 222, 227, 366, 381
Silva Carbonaria, 24
silver, 193–199, 206, 209, 214, 216, 226, 267–68
Sint-Pietersmannen, 105
Sint-Servaas, 61
Sint-Truiden, 103, 105, 110
slagen, 140
slagturven, 45
slaves
  Christianity and, 77, 80–81
  Frisians and, 77
  improved position of, 76–77
  industries and, 156
  land reclamation and, 83–86
  Lex Frisionum and, 60–61
  Lex Salica and, 60
  Lex Saxonum and, 60
  manorial organization and, 76–80, 84
  regional frameworks and, 59–61, 76–80, 84
  socio-institutional factors and, 397, 405
  trade in, 77, 215–19
Slavs, 50
Sluis, 227, 238
social change
  bureaucracy and, 263–70
  burghers and, 243, 251, 259–60, 265–66, 269–70, 273–78, 290, 303, 309, 314, 319, 322–23
  conflicts and, 271–78
  corporatism and, 253–58
  farm size and, 244–47
  fiscality and, 263–70
  long-term economic growth and, 372–409
  ownership and, 242–52, 257, 260, 272, 276–77, 285, 291, 296–97, 301, 323
  rural transformations and, 242–52
  state formation and, 263–70
  urban transformations and, 252–63
  welfare and, 303–24
social conflict
  Anabaptists and, 276–77
  assessing effects of, 277
  brotherhoods and, 275
  capitalist market and, 275–76
  Dutch Revolt and, 12–13, 261, 277–78, 387, 397
  feuding and, 288–89

Index

guilds and, 274–75
lessening of, 273–74
Peasants' Revolt of 1381 and, 273
rural, 271, 274
urban, 271–75
social development
  agriculture and, 124–46
  average life expectancy and, 143, 289–90, 309, 372, 377
  Black Death and, 37, 86–87, 173, 177, 192, 273–74, 279–81, 304–5, 329–31, 345, 373–77, 383–84
  communal organizations and, 136–40
  customs and, 136–40
  fiefs and, 52, 68, 73, 164, 171, 269
  flourishing culture and, 375–76
  friction in, 271–78
  land reclamation and, 32–50
  Lex Salica and, 60
  manorial organization and, 75–93
  markets and, 162–241 (*see also* markets)
  military and, 260, 265–66, 270, 274, 276
  proletariat and, 2 (*see also* proletariat)
  property rights and, 389–93, 399–403, 408
  Reformation and, 277
  regional diversity and, 6–7 (*see also* regional diversity)
  research approach to, 8–14
social power, 10, 92, 389, 396–97
social structures
  bureaucracy and, 263–70
  class relations and, 6, 92, 389, 396–97
  conflicts and, 271–78
  fiscality and, 263–70
  land reclamation and, 242
  marriage and, 66, 165, 176, 208, 246, 264, 267, 284–87, 290–93
  position of women and, 292–94
  principalities and, 266–67
  rural, 242–52
  social change and, 242–78
  state formation and, 263–71
  urbanization and, 13, 110–17, 252–63
  village communities and, 93–103
socio-institutional factors
  chronology and, 393–94
  economic growth and, 387–409
  guilds and, 390–94, 399–405
  land reclamation and, 388
  in perspective, 406–9
  regional path-dependency and, 387–87
  Roman era and, 387
  slavery and, 397, 405
Soignies, 256

soil, 51, 328
  aeolian, 15, 23–24
  coal deposits and, 24
  desertifaction and, 48
  ecological effects and, 44–50
  economic growth and, 372, 381–84, 389, 407
  effects from civilization upon, 44–50
  erosion of, 19, 44, 47, 340, 342, 357–58, 382
  fertile, 23–24, 32–33, 37–38, 80, 83, 134–35, 177–78, 284
  Frankish methods and, 32–33
  geographical diversity of Low Countries and, 15–27
  Holocene, 25
  Ice Ages and, 15, 18
  land reclamation and, 38–50
  loess, 15, 23, 25, 30, 32, 39, 76, 82, 131, 134–35, 141, 372
  manorial organization and, 80
  occupational choices and, 32–50
  oxidation and, 45
  palynological research and, 19
  peat, 15, 24 (*see also* peat)
  Pleistocene, 25
  population growth and, 25
  river clays, 20–23, 32, 46, 56–57, 134–35
  Roman methods and, 32–33
  salt marshes and, 20
  sand, 15, 19, 22–23, 25, 32, 37
  sea clays, 7, 15, 20, 36, 47, 128, 172, 244–45
  silt, 19–22, 149, 222, 227, 366, 381
  sustainability and, 340–41
  trade and, 214
  water and, 20–22
Solari family, 193–200
soldij, 202
Spain, 225–26, 298
specialization, 1–7, 10–13
  agriculture and, 109, 132–33, 140–41, 325–42
  changing social structures and, 245, 247, 251
  commercialization and, 294–302
  economic growth and, 372–80, 389–92, 395–408
  fishing and, 338–40
  industries and, 146, 149–61, 343–45, 362–70
  land reclamation and, 44
  livestock and, 132
  long-run economic growth and, 372–75, 379–80, 389–92, 395, 398–408
  regional, 364–67

specialization, (cont.)
    trade market and, 230, 237
    urbanization and, 282, 285–86
    welfare and, 309
spelt, 127, 130, 132
spices, 214–15, 226, 240
spinning wheels, 347–48
standard of living
    agriculture and, 140–46
    living conditions and, 320–24
    population growth and, 140–46, 279
    real wages and, 376–80
    welfare and, 304–7
state formation, 263–71
stature, 143, 146, 378, 407
Stavelot, 61, 314
Stavoren, 220
steken, 338
Sterksel, 325–26
stinswieren, 41
Strasbourg, 215
stream ridges, 21–22, 32–33
sub rosa arrangements, 170
subventione pauperum, De (Vives), 311
surveyors, 169
sustainability, 340–42
Switzerland, 72–74
Syrians, 214

tables of the Holy Spirit, 308
Tacitus, 21–22, 33
tailors, 120, 207, 277, 302, 364
Tanchelm, 62–63
tapestries, 257, 295, 362, 364
taxation
    agriculture and, 128, 342
    annuities and, 187
    capital market and, 185, 187, 189–91, 196–198
    changing social structures and, 253–56, 262–76
    commercialization and, 301
    economic growth and, 386, 392
    elites and, 118–21
    excise, 66, 72, 107–9, 112, 119, 170, 190–91, 198, 230–31, 270, 272, 274, 368
    homines franci and, 58
    indirect, 231
    industries and, 363, 368
    labour market and, 202
    land market and, 166–69
    levies and, 9–10 (*see also* levies)
    royal properties and, 58, 66, 72
    soldier's pay and, 202
    state formation and, 266
tallia and, 66
    trade and, 215, 228–34
    urban communities and, 112, 292
    village communities and, 95–96, 102
    water boards and, 43, 47
    welfare and, 305
technology
    agriculture and, 77, 84, 126–27, 131–36, 141, 323, 327, 335, 373, 397
    Carolingians and, 158
    economic growth and, 373–74
    horizontal loom and, 155–56
    industrial, 157–61, 347–55
    labour and, 158–61, 208, 245–47
    land transport and, 222–23
    land use and, 245–46
    looms and, 157–58, 208
    mechanical clocks and, 351–52
    Merovingians and, 158
    mills and, 158–60
    Rhine and, 157–58
    shipbuilding and, 158
    spinning wheels and, 347–48
    textile industry and, 347–48
    transportation improvements and, 234–38
tenant farmers, 332–35, 342
    capital market and, 181, 188
    changing social structures and, 244–47, 251, 258
    commercialization and, 295–96
    economic growth and, 377, 390–94, 403
    labour market and, 201
    occupational differentiation and, 301
    urbanization and, 285–86
    welfare and, 304, 306, 312, 323–24
tenant rights, 176
Ten Duinen, 43
Ter Doest, 43
terpen, 41, 79
territorial lords
    abbeys and, 71
    advocacy and, 71
    aspiring to being, 71–72
    banal duties and, 66–68
    bannum and, 66, 95
    bureaucracy and, 263–71
    capital market and, 202
    Carolingian, 69–70
    coin production and, 195–200
    communes and, 111–12
    counts and, 70–74, 97
    disintegration of central rule and, 64–75
    economic growth and, 386
    feudal system and, 68–69
    feuding and, 288
    Flanders and, 72–74, 108
    fortification and, 64–65, 202

Index

Hansa and, 114
jurisdictional rights and, 68
labour market and, 206–7
land market and, 164, 168
land reclamation and, 83–86
leasing and, 172–73
levies of, 66–67
loss of control over labour and, 90–91
malae consuetudines and, 66
military and, 66
Peace of God movement and, 69
properties of, 72–73, 167
social conflicts and, 271
state-building and, 73–74
trade and, 217–18, 221, 232
urban communities and, 110–17
Vikings and, 64, 70–72
textile industry, 113
  bleaching and, 362
  cloth production and, 153, 252, 254, 299–300, 343–48, 361–63
  drapers and, 156, 205, 207, 210, 252–57, 297, 303, 347, 362–63
  dyes and, 153, 155, 157, 257, 327, 354
  fashion and, 364
  flax and, 126, 147, 214, 249, 251, 326, 333, 336, 361–62, 370
  fullers and, 147, 209–10, 273–75, 306, 347, 363, 368
  iron carders and, 347–48
  labour market and, 205
  linen and, 146–47, 153, 249, 261, 295–98, 306, 326, 343–46, 349, 361–62, 366
  looms and, 153–57, 208, 253, 257, 300, 344, 346, 352, 363, 367
  power of, 205
  quality control and, 347–49
  rise in production and, 362–63
  sayatterie and, 362–63
  silk and, 214, 226, 261, 295, 363
  spinning wheels and, 347–48
  technology and, 347–48
  weavers, 153–57, 208, 253, 257, 272–74, 295, 300, 302, 306, 344, 346, 352, 362–64, 367
  wool and, 113 (*see also* wool)
Theux, 53
Thorn, 62, 351
three-field rotation system, 133–34, 137, 138
Thuin, 189
Thunensian model, 3
tide mills, 159
Tiel, 56, 81, 193, 215, 219, 221, 398, 401
time preference, 186
tin, 156
tithes
  changing social structures and, 272

community structures and, 94, 97, 103, 105
economic growth and, 398, 400
land use and, 39–40, 83–84, 138, 166, 170
manorial organization and, 83–84
religious institutions and, 62
tolls
  capital market and, 183–84
  changing social structures and, 264, 268
  community structures and, 106, 108–9
  economic growth and, 373, 386, 398
  land use and, 58, 171–72, 334, 337
  manorial organization and, 77
  royal, 56, 106
  territorial lords and, 66, 69, 72
  trade and, 216–20, 222–36
Tongeren, 28, 53, 102, 401
Tongerlo, 38–39, 71
Torhout, 221, 224
Tournai, 29, 70, 108, 111, 154, 185, 308, 351
towns
  castellum and, 102
  changing social structures and, 252–63
  civitates and, 102
  counts and, 108–9
  currency issues and, 198–200
  education and, 317–19
  fortifications and, 107–9
  industries and, 153–57, 343–49, 361–64
  leasing and, 172
  life annuities and, 185–86
  living conditions and, 320–24
  Middle Age founding of most, 102
  military and, 95, 106–8, 110, 391
  pagi and, 102
  population growth and, 285–86 (*see also* population growth)
  protection in, 107–8
  regional frameworks and, 103–10
  rights of, 107–8
  Roman antecedents of, 102–3
  royal tolls and, 106
  socio-institutional factors and, 387–409
  street patterns and, 322
  territorial lords and, 63–75
  trade and, 105–7, 110, 218–34
  urbanization and, 278–94
  wealth distribution in, 253–56
trade
  Antwerp and, 226–28
  artificial lower prices and, 229
  Carolingians and, 213–20
  cartels and, 232
  coins and, 214
  commercialization and, 294–304
  compulsory staples and, 229–30
  compurgation and, 220
  concentration of, 229–30

trade (cont.)
  excises and, 230–31
  fairs and, 221–22
  fixed prices and, 230
  Frisians and, 214–20
  government influence on, 228–34
  grain policy and, 216–17
  Great Famine and, 279
  guilds and, 218–19, 226 (*see also* guilds)
  Hansa and, 113–14, 225–26
  increased security for, 219–20
  indirect taxes on, 231
  information costs and, 230
  institutional organization of, 213–18
  Jews and, 214
  judicial duel and, 220
  just price and, 217
  land transport and, 222–23, 233, 234–36
  luxury goods and, 214–16
  market growth and, 234–41 (*see also* economic growth)
  merchant organizations and, 218–19, 226
  nobility and, 214, 217–19, 231
  North Sea and, 214, 216, 234
  open competition and, 232
  portus and, 214
  price-setting and, 216–17
  professional merchants and, 214
  protectionism and, 231
  religious institutions and, 214, 223
  river sites and, 221
  Roman era and, 217–18
  security for, 233–34
  share shipping companies and, 237–38
  slaves and, 77, 217–21
  soil diversity and, 214
  taxes and, 215, 228, 231–34
  territorial lords and, 219–21, 232
  tolls and, 214–18, 222–36
  towns and, 105–7, 110, 218–34
  transaction costs and, 216, 230
  transport improvements and, 234–41
  urbanization and, 223–24
  vicus and, 214, 215
  Viking raids and, 218
  water transport and, 213–16, 221, 223, 227, 233–40
  weights and measures standards and, 216, 234–35
  year-on-year price differences and, 236
trading posts, 105–6
Trajectum, 33
transporters, 206
tree ring research, 18
Tricht, 33
truck system, 209

Tuil, 56
Turnhout, 326
Twente, 28, 246, 297

Ukraine, 23
Upper Normandy, 171
Urals, 23
urban communities
  burghers and, 108–15, 119, 121
  capital market and, 187–93
  charters of, 112
  comital power and, 114–15
  communes and, 111–12
  elites and, 110–11, 117–23
  factories and, 204
  German Hansa and, 113–14
  guilds and, 111, 113–14, 117–23
  industries and, 343–49, 361–64
  labour market and, 202–3, 208
  living conditions and, 320–24
  military and, 115, 121
  power plays in, 110–17
  public works and, 202–3
  self-government and, 111
  socio-institutional factors and, 387–409
  territorial lords and, 110–17
  threat to princely authority and, 113
  trade and, 218–34
urban graveyard effect, 284
urbanization, 1, 13
  demography and, 383–85
  economic growth and, 383–85
  population growth and, 278–94
  position of women and, 292–94
  regional diversity and, 282–91
  socio-institutional factors and, 387–409
  Viking attacks and, 280–81
urbanization ratio, 1
usury, 182–86, 232
Utrecht, 12, 40, 53, 56
  capital market and, 190
  concentrated habitation and, 129
  elites and, 120
  industries and, 344, 359
  labour market and, 210
  Lombards and, 193–200
  manorial organization and, 78, 82
  religious properties and, 61–62
  royal properties and, 56–57
  social conflict and, 271, 276
  territorial lords and, 64, 72–74
  tithes and, 63
  towns and, 102
  trade and, 217, 222, 235
  urbanization and, 291
  welfare and, 304, 309, 312–14

Valenciennes, 111, 279, 292, 314, 318, 327, 337, 343, 351–352
Valkhof, 56
van Artevelde, Jan, 265
van Aytta, Viglius, 269
van Delft, Jan, 352
van Herwijnen, Bruisten, 266–67
van Houtte, Jan, 275–76
van Leiden, Jan, 277
van Metz, Alpertus, 219
van Oudenaarde, Jan, 253
van Schoonbeke, Gilbert, 207, 258–59, 276, 322
Varik, 56
Veluwe, 2, 25, 262, 368
   communal organizations and, 137
   deforestation and, 48–49
   iron production and, 151
   soil conditions of, 22–23, 177–78
Venetians, 226, 237
Venn, 24
vertical loom, 155–56
Vesdre, 247, 262, 347, 354, 363–364, 370, 402
vicus, 214–15
Vikings, 37
   Carolingians and, 64
   economic growth and, 385–86
   fortification building and, 65
   market issues and, 202, 218, 280
   military conscription and, 202
   political issues of, 385–86
   population growth and, 280–81
   regional frameworks and, 37, 64, 70–72, 107, 202, 218, 280, 385–86
   territorial lords and, 64, 70–72
   trade and, 218
village communities
   agriculture and, 94, 98–99, 126–29
   aldermen and, 103
   bylaws of, 95
   changes in farm size and, 244
   community charters and, 99
   customs of, 136–42
   development of, 93
   industries and, 343–45, 367–68
   justice administration and, 95
   land market and, 163
   laws of the commons and, 99, 102
   leasing and, 170–78
   living conditions and, 320–24
   loss of cohesion in, 244
   motivations of, 94
   organizations of, 136–40
   population growth and, 285
   power balance in, 102–3
   primitive communism and, 98
   property rights and, 98, 103
   regional framework of, 93–103
   religion and, 97
   social conflicts and, 271
   socio-institutional factors and, 387–409
   strength of, 94–95
   towns, 271–72
   water management and, 43–44, 97–98
Visé, 189
Vives, Juan Luis, 311, 317
Vleuten, 78
voting rights, 179
vroonten, 98

Waal, 21, 56
Wadenooijen, 33
wage labour. *See* labour
Walcheren, 20, 64–65
Wales, 26
Walloon Flanders, 135, 149, 281, 353, 355, 370–71, 399–402
warven, 74
Waterland, 263, 277
water management, 43–44, 47, 97–98, 300–1
water mills, 147–49, 156–57, 358–59
water privatization, 66
water transport
   commercialization and, 298–301
   shipping and, 298
   trade and, 213–16, 221, 223, 227, 233–41
weapons, 353–54
weavers, 270–72, 302, 306
   looms and, 153–57, 208, 253, 257, 300, 344, 346, 352, 363, 367
   tapestries and, 257, 295, 362, 364
Weesp, 235
weights and measures standards, 216, 232–33
welfare
   beggars and, 311–13
   Black Death and, 304–5, 373
   education and, 313–19
   food and, 305–7
   hospitals and, 142, 222, 308–10, 316, 351, 377–78
   kin and, 307–8, 308
   labour and, 304–6, 309–13, 316, 318, 323–24
   lepers and, 308–9, 377
   literacy and, 313–19
   living conditions and, 320–24
   negative view of, 311–12
   poor relief and, 307–13
   standard of living and, 304–7
Werden, 62
Werven, 41

Weser River, 31
Westergo, 36
Westerschelde, 20
Westerwolde, 28
Westphalia, 29–31, 58, 277
wheat, 126–32, 148, 236, 305–6, 327, 330–32, 336–37
Wichman II, 71
Wichman of Hamaland, 71
Wijnaldum, 132
Willibrord, 56, 62
windmills, 357–59
Wismar, 113
witch hunts, 294
women
  capital markets and, 208
  education and, 317
  husband's authority and, 293–94
  labour and, 207–11, 292–93
  manorial organization and, 292
  marriage and, 291 (see also marriage)
  money changers and, 197
  position of, 292–94
  witch hunts and, 294
wool, 113, 257, 381
  agriculture and, 125, 127, 133, 328
  capital market and, 198
  commercialization and, 297
  industries and, 146–47, 153, 155–56, 343, 346–48, 352, 362–63, 370
  trade and, 214, 216, 223–24, 229–30, 236
  urbanization and, 293
  welfare and, 306
Wormhout, 224
Woudrichemmerwaard, 267
written documents, 314–16

Xanten, 89, 152

Ympyn, Jan, 200
Ypres, 108, 155, 268
  architecture and, 351
  capital market and, 184–85
  cloth industry and, 343
  education and, 318–19
  social conflict and, 271
  trade and, 222
  urbanization and, 281
  welfare and, 308–9, 312

Zaltbommel, 56, 401
Zanden van, Jan Luiten, 8
Zeeland, 30, 57, 171, 190
  agricultural economy and, 338–39, 342
  cereal cultivation and, 132–33
  changing social structures and, 267
  cloth production and, 153
  commercialization and, 298
  disintegration of central rule and, 65
  ecological effects and, 47–48
  economic growth and, 372, 382, 399
  geographical diversity and, 18–19
  hydrological projects and, 41, 43
  industries and, 366–67
  labour market and, 208
  land reclamation and, 28, 40
  living standards and, 140
  salt production and, 149–50
  sea clays and, 20
  territorial lords and, 64, 67, 72–74
  tithes and, 63
  trade and, 214, 216, 226, 234, 237
  urbanization and, 280, 288
  welfare and, 314–15
Zeeuws-Vlaanderen, 47–48
Zeevang, 188–89, 193–94
Zelhem, 135
Zierikzee, 266
zinc, 156
Zoelmond, 86
Zoniënwoud, 24
Zuiderzee, 20, 23, 340, 372, 382
Zutphen, 205, 237
Zwin, 20, 227, 381
Zwolle, 113, 323, 381